THE
BROTHERHOODS

THE TRUE STORY OF TWO COPS
WHO MURDERED FOR THE MAFIA

Guy Lawson and William Oldham

SCRIBNER
New York   London   Toronto   Sydney

SCRIBNER
1230 Avenue of the Americas
New York, NY 10020

The names of some individuals in this book have been changed.

Copyright © 2006 by Guy Lawson and William Oldham

SCRIBNER and design are trademarks of Macmillan Library Reference USA, Inc., used under license by Simon & Schuster, the publisher of this work.

For information about special discounts for bulk purchases, please contact Simon & Schuster Special Sales: 1-800-456-6798 or business@simonandschuster.com

Text set in Stempel Garamond

Manufactured in the United States of America

1   3   5   7   9   10   8   6   4   2

The Library of Congress Cataloging-in-Publication Data is available.

ISBN-13: 978-0-7432-8944-3
ISBN-10: 0-7432-8944-7

Credits appear on page 510.

For Maya, always

—GUY LAWSON

Dedicated to my brothers

John Rochester
b. December 28, 1955; d. September 1, 1983
Sea of Japan

Benjamin Butler
b. February 16, 1958; d. January 4, 1976
Katmandu, Nepal

Please rest in peace.

And to my sisters
Charlotte Bowman and Nancy Patton
and my angels, my daughters,
Olivia Grace and India Pearl.

And to L.

Please live in peace and with my eternal love.

WILLIAM OLDHAM
New York City, September 12, 2006

CONTENTS

CHARACTERS IX

PROLOGUE 1

CHAPTER ONE
THE HOOK 7

CHAPTER TWO
THE PRINCE OF DARKNESS 25

CHAPTER THREE
SNITCHES AND LEAKS 43

CHAPTER FOUR
THE CRYSTAL BALL 73

CHAPTER FIVE
MOBLAND 95

CHAPTER SIX
"GODFATHERS OF THE NYPD" 111

CHAPTER SEVEN
THE AMAZING LIFE AND TIMES OF "GASPIPE" CASSO 143

CONTENTS

CHAPTER EIGHT
QUEEN FOR A DAY   177

CHAPTER NINE
DOWNTOWN BURT   215

CHAPTER TEN
EAGLE ON THE LAM   251

CHAPTER ELEVEN
OFF THE BOOKS   267

CHAPTER TWELVE
THE CADRE   297

CHAPTER THIRTEEN
FLIPPING BURT   323

CHAPTER FOURTEEN
MOB VEGAS   351

CHAPTER FIFTEEN
THE CIRCUS COMES TO BROOKLYN   389

CHAPTER SIXTEEN
TRIAL FOR THE AGES   415

CHAPTER SEVENTEEN
CORROBORATION   445

CHAPTER EIGHTEEN
THE RULE OF LAW   483

ACKNOWLEDGMENTS   507

CHARACTERS

THE CRYSTAL BALL

Detective Stephen Caracappa. Assigned to the Organized Crime Homicide Unit in the elite Major Case Squad. Attained the rank of first grade detective, a rare and distinguished achievement in the NYPD, while under the hire of the Luchese crime family. Retired to Las Vegas—to a house in a cul-de-sac in a gated community directly opposite Eppolito's.

Detective Louis Eppolito. Brooklyn detective assigned to the 62nd and 63rd Precinct, the heart of Brooklyn's mobland. Claimed to be the eleventh most decorated officer in the history of the NYPD. Son of a Gambino mafia soldier. Author of *Mafia Cop,* his life story, and aspiring Hollywood actor and screenwriter.

THE CADRE

Detective William Oldham. Investigator in Violent Criminal Enterprise and Terrorism unit of the U.S. Attorney's Office for the Eastern District. Former NYPD detective assigned to the Major Case Squad in 1989, where he worked with Detective Caracappa. Lead investigator on multiple major organized crime investigations through 1990s. Pursued investigation of Detectives Caracappa and Eppolito for more than seven years.

Joe Ponzi. Chief investigator in the Brooklyn District Attorney's Office, in charge of more than a hundred criminal investigators. Son of a legendary NYPD detective supervisor. Polygraph expert and highly experienced interrogator.

Detective George Terra. Former NYPD detective working for the Brooklyn DA. Quiet, unassuming, good undercover.

Detective Tommy Dades. Ex-boxer, ex-NYPD precinct detective. Organized crime specialist. Great street cop with a citywide reputation for busting wiseguys.

Detective Bobby Intartaglio. Brooklyn district attorney investigator and former NYPD organized crime cop. Mafia expert, particularly on Staten Island. Thinks of himself as "the old man."

Detective Doug LeVien. For decades involved in NYPD strike forces against mafia. Deep institutional memory of the battle between law enforcement and organized crime.

Detective Joe Campanella. Ex-NYPD intelligence detective, now an analyst with Organized Crime Section of the U.S. Attorney's Office for the Eastern District of New York.

Special Agent Mark Manko. Hardworking younger case agent from the Drug Enforcement Administration.

THE MAFIA

Anthony "Gaspipe" Casso. Underboss of the Luchese crime family. Confessed to complicity in thirty-six murders. Paid "the crystal ball" for information about law enforcement investigations. Inmate serving time in U.S. prison, Florence ADMAX in Florence, Colorado.

Vittorio "Vic" Amuso. Luchese crime family boss and Casso's partner. Prisoner in Allenwood Federal Penitentiary, serving life.

George "Georgie Neck" Zappola. A leader of the Bypass gang, a notorious Brooklyn burglary ring, and experienced Luchese hit man.

Alphonso "Little Al" D'Arco. Former acting Luchese boss and owner of La Donna Rosa, Italian restaurant in Manhattan. Turned himself in to law enforcement, providing evidence that led to dozens of mafia convictions. Now living in Witness Protection Program.

Peter "Fat Pete" Chiodo. Luchese captain, real estate developer, trade union shakedown artist. Shot and wounded multiple times in attempted murder ordered by Amuso and Casso. Living in Witness Protection Program.

Sammy "the Bull" Gravano. Gambino underboss and author of *Underboss*. High-ranking mafia informant.

Sal "Big Sal" Miciotta. Former Colombo capo, hit man, and businessman. Cooperating witness living in hiding.

"The Right" Nicky Guido. Member of the hit team that attacked Casso. Ran to Florida after learning of murder of wrong Nicky Guido. Convicted of assault with a dangerous weapon.

Bob Bering. Ex-NYPD cop involved in attempt on Casso. Turned himself in to cadre member Detective George Terra after learning of wrong Nicky Guido's murder.

THE VICTIMS

Israel Greenwald. Orthodox Jewish jewelry dealer in midtown Manhattan caught up in stolen Treasury bill deal gone bad. Disappeared in 1986.

Jimmy Hydell. Gambino associate and known tough guy. Part of a plot to kill Casso that failed and sparked a spate of retaliatory murders, including his own. Body never found.

"The Wrong" Nicky Guido. Complete innocent misidentified as wiseguy Nicky Guido. Shot and killed in front of his house Christmas Day 1986.

Jimmy Bishop. Trade union official and Luchese associate. Confidential informant exposed by "the crystal ball." Subsequently murdered.

Otto Heidel and Dominic Costa. Members of the Bypass burglary gang, suspected of being informants. Heidel was murdered. Costa survived an attempted murder.

Anthony DiLapi. Member of Bronx faction of the Lucheses. Murdered in Hollywood, California.

Pasquale Varialle. Wannabe mobster. Shot in a Brooklyn garage on Valentine's Day 1987.

Eddie Lino. John Gotti confidant and Gambino made man. Shot and killed on the Belt Parkway.

Larry Taylor and Al "Flounderhead" Visconti. Lucheses shot and killed on Casso's orders in murder spree of 1991.

THE LAWYERS

Bruce Cutler. Loquacious mob lawyer, represented John Gotti for years. Author of memoir *Closing Argument* and fierce defender of mafia traditions. Represented Eppolito.

Eddie Hayes. Celebrity lawyer, sharp dresser, played the mafia lawyer in the closing credits of *Goodfellas*. Author of autobiography *Mouthpiece*. Inspiration for lawyer character in Tom Wolfe's *The Bonfire of the Vanities*. Represented Caracappa.

Mark Feldman. Chief of Organized Crime Section in the U.S. Attorney's Office for the Eastern District of New York. Longtime Brooklyn prosecutor experienced in mob cases.

Robert Henoch, Mitra Hormozi, and Daniel Wenner. Prosecutors charged with presenting the case against Eppolito and Caracappa.

THE JUDGE

Jack Weinstein. Eighty-four-year-old legal legend and author of leading reference on federal evidence. Presided over dozens of organized crime trials.

THE WITNESSES

Burton Kaplan. Seventy-two-year-old millionaire businessman, degenerate gambler, and longtime mafia associate. One of the most successful "fences" of stolen property in New York City. Convicted of dealing tons of marijuana and sentenced to twenty-seven years but still refused to cooperate.

Tommy Galpine. Pot dealer, cokehead, and Kaplan's right-hand man. Federal prisoner and cooperating witness.

Judd Burstein. Criminal defense attorney who represented Kaplan for many years. Told Kaplan when Casso became a cooperator.

Peter Franzone. Owner and operator of Brooklyn garage. Kept a murder there secret for twenty years.

Steven Corso. Convicted former certified public accountant from New York City, sent by the FBI to work as cooperating informant in Las Vegas. Purchased crystal meth from Caracappa and Eppolito and devised a plan to finance mafia-themed feature films written by Eppolito.

THE
BROTHERHOODS

PROLOGUE

At twilight on the evening of March 9, 2005, William Oldham sat in a rental car in a parking lot off the Las Vegas Strip. Oldham, a twenty-year veteran New York Police Department detective now working as an investigator with the U.S. Attorney's Office in Brooklyn, had traveled across the country to arrest Stephen Caracappa and Louis Eppolito, two former NYPD detectives who had worked as hit men for the mafia in the eighties and early nineties. Across the street was Piero's, an upscale Italian restaurant decorated in a style known as Mob Vegas and frequented by local wiseguys as well as by Robert De Niro and Joe Pesci during the filming of *Casino*. Oldham watched the exterior of the single-story restaurant patiently—the red neon sign, the two attendants standing at the valet parking stand, the sun setting in the cloudless desert sky. Oldham could wait. He had been investigating Caracappa and Eppolito for seven years, the longest case of his career. Oldham was fifty-one years old, drank too much, depleted, done. For years no one else had worked the case against Detectives Caracappa and Eppolito. Oldham had refused to drop it. No investigation had demanded as much from him—time, tenacity, every trick of the trade he'd acquired during a lifetime spent chasing criminals. If this was Oldham's longest and best case, it was also likely to be his last.

As Oldham watched, Caracappa and Eppolito pulled up to the valet parking area in an SUV with tinted windows, palmed the valet a few bucks, and walked toward the restaurant. Caracappa was dressed in a black pinstripe suit with wide lapels and a gold handkerchief tucked into the breast pocket. He walked with the self-conscious stride of a sixty-three-year-old mobbed-up dandy. Eppolito, a bodybuilder and a Mr. New York in his youth, was now nearly sixty and hugely overweight. He wore a tight-fitting double-breasted olive suit. He moved slowly but with a vestige of the strut he'd affected as a street cop. Oldham caught a glimpse of Eppolito's large gold-and-diamond pinkie ring with

1

the NYPD detective shield embossed on it. Oldham hadn't seen either man in more than a decade, since he had worked with Detective Caracappa in the elite Major Case Squad. But Caracappa and Eppolito looked the same to him, just older and paler, dressed like aging gangsters. The two retired detectives had no idea they were about to be arrested. As far as they knew, they were going to a meeting with a Vegas accountant with underworld connections to talk about drug money to be used for financing a feature film about the mafia that Eppolito had written.

Before Caracappa and Eppolito reached the restaurant's door, Oldham put his rental car into gear and lurched across the avenue, pulling up behind the SUV, blocking its escape. Three chase cars from the Drug Enforcement Agency screeched to a halt and blocked the driveway. Four DEA agents planted in the vestibule of Piero's rushed the two from the entrance. At the briefing that morning, when the protocol for the takedown was planned, Oldham had urged the agents to be careful. The targets were in poor health, Oldham said. Eppolito had undergone open-heart surgery weeks earlier. Caracappa had only one lung remaining. Oldham wanted to be sure the agents didn't scare Caracappa and Eppolito to death before they had a chance to go to jail. At Piero's, Eppolito and Caracappa were sprawled against a wall within seconds. Two DEA agents took Eppolito and spread his hands against the wall. Patting him down, they found a stainless-steel .45 semiautomatic tucked into his waistband. Eppolito was plainly dazed and disoriented. Caracappa, the tougher of the two, was impassive as he raised his arms above his head and turned in a circle. Oldham went for Caracappa's ankle, where Oldham knew from their time together in the NYPD he kept a pistol.

"It's been a long time coming," one of the DEA agents said to Eppolito.

"Yes, it has," Eppolito replied.

The supervising DEA agent began to recite the charges against Caracappa and Eppolito, a formality Oldham had never heard before. He had made hundreds of arrests over the years, a number of them involving some of the most dangerous criminals in the country, but he had never experienced anything like this takedown. There was a theatrical aspect to it, the submachine guns, the dozen agents now swarming Piero's, the elaborate radio communications. The federal agents were triumphant, thrilled to be part of the arrest of the two dirtiest cops in the history of the NYPD. But Oldham had worked on the case far too long to feel elation. As a detective, he loved the chase. Capture brought out more complex feelings. Caracappa and Eppolito were "Steve" and "Louie" to Old-ham—fellow NYPD detectives, no matter the crimes they had committed. Now he watched the two being led away by federal agents.

As headlines around the world reported the next day, the two "Mafia Cops" were killers who had used their detective shields to facilitate their crimes. Caracappa and Eppolito were indicted on eight counts of murder, as well as conspiracy to murder, attempted murder, obstruction of justice, kidnapping conspiracy, witness tampering, bribery, money laundering, and drug trafficking. The allegations defied belief. The detectives had been on the payroll of the mafia for more than ten years. Witnesses, cooperators, mobsters, and innocents had been murdered as a result of their criminal actions. Detectives Caracappa and Eppolito weren't beat cops. Caracappa had been one of the leading detectives in the forty-thousand-strong NYPD. He was an authority on organized crime, and had been assigned to the Organized Crime Homicide Unit. Amazingly, audaciously, he had been the self-appointed detective in charge of gathering intelligence and monitoring the activities of the Luchese crime family—*the very family for whom he secretly worked.* Eppolito, a former detective in the 62nd and 63rd Precincts in mob-dominated sections of Brooklyn, claimed to be the eleventh most decorated cop in the history of the force. He was also the son of a Gambino "made man" and wore the heavy gold jewelry of a wiseguy while he was a detective. Eppolito had been accused and found not guilty in 1984 of providing police files to a Gambino capo under investigation—an experience Eppolito described in detail in *Mafia Cop,* the book he wrote after retiring from the NYPD. For decades Eppolito flaunted his association with organized crime, proclaimed his innocence, and defended the honor of *cosa nostra.* Eppolito had even played a bit role as a mobster in the movie *Goodfellas* before attempting to make a career as an actor and writer specializing in mob tales.

The case against Caracappa and Eppolito dated back more than a decade. The investigation Oldham led had proven to be a complex weave of dogged detective work, patience, luck, and finally the persuasion of a criminal mastermind to turn against the two cops he "ran" for the mafia. Finding proof was maddening and irresistible—evidence always seemed close enough to touch but just out of reach. Suspicions about the cops first crystallized in the spring of 1994 when Luchese underboss Anthony "Gaspipe" Casso "flipped" and started to cooperate with the federal government while in custody awaiting trial on multiple murder and racketeering counts. Casso explained the deal he had struck with Detectives Caracappa and Eppolito. In return for a "pad" of $4,000 a month, Casso told FBI agents and prosecutors, the two NYPD detectives had provided him information on law enforcement investigations and informants. Casso explained that he had also hired Caracappa and Eppolito as hit men, ultimately paying them more than $350,000 in total on behalf of the Luchese crime family. The money was paid through a go-between, a millionaire mob associate named Burton Kaplan. "The cops," as they were known to the leadership of the Luchese family, gave up snitches, tipped off raids, and shared the most sensitive police intelligence with the mob. Casso called Detectives Caracappa and Eppolito his "crystal ball" because they could foretell the future: who was informing, who was going to be arrested and indicted, who needed to be killed.

The allegations appeared in the New York tabloids in 1994, and became infamous in law enforcement circles. It was widely known throughout the NYPD that there had been leaks in a large number of organized crime investigations over the years. The problem was endemic, and deadly. The suspicions divided the department. Speculation circulated in all quarters about who might be responsible for the leaks. Theories ran the gamut, from mailroom employees in headquarters to detective squad commanders on Staten Island. Some detectives thought Caracappa or Eppolito were guilty. Some refused to believe that any of their brother officers would commit such crimes. Like many other cops at the time, Oldham assumed justice would be sure for Detectives Caracappa and Eppolito. Yet year after year, no charges were brought. Oldham watched as cases were started and abandoned. Incredibly, there were no methodical investigations of Casso's allegations—not by the FBI, the U.S. Attorney's Office in New York, or the NYPD itself.

Detectives Caracappa and Eppolito eventually retired to Las Vegas, to homes across the street from each other on a quiet cul-de-sac in a gated community—each under the watchful gaze of the other.

They had appeared to have gotten away with murder—they had "skated."

Finally in 1997, Oldham took up the case himself, figuring that if he didn't pursue Caracappa and Eppolito no one would. Working alone, for the most part, he gathered evidence and interviewed witnesses and chased down leads. Within months he was convinced that Caracappa and Eppolito were guilty. But there was a difference between knowing "the cops" were guilty and being able to prove it beyond a reasonable doubt. The case held many mysteries. How did Detectives Caracappa and Eppolito operate? Why did the FBI never bring charges? Gaspipe Casso was a psychopath and a professional killer, but did that mean he was a liar? How could Oldham convince Burton Kaplan, serving a long stretch in federal prison on a drug conviction, to cooperate? For years Oldham accumulated evidence, storing it in cardboard boxes stacked in the corner of his office. The boxes were filled with murder files and arrest records and a beaten-up copy of *Mafia Cop*. Tapes of prison telephone calls and surveillance videos were stored in the boxes, as well as thousands of pages of confessions of wiseguys who had flipped and become witnesses for the government—men with names like "Fat Pete" Chiodo, and "Little Al" D'Arco. Each document was potentially essential to solving the enormous puzzle—but a piece was still missing.

When Oldham retired from the NYPD in the aftermath of the attacks of September 11, 2001, he took his files with him to his new job with the U.S. Department of Justice. Oldham was now an investigator in the Violent Criminal Enterprise and Terrorism unit. He was one of the most senior and seasoned law enforcement investigators in the country, with the freedom to pursue cases he thought worthwhile. Oldham worked on domestic and international organized criminal conspiracies—all the while quietly continuing his long-term investigation of Caracappa and Eppolito.

Finally, in the spring of 2004, a small group of detectives and investigators, experienced in Brooklyn and most retired or nearly retired, came together to work on the investigation. Oldham called them "the cadre." They all had a personal connection to the case. They knew Detectives Caracappa and Eppolito, or their victims. The men in the cadre belonged to the generation of New York City law enforcement betrayed by their brother detectives in the most profound way possible. They were determined to see that justice was done. All of the voluminous information Oldham had gathered over the years was examined anew. More evidence was uncovered. Compelling connections between "the cops" and long-forgotten murders were unearthed. Even with the accumulated facts, Oldham knew the case needed someone inside the conspiracy to describe how it had really worked. He needed a cooperator to take the disparate strands of the case and pull them together. He needed a storyteller.

Oldham got one. The arrests of Caracappa and Eppolito soon followed. A year later their trial was held in a courtroom on the fourth floor of the federal courthouse in Brooklyn. Detectives Eppolito and Caracappa protested their innocence. Press from around the world gathered to watch two famous New York City defense lawyers try to match wits with federal prosecutors and expose holes in the government's case. For a month, NYPD detectives and federal agents testified, as did wiseguys, wannabes, parking lot attendants, a crooked accountant, Eppolito's former mistress, a defense attorney, and Burton Kaplan, the man code-named "The Eagle" by Caracappa and Eppolito. On April 6, 2006, the jury read its verdict aloud in court: guilty on all counts.

This book is the inside account of the successful investigation Oldham led into the worst corruption case in the history of the NYPD. It is also an account of the last great mob conspiracy. It is a tale that goes to the hearts of two brotherhoods—the police and the mafia—and the two cops who belonged to both.

CHAPTER ONE

THE HOOK

On the morning of Sunday, November 27, 1989, just after first light, the call came over Detective William Oldham's radio. "Ten-thirty," the dispatcher said. "Robbery in progress, 560 Wadsworth Avenue, cross streets 183 to 184, apartment 5G." Oldham was pulling out of the precinct parking lot on Broadway and 182nd Street in the Washington Heights section of upper Manhattan on his way to breakfast at his favorite diner. A Sunday-morning robbery was unusual, Oldham knew, and 7 a.m. was far too early for most criminals to be out and about. The call sounded like it matched a pattern of impersonator robberies he had been working for months. Two male Dominicans, mid-thirties, one short and muscular and carrying a large black automatic, the other tall and skinny and armed with a silver revolver, were robbing drug dealers by impersonating NYPD narcotics detectives. They operated first thing in the morning, like real cops out to hit a stash house, giving themselves the element of surprise and the appearance of authenticity. The performance of the impersonators was so convincing that the victims sometimes couldn't tell if they were being stuck up by cops or robbers.

Oldham turned uptown and picked up his radio. "Three-Four RIP responding," he said. The 34th Precinct, or Three-Four, covered the west side of upper Manhattan in a stretch from 155th Street to 225th Street, making it one of the largest precincts in the city. Oldham was assigned to Three-Four RIP, the Robbery Identification Program. In the late eighties, the area known as Washington Heights was the cocaine capital of the United States, making it one of the most dangerous and crime-ridden places anywhere. Crack, the admixture of baking soda and coke that makes a crackling sound when cooked (thus the name "crack"), was invented on the streets of Washington Heights. A predominantly Hispanic neighborhood, the avenues were lined with grand old nineteenth-century apartment buildings fallen on hard times. Known as Little Dominica, the area was densely populated, saturated with restaurants, money remittance shops, and bodegas, many of them fronts for laundering illegal money made by peddling cocaine. Dealers were everywhere, operating openly on stoops and in lobbies and on street corners. The police in the Three-Four were overwhelmed, so there was no shortage of action for an ambitious young detective like Oldham.

A "pattern" amounted to two, three, or more robberies with the same modus operandi and physical descriptions of the suspects. Oldham had been investigating these particular impersonators for months. The last robbery in the pattern had occurred a week earlier, another dawn raid of a drug dealer's residence. Oldham had arrived at the scene of that crime as the ambulance pulled up. The dealer was discovered dead, his back welted with burn marks. His daughter, a five-year-old, had her mouth and eyes duct-taped, and had been hog-tied by her ankles and wrists. Oldham had tests run on the hair and fibers on the duct tape. He had canvassed the streets for witnesses. He had talked to his CIs—confidential informants. He had used the descriptions of the perps to eliminate other robberies he thought were unrelated—some of them possibly the work of real cops, in particular a police unit nicknamed "local motion."

The investigation revealed that the pattern crew operated like narcotics detectives. They talked to their snitches in the neighborhood, gathered intelligence on dealers, sat in cars on upper Broadway running surveillance. They went after crack dealers, money launderers, people who ran the local *su-sus*—the informal banks where the poor people of Little Dominica borrowed small sums of money. The impersonators were often mistaken around the neighborhood for real plainclothes cops. They had detective shields, scanners, NYPD raid jackets, bulletproof vests in case they got in a shootout with the drug dealers—or the cops who came to arrest them. They often forced the doors of apartments, weapons drawn, and entered with the speed and precision of experienced detectives. Once inside, they rousted the bleary-eyed dealers and worked methodically. First they cuffed their victims with the cheap toy metal cuffs for sale in local bodegas—the cops called them Mickey Mouse cuffs. They duct-taped the dealers' mouths. They gathered the occupants into one room, leaving a member of the crew to guard the prisoners while the others conducted the search for a "trap"—the compartment built under the floorboards or into a closet or wall where cash and cocaine were stored. *Dondé están las drogas*? they yelled. Where are the drugs? *Dondé está la caja*? Where is the money box?

Impersonator robberies had become a plague in Washington Heights in the late eighties, going down once or twice a day. It was impossible to know the true numbers because the victims were often drug dealers and they would rarely report a robbery, unless a neighbor called 911 or they were shot or stabbed or a large amount of money or drugs was taken — and the sums involved were frequently huge, involving hundreds of thousands of dollars and kilograms of cocaine. For the most part, the so-called victims would take care of the problem themselves by trying to find out who had ripped them off and going after them themselves. The main reason the robberies came to the attention of the police at all was that midlevel dealers needed to get a complaint report number from the police so they could prove to their suppliers they had truly been stuck-up. Having been fronted drugs with little or no money down, as was a common practice in the cocaine business, the dealers were terrified that their wholesalers would think they had staged the robbery themselves to avoid payment.

Oldham's crew of impersonators were particularly vicious. If the dealers resisted, or refused to give up their trap, the crew tortured them. The Dominicans — "Domos," cops in the Three-Four called them — used hot irons and knives heated on stoves to burn the backs of the dealers. Once, they drilled a three-inch drill bit into the back of a man's head and left it there after they fled with his stash. In the end, if the dealers still wouldn't give away their trap, the perps might shoot everyone in the apartment, murdering three and four people at a time.

By mid-November, the impersonator pattern had gone fallow. It was one of three patterns Oldham was working, along with a dozen single robberies of liquor stores and bodegas in the neighborhood. Cases came and went in the normal rhythm of the robbery squad in the Three-Four. Waiting for a break was a big part of police work. There was pressure from superior officers to close cases quickly — to say a complainant was uncooperative, or all leads had been exhausted, or to reclassify the pattern as larceny or burglary so it was no longer on the books of the Robbery Squad. But Oldham dragged cases out. It was his nature. He didn't see the point of getting rid of cases. The aim was to solve the problem, not accumulate good stats or impress the bosses. The longer he had to look at a case the more he would understand the pattern and its elements. Playing for time gave him greater odds of getting lucky. Not an early riser, Oldham had come to work early that Sunday morning by chance but he was still thinking about the pattern and he was ready to take advantage of a break. Luck was like that: you make your own.

The call to Wadsworth and 183rd Street was only three blocks north of the precinct house. Oldham sped through the deserted Sunday-morning streets, making it to the job in under sixty seconds. The building was an eight-story tenement, with a dingy, cavernous yellowed marble lobby covered with graffiti. There was an elevator but Oldham didn't take it; he didn't want the elevator to open and find himself face-to-face with the bad guys. Oldham drew his gun, a five-shot Smith & Wesson, and took the stairs up five flights. He stood outside the door of apartment 5G listening. Inside, a man was screaming in Spanish. He was being beaten and pleading for his life.

Waiting for backup, Oldham had no way of knowing exactly what was going on inside the apartment. Two uniformed officers responding to the call emerged from the stairway and joined Oldham in the hallway. Oldham banged on the door loudly and identified himself: *Police! Policía!* The screaming stopped. A few seconds passed and then the door opened. Oldham and the two other cops backed away, guns aimed at the door. A heavyset Dominican man, bleeding profusely from the head, his hands cuffed behind him, was shoved out and fell to the floor. The door shut again. One of the uniformed cops started kicking and beating the victim for no apparent reason other than the fact that he was probably a drug dealer and, therefore, no victim at all. Oldham turned for a moment and watched the random, brutal violence—the kind of thing that happened in the Three-Four all the time—and returned to the door and the job. Usually, when the police arrived at an apartment, the perps knew there was no way to escape and would give up. This time, it was going to take force to get whoever was in there out.

Oldham signaled and stepped aside and let one of the uniformed cops kick the door open with one sharp blow near the lock. A dimly lit twenty-foot hallway lay ahead, bathroom to the left, living room at the end. Oldham and the other cop entered the hallway. Police working Washington Heights made forced entries often. The frequency and routine led to a dangerous nonchalance. Oldham had not waited for more backup. He did not gain cover by taking the bathroom first. The truth was that he was half expecting to find real narcotics detectives in the apartment. Making his way along the hall, the last thing Oldham wanted was to get in a shootout with fellow officers.

As Oldham neared the living room, a man stepped into the hallway and pointed his gun at Oldham's chest. Oldham registered nothing about the man's appearance: he stared directly at the mouth of a black automatic. The man pulled the trigger.

Click. The gun misfired.

It was the clearest sound Oldham had heard in his life.

In a panic, he turned and ran. He had been shot at four times as a cop, and he had shot at perps twice—and it wasn't the first time he had run away from a man with a gun—but there was no time to feel anything but blind terror. Tripping on one of the uniformed cops as he fled, Oldham shot wildly over his shoulder in the direction of the bad guy and leapt through the door.

In the hallway, Oldham called the dispatcher. "Three-Four RIP shots fired," he said. "Shots fired."

In minutes, the building was swarmed by police. "We fucked up," Oldham said to the uniformed cop who had followed him into the apartment, both of them out of breath from the close call. The police sent to cover the rear exit radioed Oldham and said they had found an injured male lying in a bloody heap in the courtyard facedown on top of a silver gun. One of the robbers had climbed out the window of the living room onto the ledge in an attempt to hide; he had lost his grip and fallen five floors. So there was one less bad guy in the apartment. "We have to go back in," Oldham said to the two uniformed cops. Reluctantly, they reentered, this time creeping along the hallway and taking cover in the bathroom. *Policía*, Oldham yelled. *Dame la pistola!* Give me the pistol!

A gun skittered across the floor of the living room into the hall—a black automatic.

Oldham entered the room and found Jorge Ramone standing with his hands raised toward the ceiling. An NYPD raid jacket and bulletproof vest and detective shield were on the floor. Ramone was cuffed and taken away by the two uniformed cops, who beat him as they left the apartment. Oldham sat by himself on a plastic-covered love seat and waited for the duty captain to arrive. After an officer discharged his weapon there was always an investigation to ensure the officer wasn't drunk, drugged, psychotic. Oldham felt blessed. He was alive. No one had been shot. The bad guys were going to jail. But he also wondered how his job had turned into such a swirl of contradictions.

"I loved being a cop. I loved everything about it. I loved the uniform when I was in uniform. I was an armed social worker, psychologist, vigilante. People come to New York City from all over the world to become actors and musicians and Wall Street brokers. I didn't want to be famous or rich. I wanted to put people in jail. The attraction for me was the crime. New York was the financial and cultural center of the world, but it was also the criminal center of the world. What made people afraid of the city was the draw for me. Crime was everywhere, but in New York City it was for real. Criminals were smart and resourceful and determined. Crime was *organized*."

Oldham was an unlikely cop, by class, culture, and education. He had spent his earliest years in the leafy suburbs of Haverford, Pennsylvania, a town along Philadelphia's Main Line, one of the wealthiest areas in the country, while his father went to medical school at the University of Pennsylvania. The family then moved to the suburbs of Washington, D.C. He attended the prestigious Quaker school Sidwell Friends, along with Bobby Kennedy's kids, and spent his summers at an exclusive suburban country club, which he boycotted as a teenager because it excluded blacks from membership. In the early sixties, Oldham's father went to work for the U.S. Agency for International Development (USAID), the goodwill arm of the State Department, and moved to Vietnam to set up hospitals for wounded civilians. Oldham was sent to high school in Taiwan, where he learned to speak Mandarin, and afterward to boarding school in New Delhi, India. Upon graduating from high school in 1971 and returning to America, Oldham learned his younger brother, Ben, was dying of brain cancer. The two set out with Oldham's best friend, Bim, to travel through Europe together. Always an outsider, required by circumstances to take on the responsibilities of an adult while still a boy, Oldham was forced to learn hard truths early in life. "My brother didn't die quietly. He was angry and difficult and headstrong. I loved him and I knew he deserved better care than I could offer, but that wasn't going to happen. At a young age I was disabused of the romantic ideas of youth." A year later his brother went on to Nepal to die in his father's home.

Back in America, an eighteen-year-old cut loose from his family, Oldham drifted and wandered through the early seventies. He got a job refurbishing antiques for the White House and Smithsonian. He dodged the draft for the Vietnam War, refusing to register. He painted houses and waited tables and managed a stereo store. In 1974, after he was arrested for having an open container of alcohol in a public place, Oldham served three days in county jail in Florida. Soon thereafter, his life took a sudden and unexpected turn. In 1975, he joined the Washington, D.C., police force. "To this day I really don't know why I did it. All I knew about being a policeman came from the movies. I had barely met a cop in my life. I've thought about it a lot and never figured it out. I knew I didn't enjoy being arrested, I wanted to do the arresting. Public service work was ingrained in my family. Doing good, as corny as it sounds, mattered. As soon as I got on the street, I found being a cop was fascinating, especially for a young white kid in a city where black and white rarely mixed—it was the chocolate city and its vanilla suburbs."

In the seventies a heroin epidemic was burning through Washington, D.C., and people were dying left and right—Oldham once handled three murders in a single night. He was young-looking, five-eleven, and only 125 pounds. He had the body of a starving junkie. He volunteered to go undercover. Oldham bought heroin from dozens of people. Some of the heroin was so pure the Drug Enforcement Agency started surveilling him to see where he was buying it. "The DEA almost got me killed. They were so obviously set up on me that it tipped the dealers off I was a cop. By the time I was done with that case, thirty-three people were in jail and I had shut down a Thai distribution network operating out of a gas station. But I hated undercover work. I got tired of lying to people and pretending to be friends to people I wasn't. I went back to patrol. Pretty soon I began to see that in D.C. crime wasn't interesting enough. It was the same murders over and over again. Domestic disputes ending in violence. Fights over small amounts of drugs. Killings over street dice games. There was no variation, no story to it. Crime was rampant but organized crime was nonexistent. I wasn't learning anything. I started thinking about moving to New York or Los Angeles, the crime capitals. I applied to both police forces and was accepted by both, but it really wasn't a close decision in the end. L.A. was attractive but the pull of New York was too strong. The close urban structure of the city was appealing. Cultures rubbed up against one another—legitimate and criminal. If you did a Chinese gang case in New York, it was like traveling to a foreign country. You ate the food, met the women, got immersed in the culture. New York had diversity, variety, and scope."

Oldham joined the NYPD in 1981 and moved to an apartment in Hell's Kitchen on the west side of Manhattan. The modern age of the gangster was at its peak in the early eighties, before law enforcement and drugs took their toll on organized crime. The city was carved up into territories. Rackets overlapped—drugs, gambling, loan-sharking, extortion—but ethnic gangs catered to their respective ethnic populations and the turf boundaries were clear. The Westies, an extremely violent Irish gang who sometimes did "wet work" for the Gambinos, controlled Hell's Kitchen. Uptown, in Harlem, the West Brothers, the Vigilantes, and PC Boys fought for streets and corners. Colombians ran College Point and Elmhurst. The Ghost Shadows and Flying Dragons dominated Chinatown. And in Brooklyn and Staten Island and Little Italy and the

Bronx and Queens—everywhere in the city, and in every racket worth working—there were the five families of the New York mafia, by far the largest, most sophisticated organized crime enterprises.

From his first day in the police academy in New York, Oldham was an outsider. He wasn't a native New Yorker. He wasn't Italian or Irish, and therefore didn't belong to either of the tribes who ran the law enforcement establishment. As a general rule, uptown and the Bronx were predominantly policed by cops with Irish blood, and Brooklyn and Staten Island were considered Italian territory. Queens was a mix. The smaller but important groups in the force—black, Hispanic, Asian, women—all had benevolent associations to look out for their own. As a young WASP male, Oldham was in a tiny minority. He rarely socialized with other cops. Broke, he spent his days off in the reading rooms of the New York Public Library and he went to night school at Hunter College to take courses on logic and Shakespeare and Milton's *Paradise Lost*—and to meet girls. Oldham didn't go to bars like the Seventeen Steps, so named because it was precisely seventeen steps from the front door of the Three-Four station house. He didn't go to the parties they called ten-thirteens—radio code for "officer in distress." He didn't go to funerals or barbecues. He kept his work and private life separate. Oldham knew what he didn't want to be under any circumstances—a rat!

"In the academy in New York, when you're training to become a cop, sometimes 'the brass' takes you aside and asks if you to want to be what they call a 'field associate.' They make it sound like you're going to be a special undercover cop, the eyes and ears of the department, a crusader fighting corruption. They promise you'll quickly become a detective. But really you'll just be snitching on other cops. You'll tell them cops are drinking beer in the locker room. Cops are taking money. Getting laid at lunch. Sticking up drug dealers. I passed. I didn't join the police department to police the police. All I knew was I wanted to arrest bad guys. And New York City had plenty of bad guys."

Oldham's first assignment was foot patrol in Times Square. The area was radically different in the early eighties with 42nd Street—"the quarter and the deuce"—packed with peep shows and perverts and junkies. There were more than two thousand murders a year in New York City in those years, and twenty thousand shootings and stabbings. "I was afraid to walk along 42nd Street—and I was carrying a gun," Oldham recalled. "Organized criminals weren't the danger. It was the wolf packs gone wilding in the streets, or kids on a crack attack. They would kill you if you weren't careful and smart. I had a six-shot in my holster and I had a five-shot in my pants pocket, but that wouldn't be enough against a wolf pack if they wanted to wrestle you for it. I always had my hand on my pocket gun when I walked patrol."

After six months on a foot beat, Oldham was transferred to the Two-Four, a precinct that covered the Upper West Side of Manhattan from 86th Street to 110th Street. It was supposed to be a favor for a young cop, with the neighborhood's singles bars and reputation for pretty women. The Two-Four had crime but it was tame compared to other parts of the city, and Oldham agitated for more action. Farther uptown, in Harlem, the Two-Eight was the smallest precinct in the city, but in 1983 it had the most murders. The two precincts shared a radio band and Oldham listened longingly to the calls coming in from the Two-Eight—shootings, stabbings, beatings. He was dying to be in the thick of it. "Then I got lucky. A female officer I knew in the Two-Eight, the only woman in the precinct, was being dogged to death by the other cops. They would give her bad posts, like standing on the corner of 116th and 8th Avenue by herself, which was a truly frightening place to be then. Her partner would take off in the car from a call, as a joke, and leave her standing alone at the scene to walk back to the precinct. If there was a DOA in an apartment, she would be assigned to guard the corpse, and in those days that meant sitting with a putrefying body for twenty-four hours or longer before the meat wagon turned up. The stench was awful. Eventually, this woman took herself hostage in the 'ladies' locker room of the precinct. It was a break for me. I offered to do a 'mutual' with her—to swap precincts. Nobody was trying to get into the Two-Eight. Everyone was trying to get out. But I wanted to be there. I wanted to be busy. Cops were called 'rollers,' and I wanted to rock and roll."

The Two-Eight station house was at 121st Street and Adam Clayton Powell Boulevard, a new concrete, prisonlike, triangular building that took up the whole block; the previous precinct house had been burned to the ground. Inside, the station was a madhouse. A uniformed cop working station house duty at the door named Spuds McCormack would pull his gun on Oldham when he arrived for a shift. "Slap leather or draw!" McCormack would call, with a beer in one hand, and then he actually drew and Oldham was supposed to beat him to the draw. At the desk, neighborhood residents would argue their cases in front of the desk lieutenant who served as the judge and jury. "He decided there and then who was arrested and charged and who was let go. Screaming and fighting and crying and domestic disputes constantly echoed through the precinct house. In the back there was a kitchen where cops drank beer and ate hot dogs. The commanding officer of the precinct was only seen when he would turn up once a week, dressed in a Hawaiian shirt, to collect his pay. Downstairs there were bunk beds and lockers and showers, where cops estranged from their wives lived for months at a time. In the basement next to the lounge was an escape tunnel, built in anticipation of the station house being burned down again.

"There were shootouts on the street all the time. 'Exchanges of gunfire,' as we said in police reports. If a perp in a cell was taking a beating, no one would even look up. If a cop was troubled—too violent, drunk, burned out—he would be taken off the street and assigned to sweep the floor or work security in the station house. Every precinct had two guys like that—the Mop and the Broom, they were called, the Man on Post and the Station House Sweeper. It was a different time. Cops looked after cops, even if that meant looking the other way. The truth is that I liked cops. A lot made substantial sacrifices. They were away from their families. They got shot. Many of them got hurt really badly—hit by a car, stomped by a gang, stuff like responding to a domestic disturbance and the old lady throws hot grease on you because she doesn't like the way you're beating her husband who just got through beating her. They weren't heroes, you don't get a medal or a promotion for that, but I really admired those guys."

The NYPD was a society within a society, forty thousand cops living in their own city-size world. In many parts of New York, particularly black and Hispanic areas, the NYPD was an army of occupation. Most of the cops were white, many from towns outside the city, and they had no clue about urban life, few street smarts, and little sense of proportion when dealing with humanity in all of its complexities. Oldham immersed himself in the city, living in Harlem and Chinatown and the East Village. He felt at home. He liked the pace of the streets, the Indian and Chinese restaurants, new-wave clubs on the Lower East Side. His friends were reporters, artists, and dancers—circles that few cops moved in. He hated it but he was always known as "Bill the cop" by his Manhattan friends. The precinct houses, courts, and Rikers Island jail were part of New York's underworld, little known to outsiders, but Oldham was interested in people of all kinds—Wall Street brokers, fashion designers, chefs. The endless supply of characters and contradictions drew him ever further into life in New York.

But being a cop in the city did not protect Oldham from the dangers elsewhere. On September 1, 1983, he lost his second brother, John, who was a passenger on Korean Airlines Flight 007, the airplane infamously shot down by Russian fighter jets over the Sea of Japan. "John was a Fulbright scholar. He was a star student at Andover, Princeton, and Columbia Law School. He was flying to China to teach for a year. He was my second brother to die—I had no others. My brothers meant everything to me. John and I had a close relationship. We were competitive. He was a straight arrow, the smartest kid in class, the one you could rely on. I was wild, lost. I was stricken. They took me off the street until I got better."

In the Two-Eight as part of the duty chart for NYPD patrol, Oldham had to work midnights one week out of every six. Historically, cops who chose to work steady midnights wanted to operate without supervision. The midnight shift at the Two-Eight was no different. Drug robberies, or "rips," by the police were common occurrences and many of the cops on the midnight shift in the Two-Eight wound up in jail. "If the cops knew there was a dealer doing business and there was a lot of money in a particular apartment, they had to invent probable cause to gain entry. They would have their wives or girlfriends call 911 and report, 'There's a man beating his wife in apartment 3D.' The cops sat in their car in front of the building for a couple of minutes. The call went out from the radio operator for a 10–34—assault in progress—in apartment 3D. The cops would pick up the radio and say, 'I'll take it.' One minute later they're in, no warrant, no probable cause, no witnesses. They'd clean it out and take off."

Oldham knew what was going on, or at least he had a good idea, but he was never invited into the inner circles. The truth was that he didn't care. Not really. There was a difference between stealing a drug dealer's money and a cop taking the dealer's drugs and becoming a dealer himself. Even so, Oldham had never snitched on another cop, just as he had never worked on an investigation into police corruption. He didn't aspire to be Frank Serpico, the NYPD undercover cop who risked his life to reveal pervasive corruption on the force in the late sixties and early seventies. *Serpico,* the movie, had been part of Oldham's inspiration to become a cop. It was the man's independence and integrity he admired, not his self-righteousness nor the crusade to free the NYPD of corruption. The distinction came naturally to Oldham. "I thought of myself as honest. There were plenty of cops sticking up dealers, but most of them were pretty good cops. I know that doesn't make sense, but there was a lot of gray area and that's where most of us had to live. I didn't have a family, four kids, trying to survive on a patrolman's salary. I wasn't holier-than-thou."

The cops on midnights at the Two-Eight were always on the lookout for any clue that there was a field associate in the precinct who might rat on them. Oldham seemed a likely sort. He was a loner. They nicknamed him Sid Vicious. He had spiked hair and he was skinny and he had a reputation for being unusual upon arrival. Oldham and his partner were constantly waved off jobs when they worked midnights. It happened so often that Oldham took to keeping a small black-and-white television set in the patrol car. His partner was straight as well, as clean as the night was long, and the two of them would watch movies to while away the hours, biding their time until they were cycled out of midnights.

While he was responding to an overdose in a building at 116th Street and 8th Avenue one midnight, Oldham's TV was stolen from the patrol car. It had to be a desperate junkie; no one in his right mind would be foolish enough to steal from a police car in the Two-Eight. When Oldham's shift ended, the cops going out on the day shift got word of the theft. They shut down 8th Avenue for four blocks and went into the street with "hats and bats"—helmets and sticks. The cops beat everyone: junkies, dealers, kids hanging out on the corner. Oldham's television wasn't the point. Power was the point. The precinct cops were telling the dealers and junkies that they were never ever to fuck with the police. *Never. Ever.* Oldham got a call that morning from the desk sergeant saying that he had received calls offering expensive color TVs and cash for a replacement. The upheaval in the neighborhood was interfering with the drug trade and the dealers wanted to get back to business. Oldham told the sergeant he just wanted his TV back. He didn't want more than had been taken. Later, there was another call and a cop was sent to an apartment building on West 117th Street. The cop knocked on the door of the apartment. A door down the hall opened and a black hand emerged with a bag containing a small black-and-white TV, brand and size matched exactly to Oldham's. Inside was a note, "If you need accessories call this number."

Corruption was pervasive in the force despite occasional attempts at reform. As a result, corruption inevitably became a factor in Oldham's career path—not as a temptation but as something he had to be careful to avoid. He had long accepted that promotions in the NYPD were based on politics, connections, connivance. To get ahead, a cop needed a "hook"— someone higher in the hierarchy to pull him upward. Oldham's hook was his lieutenant in the Two-Eight. In 1983, the Two-Eight came to national attention when a black Baptist minister was pulled over by the police and badly beaten. A federal congressional inquiry into police brutality followed, which led to the revelation of the corruption of the midnight shift. But before the inquiry began, Oldham's hook had him transferred to the Manhattan North Task Force. It was a way of protecting Oldham from the coming scandal, which could hurt the young cop's reputation. Oldham was moved to the Intelligence Division, working on desks assigned to monitor violence in the Jewish and black communities, and then transferred to the Diplomatic Protection Unit guarding heads of state. He had a spell in the robbery squad in Queens and was shifted back to Manhattan Robbery before returning to the Three-Four RIP.

Oldham was thought of as someone who moved around a lot. He was restless. But he had good numbers—he had jailed more than a hundred criminals since he joined. Oldham knew the force wasn't a meritocracy. Politicking was how officers frequently got ahead in the NYPD. The way a cop got a decoration or medal was to write a report about his own hero-ics. The identity of an officer's hook was a closely guarded secret. Oldham did well in the force but he didn't play the game.

Throughout the seventies and eighties, the government of New York City lurched from financial crisis to crisis. The NYPD was often short-changed, with the consequence that fiscal constraints determined the number of promotions given out. Finally, in June 1987, Oldham was pro-moted to detective. He had not campaigned for the promotion, as many officers did. He enjoyed uniform work and patrolling the streets. But as soon as he started working as a detective, he discovered he had found his true calling in life. "I was born to be a detective. In my family nothing was ever quite the way it seemed. My father set up hospitals for civilian war casualties in Asia during the Vietnam War. It wasn't said but clearly the projects were funded by the CIA. He had two families, one family in Viet-nam and one in a safe haven. My mother later worked for a naval intelli-gence agency in Washington. She was a Southern belle, with genteel manners, but she knew how to find weakness and exploit it. That is a very useful quality to have as a detective. All the moving around as a kid taught me to size up new environments quickly. I listened, watched, tried to figure how things worked. What piece was missing, or hidden, or illusive. How to lay down the last piece of the puzzle."

Cops and criminals were supposed to be enemies, but in many ways they reflected one another. For generations, the most corrupting influence on the police was crime that seemed victimless: gambling, prostitution, bootlegged liquor. Some cops were grass-eaters, paid to graze on the bribes and look the other way. It was easy for an officer to convince him-self that no harm was done by allowing a willing adult to lay a bet or take a drink, and so it followed there was no harm in skimming a few bucks from the enterprise. But every wave of drugs that washed over the city came with its own particular flotsam of crime. By the end of the eighties, the drugs and cash in Washington Heights had brought out the worst in people. Blood and money flowed in the gutters. The sums of money involved in illegal drugs were enormous. While neighborhoods and lives were torn apart, for some it was a gold rush, including members of the NYPD. Grass-eaters became meat-eaters, out on the street hunting money and coke like the criminals.

"The sentences for drugs were severe. If a dealer got banged out for drugs, he was going away for twenty years. This changed the way dealers did business. People snitched and gave people away to save their own skin. In response, dealers went to work in cells. The same thing happened with cops. Guys hung tight in small units. They didn't rely on a pad paid to everyone in the precinct the way it had gone for decades. Corruption was entrepreneurial. It was every cop out for himself. If a cop took a hit and was arrested, he couldn't rat out a whole precinct or shift. The stickups were secret—but an open secret. I didn't know for sure who was sticking up dealers, and no one was going to tell me. I wondered how many cops came to the Three-Four to make money.

"The atmosphere of corruption infected the force, and cast suspicion over a lot of innocent cops. I never took a dime but was accused of taking money from a drug dealer, after I arrested a dealer named John John Smith at 156th and Broadway. He was one of the original crack dealers, one of the first to use closed-circuit TV to watch us watching him. I fucked with him unmercifully. We would paint the lenses of his cameras. Roust his street touts. His mother was part of the crew. She ran a little candy store on Amsterdam Avenue and I'd spend time there just to disrupt their routine. After a while, when their patience ran out, Smith decided he wanted to get rid of me. The easiest way to get a cop was to make an Internal Affairs complaint, saying he was dirty. His mother made the complaint. She said I had stolen money from the candy store. The complaint was unsubstantiated. That didn't mean it was false, or that I was found not guilty. The finding meant it couldn't be proved or disproved. A lot of things went like that in the Three-Four."

By the end of 1989, Oldham had learned to appear to be turning a blind eye to his surroundings while keeping both eyes wide open. Earlier that year he worked a pattern of knifepoint robberies on the west side of Washington Heights. The perp waited inside the lobby of large apartment buildings standing at the top of the steps to the basement. As a woman entered alone he would run to the basement and push the elevator button.

When the woman got on the elevator it would first go down to the basement. The robber would be waiting, knife out, as the doors opened. The pattern included opportunistic rapes and sexual abuse. After a particularly vicious attack, Oldham questioned the victim. He showed her the mug shot books in the Three-Four. She was an extremely motivated witness. She wanted her attacker caught and punished. After an hour of looking through photos she picked a light-skinned Hispanic man named Hector Moreno. Oldham didn't like using the photo books for IDs as a rule; the books were filled with photographs of neighborhood criminals, and the sight of faces was highly suggestive to witnesses. He believed victims too often selected the face in the mug book that most resembled the perp, and not the actual perp.

Oldham found Hector Moreno and arrested him. It seemed a straightforward case. Oldham did a lineup at the precinct. Five "fillers" of similar age and race were collected from a homeless shelter and brought into a room with a two-way mirror. The witness viewed the lineup and identified Moreno. Oldham interviewed Moreno after the lineup. He told Oldham he was a drug dealer—a rare confession—but not a robber or rapist. Oldham checked out his story. Everything he said appeared to be true. Moreno had a nice car. He lived in a nice apartment. He had no reputation in the neighborhood as a stickup guy or a sexual predator. The lineup identification by the victim was persuasive but not decisive. Just because Moreno was a drug dealer didn't mean he was a liar, or Oldham's knifepoint-pattern perp.

"I asked myself, 'Why would a drug dealer with money be doing small-time robberies of women in elevators?' The answer was he wouldn't. In all walks of life, in my experience, people stay with what they know. A knifepoint robber may go to guns and murder, but a drug dealer is a businessman. He might escalate to heroin or try dealing pot or go legitimate. But he's not going to do knifepoint robberies. Running a successful drug operation isn't for morons. Moreno would know he faced five to fifteen years for stealing the twenty-five or maybe fifty bucks the victim was likely to have in her purse. Perps who do knifepoints tend to be desperate junkies, teenagers, or idiots. The thing about robbery patterns is you can look at them and know what you're dealing with. If the robberies are daily and sloppy, your perp is probably a crackhead on a mission. If it's more sophisticated and organized, it's probably a professional stickup artist. If the pattern dies, you wait to see if your guy was killed or jailed or moved or hurt. Moreno didn't fit the elevator pattern other than race and gender and resemblance in appearance. It was a case of bad identification. I didn't have a reasonable doubt, I absolutely knew he didn't do it."

Oldham went to see the young Manhattan district attorney who had caught the case and told him he didn't think Hector Moreno was the robber. The DA promised to talk to his supervisor. Before going in front of the grand jury to testify in the Moreno case, Oldham asked the DA what had happened. The DA said they weren't dropping the charges. Oldham asked to see his supervisor, the chief of Trial Bureau 20. The bureau chief suggested they offer Moreno a polygraph. Moreno took the polygraph and passed. Oldham thought the case was done. Days later, Oldham asked the bureau chief if the charges had been dropped. He looked at Oldham and said no.

"The bureau chief was a jerk. In retrospect, he wasn't that old, maybe thirty-five. He thought he knew better than the man on the street, which was impossible because he only knew what we told him. He was convinced he was right. He said the polygraph was for my benefit, to convince me, not them. He said Moreno may have passed the lie detector, but he must be a liar because he said I hadn't read him his rights, and I had testified under oath that I had read him his rights. It put me in an impossible position. If I hadn't read him his rights when I arrested him, and of course I hadn't, I couldn't say that. I was being sandbagged. I knew it. He knew it. Moreno's guilt on the robbery didn't matter. He was a drug dealer and he was going to jail. The one thing prosecutors hate is dismissing an indictment. They think it reflects on them badly because they have presented the case to the grand jury. It's an institutional sensibility and it has nothing to do with reality or justice."

As the trial neared, Oldham approached the judge and told him that as the detective on the case he didn't think Moreno was guilty. The judge said he couldn't dispose of the charges; they would have to let the jury decide. Moreno took the stand and offered the defense that he was a drug dealer not a small-time stickup artist. "The jury was not sympathetic to that argument. He was trying to say he didn't commit one kind of crime by explaining he committed another kind of crime. To the average juror, all they heard was that he was a criminal. They found him guilty of robbery in the first degree. He got five to fifteen years though I was sure he hadn't done it, and the elevator-knifepoint pattern continued without interruption. It was disheartening and instructive. When I started out as a cop in D.C. I was unbelievably naïve. For a long time after I came to New York, I put on the NYPD uniform and I went out to do battle for 'truth, justice, and the American way.' But life doesn't always work out like that. Washington Heights muddied my view of police work."

The day before Thanksgiving in 1989, the day after he was nearly killed by the impersonator, Oldham was sent to a department psychologist as required by the department after a shooting incident. He told the psychologist he was feeling fine. But on Thanksgiving Day he was depressed. "I don't feel things a lot of other people do. You don't last in this business if you do. You become pathetic if you're overly empathetic. You're supposed to be someone other people can look to when they need strength. I always thought of myself, rightly or wrongly, as being capable in these situations. I thought I was good at police work. But I realized the bad guy could have killed me. I had lost control of the situation. The adrenaline rush of surviving the raid on the apartment had been replaced with thoughts of how close I had come to death."

The next week, Oldham went to collect the two impersonators in lower Manhattan to take them to be arraigned. The perp who fell five stories was in a wheelchair, paralyzed from the waist down. The one who had tried to kill Oldham was so badly beaten his head looked like a purple baseball—his head was shaved and laced with stitches. "He didn't recognize me and I didn't recognize him. It was as though we had never met. It was eerie. It was clear to me that cocaine wasn't worth dying over. I wanted to work for victims who were innocent, not act as a mediator for drug dealers' disputes. I wanted to make my own cases."

That afternoon, Oldham got a call from his lieutenant in the Two-Eight. His hook was now in the police commissioner's office. He had the power to influence the direction of careers, to help a detective rise to an assignment in headquarters or be sent to one of the precincts reserved for malcontents or cops with bad reputations. For years Oldham's hook had been watching his progress. "I see from the twenty-four-hour sheets you were in a shootout the other day," he told Oldham. "You don't want to be running around like that anymore. We want you downtown. Pick a command and call me tomorrow."

Oldham knew the offer was both an order and a reward. He called back the next day. He had decided where he wanted to be assigned. "I'd like to go to the Major Case Squad," he said.

CHAPTER TWO

THE PRINCE OF DARKNESS

One Police Plaza was nicknamed the "puzzle palace" by members of the NYPD. For Oldham, it represented both a mystery and an opportunity as he arrived for his first day at the Major Case Squad. Riding the elevator up to the Special Investigations Division office on the eleventh floor, Oldham chafed in the new suit he was wearing. He had bought the midnight blue, single-breasted suit off the rack at Moe Ginsburg's, a discount menswear store on 5th Avenue, and it felt awkward. Oldham had worked plainclothes for years and he was used to dressing for the streets. Headquarters was for suits. There were four thousand detectives in the NYPD, but only forty made it to Major Case. It was a select group, one of the hardest assignments to get. "Elite" was the cliché used to describe Major Case. The big time was how Oldham imagined the squad.

"The detectives in Major Case were the sharpest-dressed cops I had ever seen. They were wearing Armani, Hugo Boss, high-end designer suits. The reason, I learned, was that Major Case had a satellite office in the Garment District. There were a lot of burglaries and truck hijackings in that part of the city. When stolen merchandise was recovered there were substantial discounts for 'New York's finest' on the finest in men's clothing. It was against police regulations but that didn't stop anybody. It was the way the job was. Police work didn't pay much but you didn't have to spend much, either."

According to the NYPD detective investigator's guide, the mandate of the Major Case Squad included the most important cases to every cop on the force: the investigation of the murder or wounding of a police officer. Major Case also handled many of the more significant crimes: kidnappings, bank robberies, art theft, burglaries over $500,000, truck hijackings, and safecrackings in excess of $250,000. The squad had the discretion to pull other cases for further investigation—"enhancement," as it was called. High-profile cases not included in the mandate were often classified as "major." So were seemingly minor cases that had special signifi-

25

cance to NYPD bosses, like the theft of the dress Marilyn Monroe had worn in *Some Like It Hot.* The squad had been formed in the late seventies in response to the ambush and murders of two young officers, Patrolmen Gregory Foster and Rocco Laurie, by a group called the Black Liberation Army. Major Case was designed to give the department a unit able to undertake complex, long-term investigations of crimes that transcended geographical and jurisdictional boundaries. The squad also took cases as directed by the chief of detectives, which could mean almost anything from a shadow investigation of another detective unit's investigation to acting as liaison to foreign and domestic law enforcement agencies.

Major Case detectives were given the luxury of time and freedom to develop expertise in specialized areas of crime. Some were detectives who concentrated on the high-tech aspects of investigations, putting up wires and pole cameras and triggerfish (a device that can capture the electronic serial number of cell phones). There were surveillance specialists. Some detectives ran stables of informants from phone companies, banks, cable companies—people willing to give information or pull up records without a subpoena. Oldham considered his capabilities to reside in the human aspect of police work: talking to people, getting people to talk, measuring character, understanding motives.

"As a rule, NYPD detectives investigate crime reported to the police, reacting to events on the streets. Major Case was about creating cases. We were expected to be entrepreneurial. We went looking for crimes. The bread and butter of racketeering enterprises—gambling, loan-sharking, extortion, bribery, drug robberies, pension rip-offs, no-show jobs—were crimes usually not reported to law enforcement. The victims were often guys operating on the margins, borrowers on the balls of their ass, who would never turn to law enforcement. Frequently they themselves had gone to the mafia, as the lenders of last resort, and then found themselves in financial quicksand. They'd end up with a wiseguy partner in their business, big vig on a small loan, maybe broken arms. In some ways the crimes were consensual—they were participants in their own victimization. In Major Case we went prospecting for people in with the mob and in trouble with the mob. We were looking for the man on the ropes. We were looking for the organized crime associate caught with a bag of heroin who could be convinced to flip and become a cooperator in return for a light sentence. We were looking for the guy who wanted out of organized crime before he got killed or arrested. Snitches were the lifeblood of detectives like me. There was nothing more valuable than an informant who could connect the dots. The art was to find someone like that and convince him to cooperate. My strength lay in identifying other people's weaknesses."

Major Case cops operated citywide. They could go into any precinct or borough detective squad room, and there was a good chance they would be recognized by name or reputation. Considered dilettantes by many in the Detective Bureau, peacocks not burdened by the heavy caseload and onerous supervision of a precinct detective, they were flexible, resourceful, experienced, and, indeed, often arrogant. Investigators of the first and last resort, inside the force they were known as the chief of detective's detectives. Major Case had offices in all the five boroughs, and the detectives had a degree of autonomy far greater than that enjoyed by most cops. The squad room on the eleventh floor was open plan, with twenty or so desks arranged in rows in the middle and a wall of windows overlooking City Hall and the Brooklyn Bridge. The floors were linoleum, the lighting harshly fluorescent, the walls painted a generic police department blue. Captain Barry Noxon, a muscular, red-headed boss, had a corner office. A bench was placed on one side of the room with handcuffs bolted to the wall. It was far from glamorous by nearby Wall Street standards but still upscale for the police department. Normally most detectives were out, apart from whoever was assigned to "catch cases" that day—to take the next case referred to Major Case.

Oldham spent his first week in the squad attending latent-print school, learning to lift fingerprints at crime scenes. He was taught the rudiments of investigating bank robberies: analysis of demand notes, bait money, the mechanics of dye packs triggered to explode as the robbers leave the bank. Banks set their alarms with a delay of three or four minutes to ensure the police didn't arrive while the robbers were still in the bank; losing a few thousand dollars was far less important than avoiding a shootout and bad-for-business bloodshed. Oldham was scheduled to take the two-day kidnap course at the end of the week.

Before he reported for the class he was grabbed to work on his first truly major case: a kidnapping. Twelve-year-old Donnell Porter was walking from home to grammar school on the morning of December 5, 1989, when he was snatched from the street. Donnell had the misfortune of being the younger brother of a crack dealer named Richard Porter who ran a crew on West 132nd Street. The older Porter had the misfortune of being involved with a major dealer who went by the name "The

Preacher." The Preacher had backed Rich Porter in the drug business, providing him the crack to get started, but the relationship had gone bad. The Preacher used kidnapping as a way to collect outstanding debts or extort money, snatching drug dealers or their girlfriends or children and demanding large sums of cash for their safe return.

The Preacher, whose true name was Clarence Heatley, led a gang in Harlem called "the family." He was known as a compelling orator and persuader, and he had a reputation for brutality even in the violent world of crack and heroin dealers. The Preacher's chief lieutenant was a New York City cop named John Cuff. Cuff went by the nickname "Captain Jack Frost," supposedly because he was so coldhearted. Off duty, Cuff was Preacher's bodyguard and driver. On and off duty, he collected drug money. Cuff was the Preacher's enforcer. Cuff strangled his victims, dismembered their bodies. He was said to be the only man the Preacher feared. "It makes you wonder why Cuff joined the police department in the first place. It wasn't like he was ground down by low pay, long hours, watching drug dealers riding around in luxury sedans while he drove a shitbox Datsun. Cuff was never a straight cop. The most insidious cops were the ones who became cops as cover. How often did guys join the police department with the knowledge and the forethought that they were going to use their position as police officers to commit crimes? It was not *that* easy to become a cop. There was a background check. Six months in the academy. The first assignments could be miserable, walking a foot post in Hunt's Point, a rough neighborhood in the South Bronx, or something equally awful. Internal Affairs had profiles to ID guys who went bad. They looked at cops whose patterns of behavior radically changed—more absences, complaints of violence, sudden wealth. But it was tough nabbing a guy like Cuff. He started out bad and never changed his ways. The system was vulnerable to a cop like him."

The night of Donnell Porter's disappearance an unidentified caller contacted his mother. The man said they had Donnell. He told the family to wait for another call and warned them not to go to the police. At one o'clock in the morning he called again. This time the kidnappers made a ransom demand of half a million dollars. Richard, the older Porter brother, refused to pay. During yet another call, Rich bargained for a lower ransom and the demand was dropped to $350,000. The kidnappers told the family to go to the McDonald's at 125th Street and Broadway to get proof of life—proof that Donnell was in their possession and alive. The Porters sent a family friend to a bathroom in the rear of the McDonald's, as instructed. A coffee can was taped under a sink. Donnell's severed right index finger lay in the can. There was also a cassette tape. Donnell's voice was heard on the tape. "Mommy, they cutted my finger off," the boy cried. "Please help. I love you, Mommy."

The Porter family went to the police. Detectives in the Two-Six referred the case to Missing Persons who sent it on to the Major Case Squad. Inside One PP, the political implications of the case were immediately apparent in a city suffering tense race relations. If it emerged that an all-out effort had not been made to save the life of a twelve-year-old black child, there would be an outcry. The mayor, police commissioner, and the district attorney were notified of Donnell Porter's kidnapping. They decided to seek a ban on media coverage. Local newspapers and TV stations agreed not to report the snatch in order to avoid revealing the fact that the family had turned to the police. A team of over fifty detectives was assigned, including Oldham. The investigation needed to be led by an investigator with the ability to manage complexity and maintain secrecy.

The case was assigned to Detective Stephen Caracappa. The choice was an obvious one. Caracappa was older, in his late forties, a detective with a reputation for discretion and excellence. Straight-backed and thin, with a neatly trimmed mustache and dark eyes, he dressed in dark, tailored suits with a handkerchief in his breast pocket. The natty appearance was completed by a gold-nugget pinkie ring emblazoned with the NYPD detective shield as the setting for a multicarat diamond. Caracappa was quiet and watchful. He was called "the Prince of Darkness" by the other detectives in Major Case because of his grave, almost funereal presence. He was considered one of the best detectives in the city.

"Caracappa was the go-to guy in Major Case. He was a mafia specialist but he also had a breadth of experience and knowledge. Caracappa had contacts in federal, state, and local law enforcement. He had access to snitches of every kind, from crackheads to investment bankers. He kept a desk at the FBI office in Manhattan. When people were dying of heroin overdoses in Harlem, when John Gotti whacked 'Big Paul' Castellano, when a cop killed himself in his precinct house, the chiefs went to the commanding officer of Major Case and he then went to Caracappa. The younger guys in Major Case tried to emulate his style—aloof, street smart, inscrutable."

Organized crime was one of the most desirable assignments in the NYPD, attractive for the mystique and complexity of the investigations it sparked. Detective Caracappa concentrated on gathering intelligence on the mafia and was highly regarded in the world of organized crime investigations. But he could work virtually any kind of case. To succeed in Major Case, detectives had to be able to transcend stereotypes. In this, it was known in the squad room, Caracappa was a master. His ability to take on roles led him to be assigned unusual and difficult cases, such as the theft of a rare Baroque painting. The work, by Giambattista Zelotti, an Italian master of the sixteenth century, had been stolen from an investment banker's mansion on Long Island and was said to be for sale. Entitled *The Mystic Hunt of the Unicorn/Annunciation to the Virgin,* the painting depicted Gabriel blowing a small curved horn and the Virgin Mary holding a unicorn to pay tribute to the virtues of the mother of Christ. The allegorical combination of Mary and the unicorn, replete with phallic symbolism, made the piece unique. It was valued at a quarter of a million dollars at the time. The price being asked by the man in Chicago fencing it was $150,000.

Detectives Caracappa and Joe Keenan were given a twenty-minute lecture on Baroque allegorical Italian art by members of IFAR—International Fine Arts Recovery, a group of volunteer art historians from Ivy League schools who loved solving cases with cops. Playing the part of experts interested in purchasing black market art, Caracappa and Keenan lured the seller from Chicago to a suite in the Gramercy Park Hotel in New York. Caracappa and Keenan were wired with beeper kels—devices designed to look like beepers and transmit voices—and an agreed-upon code word was given to signal to detectives in an adjacent room that the deal was done. As soon as Caracappa and Keenan inspected the painting and recognized it as the Zelotti, they said the word and the perps were rushed and busted. The Zelotti was returned to its owner. The NYPD received a round of excellent publicity, and legend spread through the squad room and One PP of the cunning of Caracappa and Keenan.

"Caracappa was an actor. He transformed himself into an art expert, the kind who was looking to buy obscure art. A detective could study for weeks and learn everything about Zelotti, but he wouldn't last a minute if he couldn't play the part. Caracappa clearly knew his way around. Caracappa was self-possessed, controlled, but there was some street left in him. He spoke in grammatically correct sentences, when he spoke, which was rarely, but there was still the 'dis,' 'dems,' and 'dos' of his childhood on Staten Island. Fences dealing in stolen art were wily. They had to be convinced by Caracappa. It was a skill that couldn't be taught. He knew how to make people believe him. "

In the Porter kidnapping, Caracappa quickly took control of the investigation. Three detectives manned the "nest"—the domicile of the victim.

Caracappa and his partner Les Shanahan chose the nest as the place where the most information could be gleaned. The protocol called for a Kevlar ballistic blanket to be nailed over the inside of the front door in case the kidnappers raided the apartment. The kidnap kit included a double-barrel shotgun, a tape recorder, and a pen register. The phones in the Porter apartment were wired to record all incoming calls, and call waiting and call forwarding were disabled. The Porters were asked to surrender cell phones to ensure there were no communications with the kidnappers that the police didn't know about. A command post was established in headquarters. A synopsis of the kidnap was put up on the wall charting biographical information of the victim, known associates, previous arrests and convictions ("raps"), detectives assigned, along with photographs of the hostage and family. The operation ran 24/7. The NYPD system for working kidnappings was low-tech but effective.

In a kidnapping, the nature of the ransom demand often betrayed the nature of the kidnapping, Oldham discovered. If the amount was small, a few hundred dollars, chances were it wasn't a kidnapping at all but a junkie pretending to be snatched trying to scam money from family or friends—a surprisingly common occurrence, particularly for young female addicts. In some ethnic communities, kidnapping was used as a business tool to collect debts or recoup losses on deals gone bad. A traditional ransom kidnapping of a high-profile or wealthy person was rare. Under the circumstances, Donnell's kidnap looked drug-related. Rich Porter was unemployed and lived in public housing in a poor and dangerous part of the city, but he also drove a late-model BMW and traveled to Las Vegas frequently. It was obvious Donnell had not been snatched from the street randomly. The kidnappers thought the Porters could pay $350,000 for his return, and that meant there was drug money involved.

An operational name had to be decided upon so that detectives on the case could identify themselves on citywide radio. "Thunderbird" was the name given to the Porter case. No matter how complicated a kidnapping case became there were three key moments: the pertinent call, the money drop, and getting the victim back alive. Ideally, the victim would be recovered alive before the drop. After the drop, police were working on borrowed time. The kidnappers no longer had a motivation to keep the victim alive. They had the money. The only thing releasing a victim did was provide the cops with a live witness. The penalty for kidnapping and for murder were pretty much the same: twenty-five years to life. The kidnappers needed to make a business decision whether to release the hostage or kill him.

Over the next decade, Oldham would work dozens of kidnappings, but watching Caracappa on the first case made a deep impression. "Caracappa had an imperious quality that came across as self-assuredness. He wasn't a quiet guy in the sense of being shy or dumb or having nothing to say. He rarely spoke. You could spend a twelve-hour shift with him and not exchange a single word. He was the first person to arrive in the office every morning. He got in at five, before dawn. He had the opportunity to go over the previous day's reports before everyone else. They were called 'unusuals.' They were like the NYPD's daily newspaper. The unusuals recorded arrests, injured cops, robberies, murders. It was a way of keeping on top of crime in the city. Caracappa had the jump on everyone."

As a new member of Major Case, Oldham was assigned boilerplate detective work on the Porter case. He was sent to surveil the Porters' apartment building on 132nd Street. He sat in an unmarked van outside the nest—the shifts were twelve hours on, twelve off—and watched and waited.

On the third day, Caracappa and the detectives working Thunderbird gathered around a table in the Major Case squad room to listen to the tape recording of Donnell pleading and weeping. There was no purpose in butchering the kid's finger, thought Oldham. It seemed more likely to be proof of death than proof of life. No kidnapper would want to sit around all day with a twelve-year-old crying in pain about his finger. "Caracappa played the tape and we all heard the boy weeping and terrified. It was awful. I looked at Caracappa and not a muscle in his face moved. As the tape ended, he smiled and turned and walked away from the table. He didn't say anything. Nothing about canvassing hospitals. Nothing about the urgency of the case. Nothing about how the kid might be killed at any time. It was a small moment but it struck me. As detectives, we had to dissociate ourselves from the victim. Cutting the boy's finger off was an audacious move. Reports from the nest were that the family had little affection for the detectives from Major Case. Caracappa seemed detached from the human component of the case. I didn't know if that was a good thing or a bad thing. The tape rattled me. Usually investigations started after the crime was over. In murder cases, you go home at night and come back in the morning and the guy is still dead. In kidnappings the victim is always still out there waiting for someone to come and get him—if he is still alive."

Oldham lived in Harlem at the time, a few blocks from the Porter apartment and around the corner from the McDonald's where Donnell's finger had been found. He started to freelance the case off duty. He questioned the kids working the counter at McDonald's. He went to the snitches he had developed when he worked in Harlem and Washington Heights, probing into Rich Porter's crew on 132nd Street. Like the other detectives assigned to Thunderbird, Oldham assumed the older Porter knew more than he was willing to tell about who had snatched his brother. NYPD policy left the decision to pay or not pay the ransom in the hands of the family. Unknown to the police, Rich Porter was negotiating secretly with the kidnappers. Porter considered himself savvy and tough. Oldham followed Porter once when he left the nest but lost him in traffic at the entrance to the West Side Highway at 125th Street; Porter knew he was being tailed and shook him.

Oldham was conducting a shadow investigation, an attempt to retrace steps already taken to see if any stones had been left unturned. Ten days went by and there were no new leads, from the main investigation or from Oldham's. Every passing hour and day the chances of Donnell Porter's surviving grew smaller. The next communication from the kidnappers came on December 10. A boy playing in the street in the Bronx was given a note by a strange woman and told to deliver it to Donnell's aunt. The aunt lived in an apartment across the street. The stranger slipped the kid two dollars and the boy delivered the note without thinking to take notice of the woman's appearance. The note repeated the demand for money. It also said that Donnell needed medical attention. Oldham took this as a further signal the boy was going to die soon, probably painfully and awfully. After the note, there was only silence—ominous silence—as a blizzard blanketed the city and the Christmas season arrived.

That year the Major Case Squad holiday party was held at a restaurant called Two Toms on 3rd Avenue in Brooklyn. Situated in an Italian neighborhood near the Gowanus Canal, neighbors with two mob-frequented social clubs and the South Brooklyn Casket Company, whose motto read, "Experience a world of difference," Two Toms was popular with gangsters and off-duty detectives. It was a place known for the size of its portions and low prices, not the quality of the food. "I didn't want to go. I wanted to keep working on the Porter kidnapping, but I had no choice. The party was held during duty hours and attendance was not optional. When I got there it occurred to me that this was the only time of year all the detectives in Major Case were together in one room. The detectives gathered in that room knew every trick in the book. They could get a baby out of a parked car on a hot summer day in under five seconds. They could make a rapist rat on himself by questioning his masculinity. They could run a racketeering case without leaving the office. The guys in that room would chase bad guys to the ends of the earth and never take a hard breath."

Oldham elbowed his way to the bar—"the trough." Two detectives, Irish guys both with the last name of Henry, were giving a roast. They were known as the "two Henrys." As the new detective in Major Case, Oldham was the butt of their jokes. The two Henrys presented Oldham with a statuette of a looney bird on a tiny skating pond. "Skating" was the cop term for avoiding work; it was also the term for criminals getting away with crime. Ridicule was part of the hazing process. In truth, Oldham was already known as a worker.

"I looked around Two Toms and realized I was keeping company with the best. There were legends standing at the bar—detectives who worked the biggest cases in the country. There was Jimmy Graham, who weighed four hundred pounds. He was holding forth on how to bring a hijacked tractor trailer to a halt without firing a shot—a feat of singular difficulty. He was the only one of us not wearing a suit because they didn't make suits in his size that he could afford. He wore blue jeans with elastic waistbands. He looked like a farmer who had wandered in from the tobacco patch. But he was one of the smartest and most capable detectives I ever met. Detective Gil Alba broke the Son of Sam case in the mid-seventies. A serial killer had terrorized an entire city by sending demented notes to the police after shooting his victims with a .44-caliber handgun—until Alba tracked down David Berkowitz.

"In that company, Steve Caracappa was known to be a connoisseur of organized crime—the master of its history, politics, and culture. Caracappa had an appreciation of the Byzantine. He understood plots and subplots and vengeance and betrayal and all the good things that go into a Shakespearean drama. Caracappa had a gift for making the connections. He understood the language, the meaningful silences, the shrugs and gestures. In organized crime things often weren't what they appeared to be."

The party was filled with veteran detectives—men worn out by long hours and bad diets and too much alcohol. Caracappa looked nothing like a detective. He was dressed in a black suit, with a black tie with a pearl tie tack. He had a mantello draped over his shoulders—a black silk cape with a drawstring tied in the front. Light on his feet, he possessed a certain kind of Fred Astaire–like elegance and could have passed for a suit salesman in an upscale haberdashery or a professional ballroom dancer. "He was a watcher, a noticer, smoking a cigarette and surveying the room. Our eyes met. He was like me in a way, always watching, always looking around. His face was expressionless, unless he was whispering and sharing a private joke with another detective. He was surrounded by the small circle of organized crime detectives—Jack Hart, Les Shanahan, Chuck Siriano, Richie Puntillo, all excellent guys. They were their own exclusive subuniverse in Major Case, the detectives who knew the mob's secrets."

On January 4, Rich Porter's dead body was found near a horse stable in Orchard Beach in the Bronx. He had been shot once in the head and once in the chest. His wallet contained $2,239 in cash, ruling out robbery as the motive. In an attempt to raise the ransom money, Porter had met with another drug dealer who owed Porter hundreds of thousands of dollars. The dealer, a hard case known as Alpo, recognized the opportunity to erase the debt. Rather than repaying Porter, he murdered him.

After Rich Porter's death, day after day passed with no further developments. No word was heard from the kidnappers for nearly a month. The slim chance the boy would be recovered alive was evaporating. Operation Thunderbird was downsized. Caracappa and his partner were the only detectives working the kidnapping full-time. Oldham was reassigned to catch cases. Still new to Major Case, Oldham struggled to find his place. Within a week he was deluged with a pile of the least desirable cases; his supervisors considered it a rite of initiation to inundate a newcomer. In quick succession he was given an armored car theft, a burglary at the Izod Lacoste showroom, and a series of ATM heists by a gang of young Albanians using tow trucks to literally yank the machines from the walls of banks and tow them to a safe haven to be cracked. That year there was also a spate of pre-Christmas bank robberies in Manhattan. Bank robberies, in particular, were considered grunt work by Oldham.

"In some popular movies, bank robbers were portrayed as daring and romantic. But they are mostly crackheads, psychotics, rank amateurs. Bank tellers are trained to offer no resistance. The robbers walked in off the street and wrote a note on the back of a deposit slip—they didn't even have their own pen and paper. They were often illiterate. They handed over notes to the teller saying 'I have a gub,' like the line from the Woody Allen movie *Take the Money and Run*. They had no guns—they couldn't afford them. They left fingerprints all over the place. They were plainly recognizable on videotape. The local television stations reported a rash of bank robberies as though Bonnie and Clyde were tearing across New York City, but actually it was some guy having a crack attack going from bank to bank as if he were making withdrawals from his own accounts. There wasn't much to working those cases."

The real action in Major Case was taking place on the far side of the squad room, opposite Oldham's desk, in a small office that was kept locked. The room housed the Organized Crime Homicide Unit (OCHU), a secretive group dedicated to collecting intelligence on mafia murders. Oldham, like other detectives not assigned to the OCHU, was not permitted access to this room, which contained the most sensitive information held by the NYPD. Inside the OCHU room stood five filing cabinets, each dedicated to one of the five New York mafia families. A single desk faced the door. Large metal Rolodexes with OCHU contact numbers were kept on the desk; they were locked as well. The room was Spartan—no paper or mug shots were in sight, the walls were bare, nothing to give away the purpose of the office as the collection point for intelligence from the entire NYPD. The drawers and filing cabinets contained information on active cases and mob homicides under investigation—locations, cars, perps, telephones. All were under lock and key. A phone was also locked in one of the drawers. It was what was known in law enforcement as a "hello phone"—to be answered by saying "hello," not "Major Case" or "NYPD."

Detective Caracappa had been instrumental in forming the OCHU in the mid-eighties. The unit was comprised of five or six detectives and a sergeant. It was designed to gather and disseminate sophisticated information on mob murders. Members of OCHU were assigned to assist local precinct detectives saddled with organized crime murders. OCHU detectives each concentrated on one of the five families of New York—Genovese, Gambino, Colombo, Bonanno, Luchese. They were regularly detailed to other agencies—U.S. Attorney's Offices, the district attorney's offices, FBI, DEA, Joint Organized Crime Task Force. Productivity wasn't measured by arrests. What mattered was knowing the inside story.

"Caracappa and the other detectives in OCHU were experienced. They knew better than the mobsters themselves who attended whose mob weddings, dinners, and funerals. They kept scrapbooks on their assigned families, clipping and pasting newspaper stories and adding snapshots as though they were preserving the history of organized crime for future generations. Nearly all the detectives in OCHU were Italian. Most had grown up in the same neighborhoods as the mobsters in Brooklyn, Staten Island, Queens, and the Bronx. Detectives and mobsters often knew each other all their lives. They went to the same high schools, hung out in the same parks, chased the same girls. Some of the OCHU guys looked like mobsters once removed. Double-breasted suits, gold bracelets, street attitude. Understandings and boundaries and even mutual respect between certain wiseguys and the police made for a working relationship. Cops and mobsters came from working-class neighborhoods where there weren't many options in life. All it took was getting busted as a teenager out one night with your buddies, or falling in with the wrong crowd, and it could lead down the path to hooking up with a gang. A lot of gangsters had family who were cops and vice versa—cousins, uncles, brothers. The choice for many Irish and Italian kids was the police department or organized crime."

On weekends and holidays, when the banks were closed and Oldham found himself alone in the office, he would borrow the keys to the OCHU room from the captain's desk drawer and pull old cases from the cabinets. "I came to New York to work on organized crime, not necessarily Italian or traditional OC, but sophisticated long-term cases. I hadn't gotten my chance yet. I was fascinated by the OCHU murder files. Detectives will tell you how much pleasure there is in going through a good murder file. They are written in a language the civilian reader wouldn't comprehend. It isn't technical, it is arcane. If you have worked cases, it is clear what the writer meant. 'The witness was offered a polygraph and declined' is meant to transmit that the guy they questioned is a fucking liar. 'The prisoner was subdued without unnecessary force' means they beat the hell out of the suspect. 'The facts were insufficient to support the evidence of guilt' means there is no case, but the suspect named did it. Closing a case under the designation 'all investigative leads exhausted' means it is the detective who is exhausted by the case, not the leads.

"The OCHU files had a narrative thread. The murders had more life to them than the usual homicides. Reports from outside agencies were included analyzing the particular mob family involved and what preceded the murder—rivalries, motives, intrigue. Speculation was common. The detectives reported what their snitches said. Many times detectives would know who did it but couldn't prove it. Sometimes you could see a rough sense of justice. How organized crime and law enforcement got tangled up in each other's affairs and interacted. Like the murder of Everett Hatcher. I knew the case. Every cop and federal agent in the city knew the case."

Just as criminals impersonated cops on the streets of New York, it was common for cops and federal agents to impersonate gangsters. Undercover work was one of the more effective tools available, as an FBI agent posing as a small-time hood named Donnie Brasco had proved in the early eighties by nearly destroying the Bonanno crime family. The success of undercovers made mobsters paranoid about law enforcement penetrating their organizations. Performances, Oldham knew, had to be perfect if an agent or detective was to survive. Hatcher was a DEA agent with seventeen years' experience who had taken an assignment as an undercover in a mafia-run cocaine-dealing operation. Hatcher had managed to infiltrate the crew of "Jerry" Chilli, a member of the Bonanno family. Late one night in February 1989, Hatcher and a team of five agents backing him up were on their way to buy drugs from a small-time gangster named Costabile "Gus" Farace at a diner on Staten Island. In a remote corner of the island, past the vast landfill called Fresh Kills, Hatcher lost radio contact. Panic ensued. The backup agents finally found Hatcher in his car, stopped on an overpass on a desolate stretch of highway. Hatcher had been shot four times through the driver-side window, once in the head.

The murder immediately brought national attention. Hatcher was the first DEA agent murdered in New York since the early seventies. President George H. W. Bush had just instituted a mandatory death penalty for the murder of federal agents. A reward of $250,000 was announced, at the time one of the largest ever offered. More than thirty DEA agents were put on the case, as well as scores of detectives from the NYPD. On the streets, law enforcement of every stripe came down hard on the mafia—not just Bonannos but all five families. Through snitches and informants, it was learned that Farace was the killer and that he had acted without sanction from his bosses. Soon Farace was being hunted by both law enforcement and the mafia. It took a while, but in November 1989, Farace was found dead in a car in Bensonhurst, Brooklyn. He was unrecognizable from his mug shot. He had grown a beard and dyed his hair red. He had lost weight. Farace had been shot nine times. "There were no suspects in the Farace case. It wasn't clear why Farace killed Hatcher—if Hatcher's cover had been blown or if there was some other reason. But the mob didn't want their operations interrupted by constant surveillance and attention from law enforcement. Farace was killing business so he had to be killed. Everyone in law enforcement in the city knew we forced a result. And frankly, no one was unhappy. Gus Farace got what he deserved. There wasn't going to be a huge multiagency manhunt for the killer. Whoever did him did us a favor. The Hatcher case was closed."

Oldham understood that the most important truths in a homicide file were often not in the file. Reading between the lines was crucial to advanced detective work. Oldham found a copy of the OCHU handbook for organized crime homicides on the captain's bookshelf. Detective Caracappa had compiled the handbook. Oldham took a copy home to continue his education. The NYPD shield graced the cover of the 175-page compendium of all mafia murders known to the Major Case Squad. Typed in uppercase and written in terse police prose, the book contained the blunt tales of the lives and deaths of hundreds of mob murder investigations, arranged chronologically and divided into years and families. All known mob murders from the 1980s were included.

The book began on January 5, 1980, with the murder of a Genovese associate named Norman Brownstein in Fort Lauderdale, Florida. The entry for Gus Farace used law enforcement shorthand for time and place of occurrence in 1989: "AT T/P/O THE VICTIM WAS SHOT TO DEATH WHILE SITTING IN A PARKED CAR ALONG WITH JOSEPH SCLAFANI WHO WAS WOUNDED. REMARKS: THE VICTIM WAS ASSOCIATED WITH BONANNO SOLDIER 'JERRY' CHILLI, AND AT THE TIME OF HIS DEATH WAS WANTED FOR THE HOMICIDE OF SPECIAL AGENT EVERETT HATCHER OF THE DRUG ENFORCEMENT AGENCY."

"Caracappa had literally written 'the book' on organized crime murders in New York. If a wiseguy was killed in Queens or the Bronx and the homicide detective who caught the case wanted to know how his victim fit in the mafia, he would look in Caracappa's book for connections. It wasn't a narrative in the conventional sense. There was an index in the front and then a brief synopsis of each murder. It was a reference work. It contained intimate knowledge of the mafia and how it functioned. In organized crime killings, motives were often obscure. Wiseguys routinely lured members of their own families to their deaths. The victim might be told he was going to kill another mobster or to a sit-down or a card game. 'Copping a sneak,' it was called. Plots were hatched over years, or in a moment of anger. Business reasons were disguised as personal grudges, and personal grudges were dressed up as matters of honor. The manner of death was meant as a message in many cases. A bird stuck in a dead man's mouth signified he was a stool pigeon. Body parts were sent to family members. The victim might be left in the street, for all to see, or chopped up and thrown into a landfill and the dead man listed forever as a 'missing person.'"

In January 1989, Oldham was in the office early one morning, going through rolls of stop-action videotape from a bank robbery, when Caracappa and a couple of other detectives came into the squad room. Caracappa was talking about the Porter kidnapping. He was planning a strategy for continuing the investigation: sending undercovers uptown to buy from Rich Porter's crew. Oldham was surprised the investigation was still in Major Case. Everyone knew Donnell Porter had to be dead. It was certain the kidnappers weren't getting any money from Richard Porter and there was no other way the Porters could pay. Oldham assumed the case had been reclassified as a murder and assigned to Bronx homicide.

"I was new to Major Case and low in the pecking order. Caracappa had made it plain he wasn't interested in hearing from me. I said to Caracappa's partner, Les Shanahan, that the kid was probably dead. I offered to search for the boy's body. It seemed to me that the body had likely been dumped near where his brother's body was found. Orchard Beach in the Bronx was deserted in winter. Caracappa looked at me and shook his head, like I was one sorry sack of shit. Shanahan said they were going to keep the case a kidnapping. On one level, I understood how the thinking went. The family lived in the ghetto, Rich Porter was a drug dealer, so fuck 'em. As lead detective you develop a proprietary claim to your cases. You don't want anyone touching your investigation. If Donnell's body was recovered, the case would be a homicide and Caracappa and Shanahan would no longer be the lead detectives. They would be assisting Bronx homicide detectives. As a kidnapping it stayed in the Major Case Squad. Caracappa and Shanahan kept control. If collars were going to be made, they had decided that they were the ones who were going to make them."

In late January, a homeless man out collecting cans found Donnell Porter's body stuffed inside two black garbage bags less than a mile from where his brother had been dumped. The boy had been dead for nearly a month. A search of the area would have uncovered his body weeks earlier. "I didn't feel any sense of vindication. The boy was dead. We had failed. The Preacher wasn't arrested until seven years later. The case was made by Detective Vinny Flynn, who was in a unit called Redrum that concentrated on drug murders."

Facing the death penalty, the Preacher made a deal with prosecutors to testify against the other members of his gang, including Cuff. The case became famous in black gangster culture. Rappers rapped about it and a movie was made called *Preacher: The Black Hand of Death*. The movie's poster proclaimed, "They terrorized Harlem and used it as their playground." But the story of Donnell Porter wasn't in the film—the brutality was too much even for an ultraviolent movie. The Preacher did tell federal prosecutors about his role in the killing. Despite his confession, the

Preacher was never convicted of the murder of Donnell Porter and no one was ever charged with his murder. The federal government wanted to use the Preacher as a witness.

"My belief is that prosecutors realized they couldn't put him on the stand if it was brought out in court that he was responsible for kidnapping, butchering, and murdering a twelve-year-old boy. Such a man could not be rehabilitated before a jury. The jury wouldn't care how true his testimony was if they knew about Donnell Porter. But the Preacher didn't lie about the murder. He told the government all of the grim details, they just chose not to charge him. It was one of the deals with the devil the government makes all the time, in the interest of the greater good. It was one of the paradoxes of law enforcement. The most despicable killers were often the most sagacious tellers."

Oldham had wanted to work on organized crime cases when he arrived at Major Case, but it was clear he wouldn't get the chance, at least not while Caracappa was around. Caracappa was a powerful influence inside Major Case. He was a leading candidate to be promoted to first-grade detective. First grade would be acknowledgment that Caracappa was the best of the best. He would receive lieutenant's pay. Only two hundred of the four thousand detectives in the police department made first grade. Caracappa's reputation remained very high in Major Case, and throughout the NYPD. It was a view Oldham did not share. "I didn't trust Caracappa. There was something wrong with him, something cold and calculating and evasive. I didn't consider it paranoia, at least not any more than usual for me. I didn't like him, and I assumed the feeling was mutual. Caracappa didn't want anyone in the OCHU room he didn't know and have the measure of. He wanted to control OCHU. He didn't want anyone looking at him—and he surely knew I was watching."

CHAPTER THREE

SNITCHES AND LEAKS

Detective Stephen Caracappa may not have liked Oldham, and he may not have wanted him to be involved in organized crime cases, but that didn't mean Oldham couldn't look, listen, and learn. Before he came to Major Case he had observed OC—organized crime—investigations and been fascinated by the intricacy and complexity they presented, the power struggles and personalities and plots. Now he was a member of the premier law enforcement squads engaged in the war against the mafia. He was at the fulcrum, the place where the worlds of the police and the mob met, an ideal spot to observe the unfolding drama.

As Oldham surveyed the landscape of organized crime in New York, it was plain that no one family dominated any particular borough or section of the city. Genovese and Gambino and Luchese wiseguys planted themselves and their operations wherever the opportunity presented itself. The same was true for law enforcement, Oldham knew. Competition was a way of life for cops and federal agents and prosecutors. Jurisdictions overlapped, just as mob territories overlapped. Officially, the U.S. Attorney for the Southern District covered Manhattan, the Bronx, and Westchester. The U.S. Attorney for the Eastern District included Brooklyn, Staten Island, Queens, and Long Island. There were also five district attorney's offices, one in each borough, in charge of state cases, as well as a citywide special narcotics prosecutor. In addition, the FBI, ATF, DEA, Customs, IRS, Labor Department, and Immigration all had major presences in New York. Jurisdictional boundaries had little practical importance—bad guys didn't care about law enforcement power struggles.

"Offices all over the city were filled with young, ambitious prosecutors, agents, and detectives looking to make their reputations. The competition bred excellence. The appetite for cases was insatiable. In a lot of cities there were only one or two venues. In New York there were dozens. You had to be ready, willing, and able when a case came down the pike. If you didn't seize the moment, someone else would."

Oldham, at thirty-seven, began his own real-world, real-time immersion course in organized crime and its relationship to law enforcement. The story of the two had been entwined from the very beginnings of the mafia in New York, each side adapting to changes in the other for nearly a century. At the heart of the tale was greed. Information and deception were the instruments of power. The mafia had been restructured in the 1930s by Lucky Luciano to exploit a central tenet of criminal law: a man could only be charged, tried, and convicted for crimes he had personally committed. Historically, common law held a defendant responsible only for his own actions. If a mob boss did not pull the trigger—if he could plausibly deny instructing a hit man to murder the victim—it was hard to make a case against him. There were conspiracy laws, but they were extremely difficult to prove because of strict rules of evidence and hearsay. *Omertà,* the mafia pledge of silence, was more than a cultural imperative created by Sicilian landowners resisting foreign occupiers for centuries. It was a sophisticated means of circumventing criminal liability.

For decades the mafia operated as a state within a state, with a rigid hierarchy of boss, underboss, counselor *(consigliere),* captains *(capos),* and soldiers *(soldatos)* created by Luciano. Families referred to themselves as "administrations." The structure was designed to impose order and discipline. The "commission" was the name given to the secret body overseeing the five families of New York. Territorial and business disputes were settled by the commission. Murder contracts on made men were sanctioned, or not. Above all else, the commission was created by the bosses to mediate interfamily disputes to protect themselves from rivals and law enforcement. "We went after the usual mob rackets for generations—loan-sharking, narcotics, gambling. For the most part we only nabbed low-level street gangsters. The war would never be won that way, no matter how many wiseguys we put away. The target had to be the guiding lights of the family. The executive branch. We needed a new tool."

In 1970, the Racketeer-Influenced and Corrupt Organizations Act was signed into law by President Richard Nixon. RICO, as the statute was known, did more than change the rules of the game. It attacked the mafia's code of silence with a new legal paradigm. RICO took its nickname from a mobster movie character named Caesar Enrico "Rico" Bandello played by Edward G. Robinson in the 1930 film *Little Caesar.* The movie was based on Al Capone, the Chicago gangster of the twenties, an era when urban outlaws were tabloid celebrities. The author of the law, a proselytizing Notre Dame professor named Robert Blakey, held seminars introducing RICO to federal agents and prosecutors, to little effect. Blakey tried to demonstrate how he had created an intricate system of rewards and punishments to entice wiseguys to turn into snitches. Prosecutions would then go all the way up the chain of command. But the practical advantages and opportunities presented by the law were not understood by his most important audience. Trapped inside an old way of thinking—trying to tie mob bosses to specific crimes instead of going after the organization itself—law enforcement was unable to see how it needed to reconceive the war against the mafia. The law sat unused for more than a decade.

The first time RICO was employed in a major prosecution was in 1986. A young U.S. attorney for the Southern District of New York named Rudolph Giuliani aimed to convict and jail the bosses of all five New York crime families at once. The Commission Case, as the prosecution was known, was the beginning of the end for the modern mafia. In the hands of prosecutors from the Southern District, RICO's devastating implications were finally recognized. It was a law designed to allow the prosecutors to weave the disparate elements of a criminal enterprise together—to tell the inside story. RICO wasn't about convicting a lone defendant. The purpose was to cripple the organization. Multiple charges could be brought against multiple defendants. Hearsay evidence became admissible. Associative evidence was allowed—the demonstration of guilt by association. Previous convictions and charges were used to color the character of the defendant. "Mobsters despised RICO. The gloves were off. The deck was stacked in our favor. Organized criminals couldn't rely on the old dodges to disguise their activities. RICO revolutionized criminal law in fundamental ways. It reimagined the whole idea of crime and punishment."

Over the next five years, RICO was used to prosecute mafia corruption in a series of mob-controlled industries in the city: construction, garbage hauling, concrete. In the commercial painting industry, for example, the Luchese family ran a lucrative racket through a local union official named Jimmy Bishop. The Painters Union Case, as the prosecution came to be known, was a textbook example of mafia methods. To corner painting contracts, the Luchese family used the threat of wildcat strikes to rig bids for jobs and eliminate legitimate operators. With Bishop's backing, major painting contractors in New York and Long Island were forced to buy their paint from a mob-controlled company. For every gallon sold a dollar was paid to the mafia—netting millions over the years. Jimmy Bishop, in turn, promised and provided cheap labor to contractors by ensuring that a sweetheart deal disregarding union rules and rates was in place or else his union stayed away from the construction projects. In this way, cartels of mobbed-up outfits drove everyone else out of the business. The impact of organized crime on the union movement was ruinous. Wages and working conditions suffered, jobs were lost, pension funds were pillaged. Protecting skims and scams became Bishop's priority. Public and private jobs were subject to the racket, including contracts to paint many of the city's 460 subway stations, 1,500 public schools, and 150,000 public housing units.

"The mafia knew how to take their one percent and make it seem like they were doing you a favor. The so-called tax the mafia put on deals was enough to trim profit margins but not enough to kill business. The mob knew how to calibrate its take to the size of the deal. They were parasites. They latched on to a healthy organism and didn't let go. They contributed nothing to the survival of the organism. The 'black hand' had its fingers in all parts of the economy where the work was dirty and hard, where honest working people were breaking their backs to make a living. The money the mob took didn't look big. How much was there in a contract to pick up the trash from one restaurant? How much was a mafia markup on a truckload of concrete? It looked like nickel-and-dime stuff, but one percent of everything is fucking huge."

But under RICO, first dozens and then scores and finally hundreds of gangsters were found guilty of racketeering charges. The RICO convictions resulted in unprecedented penalties. In mafia lore, a stretch in an upstate prison was no big deal. The state prisons were so corrupt—the booze and drugs and prostitutes so plentiful—mobsters regarded it as little more than a rite of passage. A few years in jail was a way to prove your loyalty by remaining silent. Prison was a place to make friends, network with wiseguys, and study crime at an institution of higher learning. Under RICO, federal convictions had dire consequences. Assets were seized, turning mobster millionaires into penitent paupers. Sentences were meted out in decades not years. The prospect of life in jail was not enough under the guidelines. Life sentences multiplied for every murder count, lives mounted on lives unto eternity.

The biggest change brought about by the law was the sudden deluge of snitches. Supposed tough guys, sworn to an oath of *omertà*, now tried to make deals with the federal government en masse. If a mafioso cooperated he had a chance for a new life. The blend of punishment and incentive created by RICO and the Witness Protection Program was designed to render the logic of cooperation overwhelming. Time in federal prison would be hard and lonely, year after year staring at a wall in Marion, Illinois, or in super-max cells dug into the side of a mountain in Florence, Colorado. A wiseguy who got in trouble with the law had to decide: rat or rot. Betrayal begat betrayal, as the layers of secrecy enveloping the mafia were peeled away.

"Mobsters were supposed to be tough. A few old-timers actually lived by the code. They were the last of the hard cases. Some would do serious time in jail rather than talk to us. They respected the code of silence. You had to admire them for it. But most wiseguys were looking for a deal, and sometimes you had to stuff a sock in their mouth to shut them up. If you caught a mobster and you could string together a couple of RICO predicates—extortion, loan-sharking, gambling, assault—it meant he might be looking at life. If he cooperated, if he wore a wire and collected evidence and testified, he might do five years or he might do no time at all. By the mid-nineties, snitching was the rule, not the exception. The expectation that a guy would keep his mouth shut vanished. Mobsters assumed a busted wiseguy was a snitch."

Of the five New York families, none suffered more than the Lucheses. The entire leadership had been convicted in the Commission Case—boss, underboss, consigliere. Anthony "Tony Ducks" Corallo, the long-time Luchese don, had earned his nickname for his uncanny ability to "duck" indictments and convictions. After his RICO conviction in the Commission Case, he was sentenced to one hundred years in a federal penitentiary. Before he went in, Corallo elevated Vittorio "Vic" Amuso to acting boss of the Luchese family. This decision caused resentment in the ranks. Amuso and his partner Anthony "Gaspipe" Casso were brutal gangsters, but they were from Brooklyn and had no particular cachet with the outfit's remaining elders in the Bronx. The Bronx crews of the family, always dominant financial contributors, wanted to install their own captain as boss. The New Jersey crew, indicted on RICO charges and fighting their own internecine feuds, failed to pay their respects to Amuso and Casso after their ascension to leadership, and then suddenly moved to Florida without consulting the new bosses. But once Amuso and Casso were in charge, they were ruthless in protecting their power. Soon, factionalism was ripping the Lucheses apart.

In the late eighties, the mafia suffered a general failure of management as a new generation of leadership bickered and plotted to kill one another. Before it had been unthinkable that a captain would murder the head of a family, the way John Gotti killed Gambino boss "Big Paul" Castellano in front of Spark's Steakhouse in 1986. After Castellano was killed, the

Luchese and Genovese families put out a contract to kill Gotti. Gotti, in turn, held a grudge against Vincent "Chin" Gigante, the Genovese boss. Gigante was facing multiple RICO indictments, as well as state prosecution, but to avoid trial—and conviction—he pretended he was mentally incompetent. Gigante maintained the act for years, walking the streets of lower Manhattan in a bathrobe, unshaven and muttering to himself.

"The mafia was becoming a public spectacle. The old mafioso knew better than to provoke or embarrass law enforcement. For generations, when a candidate for the mob was 'straightened out'—when he was inducted into a family—he more or less subscribed to the rules. Loyalty and honor were the binding myths. 'The life' wasn't a regular nine-to-five job, but there was structure. Not with the new bosses like Gotti and Amuso and Casso. Most of them were second-string gangsters. They were put in charge of complicated commercial enterprises worth millions and they had no clue how to run a business. They failed to appreciate the usefulness of discretion. Chin Gigante urinated in the streets in Greenwich Village to prove he was crazy. John Gotti strolled around Little Italy in two-thousand-dollar suits as though he were a movie star. Gotti talked to his underboss, Sammy 'the Bull' Gravano, about 'his public.' He was a stone-cold idiot."

For the new Luchese administration, killing seemed the solution to every problem. The reason didn't matter—a suspicion, a grudge, a mood. It was no way to run an organization, not to mention that it was not going to breed loyalty or esprit de corps. Murder, however, was what Amuso and Casso knew. The pair had started in the mafia together in the seventies as hit men. The "work" they did for the family, contract murders, forged a tight bond. Known as tough and canny gangsters, Amuso and Casso were also rich. But they didn't flaunt their wealth like Gotti. Operating out of a social club called the 19th Hole near the golf course in Dyker Beach Park in Brooklyn, Amuso and Casso were major drug dealers. "Together, Amuso and Casso possessed a toxic combination of incompetence, violence, and paranoia. They were born connivers. They thought they were going to be the exception to the rule under RICO— they weren't going to give anyone the chance to snitch on them. As law enforcement closed in on the Lucheses and their backs were pushed to the wall, Amuso and Casso gave up any vestige of mob ideals. They killed anyone they suspected of snitching, or having the potential to snitch. Simply being in a compromised position was justification. Amuso and Casso thought everyone was a rat—and mostly they were right."

THE MURDER OF JIMMY BISHOP

As the Lucheses and the other mob families tried to adapt to RICO, a new organized crime pattern emerged with bloody and brutal regularity: the murder of secret mob informants. Oldham was in the Major Case squad room on the day of May 17, 1990, when the problem reached another new low. That morning the painters union official named Jimmy Bishop had left his girlfriend's apartment building on Powell's Cove Boulevard in Queens and walked into a Luchese ambush. Bishop was sixty years old, a hard-drinking, loud-mouthed union leader. He had been the secretary-treasurer of the eight thousand–member New York chapter of the International Brotherhood of Painters and Allied Trades for sixteen years. Bishop had also been an associate of the Luchese crime family since the late seventies, when he turned to the mob to run off a rival union official who had been appointed to clean up Bishop's notoriously corrupt district.* From then on Bishop was "on record" with "Fat Pete" Chiodo and the Lucheses, protected but also vulnerable to the whims and machinations of the family.

Bishop's troubles with the Lucheses dated back months before the May 1990 ambush. At the time, for reasons the mob felt no need to explain, the Lucheses had blocked Bishop's bid to be elected to the board of the International Brotherhood. Bishop was told to bow out of the race or face physical harm. The message came from the heads of the Luchese family: Vic Amuso and Gaspipe Casso. "Amuso and Casso wanted their own man. They liked the way their new man dressed and conducted himself. Bishop was a blowhard boozer whom they considered unreliable. It was as simple as that: leave or we will kill you. Bishop resigned from the union. Amuso and Casso didn't expect what happened next. Bishop went to the NYPD. He wanted protection—and revenge."

When Bishop turned to the NYPD, the Organized Crime Investigation Division (OCID) and the Manhattan DA's Office were conducting

---

*In that instance, Bishop had reached out to a friend with a wiseguy contact who knew a Brooklyn barber who knew "Fat Pete" Chiodo of the Luchese family. Bishop arranged to have Chiodo and Tommy "Irish" Carew beat down the rival official early one morning in the stairwell of the union headquarters on West 14th Street in lower Manhattan. Chiodo and Carew used pipes; the man ended up in the hospital in a coma. Within weeks, Bishop was restored to his position as secretary-treasurer and the attempt to reform the union was abandoned. Two Luchese associates were then given powerful positions in the union.

an investigation of corruption in the painting business. Bishop became a confidential informant (CI) and gave them the insider account of the scam. In return, they promised to keep him alive. But confidential informants presented a serious challenge for state authorities. Because of RICO's effectiveness, the federal government had developed an elaborate Witness Protection Program to safeguard cooperators. The state had no equivalent. The NYPD had to improvise, with little money, support, or expertise. The department's procedure was to assign a team of detectives to take the CI to a cheap out-of-town motel and stay in hiding until the danger passed.

"Bishop was an exception because of his importance to the case and his ability to reveal how the mafia really functioned. Bishop was taken to Montreal. He sat in a room for a couple of weeks with some cops watching Hockey Night in Canada. A union thug with a reputation like Bishop was used to intimidating other people. Bishop was a swaggering ex-Marine. Hard men don't like to admit they're afraid. Bishop couldn't conduct his business. He couldn't see his girlfriend. There was no end to the threat in sight. He had to hide until Fat Pete Chiodo and Vic Amuso and Gaspipe Casso were put away. That could take years or it might never happen at all. The truth was that the idea of police protection was an illusion. In most cases, the state offered little more than a bus ticket out of town and a dream. There was no way to ensure a CI's safety. Bishop, like a lot of witnesses who flip and become cooperators, had to choose. He had to decide between fear and freedom, between living and having a life. Bishop took his chances and came back to New York."

The Jimmy Bishop murder file recites the known facts from that May day: "At approximately 1100 hours, the victim was operating his 1988 Lincoln automobile in the parking lot in the rear of 162–01 Powell's Cove Blvd. While driving out of the parking lot he was shot numerous times in the head and body. Thereat he expired from his wounds." Bishop was leaving his mistress's apartment that morning. Within half an hour of the murder, detectives from the 109th Precinct found and interviewed a schoolteacher who had been having an affair with Bishop. She told the detectives Bishop had been secretly cooperating with the Manhattan District Attorney's Office in an investigation into organized crime. The teacher described a warning Bishop had just received from the mob. She knew that Bishop had spoken with a detective named "Eddie" the day before. Eddie was with OCID. Eddie had told Bishop that the police had intercepted phone calls with mobsters talking about killing Bishop.

Precinct detectives contacted OCID. Like detectives in Major Case, the members of OCID recognized that Bishop's murder suggested more than just another organized crime dispute. Bishop was, in fact, one of their CIs. Only days earlier Bishop had appeared before a grand jury inquiring into organized crime control of trade unions. This murder fit into a larger pattern. "Bishop's death was just the latest in a series of loosely linked mob-related intelligence failures. It was widely believed there was a leak in law enforcement that was proving fatal to snitches and cooperators. Cases were compromised with alarming regularity. The source, or sources, were unidentified. There were suspects, too many suspects. There was a pattern but it was extremely difficult to see its shape or size."

When Bishop turned up in the internal Major Case staff assignment log, Oldham called Chris Dowdell in the 109th Precinct, who was the catching detective for the murder. The assignment log showed that Major Case and OCHU were assisting the precinct detectives in the investigation. Helping investigations of OC homicides like Bishop was one of the reasons OCHU had been formed in the first place. But it was standard practice for OCHU to appear to aid a precinct cop and at the same time withhold information. Mafia investigations in different precincts often overlapped, with felonies and murders forming part of larger investigations. Citywide squads like OCHU and OCID pursued overarching cases, sometimes at the expense of the precinct cop working one murder.

In the Bishop case, the Major Case Squad homicide book kept by Detective Caracappa was opaque to the point of being positively misleading. In the "remarks" section of the page recording the homicide it said, "The victim was an official of the painters union. Confidential information disclosed that he had a conflict with Luchese underboss Anthony Casso." There was no mention of Bishop's status as an NYPD CI, although the information would be known to Detective Caracappa and OCHU and—since Bishop was dead—there was no further need for keeping his status as a CI confidential. It was clear to Oldham that Detective Dowdell was not going to get straight and comprehensive assistance.

"I had left the 109, where Bishop was killed, a year earlier. I knew Dowdell well. When I was in the 109 he had taught me plenty about being a detective. Simple stuff like how to stop a perp from slipping out of his jacket before you cuffed him. He also taught me to be careful about who I talked to in the precinct house. The 109 was a party house, which meant there was lots of drinking and little discipline. Dowdell was a first-grade detective and police union delegate. The union delegates were the guys cops went to when they were in trouble—they were the intermediaries between the bosses and line officers. Dowdell steered me away from trouble—the karaoke bars where girls were for rent, the restaurants where you could eat for free but maybe wind up on an Internal Affairs surveillance videotape. He wasn't my mentor but he had taken an interest in seeing that I didn't step on any land mines.

"I offered to help Dowdell in any way I could. Dowdell said the 'secret squirrels' in OCHU were driving him nuts. He wanted to know everything he could about Bishop but it was hard to come by information about a CI that was supposed to be kept secret. This was true even after the CI was dead, sometimes especially after he was dead. I told Dowdell that Caracappa and the OCHU guys didn't usually talk to me. I said I would keep my ears open. I would let him know if I heard anything around the squad room. I was trying to establish myself as someone with value to detectives in the precincts. I didn't want to do bank robberies anymore. I knew I wasn't going to be selected for OCHU, particularly with Caracappa around, so I was starting to figure a way to get myself into the game. I wasn't going to work on the Bishop homicide, but I was in the right place to gather intelligence. Dowdell wanted me to pass along whatever OCHU learned."

Twenty-three investigators were assigned to the murder of Jimmy Bishop, including precinct detectives, OCID, the Manhattan DA, and the U.S. Department of Labor. The obvious inference was that Bishop had been killed because he was cooperating with law enforcement. The difficulty was turning suspicion into evidence, indictments, and convictions, while keeping an open mind and allowing the facts to lead wherever they led.

The Bishop murder file contained dozens of "DD-5s"—NYPD Detective Division Form 5, the record of detective activity and information received during an investigation. Major Case detective Larry Milanesi submitted the slugs recovered from Bishop's corpse to ballistics to check against other murders in which a .380 automatic had been used. Ballistics reported no matches, but OCHU found there had been six organized crime homicides in the city in the past year with that caliber handgun. A detective from the 109th Precinct interviewed Bishop's wife, Frances, but she appeared to know little of her husband's life outside their home. "Mrs. Bishop was too distraught to continue this interview," the DD-5 reported. Bishop's brother-in-law and son were brought to the morgue to identify the body. A friend of Bishop's told the police that Bishop was having problems with someone with the nickname "Gaspipe." The friend said Bishop had been advised to "disappear for a while."

Finally, in early June, nearly a month after her husband was killed, Bishop's widow presented the lead detective with a letter. Bishop had written the letter a year earlier, leaving instructions that it was to be opened in the event of his death. It described a meeting in a Staten Island motel with Fat Pete Chiodo. Chiodo had told Bishop he would be killed if he opposed the candidate of the Luchese family in the upcoming union election. The DD-5 read, "The said letter contained a declaration by Bishop that if he or any member of his family should be killed, it was because of his dealings with members of Organized Crime who infiltrated the union. Bishop wrote that he was forcibly removed from his position in the union and recounted the threats on his life. The letter listed names, dates, and places these threats were made and the individuals behind what he described as a 'conspiracy.'"

The Bishop murder provoked an enormous response from the NYPD. But the investigation was quickly entangled by the complexities and paradoxes of trying to catch killers and at the same time catch the leaker who had aided them. In truth, there were two investigations under way. The official investigation of Bishop's murder reported in the DD-5s showed detectives doing their duty and working the expected angles. The parallel investigation only existed between the lines of the murder file. The receipt of Bishop's letter was cited in the DD-5s but not the names it contained. There were records of meetings between detectives from OCID and the precinct detectives, but no record of what they discussed. The parallel investigation was not documented. It unfolded in the minds of the detectives working the case. The subject was not who had killed Bishop. The triggermen didn't much matter. They were pawns in a larger game. The crucial question was why Bishop had been killed. Was it because he was a CI? Bishop knew enough to do serious damage to the Luchese family bosses. It was a clear motive for murder. Did the Lucheses know about Bishop's cooperation? If so, how did they find out? There was no suggestion in the DD-5s as to who may have been suspected. For the detectives assigned to the Bishop homicide, in the 109th Precinct and in OCHU, playing it close to the vest was the smart move. They knew that creating a paper trail left the investigation open to compromise. If they committed a lead to paper, there was a good chance the Lucheses would learn of it.

"At the time, everything leaked in the police department. It was why the feds hated working with us. The NYPD had a command structure that required us to send information up the chain. Reports from a detective in the field passed through a sergeant, then a lieutenant, captain, all the way up to the chief of detectives. DD-5s were filed in triplicate. Two of the copies were distributed outside your precinct or command. It was a way of ensuring good communication, but it was terrible for maintaining confidentiality. To have accountability in the force, there was no real accountability. No detective wanted to be accused of withholding important information. No supervisor wanted to be out of the loop. The internal mail system was a joke. Reports were lost, mishandled, and misplaced. Cops assigned to do the mail were confused by poor handwriting and acronyms like OCID and OCHU. There was no effective means of tracing the movement of documents. Once the file left the office there was no way of knowing who had read it. Cooperators like Bishop were supposed to be known only to a few essential people, but controlling information was impossible. One Police Plaza was a sea of paperwork and rumors. Information was traded like currency. Cops kept track of each other. The most sensitive cases were the ones cops most wanted to know about. If a mobster flipped, or a cooperating informant like Bishop came forward, it was news inside headquarters. The result was that the 'puzzle palace' was a gold mine of information. Everyone knew everything, and everyone knew everyone knew everything.

"To make matters more complicated, gangsters and cops often came from the same neighborhoods. When they grew up, cops married women who were friends with the wives of wiseguys. They took their kids to buy clothes at the same places. They worked out at the same gyms. Their kids went to the same schools. The police and the mob were part of the fabric of society, like a reversible jacket. Even for the most honest cop in the world, the rules weren't always entirely clear. If a wiseguy got in trouble with a traffic violation or needed a pistol permit, he would turn to a precinct cop he knew. A cop might run a license plate in the DMV computer to get the registered owner of a car. If a made man had been arrested and not reported the collar to his bosses, the family would be interested in learning what the charges were—the failure to inform his superiors about the pending case could support an inference that the man had become a cooperator. A detective could help find somebody by doing power company checks, looking through probation rolls, parking tickets. Favors started small and appeared meaningless.

"The kindnesses were often returned by mobsters. If there was a crime in the neighborhood—if a girl got raped, or an old lady was injured in a hit and run—the people who knew the most about crime were the professional criminals. Nothing happened in the streets without them knowing. If the incident didn't relate to organized crime, if it shocked the conscience or could win a little influence, a gangster would do his police-man friend, society, and himself a favor and point the NYPD in the right direction. Cops were also a great weapon for wiseguys. If they didn't like another guy, if they didn't like the competition, they would tell their cop contact the guy was dirty. Every wiseguy was half a snitch. The police could be used as a business tool, or a way of getting revenge, or protecting yourself. They would turn in a rival, borrowers behind on their vig payments, a guy who was threatening them. Detectives constantly had to balance what we were being told with who was doing the telling and why.

"If you were investigating the mafia, if you were any good at it, you adopted the culture. You were an anthropologist, after a fashion. If you couldn't figure out the motivations and weaknesses and strengths of your criminals, you weren't going to be able to predict or understand the things they did. It usually made sense to assign detectives from the same ethnic background as the gangsters to the squads doing the investigations. Italian cops chased Italian criminals, black cops chased black criminals, Dominicans chased Dominicans. They talked the same language. They laughed at the same jokes—and at the stupidity of the other side. Over time, a lot of detectives started to empathize with their prey. Friendships formed, even as detectives were busting mobsters.

"Most goodfellas were likable, at least superficially. To get ahead they had to have a certain way with people. They were charmers—until they whacked you. Wiseguys were sharks. They knew how to be fast friends, how to manipulate people, how to turn a tiny opening into a major opportunity. Once a cop did a little thing for a gangster, the unspoken threat that it might be revealed could lead the cop to do more favors—and more and more. It was a trap. Mobsters understood the shortcomings of life for a police officer. Wiseguys drove Mercedes sedans and had box seats at Yankee games. They carried wads of cash. They didn't have to operate by the rules. For cops, half our lives were spent doing paperwork and fol-lowing bullshit regulations. Overtime was how most guys survived. Detectives took second jobs and saved money in jars to put their kids through college. They didn't go to the Caribbean for holidays. They didn't eat in fancy restaurants. There was a structural discrepancy between life in the mob and life in the law. Stay in it long enough as a cop, if you lacked character, there would be a problem.

"There was a lot of gray area but there were also bright lines—lines not to be crossed. Giving away a cooperator like Bishop was beyond any real cop's comprehension. Understanding the mind of a cop who would leak was not easy. Some wanted money. Others considered it a way to make friends and influence gangsters so they could make future cases. There was also the widespread belief, in the mafia and in law enforcement, that a different standard of justice applied to mobsters. None of us wept ourselves to sleep when a Gambino or Luchese took two in the back of the head. Live by the sword, die by the sword. Put Bishop into the equation, the dirty union official turned rat, and it was possible to see how a cop with a gangster mentality might convince himself Bishop got what he deserved. No one liked a snitch. Bishop's death wouldn't elicit much sympathy from any corner, apart from his immediate family.

"By the spring of 1990, it was clear we were in the middle of a new phenomenon. Talking shop about police work with other cops could be fatal. You never knew who the leak might be. It was becoming increasingly clear that there was a problem unprecedented in its complexity and implications. The NYPD, like the mafia, had the rites and rituals of a brotherhood. We had a sworn oath, a code of honor, a common interest. Giving up the existence and identity of a CI betrayed the beliefs that united us. It was also bad for business. Lose one CI and you lost a dozen potential cooperators. Word got around about what happened if you talked to the NYPD. Bishop's death was a deterrent to others who might come forward. There was an unspoken but agreed-upon line that no cop would cross. At least there had been. Identifying Bishop as a cooperator was tantamount to putting a gun to his head and letting someone else pull the trigger. It had to go deeper. The source of the leak had to believe, on some level, that Bishop deserved what he got. The source had to believe a primitive form of tribal justice was acceptable."

THE MURDER
OF JAMES "OTTO" HEIDEL

Oldham had been trained to work on criminal patterns. Like the other detectives in Major Case, he knew that seemingly unconnected homicides were adding up to more than a collection of security lapses. There were dozens of organized crime homicides every year in New York City, as illustrated by the homicide book maintained by Caracappa for OCHU. Every murder contained its own story, with its own matrix of motives and senselessness. But it was crucial to making OC cases to find the connections that reordered seemingly chaotic and unrelated events. Oldham knew the murder of Jimmy Bishop in the spring of 1990 was just the latest in a string of homicides and attempted homicides involving cooperating informants and witnesses.

The pattern appeared to have begun three years earlier with the murder of James "Otto" Heidel, a Luchese associate. Heidel was a master burglar who had pursued a long and varied career as a criminal. He had been a cooperator for the FBI since 1974, when he was busted for possession of stolen goods. A former prizefighter, he was a member of a truck hijacking outfit that stole whatever they could—washing machines, liquor, tobacco. Within minutes of being arrested, when presented with the opportunity to gain leniency in return for information, Heidel snitched—a fact the Bureau had managed to keep secret for more than a decade. After being dropped by the FBI in the summer of 1987, Heidel became a cooperator for the NYPD. Weeks later he was killed. The homicide occurred on the afternoon of October 8, 1987. Heidel was shot and killed near Avenue U and East 35th Street in the 63rd Precinct in Brooklyn.

Like the NYPD, the FBI had designations for categories of criminals cooperating with law enforcement. According to the FBI there were two kinds of cooperators. "CIs" were criminal informants, who, in return for money, provided agents with intelligence about ongoing conspiracies and planned crimes of the mafia. The amounts paid varied, at the discretion of the FBI Special Agent running the CI. Tips about an impending bank robbery might net Heidel $1,000, while a tidbit about a wiseguy plotting smaller offenses would fetch a couple of hundred dollars. The explicit agreement was that the CI would not be called to testify in court. All information provided by a CI had to be corroborated if it was to be used in a prosecution. Cooperating witnesses, or "CWs," were a separate class of criminal expected to testify in court. The difference was significant. CIs had freedom of movement, together with the belief that the betrayal of their friends and co-conspirators would never be revealed. CIs were usually not facing any charges, while CWs were hoping for future protection and "consideration"—a lesser sentence, or no time at all. CWs understood that eventually they would have to take the stand against their compadres.

According to FBI policy, a CI was not allowed to commit crimes during their cooperation. If the FBI discovered a CI's complicity in a crime, the agreement would be "breached," the cooperation would cease, and charges followed. "That was the theory. The whole idea of CIs not committing crimes was a charade. CIs like Heidel were criminals—after all, the *c* stood for criminal. They didn't have jobs. They spent all of their

time consorting with criminals. The only difference was that they had figured a way to stay out of jail. Leopards don't change their spots, nor do
burglars. Using CIs was one of the many necessities of investigating
organized crime. Compromises had to be made. Heidel was an enforcer
but he wasn't going to kill anyone, probably. He wasn't going to get other
people to kill for him, probably. There was no way to know for sure if
you were dealing with the devil or a lovable rogue. To catch bad guys you
had to deal with bad guys. The FBI didn't really want to know what its
cooperators were up to. As long as the CI didn't get out of hand and start
shooting people, the agents weren't going to give up their prized possession. CIs had a pretty free hand as long as they didn't get caught. Get
caught and all bets were off. Which was precisely what happened."

For more than a decade, Heidel was run by FBI Special Agent Patrick
Colgan. Speaking regularly—ten times a day when a bust was coming, a
few times a month during lulls—Colgan and Heidel built a productive
relationship. As a criminal and informant, Heidel's specialties were bank
burglaries, shylocking, and strong-arming. Connected to the Luchese and
Colombo and Gambino crime families, he was used as muscle to collect
money owed to loan sharks. Heidel also had a reputation as an electron-
ics buff who monitored NYPD and FBI communication frequencies. He
was an expert with radios and had a collection of minicassette recorders
and wires he hid on his body to secretly record conversations. His surveillance interest made him good at the work of gathering intelligence. Over
the years he made more than $100,000 as a CI, paid in cash, the amounts
neatly and duly accounted for in FBI files. To protect his identity, the
name Otto Heidel was not used. His name was known only to Colgan.
Like hundreds of other informers, Heidel was referred to only by his CI
number, "12872-OC."

Special Agent Colgan had run dozens of CIs over the years, but Heidel
was one of the best. In 1986 a Gambino associate and tough kid named
Jimmy Hydell had suddenly disappeared. There was talk on the street
about his disappearance being connected to Gaspipe Casso of the Luchese
family, but nothing that amounted to proof, or even evidence. Heidel
told Colgan in graphic detail how Jimmy Hydell had been killed by
Casso. Heidel's and Hydell's names were pronounced the same way and
both had reputations for violence, but they were of different classes of
criminal. "Otto Heidel was all bluster and swagger. He didn't have the guts
to kill. Jimmy Hydell was a killer, plain and simple. Hydell had been
behind an attempted murder of Gaspipe Casso in front of the Golden Ox
restaurant in Bensonhurst in September of 1986. Trying to kill Casso

and missing was worse than bad luck, it was a fatal mistake. Heidel told Colgan how Jimmy Hydell had been tortured by Casso. He said that Hydell's body would never be found. It turned out to be true. Hydell had gone out one afternoon in October 1986 and was never to be seen again. He was presumed dead. Colgan knew what had happened to Jimmy Hydell, but he couldn't prove it. As a CI Heidel wouldn't testify, and his account of events wasn't enough to indict Gaspipe Casso.

"We were always aware of a lot more crimes than we could charge. People do get away with murder. It was a hard thing to swallow as a detective. Part of what drove me to look at cases no one else had closed was knowing that everything had been done to catch bad guys who thought they had got away clean. When I arrived at Major Case, I was always on the lookout for cases like Jimmy Hydell—cases where we knew something but couldn't prove it."

By the mid-eighties, Otto Heidel was operating as a member of a crew of burglars known as the Bypass gang, although he told the FBI that he had only a social connection with them. At the time, the gang was legendary for its cunning and success. Participants came from all five families, but few in the mafia knew the identities of the fifteen or so wiseguys who belonged to the crew. After Amuso and Casso were sworn into the Luchese family in the 1970s (after the team carried out their first hit and met one of the qualifications for membership) their first assignment was the Bypass gang. They were to make sure the Lucheses got their cut of the loot—an estimated $100 million over a decade. The name "bypass" came from the gang's ability to override and disarm sophisticated security systems. The crew consisted of locksmiths and safecrackers and alarm men. They approached their work with precision. Jobs were cased and rehearsed for weeks. The gang often bribed employees of the security companies hired to install and run the alarm systems to disarm them before they went in. Break-ins were scheduled for three-day weekends, providing maximum time to get into safes and safe-deposit boxes with minimum risk. Sunday morning before dawn was their preferred moment to strike.

The Bypass gang was a loose affiliation, with members who cycled through as active and inactive participants on various jobs. A small core of criminals led the gang and recruited specialists for specific jobs. Some heists required safecracking ability, others expertise with alarm or communications systems. The part-time participants were kept from meeting one another in order to minimize the chance they might snitch. Vinny Zappola and his brother Anthony, a former NYPD officer, were two of the inner circle. Over the years, the Bypass gang made scores of scores: banks, department stores, supermarkets, a warehouse in Queens filled with Bulova watches. In the middle of their run, the gang burgled a branch of Citibank in Bensonhurst. A large number of Brooklyn wiseguys kept safe-deposit boxes in the subground floor of that particular Citibank. When the Bypass hit the bank they got away with a huge amount of cash and jewelry, much of the loot owned by the mob.

"Bypass was the Roadrunner to law enforcement's Wile E. Coyote. Detectives loved to tell war stories about them. Once the Staten Island District Attorney's Office set up a sting on the gang. Bypass had a source at a florist on Staten Island. Detectives reasoned that the source would tip off the gang if there was a large amount of money in the safe. Memorial Day weekend was coming up. The florist had a primitive security system. It was perfect, too tempting to pass up."

The Staten Island DA's detectives instructed the owner of the shop to let the source know he had a big win at the casinos in Atlantic City. It was Friday afternoon, too late to get to the bank, so he said he was going to leave $60,000 in the safe over the long weekend. The trap was laid. Fifteen detectives set up on the store and waited. Surveillance cameras with sound-sensitive devices were secreted in the ceilings. Police were stationed in vans outside. A command post was established in a nearby high school. The florist shop was surrounded and locked down. There was no way the Bypass gang could get in undetected.

"On Saturday night the fog rolled in. Sunday morning, before dawn, the building disappeared into the mist, like a ghost ship. Everyone on the police detail sat in silence and watched. Time passed slowly. The cops got edgy. A detective spotted Vinny Zappola drive by. The detectives outside couldn't stand the wait anymore. They moved in. They couldn't believe what they found—or didn't find. A hole had been cut in the roof. The phone lines and alarm system were disabled. The safe was open and empty. The Bypass had done it again. The guys working the case had fun chasing them."

On February 14, 1987, St. Valentine's Day, Heidel met with Special Agent Colgan and reported that he'd recently had a conversation with Casso. Heidel said that Casso had told him that he had a detective in the 63rd Precinct who was working for him. Casso told Heidel he would contact the detective and solicit information on ongoing investigations, including cases outside the jurisdiction of the NYPD. Heidel didn't know the name of Casso's detective, and he didn't dare try to find out. Asking too many questions could get him in trouble. Part of Heidel's tradecraft as a CI was balancing the value of collecting information against the chance of getting himself killed. Heidel was extremely concerned that Casso's source in the Six-Three might learn of his cooperation and tell Casso. Colgan assured Heidel that his identity was confidential and could be kept that way.

Special Agent Colgan put in a report of Heidel's account. Colgan was assigned to white-collar crime at the time, so he couldn't investigate the allegation himself. The "memo," as reports were known in the FBI, was reviewed by the supervisor of the squad. The process of integrating intelligence in the FBI was hourglass-shaped, with information from agents passing through the supervisors before being assessed and disseminated to agents working in the field. In writing his memo, Special Agent Colgan had fulfilled his duty; he never heard if there was a resulting investigation of the detectives in the Six-Three to determine who was on the Luchese payroll, or if other agents had written memos on the subject. The hourglass could also be a black hole.

By the summer of 1987, the Bypass gang had spent months planning to burgle the Atlantic Liberty Bank on Avenue J in Bensonhurst. Information on the heist had come in to Special Agent Colgan from a number of sources. Heidel was one of the informants. Heidel told Colgan that Casso was the head of a group targeting the vault of the bank. Casso and Vic Amuso and Sal Fusco and Vinny, Anthony, and George "Neck" Zappola were going to break in over a three-day weekend. The gang had an insider working at the alarm company that monitored the bank. Their inside man would disarm the alarm, thus allowing Casso's crew to bust into the vault. But, Colgan wondered, how would Heidel know about the job in such detail if he wasn't involved? Heidel denied to Colgan he was in on it. Heidel said he had only "overheard," not participated in, these discussions, a claim Special Agent Colgan considered dubious.

"In August of '87 the Atlantic Liberty was hit. The FBI knew about Heidel's participation in the job through another snitch. There was no way Colgan could keep Heidel as a CI now—Heidel was burgling banks, and worse yet he got caught at it and arrested. Predictably, just as he had in 1974, Heidel wanted to make a deal. He was known as a real tough guy on the street, but he was a wimp when it came to law enforcement. Heidel rolled over right away. He was terrified of jail. It was his personality. He couldn't do the time. He was going to prison, and he knew it, but he was postponing his reservation and hoping for a miracle.

After the bust, it was impossible for Heidel to remain a CI. Special Agent Colgan closed his CI file. But Heidel was desperate. He agreed to become a CW, cooperating witness. He would testify as a witness at the trial of anyone he implicated in return for the hope of a reduced sentence. More important, more perilously, Heidel forfeited the security of being a CI. Instead of working exclusively for Special Agent Colgan, Heidel became a CW for the FBI/NYPD Joint Bank Robbery Task Force. The system that had kept his identity confidential was no longer in place. A group of FBI agents had access to his name and pedigree, but so did OC detectives in the NYPD—and the department leaked like a sieve. Within a month he would be dead.

In the hyperparanoid world of the mafia, it was not surprising that Heidel had raised the suspicions of more than one Brooklyn gangster. Burton Kaplan, a businessman in the clothing industry and a Luchese associate who was close friends with Casso, was at a high-end catering hall and cabana club in the Mill Basin section of Brooklyn called El Caribe shortly after Heidel was arrested. El Caribe was a meeting place for wiseguys who wanted to stay in shape, with two racquetball courts and a swimming pool in back with chaise lounges where card games were played in the summer. Favored by Gambinos, it was also used by Lucheses for special events. El Caribe in fact served as the location of the wedding of Gaspipe Casso's daughter.

Kaplan was a well-known organized crime figure. Referred to as "the Jewish guy" and "Downtown Burt," Kaplan was one of the most prolific and deft dealers in stolen goods in New York City. Most fences specialized in particular types of goods because they had customers to buy the swag. Tobacco, alcohol, clothing—distribution channels paralleled legitimate businesses and it paid to concentrate in one area. Uniquely, Kaplan could handle everything. Designer watches, counterfeit Calvin Klein jeans, women's leisure suits, Peruvian passports, hot Treasury bills, tons of marijuana, every and any fungible item could be brought to Kaplan and a good price received.

One afternoon in the summer of 1987, Kaplan was having lunch at El Caribe when he ran into a vicious mobster named Tommy "Karate" Pitera. Otto Heidel walked over to the lunch stand to join them. Heidel had been playing racquetball. Kaplan knew Heidel from around. He also knew Heidel was close to Casso. He had the feeling there was something wrong with Heidel. A few weeks before, Kaplan had been the fence for the mother lode of Bulova watches the Bypass gang had stolen from a warehouse in Queens. Heidel had been given the job of delivering them to Kaplan. He had rented a truck and filled it with the Bulova watches and gone to a house on Staten Island that Kaplan used to stash swag. Heidel was accompanied by three other men. Kaplan felt uneasy after Heidel and the others left—it didn't seem right to have so many people know about a deal like the watches and their whereabouts. There was something about Heidel that Kaplan didn't like, something unsettling. Nervous, Kaplan got his right-hand man, a hanger-on named Tommy Galpine, to wipe the watches for fingerprints and move them to another hiding place. The next day, federal agents turned up at Kaplan's stash house looking for the watches. A few days after that, Luchese wiseguys were busted for the Bulova watch heist. Suspicion of Heidel wasn't something Kaplan could prove, but his radar was up.

Tommy Karate Pitera was a member of the Bypass gang and felt the same way as Kaplan. As Heidel stood in El Caribe ordering lunch, Pitera accused him of cooperating with law enforcement. Pitera said he thought Heidel was a traitor. In mob circles it was the ultimate accusation of betrayal. Heidel denied the claim. Affecting outrage, Heidel demanded to know how Pitera could suggest he was a rat. The confrontation escalated. Heidel, the ex-boxer, was furious. Pitera didn't back down. He said that every time Heidel was involved in a heist it seemed like people were pinched, or the police knew the Bypass gang was coming before they arrived on the job. Something always went wrong. "Personally," Pitera repeated, "I think you're a stool pigeon."

"The exchange was extremely dangerous for Heidel. Pitera was what they called 'capable' in the mafia—capable of murder, capable of anything. There were always euphemisms in the mob. Killing someone was 'doing a piece of work.' Pitera was the kind who liked that kind of work. Heidel was supposed to be a fighter, an enforcer. He depended on intimidation to make his name. But Kaplan was too smart for Heidel. That day at El Caribe, standing at the lunch concession about to buy a sandwich, Kaplan saw fear in Heidel's eyes. Fear was one emotion you didn't show around a canny gangster like Kaplan. He could smell fear and weakness, no matter how faint the scent."

"To me it didn't look right," Kaplan told Casso when they met after the Heidel encounter. Casso was not convinced. He had known Heidel for many years.

"We never had no problems with him," Casso said to Kaplan.

Casso knew that Kaplan had sources in law enforcement who might be able to confirm or deny that Heidel was a cooperator.

"Why don't you ask your friends to find out what they can about Otto?" Within days, Kaplan passed along word from his sources that Heidel was "hot"—he was a rat.

"Are you sure?" Casso asked. "I've known this guy a long time. Do you think your friends are accurate?"

Kaplan was adamant. "They haven't told us anything that wasn't accurate yet," Kaplan said.

Armed with the tip from Kaplan's sources, everything about Heidel began to appear questionable. What might have gone unnoticed before suddenly attracted attention. The gang had just failed in an attempt to break into a jewelry store on Mill Avenue in Brooklyn. They had started to ax their way through the ceiling when the alarm tripped and they were forced to flee. After the attempt, the owner installed razor wire around the roof's perimeter. A few weeks later, Heidel suggested to Vinny Zappola that they try to burgle the store again. When they went to look the place over, Zappola noticed that the razor wire had been removed. He started asking questions about Heidel. Why go back to the same place when there were hundreds of places to hit? Why did the owners pull down razor wire they had strung up only weeks earlier? It looked to Zappola like the wire was removed to make the job easier to entice the Bypass gang back, to catch them red-handed. Zappola decided against attempting to break into the store. Zappola began to think that Heidel might be setting them up.

"That same day Heidel had lunch with Casso at a Chinese restaurant called Joy Teang. I never understood why, but Joy Teang was a Benson-hurst favorite of mobsters and detectives from the Six-Two and Six-Three. The chop suey was the chef's specialty—slop suey." Heidel talked about past and future jobs in a manner that made Casso wonder if he was trying to lure him into saying something incriminating. Casso thought Heidel might be wearing a wire. Casso put out a hit on Heidel.

The murder was set for a Thursday afternoon in October 1987. Heidel was known to be extremely fit, often lifting weights at a local gym fre-quented by cops and ex-cons. The men on Casso's crew were aware that Heidel played paddleball, a variation of handball popular in the public parks of Brooklyn. They would surprise him after he finished his game. On the day of the murder, one of the hit team was late, caught in traffic on the Staten Island Expressway. His associates located Heidel's car and let the air out of one of the tires. Leaving the paddleball court, Heidel discovered the flat. He opened the trunk, took out his jack, and started to change the tire. As he bent down, Heidel saw a man walking toward him with a gun drawn. He turned and ran against traffic on a one-way street. It was late afternoon and kids from the grammar school down the block had just been let out; the park was filled with playing children at that time of day. The hit men started to shoot. Heidel dodged cars while he fled. Struck in the buttocks and back, he kept running west on Avenue U and north on 35th Avenue as the attackers continued firing, hitting him in the back. Desperate, bleeding, and breathless, Heidel jumped on the back of a passing motorcycle and commandeered it. By then, his pursuers had caught up to him. Heidel was shot again and again, his back pierced with more than half a dozen slugs; amazingly, the motorcycle rider was missed. Finally succumbing, Heidel fell to the ground. Casso's hit man stood over him and finished him with a single bullet to his chest. At the time, the murder in broad daylight barely registered in the press. On page five of the Metro section the next day the *New York Times* reported: "Another Man Slain in Mob-Style Killing."

"Mob murders were happening all the time in those days. The Colombo family was at war. The Bonanno family was falling apart. Genoveses and Gambinos and Lucheses were whacking one another wholesale. After the Commission Case in 1986, the leadership was locked up and a new generation of unsophisticated thugs took over, and the streets were littered with dead wiseguys like Otto Heidel. He could have been killed for any number of reasons. He could have been killed for stealing some mobster's jewelry in the Citibank job. There were a lot of guys unhappy about having their safe-deposit boxes emptied. He might have been killed for welching on a bet, or a drug deal gone bad. For precinct detectives who caught mob homicides, there was often no way of knowing precisely why an organized crime figure got killed. They had substantial histories. There were lots of potential motives. If you were running with the mafia, your demise came as no surprise to anyone.

"Heidel was a high-profile homicide. All of the detectives from OCHU responded to the scene of the murder—Steve Caracappa, Jack Hart, Chuck Siriano. If an OC figure like Heidel was killed, they went to have a look and help out the precinct. Looking at a crime scene was part of the job of an OCHU detective. They applied their experience as precinct detectives and combined it with their organized crime knowledge. OCHU guys might see something everyone else missed. In Heidel's case there were signs pointing in a specific direction. There was an FBI agent's card in his wallet when he was murdered—and that is not standard-issue equipment for a member of a burglary crew. FBI agents showed up at the scene and at the precinct house—and that nearly never happened. The FBI denied Heidel had been their snitch, but it was evident to everyone that he had to have been tied to the Bureau. Few people in the NYPD knew that Heidel was a CW for the Joint Bank Robbery Task

Force. Only detectives working in OCHU with access to the most confidential information knew that Heidel was an NYPD cooperator."

Detective Edward Scott from the Six-Three was assigned to investigate the Heidel homicide. He went with an FBI agent to Heidel's apartment to search for evidence. Scott found Heidel's collection of audio- and videotapes and a receiver able to monitor NYPD radio frequencies—one of the hallmarks of the Bypass gang. In the tangle of clothes at his bachelor pad, Heidel had a device to record telephone conversations and walkie-talkies and a Bulova watch. Under the floor in the bathroom they discovered a secret hidden compartment—a "trap"—containing a microcassette recorder and many tapes. Detective Scott played a few of the tapes. One contained a recording of Heidel in the process of committing a burglary, as if he was memorializing his crime as a souvenir. The rest of the tapes were placed in a large plastic bag and taken to the detective squad room in the Six-Three. The bag was placed in the supervisor's office, just off the squad room, instead of being individually tagged and vouchered as pieces of evidence. Scott wanted to listen to the tapes to see if any contained leads for his homicide investigation before they were officially entered into NYPD records.

"Within days, one of the microcassette tapes was in the possession of Burt Kaplan. His source in the Six-Three, the cop who had ratted on Heidel, gave it to Kaplan as evidence that Heidel was a cooperator. Vic Amuso's voice could be heard. Amuso was outside the bank, in a van with Otto Heidel monitoring police frequencies. The crew was inside the bank. The heist was February, in the middle of a cold snap in the city. Amuso could be heard cursing the weather and talking to Heidel about getting some hot soup. That was the tape—two cold hungry hoods talking about chicken noodle soup. But it showed that Heidel had been wearing a wire, which was more than enough to get yourself deceased in the Bypass gang. Kaplan gave the tape to Casso as proof that his cop friends were right about Heidel—and proof of how connected they were inside law enforcement."

In the aftermath of the Heidel homicide, the atmosphere in the Six-Three grew poisonous. Detective Scott was instructed to keep quiet about the case and not talk to fellow detectives. After ten days, as the implications of the homicide began to sink in, Scott was ordered to take the investigation out of the Six-Three and work from the offices of Brooklyn South Homicide. It was known that there were leaks in the precinct but it was maddeningly difficult to find the culprit, or culprits. It could be anyone with access to the offices—telephone repairmen, secretaries, patrolmen. "Trust in a small and crowded squad room like the Six-Three was vital. Cops worked twelve-hour shifts and shared desks and phones—their lives. Everyone had access to everything. If you couldn't trust your brother detectives, who could you trust? Heidel had been shot in broad daylight on a busy street but the case remained unsolved. It was the kind of case that made the rumor rounds at One PP. It became widely believed in the department that Heidel had been killed because he was cooperating with law enforcement and the mafia had somehow discovered he was a rat."

THE ATTEMPTED MURDER
OF DOMINIC COSTA

"After the Heidel hit, the Bypass gang became inactive. They stopped pulling jobs altogether. The pressure from law enforcement was so intense it was impossible for the gang members to go near a bank without half a dozen detectives trailing them. They knew they were being watched, and they knew we knew they knew they were being watched. It was the stage of the investigation where head games were played as each side was trying to fake the other out."

By the fall of 1988, the NYPD had managed to get its own snitch inside the Bypass gang. The break came in the form of a tip. During the investigation of the gang, veteran detectives had become convinced that the gang's "box man" (the man in charge of cracking the safes) had to be older, in his seventies or eighties. The standard of the safecracking was so high, and the knowledge of the design and function of old and obscure safes so deep it had to have been the work of a true craftsman. At the time, Detective Chuck Siriano of OCHU was running a cooperating informant code-named "Chicky." Chicky told Siriano that law enforcement had it wrong about the box man. Chicky was a "pick" for the gang—an expert lock pick. Even though they were both freelancers, Chicky had met the box man. He was a young locksmith named "Dominic" who lived in Brooklyn. Chicky didn't know Dominic's last name, or where he lived, but he was definitely in his mid-twenties.

Detective Siriano doubted Chicky's account. But on the off chance Chicky was right, Siriano went to the Consumer Affairs Department and pulled the files on every "Dominic" in Brooklyn with a locksmithing license. Registering for a license required the applicant to submit a photograph. Siriano presented the pictures of all the Dominics to Chicky, who identified a young Bensonhurst locksmith named Dominic Costa. With the ID, Siriano believed he had a shot at getting an informant inside the Bypass gang. For the next year, Detective Siriano worked with Detectives Frank DeMarco and George Gundlach collecting evidence on the criminal activities of Costa. The aim was to accumulate enough evidence so that when Siriano snatched him from the street he could convince Costa that he would go to jail for a long time if he didn't flip. Leverage in negotiations with a gangster was critical.

Siriano learned that Costa was, in fact, twenty-six years old. A former Marine Corps sniper, Costa moved back to New York after he got out of the military in 1981 and went to work for a trade union in Manhattan—the same painters union run by Jimmy Bishop. Costa had studied locksmithing at night school. Talented, he had been hired as a teacher at the National School of Locksmithing and Alarms on 42nd Street in Manhattan. Unknown to his employers, Costa moonlighted cracking safes for the Bypass gang. After a year of collecting evidence Siriano arrested Costa for gun possession. He presented the charges Costa was facing. "Siriano didn't have hard evidence. He had what Chicky said Costa was in on—the Bulova watch job and a jewelry store in Nassau County. It wouldn't stand up in court, but Costa didn't know that, and all that mattered was what Costa believed. Cops could lie and lie and lie to get a guy to talk. Prosecutors had to tell the truth. We didn't. The psychology of getting a criminal to talk was dependent on the circumstances. In the fall of 1988, Costa agreed to become a cooperator. As a CI his identity would never be revealed. He would go about his business and no one in the Bypass gang would be the wiser. From that moment on, it was a matter of life or death to keep Costa's name secret. If the gang heard that Costa was a rat, he would be executed."

One week later, on the night of October 10, 1988, Costa backed into his garage on Bay Ridge Parkway in Bensonhurst. It was twenty minutes after midnight when shots rang out. Costa's distraught common-law wife, Anna Carannante, stood next to Costa's car, door ajar, screaming, "Dominic, Dominic!" Costa was not dead. Six slugs were lodged in his head. His breathing was labored, and his brain damaged, but he was alive.

Detective Al Guarneri of the Six-Two was assigned as lead detective. He inspected Costa's apartment and found a police radio tuned to an NYPD frequency—the same model as had been found in Heidel's home. Guarneri interviewed Costa's wife at the hospital where Costa was being treated. Anna Carannante said that Costa had recently started getting up in the middle of the night and going out. "Annie further states that Dominic is a home type person, he don't use drugs, drink or gamble. She can't imagine why anyone would shoot him like this." After Costa had recovered enough to talk, Detective Guarneri attempted to interview him, but his mother refused to let him speak to her son. The family was eager to check Costa out of the hospital and place him in a rehabilitation program. Guarneri insisted Costa remain under police protection. Costa's mother replied that the NYPD had nearly got her son killed in the first place. There was no record in the DD-5s that Costa was a cooperating informant. The sole hint was the record of what Costa's mother told Detective Guarneri: police protection had nearly got her son killed in the first place.

Only a handful of law enforcement officials were supposed to know about Costa. Frank DeMarco worked in SLATS—the Safe, Loft and Trucks Squad, a sister squad to Major Case—and Detective Gundlach, who was with the Nassau County DA's Office were two. Another was Chuck Siriano in OCHU. One or two detectives were assigned to specialize in each of the five families. All OCHU detectives had to report significant developments in their field to Sergeant Jack Hart. Computers were new to the NYPD and were mostly used as word processors. The human component was vital in keeping track of information and building up a database. In addition to intelligence developed by OCHU, the unit was a "clearinghouse" for organized crime information. Reports came in from the FBI, the DEA, district attorneys from the five boroughs, the Organized Crime Task Force, the Organized Crime Control Bureau (OCCB), the Intelligence Division, precinct detectives—all points. Like the FBI, the NYPD had protocols for keeping the identities of CIs secret. The CI file was supposed to be accessible only to the detective who ran that CI. The documents were kept inside a locked cabinet inside the locked OCHU room. The file contained the CI's name, contact information, and criminal background, as well as information about family affiliations and known haunts and associates. OCHU detectives were required to tell Sergeant Hart if they had a CI. Caracappa was Hart's number two. As a practical matter, detectives gave their reports to Caracappa, who passed them to Hart. Everything that came into OCHU went through Caracappa and on to Hart.

"Detective Siriano was white-hot mad about Dominic Costa. Siriano was a hardworking cop who truly believed in the job—he was what we called a 'buff.' He had spent a year working on Costa. Costa was an important CI. Hart and Caracappa both knew Siriano was running Costa as a CI in the Bypass investigation. Siriano didn't accuse Hart or Cara-cappa of deliberately giving Costa away. It would be impossible to accuse Jack Hart of selling out. Hart was a classic: a chain-smoking, hard-drinking sergeant who stood up for his guys. Hart was as honest as the day was long. He would never put anyone in harm's way. Everyone knew by then that there were serious, serious problems. Something somewhere was broken. I don't think it crossed anyone's mind that someone in Major Case was a snitch for the mob."

There were other ways Costa's name could have leaked. Siriano knew that the Brooklyn DA's Office knew about Costa's cooperation and identity. Siriano confronted Mark Feldman, who was then head of Brook-lyn rackets prosecutions. Feldman said the rumor was that Siriano had given Costa up himself by mistake. The false story went that Siriano had slipped and dropped Costa's name with another CI and word had got back to the Bypass gang that Costa was a snitch. "Speculation was getting out of hand. Cops were turning on each other. Prosecutors were turning on cops. Cops were turning on prosecutors. Siriano was an impassioned detective. He was the kind of detective who didn't mind spending twelve hours a day sitting in a van sweating like a pig on a summer day because he couldn't use the air-conditioning on a stakeout—a running motor would give the operation away. Siriano was committed body and soul to the job. After Costa was nearly killed Siriano knew there was no way he could rely on the law enforcement establishment in New York to main-tain its secrets. Siriano went to see his informant Chicky. He felt that Chicky could be next. He felt an obligation to keep him alive. Siriano gave Chicky $2,000 of his own money and told him to disappear. He knew if word of Chicky's cooperation got out he would be dead."

TIGER MANAGEMENT

In the late eighties, information no longer just leaked from One PP. There was a flood of sensitive intelligence reaching the mafia. The inves-tigation of Tiger Management, a Brooklyn garbage-hauling consulting company, was an example of how dire the situation had become. Solid waste removal was one of the main rackets of the Lucheses. The industry was worth hundreds of millions and growing rapidly, with the Fresh Kills landfill in Staten Island reaching capacity. A new business emerged truck-ing trash to rural areas in Pennsylvania and Ohio. Inevitably, gangsters infested the industry, fixing contracts, bribing local politicians, and strong-arming unions and legitimate operators—the same operating procedure as in the painting industry. "Mobbed-up companies baled hazardous material, like needles and medical waste, with regular garbage to save money. Millions of tons were hauled every year. Profits were phenomenal. The Luchese end was run out of a storefront on 4th Avenue in Brooklyn. Fat Pete Chiodo was in charge. He was six-one, three hundred pounds. He was the wiseguy who had controlled the painters union and Jimmy Bishop. He had become a capo under Vic Amuso and Gaspipe Casso. Chiodo had been given the 19th Hole to operate, the social club Amuso and Casso used to run their affairs."

In the winter of 1989, a secret multiagency investigation of garbage hauling was launched. Tiger Management was one of the targets. Investigators from the Waterfront Commission of New York Harbor and the New Jersey Attorney General's Office were engaged in surveilling a trailer that Tiger Management kept in the industrial wastelands of New Jersey. Listening devices had been placed inside the trailer on St. Patrick's Day, when no one from Tiger Management was on the site. "Bugs" picked up voices in the trailer conversations. "Taps" were able to detect and record telephone conversations. Investigators set up in a hotel room across the street and half a block away from the trailer to conduct video surveillance and take photographs of all vehicles and people coming and going.

On April 18, 1989, the hotel room was manned by Victoria Vreeland, a young investigator on the first assignment of her law enforcement career. As she stood in the window watching the Tiger Management trailer, a large mobile home drove onto the property. The driver got out and started to crawl on the ground outside of the trailer. Vreeland quickly became concerned. She knew technicians had also been under the trailer installing the listening devices and there was a chance the man would see exposed wires, thereby revealing the investigation.

The man was heavyset and hirsute. He conducted himself as if he had no idea he might be under observation. Vreeland recorded the scene on videotape. In the footage, the overweight man climbed out a hatch on top of the trailer. He inspected a telephone pole. The man clearly had some expertise in wiring. He got a ladder from the mobile home and climbed up the pole. Then he got back in the mobile home and drove to the next telephone pole and did the same thing at each pole all the way down the street. He was working diligently for forty-five minutes. "That day all the wiretaps went down. The next day the bugs went down. There was no point in continuing with the surveillance. The cover of the investigation had been blown. The case against Tiger Management was compromised. No one working the case had seen such a thing happen before. No charges were brought."

By the spring of 1990, there was no question in the Major Case Squad. The Luchese family had a source inside law enforcement. The pattern was clear. The murders of Jimmy Bishop and Otto Heidel pointed that way. The attempt on Dominic Costa one week after he had become a cooperator pointed that way. The compromised bugs and taps pointed that way. There was no other explanation for what was happening to OC investigations again and again. "The problem was figuring out what to do about it. When an institution suffered a breach in its security the way the NYPD had, everyone was operating in a fog. Who could you trust? Who was suspect? How do you begin an investigation? The difficulty was figuring out how to tie events together. What we really needed was someone inside the mafia to tell us what was going on. To find our rat, we needed a rat of our own."

CHAPTER FOUR

THE CRYSTAL BALL

In the spring of 1990, Oldham moved from his apartment in Harlem to a loft on Mott Street in downtown Manhattan to be closer to the organized crime action. Mott Street ran the length of Little Italy and Chinatown, neighborhoods that teemed with criminals. There was a Gambino gambling parlor next door to Oldham's place. Down the block stood a social club with a warning sign on the wall inside saying, "This place is bugged." A few blocks east, Asian gangsters from the Ghost Shadows and Flying Dragons strutted the streets on the lookout for interlopers. On Mulberry Street mobsters sat playing cards outside John Gotti's Ravenite Social Club. The mafiosi didn't even attempt to keep a low profile. They pulled up in Cadillacs with tinted windows and Landau rooves, greeting each other with elaborate hugs and two-cheek kisses. The mafia was kind of a tourist attraction, part of the thrill and legend of New York City.

"The neighborhood was swarming with criminal conspiracy. I would walk out of my apartment and literally run into John Gotti and Sammy the Bull Gravano on a 'walk-and-talk' to avoid electronic listening devices. They were always trailed by a mob bodyguard—and an entourage of federal agents and NYPD cops trying to record their conversation. The proximity to organized crime got my juices flowing. A lot of cops lived in the suburbs. Guys would drive two hours each way every day to escape crime and the city. I wanted to be in the thick of it. I could walk to headquarters. I could go to Mare Chiaro or La Donna Rosa and listen to the wiseguys talking. I could go to New Jeannie's on Mulberry Street for the steamed sea bass and watch the Ghost Shadows enjoying their Tsingtao. What I was really doing was getting myself known in the community. I wanted the regular people running their businesses to know that I was a cop and that I lived in the neighborhood. I became friendly with the guy running the newsstand on my street. I got to know the deli owner where I bought milk and beer. Dry cleaning, shoeshine, even the beat cops from the precinct, I made it my business to get to know them. It was my version of setting up a Rotary Club. Local business owners were often the victims of organized crime. I wanted them to trust me. If they needed help, I wanted them to come to me."

Despite the omnipresence of law enforcement in lower Manhattan, the cops and federal agents working surveillance weren't apparent to the untrained eye. Oldham made a sport of spotting as many surreptitious surveillance operations as he could as he walked the streets of Little Italy and Chinatown. Easiest to see was the FBI agent in black oxfords trying to pretend he was a bum reading a newspaper in front of a flophouse at the corner of the Bowery and Grand Street. Helicopters circled overhead. Vans parked on corners had sophisticated listening instruments trained on tenement buildings and Italian restaurants. Curtained windows on apartments were set up to disguise surveillance. A mere thirty square blocks contained FBI organized crime and special operation squads, the New York state Joint Organized Crime Task Force, the DEA's Group 41, among others. There was the Jade Squad, a small unit that worked exclusively on Asian organized crime, as well as the Manhattan DA's rackets squad. The NYPD's Organized Crime Investigating Division competed with the Organized Crime Monitoring Unit of the Intelligence Division. Lower Manhattan was practically a law enforcement convention. FBI agents trailing a car outfitted with a "bird dog"—a radio transmitter attached to the undercarriage—would get their signal crossed with a detective bird-dogging a Luchese. The voice transmitters used for wiring an informant had three frequencies. Often a receiver tuned to Sicilian voices would be interrupted by a squawk of interference from another wire and the voices would be in English. Another squawk would follow and the voices would be speaking Cantonese.

"Territories overlapped in law enforcement the way they did in the mob. There were law enforcement families, each with their own history and camaraderie but also old scores to settle and divergent agendas. No one shared information. Everyone wanted to make the big busts. The FBI was the worst. They would let defendants walk on state charges to protect a federal prosecution. They weren't going to give up the glory."

In the spring of 1990, the modern age of the American gangster seemed to be at its peak. Popular culture and the mafia fed upon each other, a symbiotic relationship that conflated glamour and violence. John Gotti, celebrity killer and heroin dealer, had been acquitted of assault—again. Charged with ordering the murder of the president of the New York Carpenters Union, Gotti's third not-guilty verdict in a row established him as an outlaw hero for some, and the nickname "Teflon Don" appeared regularly on the front pages of the tabloids. *The Godfather, Part III* had just been nominated for best picture in the Academy Awards. Francis Ford Coppola's conclusion to his trilogy romanticized the mafia as the embodiment of *cavalleria rusticana* ("rustic chivalry"). Martin Scorsese's *Goodfellas* was nominated for best picture and Joe Pesci won for best supporting actor. The characters in *Goodfellas* were composites but recognizable to those in the know as real Luchese made men and associates. Henry Hill, the main character, had been a two-bit cokehead drunk and Luchese hanger-on. "A stolen print of the film made the rounds of made guys before it was released. Inside the mob it was known Hill had given away Paul 'Paulie' Vario, a captain in the family, who died of a heart attack in prison. Hill was a rat. The boys were not entertained."

THE WINDOWS CASE

By May 1990, it seemed publicly that organized crime was rebounding from the convictions in the Commission Case. The opposite was the truth. Only days after painters union official Jimmy Bishop was murdered, the FBI was planning to arrest dozens of mafiosi in a prosecution that would come to be known as the Windows Case.

The investigation revolved around a mob scam to exploit a federal Department of Housing and Urban Development plan to finance the replacement of all the windows in New York City's public housing buildings. Heat consumption and the long-term cost of subsidized public housing for the poor would be reduced by using energy-efficient double-glazed thermal panes for 900,000 windows in government apartments throughout the city. The project would cost more than $150 million and take more than a decade to complete. It didn't take long for the mob to pounce. Peter Savino, a Genovese associate who controlled Local 580 of the Architectural and Ornamental Ironworkers Union, started a scheme of rigged bids and kickbacks. The collective bargaining agreements of the union were subverted, sweetheart deals were given out to keep labor costs down, and every window installed was "taxed" by the mafia to the tune of two dollars.

"It was common practice for law enforcement to exaggerate the sums of money involved in mafia corruption cases when arrests were made. Big bucks made the bust sound big and important. The same was true of drug cases. Millions of dollars' worth of pot or Quaaludes were seized, it was said, but using made-up prices. But the Windows Case really was a lucrative business for all five families. Millions truly were made. The proceeds bought a lot of Cadillacs and Brioni suits and thick gold bracelets."

In the Windows Case the disparate strands of the leak pattern started to come together. As indictments neared, the investigation had become an open secret in the organized crime industry of New York City—both among mafia and law enforcement. In the mob, there was constant speculation about who was going to be indicted, and when. In the FBI, monthly reports on the investigation were written up tracking progress toward prosecution. FBI files were provided to the NYPD on a strictly confidential basis. Allegations, targets, action taken, and FBI actions planned were included in the comprehensive rundown of the investigation. But with so many co-conspirators it became difficult to keep intelligence confidential. The "takedown" date for arrests was set for the end of May 1990. More than a dozen wiseguys were to be arrested, including Gambino captain Peter Gotti, Genovese underboss Venero "Benny Eggs" Mangano, and Luchese boss Vic Amuso and underboss Anthony Casso. Arrests were planned to occur simultaneously in Brooklyn, Manhattan, Staten Island, Queens, and the Bronx. More than fifty NYPD detectives and federal agents were assigned to the takedown. It was going to be one of the biggest busts in the history of New York City. Timing was crucial.

Only days before they were to be arrested, Amuso and Casso vanished. Either they were clairvoyant, or they had been tipped off about the impending indictments. Detectives and agents working the Windows Case knew Amuso and Casso had to have been forewarned. In fact, Burt Kaplan's source in the Six-Three had told Kaplan the takedown was coming on the last Monday in May. Kaplan had passed word along to Casso, who then told Amuso. Going "on the lam" was a common tactic for mobsters fearing or facing indictment. It was learned that Amuso and Casso were not apprehensive about being charged with the murders of Jimmy Bishop and Otto Heidel or the attempted murder of Dominic Costa. All of those investigations were stalled and going nowhere. It was the pending RICO charges on the Windows Case that scattered them. Amuso disappeared first, leaving Casso to arrange for running the family in their absence. Casso spent the last weekend of May arranging continuity in the conduct of business for the Luchese crime family—or what passed for continuity.

On the Sunday night before he went on the lam, Casso met with "Little Al" D'Arco at "the cannon"—an antique cannon in Fort Hamilton,

Brooklyn, a Revolutionary War historical site near the Verrazano-Narrows Bridge. Casso told D'Arco about the coming indictments and instructed him on the method the bosses would use to communicate with him and the other Lucheses without revealing their location to their colleagues or eavesdropping law enforcement officials. Pay phones around the city were identified and given a designated number. When Casso or Amuso wanted to contact an underling, they would send a numeric message to that man's beeper with the designated number of the pay phone making up the last digits of the code. Thus summoned, the recipient would go to the specified pay phone and wait for a call. As he left town Casso took Georgie Neck Zappola with him, a young and proven killer who could provide muscle if Casso needed it. At dawn on May 30, the FBI arrested fifteen top-echelon racketeers in raids throughout the city, including Genovese boss Vincent "the Chin" Gigante. Only hours before the FBI was set to swoop down, Casso slipped away in the dark of night.

FAT PETE

Gaspipe Casso had not shared his intelligence with his captain Fat Pete Chiodo. At dawn Chiodo was rousted and trucked off to jail, just like the others. Soon out on bail, Chiodo knew that in all likelihood he faced a long stretch in prison. With the Luchese bosses on the run, Fat Pete started to grow more and more nervous. "Going to trial was a crap shoot that was likely to turn into a turkey shoot. It was difficult to build a defense when you were guilty. But Chiodo didn't just have to calculate what the government might have on him. He had to worry about what his own brother gangsters might do to him. In the post-*omertà* age, the charges against Chiodo made him instantly suspect to his peers. What if he ratted, in return for a lesser sentence? The mafia was looking more and more like a sinking ship as the months passed in 1990, and rats were always the first to jump ship."

Chiodo became convinced Luchese bosses were out to get him. The signs of his peril were small but telling. Before he had been arrested, Chiodo had been promoted to capo and was supposed to be the personal representative for Casso. Yet Casso had grown distant. Chiodo had run the painters union for years but Amuso had given control to another Luchese without offering a reason why. Angered and resistant, Chiodo had argued with Amuso, a rash burst of insubordination. Soon after, Amuso had shouted at him in front of other people at a gathering at El

Caribe, a sign of deep disrespect in the mafia. The past played over in Chiodo's memory. The previous Christmas, following their tradition, Casso and Chiodo had shared a lavish meal. Usually Casso picked up the tab but this year Casso had stiffed Chiodo for the bill. "Fat Pete was smart enough to put the pieces together. The language of the mob existed in gesture and implications. Measuring the mood of the bosses was a necessity. Falling out of favor could be fatal. The eye of suspicion, once cast, could not be taken away. Once a made guy started to feel like he was maybe being set up, his brain was always racing."

One thing Chiodo knew to a certitude was that Amuso and Casso would kill him if they suspected him of cooperating with the government. It didn't matter if he actually betrayed the family. A hunch was enough. The Luchese bosses would go to any length to protect themselves. He had seen firsthand their method of dealing with alleged snitches. The year before, Chiodo's crew had been given the hit on a Luchese associate named Sonny Morrissey, an Ornamental Ironworkers union official. Morrissey was good friends with Amuso and loyal to the family. But Morrissey had dealings with Peter Savino, the Genovese who had set up the Windows scam in the first place. The source Amuso and Casso had in law enforcement had told them Savino was a rat. Savino belonged to another family so the Luchese leaders couldn't kill him without starting a war. But as the Windows investigation closed in, the Luchese bosses had decided Morrissey had to go, along with three other mafia members, simply for their association with Savino. It didn't matter if Morrissey had gone bad. If Savino was a snitch it followed, in the minds of the Luchese bosses, that Morrissey had to be killed. Logical consistency, factual reality, personal history — all were irrelevant.

Chiodo had chosen "Richie the Toupee" Pagliarulo, Tommy "Irish" Carew, and Michael "Mikey" DeSantis to help with the job. The crew lured Morrissey to a housing development in New Jersey, supposedly to meet with Amuso. Morrissey never figured he was in trouble himself; he had done nothing wrong. When Chiodo and his crew got to the development they took Morrissey to a half-constructed house. Chiodo went out the back door saying he was going to go find Amuso. The Toupee opened up on Morrissey. He had a silencer on his gun but it didn't work. He shot Morrissey twice but then his gun jammed. "The Lucheses weren't the gang who couldn't shoot straight — they were the gang that couldn't clean a gun. Tommy Irish started firing. He had a six-shot but there were only four bullets in the thing. Chiodo heard the shots. He came back in to see what was going on. Morrissey was lying on the floor of the house, writhing in pain, begging to be killed. Morrissey's last words were that he wasn't a rat. In real life watching a man defend himself with his last breath is pretty goddamn convincing. Remembering this had to play on Chiodo. He had to know Morrissey wasn't a rat. Fat Pete had to know it didn't matter if he had ratted or not, he could just as easily be killed by Amuso and Casso."

After his arrest in 1990, Chiodo continued to follow the orders of Amuso and Casso. Told to report to a pay phone in Coney Island with documents related to the Windows Case prosecution, Chiodo did as he was told. But Chiodo trusted no one, not even the members of his own crew—particularly members of his own crew. The pressure was unbearable. Chiodo faced years in prison but his fear of the Lucheses made him turn his own home into a prison. He wouldn't leave the house for any reason. His health was suffering. Chiodo was grossly overweight. Finally on Father's Day in 1990—June 18, only three weeks after he'd been arrested—he suffered a heart attack. Chiodo was taken to a hospital on Staten Island. In the hospital, Chiodo was arrested again. This time, as had been predicted by Amuso and Casso's law enforcement source, Chiodo was charged with racketeering in the Painters Union Case—the same investigation the late Jimmy Bishop had been cooperating with. The concentric circles of overlapping conspiracies were starting to tighten into nooses. The suspicions about Chiodo because of his indictment in the Windows Case were doubled by the new Painters prosecution. A short time later, released from the hospital and free on bail, Chiodo met with D'Arco, who told him other Lucheses were staying away from him because of Chiodo's legal jeopardy.

"Chiodo was caught in a squeeze play—the mob was closing in on one side, and the law was closing in on the other. Every conversation was parsed by Fat Pete for hidden meanings or signs. The paranoia of Amuso and Casso was a self-fulfilling prophecy. If your mind fixed on the idea someone was going to turn against you and rat, and you started to act like he was going to turn against you, chances were good that person was going to turn against you. Fear contained the seeds of the mob's destruction—self-destruction."

As Chiodo stewed, holed up in his house, Amuso and Casso continued to roam the tristate area during the summer of 1990, a pair of wolves looking for any signs of weakness in their men. They met regularly with D'Arco at safe houses in Greenwich Village and Brooklyn. The pair arrived in a black Jeep wearing baseball caps and sunglasses, both men growing beards. Through D'Arco they tried to exercise control over the affairs of the family, but dysfunction was turning into chaos.

A simple man, with only a grade school education, D'Arco was valued by Amuso and Casso for his unthinking loyalty and obedience. Short and violent, with a broad Brooklyn accent and a quick temper, for decades D'Arco had only been an associate of the Lucheses as he ran a modest hamburger stand in Manhattan and tried to scratch out extra money from low-level crime. Finally, at the age of fifty he was "made" as a member of the Lucheses. Nicknamed "the Professor," an ironic reference to the dissonance of his preference for tweed jackets and his street thug attitude, Little Al was a reliable and ruthless killer. He had, for example, arranged for the murder of Thomas "Red" Gilmore, a Luchese associate killed because he had been overly insistent on meeting with Amuso. D'Arco had also bludgeoned a wiseguy named Mike Pappadio in the back of a bagel bakery. He had arranged for the murder of John Petrocelli, a cocaine addict who had hidden Gus Farace when he was on the run for killing DEA Agent Everett Hatcher.

"The hit list went on and on. D'Arco was the family servant who had to do all the dirty work. Amuso and Casso thought they were clever but they were suicidally stupid. If the first tool you used for every problem was a hammer, soon every problem started to look like the head of a nail. Betrayal was their leitmotif. Friends were used to murder friends, to the extent there was anything like friendship in the mob. A made man would be lured out by his closest associates. Any pretext would do. When he least expected it, before the realization could take shape in his mind, a gun was put to the back of his head and he was dead. Every wiseguy had examples of mobsters they knew who had been betrayed by their so-called buddies. For the Lucheses getting set up was more than an occupational hazard—it was how business was done."

During the summer of 1990, Casso repeatedly ordered Chiodo to report to designated pay phones to receive instructions. Chiodo refused to comply. Appearing at an appointed time at an appointed place was a good way to get oneself killed. "One of the rules of life in the mafia was that if the boss wanted to see you, you had to report immediately. Rules in the mafia were broken all the time. They lied to each other constantly. They lied to themselves. Half the time they didn't know what was true themselves. But some things about the life were known and agreed. Ignoring calls from the boss was a definite go-directly-to-the-grave move. Like laying hands on another made man—that could get you killed. Wiseguys were supposed to ask for permission if they wanted to leave town for any reason—holiday, illness, business. Close tabs were kept on everyone. Watching each other was a way of making sure the other guy didn't waver in his loyalty or go soft. It was one of the reasons for the claustrophobic atmosphere. They spent all their waking hours with each other, sitting around in social clubs conniving and scheming. The only thing they exercised was their paranoid imaginations. In a way the mafia had its own primitive form of a surveillance system. When Chiodo blew off Casso he was taking a big risk, and he knew it. The alternative was to answer Casso's call and be ordered to meet with him—and wind up dead."

In August 1990, another Luchese, Bruno Facciola, was murdered. Chiodo had known Facciola for years. He also knew that Amuso had never liked Facciola, a feud dating back to a street brawl in the seventies. The order had been given to D'Arco to kill Facciola. D'Arco was told to leave a bird in Facciola's mouth after he had been killed—not overly complex mob symbology for a cooperator who "sang" for law enforcement. The code name given to the job of clipping Facciola was "the wing." The setup was a cliché mob murder. Facciola was brought to an auto body shop on Foster Avenue in Brooklyn by his associate "Louie Bagels" Daidone. Facciola hadn't made it through the door of the shop before he glimpsed two other Lucheses waiting inside. Facciola tried to run but the three set upon him on the sidewalk with knives, stabbing him repeatedly. His body was thrown in the back of his car and driven to a street where Facciola was soon discovered by the police. There was indeed a bird shoved in his mouth—a canary.

After Facciola's homicide, Chiodo went to the Burger Palace on West Street, in lower Manhattan, to meet with D'Arco. By then Chiodo had no crew of his own and most of his money-earning illegal activities had been reassigned to other members of the Luchese. With two outstanding indictments in the Windows and Painters Union Cases, Chiodo was being ostracized by other Lucheses. He wanted to know where he stood in the family, he said. D'Arco told him that he was still a captain but that he should keep a low profile. Chiodo asked why Facciola had been killed. It went without saying that Facciola had been murdered by his supposed partners-in-crime; under Amuso and Casso every time a Luchese was killed it was virtually certain the hit had been ordered by the bosses. D'Arco said that Amuso and Casso suspected Facciola had "gone bad so he had to go."

As the weeks passed, Chiodo's terror that he would be murdered carried him to the edge of a nervous breakdown—or another heart attack.

Facing certain conviction, he pleaded guilty to federal racketeering charges in the Painters Union Case and the Windows Case. According to Luchese protocol, Chiodo should have received approval from Amuso and Casso before pleading out. Pleading guilty without permission amounted to yet another offense to Amuso and Casso. It also increased their suspicion that he was cooperating with the FBI. Under RICO, given his poor health, Chiodo was likely to spend the rest of his life behind bars. Still free while awaiting sentencing, Chiodo was at the moment of maximum pressure to strike a bargain with federal prosecutors to flip and become a CW. Whispers started to circulate in the Luchese and Genovese families that Fat Pete was cooperating. Casso beeped Chiodo night and day but Chiodo ignored him. Al D'Arco told Chiodo to report to Casso. If Chiodo didn't talk to Casso there was no doubt Chiodo would be murdered on Casso's orders, D'Arco said, and the contract would be given to him. D'Arco said he didn't want to be forced to murder Fat Pete. Chiodo would be doing them both a favor if he talked to Casso.

Finally, trapped and unable to stand the pressure, Fat Pete went on the lam himself—running away from the Lucheses, not the law. Chiodo headed south to Huntington, West Virginia, to scout an area within driving distance of the federal prison in Lexington, Kentucky, where he had been told he would serve his time. Chiodo rented a house for his family and stored his white limousine—which he reported stolen in New York to collect on the insurance. Chiodo checked into the local Radisson. He introduced himself as "Joey" and began to lay the foundations for a life after he had served his time. His fantasy of leaving the mafia forever was seductive and delusional. He would open a small chain of pawnshops, he decided, incorporating his venture as Quicksilver Pawnbrokers, Inc. Chiodo came up with a plan to purchase abandoned coal mines and use them for disposing garbage. Salvatore "Sally Paper" Buttaro, an acquaintance of Chiodo's who specialized in paper recycling in New York City, agreed to move south as well. Together they would open a paper plant and run motels through their company Lazy Boy Inns. Never one to miss an opportunity for a quick, illegal buck, Chiodo took along ten illegal Joker Poker machines to put in bowling alleys and bars. Rehabilitation and life on the straight and narrow, for Chiodo, didn't mean he shouldn't make a few dollars on the side with a harmless scam like poker machines. For more than six months, Chiodo disappeared from sight. It was a winter of deadly discontent in the mafia.

MURDER SPREE

On January 9, 1991, as reward for his fealty, Little Al D'Arco was made acting boss of the Lucheses by Vic Amuso and Anthony Casso. During the winter months the pair continued to duck and dodge around the city. The results were predictable. In February, Casso learned that wiseguy friends of Bruno Facciola in the Bronx faction were planning to take revenge against Amuso and Casso. The report of their plot had come from Burton Kaplan, who had been told by his source in the NYPD that there was a plan to kill the Luchese boss and underboss. Amuso and Casso immediately put out contracts on the plotters, Larry Taylor and Al "Flounderhead" Visconti.

On February 5, 1991, at ten-thirty at night, while sitting in his 1980 Oldsmobile on Third Street in Brooklyn, Larry Taylor was shot three times with a shotgun and once with a .38-caliber pistol. Unknown perpetrators fled on foot. On March 26, 1991, Flounderhead Visconti walked into the lobby of his apartment building at 2020 East 41st Street in the Six-Three in Brooklyn. It was nearly seven in the evening. A young man of medium height and build wearing a baseball cap stepped in front of Visconti and shot him four times. The first two slugs shattered Visconti's face, breaking his eyeglasses. The third shot hit him in the left foot. The final shot struck Visconti's penis. There were no witnesses able to ID the shooter with any degree of specificity. Detectives in the Six-Three canvassed the area and interviewed Visconti's brother and surveilled the funeral at Guarino Funeral Home on Flatlands Avenue, noting the license plate numbers of the mourners. Otherwise, the investigation went nowhere.

In the imagination of Gaspipe Casso, it seemed reasonable that he could return to normal life after the Windows and Painters Union cases ended in acquittals. Once the dozens of mobsters indicted on RICO charges in those cases were found not guilty, he believed, there would be no case for the federal government to make against him. The multiple and multiplying murders were another matter; law enforcement had no idea of the role Casso had played in those crimes; the homicides were unsolved, and almost certainly unsolvable. Amuso and Casso had no reason to fear arrest on those counts.

During the early spring of 1991, Casso continued to meet with Al D'Arco, directing the business of the Lucheses. He told Al D'Arco that when it was safe for him to come out of hiding he was going to throw a party for himself. He was going to invite a big group of his associates—Anthony "Curly" Russo, Ralph "Raffie" Cuomo, Danny "Squires" Latella, and Anthony "Bowat" Baratta, among others. They were the men who had taken advantage of him while he was on the lam, Casso told D'Arco. At his homecoming party, Casso said, he would kill all of them.

In May of 1991, after months spent building the foundations for a new life in West Virginia, Fat Pete Chiodo came back to New York to make final arrangements to move his family south. Armed and moving around town with great caution, he set about ending what little remained of his affairs and interests in the city. On May 8, the day before he was supposed to drive south and leave New York forever, he and his elderly father went out to run errands—a visit to the doctor, a stop at the bank, and last a drop by the local car repair shop to collect his father's car. At three-forty in the afternoon, Fat Pete pulled his Cadillac into a service bay of the Getty station at the corner of Fingerboard Road and Bay Street on Staten Island. Chiodo was having trouble with the fan belt on his Cadillac—it was making a noise. Chiodo popped the hood. A large black sedan, four-door, followed Chiodo into the lot. A door swung open. An unknown male, white, mid-thirties, wearing a baseball cap and a black satin jacket, opened fire as he approached; the revolver had a silencer and the only sound was the ping of bullets on the pavement.

Chiodo turned and ran. The man entered the garage's office firing. Chiodo pulled a five-shot .22 from his belt holster. Before he could return fire, he was hit in the left arm and then the right leg by another shooter who had appeared on the other side of the room. Trying to flee and fire at the same time, Chiodo emptied his five-shot. He missed. The two gunmen moved to close range, riddling Chiodo's body. Chiodo was hit twelve times in total. Everyone else in the garage had taken cover. "We've been here too long!" the first shooter shouted. The gunmen began to panic—surely Fat Pete had to be dead by now. "Let's get the fuck out of here!" he screamed. The two men ran to the waiting sedan and sped into the midday traffic on Fingerboard Road. Chiodo was barely breathing when the ambulance arrived—but he was alive. The layers of fat on his corpulent body had saved his life.

"Chiodo was not a rat. Not yet. Their attempt to kill him understandably made him reconsider his position. When someone tries to murder you it tends to concentrate the mind. Chiodo was no exception. The more the demented duo tried to intimidate their people to stop them from talking, the more likely it was that their people would talk. Violence breeds violence. Violence also breeds fear. Fear was supposed to be a motivating factor. Amuso and Casso thought they could scare loyalty into their men. All they did was increase the speed at which events were spiraling out of control."

While he lay in the hospital Fat Pete agreed to become a cooperator with the federal government. Casso had achieved precisely the outcome he most dreaded. It was the first big break in the leak investigation. Chiodo was moved to the Veteran's Hospital in Brooklyn, under heavy protection, where he was interviewed by prosecutors and the FBI. Chiodo confessed to participating in four homicides, two attempted homicides, and two murder conspiracies.

As Chiodo talked to the authorities about the inner workings of the mafia, there was a concerted Luchese campaign to convince him to shut up. His elderly father was threatened with death by two white males unless his son "did the right thing." His grandmother's house in Gravesend, Brooklyn, was torched. Chiodo's sister, a mother of three and president of her local PTA in Bensonhurst, was shot in the head in broad daylight as she returned from driving her son to school. Terrified but stuck with the deal he had made, Chiodo cooperated.

In early July 1991, in debriefing sessions with FBI agents and federal prosecutors, Chiodo became the first mobster to explain to law enforcement how deeply the Lucheses had penetrated the NYPD. It wasn't just a matter of getting tips, or asking for an occasional favor, he told them. *The Lucheses knew everything they wanted to know about law enforcement on the city, state, and federal levels.* The inside source had given Amuso and Casso information that led to the demise of Otto Heidel in 1987 and the near-death experience of Dominic Costa in 1988. The source had given away the bugs and taps placed in Tiger Management's trailer in New Jersey. The instruction had come from Casso that Chiodo should be careful what he said when he was in the trailer. Removing the listening devices was not what Casso expected. Casso didn't want law enforcement to know that they knew about the operation. "Chiodo sending the gorilla in the fedora with the mobile home to look for the wires was beyond stupid. Casso was reluctant to tell Fat Pete anything after that. Using information from Casso's source required discretion."

Chiodo told the FBI that Amuso and Casso called their source the "crystal ball." The nickname came from the ability of their source to predict the future. The "crystal ball" was a running joke for the Luchese bosses, he said. "The 'crystal ball' is expensive," Amuso joked to Chiodo. Amuso told Chiodo the "crystal ball" had cost him the price of a Cadillac once.

The murder of Jimmy Bishop remained unsolved until Chiodo told FBI Special Agent John Flanagan and Task Force Detective Thomas Limberg the real story. The "crystal ball" had played a critical part in the homicide. A year earlier, in May 1990, Chiodo said, Casso had instructed him to clock Bishop's movements. Chiodo knew from past experience with Casso that this meant Bishop was going to be killed. Chiodo had gone to Bishop's home in a leafy well-to-do neighborhood in Queens with curving streets and cul-de-sacs. He decided it would be too difficult for a hit team to make a quick escape after killing Bishop. Chiodo had gone to Bishop's girlfriend's place in Whitestone—an apartment building with a parking lot and nearby avenues where a car could easily blend in with traffic. Before the hit, Chiodo had met with Amuso and Casso in a room above a pizza parlor in Bensonhurst. Chiodo wanted to know why Bishop was being killed. Chiodo didn't think Bishop was the kind who would talk to law enforcement. He asked Amuso and Casso if they were certain Bishop had become a cooperator with law enforcement. "As sure as you're standing there," Amuso said. Chiodo told Flanagan and Limberg he knew what that meant. The "crystal ball" had told Amuso and Casso that Bishop had "gone bad." If the "crystal ball" said Bishop was a rat then as far as the Lucheses were concerned he was a rat. From Chiodo it was learned definitively that the NYPD had a cop—or cops—selling out the force.

LITTLE AL

The month that Chiodo was debriefed by the FBI about Bishop, Luchese boss Vic Amuso, still on the lam, was arrested in a shopping mall in Scranton, Pennsylvania, while talking on a pay phone. Amuso and Casso had recently been featured on an episode of the television show *America's Most Wanted* and a viewer recognized Amuso's face and tipped off the authorities. "But Amuso was not inclined to believe in the randomness of events in the universe. The reason he was caught was luck. Somebody in Scranton had seen him on TV and notified the police. But that wasn't a story Amuso could believe. He was sure he had been set up. Everything was a plot. Whoever had betrayed Amuso was in a world of woe—even though no one had betrayed him. Amuso decided he had been given away by Little Al D'Arco. There was no basis for the belief but that didn't take away from the fervor of the believer. It *might* have been Little Al became it *had* to be Little Al became *kill* Little Al. That was the mania of a murderer, the senseless sense of it."

The fate that befell Chiodo that summer and fall had not gone unnoticed by Al D'Arco—he himself had been given the contract on Chiodo and knew the rationale. Like Chiodo, D'Arco knew how flimsy the pretext could be for the accusation that a mobster was a rat. During the summer of 1991, D'Arco started to become convinced Amuso and Casso were going to kill him next. Like Chiodo, D'Arco was reading between the lines. In early July, only weeks before Amuso's arrest, D'Arco had gone to a secret meeting with Amuso and Casso on Staten Island. At the meeting D'Arco was told he was no longer acting boss. The job of boss would be taken up by a "panel" of four Luchese captains. D'Arco was included in the group but the change was undeniably a demotion. The panel would convene every Wednesday, D'Arco was told. At the meeting, D'Arco was also told he no longer controlled the rackets at JFK Airport, one of the benefits bestowed on him by Amuso and Casso. D'Arco was angry. For years he had struggled financially but as acting boss he had started to earn as much as $10,000 a week. D'Arco took Amuso aside to complain. D'Arco said he had been loyal; he had faithfully passed on money to the bosses. During the exchange, D'Arco noticed that Amuso was averting his gaze and wouldn't look him in the eye. "Not looking at another wiseguy could be worse than looking at him the wrong way. The implication wasn't lost on D'Arco but there was nothing he could do about it then and there. He was supposedly still on the panel running the family. He went to the Wednesday meetings even after Amuso was arrested. But he was watchful. He couldn't trust Amuso and Casso, and he knew it."

By September of 1991, the luck of the Lucheses was nearing the end. On Friday, September 13, Chiodo testified in the Windows Case. The gangster, now weighing more than four hundred pounds, was rolled into court in an extra-wide wheelchair. To a riveted courtroom, he told how the mafia controlled $143 million worth of contracts to replace windows in New York public housing. It was the very treachery Amuso and Casso had desperately tried to avoid.

The next week, D'Arco killed on the orders of Casso for the last time. On Wednesday, September 18, a Luchese associate and professional architect named Anthony Fava was murdered. Fava was shot in the head, chest, and leg. He was also stabbed repeatedly in the heart, neck, and brain. The architect had a reputation as a swindler but he was the favored designer of many wiseguys. While Casso was on the lam, Fava had continued to construct a large house in Mill Basin for Casso. The project was being overseen by Casso's wife, Lillian. Before Fava was shot, Chiodo was the go-between for Casso, delivering more than $100,000 in cash to Fava against the cost of the construction.

D'Arco knew Anthony Fava. He had helped D'Arco with the construction of a sun porch. Casso said Fava had to be whacked because he knew about illegal transactions related to building Casso's house. Fava was also close to Chiodo and might cooperate. "Justifications for killing were getting dicier by the day. The killing was growing more frenetic and reckless. D'Arco was not a rocket scientist, and he wasn't a professor, as Casso jokingly called him, but he wasn't a complete idiot either. Casso was on his own, with Amuso now in jail. The way he was behaving it was as if he wanted to be caught and stopped. By threatening and conniving against and then killing the people closest to him, Casso was virtually ensuring the living ones would turn against him."

The day of Fava's murder, D'Arco attended the usual Wednesday meeting of the Luchese leadership panel in a midtown Manhattan hotel. The meeting was about dividing proceeds from gambling and bookmaking with a couple of Bonanno wiseguys. It was a seemingly routine day, the bureaucracy of crime grinding on. But after the meeting ended, D'Arco began to think he was being set up to be murdered right there, in the hotel room. As half a dozen wiseguys sat together, one gangster began to ramble on incoherently about taking lithium, a drug used to treat bipolar mental disorder. The conversation didn't make sense. It seemed like the other Lucheses were playing for time. D'Arco saw that Mikey DeSantis, a longtime member of Chiodo's crew, had a handgun tucked in the small of his back under his clothes. Carrying a gun in the presence of other wiseguys was a serious provocation. DeSantis went to the bathroom and returned. D'Arco noticed the gun was now missing. D'Arco knew Casso had been spreading a rumor that D'Arco was the "rat" responsible for Vic Amuso's arrest in Scranton. D'Arco also knew Amuso would want him dead if he believed the allegation. In the hotel room, D'Arco suddenly realized he would be killed if he didn't escape immediately. The lifelong gangster leapt to his feet and fled, bolting for the door and running out of the hotel and onto the street before he could be stopped, narrowly escaping with his life.

The next day, Thursday, September 19, Anthony Fava's body was found in the trunk of a white '83 Oldsmobile Cutlass in Bensonhurst. He was naked, apart from his boxer shorts. The discovery was reported in *New York Newsday* under the headline, "Mob Informant's Friend Stripped, Shot, Stabbed." The article reported on the mystery underlying the reasons for Fava's murder. Assistant U.S. Attorney Charles Rose, prosecutor of the

Windows Case, would not comment. Federal sources said Chiodo expressed surprise over the death of Fava. "The guy was like, straight," *Newsday* quoted Chiodo. Fava had angered Casso by becoming intimate with Casso's wife after her husband left town, *Newsday* reported, "'Why else would you strip a guy before you killed him?' said one investigator. 'Clearly, someone was trying to make a point.'"

On Friday, September 20th, D'Arco received a call from his parole officer, who told D'Arco he had been contacted by the FBI. The FBI said that there was a contract out on D'Arco's life. That night, D'Arco put his family on an airplane for Hawaii and he went into hiding on Long Island.

Oldham took notice. "I figured something had happened to D'Arco right away. Little Al owned a restaurant in Little Italy called La Donna Rosa—'the pink lady,' in Italian. My girlfriend at the time worked there waiting tables. The place was clearly mobbed-up. There were rarely any customers and the maitre d' was always whispering on the phone. I would go there for the red sauce. That Friday night, my girlfriend came home pissed off and said the restaurant had been shuttered overnight. No one had told her it was closing. On Monday morning, I overheard the OCHU guys saying D'Arco and his son Little Joe had become cooperators. Within days it was confirmed that the rumor was right. The OCHU detectives always had the inside stuff first."

On Saturday, September 21, 1991, Little Al D'Arco voluntarily gave himself up to the FBI. There were no charges outstanding against D'Arco at the time and he was not the target of any specific investigation. Law enforcement quickly learned how little they knew about his activities, or what had been going on inside the Luchese family. After mobsters like D'Arco and Chiodo agreed to cooperate, they were required to sit through a long series of interviews with the FBI and federal prosecutors known as "proffers." In order to qualify for protection from the government, D'Arco had to proffer an account of all criminal activity he had engaged in during his entire life—every criminal he knew, every crime he knew about, everything. The sessions stretched out over weeks and months as mobsters searched through their memories trying to fire synapses. An enormous number of cases were closed in this fashion. Robberies and assaults and arsons were solved in astonishing numbers.

D'Arco explained how the Luchese were extorting the Italian Bread Association, driving up the price of crusty bread in New York with a 2 percent "tax" on all sales in the city. He described how the family controlled the Fruit and Produce Union and "taxed" millions of dollars' worth of fresh fruit and vegetables coming into New York through the Hunt's Point Market. The scams the Luchese ran over the decades tumbled out: gasoline tax theft, bootleg designer blue jeans, Medicaid claims, olive oil importation, vending machines, racetrack betting, heroin . . . The list was seemingly endless. Murders, attempted murders, conspiracies to murder, were recited in detail. Hundreds of wiseguys were implicated. Dozens of mafiosi would be indicted as a result of the information provided by Chiodo and D'Arco.

"If Chiodo and D'Arco told the truth, the whole truth, and nothing but the truth, they would be immune from prosecution for those crimes. If they didn't—if they shaded the truth, minimized their role, tried to leave out money they had hidden away somewhere—the deal was off. They could then be prosecuted for everything. It was a huge incentive to be comprehensive—and they were. In D'Arco's case the debriefing sessions resulted in more than a thousand pages of confessions. The professor's story made for great reading. It was longer than *War and Peace* and way more complicated. D'Arco confessed to his involvement in arranging the murder of Bruno Facciola. He confessed to conspiring in the Visconti and Taylor homicides. He explained why Fava the architect had been 'trunked'—the mafia verb for leaving a body in a car. We had no idea, not one lousy clue, that D'Arco was involved in those killings. It was often the case during proffers that mobsters would confess to crimes we didn't know had occurred. People who had disappeared and were thought to have gone on the lam turned out to be homicide victims. Bodies buried in swamps in Canarsie were dug up. Seemingly unconnected events were connected. Proffers were an extremely powerful investigative tool."

The documents generated by the proffers were called "302s" because that was the number of the FBI form used to record the sessions. The 302s were internal documents, meant to convey the version of events a cooperator gave to agents and prosecutors during their proffer. Gangsters were rarely quoted. The language was stilted and bureaucratic. The 302s were for the official record, and needed to be intelligible to lawyers in offices in Washington with no understanding how life was actually lived in Brooklyn and Staten Island. There were no references to "motherfuckers" or "cocksuckers" or "rat fucks"—the streams of expletives that were standard on the street.

Crucially, as Chiodo had done earlier, D'Arco explained during his debriefing sessions the variety of ways the Lucheses had developed sources inside law enforcement. Capo Sal Avellino paid $2,000 a month to "an agent" who provided him with FBI information, D'Arco said. They met on Long Island during the first week of every month. The money Avellino paid was on behalf of Amuso and Casso. According to D'Arco, a Luchese captain claimed he was tight with a detective in the Canarsie section of Brooklyn. D'Arco also said that an associate had a girlfriend who worked in a District Attorney's Office who was able to get information.

"There was nothing earth-shattering in this news of low-level penetration. But D'Arco also referred to another source—the one that Gaspipe Casso had, the 'crystal ball' Chiodo had described. D'Arco said Casso had access to the most secret intelligence in the NYPD. It was common for Casso to warn D'Arco where he was being bugged—La Donna Rosa, in alleyways, in his car. D'Arco's statement corroborated what Chiodo had told the FBI months earlier. The terminology was different but the substance was the same. D'Arco didn't call the cops the 'crystal ball.' He told the FBI that Casso was paying 'the bulls' for information—street shorthand for NYPD detectives. D'Arco didn't know the names or assignments of the police officers involved. But he did confirm that Casso had a double agent inside the NYPD who was effective at collecting all kinds of intelligence on our activities."

SAMMY THE BULL

The day in September 1991 that Al D'Arco became a cooperator, Gambino underboss Sammy "the Bull" Gravano sat in the Metropolitan Detention Center awaiting trial with his boss, John Gotti, on multiple RICO charges, including the murder of former Gambino boss Paul Castellano. The next day, September 22, Gravano's defense attorney came to the MDC on urgent business. Gossip ran rampant in the small world of mob lawyers in New York City as more mobsters began to betray their comrades. Speculation was rife about which wiseguy might be the next to flip. It was big news that a gangster like D'Arco had turned himself in and begun to cooperate. D'Arco could impact Gravano's case in many ways. D'Arco knew Gravano from the sit-downs at the 19th Hole when there were disputes between the Gambinos and Lucheses. D'Arco knew about Gravano's interests in the construction industry and trade unions. He knew about Gravano's extortion operations, on projects in Manhattan and Williamsburg, as well as his complicity in loan-sharking. Before Gravano and Gotti were arrested, D'Arco had carried a message from Casso that the two were about to be busted. The information, D'Arco told Gravano, came from Casso's source inside law enforcement—"the bulls."

Despite this act of loyalty, D'Arco and Gravano had subsequently begun to feud over money and territory. They vied for control of the Concrete Workers Union and the Teamsters and the lucrative construction and cargo industry payoffs they brought in. While D'Arco had served as acting boss of the Lucheses, he was supposed to meet Gravano at Garguilio's, a Coney Island restaurant, to receive $30,000 due to the family as their end of an extortion payment from a company making prefabricated houses called Deluxe Homes. "D'Arco suspected Gravano was going to try to kill him so he went to the meet at Coney Island with a team of guys armed with Uzi submachine guns. Gravano never turned up. D'Arco thought that Gravano had come for the meeting but he had seen the guns and men hiding and been scared off. There was no love lost between the two. The news that he was cooperating scared Gravano. There was an extremely good chance he would testify against Gravano."

As Gravano sat awaiting trial, he had begun bickering with Gotti, as the so-called Teflon Don instructed his underboss on how to conduct their defense. Gotti expected his underling to do as he was told. Gravano wanted to apply to have his racketeering charges "severed" from Gotti's so that the two men would be tried separately. In *Underboss: Sammy the Bull Gravano's Story of Life in the Mafia,* co-authored with Peter Maas, Gravano explained that he was certain he would be convicted if he was jointly tried with Gotti. Gravano believed, probably rightly, the boss would put the blame on the underboss and Gravano would carry the "weight" while Gotti walked again. Gotti's constant paranoia and bullying were also wearing on Gravano as he contemplated the prospect of a sentence of life without parole. For the first time, Gravano wrote, he considered the idea of cooperating with the government. In return for testifying against Gotti, he reasoned, he would go into the Witness Protection Program. He would have the chance for another life. He would be free of Gotti and the Gambinos. The logic of RICO was snaking through Gravano's mind, as it was intended to do.

On October 10, 1991, Gravano flipped. The process Gravano followed was well known to mob defense attorneys. First, a gangster client would suddenly become suspiciously unavailable. Second, the defense attorney would discover he had been fired. Third, inevitably, it would emerge that the client had made a deal with the federal government. The reason accused gangsters didn't confide in their own lawyers was to avoid word of their bargaining becoming known before they had come to terms with prosecutors. If Gravano's negotiations with the federal government leaked before he had been moved to safety he would almost certainly be killed by Gotti. Attorneys in the defense bar were notoriously loose-lipped. Gravano was not taking chances. The first thing Gravano said to federal agents was, "I want to change governments."

Flown to Quantico, the vast FBI training facility in Virginia, Gravano began to proffer. He was the highest-level mafia informant the government had ever had. Gravano had knowledge of the innermost secrets of organized crime. He described in detail John Gotti's plot to kill Paul Castellano, and how it was carried out in midtown Manhattan. He confessed to nineteen murders, most at the direction of Gotti. Gravano identified the juror that had been bribed during Gotti's acquittal on racketeering charges. Jury tampering had been suspected in Gotti's previous trials but the government had been unable to find hard proof. Gravano told the FBI that Gotti had an NYPD detective on his payroll. He told the FBI the detective had passed along information through a Gambino wiseguy who was his wife's cousin. The cop was known inside the Gambinos as "the baker."

"His real name was Detective William Peist from the Intelligence Division," Oldham recalled. "I knew Peist. I worked in the Intelligence Division in the mid-eighties with him. I was working on the Jewish desk. Peist was assigned to the mafia. He was an overweight white guy with one leg. He lost the leg in a car accident. Peist was a streetwise detective, with deep connections in organized crime from his time as a Brooklyn precinct cop. He was known as a hard worker. He was quiet, friendly. He had won medals. He had no history of disciplinary problems. No one had any idea Peist was working for John Gotti.

"Peist was making money from Gotti but that couldn't have been his true motivation. He'd gotten more than a million dollars from the insurance settlement for his injuries in the car accident, and he still sold information. Peist must have felt the NYPD didn't deserve his loyalty anymore. He didn't start as a criminal but he became one. An angry cop was a dangerous cop. He was punishing the police department. Peist denied it at first but in the end he pled guilty and was sentenced to seven years. John Gotti wasn't the Teflon Don because he had some supernatural power. He got away with defying law enforcement for as long as he did for the oldest reason in the book—he had a crooked cop in his hip pocket."

*　　*　　*

By the end of 1991, the evidence of a leak inside NYPD had grown from a molehill to a mountain. Cops were going bad. Not just thieving or sticking up drug dealers, but actively undermining the business of law enforcement. "Detectives had gone over to the dark side. From that time forward, every mobster murder was inspected for the fingerprints of the involvement of law enforcement. Casso had murdered on the say-so of sworn police officers. Major investigations were being torn apart. Conspiracy theories abounded. Denial and disbelief had given way to suspicion and anger. Chiodo and D'Arco shed light on a more serious case than Peist's. The 'crystal ball' was fingering CIs like Bishop and Heidel and Costa. 'Bulls' were conspiring to murder. Members of the NYPD were getting people killed. Something had to be done."

CHAPTER FIVE

MOBLAND

As 1992 began, Oldham was still trapped in the catching order, the list of detectives required to report to the Major Case squad room and wait for cases to be assigned to them. He was swamped by bank robberies and working the operational aspects of other detectives' cases—doing surveillance, manning wiretaps, pulling raps and mug shots. He had been at the Major Case Squad for two years and now he wanted to make his own cases—organized crime cases. But the OCHU detectives remained entrenched and sharp-elbowed. Detective Caracappa had been promoted to first grade, an exceptionally rare achievement in the NYPD. There was little, if any, chance for Oldham to start his own investigation into the mafia. He wanted to build a case from the ground up, instead of being an afterthought left to do the grunt work for other detectives.

"A roadblock had been placed in front of me. I wasn't going to be part of the inside club in OCHU. If I was going to go anywhere I had to do it on my own. I had no choice but it suited me fine. I liked working alone. I was aiming to be the best, like Caracappa was supposed to be—the go-to guy. It was egotistical but that was what you needed to be to get ahead in Major Case. I wanted to do things. I didn't talk about it with other detectives. I didn't tell the bosses what I was doing. I kept to myself. I wasn't a popular guy but I wasn't trying to win a popularity contest. I was the skinny weird young guy in the Hugo Boss suits who lived like a yuppie in the city. They considered me a loose cannon—and I was. The department needed loose cannons. There was plenty enough conformity at One PP."

Oldham needed first to learn how to use the underlying concepts involved in major organized crime investigations. That meant making federal cases, which meant knowing how to operate with the RICO statutes. Oldham had worked many successful state cases but he had never been part of a federal case. "I knew about the attractions of going federal. In federal prosecutions you could get under the skin of a conspiracy. You could really run an investigation, concentrating on one case for months at a time instead of drowning in dozens of open cases at the state level. You chose who your prosecutor would be. You didn't have to worry about crossing county or state lines. The offices were nicer and cleaner. There was more money. In state cases you were in the meat grinder. Trials lasted only a few days. They usually revolved around physical evidence, which wasn't very interesting if you were a detective. To make RICO cases, you needed to know how to investigate a conspiracy. By definition, conspiracies were secret and hard to crack. I needed to figure out how to make RICO cases if I was going to be the one who took the hardest cases and closed them."

BORN TO KILL

While Oldham continued to study organized crime and the OCHU, he became interested in another form of organized crime that had seemed to have nothing to do with the Lucheses and the mafia, but was critical to his education as a detective. Organized crime was divided in two by law enforcement. Traditional OC was the mafia—*la cosa nostra,* "LCN" in the bureaucratic acronym. There were hundreds of detectives and federal agents assigned to investigate and monitor LCN. In Major Case, Oldham decided to take a different course. Shut out of traditional OC, he turned to "nontraditional organized crime"—NTOC, or "entoc," as it was called inside the NYPD. NTOC included Russians, Colombians, Israelis, Dominicans, Albanians, virtually every immigrant group of bad guys. Newcomers arriving in America brought with them their own culture and history—as well as their particular kind of criminal organizations. Asians held a special interest for Oldham. The retail heroin trade had been controlled by Sicilians for generations but by the late eighties it was heroin imported from the Golden Triangle and wholesaled by first-generation American Chinese gangsters that flooded the city. In the Asian community in the 5th Precinct, which covered Chinatown and Little Italy, extortion and robbery and kidnapping were rampant—but commonly went unreported and therefore uninvestigated. The field was relatively open and it represented an opportunity for Oldham to find his niche.

"Everyone thought Asian gangs were inscrutable. There was the language barrier. The cultural barriers. What was intimidating about investigating Asian crime was enticing to me. Working Asian organized crime had been one of my interests since I'd come to New York to join the NYPD. When I worked in the Robbery Squad in Queens, I'd concen-

trated on Asian cases, mostly extortions and robberies. A few years earlier, I had applied to the Jade Squad and was turned down. I was disap-
pointed but I knew it wasn't the end of the line. My father had been a
doctor who worked in Vietnam for ten years during the war and came off
the roof of the American Embassy in a helicopter in Saigon. After my parents divorced, my stepmother was Vietnamese. I went to high school in
Taiwan and India and traveled around that part of the world as a teenager.
The experience gave me an interest in the Orient. I had a decent understanding of Mandarin so I had a jump on a lot of white detectives when
it came to Asian crime. They called me the Asian Caucasian."

Oldham's opening for an Asian case came on a Sunday in March 1991.
That evening a Vietnamese immigrant merchant named Sen Van Ta
decided to close his store early. Golden Star Jewelry was a booth-sized
variety store at 302 Canal Street in Chinatown. It was one in a row of similar tiny stores run by Vietnamese and Chinese immigrants. Ta sold
counterfeit watches, "I Love New York" T-shirts, novelty pens. He was
uneasy that day. For weeks a Vietnamese street gang called Born to Kill
had been attempting to extort money from him, demanding weekly payments in sums that were lucky numbers in Asian culture—$88 and $108.
Ta refused to pay. Half a dozen members of the Born to Kill came to the
store and pistol-whipped and robbed Ta at gunpoint. When the police
responded, Ta made a report and rode through Chinatown in a marked
NYPD car searching for the robbers. It was a display of bravery and fool-
hardiness. Outside 271 Canal, Ta jumped from the car, ran across the
street, and pointed to the individuals who had stuck him up. Two BTK
members—Little Cobra and Jungle Man—were arrested on the spot. A
few days later, Ta testified before a grand jury and the two were indicted
on robbery in the first degree and held without bail. Days later Ta
received an anonymous letter suggesting he recant his testimony. Ta
refused. The leader of Born to Kill, a sly and lethal gangster named
David Thai, personally came to Golden Star Jewelry to see Ta. The message could not have been more threatening but Ta still did not back
down. His wife was furious and terrified. Sen Van Ta opened for business
that Sunday with dread.

"BTK had resolved to kill the first Vietnamese who cooperated with the
law. David Thai was going to demonstrate to the Vietnamese community
the price of talking to the police. All along Canal Street, in the little booths
selling counterfeit designer goods to tourists, businesspeople were being
extorted by the BTK. The gang wasn't famous, like the mafia families or
some of the Chinese gangs, but they were one of the deadliest in New

York City. They operated below the radar. Few cops even knew of their existence and they were never reported in the press. Inside the Vietnamese community BTK was deeply feared. They aimed to keep it that way by making sure it was known that cooperating with the police meant death."

The Born to Kill gang was made up of refugees from postwar Vietnam. Many were the offspring of American GIs shunned in their homeland and sent to America by their mothers to live as orphans—"dust of the earth" they were called in Vietnam. The name Born to Kill was inspired by the motto many American soldiers wore on their helmets in Vietnam. Thai built the gang by masquerading as a father figure leading a benevolent society designed to take care of lost and vulnerable boys, and to protect all Vietnamese from the much larger Chinese population. In fact it was a cultlike moneymaking business. BTK specialized in jewelry store stick-ups but they also worked home invasions and extortion. Young and reckless, considered crazy by many who came in contact with them, they stuck up Chinese weddings, a lucrative endeavor due to the tradition of large cash gifts. The BTK traveled up and down the East Coast and even into Canada robbing Asian-owned jewelry stores, a roving band of outlaws with a herd of beat-up Toyota Corollas, armed with .38s and cheap machine guns.

"Thai thought of himself as a community leader. But he was like Fagan in 'Oliver Twist.' He put the kids up to steal things. They would return with pillowcases full of jewelry. The boys were given a pittance to live on. Six or eight would be packed into a single room in a rough part of Brooklyn. Thai himself lived in a nice house on Long Island. He drove a Jaguar. The boys recognized Thai was a manipulator. But the boys were scared to death of him."

Even by the standards of gang-ridden New York City, the Born to Kill were brutal. They had no code of honor, or pretense of obeying any standards of decency. One murder a year earlier had displayed the mindless violent streak of the BTK. There had been an altercation in a park in Elmhurst, Queens, between the BTK and three members of the Green Dragons, a rival Chinese gang also distinguished for being vicious. BTK got the worst of the fight, and were chased out of the park by the Green Dragons. The next day, the BTK had returned with guns. They pulled up in a Corolla and stalked through the park looking for Green Dragons. They had approached an Asian kid dressed in black as the Green Dragons dressed—black hat, black shirt, black pants—sitting on a park bench. "They were too chickenshit to get close enough to actually determine the identity of the person or confront him. They were clearly afraid of the

Green Dragons. A twelve-year-old girl was sitting there minding her own business. She had nothing to do with nothing. They shot her in the chest with a .38. Another shot went wild. She left a trail of blood as she ran along Queens Boulevard toward her mother's apartment. She died on her mother's living room floor."

As the months passed, the BTK acted with even more defiance of the norms of civilization. There were shootouts in the streets of Chinatown. When a tourist from Maryland—an innocent bystander—was killed in the crossfire, tourism in the neighborhood plummeted. A week later a senior BTK member named Amigo was gunned down coming out of a massage parlor on Canal Street. The gang held an elaborate funeral ceremony. They paraded through Chinatown following a hearse carrying a banner reading "Stand By BTK." Local precinct police stood on the street watching. A few of the cops started to taunt the members of the BTK and a brawl broke out. The same day hundreds of people attended Amigo's burial in New Jersey. In the middle of the ceremony, three members of the Ghost Shadows, dressed as mourners, approached the grave carrying wreaths. It had rained the night before and a sump pump was emptying a grave filled with water. The Ghost Shadows dropped the flowers and flung off their trench coats and opened up with submachine guns. The sound of the two-stroke pump engine—pum-pum pum-pum—masked the sound of the shots fired. Eight people were shot. Home video of the incident aired on television. "Bullets Fly at Gangland Funeral as New York Goes Gun Crazy," the headline in the *Times of London* read. "Bouquet-Bearing Gunmen Fire on Mourners," the Associate Press reported.

On that Sunday evening in 1991, as the sky darkened, a gypsy cab pulled up in front of Sen Van Ta's modest store. A BTK member known as Uncle Lan, the gang's foremost shooter, got out of the taxi. Tiny and thin, with pockmarked skin, Lan had been tortured by the North Vietnamese when they took over the country after America's withdrawal. He was truly psychotic. Lan told the driver to wait. The inconspicuous car would be the perfect getaway in the bustle of Chinatown. Uncle Lan walked into the store and drew his gun. "Good afternoon, Mister Owner," Uncle Lan said. He calmly fired two slugs in the back of Sen Van Ta's head and walked out of the store. He got in the cab and disappeared into the downtown traffic.

The murder of Sen Van Ta sent a terrifying message to the Vietnamese population of the city. It also embarrassed the NYPD and the Manhattan DA's Office for not providing sufficient protection for a man in Ta's situation. CIs had been lost by law enforcement in New York City—

Bishop, Heidel, many others over the years. They were criminals who had decided to flip and cooperate. Ta was not a CI. He was an innocent. He had no criminal background. He was a complainant—a citizen willing to defy organized crime. He had paid with his life. Law enforcement at all levels understood something had to be done. "The gang had never been the subject of a full-fledged investigation before. Nobody had a hook into this pack of deadly kids. The BTK were young, with no personal history or family in America—no one knew who they were. They were nomads. It looked like a tough nut to crack. It was irresistible."

Oldham took it upon himself to focus directly on the BTK. He started to meet and greet Vietnamese people in Chinatown. He ate every day in Vietnamese restaurants on Doyers Street, a dogleg block in Chinatown. He filed "wanted cards" on the BTK—a computerized notification system that meant he would be alerted of any arrests of gang members. He talked to anyone who might someday drop a dime. Within weeks, George Slater, a detective in the Eight-Four, called Oldham and said a member of BTK had been arrested for a home invasion and robbery. The defendant was being held on Rikers Island. Oldham made it to Rikers within the hour. Tinh Ngo was eighteen years old, skinny, short, his face drawn from a crack addiction. Tinh faced five to fifteen, the standard sentence for armed robbery. As an alien, he faced further jeopardy: after he served his time, he would be deported to Vietnam.

"Tinh was fidgety and uncomfortable. I thought he looked worn-out from life in the Born to Kill and Rikers Island. There was a lot of pressure being a criminal. Gangsters always looked over their shoulder. Born to Kill members couldn't move around Chinatown freely. There were many streets they couldn't walk down without getting killed by the Flying Dragons or Ghost Shadows. They had to be alert to the presence of police. Cops were constantly jacking them up on the street, patting them down for weapons, shoving them around, trying to provoke them. On top of that was the pressure of actually committing crime. Robbery is not easy. It is an intense situation going into a stranger's home or business to rob them not knowing what to expect. Most criminals will tell you sticking up is no cakewalk. Living in a world of violence is no fucking fun, unless you're insensate or psychotic. If you're smart enough to think about what you're doing, about the risks of something going wrong, your nerves erode. There's never any peace."

Alone with Tinh in a windowless room on Rikers Island, Oldham adopted a neutral approach. He was neither the good cop nor the bad cop. He didn't yell or scream during interrogations, although he would raise his voice if he felt it might work to his advantage. He didn't hit prisoners, except in extreme situations. Oldham considered that method demeaning and ineffective. The point was to gain the confidence of the interviewee and get him to talk. Interrogation was a form of persuasion, not coercion. One method Oldham developed over the years was unusual. He told his prisoners the truth, an idea so odd it amounted to a successful technique.

"Police officers nearly never tell the truth when they are talking to a suspect. They aren't required to. There is no legal requirement. You can tell him he is going to get the chair if he doesn't talk. You can say you have five eyewitnesses. The Supreme Court has repeatedly upheld our right to lie. It is useful. Lying is a tool and standard operating procedure. But my view was that if you're trying to convince someone to cooperate you have to convince them to believe in you. Criminals are expert lie detectors. If the perp catches you in a lie you're done. Telling the truth is disorienting to criminals. Cops have a hard time with the concept. I would say, 'We're going to let you go today because there's a hole in the case but we will fill the hole and then we will come and get you.' I would admit weakness in the evidence. I would explain why I needed their cooperation. I would tell people to run away if they didn't want to get tangled up with the law."

Tinh was going nowhere and he knew it. Oldham explained the options. Cooperate or you're on your own. Cooperate or you're back in a refugee camp in Thailand. No BTK, no police department, no friends in jail. Cooperate or your life as you know it is over. Oldham told Tinh to imagine he had cancer. The analogy was direct: his troubles were not going to go away. There were few Asians in Rikers at the time and Tinh was clearly at risk. After the first interview, Oldham moved him into protective custody, a dormitory atmosphere with better food and no violence. By doing so Oldham gave a practical demonstration of his power: Tinh's fate was in his hands. Tinh's situation could improve, or Oldham could also put him in a much worse situation. It seemed to Oldham than Tinh had a conscience. He was damaged but he hadn't been ruined. He had once stopped other members of the BTK from pistol-whipping a woman in Tennessee. He hadn't been directly responsible for violence. "It made a difference when I considered the prospect of succeeding in the case. Tinh had the makings of a decent witness on the stand. He wasn't a beater, shooter, or stabber. The jury could look at him and see a human being—maybe not a kid they wanted to take home but a kid who might be redeemed. Tinh felt bad about many of the things he had done. But it wasn't as though he had come forward and confessed to his sins. His primary interest in snitching was selfish but I consider that the best motive. It makes sense. You know what you're dealing with. He grew up in refugee camps and group homes, completely untethered from family, home, any kind of normal childhood. His first instinct was always self-preservation."

LEARNING RICO

The methods used to investigate organized crime were the same under federal law, whether the subject was the mafia or Born to Kill. The first priority was to construct an outline of the structure of the gang. Tinh was shown surveillance photographs to make a face book of the subjects under investigation. He also identified the cars BTK used.

Oldham had Tinh plead guilty in state court to thirteen counts of armed robbery. Tinh's sentence was deferred and he was put into Oldham's custody. As in any OC investigation, understanding the target was crucial. There was no better way to get to know the people you were looking at than to have someone on the inside tell you about them. Tinh was smart. He was able to describe the relationships and motives of the players. There were also significant gaps in his knowledge. In order to mount a case, Oldham decided it was necessary to put Tinh back on the street. Tinh would carry a tape recorder and capture David Thai and the leaders of BTK conspiring together. It was a high-stakes gamble for Tinh—and Oldham too.

"We would never do this now. We took a kid who belonged to a violent gang who had no roots in the community, who could easily have disappeared, and we let him run with the most brutal street gang in Chinatown. Suppose he had gone out and killed someone, or ran away? Suppose he was completely cooperative but we were unable to short-circuit a crime that he told us was going to go down? Looking back, I'm shocked the Brooklyn DA let us do it. Born to Kill was clearly going to do more robberies and maybe kill someone. Knowing what I know now I wouldn't do it. Everyone was so eager to get the killer of Sen Van Ta that they were willing to stretch the idea of running an informant to the absolute limits."

Finally in charge of his own major case, Oldham embarked on a RICO prosecution, which meant he had to take the case federal. The NYPD had few resources, with little money to pay for the travel and overtime necessary for a complex real-time investigation. Most important, the NYPD did not have broad enough jurisdiction. BTK committed crimes in many places, not just New York City. "BTK stuck up a company in Orlando for a million dollars' worth of computer processors and sold them on Canal

Street. They killed a man in North Carolina. They robbed Vietnamese jewelry stores in Toronto. To make a RICO case, to put the whole group out of business instead of knocking the gang out one guy at a time, we needed to be able to reach across multiple jurisdictions. It was a proactive case, moving all over the country. As a New York City detective I couldn't mount a rolling interstate surveillance operation. An expanded portfolio of resources and venue was essential."

The supply of federal agencies in New York was large. Oldham began by shopping for the right federal prosecutor. The offices of the United States Attorney for the Southern District of New York (SDNY) were located in lower Manhattan within walking distance of One PP, the FBI, and the DEA. The Southern District was like a large Wall Street law firm: there was floor upon floor of Ivy League–educated attorneys, a strictly supervised hierarchy, and an establishment atmosphere. The emphasis was on white-collar crime. The role of agents and detectives was limited. Oldham didn't think the mix would be good. He wasn't sure he would fit in. He wasn't willing to lose control of the case.

The United States Attorney's Office for the Eastern District was another story. The stepchild of federal justice in New York City, the Eastern District had one-third the staff of the SDNY and a fraction of its resources. It was housed across the river, on the far side of the Brooklyn Bridge, in a squat concrete building in a desolate area next to the off ramp of the Brooklyn-Queens Expressway. The warren of offices was crammed with battered government-issue furniture and boxes filled with documents from ongoing cases and old convictions on appeal. But what the Eastern District lacked in support it made up for in brass and ingenuity. It was where the adventurous went—people who wanted to work cases hands-on, down and dirty, with a large measure of autonomy. "I knew the Eastern District would jump on the case. The prosecutors in the Eastern District shared the background with the investigators they worked with. They were the kids of cops, not Park Avenue proctologists. They came in early and stayed late. They would pull all-nighters. They typed their own subpoenas. They weren't going to ask permission from other agencies. They were looking to get cases done. If you needed it, you got it, one way or the other. There were other agencies chasing the BTK case and I needed to move quickly. It was a race to the finish."

Oldham went to a prosecutor in the Eastern District he knew named Patricia Pileggi. Married to a cop, she had a realistic view of police work. She was young and pretty, with violet eyes, black hair, and an easy smile— and she was as tough as nails. "I needed a prosecutor with balls and Pat

Pileggi had them. She would find a way to make evidence work. In a pinch she could be relied upon and was available twenty-four hours a day, seven days a week." Oldham played her the tape recording of the interrogation with Tinh. Tinh talked about what he knew about Born to Kill and their activities. He said he thought he could wear a wire. He described some of their robberies. Tinh had a photographic memory. He promised to be an excellent cooperator. Pileggi was interested.

With Pileggi attached, Oldham needed to find a federal investigative agency to work with. The rewards of bringing a federal agency in on the case were significant, but so were the risks. Oldham's first priority was to make sure he wasn't steamrolled out of the case. "That ruled out the FBI. The FBI was notorious with cops across the country for stealing cases and credit, and were known as Famous But Incompetent or just 'the feebs' because they were so feeble."*

Pileggi suggested a young agent with the Bureau of Alcohol, Tobacco and Firearms named Dan Kumor, who quickly agreed to join in the investigation. Kumor was Oldham's opposite. "I was the classic mess-of-a-cop. The feds defined themselves against the kind of officer I was. I drank beer on the job. I didn't take orders well. I didn't do paperwork. Kumor looked straight, a Polish all-American. He was tall, muscular, clean-cut, forthright, trained and professional, the model of a federal law enforcement agent. He had never worked as a street cop. His reports ran to hundreds of pages. Dan would do the drudge work but he wasn't an empty suit. He knew what was expected but he also knew what was required to make a case—and those were two different things."

With his team set, Oldham and Kumor dropped Tinh off in Sunset Park in Brooklyn, near a BTK safe house, with twenty bucks and a cloned beeper in his pocket. Tinh was supposed to check in every day but he didn't call for two days and he didn't answer his beeper. By the third day, Oldham and Kumor were on the streets of Chinatown looking for

---

*As an NYPD detective working state cases Oldham had personal experience with the FBI's connivances trying to thieve prosecutions. Once, he had a witness in the hospital under police guard after she had jumped from a window in a housing development trying to avoid being returned to her pimp. She was one of the few people willing to testify against a major forced-prostitution ring. The FBI wanted the case badly. Oldham was determined to keep it. When the FBI tried to interview his witness, Oldham told the hospital administrator his witness was in danger and needed to be moved immediately. He registered her under a pseudonym and put her in the maternity ward. He wasn't going to take any chances.

Tinh. Finally, he called. Tinh proved to be an outstanding informant. "He was a gangster but he had the makeup of a detective."

For six months, Oldham and Kumor followed the gang as they traveled the city and eastern seaboard. They thwarted a dozen armed robberies. In order to avoid tipping the larger investigation, Oldham and Kumor used a variety of ploys: BTK's cars were towed, leaders were brought into the precinct house for questioning, Oldham put on an NYPD uniform and stood twirling a nightstick in front of a jewelry store on 6th Avenue and 21st Street in Manhattan that he knew the gang was about to stick up. Oldham and Kumor met with Tinh early mornings in a back room of a Vietnamese restaurant on Doyers Street. It was in a maze of underground vaults and tunnels housing whorehouses and gambling parlors for high-stakes mah-jongg games. Tinh would hand over his tape recordings and the scraps of paper with notes of BTK's addresses and license plate numbers.

By August 1991, Oldham and Kumor decided they had gathered sufficient evidence to make the arrests: murders, multiple shootings, stabbings, and armed robberies. Tinh was wearing out. Oldham and Kumor couldn't keep up with the gang. Events were threatening to spin out of control. The turning point came when the BTK took the equivalent of a quarter stick of dynamite, rolled it in glue and broken glass, and planted the improvised explosive device inside Pho Bang, a restaurant off Canal Street. The gang had eaten for free at the restaurant for years. The owner of Pho Bang had the temerity to suggest they start to pay for their meals. Tinh had told Oldham and Kumor about the plot. They had raced across town toward Pho Bang—but got trapped in traffic on the Bowery on the way. Kumor had leapt from the car and run. He had made it as the BTK were crouched in the vestibule of the restaurant trying to light the bomb. Oldham arrived moments later, as Kumor ran up Centre Street looking for an unpopulated place to put the bomb in case it went off. It did not.

"At that point we decided to make the BTK history. It was only a matter of time before someone got hurt on our watch. Born to Kill needed to be stopped right away. Just before we were about to make our arrests, the FBI called Andy Maloney, the United States attorney for the Eastern District. The feebs begged Maloney to cancel the planned arrests. They said they had an undercover agent in with the BTK. They said their undercover would be exposed to danger if we made our bust. Word had circulated in law enforcement circles we were about to close the case. It was another example of how nothing was secret in the law enforcement community in New York City. If the FBI had a snitch in the gang we would have caught wind of it. We knew it wasn't true."

A meeting was arranged for the following day at the Justice Department in Washington between attorneys from the Eastern District and representatives of the FBI. The FBI were going to voice their concerns about the safety of their alleged undercover agent. "They never showed up. The undercover never surfaced. It was apparent that the Bureau had wanted to buy time to make their own case and steal ours. The next week we had teams of ATF agents and NYPD detectives fanned out over the city and Long Island to arrest more than twenty members of the Born to Kill."

THE WILD WEST

The trial was held in the old federal courthouse near the foot of the Brooklyn Bridge on the third floor, before Judge Carol Amon. The docket in the Eastern District in the spring of 1992 read like the lineup to a mobland all-star team. John Gotti was appearing before Judge Leo Glasser on multiple RICO charges, including the murder of Paul Castellano, in a courtroom on another floor. In the same building, in another oak-paneled courtroom, the leaders of the Chinese gang Green Dragons were facing their own murder and robbery indictments. The Eastern District was the final destination for criminals of all kinds. Major crack dealers Lorenzo "Fat Cat" Nichols and Howard "Pappy" Mason were up on murder charges for the killing of NYPD officer Eddie Byrne. Tommy Karate Pitera, the Bonanno who'd once branded Otto Heidel a snitch at the El Caribe, was being prosecuted for six murders—the first mobster convicted on federal charges to face the death penalty. Victor Orena, boss of one of the Colombo factions, was up on murder charges for whacking a member of his own family. Vincent Chin Gigante, Genovese boss, had been indicted in the Windows Case. His co-defendant was Vic Amuso, the Luchese boss who had gone on the lam with Gaspipe Casso.

"The courthouse was lousy with bad guys. They were the same faces I had seen on the streets of Little Italy and Chinatown a few years earlier. A guy named Cow Pussy from Born To Kill would be handcuffed and belted and walking behind Frank 'Lock' LoCascio, Gotti's co-defendant. Cow Pussy was a teenage kid with bad acne and a teardrop tattoo. They called him Cow Pussy because he'd go out with the ugliest women. LoCascio was a middle-aged millionaire mobster from Queens. The

BTK kids had no family and no cash. The clothes they wore to trial were the ones they were arrested in. Wiseguys like Gotti wore a new suit every day—they were tailored, manicured, preening. It was great going to work. For decades the city had been besieged by organized crime. The tide was turning. The golden era of RICO had arrived."

With four major OC trials going on at the same time, the atmosphere in the courthouse was both electric and dangerous. Groups gathered outside in support of Gotti. A twenty-foot-high inflatable rat with a purple nose and red eyes, normally used by unions during labor disputes, was put on display in the park opposite the courthouse with a sign saying "Gravano is a Rat" hung around its neck. Bomb threats were routine. The building had to be evacuated numerous times. Unprecedented demands were placed on security. United States marshals had to be brought to New York for temporary duty from distant states like Alabama and North Dakota. "These country boys were walking around in amazement at the scene. Gangsters were everywhere. There was an intricate systems of holding cells in the basement. Elevators led up to more cells behind the courtrooms. It was the marshals' job to keep the peace—to keep them separate and keep them moving. It was an impressive collection of bad guys. The marshals would transfer our prisoners back and forth from the Metropolitan Correction Center to court every day. The vans were packed. My BTK guys were terrified of Gotti. When Gotti got in the van they would scamper off to the far seats. Gotti had 'his' seat in the van and no one else was supposed to sit in it. They were in awe of him. To me, Gotti looked like a slick car salesman—a primper. When there was a brawl down in the cell block between the BTK and the Green Dragons the marshals jumped in like it was a rodeo. They were peeling gangsters off each other, like they were wrestling calves. The marshals were from the prairies but the real Wild West was to be found in downtown Brooklyn."

When not in the BTK courtroom, Oldham passed the time in the hallways and other courtrooms in the building. He rarely talked to the press "on the record" but he was friendly with the reporters who were an integral part of the scene in the Brooklyn courthouse. *The Daily News* had a journalist named Jerry Capeci who had a column called "Gang Land." "Capeci was the best. Everyone read his column. The cops got news from Capeci, and the mobsters caught up on the news about their friends and rivals." At the time, Junior Persico, the head of the Colombos, wrote to "Gang Land" when Capeci misreported his age in a column. "You made me 57 years old. I am only 55. Don't rush these years past me.

I'll need my youth to finish this 100 years I have to do." John Gotti was furious when he thought one of his lawyers was leaking stories to Capeci. Gotti had his lead attorney, Bruce Cutler, reach out to Capeci to pass along a message. "This is not a threat now, just like a joke," Cutler said. "He'd like to kick you in the ass."

When Sammy Gravano testified against Gotti the headline in "Gang Land" read, "Give Sammy a Grammy for Song." Oldham went to the courtroom of Judge Leo Glasser to watch Gravano testify. The courtroom was packed and the air bristled with tension. The movie actor Mickey Rourke was in the gallery, claiming friendship with Gotti, and wiseguys and reporters and federal agents and NYPD detectives were packed shoulder to shoulder. "Gravano had not been rehabilitated. He pled guilty to nineteen murders. He also made an outstanding witness. I studied him carefully. He knew how Gotti operated—little things that only a true insider can know—things that make a witness completely believable. It was one of the paradoxes of RICO. The most dependable evidence was often given by the least reliable characters. More evidence was needed to corroborate what a man like Gravano said. There were extensive tape recordings of Gotti and Gravano. The two Gambino bosses were caught talking about Detective Peist, the dirty cop feeding them inside information. It was damning material. But there was no substitute for Gravano taking the stand and allowing the jury to hear the story from his mouth. In the Eastern District, it was the year of the rat."

When Gotti was convicted a chill ran through the courthouse. Hundreds of protestors from Gotti's neighborhood who had gathered in the park threatened to storm the building and free Gotti. A flatbed truck belonging to Gotti's son-in-law's wrecking yard circled the court honking its horn. Oldham went outside to see what was happening. "The protestors were chanting 'Free John Gotti,' like he was Nelson Mandela. Gotti was a heroin dealer and a killer. They were throwing rocks, trying to overturn cars. Pushing and shoving started with the police and marshals. I joined in. Reporters ran for the phones. Vanloads of cops turned up. A few of the protestors got busted and a few cops were injured but mostly it was pathetic. Gotti's 'public' weren't tough guys. They were wannabes. Gotti didn't go out with a bang. He went out with a whimper."

Two days later the BTK verdicts were read out in court. Thai and various cohorts were convicted of multiple RICO counts. Oldham was relieved—the outcome he had promised his victims and witnesses had come to pass. While Thai's conviction for conspiracy to assault was reversed on appeal, his remaining convictions were upheld. He was sentenced to life imprisonment and Sen Van Ta's death had been avenged. Some sense of order had been restored to Chinatown and the Vietnamese community. "We've crippled the BTK," Oldham was quoted as saying in the *New York Times*. "They don't have the leadership. They don't have the presence anymore." It was a moment of transformation in New York City. The mafia was being decisively defeated. Asian gangs were under siege. Criminal prosecutions of organized crime were at a zenith. The Southern District, led by future mayor Rudy Giuliani, got much of the glory in those years, but the Eastern District had succeeded where many had failed. "The common wisdom had been that Gotti couldn't be convicted, that the Born To Kill couldn't be brought down. RICO reconfigured the world of organized crime—for both sides. Now it didn't matter how clever or ruthless or connected you were—you were going to get got. I had made my first federal RICO case, and I loved the feeling of seeing justice done in the hardest cases."

CHAPTER SIX

"GODFATHERS OF THE NYPD"

Oldham's return to Major Case in the spring of 1992 after the Born to Kill prosecution did not go smoothly. Working on BTK he had learned to make a RICO case. He had pursued a high-profile OC investigation to its conclusion. He had helped destroy one of the most dangerous gangs in the city. But he had also been assigned outside the Major Case Squad and that did not sit well with his superior officers. They wanted to maintain control over their investigations. "If you're going to do another federal case, do it from here or don't bother to come back," Oldham was told by Lieutenant Joseph Pollini his first day back in the squad room after the trial was over. "Do your cases from here. Don't take them outside."

The acquisition of expertise and experience didn't necessarily mean Oldham's new skills would be put to use by the NYPD. The institution didn't operate that way. Instead of being assigned another organized crime investigation, Oldham was told to solve bank robberies and help other detectives with their cases. He would have to again find and fight for his own cases.

With the mafia on the run, law enforcement once again turned to the investigation of lower-level wiseguys—small-time scammers, bookies, loan sharks. As part of his duties assisting Major Case detectives, Oldham was routinely assigned to perform apprehensions on other people's cases. Most of the detectives in Major Case were older and overweight, and many were in poor physical shape. That spring, one had suffered a heart attack as he opened the door of his car in a parking lot in Queens. By comparison, at the age of thirty-eight, Oldham was young and fit. One of the "designated runners" for Major Case, he was sent to make arrests in the event a suspect bolted and had to be chased by foot.

That spring something occurred—seemingly out of the blue—that caught Oldham's attention and pointed to the dangerous, deep connections between the mafia and the NYPD. The event was the publication of a book about the cultures of the police department and organized crime.

Mafia Cop: The Story of an Honest Cop Whose Family Was the Mob would change the path of Oldham's career and life. The author was a retired NYPD detective named Louis Eppolito. He was the best friend of OCHU member Detective Stephen Caracappa.

The memoir, co-authored by journalist Bob Drury, arrived in bookstores with little fanfare. Inside the Major Case squad room, however, it was widely read—and even more widely reviewed. "Eppolito had retired a couple of years earlier but he was still well known by reputation as a detective who straddled the fence. He was a conspicuous cop—he dressed like a wiseguy, he was brash and brazen. Eppolito imagined himself as the man in the middle caught between the mafia and the police department. But there was no middle. There were two sides, and you had to pick a side. The book caused a stir in headquarters."

Oldham was drawn to *Mafia Cop* because of Caracappa. He knew that Caracappa and Eppolito were not only good friends but had been partners. Oldham had met Eppolito in passing. Before Eppolito retired in 1990, Oldham had seen him visit Caracappa in the Major Case office a number of times. Oldham had also seen him in the Six-Three Precinct in Bensonhurst, Brooklyn, where Eppolito worked as a detective for many years. It seemed to Oldham the attention from the book made Caracappa uncomfortable. A first-grade detective like Caracappa was the insider's insider on the mafia. "If anyone should want to be insulated from the kind of associations Eppolito called attention to, it was Caracappa. It was curious to me that a sharp cop with a reputation like Caracappa's would hang out with a schmuck like Eppolito who not only boasted about his connections to organized crime—he wrote a book about them.

"Eppolito was a 'name' in the force, like Caracappa, a detective who stood out from the pack. Eppolito was a former Mr. New York bodybuilder. He was heavyset, with a thick mustache and a taste for gold chains. He had a reputation for his love of snakes, the deadlier the better. For years he was the informal one-man Reptile Squad for the NYPD. If a call came in needing a response to snakes or crocodiles or lizards, any cold-blooded vertebrates, Eppolito got the call. Detectives Caracappa and Eppolito were inseparable but they were a study in contrasts. Caracappa was thin, quiet, watchful. Eppolito was fat, loud, foul-mouthed. Caracappa was the go-to guy in Major Case. Caracappa's discretion was his defining characteristic. It seemed he never gave anything up, or away. Eppolito didn't try to hide his mafia background. He was defiant. He strutted around like a goodfella cop."

One Sunday afternoon in June, Oldham went in search of the book.

He found it in the Strand, the used bookstore at the corner of Broadway and 12th Street. In the dank and cramped basement there was a section marked "Crime," where books about cops and criminals were shelved together—the two sides of the same story. He picked up the book and opened it. "There are no words to define my feelings for Detective Steve Caracappa, my closest and dearest friend," Eppolito wrote in his author's note. Oldham flipped to the photographs in the middle of the book, searching for one that he had been told infuriated Caracappa. The picture showed Detectives Caracappa and Eppolito as partners in the Brooklyn Robbery Squad in the late seventies. The two detectives were sitting in a squad room, Eppolito's tie undone, Caracappa dressed in a dark blazer and dark sweater. Both smiled broadly. The feeling of the photo was intimate, relaxed, confident. The caption read, "Steve saved Louie from a homicide rap by pulling him off a beaten 'perp.'" The heading of the photograph read, "The two Godfathers of the NYPD.

Oldham knew many of the lawyers and cops and reporters acknowledged and thanked by the authors—Hugh Mo, deputy commissioner of trials for the NYPD; Mark Feldman from the Brooklyn DA's Office, Doug LeVien, a retired NYPD detective described in *Mafia Cop* as "the fixer"; the journalist Jerry Capeci; and *Wiseguy* author Nick Pileggi. In the relatively small world of organized crime and law enforcement in New York they were all well-known figures. The cover of *Mafia Cop* purported to be a photograph of Eppolito's medals. It showed the Combat Cross and two NYPD Medals of Valor—two of the highest honors bestowed on police officers, often awarded posthumously. There was also a row of Meritorious Performance of Duty medals and Exceptional Performance of Duty medals displayed.

"On the face of it, the cover looked impressive. But if you understood NYPD honors it told a different story. The Meritorious and Exceptional awards had been given to him dozens of times—an extremely unusual number. Working cops were suspicious of a guy with a ton of medals. I never met a cop with as many as Eppolito. Eppolito claimed to be the eleventh most decorated cop in the history of the NYPD. It could have been true, but every cop knows what a meaningless claim that was. For a police officer to receive the medals and commendations of which Eppolito was so proud he had to spend a lot of time writing up his own Requests for Departmental Recognition. Other cops didn't recommend a cop for recognition. He had to do it himself. Eppolito had to spend hours sitting at a table documenting his heroism. There were some cops who couldn't help but write about themselves and their exploits on duty.

Traditionally, they gave their supervisor a bottle of liquor to sign the request.

"The practice got so bad defense attorneys began to subpoena Departmental Recognition Requests to impeach police officers as witnesses. The stories the cops told were at such odds with the likely truth—the accounts of police bravery so improbable—during cross-examination the police officer on the stand would quickly look either like Superman or a self-aggrandizing prevaricator. It was great for defendants. In the end headquarters stopped allowing cops to write up their requests until the conclusion of the trial. Displaying your medals as proof of valor was the kind of thing any cop looking at the book cover would instantly question."

A BOY'S LIFE

The week Oldham bought *Mafia Cop*, he was assigned to assist in the apprehension of a mobster named Giacomo "Fat Larry" Barnao. Oldham and his partner, Detective Kevin Butt, had been given the rap sheet and a black-and-white Polaroid ("a wet") of Barnao. Oldham and Butt parked under the elevated subway train in Bensonhurst at the corner of 86th Street and 18th Avenue opposite an off-track betting shop and waited for Fat Larry. Oldham read *Mafia Cop* as he sat. The neighborhood surrounding the stakeout was where much of Eppolito's book was set. The commercial strip, with low-rent storefronts, Italian bakeries, and nightclubs, seemed just another Brooklyn corner but the street was storied with mafia legends.

"I could look around and see the places Eppolito mentioned. I didn't have to work hard to imagine what he was writing about. A lot of wiseguys got killed on those streets over the years. It was the nerve center of the Brooklyn mafia. All five families were represented on 18th Avenue. At that corner, Johnny Gambino had a pastry shop where he dealt drugs. 'Baldo' Amato and Cesare Bonventre, both Bonanno associates, had a palatial marble and granite café where they held high-stakes games of baccarat. The Sicilian factions were there as well—'greaseballs' they were called, or 'zips.' The guy we wanted to arrest, Fat Larry, ran a car and limousine service, a front for his shylock and bookkeeping businesses. Fat Larry was up on a gambling charge. The collar wasn't ours. The two detectives working the case were in their own car a block away. It was just a matter of waiting for Fat Larry to turn up."

According to *Mafia Cop*, Oldham read, Eppolito's family wasn't "associated" with the mafia—it *was* the mafia. His grandfather, Luigi "Diamond Louie" Eppolito, was an immigrant who had arrived in America in 1901. Finding his footing in New York, Diamond Louie quickly became a friend of Lucky Luciano, one of the founders of the American mafia. Diamond Louie set up a stall in a jewelry store on Canal Street. The legitimate business was a front. In reality, Diamond Louie stole jewelry from Hasidic Jews, fenced swag, and ran a string of pimps and whores. In time, three of his four sons went into the family business: the Gambino crime family. Freddy "the Sheik" Eppolito, the oldest and toughest of the boys, was a flashy Tyrone Power lookalike who rose to underboss of the Gambinos. Jimmy "the Clam" Eppolito was a wiseguy and noted hit man. Louis Eppolito's father, Ralph, was known as "Fat the Gangster" on the streets of the Pigtown section of Brooklyn. After Fat the Gangster married a girl named Tess Mandelino, Eppolito wrote, mafia boss Vito Genovese bought a round of champagne in his bar to celebrate.

As a mobster, Fat the Gangster's deepest contempt was reserved for mobsters who became rats. When Genovese soldier Joseph "Joe Cargo" Valachi testified before a Senate commission on organized crime in October 1963, Valachi became the first made man to acknowledge the existence of the mafia. At the time, the Italian underworld was unknown to mainstream America. Valachi's description of the rituals and the structure of *cosa nostra* were broadcast live nationwide and caused a sensation in the press. The "mafia" became a household word. "Valachi was everything my father hated in a man," Eppolito wrote. "Ralph would sit in front of the television and have apoplexy as Valachi named names, lots of them friends of my father's. My old man used the Valachi hearings as a kind of teaching tool on what not to do. Whatever was said in our home stayed in our home." Despite the code of secrecy, Eppolito's mother, Tess, was quoted extensively in *Mafia Cop*. She told the story of her husband murdering John "Johnny Roberts" Robilotto, a nightclub owner and fellow Gambino suspected of being a snitch. "Ralph never told me in so many words, but it was Jimmy and Ralph who did Johnny Roberts. That's what got him his button. They said Johnny Roberts was a rat, and if there was anything Ralph couldn't stand, it was a rat. They were all the same that way. I guess to them, that made murder okay."

Only the NYPD received a like share of Fat the Gangster's contempt. In the fifties and sixties, South Brooklyn was "a veritable sewer of police pads and payoffs," Eppolito wrote. Bribes could buy a mobster out of most trouble. As a boy, Eppolito recalled, he carried bribes to precinct cops, payoffs to ensure Fat the Gangster's dice and poker games were left alone. "The cops were crumbs, and that's why Ralph detested them so. I don't know who he hated more, cops or rats," Tess said. Eppolito added, "The mere sight of a police officer's uniform was enough to drive him into an uncontrollable rage."

Violence was ingrained in Eppolito's life—first as victim and then as victimizer. As a child, he wrote, he was routinely beaten by his father. Eppolito described how he learned from his father how to handle himself on the streets of Brooklyn. On his way to grammar school as an eight-year-old he was attacked by a bully from the sixth grade. Eppolito said he was too afraid to defend himself. That evening, Fat the Gangster told his son to fight back. "Hit him one good shot, bloody his nose, take out a few teeth," the father advised. "A hard shot to the nose will break it all the time." When confronted by the bully the next day, Eppolito grabbed him by the throat and with his other hand broke his nose. "I kept smacking him until I thought he was going to pass out. His blood was all over the place. I had my hand on his belt and was about to punch him again when I heard a loud scream from behind me. 'Louie, Louie.' I turned around and saw my father. He looked at me for a split second before yelling, 'Fuck him up, Louie. Break his fucking face.' I couldn't believe it. So I kept on pummeling the kid, trying to break his fucking face."

Preparing for confirmation in the Catholic Church at the age of nine, Louie was slapped by his priest for making a commotion during instruction. Fat the Gangster went to the rectory to confront Father Pulio about hitting his son. At the church, Fat the Gangster sucker-punched the priest. "His jaw shattered. The teeth, everything, all over the sidewalk." Eppolito marveled at the incident and described how his father had lunged at the priest, screaming, "'You're nothing but a piece of shit priest. And if you ever, ever put your hands on my son again, I'll fucking kill you.'" Eppolito senior reportedly followed up on the bloody demonstration with some nuggets of wisdom on the fundamentals of mob semantics: "During the drive back to Midwood Street, Ralph explained to his son the difference between killing someone—that is, beating them bad—and killing someone dead. Which is exactly what it sounds like. It was another Mafia lesson for Louie."

CLASS OF '69

According to Eppolito, his father paid great attention to "honor." Life, Fat the Gangster believed, was about maintaining the mafia's traditions of silence and respect. Eppolito's mother, Tess, was more ambivalent about the attractions of the mob than her husband and son. Murder, Tess understood, was not a matter of honor or respect. In *Mafia Cop* she recalled her husband disappearing in the middle of the night. The next day, with a sense of disbelief, she would pick up the newspaper and see a story about another mob murder. She explained how she couldn't imagine her husband being involved in any of the reported murders. "I'd say to myself, 'It couldn't be my Ralph involved. He was here all afternoon. And so was his brother Jimmy.' But then I'd realize that these guys were night crawlers, and who knows what was going on while the kids and I were asleep." Tess didn't agree with Ralph's credo: "Nobody never gets killed for no reason." "But nobody has a right to take a life," Tess pointed out. "I'd mention that to Ralph. He'd just shrug me off, or say it was a 'matter of honor.'"

At the age of eleven, Louie Eppolito took a job as a pizza delivery boy. Teenagers in a gang called the Pigtown Boys hung out at the pizzeria. The prepubescent Eppolito allowed them to conceal their weapons—switchblades and zip guns—in his pizza boxes to avoid detection by the police. Soon, Louie started to help his father at the Grand Mark Bar, located at the intersection of St. Mark's Avenue and Grand Avenue in the Bedford-Stuyvesant section of Brooklyn. The bar catered to goodfellas and longshoremen. Next door the Eppolito brothers held all-night sessions playing a fast and furious Italian card game called *ziginette*. "It was here that Louie Eppolito's Mafia education began in earnest," *Mafia Cop* reported. Driving the rounds every week with his father in a black Chrysler New Yorker to collect debts and pay respects, Eppolito met the many made men of Bensonhurst. Joe Profaci, an olive oil importer and eminence in organized crime, advised Eppolito to emulate his father. "You got to grow up and have a lot of honor like your father," he said. "If you want to grow up right, grow up like your daddy." Eppolito's mother thought her son had the makings of an outstanding mobster. "Personally, I think he would have made a terrific member of the Mafia. He was fearless, and he loved to fight," she opined.

Eppolito agreed with his mother's assessment. In *Mafia Cop*, Eppolito imagined himself as a larger-than-life character. He described himself in high school as "a little fucking Casanova." At Erasmus Hall High School in Flatbush, Eppolito described himself as "the biggest stud they ever had." On one occasion, a dalliance with a girl led to Eppolito's receiving a beating from a local gang. Eppolito claimed he took seventy stitches to the face, fifty in his hands, and that a quarter of his tongue had to be sewn together. Eppolito wrote he soon sought one of the attackers and took revenge, sucker-punching a boy from the rival gang. The fact that the kid was unconscious didn't stop the brutal assault. "I knew at the moment that I was punching out this kid that I was hurting him bad. I also knew that I was going to kill him. He was unconscious. I was holding him up and smashing his face. Suddenly a hand grabbed my fist in mid-flight." Fat the Gangster told his son to stop—enough punishment had been exacted. The father was proud of his son. "You're no pussy," he said, "you blasted his face off and he never saw it coming."

Walking to high school, Eppolito was tailed by FBI agents investigating his father and his uncle Freddy and their connections to the heroin trafficking business. To young Louie Eppolito, FBI stood for Forever Bothering the Italians. When the agents accused Eppolito of withholding information he responded as he had been taught by Fat the Gangster. "I told Federal Agent Thompson to go fuck himself," Eppolito recalled. "Fucking feds. You can see how my father's irrational loathing of anyone with a badge could wear off on his son." Nonetheless, Eppolito displayed an early attraction to wielding authority himself. A sickly child, struck by rheumatic fever, he became a teenage bodybuilder who enjoyed throwing his weight around. On social occasions, Eppolito assigned himself the role of teenage party police. At a Sweet Sixteen party Eppolito said he caught a kid selling Seconals. Eppolito seized the drugs and beat the boy. The boy's older brother came to the party. Eppolito said he beat him, too. Finally Booty Romano, a twenty-three-year-old cousin, arrived and kicked Eppolito through a plate-glass window. "With typical aplomb," *Mafia Cop* reported, "Louie got to his feet, dusted the shards of glass from his clothes, and knocked every single tooth out of the front of the guy's mouth." Arrested and taken to the police station, Eppolito called home. His father answered and started to laugh as his son explained what had happened. "It turned out that, thirty years earlier, Booty Romano's old man had slugged my dad with a baseball bat, and my father had turned around and knocked the teeth out of *his* mouth. Like father, like son," Eppolito declared.

Sitting in stakeout for hours at a stretch waiting on Fat Larry, it was impossible for Oldham not to compare the books Detectives Caracappa and Eppolito had authored about the mafia—*Mafia Cop* by Eppolito and the OCHU "homicide book" Caracappa compiled at Major Case. The former partners were both deeply steeped in mafia culture. But the two books were polar opposites, like the men. The OCHU homicide book Caracappa created at Major Case was distinguished by what it didn't include. It was a compendium of a decade's worth of mob homicides ranging from the death of Colombo member Ralph Spero in 1980 to the professional hit on a Gambino captain named Eddie Lino on the Belt Parkway in 1990. The recitation of events surrounding the murders was precise and spare. The facts, and only the most basic facts, were provided in staccato police language. Eddie Lino was a notorious gangster, for example, short and tough and involved in mafia politics at the highest level; he ran a scam on New York City school bus companies, "taxing" every child's ride to class every day; he had been brazenly murdered just off the Belt Parkway in the middle of heavy traffic. The intrigue surrounding Lino's murder was directly within Caracappa's knowledge—how Lino was close to Gotti and one of the shooters in the murder of Gambino boss Paul Castellano. Caracappa could trace Lino's lineage in the Gambinos, as well as his criminal pedigree as a large-scale heroin dealer. Instead of relating any detail, the OCHU homicide book said only, "At the stated T/P/O the victim was shot to death in his auto. The victim was known to the New York City Police Department under NYSID #0765414N and FBI#445409D. The victim was a Gambino Capo who was involved with narcotics."

Mafia Cop, by contrast, reveled in the inner workings of the mafia. Eppolito celebrated his education by Fat the Gangster and the wiseguys of Brooklyn. "Eppolito held an idealized version of *cosa nostra*. In his mind, the mafia was about honor and respect and family—not money and betrayal and violence. It was a surprising point of view for a police officer to put forward."

Fat the Gangster, a chain smoker, died of a massive heart attack when Louie was twenty years old. The funeral was held at Vigilante's Funeral Parlor in Brooklyn. A fleet of black limousines filled with wiseguys came to pay respects—and the FBI took surveillance pictures to record attendance as evidence of organized crime associations. Long before he became a policeman, Eppolito had learned to meet with mobsters secretly, to avoid detection by law enforcement. At midnight, after the FBI agents had left, Eppolito opened a side door to the funeral parlor and greeted the leadership of the Gambino family with two-cheek kisses. "Slips of paper with phone numbers were given to Eppolito," Oldham said, "names he could call for work. Construction, the garment district, the docks, whatever the mafia controlled, whatever Eppolito wanted. As the son of a made man Eppolito thought he would be taken care of by the family. He felt entitled to consideration for an entry-level wiseguy gig: a no-show job, numbers running, truck hijacking. It was how the mafia was supposed to take care of their own. It was Eppolito's birthright."

As expected, a Gambino relative named Johnny "Bath Beach" Oddo set Eppolito up in a union job. Eppolito said he hadn't given much thought to becoming a "junior wise guy" but understood and accepted the choice he was making by taking a job connected to organized crime—he was setting out to be a mobster, like his father and his father before him. On his first day, the foreman smiled when Eppolito asked what kind of work he would be doing. No work was expected, and so he whiled away the morning doing nothing. His first task came at lunch, when the foreman gave Eppolito a quarter and told him to fetch coffee and the newspaper. The order outraged Eppolito. "Who the fuck you throwing a quarter at?" he growled at the foreman. "Ralph Eppolito's kid don't start out as no gofer. So why don't you take this quarter and shove it up your ass."

Eppolito's sister had married a man from the neighborhood named Al Guarneri—the same detective in the Six-Three decades later assigned to investigate the attempted murder of Dominic Costa. Young men in their twenties, Eppolito and Guarneri lifted weights together and imagined how life would look from the point of view of a cop. They talked about how they had played cops and robbers as boys. Surprisingly, Eppolito and Guarneri both decided to join the NYPD, despite long family associations with organized crime. For Eppolito the attractions of being a cop were the same as those Fat the Gangster found as a mobster. "Men could be men in this fraternal order," Eppolito wrote. "If the occasion arose where it was necessary to 'beat the shit' out of someone— a husband who battered his wife, a pimp who slashed his hooker, a purse snatcher who'd run down an old woman—those opportunities availed themselves regularly." Eppolito wrote that Fat the Gangster "would have killed me himself," had he been alive. He knew the rest of his relatives—wiseguys like Jimmy the Clam Eppolito and his son Jim-Jim— might give him the cold shoulder at first. "Blood would eventually tell," Eppolito calculated.

The paths of Steven Caracappa and Louie Eppolito first crossed in the NYPD Police Academy in 1969, when the police force was in crisis. Crime rates had doubled in the previous five years. The murder rate had tripled in the previous three years. Major riots in 1964 and 1968 displayed the department's tenuous grip on order. A wave of criminality not seen since the Roaring Twenties, when Prohibition was in force and gangsters ran speakeasies in defiance of the law, swept over the city. In response, squads specializing in homicide, robbery, and burglary were established. The "911" emergency call system was instituted. The city was under siege. Discipline and order in the NYPD were falling apart at the same time.

"The 'broken window' theory of police work holds that law enforcement tolerating a kid throwing a rock through a window encourages the criminal element in society to believe they can get away with more serious crimes. It was true, as New York discovered during the nineties when the crime rate plummeted after we started prosecuting the little things. But more important, the 'broken window' theory worked inside the police force, too. Cops who got away with taking money from illegal gambling houses concluded they could also get away with more serious crimes. In the late sixties, Frank Serpico couldn't get corruption in the force acknowledged, let alone investigated. Things had reached the point where the heroin recovered in the famous French Connection investigation was being stolen by detectives in the Special Investigations Unit. The French Connection had been one of the greatest cases in the history of narcotics enforcement. By the end of the decade, the heroin seized had been surreptitiously replaced by rotting flour in the property clerk's room in Little Italy."

The NYPD class of 1969 was the biggest in the history of the department, then or since. Thousands of Vietnam War veterans were returning to a city in steep economic decline—including Stephen Caracappa, who had served in the Army in Vietnam. Tables were set up along Broadway to entice young men walking the street to become cops. With a salary of nearly ten thousand dollars a year, the money was more than most entry-level jobs. Like all city jobs, NYPD benefits—health care, holiday pay, uniform allowance—were attractive to the children of first-generation immigrants who had worked blue-collar jobs with no social safety net. Many recruits had never considered becoming policemen, and had little aptitude for the job, but it was so easy to become a cop the offer was hard to turn down. The academy filled with veterans of a dirty foreign war—not fresh young boys out of high school, as was usually the case. Recruits who were used to Army drill sergeants and the privations of military boot camp considered the NYPD's paramilitary imitation little more than a joke. An atmosphere of near chaos enveloped the class. Fistfights were common—and more than once escalated into guns being drawn in the locker room and death threats exchanged.

"The city was desperate. If you could walk and talk, if you had two legs and two arms, you were in. Recruits with military experience were used to doing whatever they wanted even though they were in uniform. They weren't going to follow orders. The disorder of the military at the time was transferred to the NYPD and the force had a hard time coping with the culture. Authority was being questioned on every front, and that included inside the academy. As a result, more cops from the class of '69 were eventually thrown off the force or locked up than from any other year."

The NYPD application form was voluminous. It asked about family, immediate and extended, driving history, credit history, the applicant's arrest record, if any, names and addresses of neighbors, schools attended, character references. The formal interview that followed was conducted by the Applicant Investigation Unit. In *Mafia Cop,* Eppolito said he wrote a long essay explaining his family's history of association with the mafia. The recruiter was astonished at Eppolito's honesty. "Christ, you've got a lot of balls writing down this history," he said. "There isn't anybody in your family who hasn't been in jail." "Except for me," Eppolito said. He wrote, "I think the interviewer admired my audacity, because he passed me on with a recommendation."

The Police Academy was located on East 20th Street in Manhattan in those years. It was a large facility, with a swimming pool and gym, and four floors of classrooms. Recruits were taught law, social science, and police science. *Fidelis ad mortem* was the motto: Faithful unto death. The class was overwhelmingly male (female officers were known as "police matrons" at the time and carried a special caliber revolver with less recoil) and the building bristled with young men trying to outdo and impress each other. In *Mafia Cop* Eppolito described how, in one class, a diagram of the Gambino crime family (complete with mug shots) was used as a teaching aid. Eppolito recounted how another classmate called him over to the blackboard and pointed at one of the Gambino soldiers on the chart. "This cadet was a gung-ho hick from Long Island, and I could read the excitement in his face. 'Look, Lou, this guy has the same last name as you.' His mouth dropped open when I told him that he was pointing to my old man."

The class was arranged alphabetically by last name and divided into companies of approximately twenty recruits. With last names beginning with letters in proximity, Caracappa and Eppolito were trained side by side, from roll call at six-thirty in the morning to beers afterward at McSorley's Ale House. It was not hard to imagine how the two young men became friends. Caracappa also came from a working-class Italian-American quarter of the city. He had grown up on Staten Island, in the years before the Verrazano-Narrows Bridge was constructed and the only way to get to the city was by ferry. Isolated geographically, Staten Island had a high concentration of mafia. Growing up, Caracappa was known on the street as "Stevie Aces." He had dropped out of New Dorp High School at the age of sixteen and gone to work as a laborer with his father. In the summer of 1960, at the age of eighteen, Caracappa had been arrested for the burglary of a warehouse on Staten Island. Caracappa and an accomplice had rented a truck and broken into the warehouse to steal more than a thousand dollars' worth of lumber and construction materials. Caracappa was indicted on felony charges. Designated a youthful offender, Caracappa had pleaded guilty to misdemeanor charges and was sentenced to probation.

After Caracappa was interviewed by an officer from the Applicant Investigation Unit, he was disqualified from serving as a police officer because of his criminal record. "There were excellent reasons to keep Caracappa out of the force," Oldham said. "He wasn't stealing the building materials the way a kid might be caught stealing change out of a neighbor's house. It was a commercial burglary, not a boy seeking a thrill. Caracappa was eighteen years old. He knew what he was doing. He wasn't going to use the lumber to build himself a house. He had to have connections to fence the material. The likelihood was that an adult had put him up to it, promising easy money. The burglary had all the hallmarks of a professional job. He pled out to misdemeanor charges, so it wasn't like he was denying he committed the crime. The investigator looked at Caracappa and dinged him—he wasn't recommended. The decision was a strong indication of how poorly Caracappa explained his involvement in the felony. Even in the class of '69 he didn't make the cut—not until the decision was overridden by a superior officer. The reasons the investigator was overruled have been lost. Maybe the force was so desperate it stopped using common sense."

THE ROOKIES

After graduation from the police academy, newly minted Officers Caracappa and Eppolito were sent out on patrol. Eppolito's first assignment was the Six-Three, in Marine Park, Brooklyn—an area thick with the same mobsters he used to meet with his gangster father on weekends. Fraternizing with members of organized crime was forbidden by NYPD regulations. The department designated certain locations—bars, clubs, legitimate businesses known to give free goods or services to cops—as "corruption-prone locations." The reasons for the strictures were obvious: mobsters were expert at corrupting others. "A cop could easily be placed in a compromised position and thus pressured by his mafia associates to start doing a few favors in return for a forgiven gambling debt, or a night in Atlantic City in a comp suite with a couple of hookers and a few bucks for the blackjack tables. It meant that if you were sent to that kind of place on a radio run you had to be accompanied by a supervisor. If you were caught there, you would be brought up on charges. There were places that cops just shouldn't frequent, on or off duty. There were people cops shouldn't hang out with because it gave the impression you were in collusion with them."

Even as a rookie policeman, Eppolito ignored these fundamental tenets of the NYPD. He continued to pay his respects to gangsters like Colombo captain James "Jimmy Brown" Clemenza as he drove by in his patrol car. "Hell, I figured, who was it going to hurt to stop and commiserate with an old Mustache Pete about his lumbago?" From the start of his career, Eppolito began to make appearances on FBI surveillance tapes, consorting with organized crime figures.

During the course of a law enforcement career, even one lasting decades, most policemen don't use their firearms even once. Discharging a weapon in an urban environment is a last resort. In his first six months in the NYPD, Eppolito was involved in two shootouts. His policy, Eppolito wrote, was direct: "Shoot first and ask questions later." As a patrolman, Eppolito claimed he had a "sixth sense." At a glance he could tell if something was wrong with a person or a situation. Seeing a man lope across a street once, catching sight of a bead of sweat on the nape of the man's neck, Eppolito decided to pull his pistol and call the man to a halt. According to Eppolito, the instant he 'nabbed' the man, a bank alarm sounded across the street. Eppolito bragged, "I was all over the television news that night explaining my 'sixth sense' to the tabloid and TV reporters. The newsmen in New York like to think of themselves as a cynical bunch, but, in truth, they eat that stuff up."

"Doing God's work" was a common way for police officers to describe their efforts—dispensing rough justice, making sure the right thing was done, keeping the innocent safe. But in the NYPD every young cop quickly learned that sometimes the law didn't allow for justice to be done. The nature of human affairs and an imperfect legal system on occasion worked against fairness. In frustration, cops sometimes took the law into their own hands. Oldham had done it himself. But the vigilante justice portrayed by Eppolito in *Mafia Cop* was alien to Oldham. A young woman living in the Six-Three was assaulted by her spouse and Eppolito took the call. Rather than arrest the husband, Eppolito returned when he was off duty, snuck into the woman's yard, and rattled the garbage cans to lure the man out. Eppolito was wearing a ski mask to hide his face. When the man came outside, Eppolito hit him in the throat with a lead pipe. He hit the husband in the throat again and again and again, he wrote. Eppolito said he had invented a story to disguise the fact that it was a cop committing the assault. He had rehearsed his lines to make his performance convincing. "Look motherfucker," he said to the man. "My kid goes to school with your kid, and I hear you've been beating your wife. My father beat my mother to death, and any man who beats his wife has got to answer to me." Eppolito knocked the guy out and ran into the night.

"To me, that was ridiculous and insane," Oldham recalled. "Why not bust the guy? Why did Eppolito wear the disguise? Didn't he have anything better to do with his time off? Hitting a man in the throat with an iron pipe might kill him. Eppolito's story had nothing to do with police work. It had nothing to do with justice. It was about Eppolito."

When Eppolito encountered an abused wife in the course of his duties, he boasted, he immediately tried to bed her. "Every time we went on a call where a husband smacked his wife, I went back that night and smacked it to her, too. Battered wives were the most vulnerable. They needed a crutch to lean on, especially if that crutch just put the fear of God in their husbands." Once, when Eppolito was called to a domestic disturbance, the husband ripped the young cop's uniform shirt while trying to get at his wife. "I proceeded to show him what respect for the law was all about," Eppolito wrote. When the man sued, claiming Eppolito had threatened to kill him, Eppolito challenged the man to a fight in a nearby park. "He was a tough son of a bitch, I'll give him that," Eppolito reported. Eppolito claimed to have nearly choked the man to death. Incredibly, the incident offered Eppolito an opportunity to celebrate his exploits in a different area. He said he had an affair with the man's wife. "Kathy, who had a body she loved to show off, became a *Playboy* bunny. She was a cop's dream—until she'd cry and tell me how much she loved me. I knew deep down there was no way in the world I'd consider throwing a ring on this one's finger. I'd drop by her house on the way to a night shift for a quick bang, but that was as far as it got. That was as far as it got with scores of them."

Divorced early from his first wife, with whom he had a son, Louis Jr., Eppolito met his second wife, Fran, on vacation in Puerto Rico. "Louie came on to me with that I'm-going-to-marry-you stuff and I said to myself, 'Oh yeah, just you,'" Fran was quoted saying in *Mafia Cop*. "From the moment I met him I had a feeling the guy wasn't being honest with me. Just intuition." Eppolito, for his part, described Fran as "the best built girl I had ever seen, a bod that just knocked my socks off." Doo-wop music was Eppolito's passion and he courted Fran by taking her to mobbed-up Bensonhurst nightclubs like El Dante and the Gambino-controlled Plaza Suite to see the Mellow Kings and the Platters. The couple were ushered to front-row tables by dapperly dressed doormen, Fran recalled, Eppolito stopping to exchange two-cheek kisses with mafia associates of his father and uncles. Eppolito told Fran they were wiseguys he had known all his life. "Deep down I saw the longing in Louie," Fran said. "He was trying to be a good cop, he was trying to stay away, but the pull was sometimes just too strong." Their wedding was held at the Pisa catering hall in Bensonhurst, the bill reduced to less than half the normal price thanks to Eppolito's Gambino connections. There was a table set aside for organized crime figures. Eppolito had the band play the theme from *The Godfather* during the reception.

On three different occasions during the late seventies Eppolito arranged for parties to celebrate his promotion to detective, and three times the parties were canceled as he was passed over. Teamed with a slight and short patrolman named Jimmy McCafferty, Eppolito claimed they acquired a violent reputation on the streets of the Six-Three. Known as Atlas and Little Jim, Eppolito claimed the partners were baseball super-stars when it came to wielding their nightsticks. Called before the Civil-ian Complaint Review Board if a "citizen" had the temerity to register a grievance, Eppolito said he and his partner followed one rule: "We lied. Both our daddies had taught us that." Eppolito's view on the use of deadly force as a policeman was simple: "The only good perp is a dead perp." It wasn't long before Eppolito killed his first man—"ventilated the perp," as he put it. "I learned something about myself in that gun fight. I not only had the capacity to kill, I have the capacity to forget about it, to not let it bother me."

BROOKLYN ROBBERY

Finally promoted to detective and assigned to the Brooklyn Robbery Squad in the late seventies, Eppolito was teamed up with his former police academy classmate, Detective Steven Caracappa. It was with Cara-cappa, Eppolito wrote, that "I really made my bones"—the mob term for becoming a made man. Detective Caracappa had come to Brooklyn Rob-bery from Narcotics, where he worked undercover for a number of years.

"What fascinated me about *Mafia Cop* were the stories involving Caracappa. I was surprised Caracappa allowed himself to be a character in a book like *Mafia Cop*. Caracappa's job in OCHU in the Major Case Squad was to monitor the Luchese family and the mafia. Caracappa was supposed to be the ace detective. *Mafia Cop* put Caracappa in bed with a cop proud of his mob connections. Eppolito seemed to exhibit remorse at not having taken up 'the life' of a gangster. For Caracappa to be close to a figure like that didn't jibe with the sly Caracappa I knew in the Major Case squad room."

The first case Caracappa and Eppolito worked together was the investigation of a crew of stickup artists hitting black dance clubs. Known as the "Disco Gang," according to *Mafia Cop*, they were noted for using shotguns and employing extreme violence. Five of the seven members of the gang were arrested after people in their neighborhood identified them to the police. Eppolito wrote that the two members of the gang still at large were David "Big T" McCleary and a hood named "Bugs." Caracappa and Eppolito soon received a tip that Bugs had a girlfriend who lived in the Bedford-Stuyvesant section of Brooklyn. They staked out the apartment and grabbed Bugs on the sidewalk outside. Caracappa disarmed Bugs, taking away his sawed-off shotgun as they wrestled him to the ground. Eppolito then stuck his service revolver in Bugs's mouth.

The two officers transported their prisoner to the precinct for questioning. Detectives Caracappa and Eppolito demanded to know the whereabouts of Big T. Bugs refused to talk, despite the threats of impending physical harm uttered by the two detectives. "Do what you gotta do, pig," Bugs said. Eppolito rained down dozens of blows on Bugs's head. Eppolito wrote that he considered himself a tough man, an able and experienced fighter, but his blows had no effect on Bugs—he only sneered at Eppolito. This enraged Eppolito further. Detective Eppolito took Bugs to a room in the back of the precinct. There he filled a bucket with scalding hot water. He added half a jug of ammonia, a chemical that induces respiratory distress and can lead to blindness and heart failure when directly in contact with skin. Eppolito dunked Bugs's head into the water. He pulled him out. Bugs was screaming and his face was blotched and purple from the chemical exposure. "Fuck off," Bugs said. In *Mafia Cop*, Eppolito said that Bugs's refusal to give up Big T raised a grudging respect—but not enough to stop him from forcing his head into the bucket again, and again, and again.

Big T called the precinct the next day, Eppolito wrote, and asked for him by name. The sequence of events that followed was portrayed by Eppolito in detail. Big T threatened to rape Eppolito's wife and young children. Eppolito told Big T he was going to hunt him down and murder him. Detectives Caracappa and Eppolito worked around the clock for the next six days looking for Big T. The two Robbery Squad police officers questioned every informant and chased down every possible lead. Finally, a prostitute who provided tips to the police on occasion told Caracappa and Eppolito that Big T was going to meet a girlfriend in the Crown Heights section of Brooklyn. Eight detectives were dispatched in four cars. As always, Caracappa and Eppolito were together. "I'm going to eat his heart," Eppolito swore to Caracappa.

Crown Heights was an area that mixed Hasidic Jews with a large black population living in fading grand houses abandoned decades earlier during the white flight to the suburbs of New York. Detectives Caracappa and Eppolito were the first to arrive at the building where Big T was hiding out. As they pulled up they saw Big T standing in the window of a building above laughing at them.

"You're a dead motherfucker," Eppolito screamed up.

Caracappa and Eppolito ran into the building before backup arrived, and went upstairs. The raging Eppolito kicked in the front door of Big T's apartment and then another interior door. When he reached the bedroom he found Big T lying on a bed, naked, grinning. Big T had no weapons. He said he would come peacefully. Detective Eppolito ignored the offer of surrender. He jumped Big T and started to beat him, he wrote, breaking his hand on Big T's head. Within seconds Eppolito was trying to strangle Big T. Detective Caracappa struggled to pull his partner and best friend off the man. Eppolito concluded the story of Big T this way: "The public will never understand the mentality of a cop—a good cop, anyway. In a way, it's very similar to the mentality of Organized Crime. You do what you have to do and don't think twice about the consequences, because when you gotta go, you gotta go. A lot of guys couldn't hack it. Just like a lot of guys can't hack the mob."

INTERNAL AFFAIRS

More than a decade later, Oldham was sitting in an unmarked car in front of Stromboli Pizza reading about Big T in *Mafia Cop* when Fat Larry Barnao pulled up in a brown Cadillac Brougham. Fat Larry was in his late fifties, enormously obese, dressed in a suit that was two sizes too tight. Detectives Oldham and Butt crossed the traffic on Bensonhurst's 86th Street to make their arrest. Fat Larry saw the two NYPD detectives closing in on him. He tried to run. "He made it two, three steps and his knee gave out. He fell on the sidewalk. We couldn't cuff him because he was too fat and his wrists wouldn't meet. He was sprawled on the pavement cursing. He easily weighed four hundred pounds—the result of a lifetime of baked ziti and half-baked crime. It took four of us to get him up from the pavement."

During the stakeout, Detectives Oldham and Butt had started to joke about *Mafia Cop* and Eppolito's adventures. "Frankly, I doubted a lot about the book," Oldham said. "The Big T story stunk. Telling a defendant you're going to hunt him down and kill him? I have never had my face stuck in ammonia but I assume it hurts and burns. Back in those days, prisoners took unmerciful beatings in precinct houses all over the city. But you still had to take your perp to the desk sergeant before you took him downtown. You didn't want to appear with a prisoner who had just lost his eyesight. I wouldn't want to take a prisoner in that condition through the system. When you got downtown you went to Central Booking—where the guys didn't know you and had no allegiance to you. They would report a detective turning up with a prisoner in the shape Bugs was supposed to be in. After that, you have to take him to the city jailers. Prisons belonged to an agency outside the NYPD and they had actual enmity for the police. If a perp had a couple of broken ribs there would be no problem. It was common to see prisoners with their heads wrapped in gauze to stanch the bleeding from blows to the head. But dipping a perp's face in ammonia? Bugs's face was supposedly morphing into a giant purple blotch. It didn't ring true to me."

Missing from *Mafia Cop* was Eppolito's struggle to make ends meet. For most police officers, financial difficulties were par for the course. It was hard to make enough money to raise a family as a cop. Second and third jobs were common. Overtime was an obsession inside the force. There was also little in the book about the actual cases Eppolito worked, despite the fact he was supposed to be the eleventh most decorated detective in the 150 years of the NYPD. "If you were going to write a book, it seemed you would at least include the story of your best case. Eppolito didn't seem to have a best case. Clearly he was not a great detective. Smacking people around and closing a couple of robberies made thin support for a cop with more than thirty medals to his name. If the capture and beating of Big T was the summit of your career as a policeman, you should probably have turned in your detective shield."

Also missing from the book was an account of Eppolito's disciplinary record—which was substantial. As partners, Detectives Eppolito and Caracappa quickly accumulated a large number of Internal Affairs complaints. The first was from a man who alleged he was riding in a taxi at the corner of Nostrand and Foster avenues in Brooklyn when two plainclothes detectives arrested him. The man was placed in handcuffs and $300 was taken from him by the detectives—and never returned. Detectives Caracappa and Eppolito were investigated but the claim could not be proven. A short while later, jewelry went missing from the scene of a homicide. Eppolito was suspected. The charge could not be substantiated. At the same time, a confidential informant working for the DEA told the federal government Caracappa was involved in dealing drugs. The report was received by the department and inquiries were made but no action was taken. A man arrested by Caracappa in his office on Court Street alleged money and property were taken—a claim found "unsubstantiated." Yet another confidential informant for the DEA said that Caracappa and another unnamed detective showed her a copy of a homicide report in return for $10,000. This, too, resulted in no disciplinary actions or censure.

Eppolito's CPI—Central Personnel Index—betrayed even more troubles for the detective and his partner. While they were paired, a woman complained that two males robbed her. The two were "M.O.F."—members of the force—and Eppolito and an unnamed detective were investigated but the charge deemed "unsubstantiated." When Eppolito was required to testify at a complainant's pistol permit hearing, the man said Eppolito demanded money in return for changing his evidence. In a civil action relating to a car accident it was alleged that Eppolito had perjured himself. "It was difficult to make a case against a cop, unless there were witnesses or photographs or tape recordings," Oldham said. "It was the complainant's word against the cop's word. But when it came to officers constantly in trouble, the feeling inside the force was simple. Where there's smoke, there's fire. If a cop got a lot of complaints it meant he was an active cop, out on the street taking risks and making collars. The busier you were, the more arrests you made, the more complaints you got. It was the nature of the business. The easiest way to fuck with a cop was to make complaints against him. But if the cop wasn't making many arrests and the complaints kept on coming then there was something wrong. The arrest records of Caracappa and Eppolito did not look like the pair were going gangbusters. The nature of the complaints sounded authentic. Why would a man make up a story about extortion for a pistol permit? Why would a DEA CI make up a tale about a specific NYPD detective dealing dope? Why would a guy lie about two cops stealing three hundred bucks? There was specificity to the complaints and complainants. There were stories about drugs, violence, and money."

Oldham had been taught in the police academy that Mutt and Jeff teams were not unusual. The characters Mutt and Jeff were the stars of the first daily cartoon strip in America, two seeming opposites who were the precursors of Laurel and Hardy and Abbott and Costello. "Mutt and Jeff referred to a certain kind of male relationship—the fat guy teamed up with the skinny guy. One was a bodybuilder gone to pot, the other thin as a rake. The two were inseparable. It was a pairing that often occurred in organized crime. Carmine 'the Snake' Persico and his older brother 'Ally Boy' were the Mutt and Jeff of the Colombos. It happened with police partners frequently as well. Caracappa and Eppolito traded on each other's strengths and weaknesses. They complemented each other. They fed off each other. If they had never met, the characteristics they provoked in the other probably would have remained latent. Together, they brought out the worst in each other."

FRANKIE JUNIOR

After just over a year as partners, Detectives Caracappa and Eppolito were separated and reassigned. Eppolito was sent to the Seven-Seven, a precinct in Bedford-Stuyvesant known to be a dumping ground for suspect cops and malcontents. Eppolito was furious and demanded a different assignment. In the Seven-Seven Eppolito would be operating without Caracappa. He would be alone. He would be out of his element. He pleaded with the commanders to send him to the Six-Two, where his cousin Detective Al Guarneri was assigned.

Eppolito's request required the approval of a chief. Eppolito wrote that he barged into the chief of detectives' office and demanded to know why he was being sent to the Seven-Seven. "Deep down I knew what was on their minds. Uncle Jimmy. Uncle Freddy. Ralph. But I wanted to hear *them* admit it." To Eppolito's delight, and astonishment, the brass gave in to Eppolito's persistence and he was sent to the mobbed-up streets of the Six-Two. It was at the heart of mafia territory in Brooklyn. Near the precinct house where Gambino boss "Big Paul" Castellano, who was still alive at the time, owned a butcher shop. The streets were filled with wiseguys Eppolito had grown up with and knew well. "I felt like I was home," he wrote.

Once again Eppolito found himself tempted by the kindness of mobsters. The death of his grandfather, Diamond Louie, at the age of ninety-one, affected Eppolito deeply, putting him in close contact with his family as well as the Gambino family. At Diamond Louie's funeral,

Jimmy the Clam Eppolito, Eppolito's uncle and a Gambino associate, gave his nephew Louie an envelope containing $3,000 cash to take his family on a vacation to Disney World. Taking money from a known organized criminal was against NYPD regulations, Eppolito knew, but he didn't care. The money would give his family a well-deserved holiday, he felt. The pay of an NYPD detective was too modest to partake of such luxuries. He felt entitled to the extra cash; the rules did not apply to him. When he returned to New York and his duties in the Six-Two, Eppolito began to routinely drink sambuca with Uncle Jimmy and his son Jim-Jim. "I didn't give a shit about the surveillance," Eppolito wrote. "I'd played by the Department's rules long enough."

A month after Eppolito's Disney World holiday, Jimmy the Clam and Jim-Jim Eppolito were murdered. Lured to the Gemini Club in Brooklyn, headquarters of the lethal crew known as Murder Inc., the two were driven to a service road off the Belt Parkway and shot to death in cold blood. The reason for the double murder was political. Jim-Jim had been involved in an elaborate con run under the guise of a charitable organization called the International Children's Appeal. The fund was supposed to raise money for city schools during the International Year of the Child. It was in fact a money-laundering front for drug and weapons merchants. When the scam was exposed on the ABC News show *20/20*, Gambino boss Big Paul Castellano grew concerned the story would bring unwanted attention to the Gambinos. President Jimmy Carter's wife, Rosalynn, had posed with Jim-Jim for a photograph taken at a gala reception in Washington. Senator Edward Kennedy had also been taken in by the con. Powerful people made to appear foolish would, in the mind of a mafioso, use their power to exact revenge. Castellano feared that President Carter would sic a thousand more FBI agents on the Gambinos in retribution. He ordered the double hit.

After the murder of the Clam and Jim-Jim, both the NYPD and the mafia were worried that Eppolito would seek revenge, he wrote. His claim about police department concern was curious: gangland reprisals by sworn officers were neither permitted nor expected, regardless of circumstances. The Gambinos were another matter, according to Eppolito. Another wiseguy relative, cousin Frank "Junior" Santora, told Eppolito that Gambino boss Castellano wanted a sit-down—the traditional means of settling mobster disputes. A few days later, Detective Eppolito stood at the corner of 18th Avenue and 86th Street in Brooklyn as a Chrysler New Yorker pulled up to take him to a secret meeting with Castellano. It was after midnight, in order to ensure the rendezvous would not be observed.

"Some monster gets out of the car," Eppolito recalled. "He's right out of Francis Ford Coppola's imagination. Ugly, but dapper." As an NYPD officer, Eppolito wrote that he understood the consequence of having a clandestine sit-down with the man known as "the boss of bosses." "As soon as I agreed to that meeting I stopped being a cop," Eppolito wrote. Castellano lived in a white mansion on Staten Island on a rise named Death Hill by Dutch settlers. Afraid he might meet the same fate as the Clam and Jim-Jim, Eppolito relaxed at the sight of the house. Eppolito knew there was no chance he would be killed at the house of Castellano—the Gambino leader always kept himself insulated from violence.

Mafia Cop dramatized the encounter in a style meant to mimic famous cinemagraphic moments. When Eppolito met Castellano, he addressed him as "Godfather." Castellano waved him off. "I'm not Don Corleone," he said. Castellano explained that it was Jim-Jim, the son, who had been the principal reason for the murders. "The kid did a lot of bad things wrong," Castellano said. The Clam had been killed by necessity: if he was left alive he would have to avenge the murder of his son.

Eppolito adopted a grave attitude, speaking slowly, weighing his words. "I'm tremendously honored that you've chosen to respect me by bringing me here tonight," he said. He went on to say that he understood the rules of "the life" his uncle and cousin lived. As for the murders, Detective Eppolito continued, "It's not for me to say what is right or what is wrong in this matter. But I can say that I am not looking to hurt anyone. I'm not looking to come after anyone. I'm not looking for revenge. I just want the dead to rest in peace."

"The story read to me like a fantasy bordering on a delusion," Oldham recalled. "It only made sense if Eppolito was telling a story his cousin Frank Santora told him. It added up that way. Santora was a well-known guy in Brooklyn. He was connected to a few families—Luchese, Gambino, Genovese. Santora did a stretch in the early eighties in Allenwood, a federal prison. More wiseguys networked there than at any trade conference or political convention. If Castellano ordered the murder of Jimmy the Clam and Jim-Jim Eppolito it made a certain amount of sense that he would reach out to Santora and make sure the reasons were understood. No one with any sense wanted the mafia to attract the kind of attention Jim-Jim was getting. But the idea that Paul Castellano, the boss of bosses and the most discreet gangster around, would summon an NYPD detective to his house for a sit-down? Castellano would as much as confess to murder to Detective Eppolito of the Six-Two? You didn't have to be Sherlock Holmes to know Eppolito's tale lacked the ring of truth."

After the supposed sit-down with Castellano, Eppolito's wife, Fran, noticed differences in her husband's personality. Suddenly he acquired Italian mannerisms he had not displayed before, she said in *Mafia Cop,* describing his interactions with Caracappa. "The talking with the hands. The drinking of the double espressos. *Salud*-ing each other to death after every sip. And now Louie was starting to kiss everybody on the cheek." Eppolito said in *Mafia Cop* he no longer attached much importance to his job as a police officer. The glances and suspicions of other cops were too insulting. He was a different person, he said, no longer a cop, at least not in spirit. Eppolito wrote that he had come to inhabit a "moral twilight zone."

MOB JUSTICE

Increasingly in the thrall of the mafia, Eppolito started to use mob methods in his police work in the Six-Two. When a wiseguy named Frankie Carbone, wanted for breaking his wife's jaw, insulted and threatened Eppolito, the detective reacted instinctively, *Mafia Cop* related. Eppolito wrote that he fetched his sawed-off shotgun from his locker—the possession of which was itself a federal offense—and hunted Carbone down. Eppolito found him in a mafia social club on 18th Avenue. He walked over to Carbone's table and stuck the barrels of the sawed-off shotgun in his mouth and ordered him to his feet. "Suddenly I knew what it felt like to be my father," Eppolito wrote. "I was walking like a wiseguy. I was talking like a wiseguy. The power surge was comparable to what I had felt, at times, as a cop, yet somehow different. As if the police worked on the AC current, and the Mafia on the DC."

Eppolito described with relish how he'd convincingly played the role of a professional hit man.

He wrote that he instructed Carbone to report to the precinct house the next day. He explained the consequences if Carbone failed to comply: "First I'm going to throw you in the trunk of a fucking car. And then I'm going to blow your fucking brains out." As brazen as ever, Eppolito described how he would leave the body in the car near the precinct, giving it enough time to "get ripe." He would come back two days later and anonymously report a foul odor emanating from the car, and assured Carbone, "When I get to work, guess whose job it's going to be to find out who killed you?"

Over the years Eppolito worked forty organized crime homicides, by his own estimate. He allowed—"and this is a terrible knock on me"—that he didn't work particularly hard when a mobster turned up dead. One example of this cavalier attitude that Eppolito did not include in *Mafia Cop* involved the murder of a drug dealer named Frank Fiala. At approximately 2 a.m. on Sunday, June 27, 1982, Fiala was shot on the street in front of the Plaza Suite, a popular discotheque in the Gravesend section of Brooklyn. The Plaza Suite was owned by a corporation called Enjoy Yourself Inc., controlled by Sammy the Bull Gravano. The Plaza club was a large and thriving establishment, with five thousand square feet and a long bar lined with neighborhood wiseguys and party girls. On Saturday nights, Gravano featured live acts like Chubby Checker and the Four Tops. In the spring of that year, Gravano was approached by Fiala, a Czech who flaunted his wealth. Fiala said he wanted to throw himself a birthday party for three hundred guests. Fiala didn't know who Gravano "was." Fiala said he wanted no expense spared for his thirty-seventh birthday.

"Fiala thought he was a big shot, with mob connections. He was a coke dealer and a killer. He had murdered a couple of rival dealers—not just them but their entire families. He wrote a check to Gravano for thirty grand. The day of the party his check bounced. The party was a fiasco. Only eighty people turned up. Fiala had two blondes shave his head on the dance floor. Everyone was snorting cocaine. Thousands of dollars' worth of Chinese food was delivered and the crowd made a mess of Gravano's place—his pride and joy. When Fiala started dancing Gravano saw that he was packing a piece in his belt, another stupid move around a wiseguy. Gravano demanded Fiala leave. Words were exchanged and Fiala left. It seemed over."

In *Underboss*, Gravano's biography, Sammy the Bull told what happened next. First, Fiala offered Gravano $1 million to buy the Plaza Suite, $100,000 cash as a down payment, with $650,000 in gold bullion under the table, tax-free for Gravano. The price was preposterously high, and irresistible for Gravano. The deal was struck. As part of Fiala's pattern of conspicuous consumption—Rolls-Royces, yachts, two private airplanes—he owned a helicopter. Fiala started to fly over other nightclubs in Brooklyn at night hanging out the side with a bullhorn yelling at the people below to come to the Plaza Suite. The owners of the other clubs, also wiseguys, were not amused. Before the transaction was finalized, Fiala set up his headquarters in Gravano's office. Sammy the Bull stormed into the office to confront Fiala, who sat at Gravano's desk, flanked by snarling Doberman pinschers, Uzi in hand. "You fucking greaseballs, you do things my way," Fiala said to Gravano. "You think you're so tough. The Colombians are really tough. The Colombians fucked with me and I took them out. You greaseballs are nothing." Gravano was certain he was about to be killed—but Fiala didn't fire. Gravano thought, "If somebody's going to shoot you, he don't talk about it."

Later that night, Fiala exited the Plaza Suite surrounded by his entourage. He walked along 86th Street, kitty-corner to the place where Oldham would wait to apprehend Fat Larry Barnao a decade later. That night, the sidewalks were filled with people out clubbing. Gravano appeared out of the darkness. "Hey, Frank, how you doing?" he asked. One of Gravano's button men shot Fiala once in the head. Pandemonium erupted as hundreds of night-lifers ran for cover. Gravano's man stood over Fiala, bent down, placed his gun to his left eye, and fired. Then he placed the gun to his right eye and pulled the trigger. Gravano walked up to Fiala's body and spat on him. In *Underboss,* Gravano wrote that there was no doubt the entire neighborhood knew he was behind the murder.

Detective Eppolito was assigned to investigate the homicide. Press reports quoted him. "It was a methodic execution," Eppolito said. "Admitting that they had no definitive leads," Gravano said in *Underboss,* "detectives were reduced to saying that Fiala's murder was carried out very professionally." But Gravano omitted the true reason he was never charged for Fiala's murder. As he told the FBI when he flipped in 1991, Gravano paid the NYPD detective investigating Fiala's murder five thousand dollars to make the case "go away."

Oldham said, "The name of that detective was Louie Eppolito. Eppolito had solicited the payment in return for burying the case. It would not have been particularly difficult to let a murder file like Fiala's slip. Fiala was a coke-dealing moron on a suicide mission. Dead criminals littered the streets of the Six-Two at the time. Eppolito and detectives of the Six-Two never made a collar in the murder of Frankie Fiala. In the early eighties, there were dozens of OC homicides slowly cooling, turning from open cases to cold cases."

LEAVING FINGERPRINTS

Mafia Cop concluded with Eppolito's version of an event that had brought the contradictions inherent in Eppolito's worldviews to a head. According to his self-portrait, after he had become a police officer his loyalties had shifted back and forth between the two brotherhoods to which he belonged: the police and the mafia. But in the fall of 1984, while Eppolito was working in the Six-Two, an NYPD administrative trial decided the matter for good.

The trial stemmed from a discovery made during an FBI raid on a mobster's house in New Jersey in 1984. Rosario Gambino, nephew of boss Carlo Gambino, had been conspiring to sell forty kilograms of heroin. Unknown to Gambino, his customer was an FBI undercover agent. As agents searched the house, an NYPD Intelligence Division file was discovered—a serious breach in security. The file had been created by the NYPD's Organized Crime Monitoring Unit. It related to the investigation of Rosario Gambino, intelligence that the mobster should never have possessed. The FBI took the file and processed the pages for fingerprints. "Fingerprints are the product of sweat on fingertips. They can't be lifted from paper—they can only be revealed. At the time, the procedure was to place the document in a glass bell jar. It was then fumed with a chemical called ninhydrin. In this manner it became possible to observe or photograph the prints as they appeared on the paper. The upside of the process was you got to see the fingerprints. The downside was that it destroyed the original document."

When the FBI ran the latent prints from the documents, they matched Detective Eppolito's police department prints. FBI supervisors then met with NYPD Internal Affairs commanders to inform them of the identification of Eppolito's prints on the documents discovered in Rosario Gambino's house. No criminal charges were filed but Eppolito was brought up on departmental charges and suspended without pay. A trial date was set.

Within days, word of the case leaked from headquarters and then appeared in the news. Detective Caracappa was working in the Major Case Squad at the time. An early riser, always the first to work, Caracappa called Eppolito at seven o'clock on the morning the newspaper article ran. Eppolito had no idea that the story of his fingerprints on Gambino's police files had gotten out. "It's going to be a tough day, Louie, a tough weekend," Caracappa warned. "Just get the *Daily News*."

Eppolito fetched the paper. "Mob Big Got Data from Cop," the headline in the *Daily News* said. The article reported that a veteran NYPD detective had passed intelligence reports to Rosario Gambino. The detective in question was not named but Eppolito was convinced the rumor mill in the NYPD—a "huge hen party," in Eppolito's words—meant every cop in the city would soon know he was the suspect in question.

"I knew my life as I had known it was over," Eppolito wrote.

In *Mafia Cop* Eppolito wrote that a Greek proverb came to his mind as he read the story: "It is the sins we don't commit that we regret." Eppolito thought to himself that perhaps he should have joined the mafia, instead of the NYPD, as a young man.

Despite the irrefutable fingerprint evidence, Eppolito protested his innocence to department investigators. Detective Caracappa was no longer partnered with Eppolito but he visited him frequently. The way to beat the rap, Caracappa counseled his old partner, was to lie low and play it cool and see how things played out. Getting a guilty verdict was more difficult than many people understood. Predictably, the story of Eppolito's connivance with Rosario Gambino quickly spread through the force. Eppolito was isolated from his former comrades. With his pay suspended, he was running out of money—a financial crisis that deepened his resentment of the force. Before long, Eppolito wrote, opportunities in organized crime began to present themselves. Eppolito's cousin Frank Santora ran a crew in Brooklyn. A wiseguy named Red Calder belonged to Santora's outfit. Calder offered Eppolito five hundred dollars a week, tax-free, to drive a dump truck for him in Long Island where Lucheses controlled a cartel of garbage companies. A former NYPD detective named Bart Rivieccio offered to help Eppolito make unimaginable sums of money, Eppolito claimed. Like Eppolito, Rivieccio was suspected by many fellow officers of being connected to the mafia—suspicions borne out when Rivieccio was convicted of bank fraud months later.

Mafia Cop recited Eppolito's mounting indignities, from the insulting prospect of working at Toys 'R' Us to taking handouts from friends. On one occasion his son, Tony, found the former bodybuilder once nicknamed "Atlas" in his bathrobe sobbing uncontrollably. "Ten-thirteen" was the radio code for "officer down." It was also the term used inside the force for fund-raisers held to assist cops who found themselves in dire straits. Divorce and illness were often the cause, but occasionally 10–13s were held for a police officer who was the subject of an internal investigation and needed to pay for legal representation. Eppolito's 10–13 was held at Bay Ridge Manor, a Brooklyn catering hall in the Six-Two. Admission was ten dollars, with a cash bar and music from a doo-wop cop band called the Capris. Shunned by many in the force because of his deep roots in organized crime and the revelation of the Gambino connection, Eppolito expected a poor turnout. More than five hundred people attended, including lieutenants, captains, and fellow detectives. In one night, the "Louie Eppolito Defense Fund" netted nearly nine thousand dollars.

"Camaraderie among cops was strong, particularly when Internal Affairs got involved. The presumption of innocence had a different slant for police officers facing an investigation by other cops. Everyone hated cops who went after other cops. Every cop knew they could find themselves in trouble someday. We called it 'white socks-ing.' It meant that once Internal Affairs came after you, guilty or innocent, they were going to find something to charge you with—even if it was wearing white socks with your uniform. In Eppolito's case, no one trusted the FBI, for good reason. Being a member of the force was about mutual support, financial and moral, and the sense that it was us against them."

The last chapters of *Mafia Cop* offered a detailed account of Eppolito's administrative trial before Deputy Commissioner for Trials Hugh Mo. In Eppolito's telling, he was exonerated of all charges. He admitted handling the file found in Gambino's house. With the fingerprint match there was no way to deny that fact. The reason he was found not guilty, Eppolito wrote, was that the document with his fingerprints on it was a photocopy, not the original. "Bingo," Eppolito wrote.

Oldham begged to differ. "The point was that the fingerprint was authentic and original, not the document. The only way to capture Eppolito's fingerprint on that document was for him to handle the document. Eppolito's argument didn't hold water to me. It was tricky to think about, the kind of thing detectives like rolling around in their head. How do you get latent fingerprints from a document? Does a photocopier capture fingerprints on the original and transfer them to the copy? Does it matter if the document was the original or not? Eppolito had a long, contorted explanation for how his fingerprints had magically appeared on a police department intelligence document found in a Gambino's house. I wasn't buying it."

Departmental trials were not sophisticated affairs, Oldham knew. A hearing in front of a deputy commissioner like Hugh Mo wasn't like the supreme court. In Eppolito's case all of the evidence had been stipulated to. In legal terms, it meant that both sides agreed to the facts in the case. There was no way to enter evidence—or even question evidence. The only matter at issue was the interpretation of the facts. The difference between a photocopy and original had introduced confusion and doubt into the proceedings, it seemed to Oldham. The FBI was not present for the hearing to describe the effect of ninhydrin—how the chemical had destroyed the original document found in the raid, so it was impossible to enter the original in evidence. There was no fingerprint expert called to testify about lifting latent prints. Once the facts were stipulated, nothing could be expanded upon or contradicted. "The charges against Eppolito were found to be unsubstantiated. Eppolito was 'not guilty,' which was not the same thing as innocent. The waters were muddied enough for Mo to refuse to dismiss Eppolito. Reading *Mafia Cop* I couldn't figure how Eppolito was not fired on the spot. He was either lucky or smart or connected—or all three."

The day after the hearing, Eppolito wrote, he went to see Chief of Detectives Richard NiCastro. Eppolito was carrying his scrapbook, with newspaper clips of his exploits glued to the pages. He was determined to be restored to his previous assignment in the Six-Two, to clear his name and resume his work in the neighborhood he knew so well. Chief NiCastro was just as determined to keep Eppolito away from the Six-Two. Unimpressed by Eppolito's scrapbook and his claim to be the eleventh most decorated cop in the history of the NYPD, Chief NiCastro declared that Eppolito would never be sent back to the Six-Two. "I know all about you," NiCastro said to Eppolito, pushing his finger into his chest. "Your kind, and your family. I knew your father real well from Grand Avenue."

Filled with righteous indignation, Eppolito threatened to smash the chief's face flat. "I told him he didn't know my father. The only cops who knew my old man from Grand Avenue were the cops he was paying off." In sum, Eppolito offered the reason he had been persecuted by the police. "The main purpose of the entire affair was to shitcan me," Eppolito wrote. "Why? I guess the name Eppolito was enough."

Eppolito served nearly five more years in the NYPD. He never returned to the Six-Two but a compromise was struck. He was assigned to the Six-Three, the next precinct over and another mafia neighborhood. Eppolito described himself as a "bitter man." He filed a $5 million defamation suit against the NYPD, an action that went nowhere in court. Eppolito's remaining time in the NYPD was seemingly uneventful. He appeared to be waiting for the day he could retire, like many disgruntled cops have in the past. The only surprise occurred in 1988, when Eppolito was promoted to detective, second grade. "Eppolito averaged barely one arrest a year in the Six-Three—a total that put him in the extreme low end of arrest rates in the city. It was a pitiful record. By his own admission, Eppolito wasn't a cop anymore. He had sworn to get revenge. The force had treated him badly. He wrote that he had taken out a blood vendetta against the NYPD. It was curious that he was promoted to second grade. Eppolito had to have a powerful hook somewhere in headquarters."

In 1989, while on a stakeout in Manhattan, Eppolito wrote, a Hollywood casting director spotted him and was struck by how precisely the cop looked like a stereotypical New York mobster. The casting director introduced Eppolito to Martin Scorsese, the movie director. "On the spot, Scorsese hired the son of Fat the Gangster to portray, ironically, the Gambino family capo Angelo Ruggiero in the movie *Goodfellas*," *Mafia Cop* reported. The part had no lines but Detective Eppolito played a mobster, dressed in an expensive suit, grinning as the camera panned the mob bosses assembled in a New York nightclub; Eppolito's wife, Fran, also appeared as an extra dressed as a mobster's wife. During the shoot, Eppolito wrote, he became friendly with the movie's star, Robert De Niro. On the set the actor invited Detective Eppolito to his trailer for meals in exchange for tips on how to act like a mobster. Eppolito said pretending to be a wiseguy was simple. Live your life according to a code: honor and loyalty. "As frightening as it may sound," Eppolito wrote, "I found more loyalty, more honor, in the wiseguy neighborhoods and hangouts than I did in police headquarters. The bad guys respected Louie Eppolito. Unfortunately, I cannot say the same for the good guys."

"Eppolito retired in 1990 and pursued a career in acting," said Oldham. "It made sense. He had been acting the entire time he was a cop. Soon after *Mafia Cop* was published, Caracappa retired from the police department. It had to be because of the book. His best friend had publicly cast his lot with the mafia. At that point Eppolito had retired and Internal Affairs only investigates active members of the service, so they wouldn't be setting up on Louie. Caracappa was a different story and he had to know it. Internal Affairs would almost certainly want to know more about a first-grade detective in the OCHU who'd had his picture featured prominently in a book celebrating organized crime. Caracappa had become a lightning rod. Once Internal Affairs launched an investigation, Caracappa would not be permitted to retire until the investigation was concluded and closed. This practice stopped cops caught under the microscope from taking their pensions and running before they got caught. Caracappa managed to get out before an investigation began. I watched his hasty exit with interest. There was a retirement party attended by most of the big-name guys in Major Case. I did not go. Soon after I took a pair of scissors and clipped the picture of Caracappa and Eppolito from *Mafia Cop* and slipped it into my desk drawer."

CHAPTER SEVEN

THE AMAZING LIFE AND TIMES OF "GASPIPE" CASSO

The publication of *Mafia Cop* in the spring of 1992 caused a commotion in the NYPD, but did not trigger an official investigation. Eppolito was retired from the force and Internal Affairs did not start cases against former officers who were no longer members of the service. But Oldham's curiosity was piqued. He found himself brooding on the book's bizarre mix of braggadoccio, fantasy, falsehood, and naked confession. *Mafia Cop* took as its subject the relationship between the NYPD and the mafia. Incredibly, Eppolito preferred the moral code of organized crime to that of law enforcement, a perspective that was not only perverse—it suggested a deeper connection to the ways the mafia had infiltrated the police department. "As a detective in the Six-Two and Six-Three, Eppolito was on the frontlines of the war against organized crime," Oldham recalled. "As the best friend of Stephen Caracappa, Eppolito potentially had access to the most sensitive intelligence we possessed. It seemed to me that Eppolito had left the most interesting material out of *Mafia Cop*. What did a malcontent like Eppolito do for the last five years he was in the force? Those years weren't mentioned once. All the lies in the book made me wonder what the truth was about Eppolito and Caracappa and the 'Godfathers of the NYPD.'"

Early in 1993, the arrest of Anthony "Gaspipe" Casso began the process that revealed the secrets Eppolito had omitted from his memoir. On the morning of January 19, Casso rose late and had a shower. He was living in a spacious split-level house set back on a wooded parcel on Waterloo Road near Budd Lake in Mount Olive Township, New Jersey, a quiet suburb fifty miles from New York City. The sightlines of neighbors were obscured by shrubbery and landscaping. The house was owned by Rose Marie Billotti, Casso's high school sweetheart, purchased with a down payment of $100,000 in cash. Casso and his girlfriend lived reclusively. The house was lavishly appointed, with another $100,000 worth of renovations completed to ensure Casso was comfortable in his hideout: swimming pool, decks, hot tub.

Casso had been on the run for thirty-three months, acting with the same audacity as a fugitive as he had when he was free to roam the streets of Brooklyn. He was one of the country's most wanted outlaws, but he was little known to the general public. Inside the universe of organized crime—both mafia and law enforcement—he had a fearsome reputation. The Luchese underboss was rich, ruthless, and extremely dangerous. "Casso was Moby Dick for federal prosecutors—the great white whale. Cops postponed their retirements to nab him. Mob killers like Fat Pete Chiodo and Little Al D'Arco and Sammy the Bull Gravano were terrified of Casso. When Gravano flipped the only person he said he wouldn't testify against was Casso. No one wanted to take the stand against Gaspipe Casso. No one in the mob knew the reach of his power. No one in law enforcement knew the reach of his power. The man was a force of nature."

For the FBI, Casso represented a profound embarrassment. For nearly three years he had stalked the tristate area, killing rivals, running Luchese rackets, and making hundreds of federal, state, and local law enforcement officials appear foolish. Back in New York City the mob was being destroyed in humiliating and public fashion. Luchese boss Vic Amuso had been found guilty of dozens of RICO counts. The convictions of John Gotti and Victor Orena, leader of the one of the warring Colombo factions, had also been secured in the previous year. Casso was a particularly important piece of unfinished business. His orchestration of the attempt on the life of Fat Pete Chiodo and the shooting of Chiodo's sister made it clear that no Chiodo was safe while Casso eluded capture. "Turning yourself in had become a viable option for mobsters trapped between the homicidal paranoia of Casso's generation of mob bosses and other wiseguys ratting. The mafia was imploding. There was no escape for wiseguys—no one to trust, nowhere to hide. Casso was the exception to the rule."

That January morning, a twenty-five-man SWAT team waited until Rose Marie Billotti drove away in her Jeep Cherokee. They surrounded the house and entered using a battering ram, prepared for the worst. Armed to the teeth and wearing black combat fatigues, they screamed "FBI" and spread to the four corners of the house, weapons drawn. Casso appeared in the stairway, wearing nothing but a towel around his waist and a pair of glasses. "Casso was taken completely by surprise. It was a situation he had not encountered before. For once his source inside the NYPD had let him down. Gaspipe Casso was no longer the omniscient gangster who anticipated every move we made. He was naked to the world—another casualty in the war."

Agents searched the house and found a rifle, a machine gun, and briefcases containing more than $250,000 in cash. Casso had three sets of false identification. He had a stack of FBI files, including the proffers of wiseguys like Chiodo and D'Arco, which were extensive and, at the time, highly sensitive. This was a staggering discovery. Many of the people named in the statements were still on the street—including Casso himself. In the wrong hands—in Casso's hands—the FBI files provided motive for murder. It seemed to the FBI that Casso had possessed an uncanny ability to obtain sensitive information. They didn't know how.

Inside the New York City law enforcement community, Casso's capture was met with jubilation. Casso had been caught as a result of good fortune and excellent detective work. The pay phone system he had utilized for maintaining contact with his underlings had worked well for many months. Tracking Casso was impossible because there was no way to know in advance which pay phone to watch. "Lady luck smiled on us when a sharp investigator in the Brooklyn DA's Office noticed a pattern in the calls received by a high-ranking Luchese, Frank Lastorino. Brooklyn DA investigators traced the calls to a cellular tower an hour north of the city—Mount Olive Township, New Jersey. There was a good chance Lastorino was talking to Casso, Brooklyn DA investigators believed. It was a major breakthrough. The story took a typical twist in New York City law enforcement turf battles. The DA notified the FBI. The FBI rushed to make the bust and took the credit. Classic FBI."

The arrest of Gaspipe Casso captured the attention of the press. "Flushed-out Fugitive" was the headline of mob reporter Jerry Capeci's article the next day in the *Daily News*. "Another day, another don," James Fox, the head of the FBI in New York, was quoted saying. Recalled Oldham, "As Casso was cuffed and taken to the Metropolitan Correctional Center in New York City to await trail, we had a laundry list of crimes with which to charge him. Murder, attempted murder, conspiracy to murder. Now we had Casso and Amuso and Chiodo and D'Arco. Everyone in Major Case knew it was a huge breakthrough."

Gaspipe Casso would be doomed, it appeared, to spend the rest of his life in a prison cell, replaying his life story over and over against the wall of his cell. It was a story that mirrored the rise and fall of the mafia in the second half of the twentieth century. In Casso, the traits of the archetypal Brooklyn mobster achieved a monstrous zenith. He was violent, amoral, deceptive—the personification of evil. Casso was no rat but everyone knew if he were to cooperate he would bring down the house.

THE PROSPECT

Where does such a man come from? At the time of Casso's arrest, much was known about him but much more was not known. He was born in 1942, the youngest of three children and the son of a longshoreman on the waterfront of Red Hook, Brooklyn. Casso's street nickname "Gaspipe" was said to have a number of possible origins. Some speculated his father worked for the gas company, others that Casso had murdered a man in a gas station. The true story was that it came from his father, an enforcer for the Genovese family on the docks of New York during the era in the fifties dramatized in the film *On the Waterfront.* The mob preyed on the immigrant working poor who loaded and unloaded ships in the vast yards along the Brooklyn shore. Gaspipe was the elder Casso's dockhand name because it was his preferred weapon to use against wayward or noncompliant union members. "Many mobsters spent their lives trying to keep their sons out of 'the life.' They knew too well the price paid for belonging to the mafia. But many others groomed their boys in the family business. In the Luchese family in the early nineties, virtually every crew had a kid apprenticing with the mob while his old man sat in a federal penitentiary doing time. In a lot of cases cautionary tales didn't take. Gaspipe Casso the elder wasn't a made guy but he knew the life and his legacy to his son was an aspiration to join the mob. Father to son, the mafia was passed along like a poisoned chalice.

"Psychology books are packed with studies of the personality traits of men like Gaspipe Casso. They often possess a superficial charm and above-average intelligence. They rise to the top of large organizations, even nations. They usually aren't obviously irrational, at least at the beginning. They are shameless liars, as long as the lie serves their purposes. Among their characteristics are glibness, lack of empathy, an inability to accept responsibility or recognize the impact of their behavior on others—the things that make a narcissist. Casso had a short attention span. He couldn't make a long-term plan that had any realistic chance of actually happening."

As a young criminal, Casso showed great versatility, as if he had been genetically engineered to fit into the burgeoning enterprise of organized crime. He was reared near the Gowanus Canal, in an industrial area near the now gentrified neighborhoods of Park Slope and Carroll Gardens. Brooklyn was one of the five boroughs of New York City but it was also a city unto itself. The borough had a largely immigrant population of nearly three million and enjoyed the self-image as the land of new beginnings. Prospect Park, a five-hundred-acre public park designed by Frederick Law Olmsted and Calvert Vaux in the late nineteenth century after they had completed Central Park, was the heart of the borough for teenagers. "Brawls, drinking, sex, it all went on in Prospect Park. Cops were jumped by gangs. Women were raped. Teenagers ran wild in the fifties and sixties—the original wilding."

Like young Louis Eppolito, who grew up on the other side of the park in Pigtown around the same time, Casso got caught up in gang violence from an early age. Like Eppolito, Casso's first job was working in a pizzeria. Like Eppolito, he conspired with teen gangsters to help move zip guns and switch blades around the area in pizza boxes when there were brawls coming up, or the police were trying to disarm the gangs. Eppolito and Casso were both the children of organized criminals who had to learn how to navigate the streets during a time when the mafia was making the choices they faced stark.

As a teenager Casso ran with a gang called the South Brooklyn Boys. He owned a .22 rifle, equipped with a silencer, which he used to shoot hawks that were hunting the homing pigeons housed and trained on the roofs of many apartment buildings at the time. Casso was such an expert shot he was hired to gun down birds preying on the prized pigeons. A high school dropout, Casso quickly graduated from street thug to organized criminal. Working as a longshoreman in Red Hook in the early sixties, Casso met Luchese capo Christopher "Christy Tick" Furnari. Casso's father was "with" the Genovese, a term used on the street to indicate mob affiliation of people associated with a family. Despite such an association, it was not uncommon for the son of a mobster to take up with another crime family. Affiliations occurred through a combination of chance and circumstance and so it was with Casso.

In the summer of 1965, Casso was in his early twenties when he learned firsthand how entwined the worlds of crime and law enforcement were. As Casso was driving his car through the streets of Carroll Gardens in Brooklyn, he saw a man trying to wrestle a baby from the arms of a young woman. Casso pulled over and intervened on the woman's behalf. Casso recognized the man from the neighborhood as a local junkie. A fight ensued. The woman ran into a nearby house with the baby. Casso told the junkie he knew the woman, warning him off. The matter was over.

The next day Casso was at the 19th Hole when a friend told him two brothers were looking for him. The two men were carrying sawed-off shotguns in a bag. Casso grabbed a long-barreled .38 revolver he kept stashed in the kitchen of the 19th Hole and went in search of the two brothers, to no avail. The following day, Casso went to the junkie's house on Carroll Street just off Brooklyn's 5th Avenue. Casso held a tiny .25 handgun hidden in his palm. As he arrived, Casso heard a voice coming from above. An older man Casso recognized from card games at the local Democratic Party Club rooms was calling to Casso. The man said he was the father of the man Casso had fought. As they talked, the junkie approached along the sidewalk cursing at Casso. Casso spoke calmly and attempted to reason with the junkie. The junkie reached for a gun he had shoved in his belt. Casso started to wrestle with the junkie. Unable to disarm the man, Casso shot him with the .25.

Fearing arrest, Casso hid out for four months. In the fall of 1965 Christy Tick Furnari, the Luchese captain who had shown an interest in Casso's promise as a mobster, tried to reach a deal that would enable Casso to avoid prosecution. The junkie was hospitalized in critical condition but he was recovering and he and his father would be able to identify Casso. Trial and conviction would quickly follow. If Casso was to return to the streets of Brooklyn the shooting incident needed to be forgotten. Furnari contacted an NYPD precinct detective. The detective was known to Casso and his friends for a scam he ran: the detective confiscated burglary tools from Casso and the others and then sold the tools back to them. He was the kind of crooked cop who might find an accommodation. Furnari asked the detective what it would take to make Casso's problem disappear. The detective said he wanted $50,000 to "fix" the case.

"Fifty grand was a huge amount of money in those days. The annual salary for a detective was less than ten thousand dollars. Normally a low-level thug like Casso would have a hard time raising that kind of money. But Casso was a comer. The Genovese family offered to lend Casso the cash. The Lucheses were interested too. Christy Tick told Casso that would mean the Genovese would have a claim to Casso when he was 'made.' Furnari wanted Casso to be a Luchese in the 19th Hole Crew. Young Gaspipe was like a budding baseball prospect with a ninety-five-mile-an-hour fastball—teams were bidding for his services. Furnari offered to provide the money Casso needed."

The detective arranged for Casso to come into the precinct for a lineup. As agreed, the junkie's father didn't ID Casso. But then the detective overplayed his hand. He started telling the father he could be charged for falsely naming Casso in the report of the shooting. He was showing off for the other detectives, making sure there was no suspicion he was brokering a deal between Casso and the junkie's family. The father wasn't amused. He changed his mind and fingered Casso. Gaspipe Casso was placed under arrest. The deal was falling apart, with Casso facing serious jail time, if something wasn't done quickly. "When Furnari found out what happened he sent word to a relative of the junkie's. The shooting should be forgotten, Furnari said. Casso was only trying to stop the junkie from stealing a baby. The junkie had it coming. Casso was willing to pay fifteen grand in restitution. The hatchet had to be buried—but not in Casso's back. Casso appeared in court. The junkie said he didn't recognize him. The charges were dismissed. Casso had learned how pliant the law could be. Having someone inside the police department was invaluable."

THE 19TH HOLE

The fact that the 19th Hole was the setting for the beginning of Casso's troubles would not have surprised anyone who knew the neighborhood in the seventies. A small nondescript bar at a nondescript corner in Bensonhurst near the Dyker Heights golf course, it was on a block of low-rise commercial buildings including a Chinese restaurant and an American Legion hall. Across the street stood the Scarpaci Funeral Home. Joe Colombo sold Chevrolets a few blocks away along 86th Street as a front for his illegal activities. Inconspicuous to those not in the know, the 19th Hole was a major meeting spot. The neighborhood was busy, with a lot of foot traffic, making it difficult for an observer to keep track of the comings and goings of wiseguys. The area was 99 percent Italian. Lucheses were at the club every day, conducting business among themselves, receiving members of other families, and lubricating relations with food and drink.

Salvatore "Big Sal" Miciotta, once a Colombo capo and today living under an assumed identity in an undisclosed location somewhere in the Midwest, knew the 19th Hole and Gaspipe Casso well.

As a cooperator Big Sal had a mixed record. As an expert on the inner workings of the mafia, his knowledge was unparalleled. The 19th Hole was a regular stop for him. "In the front it was regular bar and grill," Miciotta said. "Wiseguys and knockaround guys and mob wannabes drank there. Real business was conducted out of sight. In the back there were tables and chairs laid out like a restaurant. It was where sit-downs were held. I went there with a beef a number of times. Usually it was about my shylock customers who weren't paying and claimed they were 'around' Christy, which meant I was supposed to leave them alone, violence-wise. A lot of decisions about the painters union were reached in the back of the 19th Hole. I had a spray painter who had a problem with Jimmy Bishop about using nonunion labor. Christy let us finish the jobs that we had open but then we had to stop because it was creating problems.

"I met Casso in the mid-seventies, when I got made." Miciotta said. "The bosses would talk in the back. I would sit in the front talking to Anthony. Casso was short, a little funny-looking. His nose was pointy, his hair was black and slicked back and greasy. He was afflicted with the Napoleon complex—he had to portray himself as a tough guy. Casso was usually the first guy to resort to violence. He dressed well, shirt and tie, clean-shaven like everyone else. The 19th Hole was dingy with a couple of televisions blaring all the time. Casso smoked cigarettes, had a few drinks. He had an attitude, constantly demanding respect. He talked fast, like a con man. The bad thing about him—his undoing—was that he thought he was smarter than everyone else.

"Casso dropped out of high school at sixteen but that didn't mean he wasn't educated. The 19th Hole was the Yale University of crime. In the Colombo family, we had our own institution of higher learning in a bar called The Diplomat over at 3rd Avenue and Carroll Street. Our place was like Harvard meets the Wild West. If you walked in with a problem, chances were you weren't walking out. But if you knew how to handle yourself, and you were one of the lucky few who got in—either on your own merit or because you were a legacy—you learned a lot. The five families were like the Ivy League. There were many imitators—guys who dressed like us, talked like us, acted like us. Brooklyn was filled with wannabes. Polacks, Jews, Italian guys who didn't get the tap. If you were the real thing you learned at the feet of master criminals. Casso's professors were guys with names like Benny 'Squint' Lombardo—he was called that because he had one eye. Joe 'Porkhead' Monteleone had a head like a pig. Joe 'Black' Gorgone was an expert in the ways of 'the black hand.' Those guys really knew about 'this life.' Every day was a rolling seminar. But you had to be careful as you learned. You didn't get a second chance, and you couldn't make a mistake. A lot of guys never got out of their freshman year. Not many made the honor roll.

"Courses included History—how and why Albert Anastasia got whacked in a barber shop in midtown Manhattan while he was getting a shave. Economics class gave an overview of techniques for extortion, shylocking, bankrolling a gambling business. Assessing a potential client's creditworthiness was important, but so was assessing his susceptibility to pressure if he was broke or tried to welch. In Social Studies we learned there were three branches of government. The executive was the boss. The judicial was the Commission. The legislative branch was enforcing the laws—and that was done by enforcers like me and Casso. There was an anatomy lab in the room in the back of the 19th Hole where a candidate learned pain points and how to chop up a body. We were taught where to shoot him, where to stab him, how to stab a guy in the lungs so when you threw him in the water he didn't float.

"The only second language offered in *cosa nostra* was Sicilian. *Amigo nostra* was 'friend of ours,' which was what you said when you introduced a member to a member. Curse words were like a kind of punctuation, which most guys had down to a fine art. *Gombata* was the guy who stood up for you. He baptized your kid, was your best man, supposedly took care of your family if you went away. *Gavoona* was a slob, a dope, an idiot—and there were a lot of them at the 19th Hole. *Conooda* was the worst thing you could call another guy. He was a disgrace, the kind whose wife was sleeping with another man and he did nothing about it. *Malendrina* was the best thing you could call another mobster. It meant tough guy. It meant bad man.

"Politics in the mafia was a deadly game. If you made a mistake you didn't lose an election—you lost your life. Protocol had to be strictly followed. If you went around your captain you were in a lot of trouble. He might not kill you immediately but three months down the line you were dead. If you talked badly about another guy all it meant was that you were the kind of guy who talked about other people—and couldn't be trusted. The guys who were going to make it to the finish line—the guys who were going to make it to a ripe old age—learned to watch for patterns of behavior. If a guy drank too much, used drugs, womanized, it was a character flaw. Everything had to be watched and then you set your course according to the observations you made. A lot of guys didn't have the cognizance to even think about things, but it was a very serious game.

"No subject received closer attention in the mafia than the inner workings of law enforcement. The ramifications of certain kinds of crime were studied. Federal crimes like counterfeit money and drugs were to be avoided. The rule was not to deal drugs, but pretty much everyone dealt drugs. There were a lot of contradictions. You weren't supposed to have dealings with the police but most wiseguys had connections inside the NYPD. Wiseguys would have a local precinct cop who could squash a bullshit charge like a traffic ticket or fireworks possession. It had to be within the 'reach.' It had to be at the level where they could rip up the paper and be done with it. They didn't have to talk to the DA, or the desk sergeant. As far as cops went, you never knew when you might need a favor. But if you were arrested you didn't say a word—not even your name. The first thing you learned was *omertà*—silence. Call your lawyer and we'll get you out of there. Learning the rules was a prerequisite for getting made. Before you were sponsored you had to learn what was expected in adverse situations.

"In them days there were a lot of dirty cops. Half of them seemed to have a price. But you treated them respectfully. You didn't want to create animosity. You wouldn't shoot a cop, same as you wouldn't shoot a newspaper reporter. Too much attention from the cops or the press was bad for business. Mob guys were tolerant of law enforcement, as long as the bosses weren't getting busted. At the street level the two societies coexisted. You didn't want to burn bridges. Most of us had family in the NYPD. I had a cousin who was a precinct detective in Brooklyn's Six-Three but I never asked him for anything. There was no reason to. Also I didn't trust him. I didn't believe in messing with cops because I figured it would get messy.

"Philosophy in the mafia amounted to an exploration of the writings of Niccolo Machiavelli. The mafia was formed by insubordinate Sicilian landowners, and the whole life—the chain of command, the ethics, the ways of maintaining order—came from the Italian monarchy. Man is greedy, cruel, deceitful—so the belief went. Anthony Casso wasn't a book kind of wiseguy like I was, but he knew exactly what Machiavelli was talking about and conducted himself accordingly. In the mob, the ends justified the means—and the end was money. That was the name of the game.

"But the most important thing about the 19th Hole wasn't what you learned. That wasn't as important as the people you met. Networks were established. Favors could be asked. Relationships were cemented. Hundreds of wannabes came through the doors of the 19th Hole every year hoping they would grab his attention. Casso got more than Christy Tick's attention. Christy Tick became his mentor. Gaspipe Casso was his prize pupil."

GAS AND VIC

Seasoned mobsters in power needed to identify young talent. Membership in the five mafia families was closed in the fifties to protect against the dilution of the "purity" of the lineage of the mob, and to ensure that no one ratted on the organization. But over the years mobsters like Fat the Gangster Eppolito were killed or died of natural causes. The numbers became dangerously low by the early seventies. The Commission decided to "open the books" to a new generation of aspiring mobsters. The five families would be able to reward their young stars with a "button." It was at this time that Big Sal Miciotta was made by the Colombos, and Anthony Casso was made by the Lucheses.

With his understudy now officially in the mob, Christy Tick Furnari teamed Casso with Vic Amuso, a thug ten years older than Gaspipe. Amuso was taller than Casso and better looking but he too slicked back his dark hair and adopted a thuggish attitude. Together they looked like a formidable team. The pair ran a bookmaking operation and collected debts for Furnari. Casso was arrested numerous times but avoided conviction, apart from one $50 fine and five days in a city jail. The charges varied, reflecting the varied life of a gangster on the rise, including bookmaking and bribing a parole officer to secure the release of a friend. There was a lot of sitting around the 19th Hole trading gossip and trying to come up with angles. Anyone outside the organization was fair game, as in the ripoff of David Stein in the mid-seventies.

Oldham recalled, "Stein was a major drug dealer doing time. Stein was tight with the 19th Hole crew. He had a girlfriend who lived in Brooklyn. She was dealing drugs for Stein while he was away in prison. A canny Luchese found out she was holding a huge amount of money in a safe-deposit box for Stein. The girlfriend had an eighteen-year-old son who was dealing on the street. Casso decided to kidnap the kid and demand the cash from Stein's girlfriend as ransom.

"Casso was friendly with a drug dealer named Danny Miller. It happened that Miller had a connection inside the NYPD. The connection was relatively small-time." Miller's source was a cop in Chinatown. In return for money, the cop was willing to provide access to NYPD files. Miller obtained a police shield and handcuffs from the cop to use in the scheme the 19th Hole crew had cooked up. Impersonating a police officer, Miller pretended to arrest Stein's girlfriend's son as he was selling drugs in Brooklyn. "They forced the kid to call his mother and demand $2 million or he'd be killed. This was in the days before caller ID. She wasn't going to go to the cops. She wasn't going to protect Stein's money at the expense of her son. She was vulnerable.

"Desperate, she reached out to the most powerful people she knew—Casso and his crew—the ones who were ripping her off in the first place. Two Lucheses drove her to the bank where she took the money from a safe-deposit box. After coming out of the bank the kid's mother got another call from the supposedly mysterious kidnappers, who told her to drop the money in a suitcase at a hamburger joint. One of her escorts convinced Stein's girlfriend that he should spare her the danger of delivering the cash to her son's kidnappers. A real gentleman, he would take the money to the thugs himself. The distraught mother took the bait and she never saw the chivalrous Luchese pass the suitcase off to Casso. The boy was released. She was promised that the guys at the 19th Hole would do everything in their power to catch the low-down scoundrels who kidnapped her son. The circle was closed. The girlfriend got her son back. The 19th Hole crew got $2 million belonging to David Stein—drug money he couldn't and wouldn't report stolen. No one was the wiser—and Casso and the 19th Hole cut up two million bucks."

To be in "the life" Casso still had to prove he was willing to take a life. Once an aspirant like Casso had killed, not for personal reasons or as an act of passion but on the order of others, it was believed there was no way to turn back. "Murder was the point of no return. Killing forces a man to see himself in a new light—morally and spiritually. No matter how much bullshit bravado there was about murder, taking a life has an impact on most people. You became a different person. They owned you."

In the mid-seventies Casso committed his first murder. The victim was a small-time drug dealer from Brighton Beach named Lee Schleifer, who was suspected of cooperating in the investigation of a large cocaine distribution network the Lucheses were running in Brooklyn. The hit was ordered by Christy Tick. Still in his early twenties, Schleifer had been kicked out of medical school for cheating. He was studying to be a pharmacist and worked on the side cutting cocaine. Schleifer was short and loudmouthed. Word got out that Schleifer was cooperating with the DEA. His death warrant had been signed.

To make sure the kill was clean, Casso needed to get Schleifer someplace safe and quiet. Casso had the kid brought to a Bonanno social club on 15th Avenue. On the day of the hit, Casso's fellow Lucheses went to the International House of Pancakes to wait while Casso "broke his cherry" with his first murder. The social club was simple—a bar and a card table in a basement. It was snowing outside but Schleifer arrived dressed like a cowboy. "Probably stoned out of his mind. He had no idea about what was about to happen. He was forced to the ground and handcuffed. Casso pulled out a .22 handgun with a silencer and shot Schleifer. He was rolled up in a tarpaulin and lugged to the trunk of a car and dumped in a dead-end street near Avenue U—by chance in front of the house of the mother of a Gambino capo."

Once Casso and Amuso were made, they were assigned to oversee the Bypass gang. Their job was to ensure that the Lucheses got their end of the millions that the burglary outfit was bringing in during the seventies and eighties. As a made member of the Lucheses, Casso quickly started making serious money from the various rackets and scams the family ran. But from the beginning, despite his newfound wealth, he lived a modest life in a working-class area in the Flatlands in Brooklyn. His wife, Lillian, opened a lingerie store. Casso portrayed himself as a sales representative for a construction company. The Cassos had two children. "From the outside the Cassos looked like any other Italian-American family trying to get ahead. Smart mobsters were discreet. To avoid attention from the Internal Revenue Service they didn't spend their money on property but on fixtures—they bought modest houses befitting the blue-collar work they supposedly did and appointed them with marble floors, gold-plated faucets, the flashiest television on the market. They couldn't buy nice cars for tax reasons so they leased Cadillacs or Mercedes-Benzes, new, loaded with the extras. They ate at the best Italian restaurants and went gambling. It took imagination to spend all the money they made."

Open secrets about organized crime were commonplace in certain sections of Brooklyn and Staten Island. Everyone "knew" who was connected. Everyone "knew" who was a wiseguy, but no one talked to outsiders about it, if they knew what was good for them. No one talked to the police. No one testified in court. It was understood that *cosa nostra* was "our thing," as the Italian translated. "Justice was supposed to be available to the little guy. Traditions were supposed to be upheld. Honor protected. But the truth was that the so-called mafia 'code' was about money and control and ego. Regular people shook hands with the devil when they dealt with the mafia. The 'favors' they did for people always came with strings attached."

In the neighborhood Anthony Casso was "known" to be a man who could dispense such favors. When Casso's neighbor's daughter got date-raped by a controlling and jealous ex-boyfriend, the parents told Lillian Casso. Rejected by the girl, the boyfriend had then come to the house and menaced the family. They asked Lillian Casso if there was anything her husband could do about it. They knew who Casso was, without having to say it. Lillian told her husband. He went to see the neighbors and asked for a photograph of the guy. Casso could have had the kid beaten, or scared him away. That wasn't his style. Casso put a hit out on the kid. He gave the job to Fat Pete Chiodo. Two weeks later the kid was discovered shot in the back of the head sitting in his Camaro in Park Slope, Brooklyn. "The matter was never discussed between the Cassos and their neighbors. The problem was solved. The case was never closed by the NYPD. The family was now beholden to Casso."

In 1980, Christy Tick Furnari moved up the family hierarchy to become *consigliere,* counselor. Casso was offered Furnari's place as captain. The promotion was an honor in the mafia. As a capo he would be entitled to a piece of all the money brought in by the members of his crew. He would have increased authority. He would be on his way to bigger things inside the Lucheses. But Casso turned it down. He put Vic Amuso forward to be captain. "Casso wasn't interested in titles or rank. He was smart enough to know that it would only attract unwanted attention, from law enforcement and rival mobsters. Casso wanted power. He wanted money. But he didn't want to call attention to himself. He appeared to be an average guy. He sold construction materials. For law enforcement Casso was barely a blip on the radar screen, some flunkie hanging on the coattails of Christy Tick and Vic Amuso. But he was a major mafia mover, without question."

Big Sal Miciotta remembered Casso well from the early eighties. They saw each other often at the 19th Hole. Casso was happy and easy to get along with, Miciotta recalled. "At the time, Casso was a traditional kind of gangster. We all operated under the same rules—even if they were broken half the time. The tradition went that murder in the mob was for honor, never for money or paranoid insecurities about suspected snitches or power plays. By the early eighties, I had killed a few guys. The first man I killed was named Scotty. He was just a street kid, nobody. I was ordered to whack him because he slapped a goodfella's brother. I thought maybe we should just break his legs, but it wasn't my call."

Like Anthony Casso, Big Sal Miciotta was part of the new generation. By 1983, he was beginning to thrive in "the life." He owned a pet store and newspaper stand on 86th Street to front for his shylocking business. Business was good for both men. Shortly after Miciotta had moved to Mill Basin, one of the best addresses for a wiseguy in Brooklyn, Casso moved in a few blocks away. "It was still a golden moment for the mafia.

It was an era of opportunity. Once you were made you could move around and do almost anything you wanted. In the twenties, there was gold in the streets for the original gangsters: bootleg liquor, unions, drugs. No one had brought organized crime to America before. When me and Casso came up a lot of businesses were already taken and the openings were few. We did pretty good, but we didn't become millionaires. Casso was the exception. He was running drugs in huge volumes. He was tight with Christy Tick. He was rolling in cash."

During this time Miciotta was beginning to realize that life in the mob was filled with treachery. The contract to kill Colombo associate Larry "Champagne" Carrozza in 1983 was a case in point. "Larry was a nice young guy. Twenty-nine years old, two kids, not made yet but proposed as a member. He drank champagne everywhere he went. Then one day, out of nowhere, I'm told he's got to go. I was told he was sleeping with the sister of a wiseguy. Supposedly he was seen coming out of a motel on Long Island with her. Larry should have known better, if it was true. But what if the allegation was bullshit? I thought he should at least get the chance to defend himself. Put him in a basement, beat him, see what he said. Did anyone even ask the kid? I had no say in the matter. My wife was in labor at the time. They came and found me in the hospital waiting room. I was told the job had to be done immediately. I said, 'What it can't wait? Nobody else in this family can kill somebody no more?'

"Once I was given the piece of work, I wanted to do the shooting. If you're the shooter you got a gun so at least you know you're not going to get shot yourself. That was a real possibility in a job like this. Your own crew would cop a sneak on you. I had a .38 revolver. I cleaned the weapon and dry-fired it twice to make sure it didn't misfire. Most wiseguys didn't have a fucking clue what to do with a gun. I went to the shooting range and practiced. I became an accomplished shooter that way. It's like being a ballplayer. You better take batting practice."

To get Larry Carrozza to come with them, Big Sal and the crew told him he was going to be tested to see if he deserved to be "made" by the family. Another Colombo was owed money and they wanted Carrozza to collect the dues, they told him. Carrozza was too green and trusting to realize what was about to happen. The crew of three met him at the candy store he owned. They told him his car would be best for the job. It happened to be Carrozza's mother's Cadillac. Miciotta sat in the backseat. He pulled on a pair of surgical gloves he had in his pocket and he put his gun in his lap as they drove through Brooklyn. Off the Belt Parkway near the Verrazano-Narrows Bridge, they pulled over opposite a block of low-rent apartments. Miciotta's partner, Jimmy Angellino, said he would fetch the guy who owed money and bring him to the car. "I waited about two minutes. Then I took the gun and I shot him twice in the back of the head. His head exploded all over me. I was covered in blood. We left Larry Champagne right there, in his mother's car. The guns went in the sewer. I went back to my house and took off my clothes and put them in a garbage bag and buried them. I took a shower and cleaned up. The next morning I picked my wife and new baby girl up from the hospital."

Two weeks later, an NYPD detective from the Six-Two left a business card for Miciotta with a note on the back asking him to contact him at the precinct house. Miciotta had never heard of Detective Louis Eppolito. But Big Sal knew a local woman had seen the flashes from the gun when he shot Carrozza. Miciotta asked around about Eppolito, to see if there was any dangerous evidence in the investigation, and he was told he had nothing to worry about. With trepidation, Miciotta went to see Detective Eppolito. The NYPD officer with a large gut and dark mustache was in the detective squad room. "Up on the wall there were photographs of all 'KG's,' known gamblers, and there I was looking at myself. There was a clipboard up on the wall saying 'Unsolved Homicides.' There was dozens of names on the list. Larry Champagne was one of them. I says, 'Wow, you're getting busy around here.' Eppolito started laughing. He says, 'I just need to talk to you. It's my job. I got to go through the motions.'

"I knew him from before. I had seen him at Ruggerio's, the Italian restaurant next door to my pet store on 86th Street. Wiseguys ate at Ruggerio's all the time. Detectives from the Six-Two went there once a week to eat in a back room. Eppolito had come in to my store a couple of times and looked at my boa constrictor. He was always shaking hands with everyone like he was running for fucking mayor. I knew he was a knockaround-type detective. He was a detective who could help if it wasn't something major or out of his control. We sat and talked for twenty minutes. How the neighborhood was changing—drugs on 25th Avenue, drugs all over the place. Then he asks what I know about Larry Carrozza. 'You know what happened to him?' he asks. I says, 'Yeah, I know. It was in the newspapers.' He says, 'I got a signed statement from Benny 'the Sic'—that's short for Sicilian—saying that you were the last guy to see Larry Champagne alive. The statement says he told his wife he was going out to get bagels and then he was going to see you.' I says, 'I really don't know anything about it. He didn't go and meet me. I don't know what the fuck he was talking about.' I could see the letter 'B' in the signature on the statement across the desk. Benny the Sic was a fucking idiot. It was a stool-pigeon move to give my name over. He should have kept his mouth shut. 'Don't worry about it,' Eppolito says to me. I was paranoid for a long time, but I never heard another word about Larry Champagne. The case wasn't solved until '93, when I flipped and told the FBI everything—including about Louis Eppolito's so-called investigation.

"Years later, I find out the real reason Larry Champagne got killed. He had hooked up with some Russian gangsters in a scam to rip off gasoline taxes. When Larry told other guys about the deal, they wanted it all for themselves. The gas tax scam brought in more than forty-five million bucks. I should have had a big piece of that, for killing Larry, but I didn't get a dime. Casso got paid. He made millions out of the partnership with the Russians. Wiseguys like Casso never missed out on a big payday. Guys like me and Larry Champagne were on the outside. Casso was an insider."

By 1984, Casso had become a major force in the mafia. He had his hands in all varieties of illegal conduct in addition to the gas tax—extortion, loan-sharking, and union scams. A measure of Casso's increasing influence could be seen in the way other gangsters treated him. When Gotti, Gravano, and a wiseguy named Frank DeCicco plotted to murder Gambino boss Paul Castellano they first went to Casso to ask if he had any objections. Riling Gaspipe was a risk the rebel Gambinos weren't willing to take. "I don't give a fuck," Casso said. But his stated indifference only lasted as long as it suited him. A month after Castellano was killed, Casso was sent to pick up Genovese boss Vincent Chin Gigante in front of Victory Memorial Hospital in Brooklyn. For decades Gigante had been pretending to be mentally incompetent in order to avoid trial. Casso took Gigante to Christy Tick's house in Staten Island. At the meeting of Genovese and Luchese leaders it was agreed that Gotti and his suspected co-conspirator DeCicco had killed Castellano without the permission of the Commission. At the time, Gotti was trying to convince other mobsters that he had nothing to do with Castellano's murder.

"Gotti wasn't fooling anyone with his crocodile tears," said Oldham. "Gotti was shocked, shocked at the untimely demise of Castellano. He was crestfallen. He was going to see the killer was caught. It was like O. J. Simpson pretending he was going to hire private detectives to find out who killed his wife, Nicole. No wiseguy was going to buy that load of crapola. Gotti whacked Castellano so he could take over the Gambino family and deal heroin without having to bother pretending to Castellano that he wasn't."

Revenge was plotted by the Lucheses and the Genoveses. The Lucheses assigned their best team, Gaspipe Casso and Vic Amuso. Both knew Gotti and his crew well. But it would be difficult for them to clock the movements of Gotti and DeCicco without being noticed. A Genovese associate trained in the military as a munitions expert was seconded to the Luchese for the hit. Casso and the associate had frequently helped each other with work. He set up on DeCicco's house trying to learn his routine. He couldn't find a place to kill the pair. Gotti was always surrounded by his own unique entourage: a mob security detail, law enforcement officials—hidden in vans and working undercover surveillance—and not infrequently paparazzi and local news cameras.

In April 1986, Amuso and Casso discovered that Gotti and DeCicco were planning to meet on the following Sunday with some "zips" (native Italians) on 18th Avenue. Casso dispatched a junior crew member to Florida to collect a load of C-4 explosives buried in the yard of a house once owned by a Luchese wiseguy. The Genovese army vet took the C-4 upstate to his place in the Catskill Mountains to build a bomb designed to detonate by remote control. He was a machinist and knew how to manipulate the rubbery, high-yield plastic explosive. The next day, Casso and Amuso drove up to the Catskills bearing a MAC-10 machine gun as a house gift. The three spent their afternoon in the country improvising explosive devices and firing 9mm handguns and the MAC-10 in the bucolic surroundings.

The day of the hit, Casso and Amuso parked on 86th Street in Bensonhurst across from a lumberyard near the 19th Hole. The Genovese drove up in a gray Oldsmobile Toronado and parked near Scarpaci's Funeral Home. He got out of the car carrying grocery bags and Italian bread—or what appeared to be food and bread. DeCicco arrived at the social club, parked, and went inside for his meeting. The Genovese wiseguy walked by, and pretended to drop something. Bending over, he slid the bag containing the explosives under DeCicco's car. An hour later, DeCicco came out of the social club on 86th Street with another made man, Luchese soldier Frankie "Heart" Bellino. The two got into the car. Mistaking Bellino for Gotti, the munitions expert drove alongside the car and pushed the detonator. DeCicco was killed instantly; Bellino was seriously injured. Casso and Amuso monitored the police response over a scanner. They all met up shortly thereafter at Caesar's Bay Bazaar, a store on the Belt Parkway. The Genovese man's ear was bleeding. His car was damaged from the blast. He said he might have been seen by locals but he wasn't worried; no one from that neighborhood knew him or would recognize him.

By the end of 1986, Amuso and Casso were no longer rising stars in the Luchese family. They were proven killers, big earners, and a potent force in both intra- and inter-family mafia politics. The verdicts in the Commission Case were drawing near. The prosecution was moving toward a conclusion that everyone knew to be inevitable: multiple convictions and massive prison sentences for the defendants. The outcome presented the Lucheses with the problem of resolving succession to the present leadership. The family was divided into three factions. Amuso and Casso belonged to the Brooklyn faction, the home territory of boss Tony Ducks Corallo and the traditional base for the family. The Bronx faction was led by Tom "Mix" Santoro, his street name derived from his resemblance to the original Wild West Hollywood movie star Tom Mix. The third faction in New Jersey was run by Anthony "Tumac" Accetturo, who also took his nickname from the cinema—in his case, the lead character in the 1940 caveman classic *One Million B.C.*

As boss, Tony Ducks Corallo decided who would take over the family. In November 1986 Amuso and Casso were summoned to a meeting in Staten Island with the leaders of the Luchese family. Casso was still recovering from the Gambino-backed attempt on his life. Verdicts in the Commission trial were imminent. Arrangements needed to be made to ensure continuity and order. There were more than half a dozen *caporegimes,* or captains, in the family, and more than a hundred made men. But one pair stood head and shoulders above the rest in the ways that mattered: moneymaking, imagination, intimidation. The choice was obvious to Corallo. Gaspipe Casso and Vic Amuso. They had repeatedly shown themselves to be "capable" in every sense of the word. At the meeting Tony Ducks asked Christy Tick Furnari to decide between Casso and Amuso. The three members of the 19th Hole Crew retired to another room to discuss the matter privately. Once again, Casso turned down the chance to be promoted. But with the Luchese bosses all facing life in jail, Casso had no choice about taking on a greater level of responsibility. Amuso was named boss. Casso was his number two.

"The meeting was supposed to lead to a peaceful transition. It had the opposite effect. Casso didn't want to take on the title of boss, but that didn't mean he didn't want power—or understand how to use it. The first step the pair took as bosses was to decide what to do about their main rivals—the Bronx and New Jersey factions. Underboss Tom Mix Santoro was from the Bronx. He and Tony Ducks weren't getting along. Tom Mix had his own ideas for the Luchese leadership. He wanted Buddy Luongo, one of the captains from his Bronx crew, to take over. It was decided by

Amuso and Casso that Luongo had to go. Adhering to an effective if demented mafia protocol, it was Tom Mix who was given the job of luring Luongo, his right-hand man, in to be killed."

Santoro told Luongo to come to a meeting at the house of "Swaggy" Carlucci, a friend of Casso and Amuso. Greetings were exchanged when Luongo arrived, unaccompanied, and they all sat at the kitchen table. Amuso excused himself and went to a bedroom. Casso had placed a gun with a silencer under a pillow. Amuso retrieved the gun, came back to the kitchen, and shot Luongo three times in the face. "The new boss murdering his rival in front of the outgoing bosses was a strong message, if lacking in subtlety. There was a new sheriff in town—a pair of them in Amuso and Casso. Luongo's body was dumped in the wastelands of Canarsie. His car was taken to JFK Airport and dropped in the long-term parking area where it wouldn't be discovered for weeks."

As the leaders of a new administration, Amuso and Casso quickly asserted control over Luchese interests. The family had a strong presence in the Garment District, using its sway over the Ladies Garment Workers Union to extort manufacturers and auction off trucking contracts to the highest bidder. Fat Pete Chiodo was put in charge of running a large scam in the concrete industry controlled by a group of Greeks. Amuso and Casso inherited union insiders at JFK and Newark airports, a large garbage collection concern on Long Island run by Luchese capo Sal Avellino, and a scheme to rip off laborers in the asbestos removal business. The gasoline business, run primarily by Russian gangsters, was netting millions and the new Luchese leaders took a slice for their family. As the pair grew richer they continued to consolidate power and ensure their rule remained unquestioned.

ON THE RUN IN HOLLYWOOD, FLORIDA

The ascension to power of Vic Amuso and Gaspipe Casso was not met with jubilation inside the other factions of the Luchese crime family. By overlooking Luongo, who was older and respected across the Luchese factions, as the heir apparent, Ducks and Furnari had put the future of the family at risk. The New Jersey faction, centered in Newark and known as "the boys from Jersey," had grown increasingly independent from the Brooklyn leadership over the years.

The New Jersey faction was caught in the middle of its own debilitating racketeering prosecution. The captain of the faction was Tumac

Accetturo. A sixth-grade dropout, street thug, and ferocious fighter as a young man, Accetturo was a highly respected and successful mobster. The usual procedure when a new boss was appointed in any of the five families was for the captains to visit and pay homage to him and swear fealty. Accetturo didn't want to make a gift to prosecutors of surveillance footage of him associating with known mob figures like Amuso and Casso during his trial. He suggested they meet clandestinely at the Sheraton hotel near the Newark Airport. The New Jersey faction gave the new bosses five to six thousand dollars a month of their earnings from scams at the airport. The amount was chump change, Amuso and Casso believed, compared to the money the New Jersey faction was really making.

At the Sheraton, Accetturo said that he wanted to move to Florida. He asked for permission. Casso said he would talk to Amuso and get back to him; it was against mob rules to move away without the agreement of the bosses. A short while later, Casso learned from Accetturo's son that Tumac had moved to Florida without waiting for approval. The son said his father feared another prosecution. The younger Accetturo said his father was "in the bag," adapting Vincent Chin Gigante's tactic of acting crazy and thus mentally incompetent to stand trial.

Casso made his own inquiries. He learned that Accetturo's faction was involved in its own internecine feud. Serious problems had developed. Accetturo had left to avoid the fight. The reason didn't matter. The New Jersey faction of the Lucheses was known to be wealthy. Cocaine from South America was a main source of revenue, including sales to many coke-addicted celebrities, but the New Jersey Lucheses were also involved in labor racketeering, Joker Poker machines, bookmaking, loan-sharking, extortion, and theft. A more significant piece of the New Jersey money was part of their due as bosses, Amuso and Casso believed. Eyeing the profits, Amuso and Casso adopted the strategy of dreaming up reasons to kill Accetturo. Accetturo's disobedience was said to reflect ancient familial grudges. A twenty-year-old pot deal gone sour was recalled by the new Luchese bosses. There were rumors circulating that Accetturo was inducting members into his "family," usurping one of the most exclusive and sanctified rights of a boss according to mafia tenets. If the New Jersey faction considered itself a stand-alone "family," Amuso and Casso would have no claim on them. "Breaking away," as such a move was called, was an offense justifying death.

"The complaints were tenuous and unproven but valuable as cumulative justifications for the radical step Amuso and Casso proposed. Accetturo and the Jersey crew were widely respected in the underworld.

There had to be a relatively good reason for killing a captain of Accetturo's stature. Accetturo was a rat, they said. It was the same ploy Amuso and Casso later used with Fat Pete Chiodo and Al D'Arco. Proving a negative—Accetturo showing that he wasn't cooperating—was difficult if not impossible. But he wasn't going to get a chance to prove anything. Rats were dealt with the predictable way—extermination."

In December 1988 Casso planned to lure Accetturo and his son to Staten Island on the pretense of having a sit-down at the house of Tommy Irish Carew. Accetturo's son was added as a target in the murder plot to forestall the possibility that he would try to retaliate for his father's murder. Arrangements were made. It was ensured that Tommy Irish's wife would be out of the house that day. Fat Pete Chiodo was sent to pick up the father and son at Newark Airport. Casso was waiting in Carew's house. Casso's plan was to shoot them as they were eating a salami sandwich; Casso told his crew he wanted to kill them between bites. But the Accetturos were too wary to fall for such a trap. They didn't fly north from Florida for the meeting. Accetturo sent word through his son that he was "back in my bag," meaning he was acting crazy again to avoid prosecution. "He's got that right," Casso said to Chiodo. "He'll be in a real bag soon."

But Casso was impatient and sought out backup. Just before Christmas, Casso dispatched Chiodo to Florida with a package wrapped to look like a Christmas present and an envelope with a card inside. Casso strictly forbade Chiodo from opening the present. Fat Pete was to give it to a man named "Junior" who would meet him in the lobby of the Coconut Grove Hotel in Miami. Chiodo couldn't resist opening the Christmas "present." Inside he found $50,000 in cash. There was no writing on the card but the envelope contained a newspaper clipping with a photograph of Tumac Accetturo. Chiodo carefully rewrapped the package and traveled to Florida. Chiodo beeped Junior and they met. Junior was in his early forties, Cuban, well dressed, and distinguished in appearance. He didn't open the package when Chiodo handed it to him.

Days before Christmas, Amuso and Casso attempted to arrange a meeting to reconcile with three other members of the New Jersey faction. A meeting was set for the Walnut Bar, on Flatlands Avenue in the Canarsie section of Brooklyn, with a closed-door session at a private house around the corner. They never showed up. "The three wiseguys weren't stupid. They weren't going anywhere to be alone with Amuso and Gaspipe. This infuriated the Luchese bosses. Now they weren't just going to kill the two Accetturos. They were going to whack the entire

New Jersey faction the first chance they got. In the mob, just like the police department, Christmas parties were a big deal. Old grudges were put aside. A feast was held. Camaraderie was restored. But that year the Lucheses had two separate Christmas parties. The Bronx faction had a party. The Brooklyn faction, which Amuso and Casso ran, had their own Christmas party. No one from the Jersey faction turned up for either one."

After the turn of the New Year, Chiodo was sent down to Florida again. Casso was frustrated that Junior had not been able to find the Accetturos. The only leads Junior had were the long-distance telephone records of calls made by the elder Accetturo, which Junior had obtained from a contact with the local phone company. He had only seen Accetturo once, driving a gray Lincoln by Miami's Fontainebleau Hotel.

In January 1989, Chiodo set out to do his own detective work in finding the Accetturos. He purchased a Panasonic camcorder for video surveillance. He got cameras with high-powered lenses. He bought a car and rented an apartment in the Galahad, a building diagonally opposite the Diplomat Hotel, a seaside resort in Hollywood, Florida, half an hour north of Miami. Accetturo was known to frequent the hotel. Chiodo had a crew with him, including George Neck Zappola and Richie the Toupee Pagliarulo. "They set up on the Diplomat Hotel like they were FBI agents on a stakeout. It went on for weeks. Guys from New York cycled in and out of the apartment. It was a great assignment. New York was going through a cruel winter that year. January was brutal. Chiodo brought his wife down so she could have a vacation while he attended to business."

Chiodo tried everything to find his quarry. He purchased a house three doors down from Tumac Accetturo's, paying $60,000 as a down payment, and using a local air-conditioning contractor as a front. The Accetturos were nowhere to be found. They failed to come to the Diplomat in Hollywood. They didn't go to the house they owned and had once lived in. The operation was costing a fortune. Finally Chiodo flew up to New York himself and met with Amuso and Casso at Le Park Lounge, their preferred watering hole in Manhattan. Chiodo described the failed attempts to find either Accetturo. "This guy is never going to surface," Amuso said. "He's got to be on to us by now." The manhunt was called off.

But in the summer of 1989 there was a sighting of Anthony Accetturo Jr. On the orders of Amuso and Casso, Chiodo immediately flew to Florida with various cohorts, including Richie the Toupee. They rented a red van from Budget and patrolled the streets of Hollywood, Florida.

As they drove around they spotted Accetturo junior in a car with his girl-friend. Chiodo tried to follow but he lost them in traffic. "As they continued to search that night they realized they were now being followed themselves—by a police car. To shake the cops, they turned into a movie theater parking lot. The cruiser pulled in behind them. *Dead Poets Society* was playing. The theater was nearly empty. The four hoods, all of them packing guns, sat and enjoyed half an hour of upper-middle-class boarding school ennui.

"As they sat in the theater watching Robin Williams emote, Fat Pete and Richie the Toupee saw two men enter. One of them was none other than Anthony Accetturo Jr. Two of Fat Pete's thugs were sitting a couple of rows back. All of their eyes met in the dark. Accetturo immediately got to his feet and walked out of the theater. His friend came over to Chiodo and said Accetturo wanted to talk to him. Chiodo went out to the lobby. The cop in uniform who had been tailing Chiodo was using a pay phone in the lobby. Accetturo wanted to know what Fat Pete was doing. Chiodo lied. Accetturo knew he was lying. Accetturo told Chiodo he was 'loaded'—and that didn't mean drunk, it meant Accetturo and his friend were armed and willing to shoot it out."

A plan for Accetturo to call Casso was discussed but it was little more than a formality. Reconciliation was talked about but all parties involved understood what was really going on. Tumac Accetturo and his son Anthony vanished again, for good it seemed.

At the same time, the Lucheses from the New Jersey faction who had relocated to Florida had been contacted to see if they were loyal to Amuso and Casso or to the Accetturos. A lone New Jersey partisan flew to New York and pledged allegiance. He was told to return to Florida and send Joseph "Uncle Joe" LaMorte up next. LaMorte booked a flight but failed to report. "To Amuso and Casso that meant LaMorte had decided to remain loyal to the Accetturos. It was probable, the Lucheses reasoned, that Uncle Joe was in touch with the Accetturos. Finding Uncle Joe and following him would lead them to Tumac and his son. At least that was the hope. Persistence was a hallmark of Casso when it came to killing."

In the fall of 1989, Burton Kaplan approached Casso with a lead on the whereabouts of the Accetturos from "the cops." Kaplan said father and son had left Florida and set up in North Carolina. Casso ordered Chiodo to Sugar Mountain, North Carolina. Accetturo and his son were running a pizzeria, according to "the cops." Chiodo drove to North Carolina, and found the pizzeria, which was under construction. There was no sign of either Accetturo.

Chiodo continued south to Florida. Once more, he set up his surveillance operation with his crew of gangsters who had flown to Miami to soak up the sun and kill the Accetturos. Casso had instructed Chiodo to purchase additional supplies: a propane torch, handguns, stun guns, handcuffs, and phony police identification. Chiodo and his crew found Uncle Joe's house. Casso instructed Chiodo to kidnap Uncle Joe and torture him until he gave up the location of the Accetturos. Kill him if necessary, Casso told Chiodo. They tailed Uncle Joe to a junkyard run by a guy named Nicholas "Nicky Skins" Stefanelli. They went to Uncle Joe's workplace and recorded his usual stops. "But he didn't lead them to either Accetturo. The orders were changed. Months had passed. Casso was frustrated, his patience pushed to the limit. Someone in Florida had to die already."

On November 11, 1989, Chiodo and his crew drove to the entrance to the housing development where Uncle Joe lived, and waited. They rehearsed the plan, practiced their escape route, and tested their walkie-talkies. At twilight, Chiodo was stationed at the entrance to the housing development to act as the "crash car" if there was any pursuit of the shooters. A pair of Lucheses were assigned to murder Uncle Joe. They followed Uncle Joe as he arrived home from work. Ninety seconds later, the two thugs came speeding out of the development. No one was chasing them. A mile and a half to the west they pulled over and threw their guns in a stream. Their car was abandoned in a bank parking lot. They got into Chiodo's rental car. "We got him real good," Chiodo's crew member said. They said they had hit Uncle Joe multiple times. Uncle Joe's leg was shaking and then it stopped moving. They were sure they had killed him.

Two weeks later word reached Casso in New York. Uncle Joe LaMorte was alive and well. He had been hit once, in the stomach. "The failure was another mark against Chiodo as far as Casso was concerned. The reason Chiodo's crew wasn't assigned to kill Jimmy Bishop was their failure in Florida with LaMorte. Casso wanted reliable shooters."

There was no time to worry about the Accetturos after that.

ON THE RUN IN HOLLYWOOD, CALIFORNIA

By the start of 1990, the Luchese family was in disarray but still a potent force on the streets of New York's five boroughs and New Jersey. The "Prince Street Regime," headed by Anthony Tortorello, was active. "Big" Frank Lastorino had taken over Fat Pete Chiodo's crew, and

Steven Crea was running "Sammy Bones" Castaldi's unit after Castaldi's health deteriorated. Anthony "Bowat" Baratta was active on the street, along with Sal Avellino, who still managed to rake in money from his garbage collection operation on Long Island.

At the time, Little Al D'Arco was captain of a crew that included his son. Like his father, Joseph "Little Joe" was diminutive but filled with large ambitions. In Little Joe's case his heart's desire was to "make his bones," as his father before him had, and become a full-fledged member of the Lucheses. He had achieved his goal but there was something keeping him from truly living up to his father's accomplishments: Little Joe had yet to kill a man. Sometime early in 1990, the opportunity presented itself. "Waiting around for a murder contract to come up wasn't a problem under Amuso and Casso. Little Joe could have had his choice. The Lucheses were plotting multiple murders at the time. Multitasking was no problem to Gaspipe Casso. While he was pursuing the Accetturos and the New Jersey faction, he was still settling the score with the Bronx faction. Tom Mix Santoro was in prison. Buddy Luongo had been shot in the face by Vic Amuso as his first act as boss of the Lucheses. But there was still one Bronx Luchese wiseguy out there hiding who had allegedly plotted to whack Amuso and Casso."

"Fat" Anthony DiLapi was the nephew of Tom Mix. A well-liked mobster from the old school, DiLapi handled a Teamsters union local for the Lucheses, a bookmaking business, and had a percentage of a Brooklyn vending machine company that owned jukeboxes, cigarette machines, and Joker Poker machines. Hugely overweight, he was known to be sharp and calculating. After the murder of Buddy Luongo in 1986, DiLapi had been ordered to report to Amuso and Casso. The new leaders wanted to know the nature of his businesses so they could figure out how much they could demand from him. Sensing danger, DiLapi wasn't willing to report as commanded. He told Amuso and Casso he would see them the following week. He sold as many of his holdings as he could and vanished. "DiLapi had rapidly added up the possibilities and understood that he would be next to go. Like Chiodo would later do, DiLapi went on the lam. For years Amuso and Casso waged a campaign to find him.

"Years went by and there were no sightings of DiLapi. But Casso didn't give up. The ace up his sleeve was Burton Kaplan. DiLapi had done time in Allenwood Federal Prison Camp with Kaplan in the early eighties. They played pinochle together. From Allenwood 'Camp,' they invested in Commodore 64 computer stocks, following the tip of a Wall Street convict, and made millions. Kaplan knew DiLapi, and he probably liked him. Most people did. It was how DiLapi had managed to stay alive for nearly four years during the reign of terror of Amuso and Casso. But liking and respecting a guy didn't mean Kaplan wouldn't help Casso. Kaplan wanted to stay alive himself, and that meant keeping Casso happy—or at least not in a murderous rage when it came to the well-being of one Burton Kaplan. When Casso asked him to see if 'the cops' could help find DiLapi that was precisely what Kaplan was going to do.

"Finding someone is extremely difficult. If a man wants to disappear he can disappear. If a man needs to be disappeared he can be disappeared. Finding people is a big part of what law enforcement specializes in. In 1990 the digital age had barely begun. The NYPD had constructed an enormous bureaucracy, with vast basements filled with filing cabinets dedicated to locating people. There were various methodologies open to a detective looking to find someone. One was putting out an All Points Bulletin, or APB. Such a bulletin meant that all law enforcement officials throughout the country were to notify the NYPD if the person in question came to their attention. A traffic stop was enough. Anthony Casso didn't have an APB. But he had Burt Kaplan and the 'crystal ball.'"

Kaplan said he had an idea. Kaplan was still on parole so he reasoned DiLapi would be on parole too. If a former prisoner on parole with the federal government moved to a different jurisdiction he was assigned to a local parole officer. Perhaps "the cops" could contact DiLapi's parole officer and find his address that way. The reply came back quickly: DiLapi was in Reseda, California, a suburb of Los Angeles in the San Fernando Valley and known as the heart of the area's porn industry.

Little Joe D'Arco was called to the Walnut Bar by Amuso and Casso. The meeting took place in a room in the back of the bar. Little Joe was told that Fat Anthony DiLapi was to be killed. Amuso said he "wanted this one bad." The junior D'Arco was handed a slip of paper. The word "adeser" was written on it, Reseda spelled backward, it was explained, in case the paper got into the hands of law enforcement officials. An address on Saticoy Street was provided. A day later, Al D'Arco drove his son Joe to the house of Vic Amuso. The older wiseguys knew Little Joe had never killed before so they took special interest in his well-being. They told him to be careful. Amuso asked if Little Joe had enough "crackers"— money—to make the trip. The younger D'Arco said yes. Little Al D'Arco gave his son a photograph of DiLapi. Little Joe embraced and kissed Vic Amuso. "Vic Amuso was avuncular in his care for the young man about to take his first life. Little Al D'Arco drove Little Joe D'Arco to the airport. In mafia terms, it was a fatherly touch."

In L.A., Little Joe rendezvoused with an associate. Little Joe and his associate went to Saticoy Street, a main thoroughfare in the middle-class suburb. They soon realized they had the wrong address. Little Joe D'Arco staked out a used-car lot on Saticoy Street on a hunch. He knew DiLapi had relatives who lived on the street so it seemed plausible they might be involved in that business. In order to remain unobtrusive, D'Arco dressed as a Mexican. Blending in with his surroundings, he hoped, D'Arco sat in a laundromat across the street from the car lot for a week. He was carrying a knife. The plan, to the extent that he had formulated one, was to stab DiLapi to death. But he failed to sight DiLapi and, at the end of the week, had to return to New York to report to his own parole officer.

Little Joe D'Arco owned a coffee shop at the corner of West and Laight streets in Tribeca in Manhattan, a few neighborhoods south of his father's restaurant La Donna Rosa in Little Italy. The day after he got back to New York Amuso and Casso went to see him. Little Joe told them he hadn't spotted DiLapi but that he had planned to stab him. The Luchese leaders weren't discouraged. Weeks later, Casso gave Little Joe another address on Saticoy Street in Reseda. Little Joe was instructed to meet with another auditioning wiseguy at the Nathan's hot dog stand on 86th Street near 7th Avenue in Brooklyn. Little Joe and his cohort flew back to California, this time under assumed names.

In Reseda, D'Arco and his collaborator used bicycles and a car to surveil the new address on Saticoy Street. Once again, they discovered they had the wrong location. Down the street, however, there was a large house with wrought-iron gates and floodlights. The security suited someone who was hiding, or living in fear. They realized that, if they transposed the numbers of the address they had been given, it matched the address of this house. A Volvo station wagon was parked in the driveway. The car matched one parked in the used-car lot that D'Arco had observed on his prior trip. After a week, they had not seen a sign of DiLapi. Little Joe returned once again to New York to see his parole officer. He returned to L.A. immediately. The surveillance resumed. This time there was a red pickup truck parked in front of the house. Another week went by without a sighting. D'Arco flew back to New York. When he returned to L.A. the third time he discovered that the house he'd had been watching was deserted. "DiLapi had made them. Riding bikes and dressing up as Mexicans may have seemed like a way to avoid attention, but it had the opposite outcome. DiLapi knew Amuso and Casso were looking for him and made himself scarce."

When Little Joe D'Arco returned to New York yet again, he met with Casso at the Castle Harbor, a surf-and-turf restaurant in Sheepshead Bay decorated with mounted animal heads and a large stuffed lion. Casso told Little Joe he had a new lead on DiLapi. During the time D'Arco was flying back and forth, Casso had continued his inquiries into DiLapi. During that time as it happened, Kaplan told Casso one of "the cops" had to travel to L.A. on business. While he was there he had inquired about DiLapi's whereabouts with the federal probation authorities. "Kaplan's 'cops' gave Casso a bead on DiLapi. Casso told Little Joe that DiLapi was the manager of a nightclub called La Cage Aux Folles on La Cienega Boulevard in Los Angeles. Back in L.A., Little Joe and his cohorts set up on the place. The Volvo was parked outside. Soon they spotted DiLapi. For the first time, Little Joe laid eyes on DiLapi. He tried to set up an ambush. He sent his associate to be the look out and he went to hide. Little Joe had a .380 Beretta his father had given him. DiLapi walked by but Little Joe's lookout panicked. DiLapi got away without a shot being fired."

Colombo capo Big Sal Miciotta was a close friend of DiLapi's. During the time DiLapi was on the lam, Miciotta kept track of him through DiLapi's brother. "Anthony was a genuine tough guy," Miciotta recalled. "He was goodhearted. He had good morals, good backbone, good character. He was lethal, if pushed, or ordered. We met in Allenwood Federal Prison Camp. I was in there with Burt and all them guys. Al D'Arco was there at the same time. D'Arco and DiLapi were like oil and water. D'Arco played the tough guy in the can. He slapped around stupid white-collar kids in on bullshit beefs like marijuana or bank fraud. They weren't made guys. They couldn't defend themselves. Beating on them was like beating on nine-year-old children but D'Arco would beat on them anyway. DiLapi would tell him to leave them alone. Little Al was tiny. He was always trying to prove how tough he was. A bona fide tough guy doesn't have to do that. DiLapi and D'Arco had screaming arguments. They were in the same family but there was a serious feud—and as a made guy you should never do that in public. DiLapi made D'Arco look like an asshole and D'Arco knew it. D'Arco developed a severe grudge against DiLapi. He hated Anthony because Anthony saw him for what he was—a bully. That was why he had arranged for his son to be the one to kill DiLapi. He wanted to make sure his son did it. You have to wonder. What kind of person would send his son on a piece of work like that?"

Once again back in New York to report to his probation officer and the exasperated Vic Amuso and Gaspipe Casso, Little Joe D'Arco was told that he would have to take along an experienced and reliable shooter the next time. Georgie Neck Zappola was in Florida at the time, part of Chiodo's crew looking for Tumac Accetturo and his son. It was arranged for Little Joe to meet Zappola in L.A. Little Joe and Georgie Neck staked out the bar where DiLapi worked once again. Zappola told Little Joe he was going "to do the hit." "Little Joe hadn't come this far to give up his chance to kill DiLapi. He had logged a lot of miles trying to make his bones. No way he was going to be denied. He told Zappola that Casso had specified that only he, Little Joe, was to kill DiLapi. It was a lie—a little white lie, maybe, although telling any untruth about Gaspipe Casso was a potential hazard to one's health. Under no circumstances was D'Arco going to disappoint his father."

Another week passed and they failed to find DiLapi. Little Joe flew a car thief he knew and used in New York out to L.A. to steal a car for them. Yet another week passed. D'Arco had to go back to New York for yet another probation meeting. While D'Arco was back in New York reporting to his probation officer that he was conforming with the terms of his probation—which did not include flying back and forth across the country to try to take a guy out—Zappola spotted DiLapi and tailed him back to an apartment complex in Hollywood. Little Joe flew back to L.A. at once. Finally, with Little Joe in town and everything set, they drove to DiLapi's apartment building and into the underground parking garage. D'Arco and Zappola were dressed in hooded sweatshirts. Little Joe had the .380 Beretta and a .357 Magnum. Zappola remained hidden, supervising Little Joe and ensuring that DiLapi was actually, finally, murdered. It was five o'clock in the afternoon on February 9, 1990. DiLapi came into the garage carrying a garment bag. Little Joe stepped out of the shadows. DiLapi screamed. Little Joe shot him. As DiLapi collapsed, D'Arco walked over to DiLapi and delivered the coup de grace, firing a shot directly to his head.

"Little Joe D'Arco had finally killed. He was now a man, in his father's eyes. The hit squad burned their clothes and made their way back to New York. The next day Little Joe's father and Amuso and Casso came to Little Joe's coffee shop in Tribeca to congratulate him. He told them about his daring deed. The vending machine percentage DiLapi had was passed on to Little Joe and Georgie Neck Zappola. By doing a made guy like DiLapi the killers were entitled to his money. Casso made a fortune that way. Vic Amuso told Little Joe he had done a good job. *Buona fatiga*—good work—he said. Little Joe didn't understand Sicilian, not even the smattering most wiseguys did. His father translated for him."

CAPTURE

Casso was on the lam, but that did not mean he couldn't throw his daughter, JoLynn, a lavish wedding—as lavish as a wiseguy on the run could afford. As a Colombo captain, Big Sal Miciotta was invited. Miciotta went to the wedding with fellow Colombos William "Wild Bill" Cutolo, Joseph Scopo, and Vinny Aloi. The reception was held at El Caribe in Mill Basin—the place where Otto Heidel had been confronted by Tommy Karate a few years earlier. "Casso was on the lam so he couldn't come," Miciotta recalled. "I thought the wedding was going to be a little more extravagant than it was. Casso was a big earner. All the guys he killed, he scooped up everything they had. He killed a couple of big shylocks in the Bronx and grabbed their money. We all knew he was renovating a house in Mill Basin. I was looking forward to a real top-notch wedding but it looked like Casso was feeling the financial strain of being on the lam.

"The big-time mob defense lawyers were there. There were Gambinos, Colombos, all the Lucheses, all of us brought envelopes. Five hundred bucks in cash was the right amount for a guy of Casso's stature. The smorgasbord had the routine stuff. Calamari, clams, oysters, shrimp. The dinner was prime rib, cornish hen, grouper fish. Regular table wine was served. For the toast Casso had a bottle of 'DP' at every table—Dom Perignon champagne. I thought that was a nice touch. There were cigars for the guys—Cuban Macanudos. I sat in the mob section, the tables where it was all wiseguys, no women. We could talk business. We were in the middle of the Colombo war. The Lucheses were on the fence—playing both sides against each other. Gaspipe wanted to side with us. There was talk at the time about merging our faction of the Colombos with the Lucheses. But none of the wiseguys missed Casso, as far I could tell. Casso wasn't a beloved figure. He made enemies on his way up. People were there because they were afraid of him. Everyone associated with Casso was petrified of him."

Fear was the underlying motivation for dealing with Casso as he continued to hide. One associate he maintained steady contact with was Burton Kaplan. Casso went to Kaplan's house in Bensonhurst on two occasions while a fugitive, a rare risk for Casso. Kaplan was one of his closest and most trusted associates. He also owed Casso a huge amount of money and thus provided a steady source of funds. While Casso was on the lam, Kaplan had repaid Casso tens of thousands in cash as partial satisfaction of his debts. Kaplan had helped supervise the construction of the house in Mill Basin. Casso was pouring his fortune into the house—twenty thousand dollars for the front door alone. When Casso decided to upgrade his lifestyle and move to the grander house, he had come to Kaplan and suggested he buy the place Casso owned at the time. He said he needed the money for construction costs. He sold the house for $250,000, what Casso claimed was a discounted price. Kaplan became the owner of record but Casso had continued to live there. When he went on the lam, Lillian Casso stayed on—for free.

"As always with Casso, there was an implied term in the proposition," Oldham recalled. "It was an offer Kaplan couldn't refuse. The house deal was the kind of thing wiseguys did to and for each other all the time. Kaplan paid the mortgage year after year. He 'owned' the house but there was no way he was going to ask Gaspipe Casso to vacate—or turn up with the sheriff to evict Lillian Casso. Their economy was fluid. Generally speaking, wiseguys had wads of cash but no assets, or savings, or safety net. A lot of those guys gambled, snorted coke, kept a girlfriend in a condo and still had to maintain the lifestyle of 'the life' with their wives and kids. Money poured through their fingers but most of them were incapable of accumulating real wealth. The sums they were supposed to be making sounded astronomical. Millions upon millions. But for the average guy the take was chopped up into so many pieces, with the bosses reserving the biggest slice of cake, they were always scrambling to make a buck."

In January 1993, Casso rendezvoused with his wife, Lillian. She was brought to him by Burt Kaplan. They had a routine for such encounters. Kaplan booked a room in the Parsippany Tara hotel in New Jersey under his own name using a credit card. When he arrived Kaplan paid cash. He would bring Lillian Casso to the hotel and leave the married couple alone for the afternoon. This time Kaplan and Casso had arranged to meet in another place—a parking lot in a shopping mall. Kaplan had already booked the hotel room. As Kaplan and Lillian Casso were driving through New Jersey they passed the hotel. Kaplan had to go to the bathroom. He asked if Lillian Casso would mind if he stopped. She agreed. Kaplan entered the hotel. On the way he spotted two men who resembled FBI agents: sunglasses, unmarked car with the telltale law enforcement antenna, the stereotypical trappings of federal agents.

Kaplan got back in the car and told Lillian Casso he thought there were FBI agents set up on the Tara. The hotel was no longer usable for the Casso trysts. There was now also a danger that they were being followed. Kaplan and Lillian Casso drove around for half an hour, Kaplan checking for a tail. Satisfied he was in the clear, Kaplan took Lillian Casso to a parking lot in a suburban shopping mall. He let her out of the car and told her to tell her husband what had happened. Kaplan said he wasn't going to go with her to the meeting place with Casso. He was going to drive away and leave her to go meet her husband. If they were being followed, the tail would go after Kaplan, not her.

"On Monday Kaplan went to collect Lillian Casso at the prearranged place. She was supposed to be on her own, but this time Gaspipe Casso was there. Kaplan told Casso about the FBI agents. Kaplan said he had spotted the agents at the hotel. He told Casso that he should be careful because it definitely had appeared to him that the FBI was closing in on Casso. In fact, the FBI was closing in.

"Casso was incapable of really going on the lam. If he had run to Tijuana or Timbuktu there was a decent chance he would get away. But that wasn't in Casso's DNA. He'd continued to run the family while he was on the run. He was incessantly calling Luchese captains, micromanaging every move the family made. Instead of using the pay phone system, which was time-consuming and awkward, Casso got sloppy. He called Frank Lastorino's cell phone one too many times. Gaspipe Casso was the author of his own fate."

By the next day, Tuesday, January 19, 1993, Casso had returned to his "safe house" on Waterloo Road in the woods of New Jersey. That cold winter morning, after his girlfriend left for work in her Jeep Cherokee, Casso took a shower. The FBI came through the doors with battering rams. The Luchese boss stood at the top of his stairs as the FBI stormed the house. Life, as Gaspipe Casso had known it, was over.

CHAPTER EIGHT

QUEEN FOR A DAY

In custody in the austere high-rise Metropolitan Correctional Center awaiting trial and faced with the prospect of spending the rest of his life behind bars, Casso was consumed by two thoughts: figuring out who was responsible for his capture, and coming up with a means of escaping. Prosecutors in the Eastern District had charged Casso with sixty-seven counts, encompassing his orchestration of fourteen murders, racketeering, and extortion. The case was similar to the one against Vic Amuso, who had been convicted in 1992. Casso knew the deal. He would be tried, convicted, sentenced to an eternity in prison, and shipped to a maximum-security concrete hell in Leavenworth, Kansas, or Marion, Illinois, or Terre Haute, Indiana, where Amuso was rotting away. His wife wouldn't come to see him. She had a phobia about prisons. Casso would be another forgotten former tough guy shuffling down a prison hallway. He had to find a way out.

Soon after Casso arrived in the MCC he caught a whiff of marijuana wafting through the cells. Applying his investigative skills, Casso discovered that there were some black inmates who came from the same neighborhood as one of the guards. FBI agents would later learn that the guard smuggled pot and heroin into the MCC for the men, who were facing drug charges. The guard was paid to bring food and alcohol in from a nearby Italian restaurant. He would carry the food into the MCC in an "I Love New York" plastic shopping bag. He placed it in a garbage can, where it would be retrieved and the liquor and food would be gratefully consumed.

Casso became friendly with the guard. While they were talking one day, Casso asked jokingly if the guard knew of a way to escape. The guard said he did. The garage of the MCC, from which prisoners were transported to and from court hearings, had weak security, he said. On the far side of the gates, there was the bustle of Wall Street. Casso could easily disappear into foot traffic if he were able to make it to the street.

A plan was hatched over the weeks and months that followed. Guards in the MCC were rotated through the jobs in the institution every three months to avoid any close relationships developing with prisoners. Shifts also rotated, ensuring no routine would set in that could be tracked and prodded for holes by inmates. Casso would wait until the guard was taking his turn working the midnight shift in the control room.

In the meantime, Casso's guard smuggled in a set of civilian clothing, which Casso stashed in his cell. Casso would impersonate a police officer as he made his way out of the MCC. He would be given a neck chain with an NYPD detective badge to wear along with his civilian clothes. Clay impressions of keys were made for the series of locks Casso would have to open to gain access to the garage area—his cell, the Counselor's Room, and finally the visitor's room. Once Casso got there, the guard could buzz him out using the remote control in his post in the control room. There was only one guard assigned to patrol outside the garage, and Casso's man said he could make sure that the guard was on the other side of the building when Casso came out. Handcuff keys were obtained from a locksmith for the escape, so Casso could free his hands. Casso hid the handcuff keys in the light above the mirror in his cell.

Payments for the preparations were made through a florist in Brooklyn. The guard would pick up a dozen long-stem red roses, wrapped in floral paper, together with a package waiting under the name "Mr. Anthony." In the same way, Casso arranged to have two guns smuggled in for his use—a .380 Colt Mustang, and a 9mm. Casso's guy complained that the pistols were too large to be safely smuggled into the MCC. A .25 Beretta was in the roses the next time. The guard told Casso he had succeeded in getting the gun into his locker.

Despite the intricate preparations, external events forced Casso to abandon his approach. After the first attack on the World Trade Center in 1993, the ringleader, Sheik Omar Abdel-Rahman, was held in the MCC awaiting trial and security was greatly increased. A cage door was installed in the garage area that could only be opened with a key. It was no longer possible for the guard to buzz Casso out from the control room.

Casso turned to a second plan. The proposal was to have two people posing as FBI agents come to collect and transport Casso to an attorney meeting. The first Saturday morning of the next calendar quarter of 1993 was selected as the date. The rotation of guards began on that day so it was reasoned the guard would not be familiar with procedures.

"Casso gave the guard a sizable down payment and waited. George Neck Zappola was still on the lam so he arranged for payment. One Saturday morning, Casso was sleeping in his cell when a guard came and let him out of his cell. He told Casso he had an attorney conference and handed him a pass to the third floor. Casso had no such meeting with his lawyer planned. He knew it was his chance—the corrupt guard had set up the breakout. But Casso had not got the note telling him it was on. Casso wasn't ready with an answer when another guard coming off the elevator asked him what he was doing roaming the halls with no escort. He hadn't even made it off the floor. Furious, Casso asked his guy why he hadn't been warned. The guard said he'd left a note at the florist shop, but the girl working that day put the note in the cash register. She was supposed to give the note to a guy who would get word to Casso through another inmate. Casso's guard was caught taking bribes and put on probation before they got another opportunity."

Talk of escape was constant among the dozens of wiseguys awaiting trial. Prisoners were shuttled by bus between the courthouses in New York City and a medium-security federal prison in Otisville, a small village an hour north of the city set in the rolling horse country in the foothills of the Catskills. Mikey DeSantis, another Luchese detainee, said he had a friend who owned property in the area. DeSantis said that the guy kept horses on his land. The plan DeSantis conveyed to Casso involved a trustee, an inmate allowed to work with less supervision. The Otisville trustee was on a work detail that labored outside the prison every day. On an agreed-upon day, the trustee would substitute DeSantis for a member of his work crew. Once outside the jailhouse walls, DeSantis would cut away from the group and meet up with his contact— who would be waiting with an extra horse. Together they would ride into the dense woods surrounding the prison. DeSantis said that Casso could join in. "When Casso was sent to Otisville for the Labor Day weekend he checked out the plan—the lay of the land, the trustee, the chances of success. It was going to be Catskill Cowboys, a real old-time bust-out. But there was one problem. Gaspipe Casso was from Gowanus in Brooklyn. He knew how to shoot pigeons but he didn't know how to ride a horse. In fact he had never ridden a horse in his life and they weren't offering lessons in prison. With great regret, Casso was forced to turn down DeSantis's offer."

As winter of 1993–1994 set in and Casso's March trial date neared, he grew even more desperate. Casso dreamt up the idea of ambushing the bus that transported prisoners from the MCC in lower Manhattan to the Brooklyn federal courthouse. Casso instructed George Neck Zappola to surveil the area. Recently promoted to captain, Zappola had hidden out in California and Florida for a time before returning to New York City to assist Casso and oversee his various business enterprises—a bagel bakery that supplied McDonald's restaurants, numbers rackets, slot machines. Zappola was a restless fugitive, frequently watching baseball games and fights in bars around Brooklyn and going to Bruno's Hair Salon on 86th Street in Bensonhurst to get a massage and pedicure. Fastidious about his appearance, obsessed with his weight, Zappola walked six miles every day. The gold watch he wore was a gift from Casso and it was inscribed, "To George, a true friend, from Anthony." Zappola carried a cell phone, and only Casso had the number. Zappola was Casso's favored killer, now entrusted with coordinating his breakout.

After studying the path the bus followed, Zappola decided the optimal place for an assault was opposite the Jehovah's Witness Watchtower building a few blocks from Brookyln's federal courthouse. The area was mostly industrial, with a warren of streets linked to a series of local avenues and express ramps. Multiple escape routes were available. Casso's crew on the outside would overtake the bus, cut the locks on its doors, and shoot their way in, to free Casso, paramilitary style. The plan for the assault on the bus caused divisions among the Lucheses incarcerated in MCC. Casso was determined to go, and so was Frank Lastorino. But Sal Avellino, another wiseguy facing RICO charges, was going to stay on the bus when the others ran. Mike DeSantis was also going to stay on the bus. DeSantis had the horseback plan in Otisville to fall back on.

The plan had a certain savage elegance but presented enormous difficulties. First, the plotters had to be sure Casso was actually on the bus on the day they struck, a difficult thing to accomplish due to tightly restricted communications with prisoners. An acting Luchese capo visited Casso in the MCC often. In preparation for the escape, Casso and his capo surreptitiously swapped running shoes during one visit. The shoes worn by prisoners were standard-issue rubber-soled laceless sneakers. There were two electronic signal devices hidden in the soles of the pair Casso kept. The crew on the outside would be able to detect the signal and know that Casso was on the bus when they hit it. Planning continued into the New Year as Casso's collaborators monitored his hearing dates.

Finally, their chance came. Early in 1994, on a cold winter day, Casso was in court by dawn. At ten in the morning the capo took up his position at the corner of Cadman Plaza and Tillary Street, outside the Brooklyn federal courthouse, waiting for the prisoner bus to emerge from the gated sally port. As soon as he received the signal from Casso's sneaker, the capo would contact one of the crew by radio. The attack would begin. But hours passed and the bus failed to emerge from the courthouse. The capo remained on his watch until two-thirty in the afternoon when he abandoned his post due to the cold. He hadn't received Casso's signal. The bus was delayed that day due to the extreme weather. Casso didn't return to the MCC until five-thirty.

There was another matter preying on Casso's mind. Sitting in the MCC, Casso replayed the sequence of events that had led to his arrest. To a mobster like Casso, there were no coincidences. The proximity in time of Kaplan's warning about FBI surveillance and Casso's arrest was nearly conclusive to Casso. Only a matter of days had passed before the FBI smashed their way into the house on Waterloo Road in rural New Jersey. There were reasons Kaplan might turn Casso in. Kaplan owed Casso a huge amount of money, a powerful motive for him to give away his longtime collaborator and thus erase the debt. Kaplan had also recently been caught up in an allegation involving the sale of Peruvian passports to Hong Kong businessmen looking to acquire an alternative nationality before the Chinese took over the legendary port city. While others had been convicted in the scam, Kaplan escaped unscathed.

"Kaplan skating on the Peruvian passport case was too much for Casso. The only way to explain Kaplan's not being in prison was that he was a rat. Casso decided to get rid of Burt Kaplan. He gave the hit to George Neck Zappola. Word was passed along the Luchese hierarchy about the Jewish businessman who had been Casso's partner for nearly a decade. Kaplan wore thick glasses and was known to have bad vision. 'Get the one-eyed guy,' Casso said."

In the MCC Casso had been able to rely upon assistance from the Lucheses still on the street. The family gave him the slim but real possibility of escape. But in February 1994 Casso was abandoned by the Lucheses, on the orders of Vic Amuso. The reasons were Byzantine but perfectly matched the logic Casso applied in ordering the murder of Kaplan. After Amuso's conviction, he had written to Casso from prison asking him to ask Kaplan to ask "the cops" how Amuso came to be arrested making calls at a pay phone in a Pennsylvania mall. The note was found when Casso was arrested. "I am still very puzzled how they nailed me on Black Sunday," Amuso wrote to Casso. "I'm surprised you never got the *true story*. That was my last call there that day. I had a new number for you. *Too late now* but I'm still looking for the correct story!" The import of the letter was plain. Casso, through Kaplan and "the cops," could access the intelligence files of the FBI and NYPD to discover who was behind the plot to reveal Amuso's location. Casso's failure to ask "the cops" raised the implication that Casso had something to hide. There was only a small leap from there to Casso's complicity in Amuso's capture. "Amuso gave the order that no Lucheses were to cooperate with Casso in his escape plans. Zappola was told to call off the plan for the assault on the prison bus. It was the prison equivalent of the Puccini aria. *Sola, perduta, abandonata*. Starring in his own soap opera, Casso was alone, lost, abandoned."

By the beginning of March, with Casso's trial only weeks away, his situation then grew even more dire. On March 2, an article appeared in the *New York Times* that offered the first public interview of a major mafia figure who had become a cooperator. Tumac Accetturo, the man Casso had so desperately wished to kill, had just been convicted of racketeering and extortion charges. He faced a sentence of thirty to sixty years. He was also still the subject of an outstanding murder contract ordered by Casso. Like so many other mobsters at the time, Accetturo decided to cooperate. Accetturo, Casso knew, would pile still more intelligence about Luchese operations atop what D'Arco and Chiodo had already given to the FBI. The case against Casso only became stronger as time passed. "Accetturo talking to the press was a new wrinkle. Law enforcement was winning on all fronts and at all levels. There was a propagandistic purpose to parsing out information from cooperators to newspapers. Gangsters like Casso felt a lot uneasier. Everyone was caving, it seemed at the time. The perception was bad for mob morale."

Interviewed by *New York Times* mafia specialist Selwyn Raab, Accetturo recited the reasons he had decided to become a cooperating witness for the government. First and foremost was the degradation of the "values" of the mafia. He said he had grown up in the old mafia tradition, when becoming a made man was "an honorable and respectable thing, like a dream, like some people want to become a doctor," he said. "In them days, we were disciplined and coordinated."

Accetturo said he had tried to avoid resorting to violence in running the affairs of his faction of the Lucheses. By contrast, Amuso and Casso were addicted to murder. "They had no training, no honor. All they want to do is kill, kill, kill, get what you can, even if you didn't earn it," the Jersey capo told the *New York Times*. When he decided to cooperate, Accetturo had turned to a New Jersey organized crime police officer who had pursued him for years—a man he'd known since childhood in Orange, New Jersey. Accetturo and Bobby Buccino had opted for brotherhoods on the opposite sides of the law. Accetturo had gone into crime; Buccino had become a policeman. "The mafia is no longer an honorable secret society," the *New York Times* quoted Accetturo saying. "There is no glamour like in the movies and most of the families are becoming street gangs. Either you wind up in the can, your life finished like me, or dead."

Prosecutors now had a mountain of evidence on Casso. His former comrades would take the stand, raise their right hand, and exact revenge on the man who had tried to kill them. The walls were closing in on him. Once he was convicted he would be shipped to some distant federal penitentiary, where he had no contacts. There would be no way to bust out. He would be finished and forgotten.

"Casso did what he always did best—he calculated. There were a lot of ways he could help the government if he became a cooperator himself. He could close the DeCicco murder for them. He could solve the murders of Jimmy Bishop and Otto Heidel and Anthony DiLapi. Casso could testify against Vincent Chin Gigante, the Genovese boss pretending to be mentally incompetent, who was about to stand trial. The chances of getting a deal were decent. Casso might get a sentence reduction. He might do twenty years, which wasn't bad considering we'd charged him with fourteen murders. But if he wanted the real deal, the Sammy the Bull Gravano deal, he would have to give up more than a bunch of mob murders. Gravano gave the federal government their number one target—John Gotti. To get what Gravano got, Casso had to give prosecutors in the Eastern District something they couldn't resist. Casso needed a bombshell—and he had one."

THE DEAL OF A LIFETIME

Arranging to become a cooperator was not a straightforward matter. In order to betray his brother mobsters Casso first had to deceive them. Casso had to engineer a way to contact the government without tipping off his co-accused. If the government didn't agree to Casso's cooperating, or if a deal couldn't be struck, he needed to be able to return to custody and trial without it emerging that he had tried to flip. Of all people, Casso understood the consequences for a made man if he ratted, or tried to rat. Casso had a trusted blood relative approach the FBI Special Agent in charge of Casso's case, Richard Rudolph. If a deal could be struck, the relative told Rudolph, Casso might be interested in becoming a cooperator.

"The offer was intriguing and revolting at the same time. Everyone in law enforcement knew about Gaspipe Casso. He was the kind of man cops become cops to catch. The government had a strong case against Casso. Amuso had just been convicted. But the first Windows Case had gone poorly. Chiodo wasn't the greatest witness. D'Arco was loud and abrasive on the stand. Prosecutors have to weigh intangibles like credibility in making decisions. Strip away all the science of organized crime cases—photographs, wire taps, physical evidence—the human component is at the heart of the law. Would Gaspipe Casso be convicted? Probably. Was there a chance he would walk and return to the streets of Brooklyn to throw a homecoming party and kill his many enemies? Maybe.

"And then there was the information Casso might give us. Casso promised he had more than even Sammy the Bull Gravano had. Gotti had been the icon of organized crime for half a decade. His conviction changed the whole tone of life in New York City. The message was incredibly powerful, to real gangsters and to wannabes. How could Casso top that?

"Casso had the answer. Casso had the 'crystal ball.' With killer cops on offer, there was no way Assistant United States Attorneys Charles Rose and Gregory O'Connell could turn down the offer. With the right structure, prosecutors could have their cake and eat it too. Casso would give them everything he had. He would plead guilty to multiple racketeering crimes. Casso might even think he was going to get five years in a special housing unit for snitches and then a new identity and life in a suburb of a distant Sunbelt city.

"Gravano's deal was an attractive fantasy for Casso—one we didn't discourage when we were dealing with cooperators. Every pitch I ever made to gangsters trying to get them to flip included mentioning the deal Sammy Gravano got. I did it with killers of many ethnicities and proclivities. I told them I couldn't promise, but I wanted them to think that if he had managed to walk then maybe they could too. It wasn't precisely a bait and switch but dealing with a man like Casso involved psychological manipulation. Some criminals respond to carrots, some respond to sticks. All the government can do, Casso was told, was promise to write a letter to his sentencing judge detailing the nature and value of his cooperation. Only the judge could decide if a lesser sentence was justified. Casso was trapped and desperate. He was eager to make a deal, and there was no point in pricking his hopes about how good it might be. The minute he became a cooperator we had him."

"'Queen for a Day' was prosecutor slang for the agreement Casso signed. In the fifties a television game show offered the winning contestant—the one who had the saddest and hardest life—the grand prize of one day with no responsibilities. She was showered with gifts—new dishwasher, vacuum cleaner, her favorite cleaning products. The same was true for criminals like Casso looking to make a deal. Casso came in for one day and told us everything he would tell us, under oath and for the record, if he became a cooperator. He pitched us. We needed to know what we were going to get before we agreed. If there was no deal, and the accused took the stand in his own defense at trial, we could use his statements as evidence to impeach him. Otherwise, he had no legal exposure for what he confessed. The arrangement allowed each side to figure out if Gaspipe Casso was the unlikely queen of the borough of Brooklyn."

On the last day of his life as a mobster, Casso telephoned his wife, Lillian. She ran a lingerie shop in Brooklyn. "Sell the store," he told her, "take the money, take the kids, and go to Florida. I'll never see you again." A sale was duly announced. "Buy 2, Get 1 Free," a sign said. "Limited Time Offer." Next a story had to be invented to provide Casso the excuse to leave the MCC without his co-defendants, Richard the Toupee Pagliarulo and Frank Lastorino. In normal circumstances, with wiseguys warily watching each other for any sign of betrayal, co-defendants moved in unison. Early on the morning of Tuesday, March 1, 1994, Casso boarded the van leaving for the Brooklyn courthouse. Five Colombos up on RICO charges themselves were in the van with Casso. "I go to trial next week," Casso said to the Colombos. "Can you believe it, I gotta give handwriting samples today." "You're kidding," one of the Colombos said. "I ain't kidding," Casso replied.

Appearing before Judge Eugene Nickerson, Casso pled guilty to fourteen counts of murder conspiracy. Then he was flown to a military base outside El Paso, Texas. La Tuna was the correctional facility where Joe Cargo Valachi had been taken three decades earlier when he became the first made man to break the mafia's code of silence.

As *New York Times* mafia reporter Selwyn Raab wrote in his magisterial history *Five Families: The Rise, Decline, and Resurgence of America's Most Powerful Mafia Empires,* Casso was housed in the "Valachi Suite." Kept in a six-by-nine cell at night, by day he had access to his own television, refrigerator, and hot plate. The temperature in the rooms in the arid desert heat was regulated by a "swamp cooler," which circulated cool water through the piping. Federal prosecutor Charlie Rose, son of an NYPD motorcycle cop and a legendary federal prosecutor from Brooklyn, conducted the debriefing along with his colleague Greg O'Connell. The lawyers were entertained by Casso's obsessive cleaning of his suite; he continuously wiped up crumbs from the cakes he enjoyed serving with tea. For reading material, Casso asked for the *Robb Report,* a magazine dedicated to the "luxury lifestyle."

Sitting with Rose and O'Connell, and a procession of FBI agents, Casso spent months recounting his life of crime. Over the years, it emerged, Casso had participated in or ordered not fourteen but thirty-six murders. Law enforcement knew that Gaspipe Casso was a dangerous man—one of the worst criminals in the history of Brooklyn—but the scale of his depravity was breathtaking. "I have done proffers with all kinds of killers," Oldham said. "I once debriefed a Cuban hit man who had murdered forty people. Casso was like that. Killing was a way of life."

Casso began by telling Rose that he had been plotting to murder him. It wasn't because Rose was trying to put him in prison; that was just his job. Casso had a personal grudge against Rose. Casso thought that Rose had been the source of the *Newsday* article that speculated that Casso's wife was having an affair with Anthony Fava, the architect whose murder Casso had ordered. As a lawman, in Casso's view, Rose should have known better than to publicly dishonor another man like that. Casso also explained to Rose that he knew Rose was a prosecutor in the Windows Case and that Rose had debriefed Fat Pete Chiodo when he flipped. Casso figured Chiodo was responsible for starting the rumor of his wife's infidelity as a way of getting at Casso.

Casso then upped the stakes. He told Rose he had employed two NYPD detectives to assist in finding out where Rose lived. Casso's "cops" had supplied him with a post office box in the Hamptons and an address on Park Avenue South. Casso said he had sent George Neck Zappola to search for Rose, with orders to kill. Zappola had set up surveillance outside the federal courthouse in the Eastern District. To Rose's colleague, O'Connell, Casso had gone too far. The government dealt with all kinds of killers but O'Connell felt plotting to kill a federal official was beyond the pale. To do a deal with Casso, to help him get a lesser sentence, put federal officials in jeopardy. Morally, ethically, politically, Casso was unusable. Rose disagreed. Using Casso was worth the risk. Casso was too valuable not to use. Casso could destroy the Luchese family. Casso could unravel the last great mafia conspiracy.

"I forgive you, Anthony," Rose said. "Let's continue."

"THE CRYSTAL BALL"

Scattered through Casso's story was the recurring, evolving, blood-soaked conspiracy involving the two NYPD detectives he called "the crystal ball." The tale didn't emerge in chronological order. Casso's story was chaotic, bouncing erratically from scheme to scam to murder conspiracy. Debriefings were done by a number of FBI Special Agents, some with little knowledge of the overarching cases. Events were recorded as Casso recalled them, or as needed to assist with ongoing prosecutions. The litany of Casso's crimes included virtually every imaginable form of criminality. Kidnapping, drug running, extortion, bid rigging, murder, murder, and murder.

Nonetheless, the conspiracy that had been hidden for nearly a decade was now revealed in all its complexity. Casso told Rose and O'Connell that he had been paying off two NYPD detectives. The officers in question were senior figures inside the force. One detective worked in the Major Case Squad, he said. The other was assigned to the Six-Three Detective Squad. "The sickening sense we had for years—the gut-wrenching feeling that something was deeply wrong inside the force—was confirmed by Casso. The tale sprawled over years, shifting from Brooklyn to L.A. and Florida, with timelines crisscrossing and conspiracies compounding in a bewildering but believable manner. Inside all the insanity, Casso's narration was devastatingly credible."

Word by word, day by day, the prosecutors and detectives assembled the chilling legacy of the "crystal ball." The beginning of the story of the "crystal ball" had been the turning point in Casso's life—the moment that divided everything that happened to him into "before" and "after." Before, Casso had been a rising power in the 19th Hole Crew in the Luchese family. Later, Casso had two members of the New York City Police Department working as informants for him. Before, he was just another mobster, albeit an unusually cunning and cruel one. After, he was one of the most connected made men in the history of the mafia. Before, he was a killer and thug. After, he was a clairvoyant, able to forsee events as if granted supernatural powers.

The tale began on the evening of September 14, 1986. It was pleasant in Brooklyn, a warm autumn breeze stirring under a clear sky. Casso had an appointment to meet his nephew Vincent "Fat Vinny" DiPierro at a strip mall in the Mill Basin section of Brooklyn. Earlier that day Fat Vinny had called Casso with a business proposition. DiPierro had been approached by a Gambino associate named Jimmy Hydell, who claimed he had a "huge" number of stolen checks he wanted to sell. One of Casso's many criminal pursuits was fencing stolen financial instruments. Through Burt Kaplan, who had connections in New York's Hasidic Jewish community, Casso was able to quickly move hot negotiables like blank checks.

A rendezvous was set for eight o'clock at a mall at the corner of Veteran's Avenue and East 71st Street in Brooklyn, not far from Casso's house. Casso arrived early, purchased an ice-cream cone at Carvel, and sat in his gold Lincoln Town Car waiting for Hydell to meet with DiPierro. "Casso knew Hydell. They were friendly. But he wouldn't deal directly with him. Always cautious, Casso used Fat Vinny as his front for the transaction so Hydell wouldn't know he was dealing with Casso. Casso was not going to give away information that could be used against him if Hydell got in trouble and became an informant. But Hydell knew Casso too. Hydell knew how Casso operated. He knew Fat Vinny would go to Casso with the deal. Hydell didn't have any blank checks to sell."

That evening, Fat Vinny waited for Hydell inside a Chinese restaurant called the Golden Ox. At seven-thirty a blue Plymouth Fury circled the intersection. Three men were inside the Fury. Bob Bering, the driver, was a former New York City transit policeman who had turned to a life of crime. A big and fierce-looking OC associate named Nicky Guido was in the passenger seat armed with a 9mm automatic and a .38 revolver. Jimmy Hydell, the Gambino associate, was in the backseat with two shotguns. "Hydell had been hired to kill Casso by a Gambino gangster named Michael 'Mickey Boy' Paradiso. Paradiso told Hydell the contract came from the Gambino family. Gotti was supposed to want revenge for the murder of Frank DeCicco. The hit was supposedly retribution. But the real reason was simple. Paradiso and Casso were fighting over money from a heroin deal."

The Hydell crew had been clocking Casso for weeks but he was far too smart and paranoid for them. He didn't follow any routine. He was expert at "watching his mirrors"—to make sure he wasn't being tailed by cops or gangsters. A few nights earlier, Casso had spotted Nicky Guido set up on him outside a Brooklyn restaurant. Casso was eating dinner when a waiter came up to him and said there was a suspicious-looking man sitting in front of the restaurant. Casso went to the window and saw Guido in a small red sports car looking like the poster child for armed thugs.

The three hunters constituted a particularly sinister trio. Nicky Guido was a standard-issue criminal: a day laborer when he had to work, a thief and hired muscle the rest of the time. Bering, the ex-cop, was a drug dealer with a bus company who'd managed to finagle a city contract to transport handicapped school kids—one of the most corrupt businesses in the city. Hydell and Bering had met on Rikers Island in the early eighties, where they were both serving time. "Bering was in his forties, Hydell was twenty-six, but they teamed up. By 1986 they were killers. Earlier that year, Hydell and Bering murdered a made man named Jack D'Angelo. A little while later, Hydell shot the manager of a school bus company, in front of his house in Great Kills on Staten Island. Joe Trinetto was caught in the middle of a disagreement with Bob Bering. Hydell had used the same trick a Luchese team used with Otto Heidel—he let the air out of Trinetto's tires and killed him as he was jacking up the car.

In April of that year Hydell discovered that his girlfriend, Annette DiBiasi, was having an affair with a married man. Hydell and Bering snatched her as she walked out the door of her house. DiBiasi was a nice girl from all reports, caught up with the wrong guy. Hydell raped her in the van. Then he and Bering wrapped her body in a tarp, naked and alive, and drove to a wooded area near the Richmond Parkway on Staten Island. Hydell had already dug a grave in the woods. As they were carrying her into the forest Bering slipped and she rolled out of the tarpaulin. Hydell sent Bering back to the car and dumped her in the grave, where he shot her five times with a .22. Hydell cut up her clothes and credit cards and wallet with scissors and tossed them out of the window of the van as they drove along the Jersey Turnpike.

As the trio circled that September evening waiting for the moment to kill Casso, Hydell and Guido were both wearing hunting camouflage, their faces covered with masks. The Fury looked like a police detective's vehicle: there was a siren and Bering had placed a "teardrop," the revolving red light used by the NYPD, on the dashboard. "The combined IQ in that Fury didn't break double digits. Hydell had purloined a set of stolen license plates to put on the car. But there was a mix-up. Bering had taken his own plates from the car and put them on top of the refrigerator at his place. Guido was staying with Bering at the time. One of the two masterminds took the plates from the top of the fridge and put them back on the Fury. As a result, Bering's own plates were on the Fury."

At eight o'clock they came upon Casso parked in the bus stop in front of the mall eating his ice-cream cone. A bus pulled into the stop. Bering didn't stop; he knew the bus was equipped with a radio. If they opened up on Casso, the bus driver would call in and police would descend with potentially risky dispatch. Minutes later they returned to the intersection. Casso was still sitting in his car licking his ice-cream cone but there was no bus in sight. The Fury pulled alongside Casso's Town Car. "There was less than a foot between the vehicles. Hydell raised his 12-gauge and opened fire. Nicky Guido, sitting on the passenger side, started to fire his 9 millimeter—but of course the gun jammed. It should have been a shooting gallery. Hydell was letting rip with a 12-gauge but he was either a terrible shot or too afraid to take aim. He nailed the Town Car. The windows were shattered. The doors were pocked with slug holes. But Bering and Hydell managed the nearly impossible—from point-blank range they didn't kill Casso."

Casso was struck by pellets in the shoulder and neck from the shotgun blasts. He rolled to the floor of the passenger side and opened the door to the Town Car and crawled to the sidewalk while the shooting continued. Once on his feet, he made for the door of the Golden Ox. He stumbled through the restaurant, grabbing a tablecloth to stanch the bleeding as he went. Casso proceeded through the restaurant, descended into the basement, and entered the walk-in freezer. No one told the police Casso was hiding in the freezer. The employees and customers were too scared. At first Casso was hiding in case the shooters came after him. After a while he was hiding from the police. He didn't want to talk to the NYPD. His wounds were painful but not life-threatening. When he was certain it was safe, he left the freezer and called Amuso and told him to come pick him up.

Fat Vinny, Casso's obese young cousin, was inspecting the damage to Casso's car as the police arrived on the scene. Investigators quickly determined that the victim of the shooting was Gaspipe Casso. The car was registered to Progressive Distributors Inc., a Staten Island clothing company controlled by Burt Kaplan. Later that night detectives found Casso in the hospital being treated for gunshot wounds. Casso didn't want to talk to the police about the attempted murder. "There's nobody who doesn't like me," he told the police. "I don't know nothing about organized crime."

But of course there were dozens of people who might want to kill Casso. Even the short list was long. Brooklyn South Homicide caught the case. Fortunately for the police, and unfortunately for the Hydell hit squad, the intersection of Veteran's Avenue and East 71st Street was teeming with eyewitnesses. Detective Thomas Kenney, a retired member of the NYPD who worked as a security guard, told investigators he heard the gunfire and then watched the blue Fury careen away from the strip mall, make a U-turn, and speed toward him. Kenney had reached for his gun but said the Fury appeared to be a police car so he didn't shoot or display his gun. He took down the license plate number: 2778TCG. The plate was registered to Bob Bering. Within days the Fury was found abandoned on Daffodil Lane on Staten Island. The fingerprints of Bob Bering and Nicky Guido were found on the interior of the car. Detective Powell was making excellent progress.

Unknown to the NYPD, there was another investigation racing toward its conclusion. Convalescing in the hospital, Anthony Casso didn't cooperate with the NYPD investigation. He wasn't interested in having the case closed by arrests. Casso wanted to close the case himself—his way. He didn't just want the lowly soldiers who had pulled the trigger. Casso wanted the man behind the man. "As a detective, Casso was resourceful and determined. He had leads. He knew better than anyone who might want him dead. The order had to come from the upper level of one of the other families. No one tried to whack a made man without approval from a boss. Casso was going to find out who came after him and why."

Jimmy Hydell, Bob Bering, and Nicky Guido were under no illusion about the magnitude of the mistake they had made. They each figured Casso would be able to find their houses and have them killed. But that was only one of their many problems. Missing Casso meant that the plot to kill him would be revealed if the three shooters weren't killed first. It followed that Mickey Boy Paradiso himself would want to make sure they remained silent. Put together, they had the Lucheses, Gambinos, and NYPD chasing them all at once. "The first night they hid out at a Holiday Inn. Guido slept with his gun. The next day, Bering packed up his belongings and moved to Long Island. Guido took to carrying a .380 automatic. Hydell grew paranoid—an attack could come from anywhere, at any time. He already had reason to be afraid of the law because of the murder of Annette DiBiasi. He was a tough, tough kid. No one was going to take him down without a fight."

After a few days Casso was released from the hospital. The Luchese underboss quickly gathered his own leads. First he was approached by a close associate named Anthony Senter, a member of the Roy DeMeo crew, which was earning the richly deserved moniker Murder Inc. at the time. Senter told Casso that a guy named Bob Bering had been asking questions about Casso's car at a bus company near Casso's home a few days before the attempt. The next day, Casso was approached by Colombo wiseguy Jimmy Angellino, who said he had information for Casso. Angellino was Big Sal Miciotta's partner, but Sal was doing a stretch in Allenwood. Angellino said he had a lead for Casso. They met at Christy Tick Furnari's mother's house. One of the Colombo family's Saponaro brothers was there, along with James "Jimmy Brown" Failla and Joseph "Joe Piney" Armone from the Gambino family. Angellino told the assembled group that the son of one of the Saponaros learned that Jimmy Hydell had been overheard talking about trying to murder Casso.

Hydell was a big muscular kid with curly blond hair, a crooked smile, and connections on his father's side to Corrado "Dino" Marino of the Gambino family. Still in his early twenties, he was already acquiring a name for being violent and dangerous—qualities that gave him cachet with Casso. "Casso liked Hydell. He had helped him get a job with a union, and they saw each other around wiseguy haunts. Keeping tabs on young guys like Hydell was part of the job description for Casso. He needed to know about kids with potential—kids who were 'capable.' With all five families operating in the same geographic space, with territories overlapping along with business interests and disputes, it was crucial to know the range of potential associates—and threats."*

The tip about Hydell was good intelligence but not evidence. Wheels moved within wheels in the mafia. The Colombos could be collaborating in a fake story to mislead Casso and start a war with the Gambinos. The possibilities baffled Casso as much as they did the investigators. Disputes were one way of measuring the range of people who might want to kill Casso. On that score, Mickey Boy Paradiso was another leading candidate. The foul-mouthed Gambino soldier had just been released

---

*A year earlier, Casso had had a run-in with Hydell. The disagreement was over a dog. On the day of the incident with Hydell, Casso had been at the 19th Hole when the owner of a Chinese restaurant on 86th Street ran into the club and complained to Christy Tick that he was having trouble. Hydell was in the man's restaurant with a Doberman pinscher. Hydell was drunk and menacing the customers with his dog. "All of the Lucheses in the 19th Hole spilled onto the street to help the man. Maintaining order was a big deal to mobsters. If someone was going to intimidate the locals it was the Lucheses, no one else. Christy Tick took control. He told a wiseguy named Angelo Defendis to talk to Hydell. Defendis had already been instructed to make sure Hydell didn't cause trouble in the neighborhood. Defendis got Hydell out of the restaurant and started yelling at him. He was pointing his finger at Hydell. But every time he gestured at Hydell the Doberman snapped at Defendis. Threatening a made man was an extremely dangerous thing to do—even for a dog. Gaspipe Casso joined the argument. He told Hydell to control the dog. Hydell ignored him. Defendis started yelling at Hydell again. The dog tried to bite him again. This outraged Casso. Casso could be counted on to escalate virtually any situation. Casso went inside the 19th Hole and came out with a pistol, screwing on a silencer. He walked up to the dog and put two slugs into its head. 'Now pick up the dog and put him in the trunk of your car and get out of here,' Casso said to Hydell."

from prison after serving eight years on a hijacking conviction. "Paradiso was nearly Casso's equal when it came to crazy. In the seventies he had slapped John Gotti in the face, and lived to tell the story. At the time, Casso and Paradiso were brawling over chopping up the proceeds of a heroin deal. Historically, interfamily arguments were resolved through official channels. Normally, Paradiso and the Gambinos and Casso and the Lucheses would submit their disagreement to the Commission. But the members of the Commission were on trial in federal court. They didn't have time to resolve disputes."

As soon as Casso was released from the hospital, Burton Kaplan contacted him and suggested he had a way of getting information that might help Casso find out who tried to kill him. Kaplan was not a "made" member of the Lucheses but he was a highly valued collaborator of Casso's. Kaplan operated by doing favors for Casso. Kaplan didn't ask for money in return. Casso's gratitude was expressed by the protection the association provided. Kaplan was "with" Casso and that meant he was not to be touched.

For the first time, Anthony Casso heard of the connection Kaplan had inside law enforcement. Kaplan said he knew two NYPD detectives who could assist Casso with his investigation. The two cops were good guys, Kaplan said to Casso. Reliable. Trustworthy. Efficient. Kaplan told Casso how he had used the pair earlier that year. Kaplan had been involved in a stolen Treasury bill scam. The deal went bad, sparking an Interpol investigation. Kaplan decided he needed to find and kill two jewelry dealers who had failed to keep up their end of the deal—and might snitch on Kaplan. Kaplan went to a local hood named Frank Santora Jr., whom he knew from Allenwood Federal Prison. When they were inmates together, Santora had told Kaplan he had a cousin who was in the NYPD. His cousin was willing to do "things," if Kaplan ever needed help.

Kaplan told Casso he had hired Santora and his detective cousin and his partner, also an NYPD detective, to find the jeweler who had kept money he was supposed to have passed along. The jeweler knew he was in trouble with Kaplan so he would be wary and difficult to apprehend. Kaplan gave Santora and the two cops the jeweler's name, address, car make, and license plate number. The three men tailed the jeweler onto the New York State Thruway and pulled him over using lights. The two NYPD detectives flashed their shields and told the jeweler he was a suspect in a hit-and-run accident. He was told to accompany them for a lineup. The jeweler complied, and vanished. Kaplan told Casso that he was impressed by the level of service provided.

"They done a piece of work for me," Kaplan said to Casso. "I can vouch for them. We can trust them."

In the normal course of business, Casso would be unlikely to agree to any dealings with NYPD officers on the take. The risks outstripped the rewards, at least potentially. There was no need to have cops working for him in the first place. He didn't need to hire hit men. Unlike Kaplan, Casso had a handy supply of killers who would carry out his orders. Less important, there was an ethic in the mafia that made men should not associate with law enforcement. The possibility of contamination was too great. The less a mobster like Casso had to do with cops, dirty or straight, the better. "But Casso was in peril. No one would have tried to kill him without the backing of some major players. Casso needed to find the people who had given the order, before they tried again. The tip about Hydell from the Colombos was a solid lead. But it didn't amount to proof, not the kind Casso needed. Gaspipe wanted rock-solid evidence that Hydell was acting on behalf of someone. Then Casso could go after his real target."

The attack on Casso occurred within the jurisdiction of the Six-Three, the precinct where Santora's cousin, the detective, worked. He would have access to information about the progress of the investigation. Kaplan suggested it was worth asking his "friends" to get it. Casso agreed. "In those days Casso trusted Kaplan as much as he trusted anyone in the underworld. If Kaplan believed the two detectives could help, Casso was willing to try. Kaplan was cautious. He didn't want to reveal to Casso the identities of his sources in the NYPD. When he told Casso the story about the jeweler, Kaplan didn't use names. Kaplan was interested in ingratiating himself with Casso, for a variety of reasons. But the less Casso knew about Kaplan's 'friends' the less risk everyone was taking."

Kaplan contacted Santora. Within days, Santora gave Kaplan a manila NYPD folder. Kaplan opened the folder and was amazed at what was inside. The crime scene reports detailed the investigation into the attempted murder of Anthony Casso. The DD-5s were comprehensive, detailing all the investigative leads chased down by NYPD detectives. There were photographs of the crime scene showing Casso's car. The license plate on the blue Fury—the plate registered in Bering's name—was recorded: "2778TCG." A list of suspects was included in the file. The names of Jimmy Hydell, Bob Bering, and Nicky Guido were on the list. The file included Hydell's criminal record, his address, and a photograph. The folder was precisely what Casso was desperate to get. Kaplan immediately went to Swaggy Carlucci's social club on 13th Avenue. He found

Casso there with Amuso. Kaplan risked toying with Casso for a moment, a rare liberty.

"Gas, you know who shot you?" Kaplan asked cockily.

Casso was indignant.

"No," he snapped. "And you don't either."

Casso was already aware that Jimmy Hydell was the leader of the crew that came after him. But letting Kaplan know that he knew was a different matter for a number of reasons. Casso didn't want word out that he was after Hydell. If and when Hydell disappeared, or turned up dead in the trunk of a car in Canarsie, the fewer people who knew about Casso's involvement the better.

"It was Jimmy Hydell," Kaplan said.

Casso feigned surprise and skepticism. "You're crazy," he said. "I just got him a union job. We made friends. We been close for the last year."

"Here," Kaplan said, handing Casso the manila folder. "See for yourself."

Casso opened the folder and found the NYPD reports on his attempted murder. He flicked through the documents that Kaplan believed provided new and vital information for Casso—priceless information. Casso pulled out the photographs of Hydell and Bob Bering. He saw the name Nicky Guido. From Casso's point of view, the NYPD file was impressive. It confirmed the version of events given to him by the Colombos. Kaplan's "guys" had done an excellent piece of work.

"What do I owe them for this?" Casso asked.

"They wouldn't take no money," Kaplan said. "They wouldn't take no money because someone was looking to hurt you and they don't want money under these circumstances. This is just to show you the kind of thing they would do."

Casso shook his head.

"Boy, that's really nice," he said. "They must be really good guys."

Dozens of mobsters now trolled the streets of Brooklyn and Staten Island looking for Jimmy Hydell. The Gambinos wanted Hydell dead before he could talk. Casso wanted him taken alive so he could talk. If Hydell was alive Casso could definitively say who had ordered him to kill Casso. If Hydell confessed—and Casso had no moral compunction about using torture to extract information—Casso could prove to other mobsters who was behind the attempt.

Weeks passed as the hunt continued, with Hydell eluding Casso's capture. Kaplan came to his associate with a startling suggestion. He said "his guys" knew "the kid Hydell." If Casso was interested they would "take care" of him. Casso recognized it was an opportunity not to be ignored. Hydell would fight to the death if any gangsters tried to take him. But if Hydell thought he was being questioned by two cops, if he thought it was a routine roust, he would have no reason to resist.

"They could attempt to arrest Hydell," Casso suggested to Kaplan. "He would go willingly with them."

"What do you want to pay?" Kaplan asked.

"What do you think they'll take?" Casso asked.

Kaplan told Casso he had paid $30,000 for grabbing the jeweler. Kaplan suggested $35,000 would be sufficient. Casso approved the offer. Kaplan called Frank Santora Jr. and they discussed the job and the price. Kaplan emphasized that Hydell was to be taken alive at all costs. Casso wanted the chance to interrogate him. Santora agreed to the job. He asked Kaplan to have Casso supply a car—one that looked like a police detective's unmarked car.

To get "the cops" a vehicle, Casso contacted Luchese soldier Patty Testa, who was in the used-car business. A nondescript four-door sedan was purchased. Kaplan sent his assistant, Tommy Galpine, to collect the car from Testa; Kaplan was on parole and had to be careful not to be seen associating with known mobsters like Testa. Casso, by contrast, had no recent criminal record and posed no risk to Kaplan's parole. Galpine delivered the car to a lot to be collected by Kaplan's "cops" and the search began.

"As if he didn't have enough to be concerned about, Hydell still had the added trouble of being the target of the investigation of the disappearance of his ex-girlfriend Annette DiBiasi. DiBiasi was not just another gangland casualty. She was an innocent young woman with a concerned family. She had been missing for six months and finding her killer had become an obsession for investigators. Detective Al Guarneri of Brooklyn's Six-Two, Louis Eppolito's brother-in-law, was working the case. Guarneri was in regular contact with Hydell but Guarneri was terrified of him—for good reason. Hydell was volatile. Guarneri had begun to take a police radio home with him, in case he was attacked by Hydell."

Without a confession or solid evidence there was no way to arrest Hydell. At the same time, Mickey Boy Paradiso's brother, Philly, agreed to wear a wire and try to get Hydell to implicate himself in the murder of Annette DiBiasi. George Terra, an investigator from the Brooklyn DA, and an FBI Special Agent named George Hanna made it clear to Philly Paradiso that if he wanted to avoid a long stretch in prison he'd better catch Hydell on tape and bring them DiBiasi's body.

With all the forces moving against Hydell, it was a miracle he was still at large and alive. He could be arrested or killed at any moment. After a few weeks Casso came to Kaplan's house on a Saturday afternoon. He was agitated. Casso wanted Hydell nabbed as soon as possible. Casso wanted to know if Kaplan's "guys" were out looking for Hydell.

Kaplan called Santora. "We gotta get this kid," he said. "Someone is going to kill him and we want him alive," he said.

"They're out looking for him right now," Santora said. He reported that the cops were in Staten Island at that moment.

The date was Saturday, October 18, 1986. Hydell's mother, Betty, was at home doing housework. Jimmy had left the house that morning. His friend Bob Bering had picked him up. Jimmy Hydell didn't tell his mother where he was going or why. He only said Brooklyn. That afternoon, her eighteen-year-old son Frank left home to go to work. Frank returned to the house after a couple of minutes. He told his mother a car had pulled up beside him after slowly passing along Bridgetown Street near the intersection with Bangor Street. Two men in what appeared to be an unmarked police car stopped Frank Hydell. They "tinned" Frank Hydell—flashed their badges to identify themselves as police officers—and said they were looking for Jimmy Hydell. Frankie told them they had the wrong Hydell.

Betty Hydell was used to dealing with the police after Annette DiBiasi disappeared and her son Jimmy became a prime suspect. If the police had questions for Jimmy, she believed, they should follow protocol, not prowl and creep along the street outside their house. "Betty Hydell was a nurse by profession but she was also street smart and tough. She wasn't going to let the cops harass her boy without an arrest warrant. She got in her car and went looking for the cops. She pulled up next to them going the opposite direction. She rolled down her window. There was a big man with black hair driving. He was wearing a white shirt and gold necklaces. The small man riding shotgun was dressed in a dark suit. Both were Italian in appearance. The driver flashed his badge."

"You should let people know who you are and what you're doing," Betty Hydell said angrily. "If you're a cop why are you hiding?"

The two NYPD detectives drove away. Betty went home and wrote down the license plate number. Something was wrong, she sensed. At two-forty Jimmy Hydell made a collect call home from a pay phone in Brooklyn. It was the last time Betty Hydell heard her son's voice. He was supposed to meet with Mickey Boy Paradiso in Bensonhurst. The rendezvous was in Dyker Beach Park at 86th Street and 14th Avenue.

Hydell's suspicions were running so high, he called Detective Guarneri of the Six-Two to tell him of his whereabouts. Hydell said he was going to see Mickey Boy Paradiso. Telling a cop was a form of insurance for Hydell. If Mickey Boy was setting him up, Hydell could say the police knew where he was and who he was with.

When Hydell reached Dyker Beach Park, "the cops" working for Casso were waiting for him. They arrested Hydell. After they frisked, disarmed, and handcuffed him, they put Hydell in their car. Instead of driving him to a precinct house, the cops took Hydell to a parking lot at 2232 Nostrand Avenue in Brooklyn.

That afternoon Kaplan received a beep from Frank Santora Jr. Kaplan left his house. The two had a system of using beepers and public phones to make sure no numbers were captured by law enforcement; Kaplan threw away his cell phones and got new numbers every month or two for security purposes. Kaplan beeped Santora with a number from a public phone. The pay phone rang moments later.

"We got him," Santora said.

"You got to be kidding," Kaplan said. "I only called you half an hour ago."

"What do you want us to do with him?"

"Frankie, I'm going to have to call you back."

Kaplan beeped Casso.

"Do you remember that toy store where we used to meet?" Casso asked Kaplan.

It was a Toys 'R' Us on Flatbush Avenue. "Yes, I remember."

"Can you bring him there? In about an hour?"

In the meantime, the cops met with Santora at the parking shed one of them rented in the lot on Nostrand Avenue. The lot had a row of two dozen enclosed parking spots in a fenced area in the rear. They drove up to the door of the shed, opened it, and drove in and closed the door. The area was cramped but large enough for Santora Jr. and the cops to pull Hydell out of the car. Hydell's hands were already handcuffed from the arrest in the park. As he started to struggle, Santora and the two police officers bound his feet with duct tape. They stuffed a handkerchief in his mouth and wound duct tape around his head. Hydell was then shoved into the trunk of the car.

With Hydell thus trussed and hidden, Santora drove the car with Hydell in the trunk. The police officers trailed him in another car they'd left on Nostrand. Hydell was kicking and screaming inside the trunk. The cops followed closely to make sure Hydell didn't draw the attention of a citizen or cop on the drive to the Toys 'R' Us. Put another way, Jimmy Hydell and Frank Santora Jr. had a police escort as they made their way to their meeting place with Burt Kaplan and Gaspipe Casso.

The Toys 'R' Us was a well-known landmark in the outer reaches of Brooklyn, popular with families shopping for their kids because of the ample parking. The large store stood at the farthest end of Flatbush Avenue, where one of the borough's main boulevards meets the Belt Parkway and beyond it the Atlantic Ocean. Mobsters liked it too, for its inconspicuousness and multiple exits. Notified by Kaplan of Hydell's capture, Casso and Amuso proceeded to the rear of the store, near a small canal. Kaplan arrived shortly afterward and parked next to Casso and Amuso. It was late in the day and the store was closed; there were no other cars parked in the back. The Plymouth Fury Santora was driving arrived next. Santora got out of the car. Kaplan got out of his car. They walked toward each other. Santora stopped fifteen feet away from Casso—keeping a respectful distance. There was no reason for them to interact; Kaplan was the broker of the deal.

"What's up, Frank?" Kaplan asked.

"He was kicking and yelling back there," Santora said. "I had to stop and pull over and punch him out to keep him quiet. You got to be careful he don't start screaming and yelling."

Kaplan took the car keys from Santora and walked back toward Casso. The arrangement was that Casso would take possession of both the Fury and Hydell.

"Who are those two guys?" Casso asked.

Kaplan turned. Two hundred feet away, standing next to their car near the entrance off Flatbush Avenue to the Toys 'R' Us parking lot, were two men. One was big and overweight, the other thin. Kaplan had not been introduced to the two NYPD detectives by Santora, but he had seen them twice and knew who they were. Kaplan walked back to Santora. "What are they doing here?" he asked.

"They followed me to back me up," Santora said.

Kaplan thought it was an excellent gesture—seeing the job through. Professional. Commendable. Beyond the call of duty.

"That's Frankie's cousin and his partner," Kaplan told Casso.

"They're backing him up."

"Okay," Casso said. "Tell them to get out of here. You get out of here."

The exchange in the Toys 'R' Us parking lot was the only time Gaspipe Casso saw "the cops" in person.

IN THE BASEMENT

Behind the wheel of the Plymouth, Casso transported his cargo to the house of an associate in Bergen Beach, who lived close to the Toys 'R' Us, reducing the possibility of being stopped with Hydell in the trunk. Casso had not forewarned his associate but he didn't need to. The guy did the smart thing when Casso commandeered his house—he left town with his family.

Hydell was bleeding badly when Casso took him from the car. He could easily have choked to death on the blood, Casso thought, curled in the trunk with his arms handcuffed behind him. Hydell was dragged down to the basement. The duct tape was removed from his head and the handkerchief taken from his mouth. The handcuffs were removed. His feet remained bound. The questioning began.

"Torture was a better word for it. Casso had a cruel streak that ran to sadistic. It was the kind of man he was. In the late seventies he was involved in smuggling tons of marijuana and Quaaludes into New York aboard a ship called *Terry's Dream.* When the boat was seized, Casso and Amuso and their posse decided the son of the captain had to be killed. His name was Dave, he was a kid, but he had been involved in bringing the drugs up from Florida and there was a chance he might talk to law enforcement. They lured Dave to a shooting range near 'alligator alley' in Florida. They shot him a bunch of times with a .22. They hadn't finished digging his grave so they cleaned up the blood at the scene and kept digging the kid's grave but the ground was rocky and hard. They only got a foot or eighteen inches deep. They dragged Dave into the hole and started filling it with dirt. But Dave was still alive. He raised his head. Casso hit him in the head with a shovel and they continued to bury him alive."

As the questioning continued through the night and into the following morning, a procession of wiseguys passed through the basement to hear Hydell recount the sequence of events. Joe "Butch" Corrao and John "Handsome Jack" Giordano of the Gambino family were brought to the basement, as were members of the Lucheses representing Tom Mix Santoro. Casso wanted them all to hear the story. He wanted permission to kill Hydell, an associate of the Gambinos and a prized young man because of his violent propensities. Hydell recited the facts of the attempt on Casso, relating details that could only be known to a participant. Hydell said he had two accomplices: Nicky Guido and Bob Bering. Fat

Vinny didn't know he was being used to set up Casso, Hydell said. Hydell's statement confirmed what Casso already knew. Casso wanted the names of the men who had ordered the hit. Hydell gave Casso three names: Mickey Boy Paradiso, Bobby Boriello, and Eddie Lino, all three senior Gambino figures.

Everyone was amazed that Casso had managed to find and then nab Hydell without firing a shot. It was the question on the mind of all the mobsters who came to the basement. How, precisely, had Casso managed to not only find Hydell but take him alive? When Sammy the Bull Gravano came to hear Hydell's confession he wasn't interested in the details of the conspiracy to kill Casso. Gravano wanted to know how Casso nabbed Hydell. The feat was the beginning of the legend of Gaspipe Casso. From that time onward, he was able to do things that appeared impossible. He knew who was a rat. He knew where bugs and taps were hidden. He knew who was about to be pinched. Casso was a sooth-sayer. There was no telling where his reach began or ended. He was a man to be deeply feared.

Gravano, a stocky, musclebound man at the time, had the temerity to ask how Casso had caught Hydell. Casso put his hand on Gravano's knee—in the mafia a gesture of contempt. "Don't worry about how we got him," Casso said to Gravano, "worry about who ordered it."

Tied up in the basement, beaten to within an inch of his life, Hydell waited to die. The Gambinos and Casso and his fellow Lucheses stepped outside for a discussion. There was no doubt Hydell was telling the truth, nor was there any doubt about what Casso was going to do. The Gambinos agreed to Casso's proposed solution. After a few minutes, Casso and Amuso went back to the basement.

"I know you're going to kill me," Hydell told Casso. "Just do one thing for me. I have a life insurance policy. It isn't much but it's all I got. Will you put my body in the street so it can be found and my mother can collect the life insurance?"

"Don't worry about it," Casso said. "I'll do that."

Casso took out a .22 automatic pistol, equipped with a silencer, and began shooting. He emptied the pistol into Hydell. He reloaded and fired again. Casso shot Hydell fifteen times. The body was put in the trunk of the Plymouth. Casso tossed in the gun. He drove to a parking lot near a boatyard. Casso gave the keys to the Plymouth to Patty Testa. He instructed Testa to get rid of the body. "Casso promised Hydell he would leave his body where it could be found so his mother could collect on his life insurance policy. Casso didn't keep his word. He found a way to punish Hydell and his family even after death. To this day, the body of Jimmy Hydell remains missing."

THE WRONG NICKY GUIDO

Casso's investigation was complete, but the punishment phase was just beginning. Casso started with the two other shooters—Bob Bering and Nicky Guido, whose names were in the manila NYPD folder Kaplan had given Casso. The file contained a photograph of Bering and his address on Daffodil Lane on Staten Island. Casso drove by Bering's house and parked outside and waited. Bering didn't turn up. Casso gave George Neck Zappola orders to continue surveillance. Zappola drove by from time to time but weeks passed and there was no sign of him. Bering had run to Long Island, displaying the good sense to make himself permanently scarce.

Nicky Guido was another matter. Information on him was thin and contradictory. Guido appeared to be a low-level newcomer to the underworld, a hanger-on used strictly for muscle. He had no criminal record so Casso didn't have a photograph of Guido nor his pedigree from the NYPD files. But Casso did have leads. The manila folder had an address for Guido near Court Street in Carroll Gardens. Casso and Amuso went by the address several times but didn't see anyone who lived there. Casso gave the contract to kill Guido to three Luchese foot soldiers. They went and watched Guido's address intermittently. While surveilling the Guido address they observed a small red sports car parked on the block. They noted the license plate number and gave it to Casso. The presence of a red sports car rang a bell for Casso. Days before he was shot he had seen a man who looked like a hood sitting in a red sports car in the street outside a restaurant where Casso was dining. The red sports car needed to be investigated.

"There was now a standard operating procedure in place. Casso gave the license number to Kaplan and asked him to have 'the cops' run a check on it. If the car was registered to Nicky Guido, Casso would have his man. Kaplan came back to him and said that 'the cops' had the details Casso was after. He said they wanted to be paid four thousand dollars for the address of Nicky Guido. This struck Casso as pure greed. The agreed price for the Hydell kidnapping had been thirty-five thousand. Casso had given Santora and the two cops an extra five grand as a bonus for a job well done. Gaspipe complained to Kaplan that the cops were asking for too much. Casso decided to take a pass. He knew the name of his target was Nicky Guido. Guido lived in Brooklyn. How hard could it be to find him? There were other contacts Casso had. Casso turned to a guy he had in the gas company. Finding Nicky Guido should be as simple as running the name through the gas company's list of subscribers. An address in Windsor Terrace came back—an area of Brooklyn nowhere near Court Street."

Casso's foot soldiers set up on the house in Windsor Terrace anyway. While watching they saw a man who vaguely fit the description Casso had given them—big, Italian-looking, young. There was a red car in the area, a Nissan Maxima. Not exactly a sports car, but it was new and had a fairly sporty design for a sedan. But the ID was weak. They didn't get much of a look at the man. The whole neighborhood was Italian-American. One of the soldiers reported back to Casso that they needed a better identification before they made a move. "Casso's crew had nothing better to do on Christmas Day 1986, than sit double-parked in a car and wait for the guy to come out of his house. That was life in the 'life'—losers wasting their lives taking lives. Late in the afternoon, they see two men emerge from the house—one older, one younger, dressed in a new white winter coat. The two men crossed 17th Street and approached the red Nissan. Two of Casso's soldiers get out of the car. They run up on the car and open fire on the driver's side. Four shots go off in rapid succession, echoing along the silent street. The kid threw himself in front of the older man, catching the hit team's gunfire. The Lucheses ran back to the car and took off. Nicky Guido was lying in the driver's seat with his eyes open and barely breathing, his white winter coat covered with blood."

The Christmas Day murder of Nicky Guido caught the attention of the press in New York City. Senseless violence on one of the holy days of the year was appalling enough to penetrate the consciousness of a city with a soaring murder rate. The investigation quickly revealed the apparent lack of a motive to murder Nicky Guido. Detective William Powell of the Brooklyn South Homicide Squad caught the case. Within hours a portrait of the victim emerged as an unlikely target of a gangland-style homicide. Nicky Guido was known in the neighborhood as a nice quiet shy kid with no affiliations with the mafia or any criminals. He worked for a telephone company on Nostrand Avenue in Brooklyn. He liked to bowl and listen to police scanners. Joe Guido, an uncle, was a detective in the Crimes Against Property Unit in the 120th Precinct. At midnight on Christmas Day he came to the Seven-Two to ask if they knew why his nephew had been killed. "All that Nicky did was work hard and live for his car," Detective Powell recorded Guido's uncle Joe saying. "Before Detective Guido came to the 72nd Precinct he talked to the Nicky Guido family and there was nothing they could tell him about why anyone would want Nicky killed. Nicky Guido's father Gabe is Joe Guido's brother and he would not hide information from Joe Guido. Joe Guido also states that Nicky looked up to Joe Guido because he was a New York City detective and Nicky wanted to be a New York City cop."

There was no evidence to suggest any organized crime connection. There was nothing pointing to another family member being behind the murder. No grudges, or disputes, or debts. Guido loved to drive his car. Local girls would go clubbing, to places like Funhouse and Players, and he would drop them at the door but not go inside. Guido claimed he wasn't dressed well enough for a nightclub but it was obvious to the girls he was too shy. He never asked the girls to go out with him. He was insecure about his appearance. Girls had "a brother-sister relationship" with him. Guido was considered a "nice kid." He didn't drink or smoke or do drugs. Lizabeth Lynott, a twenty-year-old NYPD probationary police officer Guido often gave rides to, said she had given him a white jacket for Christmas that year. None had any idea why Nicky Guido would be murdered.

Detective Powell reported in the murder file that Christmas Day had passed quietly in the Guido residence. Dinner was served at three-fifteen, with a brood of uncles and aunts and cousins in attendance. Nicky was eager to show his uncle Anthony his new red Maxima. The uncle recalled the scene, as documented by Detective Powell: "They crossed the street and Nicky opened the car door and got in behind the wheel and reached over and opened the passenger door for his uncle. The uncle got into the passenger seat and the doors were closed. Nicky started the car and was showing off the fancy dashboard. Nicky suddenly reached over, grabbed his uncle, and pulled him down in the seat. Nicky said, 'GET DOWN, STAY DOWN, STAY DOWN UNCLE TONY.' After the uncle was pulled down onto the seat, he states that he heard four shots. Nicky kept holding him down. He tried to get a look at the shooter but Nicky wouldn't let him up.

The DD-5 continued, "Uncle Anthony had only seen a white male (he could see the back of his neck) in a light-colored cap leap into a light blue car and speed away. He tried to catch the license plate but couldn't see it. He had no further details to offer on the incident—he had been engaged in admiring Nicky's dashboard. He is upset and the interview was terminated after the uncle stated he had checked Nicky for a pulse and couldn't find one. He ran into the house and told the family what had happened and they called the police. The uncle believes that Nicky saved his life by pulling him down onto the seat."

Detective Powell's leads were not promising. The only eyewitnesses were two young boys who had been outside playing that day. Neither of them wanted to get involved. They were having nightmares about the shooting. Their parents wouldn't let them assist the investigation. A neighbor across the street was a retired detective from the Eight-One. He approached investigators and told them that Nicky had no reputation for trouble—he was "well liked."

The day after the murder, Detective Powell was contacted by George Terra from the Brooklyn District Attorney's Office. Terra was investigating the attempted murder of Gaspipe Casso and had one Nicky Guido listed as a suspect. Terra didn't give Powell the context. He simply asked for the basic facts regarding the Nicky Guido killed on 17th Street—date of birth, address, criminal history. "Powell was no fool. The Brooklyn DA wasn't cooperating with his investigation. Powell continued working leads. He ran the license plates of cars parked on the street that day. He interviewed Nicky Guido's extended family. But the longer the case went the more it seemed obvious there was some kind of mistake involved in shooting an unconnected and harmless kid. There had to be something going on. Powell did his homework. He figured out there was another Nicky Guido out there—a little older, lived in Carroll Gardens, had brushes with the law. Powell decided it would be worthwhile talking to the intended victim—the other Nicky Guido."

The Guido file contained a DD-5 recording that on January 14, 1986, Detectives Powell, Semioli, and DeFranco from Brooklyn South Homicide went to see a woman named Mrs. Guido who lived in a basement apartment on Nelson Street, just off Smith Street, in a working-class Italian area where the elevated subway rattles by overhead. She was the mother of Nicky Guido—the one involved in the attempt on Casso. The detectives told her that they had heard rumors that her son was the intended victim. "Mrs. Guido informed Detectives that she had also heard the same rumors," the report said. "She further related that on 12–25–86 she learned of the murder on 17th Street on a television news show. She says she was shocked to hear the name of Nicholas Guido on the television. Her son was asleep on the couch. She woke him up and told him of the story and that the dead man was named Nicholas Guido. She stated that her son seemed shaken by the news."

The DD-5 continued, "During the course of the conversation about the rumors she had heard, it was disclosed that the trouble all comes from a friend of her son. She called this friend Jimmy. She stated that she had only met him once. He was in the house when she came home from work. She recalled that she didn't like his looks. She said that she doesn't know Jimmy's last name but that he had blond hair. She said that Nicky and Jimmy used to do small plumbing and construction jobs. She had heard that Jimmy had disappeared. She asked her son what the rumors were about and Nicky denied any wrongdoing. She was shaken by the news that the Detectives had also heard these rumors."

The three detectives told her that she should advise her son to turn himself in to the police for protection. They gave her the phone number for the Homicide Squad office. The next day, Detective Powell received a call from an attorney named Gino Singer. He said he represented a client by the name of Nicky Guido. He said Guido had called an hour before asking him to call the NYPD to see if the men who had come to his mother's house earlier that day were in fact policemen, not impersonators. "The undersigned confirmed that I was one of the Detectives that had spoken to Mrs. Guido," Detective Powell wrote. "Mr. Singer then asked what was going on. The undersigned replied that I was assigned to the murder case of a Nicholas Guido that was shot on 12–25–86. I informed the attorney that after a few days it was my belief that the 17th Street murder was a mistake. I started asking around and I was informed that there was a contract out on another Nicky Guido. Mr. Singer asked if this was coming from people who would be in the know about such things. Mr. Singer was informed that in the opinion of the undersigned his client had a problem. Mr. Singer said that Nicky had been offered police protection in the past, but he didn't like the idea. The undersigned stated that Nicky was the one to decide if he was in danger. Mr. Singer then asked if it was true that a retired cop had been found dead this morning. I confirmed this but stated that I had no particulars on the case. Mr. Singer asked if the dead man was Robert Bering. I said no. Mr. Singer said that he would convey the gist of our conversation to his client."

Detective Powell had no way of knowing it at the time, but Bob Bering had also heard the news of Guido's murder on the television broadcast. There was no photograph of the victim so Bering had no way of determining if it was the Nicky Guido he knew. Bering had called the Guido home on Nelson Street repeatedly. Guido's mother hung up on him and then Guido's cousin picked up the phone and told Bering to never call again. Bering was living on Long Island. He carried a .38 with him everywhere, including to bed. Every step he took was fraught with fear. Casso was coming after him, he was sure. On January 3, just over a week after the wrong Nicky Guido was killed, Bering met George Terra of the Brooklyn DA and George Hanna of the Joint Auto Larceny Task Force at a diner. Bering had been a New York City transit cop for seven and a half years. He knew what was required of him, if he hoped to escape with his life. He would have to snitch.

"Bering was the kind of cop who gave cops a bad name—a career criminal who almost certainly was committing crimes while he was one of us. He described his involvement in the school bus rackets. He implicated himself in tax evasion and labor union shakedowns. He told Terra and Hanna how he had been convicted of dealing Quaaludes and spent six months on Rikers Island, where he'd met Hydell. They had gone on a murder spree in 1986. He told them they could find Annette DiBiasi's body buried in the woods not far from Al Guarneri's home. Like Hydell, who killed his former girlfriend in a jealous rage, Bering had discovered that his ex-wife was living with a friend of his—Joe Trinetto. Hydell and Bering plotted his murder, and Trinetto turned up dead in October of that year, while Bering was in Chicago—on an alibi trip."

Bering provided the inside story on the Casso attempt. The hit team—Hydell, Bering, Guido—had tried to clock Casso for weeks. But Casso, in Bering's words, "passed being paranoid." He never followed the same routine and his every movement was designed to throw off any surveillance—law enforcement or mob. Bering described the license plate screwup. The blue Plymouth Fury. The bus stop in front of the Golden Ox. Nicky Guido's gun jamming not once but twice. Bering had lent Hydell a rented car one Saturday in October—the day he disappeared. Hydell was supposed to be meeting with Mickey Boy Paradiso. Bering said he had never heard from Hydell again.

Nicky Guido had gone into hiding, Bering told Terra and Hanna. As a cooperating witness for the Brooklyn DA, Bering agreed to wear a wire to implicate Guido. In April 1987, Nicky Guido was found living in Tampa, Florida. The NYPD sent Bering down to meet with him, accompanied by NYPD detectives. Detective Bernice Luhrs was assigned to pose as Bering's girlfriend. "The operation was borderline farcical. Detective Luhrs was going by the name 'Irene' but Bering kept referring to her as 'Bea'—her real first name. Bering told Guido there was a rumor going around Brooklyn that Bering was 'under'—that he was cooperating or under arrest—but he said it wasn't true. Bering and Guido talked about newspaper articles on the Casso attempt. The murder of the wrong Nicky Guido had scared the right Nicky Guido out of town. Bering suggested they go back to New York and go after Casso—'take the head off of the snake,' Bering called it. The suggestion was preposterous. The right Nicky Guido wasn't biting."

On November 11, 1987, Robert Bering pleaded guilty to the attempted murder of Casso. Bering was given fifteen to life. As a sop for his inept cooperation, and acknowledgment by the authorities of Casso's power, Bering was granted the stipulation that he would not serve his time in a New York state prison. If he were housed in a state facility he would be in far greater danger of being killed by Casso. Bering was put into the federal system.

"Nicky Guido's resolve to stay away from New York proved to be transitory. Drawn to crime like a moth to a flame, Guido came back to Brooklyn and got involved in a huge cocaine distribution network. The outfit he attached himself to was importing thousands of tons of coke from Colombia. The mafia end in New York City was run by the Genoveses and Lucheses. Four tons were seized in a container ship traveling between Honduras and the Everglades. The container was filled with wooden patio furniture and cocaine. It was the largest cocaine bust ever at the time. The operation used a civilian police administrative assistant in the 60th Precinct in Brooklyn as its own inside source—a pale version of Casso's insiders. Guido was carrying a concealed handgun at the time of his arrest. He claimed he was able to legally carry a pistol because he was a member of the Society for Prevention of Cruelty to Children of Sullivan County—a mob front designed to let gangsters carry guns."

In 1989, the right Nicky Guido was charged in state court in Brooklyn with the attempted murder of Anthony Casso. Guido's defense attorney ridiculed Assistant District Attorney Mark Feldman's references to organized crime and the conspiracy to murder Casso as "cute," paranoid, and irrelevant. Bob Bering testified in detail about the plot and Guido's role in it. "Casso was called as a witness for the prosecution. He took the Fifth on every question. He refused to answer any questions on the grounds that it might tend to incriminate him. Casso refused to admit to his name. He was the hardest of hard cases. Guido was convicted of second-degree assault.

"Even after Guido's conviction, Casso did not give up on finding and killing him. He had Kaplan consult with 'the cops' about finding the correctional institution where Guido was housed. Kaplan came back with the location. Before Casso could make a move, Guido got himself moved. By then Casso had turned his attention to getting the senior Gambinos behind the shooting."

EDDIE LINO

According to Jimmy Hydell there were three men who had ordered the hit on Casso—Mickey Boy Paradiso, Bobby Boriello, and Eddie Lino. Mickey Boy Paradiso proved to be elusive. There was no doubt about his guilt. Through Kaplan, "the cops" provided Casso with a tape recording of an interrogation of Philly Paradiso in which Mickey Boy's role in the plot against Casso was discussed. "In the aftermath of the failed attempt, Mickey Boy stopped going to his usual haunts. Casso was told by Sammy the Bull Gravano that the Gambinos were after Paradiso themselves. John Gotti assured Casso that Mickey Boy Paradiso was no longer a member of the Gambinos. But when federal prosecutors learned of Gotti's contract on Paradiso, his bail was revoked. Mickey Boy Paradiso was sent to Lompoc, a maximum-security facility in California. Casso got word of Paradiso's location to a Lompoc inmate named Anthony Senter. Paradiso was too quick for Casso. Sensing he was in danger, Paradiso requested and received a transfer to another facility."

Not all the Gambinos were so lucky, or cagey. Bobby Boriello was Gotti's driver and bodyguard, the wiseguy assigned to clean Gotti's car and escort him on his walk-and-talks through Little Italy. Using mafia logic, Casso reasoned the boss must have been in on the plot. "Casso hatched a series of harebrained schemes to kill John Gotti. Why not park a van on Mulberry Street, just like the government did for their operations, and open up on Gotti as he walked along the sidewalk? There was the problem of escape, and the inconvenient fact that a van packed with Luchese wiseguys wouldn't exactly be inconspicuous on Mulberry Street.

When Gotti was spotted eating with his girlfriend in an uptown Italian restaurant on 116th Street, Casso went to the place to see if it was possible to get Gotti there. The restaurant was on the top floor of the building. Casso told George Neck Zappola to rent an apartment across the street. Zappola tried to find a place but Gotti wasn't spotted at the restaurant again and the scheme drifted away. Casso then came up with the idea of breaking into the dentist's office across the street from Gotti's house in Howard Beach, Queens. As Gotti came out of his home in the morning they would start shooting like an old-time gangster movie—a moment that would be memorialized forever on the FBI cameras recording Gotti's every movement. Celebrity had made Gotti untouchable, to everyone but us."

Stymied on Gotti, Casso was ready to act on Boriello and Lino. Casso told Kaplan to ask "the cops" for Boriello's address. A house near 28th and Cropsey avenues in Brooklyn was provided, along with a description of the Lincoln Town Car Boriello drove. For several weeks Amuso and Casso went to the address repeatedly to look for Boriello. May of that year was a busy month for Casso. He was planning the murder of Jimmy Bishop. An indictment in the Windows Case was looming. But Casso found the spare time to plan another murder. Within weeks Boriello was dead. *Newsday* reported that he "was shot twice in the head and six times in the body" in the driveway of his home.

Eddie Lino presented yet another degree of difficulty for Casso. In the mafia and law enforcement, Eddie Lino was known as an exceptionally tough and dangerous character. A Gambino captain, Lino was short and stocky and swarthy. He was a major league heroin dealer. He was close to John Gotti. He had been one of the shooters in the Paul Castellano hit in front of Spark's Steakhouse in Manhattan. Getting close enough to kill Lino was virtually impossible. Lino wouldn't go down easily.

For more than two years Casso had a contract out on Lino. No progress was made. Like Casso, Lino was paranoid to the point of parody. A purveyor of violence himself, Lino understood the inner workings of murder plots and proceeded with appropriate caution. He never followed a pattern or routine, varying his schedule every day, watching his rearview mirrors. Frustrated, Casso came up with an idea. "The cops" might be able to take Lino by surprise. The scam had worked with Jimmy Hydell. The scam had worked for the Orthodox jeweler "the cops" had kidnapped and killed for Kaplan.

Kaplan took Casso's offer of $75,000 for the Lino hit to "the cops." Kaplan reported that "the cops" were willing to take on the murder. It was "no problem." But Kaplan said "the cops" needed two handguns and a car that resembled an unmarked police car, just as they had used in the Hydell kidnapping. Casso obtained a four-door Plymouth that had been used as a highway patrol car. The car was registered in a false name, two guns were placed in a brown paper bag in the trunk, and Kaplan had his sidekick Tommy Galpine deliver it to "the cops." For months, the two detectives tried to clock Lino. They went to his luxurious house in a wealthy area of Long Island, the rewards of Lino's success in organized crime. The pair considered taking Lino by surprise in his home but decided against it. The car they had was a junker. Casso offered to have it repaired. When the Plymouth was left at a prearranged site in Brooklyn, Casso found that the car was a wreck. A fastidious gangster, as the FBI agents later witnessed with his incessant tidying up in the Valachi suite in La Tuna prison, Casso was appalled by filthy interior and poor running condition of the vehicle. Kaplan told Casso not to worry about getting another car, or fixing that one. "The cops" would get their own vehicle.

The next time Casso heard about Eddie Lino was on the evening television news on November 6, 1990. The Gambino wiseguy had been shot and killed on the Belt Parkway in Brooklyn. Casso described the murder to federal prosecutors Rose and O'Connell as it had been related to him by Burt Kaplan. Lino was driving along the service road next to the Belt Parkway in his new Mercedes sedan. "The cops" were tailing Lino when they pulled alongside and indicated they wanted to talk to him. Lino must have recognized one or both of "the cops," otherwise he wouldn't have stopped. Seconds later Eddie Lino was dead.

"The murder of Eddie Lino caused a sensation inside the Major Case squad room," Oldham recalled. "It had all the earmarks of a gangland hit. But there were a couple of big clues that something else was at work. Lino's window was rolled down. He wouldn't have pulled over and rolled down his window for wiseguys out on a hit."

The night of the homicide, Detective Mary Dugan from the NYPD Crime Scene Unit responded. A stretch of the Belt Parkway service road was taped off. Lino's vehicle had run off the pavement and into a fence. Instead of putting the car into "park" when he pulled over Lino had kept it in "drive." There was one eyewitness to the homicide. The witness said he had seen a man running away from Lino's car carrying a gun. The man was thin, the witness said. The witness said the shooter got into a car that had a police light on the dashboard and looked like an unmarked cop car. "The report didn't necessarily mean the killer was a cop. Impersonating police officers was a common practice for gangsters. So common, in fact, that it wasn't unheard of for a wiseguy to refuse to pull over for plainclothes police if he was in a remote or unpopulated area."

The night of the homicide, Detective Dugan found and vouchered a watch in the middle of the street, sixty-six feet, nine inches from Lino's car. The watch had a broken band and the clasp was still closed. It appeared to have been ripped from the wrist of the shooter as Lino struggled to turn the gun away. The watch was a square-faced Pulsar quartz with a black face and yellow numerals. It was stopped at 6:45, the same time Eddie Lino was murdered.

"Lino's murder was a big deal on both sides of the law. The shooting was on the Belt Parkway, under streetlights, with cars driving along the freeway. The killers clearly considered themselves above the law. They thought they could get away with murder—which was what happened. There were no meaningful leads in the Lino case. The identity of the skinny shooter and his accomplice—the two men in the cop car with the teardrop light flashing—remained a mystery."

BURT'S "GUYS"

Sitting in the Valachi suite in La Tuna, New Mexico, in March 1994, Casso solved the Eddie Lino murder. After "the cops" opened fire on Lino, and his Mercedes lurched forward and hit a fence, Casso said, "Steve" had to get out of their car and run to Lino's car to make sure he was dead. Casso also said he had been delighted with the "piece of work" done by "the cops." The agreed fee was $75,000, but Casso wanted to pay $100,000, the extra a bonus for a job well done.

Over the years, Kaplan had been careful to ensure that Casso didn't learn the names or identities of "the cops," always referring to them as his "friends" or "guys." Casso, in turn, had referred to "the crystal ball" and "the cops" when describing his law enforcement sources to Vic Amuso.

But Casso had tried to figure out who "the cops" were over the years. Casso was by nature inquisitive. He wanted to know everything, despite Kaplan's instinct to compartmentalize and control information. In his own sly way, Casso had tried to solve the puzzle of the "crystal ball." Hints had accumulated over the years. According to Casso, not long after the Hydell kidnapping, Casso's son and his friends had their bicycle helmets seized by a police officer in the Six-Three, the precinct where Casso lived. He had managed to retrieve the helmets. Kaplan wanted Casso to know that his "friend" in the precinct had assisted in the effort. Kaplan used the name "Lou" for the cop. Around the same time, Kaplan told Casso that "Lou's" reach wasn't limited to the Six-Three. "Lou's" partner was assigned to the Major Case Squad. Kaplan explained to Casso what Major Case did, operating citywide with access to all manner of organized crime intelligence.

Even with these slips, Kaplan had tried hard to keep the identity of his "friends" secret. But keeping a secret from someone as observant as Casso was difficult, perhaps impossible. After the Lino hit, Kaplan described to Casso what had happened to Lino on the Belt Parkway. As he spoke, Kaplan let slip that the shooter in the murder was named "Steve." While Casso was on the run from indictment in the Windows Case in the early nineties, the final piece of the puzzle fell into place. Casso happened upon a copy of *Mafia Cop*. Casso examined its contents. On the back there was a large photograph of an NYPD officer in standard-issue warm weather patrol attire: blue slacks, short-sleeved blue shirt, silver police badge worn on his chest, holstered handgun. The man was in his twenties, muscular but running to fat, his stomach drawn in and chest puffed out for the portrait. In the background stood a row of clapboard Brooklyn houses, unmistakably Bensonhurst. The cop was leaning against an NYPD cruiser with "63 PCT" painted on the side. The picture was taken on August 22, 1969, the first day on the job for the young officer.

In the middle of the book there was an eight-page photo insert. Casso recognized some of the faces. Fat the Gangster Eppolito was in a photograph next to "Uncle Jimmy 'The Clam' Eppolito." In the bottom right-hand corner of one page was a snapshot of two NYPD detectives sitting in a squad room. One detective was large and overweight with his tie undone, the other skinny and nattily dressed in the style of the late seventies. The detectives were grinning. The names underneath were Steve Caracappa and Lou Eppolito. The caption read, "The two Godfathers of the NYPD."

"In Major Case we all knew Caracappa was furious at Eppolito for including the photograph in the book—but we didn't know why. Now it was clear. Caracappa didn't want Casso to know his name. Eppolito was the weak link in the chain in every sense—intellectually, emotionally, egotistically. The book proved that."

While he was on the lam, Casso had shown Kaplan his copy of *Mafia Cop*, he told the prosecutors. Casso had opened the book and pointed to the photograph of Detectives Caracappa and Eppolito.

"This looks like the two guys who were at Toys 'R' Us," Casso said to Kaplan. "That's really them, isn't it?"

"Anthony, I'm not going to tell you their names," Kaplan said. "You can surmise anything you want."

But Casso didn't need to surmise. He knew their names, and when he told them to the prosecutors who were listening to his life and crimes, they knew them, too.

Eppolito.

Caracappa.

The cops they had been looking for.

CHAPTER NINE

DOWNTOWN BURT

Until Anthony Casso identified Detectives Caracappa and Eppolito, law enforcement had only had a vague notion of the crimes that "the crystal ball" had participated in with the Lucheses. Now Casso connected many seemingly unconnected events. The disappearance of Jimmy Hydell was directly related to the murder of Eddie Lino four years later. The shootings of Jimmy Bishop, Otto Heidel, and Dominic Costa were part of an ongoing conspiracy designed to silence cooperators informing on Gaspipe Casso and Vic Amuso. More than simply leaking intelligence on investigations, Detectives Caracappa and Eppolito had been conducting secret investigations for the Lucheses, surveilling NYPD detectives and other law enforcement agents, and proactively seeking information that would protect Casso and enhance his underworld reputation. The bugs and wires in Tiger Management's trailer in New Jersey, Anthony DiLapi's murder in L.A., dodging the Windows Case indictments—the crimes were tied together in a complex knot that law enforcement would now have to untangle.

"In major organized criminal investigations there is not an obviously straightforward cause and effect. Conspiracies occur in parallel universes and timelines. What is the chronology of the crimes that are investigated? What happened? When did it happen? Where did it happen? Why did it happen? An order has to be given to events. Multifaceted criminal conspiracies don't work in a predictable fashion. In this case, the facts were incredibly unwieldy. Casso conspired with 'the cops' to kill snitches, Bronx guys, Jersey guys, Gambinos. Add the component of secrecy inside the mob and inside the network of Casso, Kaplan, Santora, Caracappa, and Eppolito, and the complications were compounded by an order of magnitude.

"As soon as Casso began to proffer it was a race against time. Starting an investigation quickly is supremely desirable. Over time evidence disappears, witnesses die, forget things, or are intimidated. Promising leads turn into dead ends. In this case, the events were already years old and the cases cold. There were statute of limitations issues under federal law. In RICO prosecutions, investigators and attorneys collaborate from the beginning, deciding strategy and tactics. A substantial reason that the federal government had succeeded against the mob was the realization that they needed to bring NYPD detectives into their cases. When FBI special agents ran cases on their own they had little or no street knowledge, from either side of the street. They didn't know how law enforcement operated in the real world—pulling strings, doing favors, being nimble. Most FBI agents didn't know how the mob really worked either—separating fact from fiction. In the NYPD there were plenty of problems. We didn't do paperwork like the FBI guys. We didn't follow orders or adhere to dress codes. But the force had detectives who could get inside the minds of the gangsters they were chasing—and that is critical to a successful investigation.

"Putting a RICO case together is telling a true crime story. You need to know who your characters are—their history, their motives, their connections. A case needs a beginning, middle, and an end. Pieces of evidence have to be put in context. Corroboration is sought. One danger is getting stuck on one theory and being unable to see other possibilities. An *idée fixe* can be a killer for investigators, the robotic bureaucratic lurch toward one conclusion no matter what the truth may be. The beauty of working a case like Caracappa and Eppolito is the promise that there is a truth to be found. If you do your job, everything may not be discoverable, but everything that is discovered will add up."

"GET YOUR HUSBAND OUT OF THE BATH"

Within hours of Casso's disappearance from the Metropolitan Correctional Center in March 1994, news that the Luchese underboss was cooperating shot like a bullet through the corridors of the Eastern District courthouse in downtown Brooklyn to mob defense attorneys' offices in midtown Manhattan and opposite City Hall. The government didn't announce that Casso had become a cooperator, and in fact the news was closely guarded. But in cases like Casso's the pattern was well known. When Casso decided to confess to his crimes in the hope of gaining leniency, he had no choice but to fire his current lawyer, Mike Rosen. "When a wiseguy cooperated, the wiseguy world turned its back on him, and that often included his attorneys. There were a number of reasons.

Defense lawyers didn't represent mobster informants if they knew what was good for business. Testifying against former mafia comrades was considered dishonorable. Other mob clients would be alienated and mistrustful of an attorney who acted for 'rats.' Finally, there was Casso's concern for his own safety. If word got out that he was cooperating with the government before he was moved to a safe location, Casso's life wouldn't be worth a plug nickle."

On the advice of prosecutors, Casso had hired a lawyer recommended to him by the government. Matthew Brief was a former prosecutor himself and was considered trustworthy. As soon as Casso had gotten rid of his defense attorney everyone in the New York defense bar knew what had happened. There was only one explanation for Casso suddenly disappearing. He had gone "bad." The implications for dozens, maybe hundreds, of mobsters were obvious. "Casso wasn't just another hood. He was a true insider. Gaspipe Casso was the equal of Sammy the Bull Gravano. Gravano knew secrets. Casso knew *secrets*. Casso literally knew where the bodies were buried. Casso was a player in the mafia, at the highest levels. An earthquake had struck."

Judd Burstein was the longtime defense attorney for Burt Kaplan. Burstein had worked with Mike Rosen over the years on criminal appeals. Within hours of Casso's firing Rosen, Burstein knew Casso had changed counsel. As soon as the news reached Burstein, he called Kaplan. He knew Kaplan and Casso were close. When Casso had gone on the lam in May 1990, fleeing indictments in the Windows Case, Kaplan had told his attorney that he was in touch with Casso. Burstein had told Kaplan that he was an "idiot" for associating with Casso while he was a fugitive. Burstein also knew that Casso had lived in a house that Kaplan owned. For years Burstein had implored Kaplan to cease his flirtation, as Burstein saw it, with organized crime and men like Gaspipe Casso, a known killer. Now the fact that Casso was a cooperator loomed ominously for Kaplan.

"Burstein thought he knew his client. Kaplan was one of those rare clients who was perfectly frank about his wrongdoings. If he was charged with a crime and he was guilty, he told Burstein. If he was innocent, he insisted upon his innocence. The characteristic is attractive in a criminal. But Burstein didn't know Kaplan had omitted huge parts of his criminal life. As far as Burstein knew, Kaplan was a talented and successful legitimate businessman who dabbled in the underworld. He didn't know that news of Casso becoming a cooperator was more than important to Kaplan—it was a matter of life and death."

At six o'clock on the evening of the day Casso flipped, Burt Kaplan was taking a bath. The telephone rang. His wife, Eleanor, answered. She called out that it was Kaplan's lawyer Judd calling. Kaplan asked her to tell him to call back in half an hour. A minute later the phone rang again. It was Burstein calling back. This time he insisted that Eleanor Kaplan get her husband out of the bath. He had to talk to Kaplan immediately. Eleanor conveyed the message to her husband. The sixty-year-old millionaire Brooklyn businessman and Luchese associate got out of the bath and wrapped himself in a towel. He picked up a telephone installed in the bathroom, irritated at having his bath interrupted.

"What seems to be the problem, Judd?" Kaplan asked. "You were going to call back in half an hour."

"It's very important," Burstein said. "Are you sitting down?"

Standing dripping wet in his bathroom, Kaplan grew impatient. "Don't fool around," he said to Burstein. "Just tell me what you want to tell me."

"Anthony went bad," Burstein said.

There was a pause.

"Anthony who?" Kaplan asked. "Anthony Russo?" Kaplan thought it had to be a Colombo wiseguy named Russo.

"No, Anthony Casso."

Kaplan was incredulous—and terrified. "Are you crazy?" he asked. "Are you trying to get us both killed? Why would you say something like that?"

"He fired his attorney," Burstein said. "He definitely went bad."

Kaplan sat down. He felt sick. If anyone in the world was a stand-up guy, Kaplan thought, it was Casso. Kaplan knew he was in a sea of trouble. He and Casso had collaborated in crime for years. There were dozens, perhaps many more, criminal acts they had committed together. Drugs. Money laundering. Fraud. Murder. All of that didn't matter. Kaplan knew the stakes. The government wouldn't do a deal with Casso, with the blood of his victims soaked into every pore of his being, unless Casso was able to give them something even larger than his own criminal confession.

"Thank you very much for calling, Judd," Kaplan said.

Kaplan hung up. He needed to act quickly. He dried himself off and dressed and went out to a pay phone on the street. No calls would be made from his home phones. They could be tapped by now, his house bugged. Kaplan called his second in command, longtime associate Tommy Galpine, and told him what had happened with Casso. Kaplan said he was going on the run that night. Kaplan and Galpine were in the marijuana distribution business together, grossing more than $1 million a week. To sustain himself on the run, Kaplan would need money—a lot of it. He asked Galpine if he had any cash. Galpine said he did. Kaplan told him to give all that he had to Kaplan's wife, Eleanor. Kaplan next called one of his partners in pot dealing, who also did errands for Kaplan. He repeated the story to his partner. Kaplan told him to take three thousand dollars to the wife of Tommy Irish Carew. Carew was in prison and Kaplan was taking care of her and he wanted to be sure she continued to receive at least a thousand dollars a month to survive on while he was on the lam.

"Kaplan was looking after the fundamentals," Oldham said, "the little things that have to be seen to that can make the difference between getting caught, or not. Caring for spouses when an associate was in jail was also a point of pride with a man like Kaplan. He was old-school. He believed in keeping his word—if you belonged to his inner circle. But it was also a matter of self-preservation. Keeping Carew on his side, and preventing him from snitching, was smart. One reason the mafia was falling apart at the time was the way wives and children were treated when a made man was sent to jail. Instead of seeing that they were provided for, they were abandoned and left to their own devices. A wiseguy in jail had no way to provide while inside. Their families fell into poverty. For men with an inflated sense of pride, it was demeaning to have your wife and sons and daughters penniless. It made the father and husband look inadequate— because he was inadequate. The people who paid the most for the crimes of tough guys were often their children. Kids were raised in violent households with fathers frequently absent. The veneer of being 'connected' had a certain luster in certain neighborhoods, but that wore off quickly when the old man went away and the family went broke. Kaplan wasn't going to let that happen to him."

Next, Kaplan called an associate named Michael Gordon, another partner in his drug business. He told Gordon that Casso had become a cooperator. He asked Gordon if he could stay at his place in New Jersey that night. Kaplan intended to fly from Newark International first thing in the morning and he wanted to be near the airport. He asked Gordon to collect him from his Bensonhurst home. Kaplan was going to put his car into storage. He returned home, packed a bag, and collected all the cash he had stashed in the house, along with the money his wife had saved up over the years. Kaplan would take it all as emergency money. Galpine would replenish the funds and make sure that Eleanor Kaplan received money during the time Kaplan was on the run.

Gordon soon arrived at the Kaplan residence. Kaplan and his wife got in the car and drove along the Belt Parkway toward Manhattan. He had received Burstein's call at six o'clock. It was now nine-thirty. Kaplan told him he had one stop to make. The stop was essential. Kaplan had to warn, assure, and neutralize his most important criminal collaborator.

Detective Stephen Caracappa lived with his fourth wife, Monica, in an upscale apartment building at 12 East 22nd Street in Manhattan. Caracappa had retired from the NYPD in 1992 and gone to work for the Fourteenth Street Business Improvement District, an organization dedicated to improving the "quality of life" in the area around Union Square and the commercial strip along 14th Street in lower Manhattan. Public safety, graffiti removal, and street sanitation were some of the ways BIDs throughout the city tried to rejuvenate New York. Caracappa's building was a narrow ten-story structure with a glass front and a marble lobby. Centrally located, near Gramercy Park and within walking distance of many restaurants and luxury shopping districts, the building was out of the financial reach of most NYPD officers.

Late on the night of March 1, Michael Gordon pulled up in front of the building on East 22nd Street. Kaplan left his wife and Gordon in the car while he went inside to talk to Caracappa, who lived one floor from the top. Kaplan knew Caracappa went to bed at a very early hour. Kaplan buzzed Caracappa's apartment. Monica answered the intercom. Kaplan asked for Steve.

"He's sleeping," she said.

"It's Burt," Kaplan said. "It's very important. It's an emergency. You have to wake him up. I need to speak to him."

Monica Singleton buzzed Kaplan in. He took the elevator to the ninth floor. Kaplan was embarrassed as he entered the apartment and greeted the groggy Caracappa. "Steve, we got a real problem," Kaplan said. "Anthony Casso went bad. I'm going on the lam. I'm coming here to tell you because I think there is going to be a lot of publicity in the next couple of weeks. I have come to see you because I want you to know that I'm going on the lam. I am not going bad. You can rely on me."

Oldham recalled, "The moment of truth had arrived for Caracappa—the moment he had dreaded for years. Like Kaplan, Caracappa understood the implications. With Kaplan's forewarning Caracappa could run. He had a head start. A detective with his training and know-how could make himself vanish. But unless he stared down the accusations, life as he knew it was over. He had to know his wife, a sophisticated garment district executive he'd met in the building, wasn't going on the lam with him. Monica Singleton was a successful businesswoman in her own right. She wasn't going to take a job washing dishes in Peoria. Nor was Caracappa.

"Calm was the answer. Caracappa would stay put and see what happened. There was no way to know for sure what Casso knew about Caracappa and Eppolito. If the news broke, Caracappa would hang tough. Deny everything. He would tell his wife and mother and brother that Casso had invented the entire story. Caracappa had a sterling reputation. He had friends in all areas of law enforcement. No one would believe the word of a psychopath like Casso over the word of a first-grade detective from the Major Case Squad. Guys in OCHU wouldn't be able to comprehend a betrayal of the kind Casso was alleging. Eppolito, however, was a different story. Louie was well known in the force. Louie had written the execrable *Mafia Cop*. But Caracappa had been in Major Case. For most detectives, the wound would be too deep if Casso was believed. Cops stick with cops, through thick and thin, guilty and innocent. When a cop was accused, the instinct inside the NYPD was to rally to his side. As long as Eppolito and Kaplan remained silent, there was an excellent chance Caracappa could ride out the coming storm."

"Do you need any money?" Caracappa asked Kaplan. "Do you need me to take care of your wife?"

"No, thank you very much," Kaplan said. "I have money."

"If you ever do need money in the future, just let me know," Caracappa said, "like a good friend would, and I'll take care of your wife."

"There is someone else involved in this," Kaplan said. "There's Louie. Can you control Louie? Can you take care of the situation with him?"

Eppolito was the subject that concerned Kaplan the most. Eppolito was flamboyant and potentially unreliable. Through the years Kaplan had seen how Eppolito operated. The former Mr. New York bodybuilder whined about money. He had nagged Kaplan about meeting Casso. It was an idea that Kaplan considered not only stupid but dangerous. For all Eppolito's bluster and big-belly bully-boy behavior, in Kaplan's estimation he was soft. Men who are tough don't need to brag about it, or show off. Kaplan knew Caracappa wouldn't break. Kaplan and Caracappa were self-contained men. They didn't pity themselves or make spectacles of themselves. No amount of pressure was going to get them to talk, unless they wanted to talk. Eppolito was a different story. Both knew Eppolito had to be kept in line, kept from caving under pressure. Watching Eppolito would be Caracappa's responsibility.

"Louie's been my partner and I trust him," Caracappa said. "Don't worry about it."

Caracappa and Kaplan hugged and kissed. Kaplan left. Kaplan went back downstairs and drove with his wife to Michael Gordon's house in

Edison, New Jersey. As he had prepared to leave, Kaplan told people that he was going to hide in China. He had conducted extensive business dealings in Hong Kong and China over the years, importing millions of dollars' worth of clothing from the Orient. Kaplan wanted word to circulate that he had vanished into China. If the rumor made the rounds in the mafia it was only a matter of time before it reached the FBI. Kaplan calculated that the FBI would be reluctant to commit the resources to chase him in the cantons of southern China. On Tuesday morning, less than twelve hours after Judd Burstein got Kaplan to cut short his bath, Kaplan flew to San Diego intending to vanish.

A BOY WHO LIKED TO GAMBLE

Kaplan's need to run resulted from decades of illegal behavior. But he had seemingly not been destined for a life of crime. Born in Sheepshead Bay in Brooklyn in 1933, Kaplan moved with his family when he was four years old to Vanderbilt Avenue on the edge of Crown Heights. The broad avenue was a commercial strip with merchants and restaurants and tradesmen offering their goods and services along half a dozen blocks leading up to Prospect Park. Kaplan's father was an electrician and the family ran an appliance store out of the ground floor of the five-story building. The business sold, repaired, and installed washing machines, dryers, dishwashers, and air conditioners. At a time of mass immigration in the wake of World War II, Kaplan belonged to the burgeoning working class finding prosperity in Brooklyn.

As a young man, Kaplan attended Brooklyn Tech High School, a prestigious institution with admission determined by competitive examination. Kaplan lasted only a year and a half before he transferred to Brooklyn Manual High. Promise, in Kaplan, always went unfulfilled. Weekends and evenings he worked for his father installing television antennas. By the age of thirteen Kaplan had a gambling problem. He enjoyed it—far too much. It began with trips to the racetrack with his father. In short order, Kaplan started playing cards for money. Kaplan spent his time playing in poker games around the neighborhood, running with the fast group of kids. It was the heyday for Brooklyn—the golden age after the war. Organized crime formed part of the legend of the borough. *Cosa nostra* was still an Italian secret society operating in the shadows. "Meyer Lansky was the archetype of the smart Jewish tough guy who was close to both Lucky Luciano and Bugsy Seigel. During the war,

Meyer Lansky had worked with the Office of Naval Intelligence, rounding up gangsters on the docks to watch for German infiltrators, saboteurs, and submarines—a real threat in New York at the time. To a kid with Kaplan's talents, Meyer Lansky was a major league star. Lansky made hundreds of millions over the years investing in casinos in Cuba and Las Vegas. Lansky was too smart to get caught. Kaplan had as his inspiration a Jewish legend in the underworld."

In 1952, after graduating from high school, Kaplan joined the Navy. A quick study with a steel-trap memory and a penchant for subterfuge, Kaplan was trained in cryptology and cryptoanalysis. Sent to Japan, his job was to copy secret Russian codes encrypted to make them unreadable without a cipher. Cryptology ("secret writing," from the Greek) appealed to Kaplan's nature and he excelled at his work. His last year in the Navy was spent at Fort Meade, Maryland, deciphering highly classified material. The talent he displayed led to the offer of a job at the National Security Agency, the top secret governmental organization engaged in waging the decades-long Cold War with surveillance, disinformation, intelligence, and counterintelligence.

Kaplan chose to return to Brooklyn. He continued the appliance business in partnership with his mother and brother. He married his wife, Eleanor, in 1957. But the young father, veteran, and legitimate businessman was also an addicted gambler. By the late fifties he had blown through his legal ways of borrowing money to gamble. "The pattern that followed was as predictable as it was awful. The gambler starts to borrow from finance companies, with higher interest rates than banks. After those institutions reach their limits or get wise, or the gambler starts to go into default on loans, he turns to the street—to loan sharks. At first the 'vig,' the interest, isn't excessive. Maybe one percent a week, payable every week. If you borrowed ten grand you had to pay a hundred bucks in interest each week. It seems manageable but it's not over the long haul, when your credit has no limit. Once they give you the money, they don't want you to pay it back. Not the principal. No lender does, legit or illegit. Repaying money means the shylock or financial institution has to go out and find another borrower. The difference was that the mafia had the muscle to make a borrower do what he was told. Matters only got worse the more you borrowed. The bigger the loan, the less reliable the guy getting the money became, the bigger the vig. The cycle was vicious."

A local wiseguy and businessman ran a Luchese social club in the neighborhood where Kaplan plied his trade. During this time Kaplan was called to give a quote for air-conditioning for the wiseguy's club. The elder mobster was impressed with the job Kaplan did—and the price. He introduced Kaplan to the owner of a Gambino social club at the corner of Grand Avenue and St. Mark's Place, only a few blocks from Kaplan's store on Vanderbilt. It was the place where Detective Eppolito's father, Fat the Gangster, had tended bar for years before he died of a heart attack. Kaplan went and measured the place and was introduced to the man in charge, Jimmy Eppolito—Louis Eppolito's uncle known as the Clam. Kaplan installed the air conditioners and he started to play cards in a room upstairs.

By the early sixties Kaplan was borrowing from half a dozen different loan sharks. One of them was a former New York City Police Department detective named Wes Daley. Kaplan began to borrow heavily from Daley—too heavily. When you were in debt to a gangster you were in debt in every sense of the word. When Daley came to Kaplan and said he wanted a favor there was nothing Kaplan could say, no matter what the favor might be. Kaplan was trapped. One day Daley told Kaplan there was a body in the trunk of his car. He wanted Kaplan to dispose of the body. Daley didn't say he had killed the man but Kaplan understood that he had—and that he could quickly follow in the man's footsteps if he didn't oblige the retired police officer.

"Kaplan collected the car, as instructed, and drove to Connecticut where he was to meet with another associate of Daley. The other guy was supposed to have dug a grave. It was winter. Kaplan shook all the way as he drove north. He was scared beyond belief. Kaplan was now guilty of being an accomplice after the fact to murder. He was only a gambler but that was not how things worked in the mob—events got out of hand quickly, unpredictably, permanently. When he got to Connecticut he discovered the guy hadn't dug the grave. He couldn't pierce the surface of the ground, which was frozen solid. The man told Kaplan to help him throw the body into the water. Kaplan did. He didn't know who the dead man was, or why he was made dead. But Kaplan had graduated to a new level in 'the life.'"

Kaplan was now in his early thirties. The appliance business was prospering but it didn't generate nearly enough money to repay the outstanding debts he owed. Keeping up with the interest was crushing. Kaplan approached his father-in-law, an NYPD beat cop, and asked if he could help. Kaplan wanted to consolidate his loans into a single amount to one loan shark, instead of the half dozen he owed. He wanted to repay the principal, not just keep up with the exorbitant interest payments. In order to pull off the deal he needed someone with connections to organized crime. His cop father-in-law took him to meet the gangster Kaplan had installed air-conditioning for to have a sit-down.

At the sit-down, Kaplan met Luchese captain Christy Tick Furnari at the 19th Hole in Bensonhurst. Furnari agreed to let Kaplan consolidate all his debt into one large loan. Kaplan would be able to begin paying down the principal. Furnari made it a rule not to associate himself with addicted gamblers, particularly not degenerates. He told Kaplan that if he managed to quit gambling they could become "friends."

"Furnari wasn't just doing a favor for a friend, he was also trolling for talent. To be a made guy you had to be Italian—preferably with Sicilian blood. But every gangster associated with Irish and Jewish criminal elements. It was obvious that Kaplan was a bright young man. Addicted gamblers are just as unreliable as heroin junkies—they lie, cheat, and steal to feed their need. But Furnari didn't want to let the favor go without the possibility of a kindness being repaid, with interest, someday."

By then, Kaplan's life had cleaved in two. The legitimate businessman was a husband and loving father to his daughter, Deborah. The illegitimate mafia associate was drifting further into trouble. Kaplan began fencing stolen appliances, the same ones he was selling legitimately at the store. Kaplan was a reliable contact for a wiseguy looking to unload goods he had nabbed in a truck hijacking, or a warehouse break-in. Kaplan soon branched out. He fenced a load of flash cubes for cameras—and was caught.

As a first time offender, Kaplan sought and received leniency from Judge Jack Weinstein, who had just been appointed to the federal bench by President Lyndon Johnson. Kaplan's sentence was probation, avoiding prison. His next arrest was for fencing stolen hair dryers, a case that was dismissed. "Kaplan hardly seemed like he had the makings of a menace to society. He was fencing two-bit items. But he was insinuating himself in the culture of organized crime in Brooklyn. He was learning how to move all kinds of product. In a certain sense wiseguys were just businessmen. They just didn't pay taxes, or keep accurate books. Deals were done in cash—wads of cash. Most *mafiosi* struggled like any other small-time operator running a newsstand or pet store. But a talented few made fortunes. A smart wiseguy like Kaplan understood profit margins, the importance of diversification, and how to beat the competition by associating with mob muscle."

Five years after his first conviction, Kaplan again appeared in federal court before Judge Weinstein, charged with possessing a truckload of stolen pants. Before sentencing in December 1972, Kaplan wrote a letter to Weinstein. The trend in the country at the time was toward ever more severe sentences. Nonviolent drug offenders received particularly lengthy sentences. Weinstein earned a national reputation when he refused to enforce them and then recused himself from such cases. In Kaplan's situation, with two federal convictions, a significant prison term was certain, despite Weinstein's reputation for leniency. "This arrest taught me a lesson," Kaplan wrote to Weinstein. "I started spending all my nights at home. I went to work and became successful at my marriage, and I'm home every night at 7 o'clock, and I spend all my spare time with my family." Kaplan claimed he had given up betting on horses and overcome his gambling addiction. He had developed a protective love for his mother, wife, and young daughter—and he had become fearful he would lose them due to his criminal tendencies. Kaplan told Judge Weinstein he had taken a straight job selling hosiery, earning $100 a week, a substantial sum at the time for a high school graduate with a criminal record. "I think I have a good future in this business, your honor," Kaplan wrote. "I'm not doing anything criminal."

Weinstein was unimpressed and sentenced Kaplan to four years. But Weinstein did grant Kaplan two months to continue working during the Christmas rush in order to provide for his family. When he reported to serve his sentence, Kaplan was sent to Lewisburg Penitentiary, a federal institution in Pennsylvania. The number of wiseguys housed there was so high that G Block was nicknamed "Mafia Row." Two days into his four-year term, chastened by his predicament as most convicts are when they face the reality of years behind bars, Kaplan wrote to Weinstein to plead for a reduction in sentence. Kaplan wrote that his father-in-law, a veteran NYPD police officer, had passed away. Kaplan's mother was mortified and heartbroken by her son's behavior. His wife and twelve-year-old daughter were suffering terribly. During the two-month grace period Weinstein had granted, Kaplan wrote, "I finally realized that with the proper attitude and lots of hard work it is just as easy to sell legitimate merchandise as stolen. Also a lot more morally and socially rewarding." Kaplan said he had never been involved in violent crime, or any violent acts, in deed or in word. He detested violence, Kaplan said, "and all it stands for." Kaplan concluded: "I promise you that the name of Burton Kaplan will never again come before you or the court or any court again in regard to anything that is against the law."

The wheedling letter succeeded, to a limited extent. The judge did not reduce Kaplan's sentence. But Weinstein did write to the Bureau of Prisons recommending that the promising young Brooklyn hosiery salesman with a checkered present be considered for parole at the earliest possible moment. On January 16, 1974, less than a year after he entered Lewisburg, Kaplan was released from custody.

For thirteen years, Kaplan managed to keep his promise to Weinstein to quit gambling. His promise to stay away from organized crime and violence didn't fare as well. Upon his return to Brooklyn, Kaplan went to work as an air conditioner installer for a company called Ciro Sales. As a contractor Kaplan owned his own van. Shortly after he started, Kaplan met a sixteen-year-old kid named Tommy Galpine, a stockman in the warehouse. Kaplan slipped him extra money to make sure his runs went smoothly. Galpine quickly became Kaplan's errand boy. He did chores around Kaplan's house, drove his mother to the doctor, sent messages—whatever Kaplan needed done.

In 1975, Kaplan stumbled into the clothing business. A friend from prison in Lewisburg was released and Kaplan took him to another friend's flea market warehouse to get him cheap street clothes. The friend with the flea market showed Kaplan a polyester leisure suit and asked how much he thought it was worth. Kaplan asked if the suit was legitimate or "swag"—stolen. Stolen, the man said. "Saying the leisure suit was stolen increased its value," Oldham noted. "If people were buying stolen property they thought they were getting a steal literally—a great price for a great product. Closeout or remainder goods didn't have the aura of bargain that *stolen* goods radiated. Kaplan guessed twenty bucks. The guy said Kaplan could have three thousand of them for twelve dollars each but he had to get them out of the warehouse within twenty-four hours. Kaplan saw an opportunity. He made a few calls and found a man in Connecticut with a discount clothing store who would take the suits. Kaplan needed to transport the suits first thing the next day. At two-thirty in the morning his telephone rang. A snowstorm had descended on the Northeast. The man in Connecticut said the roof of his warehouse had collapsed under the weight of the snow. He couldn't take the suits."

Forced to improvise, Kaplan rented an empty fruit store on New Utrecht Avenue in Brooklyn and constructed makeshift racks from plumbing piping. He and Tommy Galpine loaded a truck the next morning and took the suits there and started making calls. Kaplan told his friends he had a truckload of stolen leisure suits. By one o'clock that day he had sold a thousand for twenty dollars each. In three days, he sold three thousand stolen leisure suits. "But the joke was the suits weren't stolen. They'd been bought in a factory closeout sale legitimately. Kaplan marketed them as swag to spike sales and made nearly twenty-five thousand dollars in three days."

By chance, Kaplan was now in the clothing distribution business. Soon he was a successful and rapidly expanding dealer. His warehouse at 8509 Bay 16th Street in Bensonhurst became a destination for people who wanted to buy discount designer jeans and sweat suits wholesale—particularly Kaplan's friends in the mafia. It was a warehouse but also operated as a store, with the industrial appearance and whiff of swag creating the sense that bargains could be had. He sold Calvin Klein, Gloria Vanderbilt, Disco, the leading designer brands at the time. He expanded to a large warehouse on Richmond Avenue on Staten Island and started selling to huge chains like Macy's, Kmart, Nordstrom's, and discount chains across the country. He was prospering as never before, with the potential to live the life of a prosperous merchant running a multimillion-dollar operation.

But the siren call of crime was a constant for Kaplan, the devilish voice inside his head luring him toward easy cash and catastrophe. He started dealing in knockoff clothes. Imitation designer wear was manufactured in China to the specifications of Kaplan's legitimate partners, a fake label was stitched on, and the products were shipped to stores across America and into the hands of customers thinking they were buying authentic Champion and Jordache and Sergio Valente clothes. "From there the slope got slippery. The attractions of Kaplan's kind of criminal life aren't hard to see. The big payday is always just around the corner. There is the game of it. The whispering and plotting. Strategic and logistical obstacles have to be overcome, all the while playing cat-and-mouse with law enforcement. High-level criminality is three-dimensional chess combined with Russian roulette. For a gambler like Kaplan it was the best game in town."

During these years, Kaplan's ties to the Luchese crime family were renewed. Through Christy Tick Furnari at the 19th Hole Kaplan was introduced to a rising star in his mid-thirties named Anthony Gaspipe Casso. The two hit it off. They started dealing marijuana together. Casso would supply the pot and Kaplan would distribute it. The relationship played to each of their strengths. Casso was connected to a variety of suppliers of drugs. Kaplan, in turn, was a gifted wholesaler. Wiseguys all over knew Downtown Burt could move anything.

Over the years, the fine line between legal and illegal became a complete blur to Kaplan. He chased deals wherever they were to be found, no matter how improbable they sounded. By chance, he became friendly with the nephew of an African politician. Mamadou Kwaitu's uncle was a powerful official in the government of Upper Volta. The tiny landlocked nation now known as Burkina Faso, neighbored by Mali, Ghana, and the Ivory Coast, was plagued by coups and desperately poor. But there were lucrative gold and diamond mines upland, containing the promise of fabulous wealth. Mamadou Kwaitu had the concession to sell the diamonds from a mine called Bangi in central Africa. He was willing to sell them to Kaplan at a deeply discounted rate, if Kaplan could find a way to fence the dodgy diamonds himself.

"Kaplan went to Christy Tick, who put him in touch with a wiseguy who was in the diamond market on Canal Street—the former stomping ground of Louis Eppolito's grandfather, Diamond Louie Eppolito. The wiseguy introduced Kaplan to a Hasidic guy named Joe Banda who was a member of the Diamond Dealers Club. Kaplan and Banda and Mamadou formed a partnership with a three-way split. The diamonds weren't 'stolen' in the usual sense. Africa was being raped by foreign companies, and it was being raped by its own government. Kaplan was just getting in on the action."

Along the way, always looking for any angle or opportunity no matter how unlikely, Kaplan came to believe he could make money selling hair cream specifically created for the African market. Kaplan found a factory in Brooklyn and hired a chemist named Kenneth Gibbs to manufacture the hair cream. But when the product was shipped to Africa, it was discovered that the chemical composition was unstable. The cream had not been homogenized and turned brown and rotted en route. The product was unsalable. "The failed hair cream chemist then hatched another equally lame scheme. If they couldn't make African hair cream, Kenneth Gibbs reasoned, why not recoup their losses by making Quaaludes? He would reconfigure the equipment in the factory Kaplan had rented. They could make their money back. He was eager to please Kaplan—and not get whacked for his stupidity."

Kaplan was already dealing Quaaludes, along with his growing marijuana business, so it made sense to manufacture the drug himself. From a personal point of view, Kaplan had no interest in drugs, and the only time he tried an illicit drug was one toke on a joint while in prison. But Quaaludes could be big money. The drug, made from the sedative methaqualone, had the effect of a barbituate, simultaneously inducing relaxation and euphoria. Gibbs began to attempt to make the chemical formula—$C_{16}H_{14}N_2O$. Before he succeeded, Kaplan and his co-conspirators were arrested. Gibbs cooperated with the DEA. At Kaplan's trial,

Gibbs took the stand and testified against Kaplan. In 1981 Kaplan was convicted on federal drug charges of conspiracy to manufacture Quaaludes—without making or selling a single tablet. It was Kaplan's first experience of the wages and risks of betrayal.

Allenwood Federal Prison Camp in the foothills of Pennsylvania's northern Allegheny Mountains was a minimum-security facility. At the time it had a well-earned reputation as a "country club" jail. The facility had no fences, there were tennis and basketball courts, and conjugal visits with spouses were permitted. Kaplan's stretch there turned out to be highly educational.

"If the streets of Brooklyn were the prep school of hard knocks for a life in crime, and the 19th Hole was the mafia's Yale, then Allenwood was the Harvard Business School for postgraduate studies leading to a master's degree in criminality. Kaplan spent his days with an array of wiseguys and associates who formed a fine faculty. They had different tenures—three years for fraud, eight for heroin, eighteen months for assault. Little Al D'Arco and Anthony DiLapi from the Lucheses were serving time in Allenwood. Big Sal Miciotta from the Colombos was in for hijacking a trailerload of cigarettes. Inmates put on weight in Allenwood. They were eating salami and cheese. They had wine. On New Year's Eve scotch was smuggled in."

Kaplan belonged to the "smart" set in Allenwood. There were marathon pinochle games involving the other "businessmen" doing time, and the mobsters and tough guys they associated with for protection. Kaplan became particularly good friends with an organized crime figure named Frank Santora Jr. Strongly built, with a broad face and broad shoulders, Santora was an independent operator loosely affiliated with the Bonannos. Known to be violent, if required or desired, he had been caught extorting money from Frederick Lundy, the owner of a Sheepshead Bay seafood restaurant called Lundy's, a place as much a part of Brooklyn history as the Dodgers and the mafia. Kaplan and Santora slept three beds away from each other in the same dormitory. They saw each other four or five times a day and then were assigned to work in Allenwood's powerhouse together.

"Turned out they lived in the same neighborhood in Brooklyn, only six blocks apart. They had a lot in common, including old mob acquaintances. Kaplan, they discovered, was friendly with Santora's cousin, Jimmy the Clam Eppolito, the Gambino captain murdered with his son because of the scandal they caused with a scam preying on the International Year of the Child. Jimmy the Clam was Santora's cousin, as well as

Detective Louis Eppolito's uncle. Santora told Kaplan how the Gambinos had approached him after they murdered Jimmy the Clam Eppolito and his son Jim-Jim. The Gambinos asked if he was going to retaliate and Santora said he wouldn't. This was the same story Louis Eppolito told in *Mafia Cop*—only as a fantasy starring himself as the cop summoned to a secret midnight meeting with Big Paul Castellano. Santora was big and charismatic. Kaplan was drawn to men prone to violence, provided it was aimed at others."

Kaplan was released from Allenwood in 1983. He returned home determined once again to stay on the straight and narrow. While he was serving time, his clothing business had been being managed by Tommy Irish Carew—or mismanaged. There was a lock on the door of All City Distributors when Kaplan returned to his warehouse. Eviction proceedings were under way. Kaplan was justly furious. Tommy Galpine, Kaplan's young assistant, had developed a serious cocaine problem without Kaplan around to employ him. Galpine was like a son to Kaplan, even though he had led the kid into a life of crime.

Kaplan got Galpine back on track but Downtown Burt's resolve to stay away from crime again didn't last long. Kaplan needed money fast so he went after fast money. The same year he was released, Kaplan was arrested for heroin trafficking. Kaplan was outraged. He was innocent, he insisted to Burstein, who believed him. Burstein arranged for Kaplan to talk to prosecutors and explain in detail why he shouldn't be charged. A "limited proffer" was the name of the procedure. Kaplan insisted he would not implicate anyone else. He went on record and explained to prosecutors and investigators precisely how he was not involved in the conspiracy. No rat, he would only talk about his own acts, not anyone else who might be involved. It worked. The heroin charges were dropped.

In 1984 Frank Santora Jr. was released from Allenwood. Kaplan's warehouse in Brooklyn had become a kind of reunion hall for Allenwood wiseguys newly out of prison, and so Santora went there to see Kaplan, to get clothes, and to establish a connection to the outside. Santora approached Kaplan with a proposition: He could provide him help with law enforcement issues that might arise. Santora said he had a cousin who was a detective in the New York Police Department and who was willing to offer his services to Kaplan for hire, if and when the need arose. Kaplan learned Santora's cousin had a partner who was also an NYPD detective. The partner had a "prestigious" job in the NYPD. The two had access to all kinds of intelligence in police files. For the right price, Santora said, they would sell Kaplan information on law enforcement activities. Santora also said "the cops" were willing to do any "physical" work Kaplan wanted done—an underworld euphemism for violence.

"At first, Kaplan turned Santora down. He had quit gambling. He was supposedly legitimate. Kaplan didn't want to deal with cops. There were too many risks to getting involved with police officers. There was too much of a chance for the cop connection to come back in the form of an indictment—or death. Cops took an oath to uphold the law. If they turned their back on that oath, what was to stop them from turning their back on the mobsters they worked for?

"Corruption was a serious problem in precincts like the Six-Two and Six-Three. There were honest cops but there were too many cops who would take money to look the other way. Human weakness was what the mob preyed upon so they understood exactly why cops were like that. But cops who would kill for money? If Santora's cousin and his partner were capable of that they were capable of turning on him too."

According to the protocol of the mafia, Kaplan was "with" Christy Tick. The tag meant his primary association and loyalty lay with the Luchese consigliere. But with the Commission Case pending and Furnari facing the near certainty that he would be spending the rest of his life in jail, Furnari had to decide how to distribute his assets. Not only could Kaplan move large quantities of drugs—"weight," in the language of the street—but he was perhaps the single best fence of stolen property in the city or the country. An associate like Kaplan was an asset of immeasurable value.

As Furnari dealt with business matters before going to prison, appointing Vic Amuso and Gaspipe Casso to run the family, Kaplan was "given" to a younger Luchese on the rise. Kaplan was offended. He was fifty-two years old, and his new patron too young, unpolished, and unaccomplished for him. Kaplan wanted and needed to "belong" to a much more ambitious and sophisticated member of the Lucheses. He agitated for a new arrangement and was soon rewarded with a different assignment. Kaplan was given to Gaspipe Casso. The two had known each other for years. Both were regulars at the 19th Hole social club. Over the years, they had moved tons of marijuana together. The relationship they had forged was nothing compared to the deep bonds the two would build over the years ahead. Being "with" Casso offered the chance for great rewards for Kaplan, but the opportunity came with big risks.

"The first thing Kaplan did was take out a life insurance policy. In the mafia, it was known that the best way to ensure you stayed alive was to borrow money from the people most likely to kill you. If you owed enough money you became too expensive to kill. There was a running joke among wiseguys about borrowing four hundred grand from the boss as a way to make sure the boss knew your name. Kaplan took the protection provided by debt to another level. He tripled the amount of insurance most wiseguys contented themselves with. As soon as he was 'with' Casso he borrowed $1.2 million from him. Even for a wealthy mobster like Casso, more than a million bucks was serious money. Casso wasn't going to kill Kaplan with that kind of money on the line. He wasn't going to let anyone else near Kaplan, either. Casso wasn't going to let a hair on Kaplan's rapidly balding head get mussed."

The business opportunity Kaplan borrowed heavily from Casso for was a real estate venture in Scottsdale, Arizona. Kaplan formed a corporation to develop more than eight hundred acres he had acquired for $15 million, with Casso's money serving as a down payment. Kaplan bought the property with his close friend and partner, a Hong Kong businessman who had extensive dealings with Kaplan in the clothing industry. As the first outsider to represent a Chinese province under communist rule, the businessman was able to provide Kaplan access to cheap labor and materials for his clothing business. Hubei, a south-central province with a population of 60 million and the Yangtze flowing through it, was the heartland of China and an early player in the economic boom about to transform the nation. Kaplan, the canny Brooklyn gangster, was in the vanguard. The businessman and Kaplan were equal partners, with Casso the secret partner holding half of Kaplan's interest.

"Land values in Arizona tanked. But Burt and the businessman kept up payments on the mortgage for years. Kaplan had Joe Banda pledge jewels to keep the deal afloat by refinancing the bank loans. Kaplan lost four million on the deal. Along the way, he borrowed incessantly from Casso. He appeared to be digging himself a deeper and deeper hole, but on the upside Kaplan was making himself more and more valuable to Casso alive than dead. During these years, Casso and Amuso were murdering people wholesale. No one was safe with them, but Kaplan was never harmed."

In turn Kaplan was always looking for ways to enrich Casso, or at least make Casso believe he might make massive amounts of money through Kaplan. One scheme with which Kaplan whetted Casso's insatiable appetite for effortless money was a marriage of the legitimate, illegitimate, and the absurd. After the Arizona deal went bad, Kaplan told Casso he had found a way to recoup his losses. The Chinese government was going to build a "free trade zone" on the outskirts of Scottsdale near the Phoenix Airport, Kaplan said. Eighty-seven factories were going to be constructed for the manufacture of goods with workers imported from China.

"The deal was fantastical. Kaplan had Casso believing that he was meeting with the governor of Arizona all the time. Chinese officials were involved, Casso thought. All the money was being put up by the People's Republic of China. Kaplan was being allowed to take the ride because of the huge amount of money he had lost on the earlier real estate deal. Casso had no legal role in the company, but he would participate in the guaranteed windfall profits. Still obliged to repay every penny he borrowed, Kaplan was going to make Casso untold sums of money. That was the trifecta for Kaplan—insurance piled on insurance piled on insurance, Kaplan had more hedges than the Hamptons."

If Kaplan was Casso's window on the world of big business, no matter how farfetched the scheme, Casso was Kaplan's window on the world of big-time crime. Their destinies tied, they started to have dinner two or three times a week and talked to each other daily. Making money was the primary subject of conversation. Before long, Casso came to Kaplan with a proposal for an enormous score. Casso said he had found a man who worked for a company that acted as a depository for Treasury bills, or "T-bills," as they were known. T-bills were interest-paying certificates of debt issued by the federal government and marked as payable to bearer. Identification had to be provided to cash the bills but simple possession was considered legal proof of ownership, making them extraordinarily liquid. (This was before the shift to electronic handling of such securities.) Casso's contact had observed that the depository company took inventory of its stock of T-bills according to a routine. He said that there was an interval of time between scheduled inventories when he could steal the T-bills unnoticed. "The bills wouldn't be reported until they took inventory again. The plan was to cash the bills in the interim. They would be stolen but they wouldn't be reported as stolen. In other words, they wouldn't be 'hot.' If a security was hot its value plummeted."

The amount of money involved could run to millions, if Kaplan could find a method of turning the financial instruments into money before the depository noticed the T-bills were missing. Kaplan called Joe Banda and asked to meet with him. Kaplan explained the problem and opportunity and suggested that he give Banda the serial numbers and photocopies of a couple of the bonds. Banda lived in the Hasidic section of Williamsburg in Brooklyn, a densely populated area where many observant Jews dress in traditional garb. Within a few days Banda came to Kaplan and said he had found a jeweler in his neighborhood who thought he would be able to cash a stolen T-bill. The jeweler had a contact who would take the stolen bill and sell it overseas.

In the Hasidic community there was a paperless but highly structured method of transferring money similar to the "hawala" remittance system used in South Asia for centuries. The funds were transferred by a trusted third party so there were no wire records or other evidence showing large sums had been moved. Payment to the third party came in the form of percentage points of the sum transferred. Once the T-bill was sold in London, a phone call would be made to New York and the proceeds would be paid out locally, less the fee charged. There would be no way of tracing the money back to the jeweler, or Banda, or Kaplan, or Casso and the Lucheses. In theory. Kaplan wanted to test the system before he committed to attempting a large score. Kaplan told Banda he would get one T-bill worth half a million dollars and see if the method worked. Banda and the jeweler and his third party would take half the proceeds. Kaplan and Casso would get the other half—if the scam came off.

Casso received two stolen bonds from his contact in the depository. He wanted to do the test run with both $500,000 T-bills. Kaplan only wanted to use one. Determined to make sure the stolen T-bill wouldn't be stolen again, Kaplan demanded a meeting with Banda's contact. To avoid the possibility that they would be able to identify each other if the deal went wrong and law enforcement caught either of them, Banda arranged for the two men to meet in a parked car. Banda's jeweler contact sat in the front seat, looking straight ahead. Kaplan got in the backseat of the car. Kaplan couldn't tell for sure, but it appeared the man was dressed traditionally. Kaplan told the man that he wanted to know his name, address, and where he worked before he handed over the T-bill. Kaplan said he didn't want to know it himself. The man was to tell Banda, who would hold the information for Kaplan should the need arise to find the jeweler. The jeweler wrote down his name and address and place of employment. He gave his identity to Banda. Kaplan handed the man the envelope containing the $500,000 T-bill marked "pay to bearer." The man said he was going to travel overseas, to London, to cash the instrument with his banker contact.

Less than a week later, Banda gave Kaplan $130,000 in cash, and a few days later he added another $120,000. Elated, Kaplan and Casso were now ready to make an astonishing sum of money. They intended to steal $10 million worth of T-bills and cash them all at once. "A chance like that had to be hit once and for all the marbles. It would be one of the biggest heists in history. Kaplan and Casso were world-class scammers. They were within inches of the kind of money that would change their lives. But life in the mob was more complicated than that. No matter how cunning Kaplan and Casso were, no matter how sophisticated and careful, they were sailing in a ship of fools. Their great T-bill scam was undone by a wiseguy named Leo 'the Zip' Giammona, a made Luchese."

Before doing the deal with Banda's man, Casso had received two stolen bonds. Kaplan had managed to cash one. The other Casso gave to Leo the Zip, who was going to try his own method of cashing the T-bill. After Kaplan succeeded Casso told the Zip not to do anything with the T-bill. But it emerged that Giammona had already attempted to cash the T-bill, giving it to a guy he knew who worked in a bank on Avenue U in Brooklyn. The man had tried to cash the instrument, a clumsy, oafish endeavor. An investigation was under way. The element of surprise was now gone. The bonds were now "hot."

Leo the Zip Giammona was murdered driving northbound on West 3rd Street in Brooklyn one June morning by two hoods. The method of execution came straight out of the pages of pulp fiction. The hit men filled the back of a blue 1977 Chevrolet Malibu station wagon with flowers. One of the hoods drove. The other hid under the flowers. When the station wagon pulled alongside Giammona's Toyota, one of the hit men rose from the flower bed with a shotgun and let five rounds of buckshot fly, blasting through Giammona's window, killing him instantly. "The motive was dressed up as a heroin deal gone bad. Giammona was a made guy in the Lucheses, with connections in the Gambinos through his wife's family, so Casso needed to have a good reason to sanction the hit. Leo the Zip owned a place called Café Sicilia in Bensonhurst, a front for his involvement in a ring importing large amounts of heroin from Italy. When Giammona got in a dispute over the heroin, Casso took the opportunity to get revenge."

As the T-bill scam unraveled, Joe Banda came to Kaplan and said that the banker in London was being questioned by Interpol. Kaplan was upset. Banda told Kaplan that the deal had become more complicated than they anticipated. Banda's jeweler connection was supposed to take the T-bill to London himself. But he hadn't. The first jeweler had approached another jeweler and had him take the T-bill to London. The first jeweler didn't tell Banda about the change in plans. Banda learned about it when the first jeweler told him that the banker in London had not been paid the $100,000 promised to him. It seemed the second jeweler had pocketed the money. The banker had no reason to protect the first jeweler, or the second jeweler. The London banker had called the second jeweler and told him that Interpol was investigating the T-bill. The banker was talking to Interpol, Banda said. Banda believed there was a good chance the second jeweler would cooperate as well.

"Kaplan decided to put out a contract on the second jeweler. Kaplan reasoned he would be certain to snitch on the first jeweler, who would snitch on Joe Banda. From Banda the trail would lead to Kaplan and Kaplan was most emphatically not going to return to prison. Kaplan didn't tell Banda he was going to kill the second jeweler. He asked Banda to get the name, home address, and work address for the second jeweler. He also wanted to know the kind of car he drove and the license plate number. Kaplan said he wanted to put a scare into the guy—shake him up and let him know that it was a bad idea to talk to the authorities. If they grabbed the man, Kaplan said, he would know he could be grabbed—or killed."

Within days, Banda gave Kaplan the information. Kaplan called Frank Santora Jr. and told him he needed some "work" done. He asked if Santora would be willing to murder for hire.

"Without a doubt," Santora said. "I'll talk it over with my cousin. There will be no problem. It can be handled."

Santora came back shortly thereafter and said he had talked to his cousin and they were agreed to take the contract—Santora, his cousin, and his cousin's partner.

"Would you take twenty-five thousand dollars for this?" Kaplan asked. He was in financial difficulty at the time so he asked if he could spread the payment out. "I could pay it ten, ten, and five, every week for three weeks."

"Don't worry about it," Santora told Kaplan. "That's fair."

Kaplan gave Santora the particulars regarding the second jeweler. His name was Israel Greenwald. He lived in suburban New Jersey with his wife and two young daughters. Kaplan left for a business trip to Arizona to survey his troubled real estate investment in Scottsdale. Santora and Detectives Caracappa and Eppolito took Greenwald's address and drove to New Jersey to find his residence. "Israel Greenwald already knew he was in trouble. He was a diamond dealer who traveled frequently. He was under investigation by C-3, the FBI squad specializing in the theft of negotiable securities—which was a big business for criminals at the time. The FBI was looking at thefts from three different financial institutions in New York City. When Greenwald cashed the T-bill in London a source for the IRS contacted them and they in turn contacted C-3. Kaplan's fear was well founded, but not for the reasons he suspected. His free-floating anxiety was his early warning system. Greenwald was already a marked man from both sides."

Greenwald had been stopped at customs when he flew back to New York from London after cashing the T-bill. He was subjected to a secondary search. He had no cash on him; the money had already been transferred. Greenwald was told that he was under investigation for trading in stolen securities. The FBI wanted Greenwald to cooperate. He said he wanted to talk to his attorney. The next day he agreed to talk. He told the FBI that he had been given the T-bill by the first jeweler. This jeweler had told Greenwald that the T-bill belonged to a man who was trying to hide his assets from his wife during contentious divorce proceedings. Greenwald believed that the $500,000 was not stolen, and he was being paid to help squirrel money away.

"A lie to Greenwald had undone the scam. The first jeweler's story meant that Greenwald genuinely didn't know he was fencing a stolen T-bill—so why should he pay his banker in London one hundred grand for cashing a legit T-bill?"

No charges were laid against either jeweler. As fears among the conspirators rose about the T-bill investigation, the first jeweler came to Greenwald and warned him not to talk to the police. He said the deal was "a mafia sort of thing." Greenwald passed along to the FBI what he had heard. The FBI asked him to tape-record a conversation with the first jeweler. Following FBI instructions, Greenwald went to see him that day. Greenwald was carrying a tape recorder in his coat pocket. In the middle of their conversation the recording stopped. The first jeweler patted Greenwald's chest and found the tape recorder. "At least that was what Greenwald told the FBI. By now, it was unclear who to believe in the whole ordeal. The FBI didn't have a case but they knew something was going on."

On a winter morning in February 1986 Israel Greenwald rose early, dressed, and kissed his schoolteacher wife goodbye. Thirty-four years old, a devoted father, Greenwald walked his daughter Michal to her bus. As he left, he stopped and turned back for a final kiss. It was the last time his family would see him. Later that morning Greenwald was driving along the New York State Thruway when he was pulled over by an unmarked police car with flashing lights. Detectives Caracappa and Eppolito flashed Greenwald their detective shields and said that he was wanted in a hit-and-run investigation in the city. Greenwald was instructed to get out of his vehicle. They told Greenwald he had to accompany them to a lineup for identification purposes. If Greenwald was not picked in the lineup he would be returned to his car. Greenwald complied. A third man was with the two NYPD detectives—Frank Santora Jr. He drove Greenwald's car. Detectives Caracappa and Eppolito placed Greenwald in their unmarked police car.

When Kaplan returned from Arizona, he got a call from Santora, who said he wanted to come see Kaplan. Santora went to Kaplan's house, only a few blocks from his own place in Bensonhurst. Santora described what he and Detectives Caracappa and Eppolito had done with Greenwald after they kidnapped him on the New York State Thruway. He told Kaplan that they had taken the jeweler to an automobile repair shop on Nostrand Avenue in Brooklyn owned by a friend of Santora's. Greenwald was put inside a small parking shed with enough space to fit a single car. Santora told Kaplan he shot Greenwald. Santora said he had disposed of the body himself. Santora told Kaplan he didn't tell the two other guys, his cop cousin and his detective partner, where he hid the body.

"'Knowing where the bodies are buried' is one of the clichés the mafia has given to the English language, but in fact it was often true in the mob. If you killed a man you didn't want other people to know where the body was buried. When a wiseguy flipped the first thing he would do was say where the dead men could be found. Santora was giving Kaplan the comfort of knowing that no one else knew where Greenwald had been left—so no one else could rat them out. Santora told Kaplan that he dumped the jeweler's car in the long-term parking lot at JFK.

"Kaplan paid Santora thirty thousand for the job—the agreed amount with a five grand bonus. Santora pocketed the extra five grand for himself. When Greenwald failed to turn up at home, word of his disappearance reached Joe Banda. The Jewish community in Williamsburg in Brooklyn was insular and the sudden vanishing of a jewelry dealer like Greenwald was a matter of intense speculation. Banda contacted Kaplan and asked if he knew what had happened. Kaplan wasn't going to tell Banda that he'd just had Greenwald killed. Kaplan said Greenwald must have 'gone on a long vacation.' Kaplan wanted Banda to think Greenwald was living on a beach in Bahia, Brazil, or in Capetown, South Africa."

The FBI ran the usual searches—airports, train stations, the Port Authority bus terminal. An experienced world traveler, Greenwald had two passports—American and Liberian. The FBI looked for him in Tel Aviv and Switzerland. There was no sign of his existence, or clues of his whereabouts. "Finally, his car turned up in the long-term parking lot of JFK. That parking lot was a favorite dumping place for the mob. JFK was a good spot to leave a car. If a person was going to vanish, they would catch an airplane out of the country. Israel Greenwald was listed as a missing person. Presumed murdered was the more accurate description. But with no body the case couldn't be opened or closed. Greenwald could have run out on his wife and two young daughters but that seemed highly improbable. The torment for a family who knew but never really knew the fate of a loved one was dreadful. For Caracappa and Eppolito, a relationship forged in murder created a profound bond. The two NYPD detectives now belonged to each other, in the way the mafia demanded its members kill in order to be 'made.' They were blood brothers. Brothers in blood."

TO BREATHE TOGETHER

By 1986, Kaplan had not been introduced to the two cops who worked for Santora but he had seen them on the streets and in social situations. Santora took Kaplan aside at a function at the Pisa, a dinner club frequented by mobsters and cops. Caracappa and Eppolito were sitting together. Santora pointed them out. Kaplan and the two cops exchanged nods. On another occasion Kaplan went to the Vegas Diner, a burger-and-fries joint in Bensonhurst. Caracappa and Eppolito were eating together in the first booth. They made eye contact, in mutual recognition, and then they looked away. "Secrecy was of paramount importance. The three of them were outsiders to the world of the mafia, no matter how closely connected they were. They had formed their own private mafia. The root of the word 'conspiracy' is to 'breathe together.' They didn't have to talk to each other—their conspiracy was unspoken but understood."

For eighteen months, Santora brokered Kaplan's dealings with the cops. Information was passed from Detectives Caracappa and Eppolito to Santora, who passed it along to Kaplan and then on to Casso. The arrangement was awkward but effective, lucrative, and provided insulation for all participants. It was a thriving new criminal enterprise.

Until the afternoon of September 3, 1987. That day Santora was strolling along the avenue on Bath Beach with Luchese wiseguy Carmine Variale when a blue car pulled up, gunfire erupted, and Variale and Santora were shot dead. Variale was the intended target but the hit man sprayed both men. Casso had ordered the murder of Variale as a routine mob murder. He had no animus toward Santora, who was purely "collateral damage," in military parlance.

Immediately after the hit, Kaplan told Casso about the unintended

1

2

Official New York Police Department photographs of William Oldham on July 13, 1981, the day he became a police officer for New York City, and on the day he retired as a detective after twenty years of service, in November 2001.

3

Mafia Cop by Louis Eppolito sparked intense interest in Eppolito, proved useful in Oldham's investigation, and was quoted aloud by Assistant U.S. Attorney Robert Henoch in court proceedings.

4

A muscular Louis Eppolito on August 22, 1969, on his first day as a New York City police officer. This photo appeared on the back cover of *Mafia Cop*.

6

This photograph of Detectives Stephen Caracappa and Louis Eppolito looking relaxed and confident appeared in *Mafia Cop* with the caption, "The two Godfathers of the NYPD." It was a hint to William Oldham that the two men might be linked to organized crime.

5

Louis Eppolito as a young bodybuilder, 1967. As he described in *Mafia Cop,* his actions as a police officer often relied on physical intimidation.

7

8

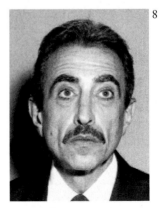

Louis Eppolito
in arrest photo,
Las Vegas, March 2005.

Stephen Caracappa
in arrest photo,
Las Vegas, March 2005.

9

Israel Greenwald was murdered over a Treasury bill scam gone bad.

Eddie Lino was murdered for ordering the hit on Gaspipe Casso. His body was found in his car off Brooklyn's Belt Parkway.

13

10

James Hydell was believed to be murdered for attempting to kill mobster Anthony "Gaspipe" Casso. His body has never been found.

Dominic Costa survived an assassination attempt in which he was shot six times in the head.

14

11

The wrong Nicky Guido was a complete innocent slaughtered in his car in a case of mistaken identity.

Anthony DiLapi was shot and killed in Los Angeles in Gaspipe Casso's 1991 murder spree.

15

12

Otto Heidel was murdered for being an FBI informant.

Alfred "Flounderhead" Visconti was murdered because he was caught plotting vengeance for the murder of Bruno Facciola.

16

17

Frank Santora Jr. was Louis Eppolito's first cousin and made the introduction between "the cops" and Burton Kaplan. He was accidentally murdered in a mob hit on Carmine Variale, another wiseguy.

18

Anthony "Gaspipe" Casso was the Luchese family boss who went on the lam before being arrested in his New Jersey hideaway. Admitting his role in thirty-six killings, he became a government informant and described his murderous activities with Caracappa and Eppolito.

19

The right Nicky Guido took part in the attempted hit on Gaspipe Casso. When he heard Casso's hit men were searching for him, he disappeared.

20

Anthony "Gaspipe" Casso, left, and Burton Kaplan, right, with their wives in happier days. The men were involved in a wide array of criminal activities and benefited from the information provided to them by Detectives Eppolito and Caracappa.

The rented garages on Nostrand Avenue in Brooklyn where the body of Israel Greenwald was dug up.

The remains of Israel Greenwald appeared as investigators carefully sifted through the earth.

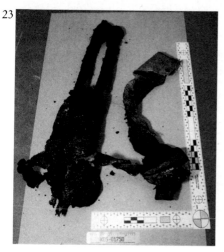

Some of the remains of Israel Greenwald.

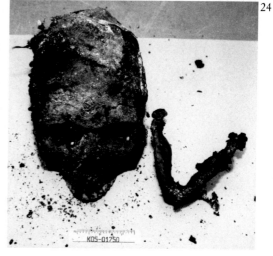

The skull and jawbone of Israel Greenwald.

Otto Heidel was murdered after he had concluded a game of paddleball.

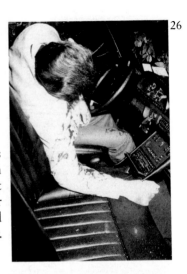

Eddie Lino was murdered on Brooklyn's Belt Parkway after "the cops" pulled him over.

Bruno Facciola was murdered and left in the trunk of his car with a canary stuffed in his mouth.

Anthony DiLapi was murdered when he fell out of favor with Luchese bosses and moved to Los Angeles.

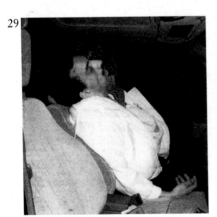

The wrong Nicky Guido was discovered murdered in his car on Christmas Day 1986.

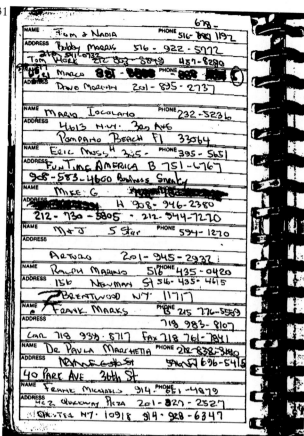

Burton Kaplan's address book, showing his entry for "Marco," his code word for Louis Eppolito and Stephen Caracappa.

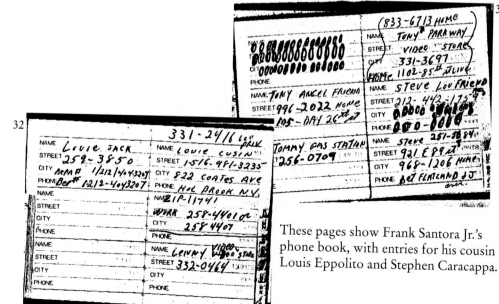

These pages show Frank Santora Jr.'s phone book, with entries for his cousin Louis Eppolito and Stephen Caracappa.

Louis Eppolito, gregarious
and talkative, protested his innocence
during the federal trial.

Stephen Caracappa did not speak
to reporters during the trial
and maintained an icy calm.

William Oldham chased
Eppolito and Caracappa
for seven years. After
serving thirty years as a
street cop, detective,
and federal investigator,
he retired in 2005.

consequence of Variale's murder. Kaplan informed Casso that Santora was their "friend"—the one who brokered the deal with "the cops."

Casso was shocked. "Geez," Casso said. "I didn't know that he was our friend. I could have stopped it."

In *Mafia Cop,* Eppolito placed Santora's murder in a footnote. In reality, the death of Frank Santora Jr. was anything but a footnote in Eppolito's life. He was overwhelmed with grief and anger. On that day, Eppolito was assigned to assist in providing security for the visit of Pope John Paul II. When he learned of Santora's death, Eppolito raced to the Six-Two precinct house in a rage. Detective Caracappa was with him. Eppolito was keening and weeping. "They finally killed the last of my family," he said.

Sergeant Joseph Piraino, acting boss of the Brooklyn Homicide Squad and formerly a Major Case detective, watched in amazement as Detectives Caracappa and Eppolito tried to find out what had happened. Eppolito had a borough-wide reputation for connections to organized crime. Santora was Eppolito's cousin. Chances were good that Eppolito would try to kill his cousin's killer himself, it seemed, or snitch to the Gambino family to get some version of vigilante justice. Caracappa physically supported Eppolito, his arms around him in consolation. Piraino knew Caracappa from Major Case. They had worked together in the OCHU. Sergeant Piraino took Caracappa aside and asked him to get Eppolito out of the precinct house. Piraino made it clear that Eppolito's behavior was inappropriate. "The scene seemed bizarre to Piraino," Oldham said. "Weeping and wailing about the death of a gangster was one thing. Trying to find out about the investigation was another. Eppolito was out of control—and out of his mind. Caracappa was trying to keep a lid on his partner."

For the NYPD and press, the deaths of Variale and Santora represented only the latest in a bewildering string of mafia murders. The mysterious murders were all "gangland-style": another Italian-American Brooklyn man gunned down on the street by assailants who disappeared and were never apprehended. William Rashbaum, then a reporter with United Press International, sought out Robert Blakey, the Notre Dame law professor who had a major role in drafting and naming RICO, to explain the rash of killing. "When the bosses get taken out, when they're facing long terms, the immunity of the higher echelons is proven to be a myth," Blakey said then. "That means the system is breaking down. One reason why you join organized crime is to avoid violence. You get in it to have disputes settled without guns. But when there is a void at the top, all of a sudden the natural environment in the underworld is very violent. The shootings are a sign that law enforcement is working," the professor added.

Santora's death should have meant the death of the conspiracy. It was a chance for the two detectives to take their money and fade away. Kaplan knew them by sight, and he knew Eppolito was Santora's cousin and worked in the Six-Three. Otherwise they were in the clear. Caracappa could have walked and no one would ever know about Greenwald, Hydell, Guido. They failed to take the chance to withdraw from their conspiracy. Caracappa and Eppolito wanted the money. Caracappa was on his fourth marriage. Eppolito was married, with young children, and a girlfriend on the side. Existing on a detective's salary was an unattractive prospect, once the pair had grown used to the extra dollars every month. They were getting away with it. There was no sign of trouble. Caracappa and Eppolito must have enjoyed the rush of knowing they were playing the NYPD for fools. Why stop when the money was so easy? Greed is a powerful motivator.

Within a month of Santora's murder, his widow went to see Kaplan at his place of business. Kaplan knew her from her visits to Allenwood, when she'd come with the couple's young daughter Tammy, and from Brooklyn when she had carried messages for Kaplan to Santora. Now she asked if Kaplan would be willing to meet with her late husband's cousin. He wanted to talk. Kaplan agreed and a plan was made. Kaplan went to the Santora residence. Detective Louis Eppolito was waiting for him in the dining room. Mrs. Santora excused herself and went into the next room so the men could talk privately. Kaplan sat at the table.

"I'm pretty sure you know who I am," Eppolito said.

"Yes, I know who you are," Kaplan said. "I've seen you on a few occasions. You're Frankie's cousin."

Eppolito asked Kaplan if he had any desire to continue the business they were doing together. Kaplan understood Eppolito to be proposing that they deal directly with each other, now that Santora was dead.

"I think we could make this simple," Eppolito said. "We could make this a business arrangement. You could put me and my partner on a pad for four thousand a month. We'll give you everything that we get on every family. Any bit of information we get about informants, ongoing investigations, wiretaps, imminent arrests."

The proposal was attractive. Four thousand dollars a month was a bargain for the quality of information Caracappa and Eppolito provided. Kaplan told Eppolito he would have to talk to Casso. As he walked out of Santora's house, along the short driveway to the sidewalk, he passed a parked car. A man was sitting in the car. Kaplan recognized him from Toys 'R' Us and the Vegas Diner. The man was thin, swarthy, with a silent brooding manner. Major Case Squad Detective Stephen Caracappa was sitting in the passenger seat of the car staring directly ahead as Kaplan passed by.

Kaplan put the proposition to Gaspipe Casso.

"What do you think?" Casso asked.

"So far they've been real good to you," Kaplan said.

"I agree with that," Casso said. "Let's do it. Tell them if they want to do this, and they want to move forward, they work exclusively for us. We don't want them giving information to other guys in other families. We don't want no problems to come back to us."

In the beginning Kaplan dealt only with Eppolito. The beefy detective would come to Kaplan's warehouses in Brooklyn and Staten Island to buy clothes. The former bodybuilder had an unusual body shape and finding clothes that fit was difficult. Kaplan would swap the pants and jackets on odd-sized suits he had in store, allowing Eppolito to match his fifty-four-inch jacket size with thirty-six-inch-waistline pants. Eppolito also owned a house on Long Island. Kaplan didn't go to the house, but he often drove to nearby locations. For meetings, Kaplan and Eppolito designated rest areas and off-ramps along the Long Island Expressway, where they met to exchange money and information.

"Kaplan and Eppolito became friends. They got along well, although Eppolito complained about money. Eppolito had an incessant need for more and more cash. He had expensive tastes—even if it was bad taste. Eppolito bought giant snakes, exotic knives, a range of rare and unusual guns. It was costly to purchase the live mice and rabbits he would feed his snakes. Kaplan worried about Eppolito living beyond his means, even with the money from the pad. It was obvious that Eppolito was not the sharpest knife in the drawer. In fact Kaplan and Eppolito nearly came to blows over one of Louie's lame-brain ideas. For years, Kaplan had shielded the identity of Caracappa and Eppolito from Anthony Casso. Eppolito was at Kaplan's house once when he said he wanted to meet Casso directly. Kaplan hit the ceiling. He threw Eppolito out of his house. He refused to deal with him. Eppolito was in danger of blowing the entire deal.

"Caracappa tried to patch things up. He went to Kaplan's house to make amends and apologize for Eppolito's excesses. Caracappa took a plate of homemade cookies. The two men discovered that they were sympatico. Both were disciplined, loyal, always two or three or four steps ahead of the game. Kaplan enjoyed dealing with Caracappa rather than Eppolito. Caracappa was too smart to shop for his clothes at Kaplan's warehouses, which were under video surveillance. He knew Kaplan was moving tons of pot every month and that the DEA, NYPD, and FBI were all set up on Kaplan's places of business."

A method of communicating was developed. Kaplan was given a code name—"the Eagle"—an apt nickname, since Kaplan had many of the characteristics of a bird of prey. It was also an inside joke. Kaplan's eyesight was poor and he was constantly squinting from behind his thick glasses. From his time in Navy intelligence, Kaplan understood encryption, how to encode sensitive information. He had Caracappa's and Eppolito's phone numbers in the phone book he carried inside his briefcase, but he was cautious about how he recorded the numbers. He had good reason to be careful. When he had been arrested in the early eighties on the heroin dealing charge, his phone book had been seized and examined. By the mid-eighties, he recorded the phone numbers of Caracappa and Eppolito under the name "Marco." He had Caracappa's beeper number, along with Eppolito's home number. Kaplan also had the number of Caracappa's mother on Staten Island. If investigators looked at the phone book to see who Kaplan was associating himself with, there was no reason for them to suspect that "Marco" was in fact two NYPD detectives.

When Kaplan and Caracappa met, they followed a protocol designed to prevent detection. Caracappa's mother lived on Staten Island near the Verrazano Bridge. Her house on Kramer Street was a modest bungalow. Caracappa often spent his weekends there. If Kaplan wanted to meet "Marco" he set a time with Caracappa. At the appointed hour, Kaplan pulled up outside Caracappa's mother's house and beeped his horn. He then proceeded down Kramer Street. There was a small cemetery surrounded by a chain-link fence. The headstones were modest, the surnames Italian. The cemetery was nearly always empty. Kaplan would get out of his car and wait for Caracappa. The two men would walk and talk along the pathways between the graves. The cemetery rolled into a small rise overlooking the rowhouses and affording a view of the Verrazano Narrows. It was the place where Caracappa passed along information that led to many murders, and received money in return. The exchanges were ghoulish—the Eagle and Marco taunting the dead.

"Over time, genuine affection arose between the two men. They were both wise in the ways of wiseguys. They recognized in each other an old-school mentality. You don't snitch. You don't ask questions, and you don't tell tales. Kaplan and Caracappa were men of honor in their own minds. They treated each other with the near-courtly formality of the old mafia. They dealt with each other for years before Kaplan even learned Caracappa's last name. Both men understood there was no need for Kaplan to know it. They believed they would take their secrets to the grave."

RATS AND CANARIES

On Wednesday, March 2, 1994, hours after Kaplan's plane had touched down in San Diego, ace mafia reporter Jerry Capeci broke the Casso story in the *New York Daily News*. "The feds hope to team the 53-year-old Luchese underboss with turncoat Gambino underboss Salvatore 'Sammy Bull' Gravano as a one-two punch against indicted Genovese family boss Vincent 'Chin' Gigante," Capeci wrote. The report said that Casso had provided information on NYPD moles whom Casso dubbed "the crystal ball."

Within hours of arriving in California, Kaplan called his lawyer Judd Burstein, who told him about Capeci's latest story. Kaplan's name was not mentioned in the press but he knew Casso would have revealed his identity and role to the FBI. "It's a big problem for me," Kaplan told Burstein. "I was the go-between for Anthony and the cops. The next day, Capeci followed with a story headlined "Two City Detectives Gaspiped." "In his first session as an informant, the latest mafia boss to sign on with the federal government fingered two city detectives as long-time moles for the mob and implicated one in a hit," Capeci wrote. "Anthony 'Gaspipe' Casso, who had jealously guarded the moles' identities from even his closest cronies, was 'extremely forthcoming' during his debut songfest with the FBI, one top law enforcement official said. 'He's told us who they are,' the official said. 'Now we're going to have to prove it.'"

Kaplan panicked. Burstein tried to reason with him, saying Kaplan hadn't been charged with any crimes and he had no indication that any charges were forthcoming. Burstein attempted to persuade Kaplan to stay put. Running now would ruin his chances of getting bail if he was charged, as the risk of flight would be amply demonstrated to any judge considering the question of allowing Kaplan to remain free before and during a trial—a period of time that often lasted years. "The exchange was a charade. Kaplan wasn't in Brooklyn. He was already on the lam in San Diego. Burstein had no idea his client was long gone. The idea that Kaplan could get bail if and when he was charged with the Caracappa and

Eppolito conspiracy wasn't going to change Kaplan's mind. If he was caught, Kaplan knew he was going away for life."

The day after Capeci's second story ran, Kaplan checked out of his hotel in San Diego and crossed the border into Mexico. A lifelong gambler, Kaplan didn't like the current odds. Casso had a huge amount of evidence against him. Detectives Caracappa and Eppolito were in a different position. Casso had never met them. Kaplan had kept them insulated from the Luchese underboss. "The question loomed—did Gaspipe know the names of Caracappa and Eppolito? Kaplan couldn't know for sure what Casso knew. He knew about Casso finding the copy of Eppolito's book. He knew Casso had seen the photograph of Caracappa and Eppolito in *Mafia Cop*. Once the truth begins to come out, facts keep coming. It's like a spool of thread, unraveling and unraveling."

The effect inside the broader organized crime circle was equally devastating. Within days of Casso's cooperation being reported, gangsters started to turn themselves in. "Six Gambino Bigshots Run for Cover—Into Jail!" was the headline in the *New York Post*. "The six feared they'd be hit with stiffer jail terms if they let mob turncoat Anthony 'Gaspipe' Casso take the stand against them, sources told the *Post*."

The story of Casso's cooperation disappeared from the news for three weeks. Finally, on Friday, March 25, the story exploded into the consciousness of a city supposedly inured to tales of corruption inside the NYPD. The headline was sensational. "Mob Boss: I Used Cops as Hitmen" was splashed across the front page of the *New York Post*. The article said that Casso had hired two unidentified New York City police officers to murder Gambino wiseguy Eddie Lino. "Casso told the feds he enlisted his two rogue cops to kill Lino because he believed Lino, a hitman himself, was too smart to fall into a trap that involved other gangland members," the *Post* reported. "Eddie Lino, whose sharp-nosed profile resembled comicbook detective Dick Tracy, always sat with his back to the wall. He never stopped his car for anyone. Not even people he recognized. But, Casso said, Lino would never suspect two police officers would be his executioners. He was dead wrong."

Detectives Caracappa and Eppolito were not named in the *Post*. The next day was a Saturday. The *Post* ran a story under the headline "Mob Canary Says Hitman Was Hero Detective." There was no mention of the names of the NYPD officers. "The *Post* is withholding their names pending the completion of the investigation." Lawyer Bruce Cutler, who had represented John Gotti for years, was quoted. "This 'Steam Pipe' or 'Water Pipe,' or whatever his name is, is a psychopath. Now they're going to ask people to rely on his word. If you ask me, Sammy Gravano's new friend 'Pipe,' or whatever you want to call him, got together with Gravano and made up these kinds of lies."

But now Jerry Capeci of the *Daily News* named names. "Hero Cops or Hitmen?" was the banner headline covering the front page on the March 26th issue. The full-page photograph was taken from Eppolito's book *Mafia Cop*. The picture was of Detectives Caracappa and Eppolito sitting in a squad room together grinning at the camera. The image was the same one Casso had seen while he was on the lam—the one that gave away their identity and began to unravel the conspiracy. "Reached in Las Vegas where he is pursuing an acting career, Eppolito first laughed off the charges as 'bull,'" Capeci reported. "'I haven't killed anybody,' he said. "My father was from a different family—the Gambinos. I don't know know anyone in the Luchese family. I have no idea why he would say that. I don't know anything about it. I never hurt nobody in my life. I don't know Eddie Lino—he don't ring a bell." Capeci interviewed "an Italian American detective who has known Eppolito for years." "I can't believe it," the unnamed detective said. "I'd been feeling that suspicion for years."

Oldham recalled, "Everyone in Major Case involved in OC investigations had known for weeks that Casso had flipped. No matter what I thought of Caracappa I didn't think he would hire himself out as a killer for the Lucheses. I didn't have access to what Casso was saying in La Tuna. The FBI 302s were top secret. In Major Case we knew little more than what was in the press. The squad was torn apart. Caracappa had worked with us until just a couple of years earlier. It was like his scent was still in the room. The OCHU had been abandoned, or disbanded, after he left. Winding down the unit made sense, in a way, with the victories we were winning against the mafia. But I started to wonder if the whole OCHU had been put together by Caracappa as a way to facilitate his criminal activities. He had agitated for the creation of OCHU. He effectively ran it, under the avuncular and unguarded supervision of Sergeant Jack Hart. It was a perfect setup."

Caracappa and Eppolito hired prominent defense lawyers. Through his friends in the Major Case Squad, Caracappa employed an attorney named Eddie Hayes. A former Bronx prosecutor, Hayes had been the inspiration for the defense attorney Tom Killian in Tom Wolfe's best-selling novel *The Bonfire of the Vanities*. Known as "Fast Eddie," Hayes had a taste for handmade suits and hand-fashioned shoes, and had a long list of celebrity clients. Eppolito engaged Bruce Cutler. Eppolito and Cutler had known each other for decades, through the streets and courthouses of Brooklyn.

They had also appeared on television together in 1992, on a show called *Nine Broadcast Plaza,* when Eppolito was promoting *Mafia Cop* and defending the mores of the mob.

"The two lawyers went on the offensive. Cutler demanded a lie detector test. He proclaimed his client's complete innocence. Hayes and Caracappa took the opposite tack. Caracappa told Hayes he hadn't committed any of the alleged crimes. And then the detective did what true tough guys do. He kept his mouth shut. Caracappa understood how many things could go wrong for the government in a case like his. They tell a little lie that becomes a big lie. They continue their criminal activity. If all prosecutors had was the say-so of Casso, they had a flimsy case. There was a good chance Casso would self-destruct."

Within weeks, the story of the "dirty cops" was eclipsed in the headlines by stories about other corrupt members of the NYPD. The Mollen Commission had been convening for a year, inquiring into the systematic corruption that imperiled the force. In late March the first indictments were announced. The "Morgue Boys," as the case was dubbed in the tabloids, attracted banner headlines. Three police officers in the 73rd Precinct confessed to using the morgue as the place to snort cocaine and have sex with prostitutes. Three other cops were charged with similarly shocking crimes, though they were later acquitted. The next week another police corruption story erupted into the news. The "Dirty Thirty" case involved a ring of detectives in the 30th Precinct, in Harlem, using false 911 calls as the pretext for raiding drug dealers' apartments yet again. The raids had been captured on videotape, scandalizing the city. Thirty-three officers from the "Dirty Thirty" were charged with perjury, assault, extortion, and large-scale drug trafficking.

"Detectives Caracappa and Eppolito were retired, lying low. I kept waiting to hear that 'the cops' were going to be charged. At the time I was working on the trial of the kidnappers of a seventy-year-old tuxedo magnate named Harvey Weinstein. Watching Caracappa's approach on the Donnell Porter case had taught me what not to do. In this case, egos were checked at the door. Drawing people into your investigation was the key, not pushing people away. This was true for the family of the victim, junior detectives, the tech guys who ran the phones—anyone who could help. Harvey Weinstein had been snatched by his own employees and kept naked in a twenty-foot-deep hole in Riverside Park, covered by dirt and a rock, for twelve days. It was a miracle he didn't die down there. The kidnappers had lowered a cell phone to him with a rope to have him talk to us. They threw bananas and oranges to feed him. He was living in his own filth. When we broke the case, when we saved his life, we dragged out one tough old haberdashery hombre. Weinstein was from a different generation. He wasn't going to crack under pressure. It was all over the papers. New York City loved him for it. And Major Case detectives never wanted for tuxedos again.

"During those weeks I read the headlines about Caracappa and Eppolito with more than passing interest. Weeks turned to months and there was no word of impending indictments doing the rounds in head-quarters. The case evaporated. It wasn't even a case—it was a surreal series of accusations that came and went. But Caracappa and Eppolito were in the back of the minds of hundreds of detectives who had worked organized crime over the years. The institutional memory of the department—the *invaluable* institutional memory—wasn't going to forget. Was it possible that Major Case Squad First Grade Detective Stephen Caracappa from the *über* elite Organized Crime Homicide Unit had been not just dirty but a hired killer? Detective Louis Eppolito, the cop-hating cop who wrote *Mafia Cop*, had actually been a gangster all along? It was hard to believe. It was perfectly plausible. I had to find out."

CHAPTER TEN

EAGLE ON THE LAM

The tourist destination of Ensenada, Mexico, a coastal city on the Baja Peninsula, describes itself as *La Bella Cenicienta del Pacifico,* or the Cinderella of the Pacific. Every day the city was visited by cruise ships with thousands of American passengers wandering the seaside promenade and markets. Here was the perfect hideout for an aging New York gangster on the run. For Kaplan, the sunburned senior citizens in floppy hats and shorts provided an excellent backdrop. Located only an hour and a half south of San Diego, Ensenada was ideal: remote and close, anonymous and populated, the kind of place that was so obvious law enforcement might never find him if they came looking.

Four months passed. By the summer of 1994, there was no more word from New York about indictments. Tommy Galpine, Kaplan's assistant in New York, took care of the thriving marijuana business. Stuck in the seaport city, Kaplan began to long for a life in America. A contact in Oregon told Kaplan he would rent him a furnished apartment there. Arrangements would take a little time, Kaplan's friend said. Over the July 4th weekend of 1994, Kaplan reentered the United States. Going back to live in the United States meant constructing a new identity, which required new identification. Kaplan obtained a library card and reinvented himself as "Barry Mayers." After that, one "Barry Mayers" also obtained a Costco card. Next, an American Automobile Association card was obtained. Kaplan then went to the department of motor vehicles and applied for a non-driving identification card. He didn't want or need a driver's license. There was no reason to risk going through the added burden of submitting to the process of getting a license, especially the vision test.

"Presto, from next to nothing, 'Barry Mayers' was summoned into existence. Kaplan had the ID. With an address and three photo identifications, no matter how tenuous or dubious, he was able to parlay nothing into a new life. He could get on airplanes, open a bank account, get back into business. Kaplan's Oregon photo identification as Barry Mayers was a piece of plastic with a photograph of an average-looking man in his sixties wearing oversized glasses. For decades Kaplan had sold counterfeit items—clothes, financial securities, whatever and whenever. For Kaplan, identity was just another fungible item. Kaplan could fence anything, and so he fenced himself back into society. As far as the FBI knew, Kaplan was hiding someplace in central China. If he wanted to, he had disappeared forever."

Nearly a year passed and there was still no word from New York about an indictment of Caracappa and Eppolito. Kaplan lived quietly in Oregon. Once a month he traveled to Las Vegas to gamble. He had stopped gambling for many years but with the vast sums rolling in from his pot business and the pressures of the fugitive life he had sought release in betting again. During this time he met and became involved with an attractive younger woman named Diane Pippa. On one of his trips, Kaplan asked Pippa to do him a favor. He wanted to look a name up in the phone book. Kaplan's eyesight was so poor that he needed her to get out the white pages and find the entry for him. "Louis Eppolito," he told her, spelling out the name. It was a long shot. Kaplan knew that Eppolito had moved to Nevada after he retired from the NYPD. Just before Eppolito left New York, in 1991, Eppolito had come by Kaplan's house in a big white van to say goodbye. Eppolito had said he was going to drive cross-country with his collection of snakes and his wife, Fran. Kaplan had felt extremely awkward at the time, as well as alarmed at Eppolito's foolhardy lack of caution—a gangster like Kaplan and a high-profile cop like Eppolito could easily be seen by prying eyes.

To Kaplan's surprise, Pippa found Eppolito's number in the book. He asked her to call Eppolito. Kaplan thought there was a possibility the federal government would be monitoring Eppolito's line and he didn't want his voice to be recorded on a wire. Eppolito's mother-in-law answered. She said Eppolito would be back at six-thirty that evening. Pippa called again and reached him. An arrangement was made to meet the next day at one o'clock at Smith's Food and Drug, just off the strip and around the corner from Tropicana Avenue. Kaplan waited for Eppolito near the row of slot machines inside the entrance to the supermarket. Eppolito pulled up in the parking lot and the two men made eye contact. Each got a shopping cart and went to the fruit section. They hadn't seen each other in years, and it was the first time they had talked since Casso had flipped and the story of their conspiracy leaked to the press.

"How are things going?" Kaplan asked. "You getting any heat? You getting any pressure?"

"In the beginning the press was awful," Eppolito said. "It's much better now. I hired an attorney."

"Who?"

"Bruce Cutler," Eppolito said.

"You made a good choice," Kaplan said.

"Steve hired a lawyer too. Eddie Hayes."

"I don't know him," Kaplan said.

"He's well known by the NYPD," Eppolito said.

When Eppolito moved to Las Vegas three years earlier, he had high hopes of finding fame and fortune. He told Kaplan he was going to live in a rented house while he built a house for himself. The price of houses in Los Angeles was prohibitively high, Eppolito explained, so he would settle in the relative proximity of Las Vegas and commute to Hollywood for auditions. Years earlier Eppolito had played a nonspeaking part in *Goodfellas*. Since then he had scraped by getting tiny roles in a series of films playing cops, mobsters, assassins, drug dealers. In Robert De Niro and Sean Penn's *State of Grace* he was credited as "Borielli's Man." In *Predator 2* Eppolito was described only as a "patrolman." In Blake Edwards's *Switch* he was "Al the Guard." With *Ruby, Mad Dog and Glory,* and Woody Allen's *Bullets Over Broadway,* Eppolito's film career put him on the sets of some of the most successful filmmakers in the country. But Eppolito never rose above the tiniest parts, little more than an extra. Now Eppolito told Kaplan what small success he had enjoyed in movies had petered out. Eppolito told Kaplan he was writing another book. Eppolito didn't say if it was fact or fiction.

Kaplan returned to Oregon. A few weeks later he came back to Las Vegas to see his girlfriend, Diane Pippa. Again, Kaplan and Eppolito set the rendezvous at Smith's Food and Drug. On this occasion, Eppolito told Kaplan that Stephen Caracappa was moving to Las Vegas. Weeks later, in November 1994, Kaplan met with the two former NYPD detectives at Smith's market. This time they went to a nearby diner for lunch. The three had sandwiches and coffee together. Kaplan was curious how Caracappa, now shopping for a house in Vegas, had coped with the pressures in New York in the time after Casso became a cooperator. The press coverage had been extensive, though the media had moved on from Caracappa and Eppolito after no action was taken by the authorities.

"Did you have a lot of problems over the publicity?" Kaplan asked.

"It was bad at first," Caracappa said. "It was hard on my mother. The only real problem I had was that my mother had to go through that."

Kaplan commiserated with Caracappa. His wife, Eleanor, had suffered for years as a result of his criminal activities.

"The worst of it is pretty much over," Caracappa said. "I've got Eddie Hayes as my lawyer."

"What about your friends in the force? How did they take the publicity?"

"Whoever was my friend stayed my friend," said Caracappa.

Caracappa told Kaplan that he had an alibi witness for the night Eddie Lino was shot and killed in November 1991. Caracappa said his wife, Monica, was friendly with a woman named Kathy Levine, who worked with Joan Rivers as an on air-personality selling goods on the QVC channel. Levine, a former high school Spanish teacher turned television shopping personality hawking everything from chintz jewelry to computer software, was the author of the books *It's Better to Laugh: Life, Good Luck, Bad Hair Days, and QVC,* and *We Should Be So Lucky: Love, Sex, Food, and Fun After Forty From the Diva of QVC.* Levine's on-air catchphrase was "Do it, try it, buy it, riot!" Caracappa told Kaplan that Levine was convinced she'd eaten dinner in Manhattan with the Caracappas on the night Lino was killed. Levine had mixed up the dates, Caracappa told Kaplan, but provided him with a "celebrity" out, if the allegations Casso made against them ever came to trial.

As always, Eppolito had money woes. He had by then purchased a new house in Las Vegas, and construction was under way, but he had found another deal in another suburb that would provide him with grand living circumstances for a lesser sum. The second house on Silver Bear Way was Eppolito's dream house, with romanesque columns in front, a pool in back, and a spacious layout befitting a man of his accomplishments. The problem was that Eppolito had committed to the first house and all his money was tied up in the down payment.

"Listen, I need a big favor," Eppolito said. "I want to get into another house but the builder isn't going to give me my down payment back until he sells the house. Can you get a shylock for me and borrow seventy-five thousand?" he asked Kaplan.

"Louie, you got to be crazy," Kaplan said.

"I'll pay a point," Eppolito said.

"How can you afford to pay seven hundred and fifty dollars a week?" Kaplan asked.

The prospect made Kaplan uneasy. That amount of "juice"—52 percent annual interest—was ruinous for an extended period. Eppolito was extravagant, in his tastes and ambitions. The last thing Kaplan wanted was

Eppolito broke, desperate, and vulnerable. He needed the weak link in their chain to hold. Kaplan offered to do Eppolito a favor. In the marijuana business, it was common for Kaplan to need a ready source of financing for large transactions. The weight he dealt in ran to tons, and the sums of cash needed were millions. He had access to large sums of money on short notice from his partners in the pot trade. The money was provided to Kaplan interest-free, as a way of facilitating the marijuana transactions. Kaplan suggested that he would borrow $75,000 for Eppolito.

"Keeping Eppolito financially afloat had been a problem since Kaplan first met the lardy detective from the Six-Three. Kaplan had tried to talk to Eppolito about his profligate ways over the years. Eppolito's need for money was insatiable—the guns and reptiles and dreams of Hollywood fame and fortune. Kaplan asked Caracappa if Louie had a drug abuse issue? Eppolito had been pulling in a detective's salary. It should have been plenty for a man who knew how to live within his means—which Eppolito did not.

While Kaplan had been hiding out and awaiting the outcome of Casso's cooperation, his marijuana business continued to thrive. Tommy Galpine, Kaplan's former errand boy who had risen to be a partner, operated the enterprise. Galpine had provided Kaplan's wife with $100,000 drawn from the drug money. He had traveled to Ensenada, in Mexico, twice to see Kaplan. While Kaplan lived in Oregon and then set up in Vegas, large amounts of cash from the pot distribution network had been forwarded to him, or delivered in person by Galpine. Kaplan suggested to Eppolito that he might be able to use the money obtained from dealing drugs to help finance his new house.

"I got a guy in my marijuana business who trusts me with a lot of money. I'll ask him if I can juggle the seventy-five grand. That way it won't cost you nothing. You won't have to pay the juice. It'll take me a few days. I got to reach out to Tommy back in New York and see."

"It'll only be for a few months," Eppolito said. "Until the builder sells the house and I get my down payment back."

By the end of 1994, Kaplan had permanently relocated to Las Vegas. He rented a furnished house in Paradise Valley, or Paradise as it was known locally, in the southeast section of the city between the Strip and McCarran Airport. He and his lover, Diane Pippa, opened a retail store selling women's suits in partnership with a couple Kaplan knew from the garment business in New York. Nothing was in Kaplan's name in the business. His partners owned the entire operation on paper. Kaplan had connections in New York who could supply him decent-quality business attire for female executives working in the casinos looking for sharp prices. "A good suit for a good value," was Kaplan's motto.

In fact, while Kaplan was on the lam he maintained steady contact with many of his closest associates in New York. Among them was Sammy Kaplan, a man unrelated to him who had served time with Kaplan in Allenwood in the early eighties. When Burt Kaplan arrived in Las Vegas, Sammy Kaplan had recommended he contact a friend of his named William Schaefer, a native of Brighton Beach. Sammy said Schaefer might be able to help Kaplan with running errands and driving. Kaplan's eyesight had deteriorated over time. In Las Vegas, it was essential to have a car, and Kaplan needed someone to drive him to and from meetings and work, as well as assist him in running errands. William Schaefer was meek and compliant, a retired food supervisor at an Air Force base who had spare time. His wife also started to work for Kaplan in the burgeoning women's suit business.

That November Kaplan met with Eppolito to lend him the money for the bridge loan on the new house as promised. Kaplan's lover, Diane, called Eppolito and told him to meet Kaplan at Caesar's Palace. Kaplan had received $75,000 from Galpine. The money had been delivered in a box wrapped as if it were a Christmas present. It was packed in the usual manner: $100 notes, the bills secured with a rubber band and stuffed in white envelopes, $5,000 in each envelope. At the casino, Kaplan gave Eppolito $65,000 and kept $10,000 for himself, for a bet on Super Bowl XXIX.

Kaplan explained to Eppolito that it was less than expected, but all that he could spare at the moment. Eppolito was pleased to receive the money. "Please, Louie," Kaplan pleaded. "I could have gotten you the money and said it was seven hundred and fifty a week. But I'm trying to keep you out of trouble. Please pay it back as soon as you can."

"You saved my life with this," Eppolito told Kaplan. "I really appreciate it. The minute I get the money back I'm going to give it to you."

The San Francisco 49ers beat the San Diego Chargers 49–26. Kaplan had backed the winner.

The following March, Caracappa left his job at the 14th Street BID in Manhattan and relocated to Las Vegas with his wife, Monica. The couple bought a house on Silver Bear Way, directly across the street from Louis and Fran Eppolito. Casso's cooperation had not resulted in charges, but Caracappa put himself in a position to keep an eye on Eppolito.

Kaplan was prospering as Barry Mayers. Constantly scouting for moneymaking schemes, he came across a business idea to manufacture and market an exercise device to mimic the workout of hitting a punching bag. The gimmick consisted of a balloon with a heavy rubber band around it. Together they formed a punching target that bounced back no matter at which angle it was struck. The product had been designed by a famous Las Vegas boxing judge who was friends with the Schaefers, the older couple working as Kaplan's bookkeeper and driver. Negotiations had begun with George Foreman to have the former heavyweight boxing champion, and promoter of the extremely successful George Foreman Grill, endorse the boxing balloon. Kaplan knew that Caracappa's wife was connected to the shopping network QVC through a friend. Kaplan reasoned that Foreman could do on-air spots for the device. Kaplan and Caracappa still saw each other from time to time. Kaplan asked Caracappa if he might be able to arrange a meeting with the people in charge of QVC. If QVC decided to sell the product on-air, the minimum order would be 100,000 units. Caracappa and Kaplan went to two meetings but the idea failed to come to fruition.

The months rolled on. The clouds hovering over the heads of Kaplan, Caracappa, and Eppolito seemed to have parted. The three men were constructing new lives under the desert sun, ready to go into business together as the opportunity arose. Back in New York, despite the universal expectation that there would be a sophisticated and comprehensive investigation of Gaspipe Casso's revelations, nothing came of it. The gambit of attorneys Bruce Cutler and Eddie Hayes to confront Charles Rose and the federal government and demand charges be laid appeared to have worked. "To my amazement, Detectives Caracappa and Eppolito skated. Hanging tough worked. The two detectives had settled into their new lives in their cul-de-sac in their gated community. Kaplan was thriving. The only ones suffering were Gaspipe Casso and the families of the victims."

MISERY, HEROIN, LOBSTERS

By the spring of 1996, Anthony Casso was housed in a witness protection unit in the Otisville Federal Correctional Facility in upstate New York. The segregated section in the center of the prison was filled with more than one hundred inmates who had to be kept apart from the general population. "Cooperators, according to the code of prisoners, betrayed the most basic tenet of criminality. Talking to the government made them uni-

versal targets for criminals of every stripe. 'Snitch jail' was another name
for the witness protection units that constituted prisons-within-prisons."

That spring, federal prosecutors were finally confronting Vincent
Chin Gigante and attempting to prove that he was competent to stand
trial.* With the "crystal ball" case stalled, testifying against Chin Gigante
was going to be Casso's ticket out of prison. During his debriefing,
Casso had told Charles Rose and Greg O'Connell about his dealings with
the Chin. Gigante was running the Genovese family, Casso said. Christy
Tick Furnari, John Gotti, Gaspipe Casso, dozens of senior mobsters
were dumbfounded or angered by Gigante's behavior—but there was no
question it was an act. "Casso described meetings Gigante held in an Italian restaurant on East 4th Street on the Lower East Side. That was where
Gigante settled disputes about chopping up the proceeds from the windows scams, demanded repayment of stolen money, and enforced mafia
punishment, including putting out the hits of John Gotti and Frank
DeCicco—which were given to Casso and his partner Vic Amuso.
According to Casso, Gigante wasn't just sane, he was a cagey con man
who insulated himself from his family solely to frustrate prosecutors. The
act had worked for years. During his proffer, Casso gave Charles Rose a
long list of people who knew Gigante was faking it. Casso was expecting
to be used by the government as a witness against Gigante in the hearings
about mental competency that spring."

Colombo captain Big Sal Miciotta had also been shipped to the witness
protection unit inside Otisville. For two years, Miciotta had been preparing and giving testimony against his former fellow mobsters. The trials
had not gone well. Miciotta was an expert on the inner workings of the
mafia, able to explain arcane practices and describe the true underlying
culture of the mob. Money, Miciotta knew, was always at the root of all
mafia matters. But on the stand, Miciotta downplayed his own role in the
murders in which he had participated. In the hope of receiving a lesser

---

* Gigante was one of the last remaining symbols of mob defiance. For years he had
been a fixture in lower Manhattan, a mumbling, unshaven, mentally unbalanced
mobster wearing a bathrobe and pausing to urinate on the sidewalk. Prosecutors were
determined to show it was an act. Throughout the late eighties and early nineties, federal prosecutor Charles Rose had targeted Gigante. In the 1990 Windows Case
Gigante had managed to have the charges against him severed from the main case. Free
on $1 million bond, Gigante had tricked law enforcement into thinking he lived with
his mother on Sullivan Street, in Greenwich Village, when in fact he had a wife and five
children living in comfort in suburban New Jersey and a mistress set up in a posh
Upper East Side townhouse with the three children the couple had together.

sentence, Miciotta misguidedly portrayed himself as less of a criminal than he truly was.

"Committing the indiscretions on the stand meant tearing up my plea agreement," Miciotta recalled. "And rightfully so. I knew I had it coming, but that only made it worse. After a lifetime of lying I could not believe that investigators and prosecutors actually wanted the truth. No one told the truth, as far as I knew. Everything was a con—everything on every level. The same had to be true as a cooperator. I didn't tell the whole truth about the money I had stashed away. I hedged on the shylock money I had on the street. I held back another guy's involvement in a marijuana deal. I was involved in a phony car accident I didn't tell the prosecutors about. When I started to cooperate I was hoping for a suspended sentence. No jail time. I was in the best possible situation. I started cooperating before I was charged with anything. But once things went wrong it snowballed. One lie leads to ten lies. Instead of starting a new life on the outside, I got fourteen years. I was at rock bottom when I got to Otisville that spring."

Anthony Casso had yet to testify in any trials. For cooperators, sentencing occurred after cooperation was complete. The Gigante trial was slated to start that spring. Casso and Miciotta were two of the few made men in the Otisville witness security unit. The unit was set up like a dormitory, with a large common area and two levels of cells. There were no windows, to avoid any contact with the general population. There were a number of fringe players, wannabes from Brooklyn and Staten Island who had become cooperators, but for the most part the section was now filled with cooperators from Latino and black gangs. Before he was allowed to enter the unit, Miciotta was put through a battery of tests by the FBI to ensure he would not hurt another prisoner or resort to violence. After a month, he was sent to Otisville. There he saw Casso, whom he knew from the 19th Hole. Casso greeted Miciotta warmly.

"In the beginning, Anthony was nice to me," Miciotta recalled. "He was able to get food in and he hooked me up with some pasta. I was thankful for it. The truth was that I never really liked him, and I don't think he liked me. But we were respectful of one another. Anthony was the same inside as he was on the street—off the wall. He said he was going to testify against the Chin. He thought he had a 'get out of jail free' card."

Miciotta settled in well. Intelligent and literate, compared with other inhabitants, Big Sal was assigned to work in the unit's law library. One of his jobs was to get the local newspapers each day and disperse them throughout the unit. Each man got half an hour with the paper. Miciotta quickly discovered that Casso had turned the witness security unit into his miniature empire. Still wealthy and able to bend others to his will, Casso had struck an arrangement with the woman who worked as secretary for the unit. She was pretty, curvy, a single mother, and a native of Puerto Rico. Casso took excellent care of her. She provided him with vodka, steaks, lobsters. When Casso received packages from the outside she would bring them into the unit. Cigars were in the packages, but the tobacco had been hollowed out and replaced by heroin and cocaine.

"Anthony had anything he wanted," Big Sal remembered. "He was ordering guys around like he was still in the street and he was still the boss. There was one Luchese guy from the New Jersey faction in the unit. Joe Marino was his name. Anthony was nasty to him. Anthony had no concept that he was in jail. There is no boss in jail. There is no more *cosa nostra*. No one cares who is *consigliere*. They don't know from that stuff. Inside, the boss is the guy who can hit the hardest. John Gotti went to jail and a black guy broke his ass. Joe Marino was a guy that worked out every day. He was in fucking super shape. Casso was a little guy. Joe would have took him apart. It would have been like throwing a fucking pork chop into a lion's den. I told Joe it wasn't worth it to take on Casso. It would only fuck up the amount of time Joe had to do, and keep him away from his family."

Miciotta was providing information on an ongoing basis to the federal prosecutors and FBI agents concentrating on cases against the Colombo family. During a debriefing session, an agent asked Miciotta about Casso. "The agent asked me, 'How's Casso doing in there?' I said that Anthony was always crazy but we weren't at odds with one another. The agent said, 'I don't think he's going to be too happy. They're not going to use him for the upcoming Chin Gigante trial.' I said, 'That's terrible.' They said, 'The psychological testing came back from the government doctors, and they marked him as a lunatic. He lied on a couple of occasions. He misled us. We aren't going to put him on the stand against Chin and weaken the case by having him cross-examined.' The government had Al D'Arco, Pete Savino, Phil Leonetti from Philly, Sammy Gravano. They had a good case.

"I left the meeting feeling I really should tell Anthony. I pondered it for a day or two. I didn't have any ulterior motive. I wasn't going to get nothing out of this. But I figured the guy should know what was going on. His hopes were high. He thought he was going get Sammy the Bull's deal. I didn't think it was right for me to not tell him. I felt guilty. It burns you not to tell somebody something like that. I went to his room. I told him what they said to me. I said they probably aren't going to use you in the

Gigante case. I didn't tell him the reasons. I didn't say you're a lying lunatic. He went off like a nut job, yelling and screaming."

"They wouldn't tell you something like that," Casso shouted.

"I'm only telling you to be a nice guy," Miciotta told Casso.

"You're crazy," Casso said to Miciotta. "You don't know what you're talking about. You're full of shit. I know more about this than you do."

"I'm just trying to help you," Big Sal said.

"I don't need your fucking help," Casso screamed. "We're not friends no more. I don't want to talk to you no more."

"You better check it out," Miciotta said. "You better call your sponsor—call Charlie Rose—and see what he says. Don't tell Rose I told you because I wasn't supposed to say nothing."

Miciotta walked out. Big Sal was a mountain of a man—six-one, three hundred and fifty pounds. Casso was five-nine, two hundred pounds, fattened by all the food he was eating. Miciotta was used to physically intimidating everyone he came in contact with, in prison and on the street. Casso represented no threat to Big Sal, he thought, as long as Casso didn't have a weapon smuggled in to the unit. The next day, Casso came to the law clerk's office, where Miciotta worked. Casso said he wanted to read the *New York Times*. The paper contained an article about the impending competency trial of Chin Gigante. It was the hearing Casso hoped to testify in. "Anthony was mad with me because I gave him the news he wasn't going to be used. He was going ballistic. He was shooting the messenger—and that was me."

"Where's the fucking *Times*?" Casso demanded from Miciotta.

"Dude, take it easy," Miciotta said. "The black guy from Florida, James, has it. As soon as he's done and he brings it down to me I'll give it to you."

"Get it for me," Casso said to Miciotta. "I don't want to have to wait for a fucking nigger."

"Anthony, we're not in Canarsie now," Miciotta said. "We're in jail. This guy has got the paper. I'm not going to go up and tell him I want the paper to give to you. You want the paper, you tell the guy."

James was serving four life sentences for murder. He was not a second-class citizen to anyone in the unit, including Casso. There was no chance he would give up the newspaper until he was finished with it. Casso was too frightened to confront James. That night Miciotta showered. He pulled on a pair of shorts, a T-shirt, and slippers, and took a seat in the common area of the unit. Friends of his were playing cards at a table nearby. One of his pals, a member of the other faction in the Colombo wars, had warned him that Casso was mouthing off about getting even with Miciotta. Sal opened the newspaper and started to read when he felt a blow to the head. "Casso had something wrapped up in a magazine. He was hitting me on the head with it. I got up and went towards him. I said, 'What are you doing, cocksucker?' He started to back away. He had the face of fear. I nailed him with a left hook. I caught him good. He hit the floor. I kept kicking him and slapping him. I was yelling at him, 'You piece of shit. You're a coward, you sneak.' He was bleeding from the side of his head. He had a gang inside—eight guys answered to him. They got in the middle and stopped me. They took him to the library."

"Casso was semiconscious. He sent a guy to my room to say he wanted to talk to me in the library. I said, 'Get the fuck out of here.' I just kicked his ass. Now he wants to talk like a tough guy again? On the street, if you raise your hands on another made guy, it's an unwritten rule that it's your life on the line. Inside there was no punitive structure. We were both rats. All the fight meant was he had to look out for me, and I had to look out for him. I put a metal cabinet in front of the door to my room. I figured him and his friends would come after me, rush the door all at once. Maybe he had a knife, because he wasn't really willing to fight. This way, at least they can only come one at a time. I could defend myself.

"Half an hour later, the prison cops knock on the door. They handcuff me and take me to the hole. I couldn't believe it. Casso starts the fight and I get arrested. Casso snitched on me. I saw the written report, signed by him. What a tough guy. His guys upstairs blocked the heat to my cell. It was winter and it was freezing in Otisville. I had one blanket. They were trying to get me sick. Three days later, they put Casso in the hole. That's when I decided to get even with him. I was scared he would poison my food. He had connections with the correctional officers and he had that secretary. I reached out for my U.S. attorney. I told him the whole story. I told him about all the contraband being brought in to the unit. I laid it all out."

The prosecutor contacted the inspector general's office and an investigation of the witness security unit was launched. The Bureau of Prisons corrections officers in the unit got wind of the inquiries being made. They told Casso that Miciotta had informed on the activities inside the unit. "Now I was in really big trouble. I was a snitch inside snitch jail. The cops hated me because I was giving up cops. The prisoners who were getting in trouble wanted to get me. It was bad—fucking bad. They were freezing me in my cell. His crew would come by my cell and threaten to kill me.

They said Anthony knew where my family was. Then one day I went to take a shower. As I come out of the shower, with my hands cuffed behind my back, the cop on duty unlocked the gym and let Casso into the hallway with me. He was carrying a weapon—a heavy brush. He corked me from behind. My feet were wet and I fell. I started kicking at him. He ran away. I was bleeding from my head. They took me to the medical department and asked me what happened. I told them a cop let Casso get at me."

A lightning raid was launched at four o'clock in the morning. All the cells were emptied. The unit secretary was locked in her office. The guards were locked in another room. The rooms were searched one by one. Contraband was rife. Cocaine, marijuana, heroin, alcohol, cigars, imported olive oil, cell phones were piled in the middle of the main room. The corruption was disclosed precisely as Miciotta described it. Casso made threats against Miciotta. Casso swore he would get Big Sal no matter what.

"Pretty soon it was clear Casso was unusable as a witness," Oldham recalled. "The agreement with him was now 'breached,' because he'd been caught committing crimes. Miciotta didn't do Casso in. Casso did himself in. It wasn't just smuggling contraband into prison. He plotted to kill Charles Rose. He plotted to kill Judge Eugene Nickerson, the longtime Eastern District judge assigned to try Casso's case. Casso was running the witness security unit like he was in the 19th Hole. His criminal life had continued in prison. Casso was a deviant wherever he was placed. Putting him on the stand meant associating the federal government with him— and that wasn't going to be pretty. Charles Rose wanted to continue to use Casso, even though Casso had wanted to kill him, but Greg O'Connell disagreed. You can't have the federal government saying this guy is our star witness when the star witness has threatened to kill a federal prosecutor and judge. You don't want to be associated with him and you don't want him associated with your case, even if he is telling the truth. The bigger problem, of course, was that now Casso could not be used to testify against Caracappa and Eppolito."

THE EAGLE LANDS

In the same way that word of Casso's cooperation had traveled through the world of mob lawyers in 1994, so did word spread that Casso had been breached in the spring of 1996. Once again, Judd Burstein contacted Kaplan, now living in Las Vegas, and conveyed the information that the government was not going to use Casso as a witness in any trial, including any potential prosecution of Kaplan and retired detectives Caracappa and Eppolito. In the time since Kaplan had gone on the lam, first to Mexico and then Oregon and Las Vegas, Burstein had remained in touch with his client. Kaplan had even started to travel under his assumed identity to New York, where he had seen Galpine and checked in on his marijuana and clothing import businesses. Kaplan had an established business and girlfriend in Las Vegas but he was eager to resume his New York life, legitimate and illegitimate. The danger appeared to have passed.

Kaplan contacted Eppolito and told him he needed to be repaid the money he had lent him as a bridge loan for Eppolito's house. Eppolito and Kaplan met. The retired NYPD detective only had $35,000 in cash. Eppolito told Kaplan that he couldn't get any more cash from the bank. He had a further $20,000 in checks. It was clear to Kaplan that Eppolito had not taken control of his finances. Kaplan wanted to help Eppolito. "Let's do it this way," Kaplan said. "Give me the total of fifty-five thousand, and forget the other ten."

Kaplan quietly returned to Brooklyn in June 1996. Moving back into his house on 85th Street in Bensonhurst, he didn't seek out attention, or tell his friends and business contacts he had returned. Maintaining a low profile did not work.

In early September, while laid up in bed feeling ill, Kaplan watched on his home surveillance system as DEA Special Agent Eileen Dinnan and two colleagues knocked on his front door. The agents weren't expecting to find Kaplan, but with a warrant for his arrest outstanding it was routine to stop at the residence of a fugitive at regular intervals. This time they got lucky. Kaplan didn't know there was a warrant out for him in a case unrelated to "the cops" and Gaspipe Casso. Kaplan's wife, Eleanor, allowed Special Agent Dinnan and the two others into the house. Shown to Kaplan's bedroom, where he was watching the surveillance camera, Downtown Burt's years of running from the law came to an end.

"We've got some bad news for you, Burt," one of the agents said to Kaplan.

Kaplan's longtime associate Tommy Galpine was also arrested. The pair was charged with marijuana trafficking.

The night Kaplan was arrested he was taken to the DEA headquarters at 99 10th Avenue on the west side of Manhattan. Kaplan was led into a room filled with law enforcement officials. Senior officers from the NYPD were present, along with DEA and FBI agents. Twenty men were in the room. Kaplan knew what they were after. Kaplan was told he could do himself a favor. The assembled brass said they wanted to talk to him about two "dirty cops." Kaplan had not been allowed to confer with his lawyers. He told the officials that he wasn't being facetious, or difficult, but he was not interested in making a deal. Kaplan said he wanted to talk to his lawyer. A ten-year-old grudge was rearing its head.

"At that moment, Kaplan could have walked on the marijuana charges without doing a day in prison. But Kaplan wouldn't cooperate with the FBI. Kaplan hated the Bureau with a passion. Why? In the mid-eighties, when he was out of Allenwood, the FBI had nearly destroyed his legitimate business. At the time, Kaplan was importing clothes on a large scale. To succeed in the business he needed large-scale financing. Kaplan was particularly close to one Fashion District factor who was willing to extend Kaplan credit for hundreds of thousands of dollars on short notice. Flexibility was necessary for a wheeler-dealer like Kaplan. He was trying to go straight at the time—or what qualified as straight for him. But the FBI was still after him. I don't know the specific reason. It was the mid-eighties, just at the beginning of RICO prosecutions and the war against the mafia. Maybe they wanted him to cooperate against Christy Tick Furnari in the Commission Case. There were many, many possible reasons for the FBI to be interested in a character like Downtown Burt. The Bureau went to the businessman and told him that Kaplan was involved with organized crime. The FBI told the man Kaplan had been in federal prison. The guy was legit. He was shocked and appalled. Kaplan presented as an honest man. Kaplan dealt with name brands, like Calvin Klein. But the mafia was ingrained in so many aspects of life in New York that the allegation was believable. People weren't used to having a face to put to the mob.

"The businessman called Kaplan and asked if it was true that he was a mobbed-up ex-con. Kaplan lied. The guy told Kaplan that if it was true he would have to stop doing business with Kaplan because the bonding company that guaranteed his financing wouldn't allow him to offer credit to a criminal. Kaplan went home that night and thought about the guy. Honor mattered a lot to Kaplan. The man was willing to take Kaplan's word against the FBI's. The man was taking on a huge risk. The situation didn't fit Kaplan's sense of right and wrong. Kaplan believed it was wrong for him to put the other guy in jeopardy. He also knew that it would be impossible to sustain the lie that he wasn't an ex-con. One phone call would result in the other man knowing Kaplan was lying.

"Five o'clock the next morning, Kaplan was parked in front of the man's office. When the guy got to work they had coffee together. Kaplan told him the truth. Kaplan said he had done time. He had friends in organized crime, he said, but he wasn't controlled by the mafia. Kaplan had a note from the guy guaranteeing eight hundred thousand dollars as security on a designer jeans deal. Kaplan took it from his pocket and offered to return it. The loss of financing would be ruinous to Kaplan, but he was going to keep his word. The guy was touched. He told Kaplan he could keep the note for ninety days. Kaplan had the time to make other arrangements and his business wasn't destroyed.

"The federal government had displayed in a vivid way its power over Kaplan. From that day forward, Kaplan hated the FBI. The FBI represented everything dishonorable and despicable to him. Now that he had been arrested in New York City, Kaplan was willing to stand trial and go to prison as a matter of principle. Snitching was not an option, not with the FBI involved. But Kaplan didn't know how steep a price he was going to pay for his silence. I didn't know how much time I would spend trying to get him to break that silence. Years of his life, years of mine."

CHAPTER ELEVEN

OFF THE BOOKS

By the fall of 1996, Detective William Oldham had become one of the "go-to guys" in the Major Case Squad—a successor to Detective Stephen Caracappa. Now forty-two years old, Oldham had been in the squad for more than six years. After the Born to Kill investigation, he had spent a year and a half investigating the Chinese Tong On gang in Baltimore, Washington, and New York, and an outfit known as the Mod Squad (a group of heroin dealers with a white kid, black kid, and two Chinese kids). His experience making RICO cases had expanded and deepened his ability to maneuver in the competitive world of organized crime law enforcement. He was fulfilling his deepest ambitions. "I had arrived," Oldham recalled. "I made my own cases. I was autonomous, to a large extent, free to pursue crimes and criminals that interested me. It was my version of starring on Broadway or making a fortune on Wall Street. The mafia had been pretty much defeated. I never made it to the OCHU— which was disbanded after Caracappa left. But I was enterprising and I was busy. I scavenged for cold cases that everyone had given up on. I wanted to take the harder cases. It was ego, to some extent. But I also perceived a need.

"There were forty thousand cops in the NYPD and I loved them and would do anything for them. There were probably two hundred detectives who carried the department when it came to serious crime. They were scattered around the precincts, in Intel, Homicide, Major Case. If a case came in that demanded the best, or a question arose that needed to be answered, no matter what, there was a small group of investigators who bosses and beat cops could approach. It was what 'go-to' meant. I could help other detectives. But I had my own cases, too. My career was thriving. But it was taking a toll. I don't know when, precisely, it began to change. Police work was muddied up for me. I got muddied up as well. It's inevitable. If you spend a lot of time around evil, it hardens you. I went looking for the worst criminals. Killers, rapists, psychopaths, men who could torture and murder children. The criminals I wanted had little pity, no remorse. I saw that bet and raised it. I was willing to push the envelope. I was a little arrogant. People I worked with called me 'Billy' because the diminution made me seem nicer than I was. I got the job done but I wouldn't win any popularity contests. I had hardened myself—heart and soul."

Oldham now operated nearly exclusively out of the offices of the Eastern District in One Pierrepont Plaza in downtown Brooklyn. Oldham wanted to be close to the action—and a good proportion of the biggest cases in the city and the country wound up in the offices of the federal prosecutors working in Brooklyn. He rarely turned up at NYPD headquarters in lower Manhattan. He clocked in for duty by gassing up at the department pump at One Police Plaza. The printout showed that he had been at headquarters at that time on that date so it couldn't be claimed that he had not reported for work. But he went weeks without going up to the Major Case Squad office. "Half the time I didn't tell the bosses what I was working on. The leaks of the eighties and early nineties had decreased but there was still the possibility of a breach in security and I didn't want my snitches hurt. If I didn't tell the bosses what I was doing they couldn't tell me not to do it. If no one knew what I was doing, word wouldn't get to the FBI so the Bureau couldn't steal my cases. It also kept people guessing. It gave me the freedom to take on cases that I thought mattered. I always had two or three or four investigations lined up to work so I wouldn't be stuck with nothing to do after I closed a case. I called it 'the back burner.' I kept cases on the back burner for years—just thinking about them, playing them out in my head, waiting for the time to work it, or a lucky break."

Oldham's small office in the Eastern District appeared chaotic, with crime scene photos and rap sheets and DD-5s scattered on every surface. The boxes he used to collect evidence related to the cases he was churning over in his mind also contained random items from his personal life: discarded ties, theater ticket stubs, hardcover novels. The assortment was, indeed, chaotic, but Oldham knew where everything was. Gathering material on lost causes and vagrant cases was more than a hobby for Oldham. It was a mania. He routinely made calls to contacts he had, ranging from the upper echelons of the Department of Justice in Washington to precinct detectives, to test theories or ask questions. Avoiding the bureaucracy of law enforcement had become a particular specialty of Oldham's. If he wanted a document, he contrived to get it as quickly as possible and nearly always by circumventing procedures. Even if it was relatively easy to use official channels, Oldham found pleasure in using back channels, keeping himself sharp and connected to the people who knew how to play the system.

"The back burner consisted of crimes I was interested in—or potential crimes, or suspected crimes, or possible crimes. If a subject or a person caught my eye, I'd start up on them. I'd gather up what was available, from newspaper clippings to surveillance reports—whatever I could get my hands on. When I was drinking, the back burner tended to go to a low simmer. But when I was sober, my mind was constantly working those cases. I kept myself from doing nothing by going through the boxes, cross-referencing and contemplating and waiting for a picture to emerge. Often I didn't know if the 'cases' I had on the back burner were cases at all. That was how it was with Caracappa and Eppolito. I saw the headlines in the newspaper in 1994 about Casso's snitching on them, like the rest of the city, and it raised my suspicions. It was why I had *Mafia Cop* in my desk drawer. But I figured the FBI would make the case, if there was a case. By then the FBI had been told four times of Casso's source in the NYPD—by Al D'Arco, Pete Chiodo, Sammy Gravano, and Casso himself. I just had that book and my suspicions of Caracappa simmering away."

In early October 1996, Oldham was walking along a corridor in the Eastern District offices when he overheard a conversation about the rap sheet of one Walter Johnson, aka "King Tut." Assistant U.S. Attorney Sam Buell was marvelling at the length of the document. Curious, Oldham stepped inside Buell's office and asked to see King Tut's rap. "It was literally several feet long," Oldham recalled. "Rappers rapped about their criminal history, but Tut's dully prosaic rap sheet showed he *was* a menace to society. Tut was an aspiring rapper but his real art was committing crime—and getting away with it. Rap sheets don't just include convictions. They include arrests. An arrest may go nowhere but it still means something to cops, who know convictions don't necessarily comport with guilt. The arrests dated back to ripping off ten-speeds when Walter Johnson was just a boy. When he was nineteen years old, he stuck up three hundred worshippers at his mother's Jehovah's Witness church, demanding their cash and valuables at gunpoint as the congregation knelt in prayer. Out on bail pending trial, Tut and his four-manchild posse boarded a city bus and robbed half a dozen passengers of their meager possessions. On and on it went: charges of assault, gun possession, involvement in a shootout with three police officers. But there were only a couple of relatively minor convictions. As I read his rap sheet, I knew I was going to take a case."

The same day, Oldham began an investigation of Walter Johnson. Oldham started by calling up the DD-5s for a shootout Tut had gotten into with the three cops. According to eyewitness reports from the day in question, King Tut had gone with his younger brother and his son to get a haircut at a three-chair barbershop in Brownsville, home turf of heavyweight boxer Mike Tyson and one of the roughest areas in Brooklyn. "Walter Johnson, starring in his own life story in the role of King Tut, walked in to find three NYPD cops in the three chairs. Words were exchanged. Voices were raised, threats leveled. Guns were produced. A shootout transpired in very close quarters. The so-called King and his son weren't hit. All three cops were wounded. Police Officer Richard Aviles was paralyzed—at twenty-four years old. Tut later denied that he had fired any shots. The outcome was not unusual for him. He was infamous in the rap community, for his violence and for the inability of law enforcement to convict and imprison him."

Oldham's work on the Tut case led him to undertake an investigation of potential connections between Sean "Puffy" Combs's Bad Boy Records and violent criminal organizations. The investigation would later stall with the murder of "Biggie" Smalls in Los Angeles, and no charges were brought. In the hyper-hyped world of gangster rap, rumors ran rampant that Tut was a member of the "Black Mafia," an organization Oldham didn't believe existed. Interviewing Tut's many victims, or the few who were willing to talk, Oldham developed an informant—a woman who was an executive in the music industry who had been robbed and brutally assaulted by Tut. She told Oldham that real gangsters like King Tut robbed "gangsta rappers."

"The faux gangstas were terrified of thugs like Tut and his sidekick Haitian Jack. Tut traveled to the BET Music Awards ceremony in L.A., high-end clubs, concerts, specifically to stick up celebrity 'outlaw' rappers. The performers looked bad on MTV, and inspired a generation of kids in the suburbs to emulate their style, but the tough talk on the TV did not impress the Brownsville boys. Victims of Tut and his posse had nowhere to turn. Law enforcement was not overly concerned about the plight of the rappers, to put it politely. The supposed gangstas were rapping about shooting cops and that didn't endear them to law enforcement officials. Stopping their victimization wasn't high on our list of priorities. It was why rappers had so much personal security."

In November 1994 Tut had accosted Tupac Shakur in the lobby of a Times Square building in midtown Manhattan. The rapper had finished a recording session and was on his way into the building for a meeting when a gun fight erupted as Tut robbed $40,000 worth of gold and diamond jewelry from Shakur. The rapper was shot five times but managed to survive—only to be murdered in Las Vegas in September 1996 by an unidentified assailant. "Before he was killed, Tupac rapped about Tut," Oldham said. "It was the usual Shakur recipe—profanity, violence, glorification of crime and mob life. What was different and interesting was the extent to which Shakur's encounter with Tut gave him a glimpse of the reality Tut represented. For Shakur it was the 'realest shit' he ever saw."

Through the month of October, with the assistance of Oldham's informant, Oldham and his Major Case partners, Detectives George Slater and Jimmy Haley, accumulated evidence on a string of robberies and extortions pulled off by Tut. The crimes were relatively minor, compared with the serial criminal behavior. But Oldham was aiming to build a federal case against King Tut. By the end of October Detectives Oldham, Slater, and Haley attended a hearing for Tut in Brooklyn Supreme Court. The unsuspecting gangster was appearing for a status conference on a state assault charge. On this day, unbeknownst to Tut, the Brooklyn district attorney would drop the state charges. Oldham and his partners planned to rearrest him under the new federal "three strikes" statute. The law provided that anyone convicted of three violent felonies was subject to a sentence of life imprisonment upon conviction of another violent felony in federal court. "It's a horrible law. I revile the law. It's repugnant. In California people get three different hub-cap theft convictions and they go away for life. But the law was custom-made for Tut. If you've got a tool and you have a bloodsucker like Tut you've got to use it. It was the first and last time I used the three strikes law."

On October 24, King Tut came into the courtroom with his lawyer. The pair sat in the second row of the gallery and continued a whispered conversation about the procedural matter on the agenda. Tut was free on bail and had little to fear from the state charges. Oldham and his partners had notified the court officers, the DA, and the judge of what they were about to do. "Before Tut's case was called, we surrounded him and his attorney—one on each side, one behind. I was on Tut's left. I leaned over and explained that I was going to arrest him. I spoke quietly, but Tut didn't appreciate the courtesy. He had been arrested hundreds of times. He started emptying his pockets, pushing his possessions to his attorney— scraps of paper with phone numbers, his wallet, his phone book, his pager, it was potential evidence. 'What did I do?' Tut whined loudly, like an innocent man. Finally I sat on his lawyer to keep him from accepting Tut's paraphernalia. He made a CCRB [Civilian Complaint Review

Board] complaint, but the people in the courtroom—the judge, prosecutors, and court officers—thought so little of the lawyer that, when they were interviewed by CCRB, 'No one saw nothing,' even though it happened in open court.

"I reported the incident, saying I attempted to sit between the attorney and client. We put Tut in handcuffs and 'leg irons' and walked him four blocks through the busy midday traffic of downtown Brooklyn to the federal courthouse. King Tut wasn't such a king after all. It was an exercise in public relations. Tut was infamous in Brooklyn and the rap community. He thought he was untouchable. It turned out he was touchable—and cuffable and convictable."

FAT BOBBY'S FRAME

On the Friday after Thanksgiving Day, 1996, William David Oldham III married Andrea Beth Rashish in a private Jewish ceremony at Alison's on Dominick, a small romantic restaurant in west Soho. Oldham had asked her to marry him on September 1, the anniversary of the death of his younger brother John. "September 1 was always a hard one for me. I told Andrea I wanted to invest that day with some joy. We lived in a loft on Mott Street on the border between Little Italy and Chinatown. We had a black standard poodle. Andrea was out walking the dog one evening. The area was dead at night in those days, before it became trendy. She used to walk down Mulberry Street because she knew the gangsters at Gotti's social club, the Ravenite, would provide some protection for a young woman walking her dog through the deserted streets. She often exchanged pleasantries with wiseguys smoking cigars on folding chairs in front of the club. On the night in question, a warm June night, she turned the corner from Broome Street onto Mott Street to find a group of young Asian men who seemed to be roughhousing—five or six guys had circled one guy. She watched as the guy in the center had his head smashed into a light pole. They were actually mugging the guy. Our trusty poodle sensed Andrea's adrenaline rush and lunged on her leash, barking. Andrea shouted out, 'Okay boys, the party's over.' The muggers scattered like cockroaches. Even my wife was fighting crime, making New York City a safer place for all."

During his investigation of Tut, Oldham learned a great deal about criminal behavior in the rap world. Tut had become the entrée to a much larger investigation. In March 1997, Oldham flew to California to attend the 11th Annual Soul Train Music Awards. He was now tagging rap superstar Chris Wallace, aka the Notorious B.I.G. Biggie Smalls, as he was also known, was involved a state gun charge that arose from a search of the house in Nutley, New Jersey, where he lived with Kimberly Jones, better known as Lil' Kim. "Prospecting for crime often meant finding small, or seemingly small, offenses like what I had on Smalls. One step at a time, you build and build until you have the makings of a major case. Police work, for me, wasn't a passive enterprise. Crimes didn't come to me, I went looking for them. It was like starting a small business. Rap was a hole I found in the market of criminal investigations and I set out to fill it."

On the evening of March 8, 1997, Oldham posed as one of the photographers on the dais outside the Shrine Auditorium in Los Angeles, where the Soul Train Music Awards were being held. Shakur had been killed six months earlier but he was nominated for Rap Album of the Year for *All Eyez on Me*. The next day, Biggie Smalls would be killed driving away from a music industry party in Mid-Wilshire's Museum Row. Hundreds of industry executives and musicians were pouring out of the building at the time, but police had trouble finding anyone who admitted witnessing the shooting. It was a murder that spawned a subindustry of conspiracy theorists alleging law enforcement links to gangster rap.

As he stood on the dais, Oldham received a call from DEA Special Agent Eileen Dinnan. Oldham had not talked to Dinnan for more than a year. She was young and inexperienced but a gung ho DEA investigator. Oldham had helped her with her first major investigation into a mob-related marijuana ring that resulted in the conviction of a number of leading Luchese killers. Dinnan was calling from New York City. She asked when Oldham was going to be back in town. Oldham said he had to return the following day to testify in a Chinese street gang case then being tried in Brooklyn.

"You remember that pot case we worked on?" Dinnan asked. "The Kaplan case?"

Oldham did remember. After Burton Kaplan was arrested, Oldham had helped Dinnan prep Robert Molini, a convicted murderer turned cooperator. As far as Oldham was concerned, Kaplan was a wealthy businessman who dealt pot. Dinnan had told Oldham about the pressure from high officials in federal law enforcement to get Kaplan to cooperate. Kaplan was connected with a significant number of serious mobsters, Dinnan explained, which was why the government was interested in getting him to talk. "Dinnan didn't know about Kaplan's role in the Caracappa and Eppolito conspiracy," Oldham recalled. "Neither of us knew anything much more than the basics that had appeared in the press and the rumors that circulated at the time but soon died down. But Eileen knew my way of working. She knew I was always on the lookout for a good case. She knew I wasn't interested in investigation of cops, per se, but she also knew if she had a lead about a leak inside the NYPD I could be trusted to look into the matter—and get to the bottom of it."

"I've got a cooperator I'm debriefing," Dinnan said to Oldham. "Her name is Monica Galpine. She was married to Kaplan's flunky Tommy Galpine. The other day she started talking about cops who worked for Kaplan and Galpine. They were NYPD. One of them was a big fat guy who wrote a book about the mafia. It sounds like these cops were pretty tight with Kaplan. I told Monica I didn't want to know anything about it, but that I knew someone who might. That's you. You can't talk to her until she's done testifying but I thought I should let you know. What do you think? You interested?"

"Fuck, yeah," Oldham said, excitedly.

"The memory is crystal clear," Oldham recalled. "The limos were pulling up in L.A. I immediately knew what Dinnan had to be talking about. Eppolito had written *Mafia Cop*. If it was Eppolito it had to be Caracappa. The moment was surreal. I was set up on gangsta musicians. I was talking about NYPD detective hit men. An old clothing wholesaler back in New York was sitting on the biggest corruption case in the history of the NYPD—and I was going to have a head start on it. Life was great. I wasn't rich. I wasn't famous. But Jesus, I loved that job. I had the best job in the world. I went around putting bad guys in prison forever. I righted wrongs. Now I had a lead on Caracappa and Eppolito—a pair that were notorious original gangsters, not in some rap song but for real."

Oldham started to follow the Burton Kaplan case closely. Jury selection for the trial of *The United States v. Burton Kaplan and Thomas Galpine* was completed in early May 1997. On May 6, Kaplan's role in the conspiracy was revealed in the press for the first time by mob reporter Jerry Capeci. "Feds Eye Rat Trap to Snag Two Ex-Cops," the headline in the *Daily News* said. The story ran on page twenty-six, next to advertisements for silk brassieres and gas barbecues. "The feds have hit a reputed mob associate with drug and tax charges in the hope of jump-starting an investigation of two retired New York City detectives suspected of being mob hit men," Capeci wrote. "Burton Kaplan, an alleged former associate of one-time Luchese family underboss Anthony 'Gaspipe' Casso, is being prosecuted in an effort to coerce him into testifying against the detectives, sources said." After a two-year investigation, prosecutors in the Eastern District had concluded that the only way to make a case against Caracappa and Eppolito was with the cooperation of Kaplan. James Orenstein, the federal prosecutor in charge of the file, had written a memorandum on the case, Capeci reported. "In the memo, Orenstein told his supervisor, Mark Feldman, that his investigation had 'been stalled for a long time and is likely to remain that way unless Kaplan flips.'"

Oldham couldn't wait for the Kaplan and Galpine trial to end. Until then Dinnan wouldn't talk to him, for fear of jeopardizing the prosecution's case. The trial lasted three weeks. The defense theory was that the government was framing Kaplan as a way of punishing him for refusing to cooperate against Caracappa and Eppolito. Two of the lead witnesses for the prosecution were Monica Galpine and the cooperator, Robert Molini.

"At the heart of a lot of criminal cases there are fundamental questions that can never be known for a fact. Scientific evidence like DNA and fingerprints provide certainty. But cases like the one against Kaplan and Galpine don't have that kind of proof. It's a matter of testimony, collaboration, credibility. The truth has to be decided. It's why there are juries. Kaplan believed Molini and Monica Galpine lied on the stand. There were certainly reasons to question her credibility. Monica Galpine was a woman who despised her ex-husband and his partner Burt Kaplan. Fat Bobby Molini had his own reasons to try to ingratiate himself with the government."

Until months earlier, Molini had been housed in the Otisville Witness Security Unit with Anthony Casso and Big Sal Miciotta. Miciotta, the Colombo captain now living in an undisclosed location, remembered Molini well. "I spent countless hours playing cards with Fat Bobby Molini in Otisville," Miciotta recalled. "He was a young guy in his early thirties, short, fat, bald-headed, a Luchese wannabe. He was from Canarsie. On the outside Molini kept a lion in his house—maybe it was a cougar, but it was an exotic cat. Inside the witness protection unit, he was a mutt, a momma's boy. Molini was one of Casso's minions. Fat Bobby was in on Casso's scam to bribe the guards. Casso was Molini's idol. Casso had a big grudge against Kaplan, because he had convinced himself that Kaplan had given up his New Jersey hideout and thus got Casso caught. It wasn't true, of course, but that didn't matter to Gaspipe. Casso had tried to get Kaplan killed. If Casso wanted to get revenge against Kaplan, Molini would be a prime candidate to help put Kaplan away."

The motive for Molini himself was strong. In September 1996, Molini had been released from Otisville as part of his cooperation agreement. But Miciotta snitching on Casso's schemes in the unit had put Molini at risk.

By the time Molini was freed, the inspector general's investigation of the Witness Security Unit had revealed the depth of corruption inside Otisville. If Molini were caught participating in Casso's scam, his cooperation agreement would be "breached" and he would be put back in prison and sentenced again, to an additional four or five years. Molini decided to confess before his role was revealed. In October he told the authorities that he had bribed a guard to bring him food and clothing. He was locked up. Stuck back in prison, a snitch undone by another snitch, Molini needed to come up with a way to get back in the good graces of the government. Molini had to find a new crime to snitch on—something big.

"Molini was a lower-level guy, but he was a conniver," Miciotta recalled. "The bribery charge was a serious offense. He was in the smuggling ring up to his eyeballs. For Molini to save his ass he had to give up a guy further up the food chain. He had to bring in the prize to get a reduction in sentence. Who better than Burt Kaplan? The government had a hard-on a mile wide for Kaplan."

In the Eastern District courthouse, Molini took the stand and testified in great detail about Kaplan's marijuana enterprise. "Kaplan listened to Molini's testimony absolutely seething," Oldham recalled. "Every day prosecutors wheeled in a shopping cart of pot that was supposed to be Kaplan's. But it wasn't. Kaplan wasn't just a marijuana dealer—he was a quality marijuana dealer. Kaplan's pot was processed into two-foot-long ingots that looked nothing like the pile of irregular and second-rate weed in court. Tommy Galpine inspected the marijuana and told Kaplan it wasn't theirs. Kaplan wouldn't sell the low-grade grass the DEA displayed to the jury. Kaplan's pot was twice as good.

"Molini testified that he knew Kaplan, which drove Kaplan wild with fury. According to Kaplan, the two had never been introduced or talked. Molini had *tried* to meet Kaplan. But Kaplan wanted nothing to do with Molini. Kaplan kept his circle small and controlled. It was the same principle he used in dealing with Caracappa and Eppolito. Everything was on a 'need to know' basis. Kaplan had seen Molini at his warehouse on Staten Island but that was as far as it went. Once, at a party Molini asked another wiseguy to introduce him to Kaplan but Kaplan refused. Kaplan said there was no reason to meet Molini and he had no desire to meet Molini. And there was Molini giving sworn testimony about the inner workings of Kaplan's operations."

The case against Kaplan and Galpine was not ironclad. Much of the evidence was circumstantial, and cooperators like Robert Molini were not always credible to jurors. Kaplan had reason to hope that an acquittal might be the outcome. If convicted, he would be imprisoned for years. If he agreed to cooperate against Caracappa and Eppolito, there was an extremely high chance he would serve no time at all. Even as the trial proceeded, as the government put on their case against Kaplan and Galpine, Kaplan was approached.

"The pressure on Kaplan to cooperate was intense," Oldham recalled. "In the middle of the proceedings, the Organized Crime Task Force went to Kaplan and suggested they come to terms. It was not too late for Kaplan to cut a deal. Kaplan refused. Kaplan and his associate Tommy Galpine were convicted. After the guilty verdict, while Kaplan was waiting to be sentenced, the government came to him yet again and asked for his cooperation—and he said no. For a year Kaplan was repeatedly and insistently offered a deal. Kaplan just as repeatedly and insistently turned the offer down. Kaplan received a sentence of twenty-seven years. The sentence was incredibly harsh. Twenty-seven years was more than a lot of murderers got.

"Burton Kaplan had chosen his life—the life. Framed, he believed, by the federal government, he would prefer to spend the rest of his life behind bars to giving law enforcement the satisfaction of wearing him down and forcing him to give in. Post-conviction, as Kaplan and Galpine waited to be shipped out to their assigned federal penitentiaries, Kaplan told Tommy Galpine how they would conduct themselves. They would not snitch. In the post-*omertà* age with made men flipping by the dozen, *omertà* would be kept by a Jewish pot dealer and his oafish Irish-American sidekick."

"We're both men," Kaplan said to Galpine. "We got to do what we got to do. We got to go to jail."

"I'm with you," Galpine said.

MONICA'S STORY

On an August afternoon in 1997, a meeting with Monica Galpine was set for the Floridian Diner, a small place on Flatbush Avenue in Brooklyn. Oldham and Dinnan were drinking coffee in a corner booth when Monica Galpine arrived. She gave the diner a long look-over, to make sure there was no one she recognized, and then joined Oldham and Dinnan. She sat with her back to the rest of the restaurant so only the back of her head would be visible to the other patrons. Introductions were made. Galpine lit a cigarette—the first of half a dozen she smoked in the next hour.

"Monica Galpine was nearly good-looking but not quite," Oldham recalled. "She was a bottle blonde with big hair, dressed in tight white with spiky boots with fringes dangling down. She was tough-looking, a neighborhood girl. From the trial transcripts I knew she and Galpine had broken up badly. He was a cokehead and she was a drinker and prone to hysterical late-night calls to the Kaplans. Her testimony was critical in the conviction of Kaplan and Galpine. She was an angry woman, a scorned woman, and a scared woman. Gaining her trust and confidence wasn't going to be easy."

She was afraid Burt and her husband were going to come after her, she said, toking on her cigarette.

"He got twenty-seven years," Oldham said. "He ain't doing nothing but staring at a wall."

"Burt's got connections," she said. "He's got power and money."

She ashed her cigarette.

"Burt had cops," she said. "Tommy had cops."

"That's why I'm here," Oldham said. "I want to hear about it."

Monica Galpine began to tell her story. She told how Tommy had met Burt when he was a teenager working for an air-conditioning company. By the time she met Galpine, he was advancing up the ranks of Kaplan's criminal and legitimate operations. Monica was working as a nurse in a psychiatric ward in the city. She believed Kaplan sapped Tommy's affections with his constant demands.

According to Monica Galpine, her husband didn't just admire Burton Kaplan. Tommy Galpine was in the thrall of Kaplan. Whatever Kaplan wanted done, Galpine did. She said her husband had no time for her, or their marriage. "Tommy was Burt's 'butt boy,'" she said. "'Tommy Tag-along.' Her contempt was palpable. She truly despised Kaplan. If Galpine had been even remotely decent to her she would have kept his secrets and been his defender forever. She was no innocent trying to see justice was done. She wanted to get back at Kaplan and then Galpine. Kaplan was too smart to ever treat one of his intimates so poorly. Kaplan kept his wife sufficiently content to keep her quiet. Not a dunce like Galpine, who didn't understand one of the little known precepts of a life in crime is keeping your loved ones happy—at least happy or sedate enough that they won't rat you out."

Monica Galpine said she used to go to Burt's house on 85th Street with Tommy to get money for the cops. Tommy made her wait in the car. He always came out of Burt's place carrying a manila envelope. He'd tell her it was for "the cops." Tommy thought it was amazing that Burt had real police officers working for him. She never met "the cops," she said. She didn't know their names or anything about them except that they worked for Burt and Tommy and they got paid a fat wad of cash.

Kaplan's caution reached so far as to try to cover for Galpine. When Monica grew hysterical and claimed Galpine was beating her—something that was never proven—Kaplan and his wife Eleanor would pick her up and let her stay with them. When the Galpines finally split up, the Kaplans allowed Monica to stay with them while she got back on her feet. Ordinarily, such gestures might have engendered gratitude. But Monica Galpine's fury toward her husband and his millionaire mentor was all-encompassing.

"Then there was the time at the Chinese restaurant," she said.

"What's that?" Oldham asked.

"New China Inn," Galpine said. "Over on Flatbush." She'd gone there with Tommy for dinner one time. He had started laughing. She had asked why. He had jerked his head at a framed eight-by-ten glossy head-shot hanging on the wall. The photograph was of a guy—beefy, with a mustache, huge jaw, dumb eyes. "That's one of our cops," he had said. "He's got his picture on the fucking wall."

Oldham discovered the New China Inn had closed a few years earlier. But he spent days making inquiries, an effort that resulted in locating the former owners, who had retired to the Sunset Park section of Brooklyn. Oldham drove out to meet Nancy Wong, an elderly Cantonese woman who was tending a neatly kept flower garden in front of a modest row house when Oldham pulled up. After a brief chat, Oldham asked if she recalled a picture hung on the wall of the New China Inn.

"That's Rouie Epporito," Mrs. Wong said. "He think he big star and stuff. He never pay for dinner."

CHARACTER STUDIES

The lead was small, and the testimony of Mrs. Nancy Wong wouldn't amount to much in a court of law, but for Oldham the identification was not just another indication that he was on the right trail. He was definitely going to start up an investigation. Others had attempted the case, he knew, and all had failed. Convincing Kaplan to snitch seemed to have been the beginning and ending of their efforts. Oldham would try another way. He would pursue the case from an oblique angle. Instead of going directly to Kaplan and pitching a deal to him—an approach that was proven to fail—Oldham would start to inform himself about the lives of the people he was investigating. Studying the character of your suspects was the beginning for any serious investigation. A hunter needed to know his prey—strengths, weaknesses, history.

The next day, Dinnan met Oldham at the offices of the Eastern District. She handed him a box from the Kaplan-Galpine trial. She said it might help him with "the cops." Oldham took it to a conference room on the tenth floor. He closed and locked the door. Alone, Oldham opened the box. Inside were financial documents, cancelled checks, pen registers, videotapes of Kaplan's warehouse, lists of associates, and memos on surveillance—evidence that turns into moldy ephemera the moment a verdict is read. Oldham picked up Burt Kaplan's phone book. It was filled with contacts—business associates, friends, family. The phone book had been seized from Kaplan's valise when he was arrested on the marijuana charges in 1996. The book had the appearance of disguising as much information as it revealed about Kaplan's web of criminal associations.

"I pored over the phone book for hours and hours," Oldham said. "There were numbers crossed out. There were numbers written over. Kaplan had been a cryptographer when he was in the Navy in the fifties. He understood how to bury a number or an identity. My mother had been in naval intelligence. It was the kind of puzzle I loved.

"I was in the neighborhood on an apprehension warrant that week so I decided to go by the 63rd Precinct house. I wanted to see if I could get Eppolito's beeper number. I wanted to look through Kaplan's phone book to see if it was in there—maybe with a number reversed or scratched out. It would also give me the chance to trace the calls that came into that beeper number. Normally, I would have to get a subpoena to find that out but I had friends in the business who would run a phone number for me. I also wanted to get a read on the precinct-level rep of Eppolito. I wanted to ask around the detective squad room—see who remembered him, what he was like. Casually. I didn't want to trip any alarms, or alert Eppolito that a Major Case detective had been in asking questions. When I walked into the detective squad room there was a photograph of Eppolito on the wall. I had half forgotten what a jerkoff he was. I told them I wanted to get in touch with him so they pulled his stuff out. I looked around, too."

Oldham discovered the detectives in the Six-Three wouldn't move the picture until something took its place. No one wanted to offend someone important. He was a great guy, they said. Oldham was not surprised.

Cops accused of wrongdoing were not given the benefit of the doubt in the NYPD—they were given the benefit beyond reasonable doubt. Police culture held that defending fellow officers was one of the foremost articles of faith. From the onset, Oldham decided not to seek permission from his supervisors in the Major Case Squad. Caracappa had left Major Case five years earlier. But word traveled rapidly in those circles, Oldham knew, and he didn't want to tip his hand about taking up the case. He would freelance for a while, fly under the radar, and see where it took him.

"CAN I TRUST YOU?"

A few weeks later, at the sentencing of Walter Johnson, aka King Tut, Oldham sat in the gallery of Judge Frederic Block's courtroom. A compact man in his forties, casually dressed, sat two rows behind Oldham scribbling in a notebook. Oldham recognized his face but couldn't remember the name. The man had a press pass hung around his neck. Oldham read the name: Jerry Capeci. "I only knew Capeci by reputation. He was *the* premier mob reporter—as a much a part of the Brooklyn OC landscape as the mobsters, detectives, federal agents, criminal defense attorneys, prosecutors, and judges. There were few people in law enforcement I could talk to but I needed guidance to navigate the waters of a mafia case. I had studied organized crime and I knew a fair bit—more than people thought I did, which was an advantage in itself—but I was looking for help. A friend of mine, Willie Rashbaum, was a crime reporter and he spoke highly of Capeci's reporting discretion and integrity. I introduced myself. Capeci had heard my name."

"You did the Plum Blossom case," Capeci said to Oldham, referring to his investigation of a Chinatown gang notorious for torturing Chinese immigrants for ransom. "That was a great case."

"Thanks," Oldham said. "Can I speak to you in the hallway for a minute?"

The two men walked out into the marble hallway on the fourth floor of the Brooklyn federal courthouse. As usual, the hallway was deserted, apart from an attorney trying to console a young mother with an infant, who was weeping at the prospect of losing her husband to federal custody.

"I don't have a story for you," Oldham said. "I need your help. Can I trust you to keep it between us?"

Capeci closed his notebook.

"I'm looking at Caracappa and Eppolito," Oldham said. "I've ID'd Louie as one of Kaplan's cops. I got him in a photograph in a Chinese restaurant in Flatbush."

"I can't believe no one has taken that case yet," Capeci said. He appeared to be offended that the prosecution had languished for such a long time.

"Well, I am," Oldham said. "You think those guys did it?"

"I know you're on the right track," Capeci said. "I've heard rumors from the other side. If I can help you, let me know."

Capeci took out a card and scribbled his cell number on the back. Oldham had another "Deep Throat" in the organized crime world to call upon.

"There were certain guys in law enforcement that I knew I could talk to. One was Matty Zeuman, a retired detective I knew from the Intelligence Division in the eighties. I knew Matty was friendly with another retired detective named Kenny McCabe. I figured McCabe was key. I had always heard no one in the city knew more about wiseguys than McCabe. Some guys call in their work, and others work hard. McCabe's life was the job. He spent his days off attending mob funerals or sitting in front of John Gotti's house taking photographs. McCabe was dubbed *cosa nostra*'s 'unofficial photographer,' a kind of cop photojournalist. Gangsters sent out wedding cake to McCabe—which he refused. McCabe didn't actually need the photos. He had a photographic memory. But McCabe figured, rightly, that there was no way to know what minor league figure, or unknown man in a trench coat with the collar turned up, could be the key to a huge case. McCabe was the detective who arrested Big Paul Castellano for the Commission Case. He worked John Gotti, more than once. McCabe was said to be able to tell the rank and standing of wiseguys just by looking at their behavior."

McCabe's office was on the seventh floor of the United States Attorney's Office in the Southern District of New York, a large room overlooking St. Andrew's Plaza in lower Manhattan. McCabe was fiftyish, large, Irish-American, jovial. He might have looked like just another beefy cop but his eyes were alive and displayed an unusual intelligence. McCabe offered Oldham a seat. An awkward few seconds passed. Oldham wasn't sure how to broach the subject of Caracappa and Eppolito. If the two detectives were guilty of the conspiracy Casso had described, it was certain that one of the people Caracappa had duped into giving him sensitive information was Kenny McCabe. "I was afraid McCabe might think I had come to embarrass him," Oldham recalled. "Nothing could be further from the truth. But the embarrassment couldn't be avoided. The case was a stain on detectives who worked in OC and dealt with Caracappa or Eppolito. In 1994, when the accusations were published in the newspapers, detectives started to take inventory of their interactions with the two 'mafia cops' and wonder if they had inadvertently got someone killed or given away a case."

McCabe was understandably sheepish when Oldham talked about Caracappa and Eppolito. The unease passed quickly. McCabe turned out to be generous, patient, and encouraging. Like Oldham and many other NYPD detectives, McCabe had mulled the matter over many times. There was an extremely good chance that Caracappa and Eppolito were guilty. He confirmed what Oldham suspected. Caracappa had often come to McCabe with questions about ongoing investigations—the Windows Case, the Painters Union Case, various snitches. Acting in good faith, never suspecting Caracappa was capable of betraying the force, McCabe had shared his vast store of knowledge. Access to McCabe's encyclopedic memory as well as his insider's awareness of virtually every significant law enforcement initiative against the mafia had amplified the harm Caracappa could wreak by multiples.

"I'll tell you one thing," McCabe said. "Steve was smart. I've thought about this a lot. There is no one moment that I can point to, but in retrospect I know he pumped me for information. I know what he was doing, looking back. I know it was him. There just isn't any way for me to prove it."

"You're not the only one with that problem," Oldham said.

"They did it," McCabe said. "Go get 'em."

PASSING THE SMELL TEST

Oldham found his copy of *Mafia Cop* stuck in the back of the middle drawer of his desk at Major Case, the photograph of Caracappa and Eppolito clipped out from the middle. He read it again, slowly this time, methodically, dog-earing pages and scribbling in the margins as he went. For Oldham the book was now an investigative tool. In *Mafia Cop* Eppolito described in detail attacking a man with a lead pipe, hitting him in the throat repeatedly. Oldham went to the Aided and Action Center on the fifth floor of headquarters. Microfiche was kept there recording instances of injury to citizens documented by the police department. It was organized by precinct, by year, and alphabetically. Oldham was unable to find any reference to a man beaten with a pipe in his backyard during the year in question in the Six-Three. Oldham pulled Eppolito's arrest record. He was surprised at how few busts were noted.

"Nothing checked out. His exploits were on nearly every page of *Mafia Cop*. Everything about his police life had to be taken to be a fantasy. Eppolito wrote that he had stopped a truck hijacking in midcourse in broad daylight while he was on foot patrol as a rookie. He wrote that he was standing at a street corner when a truck loaded with swag sped by. Eppolito interdicted the truck single-handedly. What did he do, run after it until it hit a red light? Shoot warning shots in the air? Did he leap up on the running board and ram his pistol in the driver's ear? Eppolito obviously had a tenuous relationship with reality."

In *Mafia Cop* Eppolito recounted in detail the supposedly outrageous witch hunt of his administrative trial after his fingerprints were discovered on documents seized by the FBI during a raid on gangster Rosario Gambino's New Jersey home. Eppolito had been tried before NYPD Deputy Trials Commissioner Hugh Mo.

Mo knew the name Eppolito, Oldham learned. Years before, in the mid-seventies, Mo had been an assistant district attorney in Manhattan working in the consumer affairs bureau. Mo had been involved in the investigation of a warehouse on West 47th Street in Manhattan's Hell's Kitchen area. The warehouse held the possessions of tenants who had been evicted from their apartments. The poorest of the poor, families thrown into homelessness, their belongings were meant to be stored until they were collected. The warehouse was owned by Louis Eppolito's uncle, Jimmy the Clam Eppolito. Mo's investigation revealed that Jimmy the Clam was running a scam in the warehouse. When the marshals brought the property in, it was sorted through and everything of value sold. When the evicted tenants tried to collect their possessions they were told that their things had been lost. Mo had been appalled by the sleazy racket. He had obtained a search warrant for the warehouse. When his investigators went to execute the warrant he discovered that the warehouse had caught fire that very day. The documents and records in the building had been burned, along with the property and possessions of countless of the dispossessed.

"In *Mafia Cop* Eppolito claimed he had been exonerated by Mo," Oldham recalled. "But that wasn't the same as finding him completely innocent. The standard of proof in the proceeding was supposed to be the preponderance of evidence. The question was whether Eppolito was fit to be a cop, not if he was guilty of criminal conduct. But the department was skewed toward giving cops a soft shake. The photocopied reports that Eppolito had allegedly taken played no part in Mo's decision. The evidence was stipulated to by the lawyers so there were no questions of fact before Mo. Eppolito turned up with a scrapbook of newspaper articles about himself. Mo wondered why the department had given up on the case. Why not put on evidence? Mo thought that the department hadn't proved how the documents had wound up in New Jersey. The fingerprints had nothing to do with Mo's decision. Eppolito had obtained the documents from the Intelligence Division and the documents had turned up in Gambino's house with Eppolito's fingerprints on them. The inference should have been that Eppolito had sold them to Gambino. Eppolito's family were Gambinos. His father and uncles were Gambino hit men. But no evidence was placed before Mo explaining what Eppolito had said when he went to the Intelligence Bureau and requested the document. Mo wanted to close the loop. None of Eppolito's fellow detectives were called to be questioned about how organized crime intelligence was gathered, managed, and protected in the Six-Two."

There was a difference between the degrees of proof needed by a detective and a lawyer. "A lot of old detectives are bloodhounds," Hugh Mo recalled. "They rely on the smell test to see. The detective says if it smells it must be shitty. But the smell test is not good for lawyers. For me, if it smells it could be sulfur, a rotten egg, burned rubber. Obviously, by and large, the smell test proves to be accurate in most cases. What I'm basically saying is, give me all the evidence. The department gave up. They threw in the towel. They gave me nothing. Now the question becomes why."

Mo had no answer and it wasn't his job to find out. There was outrage at the highest levels inside the NYPD at Eppolito's acquittal. Chief of Detectives Richard NiCastro was furious, Mo recalled. "You found him not guilty, but in my book he's guilty," NiCastro told Mo. "Fuck him."

"NiCastro was angry for good reason," Oldham said. "We had the chance to get rid of Eppolito. People would be alive today if the department had been able to just do the minimum necessary to protect itself. But that was part of the problem in the NYPD. The institution was dysfunctional. It wasn't able to deal with Caracappa and Eppolito's level of deviance. Caracappa and Eppolito knew it, exploited it, killed with it. Mo remembered how astonished he had been when he went to a promotions ceremony only a couple of years later and saw Eppolito being promoted to the rank of second-grade detective. After the hearing, Mo had helped get Eppolito sent to the Six-Three, another mobland precinct in Brooklyn.

The bosses wanted to send Eppolito as far away from the mafia as possible. Mo thought that wasn't fair. But Mo assumed that Eppolito would be under a cloud inside the force. The trial was damaging to his reputation. The story was reported in the newspapers. And there was Eppolito being promoted to second grade. Mo thought someone was doing some heavy lifting for Eppolito."

PHONE WORK

Oldham kept working his connections. Throughout his career, he had learned the value of tracking prisoners. Penitentiaries were not the end of the line. Oldham knew he could apply pressure long after sentencing. "Everyone has something to lose, even an inmate," Oldham knew. "It can be a tiny thing. The same is true in prison. There are good and bad penitentiaries—and then there are awful ones. For an older prisoner medical care might be a priority, so the stresses of moving and never seeing the same doctor twice can be a fearsome prospect. It could be visitation privileges."

Oldham requested and received Tommy Galpine's intake folder from the security deputy warden at Federal Prison Camp Duluth in Minnesota. The folder contained Galpine's biographical information and notes from his interview with a social worker. In the file, Oldham found the name and address for one Inez Ramirez, Galpine's girlfriend. She lived on George's Lane in the Richmond Terrace section of Staten Island. Oldham drove out to see the house the next morning.

"She lived at the end of a dirt road in a rough neighborhood. It looked more like Appalachia than New York City. The two-story clapboard house was falling apart. There were broken windows, a refrigerator on the front porch, and a gray 1977 Plymouth up on blocks in the backyard. No one was home. I peered through the window. There was a garbage can filled with empty beer bottles. The sink was filled with dirty dishes. A massive brown mongrel lunged at me, barking madly, scratching at the window trying to break the pane. I backed off, scared he might break through the windows and tear me a new orifice."

Oldham learned that Inez Ramirez worked in a city cafeteria in downtown Brooklyn, only a few blocks from the courthouse and the offices of the Eastern District. Oldham went to the cafeteria for lunch. "Ramirez wasn't hard to spot. She was short, plain, and chubby. I ordered food from her. Her pay and benefits were poor, the prospects for promotion slim, and the shifts Ramirez was able to get sporadic. Ramirez was living near the poverty line, barely holding on. I knew that Kaplan's wife's circumstances weren't nearly as bad, I had seen Burt's house and how Eleanor was living. She had a nice place in Bensonhurst. She didn't seem to suffer economically from Burt's absence. She had a nice car, neatly trimmed lawn, a comfortable but presumably lonely existence. Kaplan had means. Galpine had nothing. It looked like I might have a wedge into Galpine. I figured Galpine would give sooner or later. If there was a weak link it was Galpine."

Oldham wrote to the Bureau of Prisons at the Duluth camp, on Department of Justice letterhead, requesting the tapes for all calls made by Tommy Galpine. All calls are taped in federal prison and kept for ninety days. The first batch of Galpine's tapes arrived the next week. Oldham had a boom box in his office he used to play the tapes to determine which were "pertinent" and "not pertinent." Oldham listened as the tape captured the phone ringing and Inez Ramirez answering. A recorded female voice preempted conversation. "This call is from a federal prison inmate," the female voice said in mechanical monotone. "This call is prepaid. You will not be charged for this call. To decline this call, hang up. To accept this call, press five. To decline further prepaid calls, press zero."

Ramirez pressed five. "Hang on," she said.

"I got plenty of time," Galpine said dryly.

A minute passed and Ramirez returned to the phone.

"Every time I call, you're never home," Galpine said. "You should get a cell phone. The best way to keep this relationship going is communication. I think you know that but maybe you're just too lazy to do it."

Ramirez sighed. This was clearly familiar territory.

"What's new? Anything new?" Galpine's voice was depressed and insecure. "I really love you, " he said.

She said, "I love you too."

"I ain't going to be nobody's fool."

"You're not," she said.

Oldham had a vested interest in the future of their relationship. To his mind, the better the relationship was, the more likely he would be able to convince Galpine to cooperate and betray his promise to Kaplan in order to be with Ramirez.

"Here we are arguing again," the conversation drearily continued. "I love you but I'm willing to give that up if you don't want this. That's the signals I'm getting. You do nothing for me."

"I know I do nothing for you," Ramirez said. "That doesn't mean I don't love you, Tommy."

"We have no communication," Galpine said, sighing. "We're drifting apart. Put yourself in my position—I put myself in your position. I know your life is no bowl of fucking cherries. I keep calling you and you're never home. I got to line up for half an hour, forty-five minutes to get a phone and you're not there. It's four below fucking zero out here. I don't even want to speak to nobody else out there. I called all my family. I wished them merry Christmas."

"I got two calls for me the other day. I don't know who it is that's trying to call me."

It had been Oldham calling her.

"That's how much I love you," he said, "if you want your freedom you can have it."

"I could have been doing anything I wanted all this time. I don't want to do nothing."

"I'm a person of my word," Galpine said. "I want you to show me that. If I say I'm going to do something, I do that and that's what I want you to do. Or at least try. No more one-sided shit. I'm willing to end it if you want to end it."

Dismayed, Oldham didn't see Galpine's chances of cooperating improving. Listening to Galpine and Ramirez was excruciatingly dull. The same arguments were repeated ad nauseam. "Listening to prison phone conversations should be required as punishment for every juvenile delinquent in the country. If you ever want to know how important it is to stay out of prison, listen to the telephone conversations of prisoners. They are exercises in emptiness."

Next Oldham ordered the prison tapes for Burton Kaplan. Oldham also listened to many calls Kaplan made from Allenwood, some to his wife, Eleanor, and others to his girlfriend, Diane Pippa, who lived in Las Vegas. Kaplan's calls were in stark contrast to Galpine's. Galpine was catatonic but Kaplan still had vigor in his voice. When Kaplan spoke with Pippa, his voice was filled with nostalgia. They laughed, recalling meeting at airports, drinking together, pouring each other back onto the airplane to return to their everyday lives.

"I never was a partier," Kaplan said on one tape. "I'm certainly not partying now." He sighed. "I wasted a lot of time. Time will tell what happens. I don't want to be sad. It's a sign of weakness."

There was a series of clicks on the phone.

"It might be someone at my end," Pippa said.

"They could be listening over here," Kaplan said.

And they were. "I was listening," Oldham said. "For weeks and months and in the end years I listened to Kaplan and Galpine. I didn't listen to every conversation and I didn't listen to every tape. I've never been methodical in that way. I'm an impressionist. I wanted to create a rift between the two. I was going to play Kaplan's tape to Galpine to show him Burt wasn't suffering financially the way Tommy was. Burt was taking care of his loved ones."

The next interesting tape Oldham reviewed was a call from Kaplan to Michael Gordon apologizing for the late hour. "There's only three phones here and you got to grab them when you can because the other guys will just talk forever and you have to wait your turn."

The two old friends exchanged small talk. Pleasantries done, Kaplan turned to business. Kaplan was convinced the government was continuing to punish him for refusing to cooperate. Kaplan had no idea who Oldham was, or what Oldham had in store for him. He was paranoid that the government was intruding upon every aspect of his life, from putting him in prison for the rest of his life to even intimidating tradesmen not to work for his wife. Or so Kaplan believed. He told Gordon about a carpenter working on the renovations Kaplan was having done to his Bensonhurst home—another indication of his continuing financial well-being. One day, suddenly and for no apparent reason, the carpenter started to "act crazy" and left the work site and never returned. A short while before, a plumber was working on one of Kaplan's bathrooms when he stopped work and refused to continue with the repairs.

"In Kaplan's mind, the government was still fucking with him," Oldham said. "He probably thought it was the FBI. Kaplan knew the feds didn't mind playing hardball. He thought people were being 'talked to' and warned to stay away from him—and his wife. Of course, I was doing no such thing. I wasn't talking to carpenters and plumbers to get to Kaplan. I was trying to make a case. I was chasing him, in my way. But once a guy knows you're looking at him, you become the source of all evil. Kaplan's imagination was at work. Part of making a case like this was getting inside the head of your target. Kaplan was starting to see shadows. He heard bumps in the night. I was the ghost of conspiracies past. I was the man who wouldn't let him forget the winter night he drove a dead man up to Connecticut to bury him in the frozen earth. I wanted to be his subconscious—the buried bodies, the faces and sounds that came to him in his dreams."

Listening to Kaplan and Galpine became a hobby of Oldham's. It was toilsome but also a release from the stress of work. He had not found an opening and began to think there was little chance Galpine would betray

Kaplan and snitch on Caracappa and Eppolito. But he was preparing to get lucky.

"They're going after anybody who knew me through the years," Kaplan told Gordon. "They gotta be talking to Monica Galpine and all the names that she gave them."

Timelines were folding in on each other. Oldham's investigation was catching up with and overlapping the ongoing conspiracy to protect Caracappa and Eppolito. Listening to Kaplan talking about Oldham's investigation was more than an eerie irony of detective work. It gave Oldham the chance to measure if the pressure was having any effect, positive or negative, on Kaplan's resolve to remain silent.

For months, as Oldham and his now Major Case partner, Detective George Slater, listened to the tapes of Kaplan and Galpine, the pair were also consumed by an investigation of Republican fund-raisers. The case was slow going. Senior officials in the NYPD resisted Oldham's pursuit of the case. Oldham and Slater were reassigned to the chief of the Internal Affairs Division. The assignment to the IAD was supposed to be an insult to Oldham. The division was dedicated to investigating police officers. "I wasn't interested in IAD," Oldham said. "I didn't want to chase cops when I was in the Two-Eight. I didn't want to chase cops when I was in Manhattan robbery, in Queens robbery, and not now in Major Case. I fought as hard as I could. I had no interest in chasing down fellow officers—other than Caracappa and Eppolito."

In the late nineties, as his career stalled, the prison tapes provided Oldham with a quiet comfort.

GASPIPE'S 302s

In the winter of 1999, Oldham walked by a stack of boxes in the hallway in the Organized Crime Section on the nineteenth floor of the Eastern District offices. One of the boxes said "US v. Kaplan" on it. Oldham was intrigued. A prosecutor he had known for years from around law enforcement circles, Judy Lieb, was leaving the Eastern District to become a state judge in the Bronx. Her boxes were being sent to storage. Oldham wanted to make sure the boxes weren't shipped into the maw of the federal government's bureaucracy. "Boxes were sent to the National Archives in Missouri never to be seen again. Grabbing boxes meant that they wouldn't disappear into an abyss. I was a pack rat for documents that related to cases I was interested in. People were always coming up to me and asking if I had old homicide files or immigration folders related to a case they were working on and often I did. If I knew stuff was going to get lost—like the Kaplan boxes—I figured it was better to keep them around. I had my own archive. I had a collection of crime scene photos, raps, surveillances. I had been walking through precinct basements for twenty years collecting documents on guys I was interested in, or thought I might be interested in. I had a Chinese section, a Rap section, a Mob section, psychos. You never knew when an old file might turn into a new case."

Oldham began circling past Lieb's office hoping to run into her. Finally, on the Friday she was leaving the office, Oldham caught up with her and asked about her boxes. "A couple of them are from the Kaplan case," Lieb said.

"Can I have them?" Oldham asked.

"Sure," she said, "they're just going to archives. There's a memo in there from Jamie. Take a look at it."

Oldham did. He took the boxes up to the closet office on the nineteenth floor he kept at the Eastern District. The memo from Jamie Orenstein sat in the box on top of a pile of manila folders. It was titled "the crystal balls." In another box Oldham found a thick black binder. Inside was a 504-page document recording the debriefings of Anthony Casso. The document was a clean copy.

"I spent the next two days and nights reading and rereading Casso's 302s," Oldham recalled. "The 302s were bewildering in many ways. They bounced around in chronology. When I do a debriefing I start at the beginning and proceed chronologically. But Casso's story was all over the map. The crimes he committed and admitted were voluminous. But the telling of the tale was disorienting. I loved reading NYPD OC murder files because there was usually some life to the story. I had read plenty of FBI 302s over the years. But Casso was forthcoming in an unusually detailed way. Casso clearly didn't want to get in trouble for holding anything back. To the contrary. He was meticulously forthcoming.

"I knew Eppolito was the guy when I found the owners of New China Inn and they told me about 'Rouie Epporito,' " Oldham recalled. "When I found out Steve lived across the street from Louie in Las Vegas I knew I was onto something. When I read Casso's 302s I *knew* Caracappa and Eppolito were guilty. I just couldn't prove it—and it was driving me crazy."

On February 16, 1999, Oldham drove by a building on Vanderbilt Avenue in Brooklyn. A three-story tenement with a liquor store on the ground floor, it was the building where Kaplan had grown up, and was still owned by his mother and brother. Oldham knew Kaplan's brother ran the store. He'd found the place after listening to Kaplan's prison tapes and running searches for Kaplan's assets and past addresses. At the time the neighborhood was in a bad state, with a few bodegas open at night and clusters of young men drinking beer on stoops. The fluorescent sign in front flickered with a slogan: *Taste the Excitement.*

Oldham pulled over. He got out and stood in front of the store. It was in sorry condition, a run-down stop for drunks looking for the cheapest alcohol available. Bulletproof glass protected the man sitting at the cash register. He was in his fifties, unshaven, overweight, bald. It was surely Kaplan's younger brother Howard. Oldham waited outside while the sole customer paid and left. There was a Puerto Rican employee, with tattoos, a ponytail, and the manner of a former tough guy, who was stocking the shelves with jugs of cheap red wine. Oldham went in and a bell attached to the door chimed to announce his arrival.

"Is Burt around?" Oldham asked Kaplan's brother.

"Who's asking?" Kaplan's brother said.

Oldham pulled out his detective's shield and flashed it—long enough for its authenticity to be registered, but too fast for the man to catch Oldham's badge number. There were slits in the bulletproof window for customers to talk through. Oldham leaned forward.

"Maybe you and I could talk about Burt a little bit," Oldham said. "Maybe you and I could figure a way to try to help him. Let's go outside and talk privately."

The Puerto Rican put down the jug of wine he was shelving. The place was silent, the only sound a transistor radio playing "Oye Como Va."

The younger Kaplan made it abundantly clear that he had no intention of talking to a cop.

"You don't have to be afraid," Oldham said. "I won't hurt a hair on your head. We'll just talk."

"Why don't you go on and get the fuck out of here before I call the real cops," Kaplan's brother said.

Oldham stood back from the Plexiglas. He looked at the fat bald man. Anger rose, frustration. Oldham banged on the Plexiglas with his fist. "C'mon big boy," Oldham said. "Let's have a little heart-to-heart."

"That's it, I'm calling the real cops," Kaplan's brother said.

"I watched him dial 911," Oldham recalled. "I thought about the fact that I didn't have an authorized case against Burt Kaplan. The idiot was calling 911 and soon police sirens would start wailing. If I stuck around I would have a hard time explaining what I was doing there. I couldn't say I was investigating two retired detectives who might have been hit men for the mafia. I listened to Kaplan's brother give a description to dispatch. 'White male, five eleven,' he said, 'wearing a brown leather jacket and blue jeans.' He was talking about me. I decided retreat was in order. I waved goodbye, promising to be back, and I walked slowly to my car parked around the corner. As I got in the car I heard the yelps of oncoming sirens in the distance. As I pulled onto Atlantic Avenue, I watched a radio car whip by. The case was getting personal. I needed to pull back or I was going to get myself in trouble."

But Oldham didn't stop. He would have to be discreet and develop a strategy. The priority was gaining the confidence of the organized crime community. As the tapes continued to arrive, Oldham heard Galpine start to express the desire to move to a prairie state, someplace far from the scheming of Burton Kaplan and organized crime. Nebraska, Kansas, Wisconsin, anywhere but Brooklyn and the life of a gangster. Galpine had more than 180 months to serve, more than five thousand days of a life slowly wasting away.

"Long periods in prison have a dull and predictable dramatic arc to them," Oldham knew. "Convicts start out defiant. Then there's denial. After a couple of years the hopelessness of it all settles in. Maintaining a brave face is one thing. Being tough is one thing. Tearing up entire chapters of your life is another. The way to get to Galpine wasn't Inez Ramirez. I knew that Galpine would always follow Burt Kaplan. He was in truth Kaplan's 'butt boy.' But I heard in Galpine another kind of opportunity, perhaps an opening. It was a matter of waiting for Galpine's despair to ripen. When he was ready to rat, I was going to be ready."

A few months later, in March 1999, Oldham got another small insight. This time it came from the redoubtable Burt Kaplan. Kaplan was able to take care of his wife financially, but matters were more complex when it came to providing for his girlfriend, Diane Pippa. In order to help Pippa he had to figure a way of getting her money without his wife finding out. Kaplan had spent a lifetime assisting people in need, a form of insurance against the day he might need help. But with Kaplan behind bars, effectively serving a life sentence, it was far more difficult for him to call upon friends and associates for assistance. On the tape for March 11, 1999, Oldham listened as Kaplan called an associate again, this time to borrow money for his girlfriend.

They exchanged small talk. Kaplan gleefully reported that his old Luchese associate, Christy Tick Furnari, had been transferred to Allenwood with him. With some palpable discomfort, Kaplan eventually worked his way around to asking his associate to wire money to his girlfriend.

As Kaplan spoke it was apparent to Oldham that the very act of asking was galling to Kaplan. The conversation was demeaning. Kaplan had been a big-time gangster in New York City. Downtown Burt could get millions from Gaspipe Casso and the Lucheses on a handshake. The associate's reluctance to simply do as Kaplan said would never occur if Kaplan were on the outside. Pippa needed the money immediately, Kaplan explained, so it should be sent by overnight courier. The money would be returned within thirty days.

"Where's the money coming from?" Kaplan's associate asked.

"It's coming from a dear friend of mine, from my business."

"Kaplan paused for a full five seconds," Oldham remembered. "The fury traveled through the phone line like a spoken word. If and when I got in a room with Kaplan to talk about cooperation, the last thing I would do was play cute with him. Kaplan didn't want to play games, or have his word doubted. Straight shooting was what Kaplan demanded—whether it was borrowing money, or planning to whack a guy. There was no nonsense about him when it came to business."

"I would be very, very upset if anyone refused me anything because I've done three million favors in my life," Kaplan said.

Kaplan's associate finally got the message. He quickly changed the subject, asking, "Everything else okay?"

Next, Kaplan turned to the subject of an appeal he had pending. He was hopeful the appeal would prevail. It was based on an allegation—which he later withdrew—that Judd Burstein and other defense attorneys had failed to vigorously present Kaplan's defense. The reason, Kaplan claimed, was that the lawyers knew the government wanted to make Kaplan pay for refusing to divulge what he knew about Casso's "cops." Everything in Kaplan's life revolved around his dealings with Caracappa and Eppolito. His refusal to flip had brought the wrath of the federal government down on him. "Kaplan was defiant and defeated. He was trapped and he knew he was trapped. The consequences of keeping his word to Caracappa and Eppolito were enormous, but Kaplan seemed resigned to his fate. The feds taking him down pushed him to be a stand-up guy—to be a man. In private moments, the regret and sorrow could be heard in his voice."

"I knew this was coming," Kaplan said to his associate. "I knew this was going to happen. I'm ready for it. You know my head. I got a lot of hopes. I'm going to make a comeback. I'm strong."

There was something perversely admirable about Kaplan. He was in prison for the rest of his life and unhappy about his situation but he wasn't going to let it grind him down. Oldham believed it was highly unlikely he would be convinced to talk unless circumstances changed significantly. "If I was going to get Kaplan or Galpine to flip, I had to find ways to exert influence over one or the other of them. Just turning up at a prison and slamming the table and screaming and shouting wasn't going to get it done. I had to construct a new reality for them. I had to change their way of seeing themselves and their future."

SIMMERING ON THE BACK BURNER

"I called Kenny McCabe. I told him about the Kaplan boxes and Casso's 302s. I told him about the New China Inn and the photograph of Eppolito on the wall. Kenny told me that I should try to work from a specific case. Turned out, McCabe knew the case against Caracappa and Eppolito better than he had let on when we first met. Take one murder count, he said. He suggested I start with Jimmy Hydell. Five, six guys knew that Hydell was going to be in Dyker Heights that September afternoon in 1986."

Oldham went looking for Hydell's murder file. There was none. Hydell's body was missing, and he was presumed dead, but there was no NYPD file at all. "His mother, Betty, talked to local detectives. But she couldn't file a murder complaint and the matter didn't meet the criteria for a missing person report. Hydell was of majority age. There was no sign of foul play, other than his mother catching sight of two cops in a blue Nissan the day her son disappeared. There was no note, no body, no body parts. As far as the NYPD was concerned, Hydell could have caught a flight to Rio and started a new life."

Oldham learned that Hydell's younger brother Frank had been murdered in the spring of 1998. Frank Hydell was shot on the sidewalk outside a topless bar in Staten Island, on the orders of Colombo boss Alphonse Persico. Frank Hydell had been labeled a rat. The younger Hydell's problems had started months earlier when he called 911 to summon an ambulance for a construction foreman who had been shot in the rear during a party and was bleeding to death. The foreman had made the mistake of asking his new hire, the nephew of a wiseguy, to actually show up and work at his new construction job. The foreman was not supposed to be killed, just punished, and his unnecessary death eventually led Hydell to inform on the Colombos. It didn't take long for Persico to figure out that Hydell had flipped. When Frank Hydell was killed he was found to have a large tattoo across his back that read, "Casso is a Rat."

"I knew Casso had given an interview to *60 Minutes* in 1998 to try to get back in the good graces of the government. In the interview with *60 Minutes* Casso described killing Hydell. That part of the interview was excluded for some reason. I called a guy I knew over at *60 Minutes,* a junior producer, and he said they didn't run the piece because they had no way of corroborating Casso's account."

Oldham compiled a list of potential witnesses. It ran to nearly one hundred people, ninety-nine of whom weren't talking.

"One day I went to my supervisor's office to talk about the case. I mentioned it once and that was enough. He didn't want to hear about it. He said the words slowly, carefully enunciating them.

"'I do not want to hear about that case ever again,'" he said. "'Understand? Nothing good will come of it.'"

"I understood. Catching Caracappa and Eppolito would bang out two old retired cops whose day had passed. But it would hurt the whole department. Certain people think cops go bad every day. This would just confirm it. The feeling I got from a lot of the guys was that the case should be allowed to die. Meanwhile, I had my boxes. I had my back burner— in this case, it was a low and slow back burner. I needed Kaplan or Galpine. I needed a storyteller."

CHAPTER TWELVE

THE CADRE

In November 2001, Oldham retired from the NYPD. One of the leading detectives on the force, he took a job as an investigator with the Violent Criminal Enterprise and Terrorism Section of the Federal Eastern District—a position specifically created for him in the wake of the 9/11 attacks. Oldham had worked out of the Eastern District for years, while still attached to and paid by the NYPD, but now the relationship was official. "It was the perfect scenario for me. Most retired cops end up doing security work. It was a real job, with real investigative responsibility, a continuation of my work at Major Case. If anything the scope and sweep of my job was greater. I had autonomy and I had access to the resources to pursue cases I thought were important.

"Things were great. Andrea and I had our first child, a beautiful girl named Olivia Grace. But drinking was really becoming a problem. Alcohol numbed me. A lot of cops self-medicated. Over the years the bad memories agglomerate. The loss of two brothers never left me. Pretending not to care about what you were doing—the victims, the violence, your own health and sanity—is one of the many ways many cops act tough. I was no exception to that rule. Heroic drinking was part of the culture. When cops retire, when we lose the demands and bonds of our brotherhood, we lose the basic structure of our lives."

Working for the Eastern District provided Oldham with the opportunity to begin in a new direction. He arrived at his new job with a dozen cardboard boxes. They were his files from half a dozen cases. The array of investigations Oldham had on his mind reflected the range of his interests—they were the cases he was "looking at," the cases he couldn't let go. One investigation involved a series of suspicious deaths in the Guyanese immigrant community in New York that had drawn the attention of life insurance companies, who had turned to law enforcement. Oldham had taken it upon himself to discover if there was an insurance broker selling policies and then murdering the beneficiaries to collect the hefty proceeds. In another ongoing case, an Egyptian national named Mohammed Khalil was posing as an FBI agent in order to kidnap Arab immigrants. Oldham was also looking for Vere "Joker" Padmore, a twenty-eight-year-old armed robber working with two corrupt cops in the 77th Precinct in Brooklyn who dressed in gawdy women's clothing as a disguise. The Joker was wanted for three homicides and a string of jewelry store heists and home invasions.

Upon his arrival at the Eastern District, Oldham was also tasked with the Arab interview program in the aftermath of the 9/11 attacks on the World Trade Center towers. "I was given a list with hundreds of names from so-called 'target countries' by the Department of Justice in D.C.," Oldham recalled. "The information came from the worst database imaginable. Many of the people on the list hadn't lived in America for years. Others were dead. The government had no clue how to investigate supposed 'terrorists.' Most of the people I interviewed on the list were Coptic Christians who had been driven out of their homelands because of their Christian beliefs."

Now assigned an office with a window on the eighteenth floor, Oldham moved the "back burner" boxes from the closet he had maintained one floor up. One box relating to Caracappa and Eppolito was on top of his filing cabinet. Another was under his desk. Free from the strictures of the NYPD, but swamped with terrorism-related assignments, Oldham promised himself that as soon as he could spare the time he would conduct a comprehensive investigation of former detectives Stephen Caracappa and Louis Eppolito. Above all others, it was the case he was determined to make. For Oldham the case itself had become a "crystal ball"—a mysterious and mesmerizing prism-like object to be contemplated from all angles.

"I know this sounds crazy, but the thing that I discovered when I became a detective is that I had an ability to see how cases were going to turn out," Oldham recalled. "I'm not a fortune-teller, and I'm not deluded. In every other aspect in my life I am as clueless as the next guy. But when I looked at a case—when I looked at the evidence, the witnesses, the suspects—I could usually see how things were going to play out. It was like that with Caracappa and Eppolito. I didn't know when or how I was going to get the chance to start up on them again, but I knew it was going to happen. Stevie Aces and Rouie Epporito weren't going to go to their graves having played the entire world for suckers. Every time I collected another set of cassette tapes of Kaplan and Galpine in prison, or scavenged a Bureau of Prisons record, or ran into Kenny McCabe in the

Brooklyn federal courthouse, I wasn't letting the thing die. From time to time, I tossed in a crime scene photograph, or a DD-5 I had come across, or an interesting memo. It was how I worked."

KUBECKA AND BARSTOW

One artifact Oldham tossed into his boxes was a newspaper article that ran in *Newsday* in late December 2001. The report by journalist Steve Wick was headlined, "Used and Left Unprotected: 2 LI Garbage Haulers Betrayed by Detectives, FBI Mole." The story was nine thousand words long and represented an entire year of investigative journalism by Wick. "They met by the Surfside Three Motel in Howard Beach, three gangsters with something to talk over," Wick began. "Salvatore Avellino had driven into Queens from his mansion in quiet, exclusive Nissequogue. A captain and rainmaker in the multimillion-dollar enterprise called the Luchese crime family, Avellino had a proposal to talk over with his bosses, Anthony Casso and Vic Amuso. He wanted a man murdered."

Two men, as it turned out. Wick's feature story detailed the conspiracy to kill two Long Island businessmen who ran a small garbage hauling company. For most of the 1980s, Robert Kubecka and Donald Barstow had resisted pressures from the mob and cooperated with law enforcement. The men had been harassed, threatened, and intimidated by an organization called Private Sanitation Industry Inc. of Nassau and Suffolk Counties, a Luchese- and Gambino-controlled cartel running trash collection on Long Island. Kubecka, forty, and Barstow, thirty-five, both had families, and both of their wives had been threatened and their children followed home from school. The intelligence they had provided law enforcement proved invaluable. The pair had suggested to organized crime investigators that they place a bug in Avellino's black Jaguar. Sal Avellino often drove Luchese boss Tony Ducks Corallo on his errands. During the car rides, Corallo had given Avellino a sophisticated account of the operations of the "commission," which oversaw the five New York crime families. The information obtained through the bug was put before the jury in the Commission Case in 1985, leading to Corallo and other mob leaders receiving one-hundred-year sentences and subsequently dying behind bars.

"I knew the Kubecka and Barstow murders," Oldham recalled. "It stood as a black mark against law enforcement. There was no way the state task force should have put two businessmen in a position where they were acting as informants in an ongoing investigation of known killers. In the Born to Kill case I put a kid named Tinh on the street as an active cooperator. But Tinh was a member of the gang. He was a criminal. He knew when to ask questions and when to shut up. The task force told Kubecka and Barstow they had a network of informants feeding them intelligence on the mob in the garbage business—parallel informants who would know if their lives were in danger. But there were no other informants. They said they would protect their identities, but they didn't. They promised protection, but they couldn't provide it."

Barstow and Kubecka had no way of knowing how much peril they were in. The men were trying to balance outward defiance of the mob and secret cooperation with the government. At the time law enforcement was gaining experience in setting up dummy companies to operate in corrupt industries. Operations were established in the garment and carting industries using undercover detectives and federal agents posing as businessmen. The ruses were expensive and time-consuming but it was a necessary precaution to employ trained undercovers. Oldham said, "Kubecka and Barstow were amateurs. They must have known they were taking a risk but they couldn't give informed consent because they didn't know the way information circulated in the organized crime universe—cops and robbers. The result was inevitable, with Amuso and Casso in charge of the Luchese family and able to access sensitive law enforcement information."

In the summer of 1989 Barstow and Kubecka testified before a grand jury about the methods the mafia used to control the garbage industry: rate-rigging, dividing territory, destroying competition. On September 9, 1989, Kubecka received a threatening call. Kubecka contacted the head of the New York State Organized Crime Task Force. The official told him to call 911. Kubecka called 911. A patrolman came to speak to the two men and took Kubecka's complaint but no other steps were taken to protect the men. At dawn the next day, two gunmen appeared on Kubecka and Barstow's lot in East Northport. Frankie "Pearl" Federico and another Luchese hit man had been given the contract to kill Kubecka and his father. The hit man entered the office shooting and struck Barstow. Barstow dropped dead. The hit man fired again. Kubecka was shot but still alive.

"The hit man's gun jammed," Oldham said. "The third bullet wouldn't feed from the clip. He tried to jack the slide back to eject the cartridge. Hearing the commotion and voices inside the trailer Frankie Pearl came in. Kubecka lunged and butted heads with him. They wrestled on the floor leaving hair strands, blood, a gun. Finally Frankie Pearl and the other man ran for it. Kubecka crawled to the phone and called 911 again—and gasped that he didn't know who shot him."

Wick had started reporting the story as a little-known tragedy from the war on organized crime. Two Long Island businessmen had tried to do the right thing and paid the ultimate price. But Wick discovered basic questions couldn't be answered. Why was there no security sent to Kubecka and Barstow? How did the hit men know there were no cameras or surveillance set up by law enforcement on the tiny office? Wick became obsessed with the story. The families of the two men had sued the state of New York and won a $10.8 million judgment for negligence in the late nineties. But Wick came to believe it wasn't indifference or incompetence that got Barstow and Kubecka killed. What if there was a mole who betrayed them?

After months and months of trying, Wick was finally granted an interview by Gaspipe Casso. Wick traveled to Florence, Colorado, to the super-max prison where Casso was housed. Casso told Wick about the meeting with Avellino at the Surfside Three Motel in Howard Beach. Casso told Wick that he had a high-ranking FBI mole, but that he'd never met him. Casso said he paid and communicated with the mole through Kaplan, Caracappa, and Eppolito. Casso claimed that he had told the FBI about his mole when he was debriefed in 1994, but the FBI had refused to believe him or even record the allegation in Casso's 302s.

Oldham read the Wick articles at the time, adding them to the boxes he kept on Caracappa and Eppolito. He wasn't convinced by Casso's claim about the FBI agent; even if it was plausible, someone in the NYPD was more likely. Eppolito had lived on Long Island during the eighties, so he had physical proximity, and there was no question in Oldham's mind that Eppolito was capable of committing more crimes than Casso knew about. "There was a large likelihood that Caracappa and Eppolito had more going on than just their deal with Casso and Kaplan," Oldham said. "Virtually every criminal who flipped and became an informer surprised us by revealing crimes we didn't know had been committed—murders, assaults, extortions. It was one of the uses of RICO. Instead of attacking specific crimes, the law went after criminality. So I was open to the possibility. But by the time Wick was reporting on Barstow and Kubecka, Casso had been locked up for years. A prisoner like Casso is usually desperate for any kind of chance at improving his circumstances. While Kaplan stayed silent and did his time, Casso was like a demented canary in a cage. He sang and he sang and he sang. He would sing any song you cared to hear, if he thought it might get him a new deal with the government, or a trip to New

York City to testify in court. Any relief from the tedium of twenty-three-hour-a-day lockdown. I figured Casso was yanking Wick's chain about the FBI agent."

The *Newsday* article circulated around law enforcement circles. Bob Creighton of the Suffolk County DA's office and a homicide detective named Eddie Sandry traveled to the various penitentiaries scattered over the country housing convicted Lucheses, as well as contacting Lucheses who were hiding in the witness security program. Following Wick's lead, they went to Florence and spoke with Casso but decided to pull the plug on Casso when he told them he'd never dealt with the FBI agent in person but always through Kaplan, Eppolito, and Caracappa.

The matter seemed to go away, but another seed had been planted in the mind of Oldham. *Newsday* reporter Wick recalled his intentions in writing the article and reviving attention to a crime that was drifting into the forgotten past. "I was convinced that these families were owed more than just the settlement for the negligence suit," Wick said. "I thought they should know that Barstow and Kubecka had been betrayed and by whom. I thought they deserved to know the truth. When the article came out I think it touched off a lot of dominoes."

FRANKIE THE PEARL

On January 27, 2003, Frankie the Pearl Federico walked into a donut store in the Bronx. Federico was seventy-five years old. He had been on the run for more than a decade, mostly living in Italy, running from certain conviction for the murders of Kubecka and Barstow. The presence of his hair and blood at the scene of the murder of Kubecka and Barstow gave the government an ironclad case and a continuing interest in the aging gangster. But after so many years successfully eluding arrest, Federico had grown sloppy. His guard was down that day. Federico was expecting to borrow money from a mob contact. Federal agents were waiting for him inside the donut shop. Federico had been lured there with the promise of a few thousand dollars from agents posing as OC associates of Federico's—the law enforcement equivalent of "copping a sneak."

"Frankie the Pearl was an embarrassment to us when he was on the run," Oldham said. "He evaded justice for a long time but we got him in the end. In court Federico made an awful spectacle of himself. Rather than clinging to a sliver of dignity, he made himself look not just like a killer—

but a deluded self-pitying killer. Federico's blood was all over the crime scene, but he claimed he had been framed. Federico said the FBI had tortured him when drawing blood for a DNA test by using extra-long needles and threatening to suck all the blood out of his body. Federico claimed to have great evidence that would destroy the government's case." During the trial, he compelled the government to fly Gaspipe Casso, Vic Amuso, Georgie Neck Zappola, and a bunch of other Lucheses to New York to testify. Before they took the stand, at the last moment, Federico agreed to plead guilty and take a fifteen-year sentence—effectively life for a man his age. When the judge refused to accept the deal Frankie the Pearl collapsed and had to be carried from court. "The mob had become a cabaret, a pathetic and pale imitation of itself, with a hit man in his mid-seventies swooning for sympathy. Judge Block relented a few days later. 'You'll surely die in jail,' Block said."

The arrest and trial of Federico had, in fact, revived interest in Barstow and Kubecka once again. Like the *Newsday* article by Steve Wick, the case kept questions about past leaks and murdered cooperators alive in New York. Soon after Federico's capture, sometime in the spring of 2003, Oldham received a call from Bill Mueller, a senior attorney in the Eastern District. Mueller said that Federico's arrest had provoked inquiries about Barstow and Kubecka. Mueller wanted to know whether the failure of the NYPD to catch and fire Caracappa and Eppolito was possibly to blame for the deaths of Barstow and Kubecka. The intelligence Wick had gathered about Casso's connection to the double homicide and Casso's connection to Caracappa and Eppolito led to a rumor running around town that a civil lawsuit against the NYPD might be launched. The next day, an analyst in the Organized Crime Section named Joel Campanella stopped by Oldham's office. Campanella asked if he could look at Oldham's boxes on "the cops."

"They're not my guys," Oldham said. "There's another dirty cop out there on Long Island."

Oldham gave Campanella the "case file," a rudimentary summary of the case and its progress, or lack thereof. "I had read Casso's 302s," Oldham said. "I knew that the Lucheses had more than Caracappa and Eppolito inside law enforcement. Sal Avellino had 'cops' too, and Casso was paying two grand a month to those 'cops.' But I was pretty sure Avellino's 'cops' weren't my 'cops.' Likewise with the supposed FBI agent Casso had on his payroll. Casso lied about his law enforcement contacts when he talked to other wiseguys to protect his real source—

Caracappa and Eppolito. Casso said so himself in the 302s. In 1991 Casso said he'd once told Sammy the Bull Gravano he had an FBI agent to throw him off the scent."

Campanella returned the next day. Oldham was right, Campanella said. It appeared the Barstow and Kubecka case had nothing to do with Caracappa and Eppolito. But Oldham's curiosity was piqued. Walking down the hallway in the Eastern District soon after, Oldham ran into prosecutor Mark Feldman. Feldman was now the head of the Organized Crime Section. He was an institution in the OC industry. Before he started working for the federal government, for many years he was an assistant district attorney—ADA—in Brooklyn. Feldman had been prosecuting mob cases in New York City for decades. He was large and bespectacled and generally personable. He had married a police officer and committed his life to fighting the war against the mafia. Cops and wiseguys, reporters, judges, stenographers, court security guards, all knew Feldman. Including former Detectives Caracappa and Eppolito. In *Mafia Cop,* in his Author's Note, Eppolito's co-author journalist Bob Drury had thanked Feldman for his assistance with the book. In the book, Eppolito described Feldman as "one tough Jew."

"From virtually every angle, over two decades and including dozens of characters in the mafia and law enforcement, Feldman was woven into the fabric of this case. As a young assistant district attorney, he had been assigned to the Brooklyn Rackets Bureau as the 'riding' attorney for mob murders. The job required him to go to the scenes of crimes and begin to build a case for trial alongside detectives working the investigation. The assignment was bloody and boring, a task given to junior lawyers. As a riding attorney, Feldman had been sent to the scene of the homicide of Eppolito's uncle Jimmy the Clam and cousin Jim-Jim. In the late eighties Feldman had been the prosecutor assigned to try the attempted murder case against a thug named Nicky Guido, when Casso had taken the stand and taken the Fifth Amendment to every question. Everyone of our generation in law enforcement in New York knew about Caracappa and Eppolito, but I knew about Feldman's deep personal connections and I figured he might be interested in taking up the seemingly lost cause.

"Feldman told me that another detective had been talking to him about Caracappa and Eppolito," Oldham said. "I was surprised but not shocked. Caracappa and Eppolito were infamous—the greatest cold case of our time. It made sense that another detective was thinking about Caracappa and Eppolito, or had stumbled into a lead. I was the keeper of the boxes—and the flame—but I knew there were veteran cops out there who would love to take a shot at Caracappa and Eppolito. Feldman said the detective's name was Tommy Dades. I had heard of him. Dades was well known in the NYPD. He was said to be a great street detective and an expert on Brooklyn OC. I called him that day and invited him to stop by and say hello."

TOMMY DADES

The next day, Detective Tommy Dades turned up at Oldham's office with another NYPD detective named Jimmy Harkins—one of Oldham's favorite cops on the force. Harkins introduced Dades to Oldham—Harkins calling Oldham the "wild man" of Major Case. Tommy Dades was nearly a decade younger than Oldham, a former prize fighter with his nose flattened from years in the boxing ring, and his accent and attitude the pure "dems," "des," and "dos" of Sunset Park, Brooklyn. A twenty-year veteran, Dades had served in the Six-Eight in Brooklyn before being assigned to the Investigative Squad of the Intelligence Division. Dades specialized in the mafia and had developed a deep understanding of its culture, along with a string of great stories. Over the years, Dades's tales had been frequently chronicled by *Daily News* reporter Michelle McPhee and then turned into her book *Mob Over Miami*. "Tommy had chased a wanted gangster through St. Ann's Church on Staten Island," Oldham recalled. "A dopey wiseguy named Ronald Moran had sent Tommy a letter threatening to machine-gun his house, killing him and his family—but the half-wit licked the envelope, leaving his DNA behind. Being energetic in the law enforcement business is half the battle, and Tommy was clearly filled with energy. He was about to retire from the NYPD but looking for a way to stay in the game. Tommy was my kind of cop. Both of us were dying to start up an investigation on Caracappa and Eppolito."

Oldham told Dades he had accumulated boxes filled with evidence on Caracappa and Eppolito over the years. He told Dades the story about Monica Galpine, the Chinese restaurant, and "Rouie Epporito." Oldham was certain that Caracappa and Eppolito were guilty; the problem was figuring out how to prove it. Dades, in turn, shared his story about "the cops." Dades had no in-depth knowledge of the underlying facts. He had not read Casso's 302s, or reviewed the scores of DD-5s from the murder files, as Oldham had. But Dades had a lead he called the "golden nugget." Like Oldham, he was convinced the case against Caracappa and Eppolito needed to be reopened and properly investigated. Not by the FBI, who had proven themselves incapable of closing the case. This time, the case needed to be taken up by detectives who knew the NYPD precinct houses, computer systems, and culture. Caracappa and Eppolito needed to be investigated by their fellow detectives—the men they had betrayed in the first place.

Dades told Oldham the tale of the "golden nugget." Dades said he had gone to see a Staten Island woman named Betty Hydell a few months earlier. She'd been devastated by the loss of her son Jimmy in 1986, only to lose her other son, Frankie, a young hood who had also been an informant working for the FBI and Dades twelve years later in 1998. Dades told Oldham how when Frankie Hydell was found dead, in front of a Staten Island strip club with three slugs in his head and chest, his entire back was covered with a huge tattoo saying, "Casso is a Rat." Years had passed, but Frankie Hydell had stayed on Dades's mind and nagged his conscience. Dades felt that Frankie Hydell had been killed because he was a cooperator and that somehow word had leaked to the mob. From time to time, Dades went to see Betty Hydell to talk about Frankie. Dades had developed the habit of dropping in on his sources, victims, and families, for a cup of coffee and a chat. The visits were useful for gathering intelligence. Betty Hydell, a sixty-five-year-old lifelong nurse with the appearance of a woman who had known the great grief of losing two sons to murder, was one of Dades's regular stops.

"This time, Tommy said Betty Hydell was more interested in talking about her other son—Jimmy Hydell. She started out slowly, Tommy said. The day Jimmy Hydell disappeared she said she had seen two 'cops' circling the block outside their house. She said they were driving an unmarked vehicle, of the kind NYPD detectives routinely use. One cop was thin, she said, and the other was fat with a thick mustache. That was in 1986. Six years later, Betty Hydell told Dades she was watching the *Sally Jessy Raphael Show* and on came a retired NYPD detective talking about his new book, *Mafia Cop*. Betty Hydell bolted up from her chair. It was the cop she had seen the day Jimmy vanished. She went out and bought the book that day, she told Tommy. She opened the book to the photographs in the middle and was instantly convinced that the author was the same man.

"Dades thought it was a 'gotcha' moment, but in my view, it was pretty thin evidence," Oldham recalled. "She saw him on television and didn't report it for more than a decade? She had seen two cops acting suspiciously outside her house the day her son vanished forever and she didn't report it? From what distance? What was her sight line? Defense attorneys would have a field day with the testimony if that was all we had against Caracappa and Eppolito. But I loved Tommy. I loved the stories he told about the mob. I loved his enthusiasm. It was important to harness the ripples that were out there and turn them into a wave. It was like the butterfly effect. A small thing like Betty Hydell's accusation, of marginal use in a trial, could start a chain of events and have a big effect in the future. The *sine qua non* was flipping Kaplan or Galpine, but this could be the break I had been waiting for.

"Re-creating the timeline to be accurate and sure about what kickstarted the investigation of Caracappa and Eppolito is impossible. I was always looking at the case. Tommy Dades had the wits to act on what he had from Betty Hydell and go to Mark Feldman. The stars had aligned. Call it kismet. To me, it was the kind of confluence of events that make for the best cases. I had the boxes that would give us a huge head start in gathering materials. Tommy had the 'golden nugget.' The bosses in the Eastern District and the Brooklyn DA's office were getting serious about Caracappa and Eppolito. Resources would be applied to undertake a real investigation. I could get the manpower to build a real prosecution. If I didn't jump at the opportunity, I knew it was never coming around again. I would do whatever I could to be accommodating, come what may. I could hardly believe what was happening. Finally, at long, long last, we were going to make the case."

"READ THE BOOK"

Within days, Oldham stopped by the office of a young prosecutor named Robert Henoch. Oldham often dropped in on Henoch, ostensibly just to talk but in truth to see what he was working on and keep alive the chance of using Henoch on one of his cases. It was Oldham's manner to come at the actual subject of conversation obliquely. He would talk for a time about nothing in particular. Cutting to the chase was not Oldham's style. He liked to take the temperature of his interlocutor and measure mood. This day Oldham was carrying a hardback copy of a book. He dropped *Mafia Cop* on Henoch's desk. "I have a great case for you," Oldham said. "You're not going to believe this case. It's about cops and I know you love cops. I'm doing this one. I've been waiting to do this one for fucking years."

Henoch picked up the book and glanced at the cover. Oldham's copy of *Mafia Cop* was tattered, the jacket torn at the edges, the pages dog-eared with scrawls in the margins.

"Read the book," Oldham. "You're not going to believe it."

As the lead investigator inside the Eastern District working the Caracappa and Eppolito case, Oldham had some influence in choosing an attorney to prosecute his cases. There were dozens of bright young lawyers in the office, many of whom would leap at the chance to embark on a case as difficult and ambitious as Caracappa and Eppolito promised to be. Over the years, Oldham kept a close eye on prosecutors as they arrived in the Eastern District. He was watching for new talent and keeping track of the stable of potential collaborators. Oldham knew he had to be particularly careful with his selection in this case. The demands placed upon the attorney would be prodigious. There were major political and jurisdictional issues to be considered. The Brooklyn DA's office was going to be involved in the case. Oldham needed an attorney tough enough to stand up to the DA's office, but smart enough to know how to avoid conflict.

As with virtually all of Oldham's partners over the years, Henoch's best qualities were diametrically opposed to Oldham's. Henoch was in his early forties, thin, fit, disciplined, focused. Henoch had been born in Los Angeles and raised in the suburbs of Washington, D.C. He studied Soviet history at the University of Michigan and belonged to the ROTC. His father had been a World War II infantryman who became a nuclear physicist working on arms control. After graduation, Henoch was commissioned as a second lieutenant in the Army. As an artillery officer, Henoch was taught to rain down shells on distant targets, a skill set that would prove useful as a prosecutor planning long-term RICO cases. "I knew Bob had been an assistant district attorney in Manhattan before he took a job with the Eastern District," Oldham said. "It was the prosecutor's equivalent of having been a cop. Henoch had tried dozens of cases. He knew the state system—not just the halls of justice, but the dark alleys where detectives and street cops operate. He had been forced to make big decisions involving real lives in real time. Henoch was a colonel in the Army Reserve. Logistics were his speciality. He was crisp, precise, disciplined, all the things I decidedly am not. With the case going to the Brooklyn DA, I figured the guys in the Brooklyn DA's office would trust him. I trusted him."

Reading *Mafia Cop* repulsed Henoch. Over the years, Henoch had worked with many cops but he had never come across a cop who matched Eppolito's perverted portrait of life in law enforcement. Henoch still wasn't certain he wanted to throw himself at such a problematic case. Henoch had good reason to hesitate. Oldham was known as a loose cannon around the office. He was beyond control—beyond the control of the bosses, the rules and regulations. Working with him was known to be taking a trip into the old-school ways of NYPD detectives, for good and for bad. As delicate negotiations between the Eastern District and the Brooklyn DA began, Oldham continued to talk to Henoch about Caracappa and Eppolito and *Mafia Cop*.

"You can do it," Oldham said to Henoch. "This case can be made."

The look in Oldham's eye was childlike, it seemed to Henoch. He was sold. Oldham had his attorney. The choice was superb—but Henoch wasn't going to play second fiddle to Oldham. He was a decade younger, and vastly less experienced, but Henoch had an ego to match Oldham's. Henoch was a control freak. He was detail-oriented. As soon as Henoch touched a case he wanted power over all aspects of it. Over the years Oldham had been able to set the agenda and maintain control in his investigations. As much as the men needed each other, they were fated to clash—but not yet.

Before the investigation could begin in earnest, a decision had to be made about which jurisdiction would lead the investigation and ultimately try the two men—the Brooklyn DA or the Eastern District? Would the case be federal or state? There were a multitude of reasons to prefer a federal case to a straight state homicide case. Associative evidence and prior bad acts were admissible in a federal case. Testimony by an accomplice had to be corroborated by independent evidence under state law. There was no such requirement under federal law. RICO allows the government to put an accomplice on the stand regardless of corroboration. Thus, if Kaplan or Galpine were convinced to become a cooperator, he could testify to the entirety of the conspiracy in federal court, but only to a very limited extent in state court. In state court, there would only be fragments, which could confuse or fail to convince a jury. Under RICO, the story would be told in full.

But there was a major stumbling block. According to RICO, a federal prosecution had to be brought within five years of the cessation or fulfillment of the conspiracy. Under state law, there was no time limit on murder prosecutions. From their first conversation onward, Oldham and Henoch had discussed the time limit issue as an impediment. Oldham believed there were arguments to overcome the statute of limitations issue. Oldham was not a lawyer but that had never stopped him from making legal arguments. The truth, he believed, was that no jury would acquit Caracappa and Eppolito once it learned of the nature of their criminal enterprise. The statute of limitations might give the two retired officers technical grounds to avoid conviction, but that was not how the real world functioned.

"I knew Caracappa and Eppolito weren't going to get off because they moved to Las Vegas and too much time had passed. It wasn't going to fly. The court would find a way to do the right thing. It was a stupid law. There was no jury in the land that would let the murdering former NYPD detectives go free after getting the wrong Nicky Guido killed because they had holed up in a cul-de-sac in Vegas."

Additionally, according to RICO, it was possible for the two former NYPD detectives to offer the defense that they had "withdrawn" from their conspiracy. The difficulty, for Caracappa and Eppolito, was that the burden of proof fell on them. Oldham and Henoch didn't think Caracappa and Eppolito could prove that they had "withdrawn" from their criminal enterprise. Caracappa and Eppolito would almost certainly outright deny any involvement whatsoever with organized crime. "It was a catch-22," Oldham recalled. "To assert the defense that they had absented themselves from the Lucheses would require them to admit that they were members of a conspiracy in the first place. If that was going to be the defense offered by the two former NYPD detectives, the prosecution would be in excellent shape."

Feldman disagreed with Oldham on the issue of the statute of limitations. The crimes committed by Caracappa and Eppolito began in the mid-eighties. The last crime known to be committed was the murder of Eddie Lino in 1990. Both had left the NYPD by 1992. Saying the conspiracy lasted all the way to 2004 strained credulity. Such disputes were common in the competitive bristle of OC prosecutions. Feldman was a lawyer with a distinguished record. Oldham was a cop turned federal investigator. There should have been no room for dispute but Oldham was a determined infighter. Each man turned to the best legal minds in their section of the Eastern District for an expert opinion on the matter. Feldman had legal advisors in the Organized Crime Section. Oldham had access to legal eagles in the Violent Criminal Enterprise and Terrorism Section. The opinions came back with opposite answers. Feldman's lawyer said the time limitation on homicides meant it was too late for a federal RICO case; Oldham's lawyer said the time limit didn't rule out RICO charges. Oldham and Henoch wanted to do the case in the Eastern District. Feldman was more cautiously inclined. The risk was investing the man hours of an attorney and investigators, only to have the case fall apart or be dismissed by a federal judge because of the statute of limitations issue.

Feldman had the ultimate say. The case might still wind up under federal control, but for the time being it would be a collaboration with the Brooklyn DA's office. However the investigation played out, it was best to work the case as a team effort. In any cold case murder prosecution, access to the materials held by state and city officials is critical. The Eastern District could subpoena the documents, but it was easier and more efficient to cooperate. Keeping the Brooklyn DA on their side could only help. Oldham accepted the decision in an effort to steer any course that would finally get a prosecution mounted.

WAR ROOM

The first meeting of the investigators and lawyers who would pursue Caracappa and Eppolito was held in the offices of the Brooklyn DA. Oldham took along Special Agent Eugene Kizenko, a young Immigration and Customs Enforcement investigator who had been working with him on the Guyana life insurance murder case. Oldham wanted a witness to the proceedings. If promises were made, or undertakings given, Oldham didn't want to be the only one in the room who was an outsider. "Gene always told the truth," Oldham said. "It wasn't exactly enemy territory, but I figured it could be a minefield. I wanted someone I could count on."

A round of introductions was made. The Brooklyn DA team consisted of men who collectively had many decades' worth of mob experience. "It was like a mobster meeting. They were all Italian, slick in their suits. They were calling the meeting a sit-down, like they were *capos* and dons. Which was kind of true—they were the leaders on the side of the law, the functional equivalents of mob bosses and underbosses and captains." The "cadre" was how Oldham thought of the team. They were a motley collection of law enforcement officials in middle or late middle age, most of them retired and playing out the string at desk jobs. It was like the Clint Eastwood movie *Space Cowboys,* Oldham thought, conjuring the band of aging astronauts who came out of retirement to solve a problem that had eluded everyone else and called upon their guile and experience.

Oldham discovered that everyone in the room, except for Kizenko, had a personal connection to the case. Bobby Intartaglio, or "Bobby I." as he was known, had been assigned to the Staten Island District Attor-

ney's Office for much of the 1980s. He had worked the Bypass burglary gang. He had been involved in the electronic and physical surveillance of Burt Kaplan's warehouse. Intartaglio also had been involved in
the Dominic Costa case. He was the same age as the others: fifties and
holding on. "'The old man' was how he referred to himself. In the third
person. He would say, 'the old man's feeling good today,' or 'the old man's
losing his marbles.' I liked him fine. He was stalwart, it seemed to me, the
kind of detective who could be relied upon to keep confidences. He had
lived through the era of leaks. He knew what it was like to feel that the
mafia was a step ahead of us, and that there was nothing we could do to
catch our rat."

Doug LeVien was a veteran NYPD detective who had gone undercover in the seventies, pretending to be a Luchese associate, but was
now jockeying a desk in the Brooklyn DA's office. In 1990, when Eddie
Lino was shot on the Belt Parkway in Brooklyn, LeVien had become convinced that Lino had been murdered by a cop. The crime scene had the
markings of an NYPD pullover turned into an OC hit. LeVien had a
friend who worked in the Organized Crime Control Bureau at the time
who told him the detectives there believed Lino was a victim of a dirty
member of the NYPD. "There was an encyclopedic aspect to the gathering. Caracappa and Eppolito had woven an incredibly complicated web
of lies and murder, but it seemed like the cadre covered the entirety.
Detective George Terra was a veteran who had been working on the
investigation into the murder of Annette DiBiasi. Terra's prime suspect
was Jimmy Hydell.

"Mike Vecchione was chief of the Rackets Bureau at the Brooklyn
DA's office. He was an aggressive prosecutor and a political operator. He
had worked in the Brooklyn DA's homicide section and then in the
appeals section, before going into private practice. Politics brought him
back to public service. When his longtime colleague Charles Hynes was
elected DA for King's County, Vecchione followed him. Years of suffering under the yoke of 'the feds' had made many people in the DA's offices
deeply distrustful. Brooklyn prosecutors were foremost amongst those
fed up with the feds, I thought. It wasn't enough that justice was done in
New York City—justice had to be *seen* to be done in the boroughs.

"From the start I knew that if the prosecution was successful there
would be a brawl over credit. It was how things worked in our little
world. The DA and the Eastern District had a long history of animosity.
There were the dynamics between the NYPD and the FBI—which was
why I was determined to keep the Bureau out. On top of that, there was

the reality of life as a cop or mob prosecutor. Money was tight. Years went by before you got a shot at a major case—and this was going to be *major*, if it came off right. There weren't a lot of rewards out there for folks like us. Recognition from your fellow cops was one of the ways we measure success. Careers are made and reputations and legends established by the cases you work."

Chief Investigator Joe Ponzi seemed different to Oldham. "Ponzi was sharp, in every sense of the word. It was evident the work gave him satisfaction. His old man was a legend in the NYPD. Emidio 'Larry' Ponzi had formed the Senior Citizens Robbery Squad—one of the many things Eppolito falsely took credit for. The older Ponzi had been Louie's commanding officer. In his Author Note in *Mafia Cop*, Eppolito recognized Joe's father. 'To Sergeant Larry Ponzi, who taught me how to be a detective, I send my respect.' I figured that line had to give Joe an extra incentive to see that Eppolito was brought to justice.

"Apart from Gene and I, everyone else in the room was attached to the Brooklyn DA and seemed highly suspicious of me. I was one of them— an NYPD detective. But I was also a representative of the Eastern District so I was half a fed—and the feds are always screwing the state. I knew that. I told them I wasn't going to fuck them on this. I didn't say you're not going to get fucked because we all knew there was a good chance they would get fucked. I told them, 'I'm going to give you everything I have. I'm not going to play games and hold things back.'"

Oldham told the cadre what he had collected over the years as evidence. "I had tapes of Tommy Galpine and Burton Kaplan's prison telephone calls. I had Steve and Louis's personnel files and their arrest printouts. I had a folder with Bureau of Criminal Investigation computer printouts run by Caracappa. I had Kaplan's phone book, with its squiggles and rubbed-out numbers—I was sure the numbers for Caracappa and Eppolito were in there somewhere. There were also mortgage applications, car registrations, old phone work, documents I knew I couldn't replicate later. There were quite a few pen registers printouts—they only show the numbers for outgoing calls and they look like cash register receipts. There were 911 calls and surveillance photos, though none of Steve or Louie. I explained that Internal Affairs had lost its files on Steve and Louie. As I talked, someone said that Feldman thinks that there is no way to bring a federal case because of the time limits in RICO."

"I don't give a fuck what Mark Feldman says," Oldham told the Brooklyn DA group. "I don't think we're out of statute."

The following day, Tommy Dades and Bobby Intartaglio came to

Oldham's office in the Eastern District to collect the boxes. They were stacked in the corner of Oldham's office. Upstairs there were still more. A "war room" was initially set up in the DA's polygraph office. Dades and Intartaglio set about going through the materials Oldham had collected over the years to familiarize themselves with the evidence. With more than thirty boxes from the trial of Burton Kaplan in his possession, Oldham moved the "war room" from the Brooklyn DA's premises to a small windowless room on the fifth floor of the Brooklyn Union Gas building next door to the Eastern District. Henoch began to take control of the meetings, keeping track of assignments and constructing to-do lists. "The older guys were always joking about me trying to run the case like it was the Army," Henoch recalled. "It was a blast. I loved it. It was fun to work with extremely seasoned detectives. They knew their jobs. They were excited about the case. They understood the case and what I needed. The best retired detectives know the difference between knowing what's true and being able to prove it. They understand criminal minds. They understand how to get a criminal to cooperate. The retired NYPD detectives I worked with, who stayed in the law enforcement field after they left the force, taught me a lot. The motives of witnesses, how to get information without screwing up their testimony. They understand how the world works.

"Oldham was the risk taker, which was what I liked about him. He was a macro guy. He saw the big picture. He understood trial strategy. He enjoyed the back and forth of office politics and I don't, so he handled a lot of the stuff that I wasn't interested in. He knew the lay of the land within the office. He knew who to ask when you needed a favor. He understood people, even if he wasn't good at dealing with people. I was content with letting him guide relations with the Brooklyn DA. But the thing I liked about him best was that he was an outsider. I think of myself that way. He didn't care what people thought of him and I liked that. He was an independent thinker. Those are valuable commodities to bring to the table."

Constructing a timeline became a primary priority. Some dates were known, others weren't. Caracappa and Eppolito were both part of the NYPD class of 1969. They had served together in the Brooklyn Robbery Squad in the late seventies. But what about other landmarks in their NYPD careers? The murders they were involved in, tangentially and directly, were cataloged. What cases needed to be tracked down? Whom should the cadre talk to? When? What could be done without risking Steve and Louie finding out they were being investigated?

"Secrecy was all-important," Oldham said. "We didn't know how connected Caracappa and Eppolito still were. They had been in Vegas for years but that didn't mean they didn't have sources. Caracappa had been one of the most senior OC cops in the NYPD. He had resources inside the FBI, DEA, as well as precinct houses and One PP. All it took was one leak and our investigation could be blown out of the water. Henoch was haunted by images of Caracappa walking across the border of Mexico with a backpack on and disappearing forever. I considered it a real possibility, too—and an outcome that had to be avoided at all costs."

In September 2004, Detective Tommy Dades retired from the NYPD and took a job with the Brooklyn DA. His first case was Caracappa and Eppolito. He brought Betty Hydell into a meeting of the cadre at the Brooklyn DA's offices. "Betty Hydell was Irish, square-jawed, the kind of woman who had a tough life. She was a nurse. A nice lady. I felt for her. But watching her talk to us, I was certain she wouldn't work on the stand, certainly not as the lynchpin to any case. She believed she had ID'd Eppolito, and who could blame her for wanting him brought to justice, but would a jury believe her? If the government puts on weak evidence it can cast a poor light on the entire case. If Betty Hydell was going to testify, it was going to be in a very limited manner, as background for the jury to hear from the mother of a murder victim to ground them in the reality of Caracappa and Eppolito's conspiracy.

"I was involved in the investigation, of course, but I knew what was in the boxes and I had been pursuing the case for years. The other guys needed to get up to speed. I was also working the Guyanese life insurance murder case, and it was going well. An insurance broker in Queens was selling life insurance policies to indigent and illegal Guyanese immigrants. The coverage was relatively small, for life insurance policies. The average was two hundred thousand. But the payday was huge. Some of the suspicious deaths were taking place in Guyana and so I started to travel back and forth." The investigation would later lead to murder indictments of the insurance broker and his accomplice and an upcoming trial.

Meanwhile, Tommy Dades and Bobby Intartaglio holed up in the war room and went through the documents Oldham had accumulated. Inside the box Dades found the originals of the Bureau of Criminal Investigation checks run by Detective Stephen Caracappa during his career at the NYPD that Oldham had collected. The BCI checks consisted of the names Caracappa had run through the NYPD. Department of Motor Vehicles databases were checked as well. With a BCI check, the address, date of birth, and basic physical characteristics of the person in question were listed. It is also indicated if the person had a criminal record. Detectives were supposed to get approval from their superiors to run a name. The sergeant needed to sign the form to run a check, and detectives were required periodically to provide a list of the names they had run. The NYPD did not want its officers using the database for improper or criminal purposes. Dozens of corruption cases had been brought against cops using the computer systems to trade information for money. It was one of the most common forms of corruption in the department.

"The power of the information is the ability to find people you are looking for," Oldham recalled. "The mafia thrived on that information. Locating enemies was one of the main preoccupations of wiseguys. The NYPD understood this and strictly regulated the BCI. It was evident Caracappa had no regard for the rules. In the mid-eighties, while he was dating a young woman who lived in his building on East 22nd Street, Detective Caracappa ran a BCI search on 'Monica Singleton.' Caracappa had used the BCI system to run a criminal background on his girlfriend, soon to be fiancée and wife. There was no question that Caracappa was guilty of abusing his position. But to what extent? Was it just running the name of the girl he was seeing, to make sure she wasn't hiding anything from him? That was sleazy, and the product of a sly, mistrustful mind, but it wasn't a federal crime."

The evidence in Oldham's boxes was devastating to Caracappa. The BCI files that Dades dug out showed that on November 11, 1986, Caracappa had run the name "Nicky Guido" through the BCI database under a number for an unrelated investigation concerning a man named Felix Andujar. There were a number of other names in the search Caracappa had run. Guido was in the middle of the list. The Nicky Guido search was immediately understood to be hugely important. "It was exciting," Henoch recalled. "It established a direct connection between Caracappa and one of the victims. Because Nicky Guido was such a minor figure in the OC world, not under any NYPD scrutiny, it was highly suspicious that a Major Case detective who was not working on the Anthony Casso attempted murder did this. Caracappa had no business running the name of a small-time hood in November of 1986, weeks after Casso was shot. Major Case had no involvement whatsoever in the Casso shooting. Period."

But it was worse than that. Caracappa used a case number that had nothing to do with Anthony Casso. He disguised his actions by placing

Guido's name in a list of other names, as if Guido were just another witness or suspect in the case in question. The final fact was the most damning. The search Caracappa had run listed a Nicholas Guido born 2/2/1960 who lived on 17th Street in Windsor Terrace. The Nicky Guido who had shot Casso lived in downtown Brooklyn. Special Agent George Hannah and Detective George Terra, who were working on the right Nicky Guido case at the time, knew who the right Nicky Guido was within days of the shooting. The mistake demonstrated that Caracappa didn't know who he was looking for. The fact that he was looking at the wrong Nicky Guido showed that Caracappa had searched an innocent man's name—just before he was murdered.

The timing could only be explained in connection to Gaspipe Casso and his freelance "investigation" to get the men who had tried to kill him. Caracappa's run was done two months after Casso had been shot, in September 1986. Jimmy Hydell had been snatched on October 18, 1986. Casso had tortured and murdered Hydell, after acquiring the names of Hydell's conspirators—including Nicky Guido. Caracappa ran the search on November 11, 1986. On Christmas Day 1986, six weeks later, the wrong Nicky Guido was murdered in front of his house.

The implication of the evidence was clearly promising. Yet the claim to its discovery was contested and disheartening for the cadre. Various assertions about unearthing the BCI runs circulated among detectives and lawyers on the case. Oldham said he had put the BCI run in his boxes in the mid-nineties and knew that they contained Caracappa's search of Nicky Guido. FBI agents claimed they had run the name in 1994, when Casso first flipped. Tommy Dades said he'd discovered the Nicky Guido search. "Personalities were starting to get in the way," Oldham said. "I gave Tommy the boxes to go through. Tommy found the document and recognized it for what it was. The important thing was that we had the Nicky Guido search. We weren't going to get a conviction with that alone. It was good but we had a long way to go before we could prove the guilt of Caracappa and Eppolito beyond a reasonable doubt."

SUBPOENA

Joel Campanella, the analyst with the Organized Crime Section and a veteran intelligence detective in the NYPD, was given the task of putting the FBI 302s on compact disks so members of the cadre could read the collected criminal works of Gaspipe Casso, Little Al D'Arco, Fat Pete

Chiodo, and the other Luchese wiseguys who had become cooperators. "Reading the 302s left the guys in the cadre amazed," Oldham said. "Ponzi and Dades and Bobby I. couldn't believe their eyes. They had the same response I did when I read them. There were scores of things the FBI could have checked out to corroborate Casso. It defied belief that the feds had failed to make the case against Caracappa and Eppolito. Famous But Incompetent was given an entirely new meaning."

One lead to be pursued, it seemed to Tommy Dades, was searching the house where Gaspipe Casso said he had taken Jimmy Hydell after the handoff in the parking lot at Toys 'R' Us in order to interrogate and then murder him. Dades tracked down the address and obtained a search warrant. It turned out the house had just been renovated and was on the market. "I didn't see the point in it," Oldham said. "From an evidentiary angle, I didn't think there was anything to be gained. What if we found bullet slugs? Could we use that at trial? Not unless we put Gaspipe Casso on the stand and tried to establish that he was telling the truth. The same for blood traces. Hydell had disappeared in 1986. There was no body. But I was trying to be a team player. Tommy was full of energy and I didn't want to dampen his enthusiasm."

At six o'clock on a morning soon thereafter, Oldham, Dades, Intartaglio, DEA Agent Mark Manko, and a forensic team from the Chief Medical Examiner's office arrived at the house on 58th Street in Brooklyn. There was a For Sale sign on the lawn in front of the house. Knocking on the door elicited no reply. The house appeared to be empty. Oldham and Intartaglio walked two houses down the street, where the lights were on, and rang the front doorbell. An older couple answered. Oldham flashed his identification and said they were looking for the house where a kid was murdered twenty years earlier.

"The kid was killed in the basement," Oldham said. "He was a real tough kid, a gangster."

"Do you mean our son?" the mother asked. "Our son was murdered in our basement."

The woman told Oldham and Intartaglio that her son had gotten into debt with Manhattan gangsters and that they killed him.

"I'm so sorry," Oldham said. "I didn't know."

Even years after the mafia lost the war, the streets of Brooklyn contained the scars left by casualties long forgotten by society. Oldham and Intartaglio went back to the house shaking their heads at the coincidence. Dades had called the real estate agent but there was no sign of anyone turning up, so the men let themselves in by forcing the front door.

The house was newly decorated in gaudy Italianate fashion, with mirrors and black tile floors and ornate chandeliers. "We went down to the basement and got to work. We broke all the tiles in the basement looking for slugs and blood," Oldham recalled. "We tore the place apart. And then the owner turned up with the real estate agent. We hadn't found a thing. I was assigned the job of keeping them from coming down into the basement and seeing what we were doing. I told them it was a police matter, that they were not to interfere until the search was complete."

Meetings of the cadre alternated between the offices of the Brooklyn DA and the Eastern District. The regulars from the Eastern District were Oldham, Henoch, and Mark Manko from the DEA. Intartaglio, Dades, and Ponzi attended from the Brooklyn side. Henoch recounted the combustive nature of the encounters. Once, during a meeting the conversation turned to a certain high-ranking NYPD officer. The officer in question was prominent in the force, and controversial. Oldham said the cop was corrupt. Intartaglio went crazy. "You can't just say that, what are you talking about?" he demanded. "I'm telling you, he's no good," Oldham said. The pair stepped outside. They had a discussion. No blows were exchanged but it was evident that there were clashing egos and sensibilities.

Oldham and Henoch began to arrange conversations with Luchese made men who were living under assumed names in hiding. The first was Fat Pete Chiodo. Oldham, Henoch, Campanella, and Intartaglio sat in on the conference call. Chiodo was a seasoned cooperator. He didn't have to be persuaded to talk. "Chiodo said it was well known within Gas's crew that Gas had a 'crystal ball.' Chiodo said Casso called his source that because it could see the future. Chiodo told us about Tiger Management, confirming what Casso told the FBI in 1994. Chiodo knew about the intrafamily Luchese murders: Bruno Facciola, Anthony "Buddy" Luongo, Anthony DiLapi's murder in Hollywood. There was nothing new from Chiodo. He had been briefed about the 'crystal ball' years ago. But we were building a deeper understanding of the case.

"Chiodo said that Casso never told him who the source was. Casso was very elusive about it. As we spoke, Chiodo said no one called him 'fat' anymore. He had lost more than two hundred pounds. I was impressed. I thought he should write a cookbook—*Fat Pete's Gangster Diet.* Chiodo liked the idea, provided he didn't blow his cover. There were plenty of people who would like to get at him."

The investigation unearthed artifacts large and small from the past. Bobby Intartaglio said they were like archaelogists. In the mid-eighties, it was discovered, Detective Eppolito had answered a newspaper advertisement looking for people who had trouble controlling their rage. The company wanted to videotape people for a series on anger management. A video from this was made in 1985, just after Eppolito had undergone suspension and trial on charges of providing NYPD intelligence to Rosario Gambino. The cadre gathered to watch the footage. Eppolito addressed the camera filled with authentic rage. "I worked my ass off, I worked my fucking ass off for the city of New York," Eppolito said. "All I got was, 'You're Italian and you had family members that were in organized crime.'" Eppolito described the scene in which he was forced to hand over his NYPD detective badge. Eppolito's fury was overflowing. "I says, 'If you keep on insisting on fucking with me, I'm going to give you such a beating that your mother's going to throw up when I show her your picture.' I says, 'I'm not fucking lying to you.' I says, 'Don't try to go at me anymore.' I says, 'Because the four guys with you, by the time they get up,' I says, 'by the time they get up I'm going to break your nose and take your teeth out in one shot.'" Eppolito paused. "And then the anger started to come."

The cadre sat in silence after the video ended. There was no question that Eppolito had displayed the kind of fury that was common in criminals—the lethal combination of self-pity, self-justification, and violence that Fat the Gangster had bequeathed to his son.

DEAD END

The bickering between the Eastern District and the Brooklyn DA began to increase in the fall of 2004. Haggling over assignments and responsibilities was constant. The simple matter of where to hold meetings of the cadre became contentious. The war room was in the Brooklyn Union Gas building next to the Eastern District, but the Brooklyn DA insisted the feds walk the four blocks to their office. Henoch was tiring of the dysfunction and pettiness. He didn't want to walk to the meetings anymore. Oldham convinced him that it was better to assuage the Brooklyn DA investigators. The power plays were only a distraction, Oldham said to Henoch. It was better to be gracious and generous and hold the meetings on their home turf.

While Dades and Intartaglio concentrated on the documents, Oldham was primarily working on Burton Kaplan and Tommy Galpine. Both were federal prisoners and therefore unquestionably under the jurisdiction of the Eastern District. Getting one of the two men to agree to cooperate was without doubt the key to solving the case, Oldham and Henoch believed. The question was how to succeed where everyone else had failed. Oldham ordered the prison records for Burton Kaplan. A six-inch-thick stack of documentation arrived on Oldham's desk. It contained an accounting of Kaplan's personal possessions, including prayer oil, ten books (an unusually high number for an inmate), and dental floss. The record showed what Oldham suspected. Kaplan was tough. But he was also taking care of himself and had not given up on life.

For months, while the cadre worked their way through the boxes, Oldham tried to convince Henoch that they should consider using Gaspipe Casso as a witness against Caracappa and Eppolito. Mike Vecchione, the Brooklyn assistant DA, suggested that another way of using Casso was to charge Casso in state court with the kidnap and murder of Jimmy Hydell and make his co-accused Caracappa and Eppolito. The two former NYPD detectives would then be sitting at the defense table next to a confessed thirty-six-time murderer with the physical and mental tics that accompany solitary confinement for years on end.

"Putting Casso on the stand was preposterous. Casso's cooperation agreement with the government had been breached. Gas was considered an unreliable witness. He had conspired to murder a federal prosecutor and a federal judge. He had killed or conspired in the killing of thirty-six people. In person he managed to be even creepier. The *60 Minutes* interview in 1998 was like watching a lunatic. He reveled in killing Jimmy Hydell. It would be more than a high-stakes wager—it would be a Texas hold 'em all-in bet.

"I wanted to try. The cognitive dissonance would be a reach for a jury. The cross-examination would be brutal. But it seemed to me that if there was no other choice then there was no other choice. Reading Casso's proffers was a transformative experience. There was no question that Casso was telling the truth about Caracappa and Eppolito in 1994. The only question was the same as always. Would a jury believe Casso? To let the case go—to let Caracappa and Eppolito skate—was unacceptable. At least put it to a jury, I thought. Henoch was coming around to that view. He had the balls to try.

"Good detectives want to close their cases. I wasn't going to turn away from Caracappa and Eppolito, no matter the toll, personal or professional. That was my strength. It was also my weakness. We had the Nicky Guido BCI search, which wasn't nothing, but we didn't have much else. The case was a long way from made. We needed a break."

CHAPTER THIRTEEN

FLIPPING BURT

On a Tuesday morning in early March 2004, Oldham plugged in a cassette tape recording of Tommy Galpine calling his girlfriend Inez Ramirez on Thanksgiving Day 1999. Oldham was driving with his newly born daughter India Pearl to pick up his three-year-old, Olivia, at her day care center. The evening before, Oldham had retrieved a handful of the Kaplan and Galpine prison phone conversation cassette tapes as part of his ritual of listening to them again. The other members of the cadre had played a few of the tapes and been exposed to the grueling experience of hearing the two jailbirds wheedle on the phone. Oldham knew listening was excruciatingly dull, but there was also the chance that he had missed something critical the first time around. He listened to the conversations at work, as he did other things, in the car, at home on the boom box he had in the kitchen. The cassette tapes he had grabbed were marked "Pertinent" or "Not Pertinent" and stored in a box in Oldham's office. Oldham had deemed Thanksgiving Day 1999 "Pertinent" for a reason he couldn't recall as he listened to Galpine and Ramirez argue.

"I was mostly concerned with flipping Tommy Galpine," Oldham said. "Everybody said Burt would never flip. People had tried for years, and everyone had failed. He had been approached by law enforcement officials from the NYPD, DEA, FBI, the United States Attorney's Office. His lawyers had been contacted. He was doing twenty-seven years the hard way, when he could have avoided a single day inside by talking. There was a chance with Galpine, I thought. Kaplan was immovable, impossible."

The Thanksgiving Day tape was a particularly dreadful example of the frustrations of the long-distance relationship. Galpine and Ramirez could only talk once a week and the calls were hardly an adequate substitute for human company. The calls weren't just exhausting to Oldham, they seemed to exhaust Ramirez and Galpine as well. So far, the calls didn't seem to bode well for Oldham's strategy.

"I'm so tired," Ramirez said on the tape.

"Every time I talk to you, you sound half dead," Galpine said. "You have nothing to say. You never have anything to say."

Shaking his head, Oldham concurred with Galpine.

"I wish you wouldn't get so upset with me," Ramirez said. "I didn't do nothing wrong."

"You didn't do nothing, period," Galpine said.

Oldham turned on to the Brooklyn Bridge with a heavy sigh. India Pearl was only five months old, an angelic blonde sleeping in the baby seat in the back. Exposing her to Galpine and Ramirez's problems was something he was sure his wife, Andrea, would not approve of. Crossing the bridge, Oldham noticed an exchange he had not heard when he first listened to the tape—or perhaps he had heard it and that was why he marked the tape "Pertinent" in the first place. It was about Burton Kaplan.

By way of demonstrating to Ramirez the kind of attention he was hoping for, Galpine told her: "Burt's wife, Eleanor, wrote to me and asked me what books I like. She sent me books about improving my vocabulary, which is one of the things I want to do with my time in here."

"Oh, Tommy," Ramirez exhaled.

"Eleanor said that she and Burt have a grandchild," Galpine said. "Their daughter Deborah adopted a baby from Russia. Burt's over the moon."

Oldham stopped the tape and hit rewind and listened to the conversation again. Kaplan's daughter had adopted a child, a boy from Russia.

Burton Kaplan had a grandson.

Not only that: Oldham now knew that Burton Kaplan had considered the news important and exciting enough to have his wife share it with Galpine (Kaplan couldn't write to Galpine himself; direct communication between federal prisoners is forbidden). Kaplan's daughter Deborah, a criminal court judge in the Bronx, was his only child. The adopted boy was his only grandchild.

Oldham thought about it. Burt Kaplan, criminal mastermind and hardcore *omertà* adherent, had a grandson.

"Kaplan's grandson was probably a little thing but just maybe it was a huge thing. It was the first chink in his armor, maybe. Kaplan had forsworn all of the pleasures of life to stand up to law enforcement. In the cosmos of Burton Kaplan, keeping his word and defying the federal government came first and foremost. It was his life, and his choice. But it was clear Burt didn't just love his daughter, he felt a duty toward her. The grandkid could be the old man's soft spot. It was worth a shot. It was time to pay a visit to Downtown Burt."

For months, Oldham and Henoch had talked about flipping Galpine, Kaplan, or even both men. All that the prosecutors could do to induce them was make recommendations in the form of a letter that outlined the nature and extent and value of a defendant's cooperation. For a defendant facing charges such a document was called a "5(k)" letter and for a convict seeking a reduction in sentence it was a "Rule 35" letter. But they were the same in substance. The letter explained to the sentencing judge how the admitted criminal had come to cooperate; what had been accomplished as a result of his cooperation; how he had performed as a witness.

"For a wiseguy snitch, a letter from a prosecutor singing his praises and recommending leniency was the jackpot. The attractiveness of a 5(k) letter or Rule 35 letter presented us with a huge problem that no one in law enforcement liked to talk about, or admit. There was the real and constant chance of suborning perjury—inducing a criminal to lie. Subtle and not so subtle messages were sent to criminals about what the government wanted them to say. It happened too often. The rewards for the government for using snitches were huge—but so were the risks. An overzealous prosecutor, or an unscrupulous federal agent, could get a desperate criminal to say just about anything about anyone. The process was simple. A mobster is asked a question once and when he answers in a certain fashion the agent says he's lying and we send him back to his cell. His attorney is told to have a talk with him. It doesn't take long to become obvious, even to a moron, that there is a right answer.

"Defense attorneys love to talk about the process of flipping mobsters and who can blame them? There are real dangers—the benefits received, the pressures put on them, the unreliability of evidence obtained that way. The power of the government is formidable, and open to abuse. Kaplan was giving his life—his entire existence—over to an abstraction. The mob code of silence had swamped every other aspect of his existence. He had everything to gain from telling us what we wanted to hear. That was the beauty of Burt. He was the opposite of every two-bit jailhouse snitch and lowlife mobster looking to get out."

Oldham had not told Henoch nor anyone else in the cadre that he had decided to go see federal inmate Burton Kaplan. But Oldham needed someone from the cadre to accompany him. On the way home at the end of the day, he stopped in at the office of DEA Special Agent Mark Manko. Oldham thought well of Manko. Manko was hardworking, good-natured, and projected a steady presence. Manko was in his thirties, experienced, and not a bad detective. He could be relied upon to have the sense and discretion not to intervene in sensitive moments. Of all the members of the cadre, Manko was the most controllable. Manko's days were filled with a large degree of drudgery. If Oldham took Intartaglio, or Campanella, or Ponzi to see Kaplan there would inevitably be differences in approach and technique. Experienced detectives developed their own way of talking to criminals. The time was not right for another voice in the room with Kaplan. Oldham knew Manko would be pleased to join in such a potentially momentous and memorable encounter.

"Let's pay a visit on Burt Kaplan," Oldham said to Manko.

"Really?" Manko asked, amazed. "You think we got a chance?"

"Burton Kaplan has not had the pleasure of my company," Oldham said. "Tomorrow morning I'll be at your place first thing."

The short notice to Manko was part of Oldham's preparation. He wanted to give Manko as little warning as possible. He didn't want Manko thinking about talking to Kaplan, or seeking guidance from anyone else in the Eastern District.

Oldham walked down the hallway and stuck his head into Henoch's office. Keeping Henoch on his side and informed was important, Oldham knew. But it was Oldham's game and he was going to play it the way he saw fit.

"I'm going to give Burt a shot," Oldham said to Henoch. "Thought I'd let you know."

"That's great," Henoch said, surprised and excited. "What the fuck we got to lose?"

THE SHU

The next morning Oldham traveled with Manko three hours west of New York to the foothills of the Allegheny Mountains in central Pennsylvania. It was a crisp winter day, the rolling rural hills a pleasant contrast to the city streets. Manko drove. The Allenwood Federal Prison Complex was located in the town of White Deer, Pennsylvania. Oldham had not been to Allenwood in years. Since his last visit the facility had undergone enormous expansion, a beneficiary of the booming business of incarceration in America. Previously Allenwood had been a small federal prison camp with fewer than a thousand inmates. The camp, which had been described by the press as a country club when Nixon cronies resided there, boasted tennis courts, swimming, and a truly lax regimen. Allenwood was now a formidable federal correctional complex, the site of four prison facilities housing more than five thousand convicts. It was a vast concrete complex, with low-, medium-, and maximum-security prisons, sprouting watchtowers and sniper stands and ringed with walls strung with miles of barbed and razor wire.

Kaplan was housed in the medium-security prison. As an older man with no known history of violent crime, Kaplan was designated a lesser escape risk and a minimal risk to other prisoners. As Oldham checked in at the entrance, he was surprised to learn that Kaplan had been taken out of the general population and placed in administrative segregation. After securing their guns, Oldham and Manko were escorted by a correctional officer from the entry lobby to an interior building that adjoined an exercise yard. They followed a concrete walkway along a corridor until they reached a large orange metal door. The door was the entrance to the Special Housing Unit—the "SHU"—the section constructed to house problem inmates. A Lieutenant Stiles greeted Oldham and Manko. Stiles was in his thirties, dressed in a khaki uniform, blond, muscular, exceedingly professional. He led them into the unit, locking the door behind him. The SHU was a two-tier facility with a command post and administrative office on a landing between the floors. The cells, small and spartan, contained two concrete mattress platforms and a stainless-steel sink and toilet. No direct sunlight penetrated into the unit—the light was diffused by thick yellowed Plexiglas windows. "The atmosphere was like an intensive care ward in the dead of the night. All of the prisoners were locked down in their cells twenty-three hours a day. Whenever an inmate moved out of his cell he had to be shackled and escorted by a guard. Every door was locked. There were no televisions blaring, none of the banter and jailhouse jive. The only sounds were clanging doors and the occasional psychotic howl."

Lieutenant Stiles showed Oldham and Manko into the administrative office. The room was small, about five by ten feet. Oldham sat in a gray "Corcraft" chair (the brand of furniture manufactured by correctional inmates) by the door. Manko remained standing. Stiles went to fetch Kaplan. "I had thought about Kaplan a lot over the years. Listening to his prison tapes for hundreds of hours, watching the surveillance videotape from Staten Island, reading Casso's proffers to the FBI, I had developed a picture of the man in my mind. I knew he was a hard guy. Not muscular but temperamentally tough. I was very interested to finally meet the man behind the voice.

"Stiles came back with Kaplan, uncuffed him, and put him in the seat opposite me. Kaplan was a little shaky on his feet. He was scrawny, pale, stooped, squinting through thick eyeglasses. He looked his age—seventy-one years old. He was slightly disoriented, confused about why he had been taken from his cell, who his visitors were. Stiles seemed to like Kaplan—at least relative to the rest of the population in the SHU. The feeling appeared to be mutual. Kaplan took a seat slowly. His eyes were smart, wary."

"Who are you?" Kaplan asked.

Oldham offered an introduction in a matter-of-fact tone. "I'm William Oldham from the U.S. Attorney's Office in Brooklyn. This is Special Agent Mark Manko from the DEA."

"I was expecting my attorney," Kaplan said.

"We would like to talk to you," Oldham said.

"I ain't interested," Kaplan said. "I got nothing to say."

"That's fine," Oldham said. "You don't have to say a word. I just want you to listen."

"I want my attorney," Kaplan said.

"You're a sentenced prisoner," Oldham said. "You're not under arrest and you're not being charged with anything. Burt, you have no right to an attorney and you're not getting one."

"You're putting me in a bad position," Kaplan said. "Everyone in here is going to think I'm talking."

"Not if they don't see your mouth moving," Oldham said.

The administrative office, where they were sitting, looked out on the SHU through a large Plexiglas window. Prisoners could see Kaplan was with two men dressed in "world" clothing. Maybe the pair were attorneys, maybe prison inspectors or law enforcement officials. There was no way of telling, but prison was a cauldron of rumor and speculation and the simple act of being seen speaking with outsiders could alter an inmate's reputation—especially one like Kaplan who was known to be one of the last men in the joint who would never talk.

"Now listen to me," Oldham said. "I'm not asking you to say anything. I'm going to tell you some things."

Stiles had stepped away for a moment to get another chair. He returned and sat at the table with Oldham and Kaplan. Oldham began the pitch. He had not rehearsed the words, or his demeanor, but he followed the practice developed over many years of talking to criminals: direct language, with no adornment, just plain hard-driving unforgiving fact.

"The world is a different place now," Oldham said. "The mafia is finished. Everyone has snitched, on you and everyone else they can think of. Anthony Casso took a contract out on you for absolutely no reason. Your friends are all dead or locked up and those situations aren't going to change. The only one keeping *quiet* is you."

Kaplan began to get to his feet. "I want my lawyer," he said.

"You're in here now," Oldham said, softening his tone. "Listen up. It won't take long."

Oldham had moved his chair a few inches in front of the door, impeding Burt's path to it. Kaplan started to move for the door—or attempted to start, in the manner of a prisoner trying to assert freedom of movement. Oldham blocked his path. This was a critical moment. If Kaplan insisted, if Stiles didn't support Oldham and signal to Kaplan that it was in his best interests to stay put, he would be returned to his cell. Oldham could not force Kaplan to cooperate—or even to listen. Oldham got lucky.

"Sit down for a minute, Burt," Stiles said soothingly. "Just listen to him."

Reluctantly, Kaplan sat. Stiles had turned the momentum in the room to Oldham's advantage. The small rapport Stiles had with Kaplan—the respect Kaplan commanded from many people in law enforcement—had left the door ajar a fraction of an inch. Oldham pushed forward cautiously.

"How is your family doing, Burt?" Oldham asked. "I know your wife wants you out of here. I know your health isn't great. You've got prostate cancer. I've been listening to your phone calls for some time. I'm the guy who went to see your brother."

Kaplan sat perfectly still, face expressionless, staring. The muffled squawking of Stiles's walkie-talkie was the only sound intruding.

"I'm not going to tell you who we're interested in, but you know what this is about," Oldham said. "They are the only guys you could offer up that would interest us."

Kaplan spoke, measuring his words carefully. "With all due respect, and I do respect you guys because my father-in-law was a cop, I got nothing to say," he said. "I ain't no rat. I'm from the old school. Those other guys snitching made me sick. I never ratted in my whole life and I'm not going to start now. I'm seventy-one years old. This is my life."

"The guys we're talking about, they're outside living the good life," Oldham said. "You know they wouldn't keep their mouths shut for you."

"The guys you're talking about are good guys," Kaplan said. "I don't know nothing about them."

"You're making a mistake, Burt," Oldham said. "The world around you has changed. The life you lived is over. That life doesn't exist anymore. You're an anachronism."

"What does that mean?" Kaplan asked.

"You're a dinosaur, and trust me they don't roam the earth anymore. If Tommy Galpine talks first, you're going to be out of luck. You've got another seventeen years to go. You're going to rot and die in here."

Kaplan turned to Stiles. "I want to go back to my cell now," Kaplan said.

"C'mon, Burt," Stiles said. "I'll take you back."

"We're going to see you again. I want you to think about what I said. I'm going to give Lieutenant Stiles my number. If you want to talk to me, tell Lieutenant Stiles."

Oldham handed his card to Stiles. "Can he make a phone call?" Oldham asked.

"If he wants to make this call, he can come into my office and use my phone," Stiles said. Stiles rear-cuffed Kaplan and said he would return in a minute.

With Kaplan gone, Oldham turned to Manko. They both laughed. "He's a tough old bird," Manko said. "Twenty-seven years for pot and he still won't budge."

"It's not over yet," Oldham said, sensing a glimmer of hope.

Stiles came back and led Oldham and Manko out of the administrative office.

"Burt's a hard case," Stiles said. "Seventy-one years old and the guy is in the SHU."

"What's he in the SHU for?" Oldham asked.

Stiles explained. The story involved a bet Kaplan had placed on Super Bowl XXXVIII. New England played Carolina. The Patriots won on a field goal kicked with four seconds left. Kaplan had backed New England. But the prisoner bookie with whom Kaplan had placed the bet had welched, refusing to pay. The con who owed Kaplan money was an enormous man, Stiles said, a really tough black guy. A week and a half later the black inmate was in the exercise yard. There had just been a snowfall so the yard was blanketed in white. Four Mexican inmates approached the inmate. He ran. Stiles said the four Mexicans ran the black man down like he was a wounded antelope.

"They beat him with rocks," Stiles said. "You should have seen the blood on the snow. It looked like he was going to bleed to death. When we got to him he looked like he had fallen from a plane at thirty-five thousand feet."

An investigation had been launched by Lieutenant Stiles. It was apparent that the four Mexicans had no motive to attack the black inmate.

Inquiries in the prison revealed the dispute between Kaplan and the man.

"I knew it was Burt who paid the Mexicans to jump the guy but I couldn't figure out how he paid them," Stiles said. "I found a number in New Jersey Burt called using another prisoner's calling code. That was as far as I got." Stiles explained that although he didn't have enough evidence to criminally charge Kaplan, he had enough to put him in the SHU while an investigation was pending.

Oldham offhandedly asked for the phone number Kaplan had called. Stiles said it would be no problem. Oldham asked Stiles for a tour of the SHU. As they walked into the hallway, an inmate shuffled past, dragging chains from his arms and legs. The man was black, six-six, two hundred and seventy-five pounds. He had been beaten so badly the permanent damage was apparent from a distance. One of his eyes stared off into the middle distance, unresponsive to light or movement. He turned his head down. The shuffle, Oldham noted, was not because of the leg irons but due to the wounds that Kaplan's Mexican assailants had inflicted.

The next day Lieutenant Stiles provided Oldham with the telephone number Kaplan had called from Allenwood after the other inmate had welched on Kaplan's bet. Within a day Oldham had figured out how Kaplan had hired the Mexicans to jump the giant bookie. Oldham traced the number to a vending machine company in Newark, New Jersey. The company was associated with a Michael Gordon, a name that had come up during the investigation of Caracappa and Eppolito and the Lucheses. "It was clear how the money was paid out," Oldham said. "Kaplan sits and meets with the Mexicans in Allenwood and makes a deal—a grand for jumping the bookie. When the Mexicans beat the guy, Kaplan reaches out to an associate in the vending machine company in Newark. It was the only call Kaplan made within twenty-four hours of the beating. Once it's done, the Mexicans send someone to the vending machine company to collect the cash. Kaplan was in prison but he still had power."

The significance of Oldham's actions was threefold. First, it would display to Kaplan that his every move was being monitored, and not just at the level of prison officials. Federal law enforcement was taking an interest in his current activities. If he didn't cooperate, Kaplan would be subject to scrutiny that could make his life exceptionally difficult. Second, if negotiations went poorly Oldham could use the information he had obtained to bring an additional criminal charge against Kaplan. The amount of time Kaplan would get for hiring the Mexicans to beat his fellow inmate would not be small. At Kaplan's age, with his health issues, the numerical increase would be meaningless, but for Kaplan and his family it would be a soul-sapping step in the wrong direction.

The third significance to Oldham's discovery of Kaplan's use of the Jersey company was less obvious but legally important. In order to be eligible for a Rule 35 letter, Kaplan needed to confess to or cooperate with law enforcement regarding a crime committed within one year of his most recent crime. The one-year time limit appeared to be arcane but it provided finality for the government in dealing with convicted criminals. Instead of open-ended interaction, the period of time available to a convict to reconsider was finite. If the Eastern District were going to offer Kaplan the benefit of a letter to a federal judge describing his cooperation it had to include a "fresh" crime, not the crimes for which he had been convicted nearly a decade earlier. The assault in Allenwood fit that definition.

A DISPLAY OF POWER

Oldham waited once again. Time was now his ally. In early May, Oldham decided to make his move. He "writ" Kaplan down to New York from Allenwood. Six weeks had passed since his first meeting with Kaplan. Long enough, Oldham reasoned, for Kaplan to have had time to think over Oldham's pitch. Long enough for Kaplan to begin to wonder and worry when the next meeting would come. The writ was a court order signed by a judge requiring Kaplan to be moved to the Metropolitan Detention Center in Brooklyn, the facility designated for convicted criminals to be housed during legal proceedings in New York City. The bus trip from Allenwood to New York City was not a straight three-hour ride. Kaplan was transported by the Bureau of Prison system, which meant riding in uncomfortable buses first to St. Louis, then to Atlanta, and finally to New York. Oldham had demonstrated to Kaplan his ability to change Kaplan's circumstances for the good—or the bad.

The morning of May 24 was sunny and warm in Brooklyn. The flowers were out on Cadman Plaza. Oldham walked to work, a pleasant three miles to clear his head. For months, Oldham had felt the walls closing in on him at the Eastern District. He was buried under a pile of cases. The "crystal ball" case had yet to take shape the way Oldham had imagined it would. They still needed Kaplan or Galpine. He made his way through the outdoor farmers' market in front of Brooklyn's City Hall, stopping to buy an apple. He had dressed smart-casual: sports jacket, button-down shirt, black jeans. Maybe this was his lucky day.

"I was in a good mood. I figured flipping Burt was going to take a while, if it happened at all. But I was optimistic. I had been preparing for years for Kaplan. I knew everything that could be known about him. Moving Kaplan to the city was a show of power. I wanted him to learn the hard way the power of the government. We could put him five minutes away from his family. I wanted him to know we could disrupt his life— or change his life. For an older prisoner with medical problems like Burt, moving around in the federal prison system was a bitch. There weren't nice hotels with bellhops. I wanted him off balance and tired. I didn't wait for him to gather himself at the MDC."

The usual practice in pitching potential cooperators was to bring a prisoner to the U.S. Attorney's Office in downtown Brooklyn. The location was convenient for investigators and prosecutors. The problem with this procedure was that nearly everyone in the office knew which defendants and convicts were snitching. Oldham didn't want Kaplan to come to the federal offices. The floors were thick with FBI agents. Word that Kaplan was in the building would spread like wildfire. It was important to keep the investigation confidential. There was no way to know if Caracappa still had contacts in New York who would pass along word of the investigation. Oldham thought they would be better off hiding in plain sight in a visiting room at the MDC.

Oldham rode the elevator up to the nineteenth floor of Pierrepont Plaza. The hallways were lined with boxes from ongoing trials. There was one hallway with a series of rooms dedicated to each of the five crime families of New York City. Joel Campanella's door was open when Oldham stopped and poked his head inside.

"Let's go see Burt," Oldham said.

Campanella had never met Burt Kaplan. Oldham told him that Kaplan had been transported down to the MDC. As an analyst, Campanella was not a detective, nor an investigator. He scanned documents into the U.S. attorney's organized crime database created over the years. It was unusual for Campanella to leave the office. Going to see Kaplan was a rare treat for him. Oldham could have asked someone else in the office but he had known Campanella since the late eighties and thought he would be a reliable witness and note taker. "I'm dying to meet this guy," Campanella said. "You think he's going to flip?"

"I doubt today is the day," Oldham said. "But we're moving the ball forward, or whatever the fuck they say in football."

Oldham went to his office and called Joe Ponzi in the Brooklyn DA's office. Ponzi's secretary picked up. Oldham asked to be put through.

"What's up, Oldham?" Ponzi asked within seconds.

"You want to take a ride?" Oldham asked.

"Where you going?"

"I thought I'd go over to MDC and see Burt Kaplan."

There was a pause. Oldham hadn't told Ponzi that he was bringing Kaplan to the city.

"Really?" Ponzi asked. "Hell, yeah. I'm busy but I'm not that busy."

"I'll come get you," Oldham said.

The call appeared to be casual, the request offhanded, but Oldham had given the matter considerable thought. It wasn't like taking Special Agent Gene Kizenko to the first meeting of the cadre, or having Special Agent Manko accompany him to Allenwood. This encounter with Kaplan had the potential to be make-or-break. Ponzi was Oldham's first choice.

The reputation of Joe Ponzi as an interrogator had been established many years earlier. "He Gets Slayers to Sing," a *Daily News* profile of Ponzi in the late eighties had been headlined. "At first glance, he looks like a well-heeled real estate guy—houndstooth suit, silk tie, shoes polished a glossy ebony," reporter Mark Kriegel wrote. "Only the hair gives him up. Straight back and perfect, just like they wear it in South Brooklyn." The article enumerated Ponzi's already prodigious accomplishments, even though he was only thirty-three years old at the time. More than seventy-five murderers had confessed to Ponzi. Known as a polygraph expert, Ponzi rarely used the machine in his sessions with suspects. The device was a prop and a way of facilitating conversation. There were a few simple principles Ponzi followed, all in accordance with Oldham's practice. Adapt your performance to your audience. Be tough, when required, calm and reasonable when it played to your advantage. Don't bang tables. Don't lie. Show your man you're not afraid of him. No guns in the room. No security standing at the door. Don't let silence kill you. Keep the guy talking, or talk yourself. Let them know it's the most important day of their lives—the Before and After moment. Never give up. No matter how long it takes.

"Joe was the son of one of the best Brooklyn cops of all time. His father was known as Larry but his real name was Emidio Ponzi. Joe called his father 'the Sergeant.' In his day in the Brooklyn branch of the NYPD, Larry Ponzi had seen it all—including the act of an overweight loudmouth named Louis Eppolito. When Eppolito was in the Brooklyn Robbery Squad, Larry Ponzi was his commanding officer. Joe didn't just have expertise and the power of being a senior and respected figure in the DA's office. Joe had history. Chances were good that Kaplan would recognize the name Ponzi. Kaplan's father-in-law had been a cop. Kaplan was a bit of cop buff himself, giving deals to off-duty cops at his Brooklyn warehouse during the eighties. In Allenwood Kaplan had told me he 'respected cops' and the job we have to do. Ponzi was the personification of respect. I knew he would be respectful of Kaplan and not blow our chance with histrionics. I trusted him, and there is no bigger compliment I could give one of my brothers in law enforcement. Joe wouldn't turn on me, come what may. By this time I was in the middle of alienating pretty much everyone around me. I was drinking too much. Joe knew my kind. To succeed the way Joe did—to get so many people to confess to their most heinous acts—required a fine appreciation for human frailty."

Dressed sharply, as usual, Ponzi was waiting outside the entrance to the Brooklyn DA's office. Campanella rode in the back of Oldham's beat-up purple Dodge Omni. Oldham was always assigned the worst car in the Eastern District's pool of automobiles due to his richly deserved reputation for trashing vehicles. His purple ride distinguished itself for shabbiness with shot shock absorbers and a cracked windshield. As the men pulled onto the Brooklyn-Queens Expressway there was the unmistakable air of excitement in the car.

"How you want to approach it, Mr. Oldham?" Ponzi asked.

"We got to see who's doing the talking," Oldham said. "If he's not talking we have to keep talking at him. The way to get him to talk is to start bad-mouthing the FBI. He'll join right in. Talk about his twenty-seven-year pot sentence. That'll get him started."

"What's he like?" Ponzi asked.

"Very cagey. He's not going to give anything up before he knows he wants to do a deal. He's going to want to know where he stands. We have to dance around. Allude to what we want. We don't want Caracappa and Eppolito to come up in this session. No specificity. He's not going to talk about crime until he's proffering."

With an interrogator as experienced and adept as Ponzi, Oldham didn't need to lay out the obvious. Don't overpromise. Don't suborn perjury. Don't play games. Don't force the position or back Kaplan into a corner so that the first session becomes the last session. The tone set in the initial meeting would persist throughout their dealings with Kaplan, if there were any. Oldham told Ponzi about Kaplan's adopted Russian grandson. The boy presented a new and perhaps significant personal dilemma to Kaplan. He couldn't sit down and explain to a three-year-old why he chose to remain in prison rather than tell the truth and perhaps be free to come home. Oldham told Ponzi about the Mexicans Kaplan had hired.

"He's not without resources," Oldham told Ponzi. "He's not out of the game. He works with what he's got."

Turning off the expressway at the 30th Street exit in the industrial wasteland of the Brooklyn docks, Oldham gave Ponzi and Campanella the rundown on the cast of characters in Kaplan's life. He mentioned Kaplan's girlfriend in Las Vegas. They talked often. Michael Gordon was a convicted heroin dealer who was also close to Kaplan. Tommy Galpine was Kaplan's longtime sidekick.

Kaplan's loyalty to his old gangster friends and life had to be taken out of the equation, Oldham said. Kaplan owed no loyalty to Casso. He had to be convinced that any sense of loyalty he felt toward Caracappa and Eppolito was misguided. "There was no neutral territory. Tommy Galpine was going to pay a price if Kaplan didn't talk. Galpine had eight years left to serve—less than one hundred months. On Galpine's prison tapes he repeatedly expressed the desire to leave his life of crime behind and move to Oklahoma. Kaplan thought of Galpine as a son. If Kaplan refused to cooperate, we would tell him our next step was to take Galpine out of the prison camp in Duluth, Minnesota, and move him to a maximum-security prison. Prison camps were comparatively comfortable, when contrasted with most federal penitentiaries. Kaplan would then be responsible for Galpine's fate, yet again, just as he'd been when he brought him into the world of crime at the age of sixteen.

"You give your target a choice. One choice is good. There are benefits. The decision will sting. No one wanted to rat, especially Kaplan. But the other choice has to be so bad that it is not only irrational, it is crazy. Joe and I didn't talk about it, but it was clear that we were going to play different characters. The cliché is good cop/bad cop. There is a kernel of truth to that saying, but it disguises the complexity of the encounter. Joe represented the acceptable face of law enforcement. He was well dressed, straightforward, reliable. I was the wild card—the guy you couldn't predict. I was the hammer. The hammer drives the point home. Joe would put the case for cooperating. Joe would describe the benefits. Possible sentence reduction, witness protection, maybe a grandson bouncing on his knee. I would lay out the costs. If you don't help us, we're going to go about making your life miserable. Burt had the right to remain silent. We had the right to move him to a prison in the bayous of Louisiana."

PONZI SCHEME

The enormous Metropolitan Detention Center complex was located in Brooklyn's Sunset Park. On visiting days, the lobby entrance was filled with women coming to visit their boyfriends and husbands. The lot was deserted on this May day. Oldham parked the car and the three men entered a secure room off the lobby where their weapons and cell phones were placed in gun lockers. Buzzed first into a vestibule, Oldham, Ponzi, and Campanella surrendered their identification and had their hands stamped with ink visible only under ultraviolet light. The guard processing their entry was hidden behind smoked glass. The second buzzer sent them through to the waiting room. Oldham told a prison officer sitting at a desk that they were there to see Burt Kaplan. He gave the man a slip of paper with Kaplan's registry number. The officer picked up his walkie-talkie and called for Kaplan to be brought down from his cell.

The "Counsel Rooms" were glass-enclosed cubicles arranged along two walls of the visiting area. There was a guard located on a raised platform at the head of the area for security purposes. The place was freezing cold. Vending machines sold stale sandwiches, pretzels, and soda at exorbitant prices. Oldham spent five dollars buying a pack of pretzels and a Coke for Kaplan.

A large conference room–sized cubicle at one end of the row was occupied by a convict and two attorneys. Ponzi pointed out Joseph C. "Big Joey" Massino, the Bonanno boss known in the press as "the last Don." Once a close friend of John Gotti and one of the mafia bosses convicted in the Commission Case in 1986 but since released from prison, Massino had been arrested in 2003. The main charge was ordering the murder of Dominick "Sonny Black" Napolitano on August 17, 1981. Sonny Black was killed because he had been the wiseguy who allowed FBI agent Joe Pistone, posing as a knockaround gangster named Donnie Brasco, to penetrate the Bonanno family. Sonny Black had been found dead, with his hands cut off as a gesture indicating his punishment for "shaking hands" and trusting an FBI agent. In the spring of 2004, Massino was facing the death penalty. "The case against Massino was overwhelming. He was going to go to be executed. The only defense strategy open to him was to cooperate. Which was what Massino did a few weeks later. While we were preparing to flip Burt Kaplan, 'the last Don' was going over a defense strategy which would lead him to become the first boss to snitch on his own family—the ultimate rat."

Oldham and Ponzi chose a cubicle at the opposite end of the row. The room was small, claustrophobic. The table was gray formica-topped, the chairs black plastic, the fluorescent lights locked behind metal grates. Oldham arranged the chairs so Kaplan would have to sit on the opposite side of the room, farthest from the door. The arrangement made it impossible for Kaplan to leave the room without asking one of his interrogators to let him by. Campanella was designated to take notes, if notes were needed. Defense attorneys were entitled to all documentation created by investigators. Only the broadest outline of the conversation would be memorialized for formal purposes, unless Kaplan suddenly started to talk, a very unlikely outcome.

Kaplan entered through a gray metal door in the corner of the room wearing a standard-issue khaki prison jumpsuit. He was squinting through his thick glasses and seemed disoriented and out of his element. Kaplan had not been informed of the reason for his transfer, nor did he know who was waiting for him in the counsel area.

"You're not my lawyer," Kaplan said, standing at the doorway. He recognized Oldham and nodded his head. "I figured," Kaplan said.

"Sit down," Oldham said, indicating the vacant chair.

Oldham, Ponzi, and Campanella remained standing to give Kaplan room to get to his chair.

"This is Joel Campanella from my office," Oldham said.

"I'm Joe Ponzi, an investigator with the Brooklyn DA's office."

"Why is he here?" Kaplan asked. Kaplan was in a federal institution, serving time on a federal conviction, so he wanted to know why a state official such as Ponzi was present.

"We want to make sure whatever you tell us is covered in the state and federally," Oldham said. "We want everybody on board with this thing. We don't want anyone taking a shot at you independently."

"I thought you were FBI, with the suit and everything," Kaplan said to Ponzi.

Oldham began the discussion.

"Look, we got to work this thing out," Oldham said. "Relatively speaking, you're a pretty good guy. You're not the worst guy we've come across. The other guys did murders. They're bad guys. Casso, Amuso, they're real bad actors."

The aim, in the beginning, was to downplay Kaplan's culpability and make him feel he had been treated poorly by the authorities. The mindset Oldham wanted to create was that Kaplan had been victimized—and he and Ponzi had come to help him.

"You know the government wanted you," Oldham said. "Big Sal Miciotta, the Colombo captain, cooperated and he got five years for four murders. You got twenty-seven years for dealing pot. You do the math."

"And they never showed any of my pot," Kaplan said. "The pot they brought into court in a wheelbarrow wasn't even my pot. They lied on me."

"We're with you," Oldham said. "That's part of the reason we're willing to help you out."

"The FBI are liars," Kaplan said, visibly agitated. "I had a one hundred percent legitimate clothing business they took from me. They came to me when I got arrested in the pot case and said I didn't have to do a day in jail. All I had to do was talk. I told them to get lost. I don't want nothing to do with them guys."

With Kaplan talking, Oldham fell quiet and let Ponzi explain the situation. Regardless of Kaplan's cooperation, the Brooklyn DA was going to prosecute Caracappa and Eppolito for the kidnapping and murder of Jimmy Hydell. The investigation had revealed that Betty Hydell, the kid's mother, had seen Caracappa and Eppolito outside her house in Brooklyn the day of her son Jimmy's disappearance. Tommy Dades's "golden nugget" was not going to get a conviction without a human face telling the story of the conspiracy, Oldham believed, but it could prove priceless if it helped convince Kaplan that a state prosecution was a real possibility.

Oldham explained the immediate consequences. With the Hydell murder count in state court, Kaplan would be taken out of federal custody and lodged at Rikers Island. The suggestion of Rikers was dread-inducing for an elderly and sickly white man. Federal prison was paradise compared to state prison. Oldham didn't have to tell Kaplan that Rikers was awash in young violent kids, junkies, rapists. There was civility and control in Allenwood, even in the SHU. Kaplan could read magazines, rest, relax. There was a perverse soothingness to the routine of institutional life. Rikers, by contrast, was Dantesque.

"If you don't come across there's a good chance Tommy will," Oldham said.

"Tommy's a good kid," Kaplan said. "He don't know nothing."

Oldham let the hammer fall again. "Tommy's going to get hurt in this," Oldham replied. "We're not going away this time. I didn't put in all these years to have this case hit the wall. We're not taking 'no' for an answer."

He could feel Kaplan's anger toward him growing. Kaplan had entered

the room with a vision of himself as a tough guy willing to defy authority to live up to his ideals. Oldham wanted him to walk out furious—and
afraid. Kaplan had to believe even more suffering would befall him and his
loved ones if he continued to hide the truth.

Ponzi intervened, sensing the need to change the atmosphere,

"Burt, you've got to understand our position," Ponzi said. "We've put
together a team of guys that aren't the FBI. We're going to do this. It's
going to get done once and for all. We want you on our side."

"This is our business," Oldham said. "We've been doing this a long
time. We're not going to lie to you. We're not going to make promises to
you. I can't stay in this business if I go around lying to cooperators. I
don't have anything against you personally. You can ask around about me.
You can ask around about Joe Ponzi. Joe is as straight as they come.
You're talking to the chief investigator from the Brooklyn DA's office. He
didn't send an errand boy. We think this is important."

"I respect you guys," Kaplan said. "Ask anybody, I got a lot of respect
for cops. It's a tough job. This just isn't the way I came up."

Kaplan pushed back his chair and rose. He made for the door, trying
to squeeze by Oldham's chair.

"We understand, Burt," Ponzi said. "But you have to understand the
world has changed. The old world doesn't exist. The codes of honor are
a joke. Nobody stays silent. We have guys lining up to talk to us now."

"We respect your position but it's not pragmatic," Oldham said. "It
doesn't make sense. Why are you alone going to take the fall? You're
smarter than that."

Kaplan sat again. Not defeated, Oldham thought, but another small
step had been taken. Incrementally. Calmly. Logically. Those were the key
words, for Oldham, as he considered how to proceed.

"We will do whatever it takes to help you out, once you're with us,"
Ponzi said. "There's nothing we won't try to do. We're not allowed by
law to promise you anything. The judge decides. But we can work with
you to maximize your benefit."

"We can't tell you what you'll get," Oldham said, dropping his voice
to make it clear he was now leveling with Kaplan. "But I will tell you what
other people in your position got. Take Sammy Gravano. Nineteen murders and he got five years with three years of supervised release. With time
served, he did less than two and a half years after he testified against
Gotti."

Oldham had never conducted a pitch to a potential cooperator without
referring to the "Gravano deal." Everyone knowledgeable in organized

crime, mobsters as well as cops, considered the terms overly generous. The outcome was infamous. In cooperating, Gravano had taken himself from the near-certainty of a life sentence to a book deal and a life in a big house with a swimming pool in Arizona. The fact that Gravano subsequently started dealing ecstasy with his son and was sent back to prison for twenty years was also widely known. But it was the amazing deal Gravano had struck that stayed in the mind of every serious criminal Oldham had encountered since.

"Gravano took responsibility," Ponzi said. "He came to us. Voluntary acceptance of responsibility is a huge positive consideration for judges."

"You didn't kill anyone—" Oldham said.

Kaplan began to rise from his chair again. Kaplan met Oldham's eyes for a split second.

"—that we know of," Oldham finished.

Kaplan sat back down again.

"You're not well," Oldham said.

"We can help get you better medical care," Ponzi said. "We can keep you close to your family in New York. Your wife has put up with you being in prison for years."

"We're not interested in all your other friends," Oldham said. "We really don't care. There are two guys we're interested in. You know who we're talking about."

The moment had arrived.

"I took an oath," Kaplan said.

"They took a fucking oath," Oldham said, now angry himself. "I was a cop for twenty-five years. I was in Major Case with one of those guys. I know what a fucking oath is about. If every cop in New York City was like these two, no one could walk the streets."

"You're right about that," Kaplan said.

"Those guys didn't take an oath of *omertà*," Oldham said. "They took an oath to protect and serve. They didn't protect and they didn't serve."

The names of Detectives Stephen Caracappa and Louis Eppolito had not been mentioned. Prompting Kaplan on such a fundamental matter in any way could have serious consequences at trial. If Oldham or Ponzi mentioned the names first, an experienced and able defense attorney would elicit that information in cross-examination. Juries did not like to hear that law enforcement was suggesting evidence to its cooperators. Maintaining Kaplan's integrity for trial was crucial, even though he had not agreed to cooperate.

"You know who we mean," Oldham said. "Your 'friends.'"

Kaplan didn't speak for a moment. But he didn't feign ignorance. Engaging in any discussion was a tacit admission on Kaplan's part. Kaplan parsed his words carefully, allowing himself room to backtrack and avoiding any admission that could be used against him. The terms were set by Kaplan. He referred to the pair as the "fat one" and the "skinny one." A different formulation was the "loud guy" and the "quiet guy." No fool, Kaplan was leaving himself room to recant.

"Them guys, the fat guy and the skinny guy, they're really not such bad guys," Kaplan said. "They just got mixed up in the wrong business."

"Burt, Oldham and I respect you for standing up," Ponzi said. "But you have to know you are standing up for nothing and no one. Look at Casso. Your friend Gaspipe is trying to get you whacked and his wife is living in a house owned by you, while your own wife is just getting by. Meanwhile, the fat guy and the skinny guy are out in Vegas living the high life."

"They wouldn't do shit for you," Oldham said.

"The skinny guy would," Kaplan said.

In that moment—in defending the honor of Stephen Caracappa— Kaplan had started to shadow box. The change in stance was slight but perceptible. Kaplan was saying very little—but he was talking and the conversation was building toward an exchange. Kaplan realized the alteration in tone and stopped himself.

"I want my lawyer with me," Kaplan said. "I don't mean to be rude, fellas, but I got to get going."

Kaplan rose for a third time.

Oldham looked at Ponzi and then Campanella and then Kaplan, who was waiting expectantly for Oldham to move and allow him to pass.

"Burt, you're giving up your grandson," Oldham said. "You're going to die in jail without ever touching him. You're choosing the fat guy and the skinny guy over your only grandson's chance to know his grandfather."

Oldham knew in that instant that he had surprised Kaplan—shocked him, in fact. The distaste Kaplan had displayed for Oldham now appeared to be outright hate. How did Oldham know about his grandson? Were there no lengths to which the government wouldn't go? Bringing an innocent child into the equation? In Kaplan's mind, it seemed to Oldham, it was not just a low blow—it must have been the cruelest truth. Oldham did not spell out the cascading consequences to Kaplan. If Kaplan didn't cooperate, the boy would grow up knowing that his grandfather had had the opportunity to be with him—and finally tell the truth about his life—but he had opted to be a criminal unto the bitterest end. Kaplan's ruined life would be imprinted on the consciousness of the boy who would carry the memory of Burton Kaplan for the rest of his life.

"Your daughter would like her son to be able to know his grandfather, for you to teach him how to be a man," Oldham said. This was Oldham's play. From Kaplan's reaction, Oldham thought he might have found Kaplan's vulnerability. It matched his impression from listening to Kaplan's prison phone calls. The child struck an emotional cord with Kaplan.

"How do you know about that?" Kaplan asked.

"I know things," Oldham said.

"She brings him up to visit sometimes," Kaplan said.

Kaplan sat down. He stared directly ahead. Kaplan wouldn't look at Oldham. "Joe, can I use your pen and paper?" Kaplan asked.

Ponzi slid his yellow legal pad across the table. Kaplan scribbled on the pad.

"Joe, that's my lawyer's name and number," he said.

Ponzi replied, adopting a formal tone of voice, "Thank you, Burt."

As Kaplan rose to leave the room, Oldham allowed him to pass. Ponzi opened the door for him as Kaplan avoided Oldham's eyes. Kaplan seemed relieved, but also disgusted with himself in some way—an emotion he projected onto Oldham. "It was nice to meet you fellas," he said to Ponzi and Campanella.

As Oldham and Ponzi and Campanella walked back to the car through the parking lot they were jubilant.

"I knew we had him the third time he stood up and sat down," Oldham said.

"We got him," Ponzi exclaimed.

Oldham turned to Ponzi with a broad smile.

"Good job, Joe. I think Burt's in love with you."

PISSING MATCH

The next meeting of the cadre took place in a large conference room on the nineteenth floor of the Eastern District offices. The shift in meetings from the Brooklyn DA's quarters signaled yet further the slippage of the case from a state to a federal prosecution. Oldham, Special Agent Manko, and Campanella were in attendance for the feds. Ponzi, Intartaglio, and Tommy Dades represented the Brooklyn DA. Oldham told the assembled group that he and Ponzi had talked to Kaplan. Everyone in the room had extensive experience with the delicate matter of convincing criminals to snitch. Everyone had an opinion on how to turn the opening Ponzi and Oldham had created into a cooperation agreement. Fights in the cadre meetings were routine. The meetings were productive but often contentious as egos clashed.

As the attorney assigned to the case, Henoch tried to gain power over how it was conducted. But since he had started, Henoch knew there was no way he could dictate to Oldham when and how to approach Galpine or Kaplan. Oldham had his own style and methodology. Moreover, a prosecutor should not be the first one involved in negotiations with a criminal like Kaplan. An experienced detective like Oldham knew how to loosen up Kaplan and could speak the same language. It had to start with a cop—it had to start with Oldham.

But Oldham had argued with Tommy Dades for weeks about how to approach Kaplan. "Tommy wanted to tell Burt we had him as well as the cops on the Jimmy Hydell homicide," Oldham recalled. "There was nothing wrong with the suggestion, legally or morally. Cops lie to suspects all the time. It just wasn't a good idea. Burt would ask *how* we had him. We didn't have a good enough answer, I thought. Betty Hydell wouldn't convince Kaplan. He was a sophisticated businessman as much as he was a mob associate. Kaplan wasn't going to be bullied or bullshitted. The art of the deal was needed—persuasion, reason, self-interest."

"It's not going to work," Oldham said to Dades. "If we lie to Burt he will know we're lying and we'll be fucked. If we lie, he will lie to us. We'll fuck up the entire case."

Dades didn't agree.

In many ways, Oldham was difficult to deal with. He did not work well in team situations. He could be evasive, argumentative, combative. He could be a jerk, he knew. "Likability is one of the most overrated characteristics in fact and fiction," Oldham said. "It might be strange to say this, but it's the truth. I was not a likable character. I didn't come to work to make friends. I came to put dangerous people in jail. Twenty-five years as a cop, detective, and then federal investigator put an edge on me. Bobby I. and Campanella were different. They had been NYPD detectives for decades, but they were controlled, detailed-oriented, and patient. The team needed all kinds."

For some time there had been tension simmering between Oldham and Dades. There was no personal animosity, it seemed to Oldham, but a reflection of real institutional tensions. Oldham was attached to the United States Attorney's Office, and might have divided loyalties, despite his many years in the NYPD. Dades was working for the Brooklyn DA's office so he was technically an investigator on the state side. The two agencies were supposed to be working together but decades of rivalry and double-dealing—mostly on the part of the FBI—had left raw wounds. The investigation of Caracappa and Eppolito had started out with the local DA, but it had gradually begun to fall further under the sway of the feds—a familiar pattern that created resentment. "Our personalities were also very different," Oldham recalled. "Tommy was an ex-boxer. He was pure Brooklyn. I wasn't. I read books by Flannery O'Connor. Both of us were pretty good detectives, though, and both of us had strong opinions on most things—which we were more than willing to share."

Two versions of the case were emerging inside the cadre, one state, one federal. The Brooklyn DA account claimed that Betty Hydell and the printout of the search for the wrong Nicky Guido were sufficient proof for a successful prosecution—thus, the case had been "made" by Tommy Dades and the Brooklyn DA team. The other version held that getting Tommy Galpine or Burt Kaplan to talk would "make" the case—then and only then would convictions be the likely outcome. Both were right, and both were wrong. Every component was necessary. In the end, making a RICO case required an insider to tell the story. Corroborative evidence, such as the wrong Nicky Guido printout, was meaningless without a storyteller. The tale had to be told to a jury by a reliable narrator. Otherwise the rest of the case would lack context and meaning.

The undercurrent of tension finally erupted in a fit of anger on the part of Oldham. During a meeting to discuss tactics to try to get Kaplan to flip, Oldham insisted on controlling contact with Kaplan and his attorney.

No lies would be told to Kaplan, he told the group.

Dades got to his feet to speak. Oldham held his hand out and put it a foot in front of Dades's face to keep him from speaking; Oldham was in his face.

Dades looked at Oldham's hand, hesitated, and then angrily left the room.

Oldham rose and went after him. "I followed Tommy into the hallway, into the lobby, and then along a second hallway to the men's room. I wasn't going to let it pass. I like Tommy a lot but he was wrong about lying to Kaplan. There was no 'golden nugget.' The case had been built up over years and years. Turf wars like this did nothing to help the case. It had become a pissing match. Tommy was at one urinal, I was at the next one."

"You don't really think you made this case on your own, do you?" Oldham said to Dades. "You did a lot of important stuff. But there ain't no fucking 'golden nugget.'"

"Whatever," Dades said. He shook, zipped, and left.

"Tommy returned to the meeting and sat quietly. He never attended another meeting of the cadre. A short time later, he resigned from the DA's office. I was sorry Tommy left. He was all right. We still had a long way to go to make the case. We had to close the deal with Burt. And then we had to build a case for trial. It would have been good to have Tommy along for the ride."

Joe Ponzi gave the name and number of Kaplan's lawyer to Oldham. David Schoen was a former New Yorker who had moved to Alabama to practice capital cases, and there were many such cases in the Bible Belt states of the South. For the following three weeks, Oldham spoke regularly with Schoen. They discovered they had friends in common through their years working with convicted murderers. "Schoen was professional and thorough and courteous," Oldham recalled. "I liked dealing with him. Schoen understood this was Kaplan's last best chance to change his life. As a defense attorney, Schoen had dedicated his life to trying to save the lives of death row prisoners—a cause I agreed with. As a cop, I had dealt with killers for decades and one thing I came to strongly believe is that taking life is wrong. Period. Burton Kaplan wasn't facing a death penalty, but he was effectively doing life. Schoen agreed that Kaplan had every good reason to become a cooperator. There was no downside for Kaplan. Things could not get any worse. As for Kaplan's loyalty to Caracappa and Eppolito, they were the only beneficiaries of Kaplan's largesse—two killer cops living on Silver Bear Way in Las Vegas, doubtless steeped in ingratitude. Meanwhile Kaplan's wife, daughter, and grandson had had to make do without him."

Reaching Kaplan through a conduit such as Schoen was critical, Oldham knew. There was a limited number of times that Kaplan could be approached by law enforcement before the fine balance between persuasion and provocation was tipped. During the swelter of late August, Oldham called Kaplan's attorney every day. Over time, as the two men bargained and brainstormed, Oldham came to have Schoen's home phone, cell phone, and travel itinerary. The main subject of their discussion was how to craft a Rule 35 letter. The letter would be presented to a federal judge, after Kaplan had testified against Caracappa and Eppolito. Cooperating against the the former detectives would put Kaplan at the center of one of the biggest trials in the history of New York City. Schoen made it known that Kaplan was seriously considering flipping.

While the main question was outstanding, smaller issues arose with Schoen. Kaplan insisted that Tommy Galpine also get a deal. There was no problem with that demand, provided Galpine cooperated as well—which Oldham was sure he would if Kaplan started to sing. Galpine would probably do anything Kaplan told him to do. There was also the matter of Kaplan pleading guilty to the conspiracy to have the bookie jumped by the Mexicans in Allenwood. With Kaplan's confession to that crime, there was a felony committed within the past year—so Kaplan qualified for a Rule 35 despite not talking about "the cops" for all those years.

"But there was one huge obstacle," Oldham recalled. "Kaplan wouldn't snitch on anyone else, including himself. He would not recite and confess to every crime he had ever committed. He would not describe the criminal acts of the gangsters he had dealt with over the years. Kaplan flat refused to become a snitch, at least in the conventional sense. No one had ever got the deal Kaplan was holding out for. Casso, Gravano, Big Sal Miciotta—when a wiseguy ratted he had to rat on himself. He had to rat on all his friends. Gravano got Gambinos arrested in huge numbers. Sixty mobsters were busted after Big Sal came over to our side. Casso incriminated an unbelievable number of people. Casso's confessions read like a diabolical version of the Old Testament, with a bewildering number of names and so much senseless violence.

"Kaplan thought he understood the importance of leverage in business. He wasn't just another gangster reciting the dreary details of another brutal gangland conspiracy. For a convicted felon sitting in solitary confinement, with seemingly no hope left in the universe, he had an oversized appreciation for the power he held. Kaplan believed we were going to have to pay his price, no matter how exorbitant. He had such contempt for federal authorities he didn't figure we could be canny—that he was talking to a former NYPD detective, the kind of cop who knew his kind. I was not going to be Burton Kaplan's fool. He was going to be mine.

"I was working the negotiation solo, not with Henoch or anyone else in the cadre. It was what I had trained to do my whole life. Kaplan could think he was in control. Kaplan could believe he was getting over, again. When I talked to Schoen I was just an investigator—a guy who could say and do things the lawyers couldn't. Henoch trusted me.

"Testifying against Caracappa and Eppolito would give us the most important thing we wanted. Not ratting on his lifelong buddies would allow Kaplan to keep a shred of his dignity.

"But decades of law enforcement practice stood in the way. A cooperator has to give up everything when they flip. It was as simple as that. I wanted Kaplan to convince himself that he had found a way out. Once we had Kaplan in a room talking terms, we were talking terms, not talking about talking itself. It wasn't unusual for a potential cooperator to angle for the best deal possible. My duty was to make a deal, and convince Kaplan that he should talk, but it wasn't my responsibility to stop him from imagining that he could have it both ways. I wanted him to think he could flip and save face as a gangster. I wasn't lying to Kaplan and I wasn't misleading him. I was allowing an impression to form, however improbable the scenario. Finally, after dozens of calls and six weeks of talking, the pendulum swung decisively. I was ordering the steamed sea bass for lunch at a restaurant in Chinatown when my phone rang."

"I think we got a deal," Schoen said.

"About time," Oldham said with a laugh. "It's never too late."

Oldham was elated. He had no idea he was soon to be deflated. A crucial but little understood moment in federal criminal prosecutions occurred when the case ceased to belong to investigators and passed into the hands of prosecutors. The process was usually gradual. As investigators gathered more evidence, lawyers started to shape the mass of information collected for the upcoming trial. Tactical decisions became strategic. Handling a witness, or deciding whom to subpoena, were matters that prosecutors wanted to control. Power shifted in increments, like grains of sand slipping through the fingers of the investigators, until a new paradigm emerged.

"Henoch was much younger than most of the cadre. We were all older. But seniority was no longer important. Henoch had tried dozens of cases. He knew that the manner in which a key witness was prepped formed the foundation for that witness's entire testimony. As investigators, the cadre ran interrogations. As a prosecutor, Henoch would be running the proffers and trial preparations."

After the session at the MDC, Oldham moved Kaplan to the Federal Correctional Institution Gilmer in West Virginia. Henoch and Mark Feldman flew down to West Virginia to finalize the agreement with Kaplan and Schoen. Oldham was supposed to attend but his flight was delayed by weather and he missed the session. "I thought it was an omen," Oldham recalled. "I had been sober for months. During that time, I had been able to focus and really think through the approach to Kaplan—the staging and sequencing. With Kaplan coming on board, I knew the case was going to get done—and that Steve and Louis were going to get done. It was a personal triumph. But I hit a wall—a personal brick wall. By Thanksgiving the FBI had managed to have Special Agent Geraldine Hart assigned to the case."

In FCI Gilmer, Henoch's boss Mark Feldman began the conversation. Feldman said there would be no special favors given to Kaplan for cooperating, nor would he suffer any punishment if he decided not to cooperate.

"I was told I wouldn't have to talk about anyone but me and the cops," Kaplan said.

"That's not how it works, Mr. Kaplan," Henoch said. "That's not the deal. It's never going to be the deal."

Henceforth, Kaplan's location and cooperation had to be kept secret. Kaplan was taken from West Virginia to a small county jail in rural New Jersey. A criminal of Kaplan's pedigree would normally never be housed in such a low-security environment. That was the point. The anonymity afforded by a county jail offered the best cover for Kaplan. Prisoners were doing brief stints for drunk driving and assault. They cycled through the facility on a short-term basis. They were petty offenders, not organized criminals, and it would not occur to them that they had in their midst a criminal of Kaplan's stature in the underworld. Kaplan could be taken out and returned at night without attracting attention. Nothing truly big could be happening in Ocean County, New Jersey, during the lazy days of August. The nearby Holiday Inn in Toms River was perfect for conducting serial debriefings attended by as many as a dozen people at a time.

Henoch dictated the rules. There would be no conversation with Kaplan by Oldham or anyone else. No names would be mentioned that Kaplan did not bring up himself. Henoch would start at the beginning and proceed chronologically to accumulate the amazing but true story of Burton Kaplan's life and crimes. Oldham and the other older investigators in the cadre were invited to sit in on the sessions and listen only.

For months, Henoch and DEA Special Agent Mark Manko rose with the dawn and drove from New York to New Jersey to trace Kaplan's life from Vanderbilt Avenue in Brooklyn to secret meetings with Caracappa and Eppolito in the produce section of a Las Vegas supermarket. Oldham's choice of prosecutor had been superb. Caracappa and Eppolito were going to be tried and convicted, Oldham believed. He was on the way to winning his last and greatest case—and yet he had lost his grasp on it. Henoch was now in charge.

CHAPTER FOURTEEN

MOB VEGAS

On a June morning in 2002 a certified public accountant named Steven Corso drove to work in Manhattan from his home in the wealthy suburb of Greenwich, Connecticut. In his late forties, Corso had the look of a dissipated frat boy, with a wide jowl, ruddy face, and dark, slicked-back hair. He had been educated at New York University and Cornell. Married with two young children, Corso was a successful businessman, and a name partner in the prestigious accounting firm of Merdinger, Fruchter, Rosen & Corso. His firm had offices in New York, Los Angeles, Houston, Las Vegas, and Switzerland. His clients were rich. For a kid from working-class Hackensack, New Jersey, Corso had done very well in life.

As Corso made his way toward Manhattan, he received a call on his cell phone. His office manager told him that the FBI and the IRS were in the office. Federal law enforcement officials were picking through and seizing Corso's files. Corso thanked the office manager and hung up. It was no mystery to Corso what was going on. He called a friend who was an attorney and asked him to recommend a criminal defense attorney. The lawyer Corso contacted called the U.S. attorney in Connecticut and inquired if Corso was in legal jeopardy. "Part of the 'game' of prosecutions is withholding charges until the moment is right," Oldham said. "The attorney was told Corso was not the target of an indictment and that there were no warrants for his arrest outstanding."

Corso was no fool. He never returned to the offices of his accounting firm. There was no turning back. Flight was the answer. His life had been spiraling downward for years. Disaster, Corso knew, was inevitable. He flew to Las Vegas and hit the gaming tables. Corso was already in debt to various hotels and casinos in town for more than half a million dollars. From 1997 until 2002 Corso had stolen $5,329,000 from various clients.

Corso's theft was not a complicated financial scheme. His modus operandi was simple. Responsible for preparing the tax returns for wealthy clients, he told them that the IRS had assessed them large sums in tax liabilities. The firm was reputable, as was Corso, and there was no reason for his clients to doubt him. They wired money to cover the tax liabilities to an escrow account maintained by Corso. The sums were never paid to the IRS. Instead, Corso took the money to gamble, buy his girlfriends designer clothes and jewelry, and bankroll the life of a Vegas "high roller."

For the next six months no one from law enforcement contacted Corso. But the lawmen were closing in. Finally, in October 2002, Corso traveled back to the East Coast to answer questions and provide details about the amount of money he had stolen. There was no publicity attached to Corso's capture or crimes. "For the FBI, nabbing a man like Corso represented an opportunity to place him into the financial world as a cooperator. Corso didn't just look the part—he was the part. He understood high finance from both sides of the fence. The FBI wanted to put him into the field and see how he did. Corso would effectively be an undercover agent for the Bureau. In exchange he hoped to get the lightest sentence possible—maybe no time at all."

Corso worked on an investigation of a possible bank fraud during November and December 2002 posing as a corrupt accountant. Afterward, he returned to Las Vegas, where he owned a house. Through his contacts in the FBI in New York, Corso was introduced to two agents in Las Vegas. This Corso went prospecting for crime. Before long a friend in Las Vegas introduced Corso to two men, Joey Cusumano and Rick Rizzolo. Rizzolo ran a club called Crazy Horse Too. The men were in trouble, Corso's friend said, and needed tax advice. Corso recognized the opportunity. If the men were ensnared by the federal government, Corso could pretend to help them, while assisting the government.

The Crazy Horse Too was the Vegas imitation of the French cabaret Le Crazy Horse de Paris, which had opened in 1951 and was famed for the fact that its dancers were indistinguishable by height and breast size. The Vegas version, located in the center of the city, was packed with topless lap dancers and pulsed with ear-splitting music twenty-four hours a day. Lap dances started at twenty dollars, plus tip, with a three-song session in the "Champagne Room" running to at least one hundred dollars. "Corso was introduced as a guy who could do tax returns and give financial advice. Various dancers, bartenders, and waiters started using Corso to do their taxes. He substantially underreported their income, with the permission of the FBI. He wore a wire and recorded more than a thousand hours of conversations. Corso appeared to be just another louche Vegas character. The accountant who hangs out at a strip club, gambles, drinks.

He started on the fringe of the underworld in Vegas and gradually worked his way inward."

Corso began to frequent an Italian restaurant called Casa di Amore, a place he understood to be favored by wiseguys. Corso tackled his role as a corrupt accountant and mob wannabe with gusto, fishing for stories and reveling in tales of violence and mayhem back east on the mean streets of New York. By August 2003, the FBI had assisted Corso in opening an accounting office of his own. The five-room suite Corso occupied was equipped with hidden cameras and microphones. Next door, in a hidden one-room office, the FBI installed video and audio monitors to follow everything that transpired in Corso's firm. Corso was paid $5,000 a month, plus expenses, in return for his cooperation.

It became clear that Corso was adept at undercover work. Claiming affiliation to New York's mob families, he met many of the self-proclaimed wiseguys in Vegas, including John Conti, who told Corso he was the "real head" of the mob in Vegas, and ran the town for the mafia. The fact that Conti would boast about his "connections" was itself proof of how far things had fallen for the mafia. Corso was a newcomer. No real wiseguy—let alone the "head" of a city—would have spoken to a stranger like Corso during the mob's heyday.

"Vegas was an 'open city,' by declaration of the mafia commission; fair game for any enterprising mobster," Oldham said. "No family ran the city, and none of the five families of New York had a territorial claim. Since Bugsy Siegel moved to Vegas in the forties to build the Flamingo Hotel, it had become a major money earner for organized crime. But the Vegas crime scene had been eclipsed by RICO, as it had in New York City. The hoods and hangers-on who Corso met in Las Vegas glorified the old days back in New York. In Vegas, the real thing had become ironic, an Elmore Leonard novel populated by a pack of superannuated putzes trying to convince each other how hard and tough they were. Mob Vegas it was called. The wiseguys there were about as authentic as the gondoliers poling down the fake canal in the Venetian Hotel on the Las Vegas Strip."

But there were still crimes being committed, no matter how desultory or disorganized the "mafia" was. Crime meant work for the hundreds of FBI agents assigned to investigate organized crime. By then, the infrastructure set up by the government to bring down the mafia outmatched the size of the challenge. "The FBI was using a twelve-gauge shotgun to get the rats and gnats eating *osso bucco* at Italianate restaurants. A guy like Corso outmatched anyone he would encounter in Vegas. Corso was smart, sophisticated, a mobster's dream come true. Corso knew how to evade taxes, launder money, raise money. As far as the FBI was concerned, Corso was panning for gold. Eventually, if he was patient and convincing, if fortune smiled on him, some sap with a criminal conspiracy sufficiently large or interesting to the FBI would fall into his trap. But legally, entrapment was tricky. There were moral questions about enticing a human being to become a criminal. There were also legal issues, with a defendant being able to claim the government had enticed them to commit a crime. But if a mouse walked into a trap, eyes wide open, was it the fault of the cheese? It was a matter of character and criminal predilection. It may not be the most attractive aspect of law enforcement but it was standard operating procedure. Corso was a loathsome human being, a thief, and a liar. He sold his soul to save his skin. But if he could help us make a huge case then it was worth doing a deal with such a man."

OUT OF SIGHT, OUT OF MIND

Retired in Las Vegas, like hundreds of other NYPD cops, former detectives Stephen Caracappa and Louis Eppolito lived in houses opposite each other on Silver Bear Way. Their gated community had been built on what was the edge of the city at the time, but by the turn of the millennium the subdivision had been swallowed up by the frenzied sprawl of one of the fastest-growing cities in the country. Despite the churning, ever-swelling population, Caracappa and Eppolito were able to find and become part of a community of self-exiled New Yorkers, many of whom enjoyed Las Vegas's snowless winters, endless sunshine, and supine morality, in which gambling was the engine of prosperity, prostitution widespread, and money, especially cash, worshipped without reservation. "'There are no second acts in American life,' F. Scott Fitzgerald wrote. It's an aphorism that is precisely wrong when it comes to the mob and cops in Las Vegas. There was nothing but second acts. The NYPD and mafia of Brooklyn and Staten Island in the eighties had been turned into a rabble of fatsos pretending they were tough guys. Caracappa and Eppolito belonged to the Las Vegas chapter of the '10–13 Club'—NYPD radio code for 'officer in distress.' Caracappa and Eppolito also operated inside the world of Mob Vegas."

Despite their proximity, the two men rarely socialized. Caracappa, ever industrious, ran a private investigator agency called Argus West. Associated with Argus, a successful New York City PI agency run by former

Major Case detective Jack McCann, Caracappa found only occasional work. Over the years he did a few small things for Eddie Hayes, the attorney he had hired when Gaspipe Casso's allegations surfaced in the newspapers. Able to provide security for visiting celebrities, Caracappa was engaged by Home Box Office to protect Cher for a live concert at the MGM Grand; Eppolito was one of the nine men Caracappa used. When professional wrestlers The Rock and Triple H came to Las Vegas, Caracappa was hired to ensure their safety. "Caracappa was the brains. If muscle was needed for a job, Eppolito could be counted on, despite his age and health. But both were bottom feeding in Mob Vegas—looking for the main chance."

Caracappa found a job as chief investigator at the Southern Nevada Women's Correctional Facility. As happened at the Major Case Squad in New York, Caracappa was noted for his vampiric *sang froid* and icy drop-dead stare. Intimidating and known for his intensity and demand for "respect," now he investigated cases involving women having sex with prison guards and getting pregnant. He also walked for miles every day, circling the streets of the gated community. "Few cops back in New York knew what had become of Caracappa. In New York, in OC circles, Caracappa was considered either wrongly accused or the guy who had got away with murder. Caracappa told his mother and brother and friends he was going to move to Nevada because his wife Monica had family there and there were jobs to be had. He kept up his New York City pistol license, saying he still lived at his mother's house on Staten Island. Legally Caracappa had to be a resident of New York state to carry a concealed handgun. In Vegas he was the silent guy keeping a close watch over everything Louie Eppolito did."

Predictably, Louis Eppolito essayed a more flamboyant life. Inhabiting a reinvented persona, Eppolito became author and auteur, a streetwise, foul-mouthed Brooklyn cop turned to mobbed-up third-string celebrity denizen of the desert. He was mentioned in the gossip pages on the *Review-Journal*. The ink came infrequently, at the outermost edge of hangers-on and wannabes in local gossip columns, but it was enough for a retired detective to construct a character who was "somebody." Eppolito was noted for attending a performance of Harry Barlo, a retired policeman from Philadelphia who had taken up as a crooner said to "do justice" to Frank Sinatra and Tony Bennett. Eppolito, as a notable at the free concert at a place called Greek Isles, was described as the author of *Mafia Cop* and a screenwriter.

Along the way, Eppolito and Caracappa got involved in the case of convicted murderer Sandy Murphy. In Las Vegas the case was extremely high profile. In 1995, a twenty-three-year-old Californian surfer came to Vegas and lost her life savings in one night at the casino. Sandy Murphy didn't turn around and go home. She stayed and started to hustle. She sold lingerie to strippers at a club called Cheetahs. She would dance herself, if the money was good enough. One night the son of a casino magnate came in with a wad of cash. "Ted Binion was worth seventy-three million bucks. He started to spend it on sexy Sandy Murphy. They began to live together. The only problem was that Binion was a heroin junkie with ties to organized crime. In 1998, Binion lost his casino license because of his mob connections. Binion took eight million dollars' worth of silver from his casino and had a friend of his bury the loot in Pahrump, an hour outside Vegas. The friend's name was Rick Tabish. The two men met in the bathroom at a Vegas restaurant called Piero's. By then Binion's heroin problem was out of control.

"Before long, Sandy Murphy and Tabish were having an affair. On September 17, 1998, Binion was found dead in his home, presumably of an overdose. The night after Binion's body was discovered, Tabish was seen digging in the desert near Pahrump. By the time police arrived, Tabish had Binion's silver loaded into his truck. At trial, Binion's attorney said his client had called him the night before he died. 'Take Sandy out of my will, if she doesn't kill me tonight,' the lawyer said Binion told him. 'If I'm dead, you'll know what happened.'"

Murphy and Tabish were arrested. Murphy professed her innocence. The pair were convicted of murder and theft of Binion's silver in 2000 after an eight-week trial, involving one hundred witnesses and national press coverage. William Fuller, an eccentric Irish mining millionaire backed an appeal by Murphy because of her Irish heritage, which resulted in the murder conviction being overturned—much to the surprise of onlookers. Catching scent of Fuller's millions and the media frenzy, Eppolito saw an opportunity for a well-funded screenplay. He formed a committee of one, running a full-page ad declaring Murphy's innocence in a Las Vegas paper. Eppolito listed himself as the "spokesman," but he was the committee's only member. In prison, Caracappa was the only authority Murphy would deal with when she encountered a problem. The name of the group formed to attempt to set her free was "Citizens to Ensure Justice Is Done." The involvement of Caracappa and Eppolito in the case was typical of their activities in Las Vegas—on the edges of the spotlight, with people in the middle of big trouble, but looking for a large score.

"For someone who was retired because of heart trouble, Eppolito remained ambitious and reckless. As soon as he moved out to Vegas he took the job of sergeant-at-arms at the Senior Citizens Club of Las Vegas. The club was a front for the social club of John Conti. Eppolito fit right into the scene. He was close to an older Gambino made man named Mike DiBari. Decades earlier, back in Brooklyn, DiBari had met Eppolito when he was the son of Fat the Gangster. By then DiBari was the bartender at the Senior Citizens Club of Las Vegas. Eppolito's job was voluntary, honorary, but he loved the work. It gave him the chance to spend all his time hanging out with hoods—finally."

After his brushes with Hollywood fame, with one line as Fat Andy in *Goodfellas* ("How ya doin', buddy?") and a few nonspeaking bit parts afterward, Eppolito gradually gave up on a career as an actor, and came to consider himself a writer. *Turn of Faith* was a straight-to-video feature film made from an original script written by Eppolito. The lead role, a dirty police officer named Joey De Carlo, was played by former lightweight world champion boxer Ray "Boom Boom" Mancini. Mancini was a lightweight actor, as well. In the movie, the cop's best friends are a mobbed-up murderer and a priest. De Carlo's idea of stalwart law enforcement work is to give his gangster buddy tips on police investigations, help him beat a man in an alley, and bury tapes with incriminating evidence.

"Eppolito played a 'limp dick' union official named Victor Bruno. Safe to say he was never going to thank the Academy. His performance was so bad it was alarming. Eppolito was grossly overweight, mustachioed with a hambone jaw and hambone acting skills. He had a canny way of talking fast and seeming slow-witted at the same time. Everyone in the movie cursed all the time. 'Get your fucking hands off me, fuckface,' was a typical piece of repartee—and that was a priest talking.

"The moral universe the movie created was perverse. The cop character of De Carlo has been raised by a mobster union boss nicknamed 'Big Philly.' Charles Durning, a good actor, played the part in the lamest performance of his career. Just as in *Mafia Cop* with Fat the Gangster, this father figure was cruel, conniving, and murderous. But no matter how brutally his 'father figure' behaves the cop stands by him. De Carlo the cop is only too happy to help the gangster—until, drum roll, Big Philly betrays the cop's best buddy, also a gangster. In the end, the hero cop wants to quit the force because he is insufficiently admired for severing his links with organized crime. 'I want out,' he shouts. 'Sixteen years I've given to this job. Sixteen years I've banged my head against the wall trying to be a good cop, trying to be an honest cop, and for what?'"

Going direct to DVD, *Turn of Faith* did not change the direction of

Eppolito's life. As time passed, he slid further into failure and obscurity. His claims to fame growing increasingly tenuous, Eppolito found new ways to associate himself with celebrity. In addition to his occasional work as a bodyguard to stars, he set himself up as screenwriter for hire. He was hired to write a comedy about a homeless bag lady, supposedly to star Debbie Reynolds. Jack Gordon, the former husband of La Toya Jackson, engaged in talks with Eppolito to co-author a book about his life. Gordon, a self-styled entertainment impresario who was also dredging the sludge of society, had encouraged La Toya Jackson to perform in soft-core porn and pose for *Playboy* magazine. Gordon's clients included John Wayne Bobbitt, the man whose own fleeting claim to fame was that his infidelities had led his wife, Lorena, to cut off his penis as he slept. A fan and friend of Eppolito's on the Vegas film scene was a "B" grade movie director who has worked under the pseudonym Cash Flagg and directed horror movies like *Rat Phink a Boo Boo* before turning to pornography and films titled *Sexual Satanic Awareness, Debbie Does Las Vegas,* and *Sex Rink.*

In early 2002, Eppolito was introduced through a mortgage broker refinancing his home to a former Las Vegas call girl named Jane McCormick. The mortgage broker was friends with McCormick. He told Eppolito she had been "on the arm" of Frank Sinatra for thirteen years as a paid escort. Her life would make a great movie, the broker said. Eppolito was interested. The two talked on the phone. McCormick was living in Minnesota. She had a small domestic cleaning service in St. Paul. She sent Eppolito her unpublished autobiography. McCormick's life had been tough, involving more than her share of tragedy and suffering. He called back a week later. McCormick recalled that Eppolito said it was the most compelling story that he had ever read. Eppolito told her he wanted to meet her.

"I would love to write a movie about you," Eppolito said. "I'm sure it would be a blockbuster."

"A week later, I flew to Las Vegas," McCormick remembered. "Lou's home was gorgeous. Large Romanesque pillars were in the front. There was a three-car garage. The furniture was leather and silk, plush and expensive, with paintings of beautiful women on the walls. He had a flat-screen television, large entertainment center, and black leather reclining chair. The kitchen was peach-colored, with marble counters and a large island in the middle with a sliding glass door to the back. In the yard, there was a stainless-steel barbecue on the patio, and eight-foot tall Greek statues, and a swimming pool. He had a putting green even though he never played golf.

"I thought it was a beautiful, beautiful home. He showed me around the grounds like a cock on the walk. He was proud. He said, 'You know I didn't get all of this by being a cop in New York. I got it by doing movies and writing movie scripts.' He had a bullmastiff, a huge dog named Caesar, he was telling not to slobber on my pantsuit. We sat on the patio. I had a list of questions. He said he was well-known. He showed me his writing room. He had converted part of the garage into an office. The room was covered with wall-to-wall photographs of Louis with movie stars and directors. There was a picture with Robert De Niro. In the photo of Louis with Martin Scorsese, Scorsese's arm was around him. I was impressed. I thought he was big time."

McCormick spent the whole day with Eppolito. He said she was one of the most interesting people he had ever met. "I think you have a compelling story," Eppolito told her. "I've met a lot of people in my life. I've seen a lot of tragic things in my work as a police officer in New York. But I've never met one person who has had so many horrific, traumatic things happen and survived it and not been committed to an insane asylum."

Recalled McCormick, "He didn't mention money until four days later. Finally he said he would write the script for only seventy-five thousand dollars. He would have it done in three months. He guaranteed I would be happy with it. He said that even though he was a man he had feelings and he could sense what I had been through. I told him I could never come up with that kind of money. Not in a million years. Lou said he had come to like me in the past few days. He said he really wanted to see this happen. 'Your story needs to be told,' he said. 'Your story can help other women avoid the life of prostitution.' Louis said he really felt for me. 'Can you handle forty-five thousand?' he asked in a real gentle way."

A speed talker, with a flim-flam explanation for the financing of films, Eppolito told McCormick she would get all her money back, plus large profits, for the investment of $45,000. According to the Writers Guild of America, Eppolito said, the minimum that a feature film script could sell for was $125,000. He told her that her story would sell for more—between $165,000 and $180,000. All of that money would be hers, Eppolito said with a gap-tooth smile. She would also get back the money she'd paid him as a fee. The logic was bewilderingly circular. McCormick was unsophisticated and entranced by the chance to achieve fame and fortune. When the film sold, she would be compensated in full, he said, leaving the impression that her fee was somehow refundable. McCormick didn't know where to begin asking questions.

In addition, Eppolito continued, she would be paid $50,000 to be on the set to assist the actress playing the part of her life. Eppolito suggested Angelina Jolie as the star of the film. McCormick was hoping for Reese Witherspoon, because her looks more closely matched her own when she was young. Eppolito's deal made little sense to McCormick, but he and his family seemed sincere and trustworthy. McCormick had never read a contract for writing a screenplay, let alone the confusing document Eppolito presented to her. Eppolito gave McCormick a signed copy of *Mafia Cop*. He inscribed it, "I hope we make a great movie of a story that must be told. You are a great woman. I am so proud to call you a friend. May God make all your dreams come true. Love you, Lou Eppolito."

"I was sold," McCormick recalled. "I believed him. I thought he had a soft heart. I didn't think he would ever lie to me. He told me about his life as a cop. He said he had once found a baby in a trash can, and how all the cops were crying about 'Baby Angel.' Every other word was a swear word but he made you think he was telling the truth. He saw himself as a famous writer. He acted like he was a famous writer. He wanted me to believe he was already a famous writer. Deep down I am sure he believed it all. He loved the arts. He wanted to be Martin Scorsese. He said we were going to walk down the red carpet together. He lived in a fantasy world. I couldn't resist."

McCormick returned to Minnesota determined to mortgage her house to pay Eppolito. She had an excellent credit rating. The bank granted the loan within days. She sent a check to Eppolito the next day. For months, McCormick corresponded with Eppolito and traveled back and forth to Las Vegas. During one trip, Eppolito asked her if she would like to see his "favorite thing in life." He bent under his desk and opened a combination lock. He proudly took out a gold handgun. He talked about how his father, Fat the Gangster, beat him terribly as a child and said Eppolito was ashamed that his father was in the mafia. Eppolito showed McCormick pictures of himself as Mr. New York, posing in a bathing suit; a blown-up photo was hung on the wall. Eppolito told her about the trouble he had been in with the NYPD in 1984. Eppolito told McCormick to watch *Goodfellas*. He described to her the scene in which he played Fat Andy. His wife, Fran, was in the scene in the restaurant. She was in the back of the restaurant, in a booth, blond at the time. McCormick rented the movie when she got home and watched it three times in a week. "It was a great, scary, horrible, cold-blooded movie. Louis said he helped Scorsese with the movie—to make it legitimately believable. I didn't think at the time what that meant."

Eppolito titled the script he wrote "I Never Met a Stranger: The Jane McCormick Story." The first draft was replete with misspellings, terrible grammar, and typos. McCormick was shocked and appalled. Eppolito responded that spelling words properly had nothing to do with selling a movie. Producers didn't care about spelling, grammar, or simple competence in presentation, he said. Eppolito put his wife, Fran, on the phone with McCormick to type in the corrections. He told McCormick he always wrote a part for himself in every script so he could be an actor in the movie—like Alfred Hitchcock. In the first draft he wrote a scene with a fat man taking the character of Jane McCormick as a prostitute up to his hotel room and passing out before they had sex. "He wanted to be the fat guy running around the set with Angelina Jolie half naked—living out his wildest dreams."

During the rewrite sessions in Las Vegas, McCormick met Eppolito's neighbor, Stephen Caracappa. He slipped through Eppolito's door without ringing the doorbell, showing himself in and walking through to the back patio.

"So you're the famous Janie I've been hearing about," Caracappa said.

"I don't know how famous I am," she replied.

Caracappa laughed.

Small talk was exchanged about the old days, when Vegas was Vegas, and McCormick had been Sinatra's escort. Caracappa said he loved the heat of the desert. "I thought the poor man was a cancer patient. He was so terribly thin. He was real quiet. After ten minutes he left. Louis told me that they had been partners. He showed me a photograph of them sitting together at a desk in New York. I thought it was weird that Steve lived across the street from Louis.

"You guys were cops together in New York, and now he lives next door to you in Vegas?" McCormick asked. "You must have been close."

Eppolito smiled. "Like brothers," he said.

"I Never Met a Stranger" was structured as a biopic, but the effort was amateurish, the dialogue wooden. Characters were one-dimensional. Transitions were disjointed, both predictable and improbable. Eppolito refused to do further rewrites. He would do no further work until the movie sold, he said. Eppolito had little idea how to write a screenplay, but he understood how to prey upon the frailties of a damaged and credulous woman desperate to tell her cautionary tale.

"I Never Met a Stranger" opens in the cabin of an airplane as it approaches Las Vegas. Two women are sitting beside each other: Jane

McCormick and her longtime companion, Patti. "In the background we hear Wayne Newton singing an upbeat tune," Eppolito wrote. The camera closes in on the McCormick character. "She's a very beautiful, well-kept woman approaching sixty years old. She looks much younger than her age because of her flawless skin and well-groomed manicured hands and beautifully styled blond hair." Patti, likewise, is "a tall beautiful professional woman." The Pilot comes on the intercom to announce the descent into Las Vegas. "The temperature is a hot 99 degrees and zero humidity," the Pilot reports. "The local Las Vegas time is the bewitching hour of midnight. I have to tell you that because as you know you won't see any clocks in the casino."

The screenplay proceeds in this fashion for more than one hundred pages. In the first act, in Vegas as a tourist, the character "Jane," also known as "Janie," encounters a young woman sitting in a bar in the Sahara who happens, at that moment, to be in the middle of being convinced by a pimp-like boyfriend to turn a trick. "Jane looks towards the young couple and sees the beautiful young girl appears to be in distress," Eppolito wrote. "She can overhear their conversation." The ensuing exchange of dialogue typifies Eppolito's work.

"It's gonna be a piece of cake," the boyfriend says. "Besides with a body like you have, he'll cum in two minutes and it will be all over."

"I don't know if I can do it," the young woman says. "It makes me feel dirty."

"You told me you loved me but you sure aren't showing it," the boyfriend replies. "Now is not the time to find your morals. I told you the first one would be hard and after that it will be downhill all the way. Meanwhile with your good looks and body we'll make a fortune. In no time we'll be able to get married."

"I love you," the young woman says, "and I'll do anything for you—even this."

The boyfriend has already lined up a customer who is about to meet the girl at the bar. He departs to gamble, offering a parting piece of wisdom about becoming a prostitute. "Trust me, baby, you might even end up liking it."

Janie intervenes. She says she wants to talk to the young woman. "I know you very well," she says. "It was me sitting on that stool forty years ago." She tells the girl what they have in common: broken home, sexually abusive father, the long forlorn search for love ending in being turned out as a hooker. "The same thing happened to me, and I never told anybody about it, but I will now. I'll tell you my story."

"Why would you want to tell me?" the young woman asks.

"'Cause it could change your life," Janie softly says, "and trust me, if I had someone sitting next to me forty years ago I would have listened. I would have listened good."

Flashing back decades, we hear Janie narrate a tale that takes her to Las Vegas in the early sixties and the age of the cocktail generation and the Rat Pack. The plot follows Jane as she descends from tragedy to tragedy as a child and young woman, enduring sexual abuse, rape, spousal abuse. Her two young children are taken away from her to her in-laws, May and Clarence Heck. Trying to earn enough money to get them back, Jane turns to prostitution. Her pimp boyfriend, the handsome young Tyler Moore, is stereotypically manipulative and cruel.

The character Janie has an ambivalent relationship with prostitution. The money is great. She moves in high-roller circles, swanning through casinos and hotel lobbies. She is also despondent and desperate. Sexy and carefree in one scene, in the next she is suicidal. Eppolito the writer flits breezily back and forth between glamour and despair without considering the contradiction or the implications for the character named Jane McCormick. In its psychological dimensions, "I Never Met a Stranger" was reminiscent of *Mafia Cop*. In his memoir, the character of Detective Louis Eppolito careened back and forth between cop camaraderie and the glorification of organized crime. Beaten mercilessly as a boy by his father Fat the Gangster, Eppolito professed admiration for his father's sense of honor and respect. As a detective in the Six-Three, Eppolito thrilled when he shoved the mouth of a double-barreled shotgun down the throat of a wiseguy. The actions did not belong to a complex character, but to a man animated by self-pity. Memory, conscience, taking responsibility for one's own deeds—none of these elements were evident in "I Never Met a Stranger" or in his book *Mafia Cop*.

The script reaches its apogee one night in the Sands lounge when one of Janie's friends introduces her to Frank Sinatra.

"How you doin' baby?" Sinatra says.

Sinatra, Dean Martin, and Sammy Davis Jr. invite Jane up to a suite in the Sands.

"The Rat Pack is in the room and a group of call girls, mostly Jane's friends, are walking around the room in spike high heels, their panties and bras," Eppolito wrote. "There is music loudly playing and champagne being poured for everyone. Frank walks over to Jane and takes her hand. She puts her drink down and he leads her to his bedroom."

A montage of scenes follows, with Sinatra's "The Summer Wind" playing in the "b.g." "I was living a life few people could dream of," Jane says in voiceover. "Can anybody imagine being part of the Rat Pack!" In one scene, Jane and her girlfriends are sitting at a table in a Vegas lounge. "We see a number of tuxedo pants and patent leather shoes indicating that there are a number of the Rat Pack on stage," Eppolito wrote.

In real life, McCormick convinced herself the completed script for "I Never Met a Stranger" would bring her fame and fortune. Eppolito had promised her as much. In their written agreement, Eppolito undertook to use his contacts in show business to help McCormick sell the script. He told McCormick that the Showtime channel was considering the script and would get back to him soon. HBO, Movie of the Week, Ray "Boom Boom" Mancini, who had been involved in producing *Turn of Faith,* were all supposed to be interested. McCormick contacted Mancini. Boom Boom told her that the movie would have to be rewritten extensively.

"I didn't like the script," McCormick said. "I felt like I was being conned." McCormick was told the script wasn't right and that Louis Eppolito was a struggling writer. "I got depressed. I started calling him up, after I had a few drinks, to cuss him out." McCormick now felt she'd been duped. Eppolito didn't have the movie industry connections he'd led McCormick to believe. "I said I had to declare bankruptcy because of him. Louis got angry. 'Don't call me when you've been drinking,' he said. 'You don't know who you're dealing with.'"

That was certainly true. But it was also true Eppolito did not always know who he was dealing with, either.

THE "FOOLPROOF FORMULA"

By the fall of 2004 the fallen accountant Steven Corso had insinuated himself deeply into the inner workings of the organized crime underworld in Las Vegas with the FBI tracking each move. Dining often at Casa di Amore, in a matter of months he had become a fixture on the scene. Corso's main contact was a Bonanno associate who ran an escort agency. Convinced of Corso's promise as a financial advisor to the Vegas mob, the Bonanno associate introduced Corso as being "with Jerry of the Fulton Fish Market." The reference was to Jerry Chilli, a Bonanno mobster convicted of a wide variety of racketeering crimes over three decades in the mob, including forgery, loan-sharking, attempted manslaughter, and conspiring to sell $300,000 worth of stolen salmon fillets. Chilli was known to operate out of New York City's Fulton Fish Market, a venerable open-air market on the Lower East Side with every kind of fresh fish and seafood for sale—notoriously corrupt and later shut down by the government, it moved to Hunt's Point in the South Bronx. Wily enough to run a credit card scam while in prison in Florida during the nineties, Chilli had relocated to Florida but had interests in Vegas.

Dropping Chilli's name had a warming effect. In the mafia, "being with Chilli" meant that Corso was under the protection of the mafia. Corso was proposed and accepted as a member of the Senior Citizens Club of Las Vegas. Corso became a regular at the club's Thursday lunches, where attendance was required. He even cooked lunch there. Corso wore a recording device to capture his conversations with hundreds of people moving in suspect circles.

In October 2004, Corso was approached with a proposition. Corso was now tight with two older Gambinos: Mike DiBari, who claimed he had once been a close friend of John Gotti, and another man named John Frate. DiBari suggested to Corso that he meet their friend "Lou." DiBari appeared to be close to Lou. DiBari told Corso that "Lou" was working on a movie. "Lou" had written a screenplay and was now looking to raise money. Corso had a reputation as a man with access to money, especially illegitimate money. "Lou" was a retired New York detective who had moved to Las Vegas and gone into the moviemaking business. DiBari was to make the connection.

"Lou is one of us," Corso was told. "You can deal with him."

Until "Lou" was mentioned by DiBari and Frate, Corso had never heard of Eppolito, *Mafia Cop*, or the newspaper headlines generated by Casso's confession in 1994. In the time since he had become a cooperating witness, Corso had collected scores of such names, and there was a routine followed. Corso notified Las Vegas FBI Special Agent Kevin Sheehan, who was running Corso, and asked if he wanted him to meet with "Lou." As it happened, Sheehan was friendly with Las Vegas DEA Agent Chris Moran. Unlike New York City, where interagency rivalries were blood sport, law enforcement officials in Las Vegas often liked and trusted each other. Because of their good relations, Special Agent Sheehan knew that the DEA office in Vegas was surveilling two retired NYPD detectives as part of an investigation being run by the Eastern District of New York and that Louis Eppolito was one of the targets of the investigation. Moran had pulled the phone records on the NYPD detectives' telephone lines, and attempted surveillance. Nothing of significance was found. But when Sheehan told Moran about Corso's contact with a retired NYC cop named "Lou" who was closely associated with Las

Vegas organized crime figures, Moran passed the information on to the New York office of the DEA.

"I had been getting antsy about the Vegas side of the case," Oldham recalled. "I didn't believe the case would be made the way it should be made unless we went out to Vegas and set up on Steve and Louie ourselves."

In the offices of the Eastern District on Pierrepont Plaza, Robert Henoch knew that what Corso offered was potentially a huge break. For months, he and Oldham had prepared to take the case to trial and fight on the subject of the statute of limitations. The last known crime committed by Caracappa and Eppolito had been the murder of Eddie Lino in November 1990. Caracappa and Eppolito had continued to receive their monthly payment until Casso's capture in 1993, which amounted to evidence of their ongoing conspiracy, but otherwise there were no further crimes with which to charge them. The two NYPD officers had left New York for Las Vegas in the early to mid-nineties, absenting themselves from the geographical center of the mafia. Had they committed any crimes in their new surroundings? DEA Agent Moran's investigation had not revealed any. Oldham and Henoch recognized that using Corso could alter the entire case. If he were successfully introduced to Caracappa and Eppolito under the guise of facilitating illegal ventures, it could well be that "the cops" would incriminate themselves. Corso had been an excellent snitch for the FBI. The question was whether he could convince Caracappa and Eppolito to let down their guard.

Oldham and Henoch wanted to think through the implications carefully, and not rush into an ill-conceived sting. Meetings were held. Word was passed from New York to the Las Vegas FBI agents to get Corso to wait. In the meantime, John Frate and his son, Mike, met for a lunch with Corso. They were eager to make the connection with their friend "Lou." The Frates handed Corso a manila envelope, which Corso opened. Inside was an inch-thick movie script titled "Murder in Youngstown." The film Eppolito wanted to make was based in the crime-ridden streets of Youngstown, the same working-class Ohio city where Eppolito's flop *Turn of Faith* had been set. The Frates wanted to know if Corso might help Eppolito raise the funds necessary to make the film. Corso followed his instructions from the FBI and responded that he had a "problem" meeting with Eppolito, given his past as an NYPD detective. Corso was understood to be an accountant for underworld figures. Associating with a police officer, even a retired one, was bad for business, and potentially dangerous for a man in the business of crime. The Frates reassured Corso about their close friend. "Lou was one of us," the elder Frate said, referring to their days back in New York, when Eppolito served the NYPD. "You can deal with him. If anyone has anything to be fearful about, it would be him—with his background."

"The way cooperators often work, we flip a guy and then insert him into an investigation," Oldham recalled. "In Corso's case it was the opposite. The investigation of Caracappa and Eppolito was going forward. We were going to prosecute, come what may. We had surveillance up on Caracappa and Eppolito but it wasn't yielding anything. Frankly, I wasn't convinced that the Vegas DEA was putting much effort into the case. Corso stumbled into it. Having a CW like Corso, who we didn't plant, was unusual and a potent possibility. Eppolito was out trolling around the OC world for money. The relationship was Eppolito's idea, not Corso's, not ours. He wasn't being trapped by us, or 'entrapped' in legal lingo. Eppolito was constructing his own trap.

"But there were substantial risks in putting Corso with Eppolito. If Corso suggested criminal enterprises, all Eppolito had to do was say he wouldn't get involved in such matters and our prosecution would be in serious jeopardy. According to the rules of evidence, the government is required to provide defendants with all relevant material relating to their case. The rules include material that is exculpatory. All Eppolito needed to do was refuse Corso and there was a huge chance he could establish the 'withdrawal' defense. If Corso asked Eppolito to launder drug dealer money, Eppolito could state he would never do such a thing. If Corso asked if Eppolito would get him drugs, or hookers, Eppolito would be on tape saying no. If Corso tried to get Caracappa involved, Eppolito could say that he would never suggest such a thing to his old friend. Eppolito could say he and Caracappa were honest, decent men, retired police officers sworn to uphold the law, and that the idea they would take dirty money or deal narcotics was outrageous and ridiculous—and the whole thing would be on tape. The stakes were high for us. Eppolito could save himself, or sink himself. Henoch gave the green light. We all crossed our fingers."

Within days, word reached Corso from FBI Special Agent Sheehan. "You're good to go," he was told. A meeting between Corso and Eppolito was arranged for ten days later. Corso drove to a gas station in Las Vegas and met John Frate. He followed Frate through the Spanish Springs area of Las Vegas to Eppolito's mini mansion on Silver Bear Way. Corso was wearing a wire. When Corso arrived he was introduced to Louis's wife, Fran, and his two daughters, Andrea and Deanna. The discussion turned to business. Eppolito suggested they retire to another room out of the earshot of others. They went to Eppolito's office. The walls were adorned with dozens of vanity photographs of Eppolito smiling with celebrities. There were brass-on-wood police plaques bearing the NYPD detective shield, certificates of appreciation, a framed copy of the cover of *Mafia Cop,* and a letter from Hugh Mo, the former deputy police commissioner of trials who had heard the charges that Eppolito had leaked intelligence to the Gambinos in 1984. Eppolito's collection of knives was displayed in a glass case, some worth as much as $5,000. Two safes were packed with 113 guns. The arsenal included .45s, .44s, .357s, .38s, .32s, .22s, .25s, .380s, 10mms, gold-plated revolvers, Lugers, Derringers, double-barreled shotguns, and semiautomatic pistols. "Mafia Cop, Louis Eppolito" was engraved on the side of one pistol.

Seated behind his massive faux mahogany desk, Eppolito told Corso he needed further funding to make "Youngstown," as he called his project. Eppolito claimed to have already raised $3.5 million. He needed $1.5 million more. Eppolito told Corso that a group of investors had pledged their personal assets with the Bank of America. The idea confused Corso. He had not read the script but it struck him as highly improbable that anyone with the means to fund such a project would be idiotic enough to gamble their financial security on the outcome of an unmade movie written by a failure like Eppolito. Corso asked for particulars. They called Eppolito's producer on the speakerphone.

"Why would an individual pledge his assets and risk losing it all if the movie didn't make money, or wasn't made?" Corso asked.

There was no good answer. From a business perspective, the deal made no sense. Under normal circumstances, if Corso weren't acting the role of a sophisticated accountant dumb enough to fall for Eppolito's preposterous proposal, the conversation would have ended then and there. But Corso was playing Eppolito, seeing where events led.

A second meeting was planned for the next day. The location was Corso's office. FBI cameras and recording devices capturing the encounter showed Eppolito proudly giving Corso a copy of his book, *Mafia Cop.* Eppolito said he had mastered a question that had mystified generations of producers and auteurs. Eppolito had a "foolproof formula" for making money on movies. All that was required was for Eppolito to stick to the formula and the money and accolades would roll in. Eppolito didn't describe the formula.

Corso feigned fascination.

On November 21, the two men met again at a Vegas Italian restaurant.

Eppolito was in an expansive mood as they waited to be shown to their table. Eppolito told Corso about his supposedly burgeoning business selling his skills as a screenwriter to unsuspecting souls like Jane McCormick. As they stood at the bar waiting for their table, Eppolito told Corso how he worked deals with people who wanted to turn their life story into a movie. His price was $75,000 for a script, minimum. The deal was open to anyone, regardless of the nature of the story or how the funds to pay Eppolito were obtained. "I says, 'Put up seventy-five thousand dollars, I don't care where you get it from, and you and I will be partners.'"

The pair was joined by a client of Corso's who had funded other investments. The client had no idea Corso was wearing a wire and cooperating with a federal investigation. Over dinner, the conversation turned to the prospect of creating a film production company for "Youngstown." Instead of raising $1.5 million, Corso suggested that the amount of money being sought ought to jump to the whole $5 million. There were a couple of ways such a sum might be raised. A public offering of securities for Eppolito's movie might work, Corso said. Corso's "client" had a publicly listed company. Eppolito's existing corporate entity was called Deanntone Productions, a name created by merging the names of his children Deanna, Andrea, and Tony. The entity could be merged into the public company, and the reconstituted corporation would issue and sell shares of stock. Eppolito would be paid $250,000 a year in salary. Eppolito would retain a controlling interest in excess of 51 percent of the equity. Friends of the founders would be able to receive small amounts of restricted shares in the company in order to participate in the windfall. Such an arrangement was typical, Corso said, one of the benefits that befell a man in Eppolito's privileged position. Eppolito said he had friends who might be interested. In particular, a former "police partner" of his, named "Steve," might want to participate in such a moneymaking enterprise.

Eppolito lived far beyond his means, it was apparent to Corso. A successful screenwriter, in Eppolito's own mind, entitled to the finer things in life, he had to survive on his $70,000 NYPD pension and whatever money he could squeeze out of marks like Jane McCormick. The putting green in the backyard, the flat-screen television, the gold jewelry, and grotesque collection of knives and guns, were costly ostentation. Corso knew he appeared to be the answer to Eppolito's woes. Over a period of months, Corso ingratiated himself into every aspect of Eppolito's life. Just as Eppolito had played McCormick, preying upon her fantasy of fame and fortune, Corso played Eppolito.

"Likewise, of course, Eppolito was conning Corso. Eppolito was trying to pull Corso in, using whatever means he could—mob stories, police stories, any and all bullshit he could come up with. Back and forth the fantasies went. With Corso's expenses covered by the FBI, he bought meals and flashed wads of cash, consciously creating the impression he was rich and held the keys to greater riches."

Closely monitoring developments in Las Vegas, Henoch, Oldham, and investigators in New York held a conference call with Corso. He was asked a series of detailed questions regarding Eppolito. Corso described Eppolito's house and office. He told the agents the type of cell phone Eppolito used and the many weapons Eppolito had on display in the house, including his knife collection. Corso explained Eppolito's screenplay scam and the fee of $75,000. Corso was asked if he thought Eppolito might be interested in obtaining the desired $75,000 if it came from drug money, or a high-ranking drug boss. Would Eppolito accept the money? Corso felt strongly that Eppolito wanted the money, regardless of where it came from. Corso told the federal agents he was confident Eppolito would go for the scheme very quickly. Eppolito was to be told he could have the money fast, within forty-eight hours, if he agreed. The con man ex-cop was about to be conned by law enforcement.

In the plan devised to test Eppolito's legal and moral mettle, Eppolito would be offered the chance to knowingly launder illegally acquired drug money as a means of getting investment in his movie project.* The FBI coached Corso to put the proposal to Eppolito concisely. Corso, a skilled liar, would easily handle the deception. Eppolito, with a weak heart and a long history of corruption, would be presented with a tissue of lies, and have the chance to participate—or refuse to participate.

Corso laid the foundations of the proposal at his next meeting. Corso told Eppolito that he had found a potential investor in Eppolito's screenplay venture. On December 7, 2004, Corso and Eppolito convened in Eppolito's office, surrounded by the photographs from Eppolito's brushes with Hollywood fame and NYPD infamy. The offer, Corso told Eppolito, was from a Florida drug dealer looking for investments. The drug dealer was trying to transform drug money into legitimate ventures.

---

* The federal offense of money laundering sprang from the tax evasion convictions of Al Capone in 1931. As a result of that case, Meyer Lansky started the practice of squirreling his money in Swiss bank accounts using a series of shell companies. The cat-and-mouse game between organized crime and investigators took on the trappings and sophistication of high finance. Thus did hiding ill-gotten gains become as important and chancy as acquiring them in the first place.

Believing his own deceptions, Eppolito failed to see the larger deception engulfing him.

"The seventy-five," Corso said with a sigh, "it's going to be here next Thursday, Friday, Saturday, Sunday, or Tuesday." He laughed. "It's either going to be cash or wire. You don't care, right?"

"No," Eppolito said.

"Do you care what someone does for a living?" Corso asked.

"I don't give a fuck about nothing," Eppolito said.

"I think the same way you do," Corso said.

"Here's what I tell people," Eppolito said. "As long as you're not asking me to do it, if this is the biggest drug dealer in the United States, I don't give a fuck. But don't ask me to transport drugs for it. I don't do that. That's what I tell somebody. If you said to me, 'Lou, I want to introduce you to Jack Smith, he wants to invest in this film.' And Smith says, 'Seventy-five thousand comes in a fucking shoe box.' That's fine with me. I don't care. I've had people give me money before. That doesn't bother me, and I don't question people."

"Right, okay," Corso said.

Eppolito told Corso about an investment in a film project he had previously received from a Vegas wiseguy named "Mike" who used to drive for Joe Bonanno back in New York City. "I don't give a fuck, like I said, about that. I know him. I respect him. He respects me. I have a thing, as stupid as it is, I don't put my hand in your pocket, and I don't like it when it's done to me."

"I'm not putting the money in," Corso said.

"I'm talking about for your end," Eppolito explained, referring to the sum Corso could expect to make for putting the Florida drug dealer together with Eppolito. Brokering such a deal, it was understood in the mob, required the go-between to be compensated. Eppolito said that the wiseguy Mike and his son had presented him with $25,000 in cash.

"Mike came up, 'Ba-boom, here,'" Eppolito said.

"Cash in the cardboard box?" Corso asked.

"Yeah. When I sell the movie, the first day that they yell 'Action' on the set, they have to give me a check. So let's say I sell the movie for one hundred and twenty-five thousand. I give you back your twenty-five thousand dollars, and I give you twenty-five percent of what I made. So you make a hundred percent on your money."

"Okay," Corso said, not contesting Eppolito's misrepresentations, or the wild improbability of "Youngstown" or any Eppolito-written project being made.

During the preparation of Corso for his dealings with Eppolito, Henoch had been careful to instruct Corso to not try to massage conversations to get Eppolito to say specific things. Cooperators too often concerned themselves with trying to satisfy the terms of a criminal statute to ensure that the target would be convicted—and that the CW would be rewarded. The practice was foolhardy, Henoch believed, practically and legally. If a CW attempted to steer the target to say preordained words, suspicions could easily be aroused. Juries would be less inclined to credit an investigation that looked to have stacked the cards against an accused. Let the conversation take place naturally, Henoch had told Corso. Don't talk too much, Henoch had said, an instruction an inveterate talker like Corso found hard to obey.

Corso broached the subject of the investor's mob connections by insinuation. "This guy is very quiet," Corso said of the Florida drug dealer. "He's an Italian guy. You don't mind dealing with Italians, right? He's a strong guy."

"I don't care who it is," Eppolito said. "Listen to me, I got people from the Gambino family that call me all the time. They say, 'Louie, we have money.' I says, 'It's not a question about your money, it's you don't have enough to make the movie. You want to give me three hundred and sixty thousand?'"

"I'll take it," Corso said, picking up on Eppolito's thought. "If you want to give me three million I'll take it."

"I'll make the movie," Eppolito said. "But it's not enough just to say to me you have money. Especially when they have the mentality that they have all their lives. It's always a scam, always a scam."

Eppolito then told Corso a story about a Gambino wiseguy from upstate New York. Eppolito said he had known the wiseguy since he had been a teenager living in Brooklyn taking long drives with his gangster father as they made the rounds of Gambino social clubs. The wiseguy was now sixty-five, nearly a decade older than Eppolito, but still an earner. "A hustler, not a boss or a capo," Eppolito said.

"That would be called a soldier?" Corso asked.

"An earner," Eppolito said. "He's out there doing whatever he's got to do."

"You can educate me about this stuff," Corso said.

"He's got more clout than other guys because he brings in money. You know what I mean? He might be scamming, he might be doing this, he might be doing that."

Eppolito said the wiseguy called to make an arrangement to meet. But the mobster only said "Hello, it's me," and then fell silent. Corso laughed at Eppolito's imitation of a paranoid gangster on the phone. The mobster told Eppolito he wouldn't talk on the phone, Eppolito told Corso, because he didn't know who might be listening on a wiretap. "I said, 'What are you doing that's so bad nobody could know? If they're bugging my phone, congratulations, they get my wife talking all fucking day.' I don't talk on the phone."

Eppolito imagined himself a raconteur. He enjoyed telling Corso about New York mob culture, a subject he was an expert on. Eppolito told Corso he had made an appointment to meet the Gambino made man at the Bellagio, the landmark Las Vegas hotel with a vast fountain in front that is claimed to be "the most ambitious, commanding water feature ever conceived." Eppolito's wife, Fran, didn't want him to go. "She said, 'You don't even know if you're going to get killed.' I said, 'Who's going to bother me? I don't bother no one.' " According to Eppolito, the two men shared the bear hug and two-cheek kisses customary for greetings in the mafia. The avuncular gangster told Eppolito he had come up in a conversation at Puglia's, an Italian restaurant on Hester Street between Mott and Mulberry streets in Little Italy in lower Manhattan.

Corso hung on Eppolito's every word. "He says, 'I ran into a good friend of yours. He said you're looking for money.' I says, 'I'm always looking for money.' He says, 'Tell me what the thing is, and let me know what you need because these people have money.' I says, 'I need to raise three-and-a-half–four million dollars on a script I have here.' "

Eppolito paused and asked if Corso had taken the time to read "Murder in Youngstown." Corso admitted he had not. "I've been busy," he said.

"That's all right," Eppolito said. "I says to him, 'I got a script I can do in Vegas, it's three-and-a-half million. It's not as big as 'Youngstown.' 'Youngstown,' we have a better shot of making more money, but this shot here, we have a shot of selling this movie in Europe alone for five. That's only one group of people that's in Europe. I says, 'We sell that to fucking Europe, you're probably looking at five to seven million dollars.' Everyone who can't come here wants to see Las Vegas on the screen. There's shots of Vegas, the hotels. That's all second-unit directing. You can send out one guy and his crew, get in a car at night and go down the Strip and take both sides of the street and use, as you want, from those clips, you know what I mean?"

Eppolito went on. "He says, 'I'll give you six hundred thousand tomorrow.' I says, 'Where do we fucking fall off the train? Three-and-a-half million I need. Six hundred thou doesn't go.' He says, 'I wanna come in. I'll take a percentage.' I says, 'That is so fucked up.'" Eppolito explained the basics of movie financing, as Eppolito understood them, to the Gambino wiseguy. The investor with the majority share was paid first and foremost. Minority stakeholders were the last to see any profits. "I says, 'I want the people to make money, but whatever it is with me I want to make money.'"

"Was he insulted that you didn't want to take his money?" Corso asked

"He just doesn't understand," Eppolito told Corso. "I says, 'Let me tell you the ways the Jews do it. There's no better way. The Jews say there's four of us, that's a quarter each. The way Italians do it is to want sixty-five cents, a dime for another guy, three cents, seven cents, but always make sure I get the most.' I says, 'Jews don't care because there'll always be another dollar, and another dollar.' Italian people for some reason, and I don't know the reason, they always ask how am I getting fucked? Where I am getting fucked? It's like their assholes are puckered."

Eppolito turned to the piece of business at hand, as the two men continued their meal. The unnamed Florida investor was willing to send Eppolito the desired $75,000.

"Do I meet this guy, or no?" Eppolito asked Corso.

"I don't know," Corso replied.

"I could bring you the papers. Let him sign. He could sign it fucking 'John Wayne.' I don't give a fuck what name he uses."

Over the weeks they'd known each other, Corso saw Eppolito constantly. He went to Eppolito's daughter's college graduation party. He expressed an interest in dating her, despite an age difference of more than two decades. It seemed to Corso that Eppolito was withholding his approval of a liaison with his daughter pending the outcome of their business dealings. If Corso came through with the money, it seemed, Eppolito would encourage his daughter to see the much older, ruddy-faced, corrupt accountant.

Despite his corpulence and poor health, Eppolito was eager to impress Corso with his propensity for violence. Early in their relationship, Eppolito fantasized about an incident in which he purportedly met a sixty-seven-year-old gangster associated with Eppolito's deceased mobster father. The gangster now lived in Las Vegas. Eppolito's recollection of his conversation was recorded by the listening device Corso was wearing. "He took my kids, Deanna, Andrea, Tony, Fran, her mother, and me and he said to my family it would be an honor for me to kill anyone who fucks with your family. Just tell me who it is and I will take care of it. You will never hear about it. You'll read about it. It would be an honor because I loved your father so much."

On December 20, over another meal with Corso courtesy of the FBI, Eppolito explained to Corso the dealings he had with a man he had hired to work on his house. The contractor was a member of the Hell's Angels, Eppolito said, his voice registering clearly in the small recording device Corso wore. When a dispute about payment arose the contractor came at Eppolito with a hatchet, the retired tough guy cop told Corso. Eppolito said he grabbed the axe from the biker. "Do you think I won't put this through your fucking head, faggot?" he told Corso he said to the biker. "I says, 'You are nothing but a faggot.' I says, 'Your tattoos don't show me shit.' I says, 'If you don't finish this job today or tomorrow I'm going to personally kill you in front of your friends, then I'm going to kill your friends.'"

Eppolito told Corso he had brandished the axe as the violent Hell's Angel biker cowered in the face of the obese screenwriter in his late fifties in need of a double bypass operation. "I says, 'I'll put this right through your fucking head.' I says, 'You're not taking my kindness for weakness.' I says, 'If you ever want to push me, I will personally kill you, and I'll do it in front of your mother and father and then I'll kill them.'"

There was a profound lesson in the incident, Eppolito told Corso, an important truth about Eppolito's character revealed in his treatment of a biker who had the temerity to threaten the former NYPD mafia cop and son of Fat the Gangster. "You got to let people know the obvious," he said to Corso. If a hand or axe were raised against him, Eppolito said, following the dictates of *cosa nostra* to the letter, there was only one response possible. "You'll kill them first. That's imbedded in me."

In late December, Henoch flew to Las Vegas to meet with Corso. Eppolito's earlier mention of Stephen Caracappa had turned the FBI investigation of Eppolito into a potential prosecution of both men. The time was not ripe to move on Eppolito, Henoch decided. The story needed more time to develop. As talk of the $5 million deal continued, Eppolito insisted he needed cash right away. The sum Eppolito referred to continuously was $75,000.

By Christmas, Eppolito was growing agitated. Corso was a continuous presence in his life, in person and on the phone. But no money had arrived from Corso's Florida "connection." On December 26, Eppolito had open-heart surgery, a double bypass. Corso went to see Eppolito in the hospital. Wearing a wire, he offered his best wishes to the convalescing ex-cop.

"I don't want to die, but I'm not afraid to die," Eppolito said. "I'm not afraid of anything."

Corso continued to string Eppolito along during the month of January as Eppolito cajoled and pestered him for the money. Throughout Eppolito's dealings with Corso, Stephen Caracappa had been a subject of discussion between the two men. Eppolito told Corso that he and his former NYPD partner, Caracappa, worked together in the "protection" business and that Caracappa was Eppolito's advisor and confidant. Corso knew Caracappa read everything Eppolito wrote—original screenplays, commissioned life stories, spec television scripts. The two retired detectives living across from each other on Silver Bear Way were dear friends with a deep bond.

On January 31, 2005, Corso met Eppolito for dinner at Vegas's Il Mulino of New York, an Italian restaurant in the upscale Forum Shops of Caesar's Palace. Eppolito was accompanied by a man named Al Pesci whom Corso had met at Eppolito's daughter's graduation. Eppolito also brought Caracappa with him. Pesci and Caracappa had many questions for Corso regarding the nature and structure of the financing deal he was offering Eppolito. Caracappa, in particular, wanted details on how the public offering would be conducted.

"I'm looking out for Lou," Caracappa said. "He has been hurt on other deals."

Corso nodded.

Caracappa said, "We bring you into our group—our family, our closeness—and we don't want to be hurt by it."

On February 3, Corso and Eppolito met again in Eppolito's office. As always, Eppolito wanted to know when he was going to get his money. Corso explained that the Florida investor was nervous that the transfer of money would be detected by law enforcement officials. They were young guys, Corso noted. He said the contracts should be completed using fictional identities. "Movie names," he said. Payment would come the week of February 14. The method of payment preferred was in amounts less than $10,000, Corso said. He explained to Eppolito that the federal government tracked large transactions by requiring banks and financial institutions to notify it if a deposit or withdrawal was over $10,000. The method of notification was a currency transaction report, or CTR. The drug dealer would pay in small tranches and thus not arouse suspicion.

"This is how the money is going to come in," Corso said. "I just want to make sure you're all right with it. What a CTR is, any time you get a deposit in your account over ten thousand dollars it flags. Okay? Let's say these guys hire me, they want to buy a restaurant. They want to invest in a public company. They pay me, I don't give a flying fuck. But this is drug money that's coming. I know you don't care, I'm just saying."

"Yeah," Eppolito said.

"Just so you know," Corso said.

Eppolito understood what was happening—or thought he did.

On February 15, Eppolito received $5,000. The money was transferred by wire by the FBI, a method that created an electronic record of the transfer. Eppolito and Caracappa and Corso convened for dinner at yet another Italian restaurant. Fellini's boasted rooms with frescoes of Italian cities painted on the walls and a clientele said to include "Legends of Entertainment." As they ate and drank, courtesy of the FBI, Corso pretended to be upset that Eppolito had *still* not been paid in full. Corso said it was a matter of honor. He had given his solemn word to Eppolito that the money would be paid in full. The delays were upsetting and humiliating, Corso let it be known, growing more and more exercised. Corso was a fast talker, like Eppolito, and his red-faced outrage was exaggerated to mimic sincerity. Caracappa urged Corso to calm down.

"You got to understand one thing," Caracappa said to Corso while Eppolito was in the men's room. "Trust me when I tell you this. Don't put too much pressure on yourself. It's going to happen. You believe it's going to happen, then it's going to happen. Calm yourself down. I'll tell you why. You're going to make yourself sick over it."

Corso muttered his agreement.

"I've been in this business a lot longer than you," Caracappa said. "I know what I'm talking about here."

"Steve, if I don't have my word, I've got nothing."

"If I didn't believe your word, I wouldn't be sitting here with you. Or you wouldn't be sitting here with me and him."

"If I tell you something, it's going to happen."

"But you know what? Give it a little bit," Caracappa said.

"They're being very careful," Corso said. "They want to keep it under ten thousand dollars. I explained that to him."

Caracappa understood Eppolito's manner when involved in matters of money. "Is he being concerned about this?" he asked.

"I don't know this," Corso said. "It's none of my business. But I believe he's under financial pressure."

"Well, he is," said Caracappa of his partner.

Eppolito returned to the table.

"They're just paranoid," Corso said of his Florida connection. "But five thousand dollars is more than you had yesterday. That's the way I look at it."

"What are they so fucking paranoid about?" Eppolito asked. "They're from Florida, right? Why didn't they send a guy with a fucking car? I would have flown down there and drove back. That would not be a problem for me."

"They just want to do it this way," Corso said.

"I don't give a fuck," Eppolito said.

"I CAN GET YOU ANYTHING YOU WANT"

During the months Eppolito tried to lure Steven Corso to invest in his moviemaking schemes, Corso befriended Eppolito's twenty-four-year-old son Anthony. Tall and thin, with a shaved head and large dark eyes, Anthony was in the thrall of his father. "Anthony was a 'casino kid,' a young man trying to figure out how to make a living out of Vegas's largest industry," Oldham recalled. "Anthony was only a beginner but he was friends with another casino kid who knew the game well. Guido Bravatti, a Guatemalan immigrant, was in his mid-twenties, with a shaved head and goatee. He worked in the clubs of the Venetian Hotel on the Strip. Corso met Bravatti through Tony Eppolito. Bravatti portrayed himself as a guy who could get anything. The first time he met Corso he offered to get him hookers. Caracappa had also met Bravatti through Anthony Eppolito. Caracappa took a shine to Bravatti. The kid was a jack-of-all-trades. He came over to Caracappa's house and helped Caracappa's wife set up her computer. Bravatti could get hookers, drugs, seats to a fight. He was an operator, a facilitator, and that appealed to Caracappa. The old Major Case Squad detective took Guido under his wing.

"By the time Corso sat down for dinner at Fellini's with Caracappa and Eppolito on February 15, the ground had been laid for the next gambit. The money-laundering charge against Eppolito was complete and the linguini hadn't even been served. The tapes were irrefutable proof that Eppolito was only too happy to take drug money, in cash, as an investment. All the requisite elements had been proved. Corso had let the conversation unfold naturally. Eppolito had obliged. That charge was airtight.

"From the start we had talked about asking Caracappa and Eppolito if they could supply Corso with drugs or prostitutes. When Henoch talked to Corso he asked if he thought Eppolito might be willing to deal drugs. Eppolito said in December he wouldn't touch the drugs himself, but it was unclear if he would participate in a transaction as long as someone else actually handled the drugs. Corso was sure Eppolito would want to be in on a drug deal—any deal we offered. Eppolito said he would do anything for money, and Corso believed Eppolito meant what he said. 'Toss it out there,' Special Agent Sheehan said to Corso. If Caracappa and Eppolito had even a lick of sense, or decency, they wouldn't go for the bait. Taking money from a drug dealer was one thing. Dealing drugs was another."

During the main course at Fellini's, Corso broached a new subject. Over red wine and pasta he suggested an escalation in their business relationship. Attempting to sound offhand, his voice audible over the din of dinner, Corso upped the ante.

"The other thing I want to talk to you about," Corso said to Caracappa and Eppolito. "Don't take it the wrong way. I got these guys. These four young guys are coming in. They're young Hollywood punks. They're my clients. Two are famous. They're coming to Vegas this weekend. These are guys that are going to invest. They may need protection, but I haven't asked them about that. The reason I tried to get in touch with the Guid-ster . . . Did you talk to him today?"

"Who?" Eppolito asked.

"Guido?"

"No," Eppolito said. "I have to see my son. My son knows him."

"These guys have been my clients for three years," Corso said. "They're younger. Two of them are famous. They're coming for the whole weekend."

"How famous?" Eppolito asked "What are you talking about famous?"

"You'd know their names," Corso said.

"Are they actors?"

"Yeah," said Corso. "They're going to invest."

The Cheddar was set before the mouse. Caracappa and Eppolito were within reach of a huge windfall. All they had to do was one small thing: commit a federal felony. The movie stars Corso had dreamt up as the lure for Eppolito—the combination of fame and fortune—were going to give him money for his scripts. The amount wasn't just $75,000. The Hollywood actors, with all of the cascading contacts and opportunities such a connection promised, were going to buy *four* scripts. Eppolito would receive $300,000. The deal sounded too good to be true—because it was.

"It's not my problem," Corso continued, "but my thing is that these young guys like to party. They do things that I have no knowledge about. Basically, it's designer shit—designer drugs."

"Tony can take care of that for you," Eppolito said, referring to his younger son. "My son can bring them to all the top places."

Corso wanted to make it perfectly clear to Caracappa and Eppolito that he was talking about purchasing drugs, not getting into clubs or hiring hookers. "What they want..." Corso's voice trailed off. "This is why I was thinking about Guido. They don't want to go to the places. They want me to get them ecstasy or speed. I don't know what that is."

"You got to ask Guido," Eppolito said.

"Guido's the guy?" Corso asked.

"Guido can handle it," Caracappa said.

"Guido can handle it?" Corso asked.

"All those places, yeah," said Eppolito.

"So I just gotta get in touch with Bravatti," Corso said. "That's why I was trying to get in touch with him. That and to see if I can do any accounting with him."

After their dinner, Eppolito called Corso with Bravatti's number. Corso took the number but refused to discuss the drug deal with Bravatti on the telephone.

"I don't talk about anything illegal on the phone," Corso said.

Eppolito grunted.

Corso and Bravatti talked the next day. Bravatti had heard about Corso's dinner with "Uncle Lou" and "Uncle Steve." The story about the incoming celebrities and their needs had been conveyed. Bravatti asked if Corso was free to meet for dinner. Bravatti was going to bring his "partner" along.

El Molino on West Sahara Avenue was a Mexican restaurant specializing in fajitas and margaritas. Corso arrived at six p.m. wearing a wire and expecting Bravatti to arrive with his "partner." Just after seven, Bravatti arrived. Anthony Eppolito was with him. The former NYPD detective turned screenwriter had shown he would do anything for money, including dealing drugs, provided he didn't have to touch the drugs himself. Corso had not considered the possibility that "anything" included using his son to do the dirty work Eppolito eschewed as too dangerous.

The three were shown to the table. Drinks and dinner were ordered. Corso had rehearsed what he was going to say. Trust was the first order of business. Corso had to know that he could trust Bravatti and the younger Eppolito. "I asked Tony's dad and Steve if I could trust you," he said to Bravatti. "I know I could trust Tony because I know his dad. They vouch for you up and down. I made them swear that I could trust you. I need . . ."

Corso paused.

"These guys need to get an ounce of meth and about six to eight pills of ecstasy for their party," he said.

"No problem," Bravatti said quickly.

"I don't know how much it's going to be, but whatever it costs I'd rather do it in my office," Corso said nervously.

"Because you're Dad's friend, because of that, there's no way that anybody you would bring to us would get fucked," Tony Eppolito said. "Believe me."

"I know that," Corso said. "That's why I'm coming to you guys. But I don't want to get fucked."

"No," said the younger Eppolito.

"I got to be careful," Corso said.

"Don't worry about it," Eppolito said.

"If it's a thousand, if it's eight hundred," Corso said, "I don't give a fuck what it is. I need it tomorrow afternoon if I can."

"Do you only need an ounce?" Eppolito asked.

"An ounce of speed and, like, six to eight pills?" Bravatti asked.

"I don't know what else you guys can provide," Corso said.

"We can provide anything," Bravatti said.

"I don't know," Corso said.

"I can get you anything you want," Bravatti repeated.

"I don't know nothing about this shit," Corso said. "You tell me if there's something in addition that you like and you want them to try and I'll buy it from you. I just don't know anything about it. Okay? The reason I'm doing it is—first of all because they pay me a lot of money."

Bravatti laughed.

"No shit," Tony Eppolito said.

"Whatever they want, I want to be able to give to them. Because the number two reason I'm doing this, I want their minds to be perfect. The only thing I care about is they cough up the money. That's all I give a shit about."

"As long as you take care of my Dad I'll give you whatever you want," the younger Eppolito said. "I don't give a shit."

"There's seventy-five times four coming to your Dad," Corso said.

"To be honest, I'll make money off the deal," Bravatti said. "But as long as your deal goes through and they have a great time they'll keep coming back."

"If you got something else I'll buy it," Corso said. "I don't give a shit. They're going to be with a couple of girls, but look I don't know what they want. I don't know what you can provide. They might want girls, if you've got access to girls that are hot. These guys got money."

"We've got access to everything," Bravatti repeated again. "Do they like prostitutes?"

"They're bringing their own girls?" Eppolito asked.

"These are the type of guys, they would say to the girls go out there and have a good time."

"We got girls," Eppolito said.

"I've got porn stars," Bravatti said. "I've got access to everything."

"Are they —" Corso began.

"Top-notch?" Bravatti interrupted. "They are. I've been in Vegas twelve years so I know the town pretty well."

"These guys are coming in tomorrow night," Corso said. "Will you be able to get me the shit tomorrow?"

"I could have it to you tonight," said Eppolito.

"I could have it to you tonight," Bravatti agreed.

"Tomorrow's good," Corso said.

The next morning Corso arrived for work at nine, as usual. The meeting with Bravatti and Tony Eppolito was set for two in the afternoon. Corso worked through the morning. He was a cooperator for the FBI, but part of his deal with the Bureau allowed him to perform accounting for legitimate clients. Over the months, Corso had developed a small but promising practice. Despite the depths of his situation, Corso was attempting to claw back some version of a life to carry forward after his time as an FBI snitch was finished and he had served the sentence he was given, if any, for his crimes.

Before Bravatti and Eppolito arrived, Corso was summoned to the "other" office. DEA and FBI agents were in the adjacent room monitoring the video and audio surveillance equipment. They frisked Corso, emptying his pockets to ensure he had no cash or contraband that would sully the anticipated drug transaction. Corso was furnished with $1,400 in hundred dollar bills. Corso began to wait for Bravatti, hoping Tony Eppolito wasn't with him.

Guido Bravatti and Tony Eppolito arrived on time. Corso gave them a tour of his five-room suite, excluding the DEA and FBI office accessible through a side door. The small talk over, Corso locked the front door of his suite. The threesome made their way to Corso's office. Eppolito and Bravatti sat in high-backed chairs opposite Corso. Under the gaze of the FBI video camera, Tony Eppolito placed the crystal meth on the desk.

"From the outset, the younger Eppolito and Bravatti had been enacting an orchestrated pantomime for Corso. Bravatti promised anything Corso wanted. Tony Eppolito was the concerned and connected son of the ex-cop gangster who could be trusted. The two-bit punk drug deal was infused with an interior and unspoken conversation. Sending his son meant that Louis Eppolito was in earnest. Providing an ironclad guarantee that Bravatti was credible showed approval by Caracappa. The two young men had prepared their performance to draw Corso further into their web—as Corso drew them into ours."

In Corso's office, the younger Eppolito was about to deliver the goods. "My friend got it for eight hundred," Eppolito said as he handed over the baggie containing the drugs. "He wants nine hundred."

The surveillance camera angle was perfect: Corso was in the foreground, back to the camera, while the two young men sat on the edge of their seats eagerly as Corso picked up the drugs and inspected the baggie.

"Good," Corso said.

"It'll blow your mind," Bravatti said.

"Was it hard to get?" Corso asked.

"It was easy," Eppolito said. "They sell it to wannabes like us. Actually it's a little hard to come by an ounce. It's a large quantity. Selling smaller amounts is easier. An ounce can be chopped up and sold in much smaller pieces and make a lot more money."

With one transaction complete, back in New York Oldham and Henoch began to plan further operations. A second delivery of drugs was proposed, in order to show a pattern of narcotics dealing by the criminal enterprise Caracappa and Eppolito were still operating in Las Vegas. In Vegas Corso tried to contact Tony Eppolito but failed to reach him. Another drug delivery was attempted but a DEA agent involved fell ill and the transaction had to be postponed. Two weeks later, Corso met with Eppolito and one of his daughters. Eppolito appeared upset.

"How you feeling?" Corso asked, with concern.

"I got a panic call from my son," Louis Eppolito said. "I'm very, very fucking upset. Don't call him or Guido anymore. No more. They don't exist."

"What's the problem?" Corso asked.

"Don't call them anymore, okay," Eppolito said. "Do not call them anymore."

"They were supposed to meet me—"

"They're not meeting you."

"Why?"

"I told them not to."

"How come?"

"It's an over situation. I don't want to go into it. I don't want to discuss it. Just do not reach for either of them. If the guys from California cancel out, it's fine with me. It's not going to have any bearing on me. I don't give a fuck."

"You seem upset," Corso said.

"Very."

"You want to tell me about it? No? Okay."

A fourth meeting was set for March 3. Corso arrived as agreed. No one else turned up at the appointed time and place.

TAKEDOWN

By early March, Oldham and Henoch were growing increasingly concerned about security. If Caracappa and Eppolito got word of the investigation, there were many things that could go wrong. First, the cops could go on the run. Second, they could go after Corso. Third, there were the wild cards that got dealt in any investigation. "The most unpredictable moment is just before you take them down," Oldham recalled. "Years of work had gone into making the case against Caracappa and Eppolito. We had Burt Kaplan, Tommy Galpine, Monica Galpine, Pete Chiodo, and Al D'Arco. We had the Vegas charges—money laundering, drug dealing, hours of Eppolito bragging about his capacity to kill. We had reached that exquisite moment when things could only go downhill or wrong. Caracappa and Eppolito were still connected inside law enforcement in New York City. Most of the guys they'd worked with had left the force, but that didn't mean they had no juice."

Henoch was planning the arrest for late March. Methodical by nature, a prosecutor with the mind-set of a military logistics specialist, he wanted the angles thought through before acting. Then Henoch got a phone call that changed their plans. The call came from Bob Nardoza, a public affairs officer in the Eastern District. Nardoza said he had received a call from the Brooklyn DA's office's public information officer, Jerry

Schmetterer. Officials there wanted to know if the arrest of Caracappa and Eppolito could be arranged for a Sunday.

"If the takedown came on a Sunday, we were told, the television show *60 Minutes* would run footage from the press conference on that night's broadcast," Oldham said. "The publicity that the U.S. Attorney's Office and the Brooklyn DA would receive would be enormous. If things went wrong we couldn't have dug ourselves a hole deep enough to hide in. The stupidity of the notion was stunning."

Sensing disaster, Henoch began to record events so that he would have contemporaneous notes if the case went off the rails. The next day, *60 Minutes* reporter Lesley Stahl turned up on the front steps of Tommy Dades's house asking if he would talk to her. Dades turned Stahl down and called Mark Feldman. Now there was a real possibility that the outcome of the investigation could be altered.

Henoch had planned to continue working Corso with Caracappa and Eppolito. The two former NYPD cops had grown suspicious of Corso, but it seemed it would be worth seeing whether they would be willing to engage in more money laundering and drug deals. Now that plan was precluded. There was no time to lose. Caracappa and Eppolito needed to be arrested as soon as possible.

As the team prepared, Oldham made inquiries among doctors about the recovery time for an open-heart surgery patient. Oldham wanted to know how long after such an operation it would be considered safe to place a patient's heart under the strain that Eppolito's would face as he was arrested. "I didn't want to be handcuffing a purplish fat man as he lay dying."

Oldham flew to Las Vegas, as did Intartaglio, Campanella, and Manko. The tactical meeting for the arrest took place in the morning in the DEA's Las Vegas field office. It was in another of Las Vegas's gated communities, enclosed by a ten-foot cinderblock wall, ringed with surveillance cameras. Entry was gained to the compound through electrically operated heavy metal gates.

At noon Oldham received a call from Henoch. The prosecutor told him that Kaplan had failed a lie detector test. Henoch was no longer sure they should go through with the arrest. Oldham argued that the failed lie detector test was irrelevant. Polygraphs were not admissible in criminal trials. It had been decided by the courts that the probative value of polygraphs was outweighed by the prejudice they invited. Experienced law enforcement officials knew that the tests were useful as a threat or a tool but not as direct evidence. Kaplan's truthfulness had been verified by every traditional means possible. Henoch had spent many hours with Kaplan during the proffer sessions. Oldham knew Kaplan was telling the truth about Caracappa and Eppolito. That was the case at hand. Oldham made a raft of phone calls to senior federal attorneys to learn their views on the consequences of Kaplan failing the polygraph. The consensus was that the failure should not abort the arrests. By late afternoon Oldham and Henoch had reached an agreement. The takedown would proceed on schedule at Piero's, a "family"-style establishment owned by a local businessman named Freddie Glusman. In an advertisement, Glusman boasted, "No one gets bothered in my restaurant. I don't care who the celebrity is or what they have done. I see to it that they are allowed to dine in peace and quiet . . . No exceptions!" Known for its "awesome bucco" and spumone and as a regular hangout for the Rat Pack in the sixties, Piero's was frequented by diners who enjoyed its notoriously colorful ambience. Glusman was noted for joking, "the boys still come in here, but now the FBI follows them."

On the evening of March 9, 2005, four agents lolled in the vestibule entrance to Piero's. They knew Eppolito and Caracappa were coming. The former detectives were expecting to meet Corso for an evening of food and conversation. Traffic was light, but it was still early evening. Manko and his team idled in their car a short distance away. Although it had taken DEA Assistant Special Agent in Charge John Peluso nearly half an hour of cursing and channel surfing, the portable radios now worked properly. The designated DEA chase cars reported that a Cadillac Escalade SUV carrying Eppolito and Caracappa was a few miles away from Piero's and making good time. The parking valet leaned on a railing reading a paperback book.

"As the cars drew nearer I moved my car to a position across the street from the restaurant. Minutes passed slowly. The Escalade came into view turning onto Convention Center Drive from Country Club Lane. It slowed and turned into Piero's lot, coming to a stop under the valet parking portico. Louie left the driver's seat as Steve stepped from the passenger side, taking a second, running the flattened palms and fingers of both hands from his shoulders to his waist to smooth the lines of his suit jacket.

"Having been a policeman for approximately 10,496 days of my life, I pulled into the lot behind the Escalade, at the same time cutting off entry to the chase cars. Clearly not part of the plan, not tactical genius. I reached Steve as he was about to enter the restaurant, at the same time Louie was being pushed out of the restaurant by the four agents in the vestibule. We sprawled both men against the exterior wall of the restaurant. As I searched Steve and Peluso handcuffed him, an agent relieved Eppolito of a large silver-colored semiautomatic handgun that had been tucked in his waistband.

"That night at the DEA field office, I passed what appeared to be a reinforced concrete and fiberglass room. It gave the impression of being a fish tank of some sort. I saw Steve sitting alone handcuffed to the single bench that ran along one wall. I stepped into the room and sat down next to him. He looked at me hard for a minute. 'I know you. Where do I know you from?' he asked. 'I'm Oldham. We worked together at Major Case.' Caracappa smiled as his face lit with recognition and then he slapped and squeezed my thigh. He didn't get it. He thought he'd been arrested for violating some local ordinance in Las Vegas — spitting on the sidewalk, or something. He looked at me and asked wryly, 'Hey, who'd I kill to end up in this fucking place?' I cupped my hand and leaned over and whispered into his ear, 'Eddie Lino.' He looked stunned. He didn't ask, 'Who?' He turned away from me, leaving me staring at his back, and muttered, 'I don't know nothin' about that.'"

CHAPTER FIFTEEN

THE CIRCUS COMES
TO BROOKLYN

The arrest of Caracappa and Eppolito made headlines around the world. "Among the most startling allegations of police corruption in memory," said the *New York Times*. "Could be the last of the red-hot organized crime trials . . . equal parts titillating and chilling . . . a courtroom pageant for the ages," predicted *New York* magazine. "The most shocking scandal to hit the New York Police Department for a century," said the BBC.

The federal government was feeling triumphant in the aftermath of the bust. "This indictment is an indication that the passage of time is never a safe haven for those who violate the law," the U.S. Drug Enforcement Agency said in a press release. "With the charges announced today," U.S. Attorney for the Eastern District Roslynn R. Mauskopf said, "these defendants will rightfully face justice, ensuring that their conduct will never tarnish the reputation of a proud and honorable police department." Mauskopf emphasized that the arrest did not mean that the investigation was complete. The capture of Caracappa and Eppolito gave the government the opportunity to accumulate more evidence as people with information came forward or were found by the cadre.

News of the arrests caused a chemical reaction in the country's entertainment industries, many of them centered in the same city where the story was located. The words *NYPD*, *murder*, and *mafia* set in proximity to one another fused to become a new substance—an enticing media property. Hollywood producers, Manhattan literary agents, and newspaper reporters began to prowl around the case looking to make deals; all were claiming special access to the main players who had inside information. Detective Tommy Dades, now retired and spending evenings working with kids boxing in a gym in Staten Island, suddenly became prominent, having emerged in reports as the easy-talking sleuth who had "broken" the case. "Dades' relentless investigation of Eppolito and partner Stephen Caracappa resulted in the arrests Wednesday of two of the allegedly dirtiest cops ever—cops who thought they had gotten away with murder," the *Daily News* reported. The work of Oldham and other members of the cadre went largely uncredited.

The subterranean skirmishing between the Eastern District and the Brooklyn DA finally came into the open on national television on the CBS show *60 Minutes* on Sunday, April 10, 2005. Denied the chance to prosecute Caracappa and Eppolito by the Eastern District, unnamed sources in the Brooklyn DA's office contrived to put forward a version of events that gave credit for the case against the newly dubbed "mafia cops" to a single investigator: Tommy Dades. The *60 Minutes* segment was reported by Ed Bradley, and began with a review of the show's closeness to the case over many years. "I spoke to Anthony 'Gaspipe' Casso in 1998 in prison where he began serving a life sentence after admitting to thirty-six murders," Bradley said. "Casso's claims couldn't be substantiated at the time, so we couldn't air them until now, now that the detectives have been indicted."

The videotape of Gaspipe Casso appeared onscreen next. Dressed in an orange prison jumpsuit, Casso described the kidnapping and killing of Jimmy Hydell in 1986. "Louie and Steve made believe they were going to arrest him," Casso said. "The kid thought they were taking him to the station house. But they took him to a garage. They laid him on the floor, tied his feet, put his hands in cuffs, and they put him in the trunk of the car. The guy is kicking in the trunk, making noise. I took him to a place I had prearranged. It was somebody's house I could use. I sat him down. I wanted to know why I was shot, who else was involved, who gave him orders. After that, I killed the kid myself."

"You killed him?" Bradley asked.

"Right," Casso said.

"With just one shot to the head?"

"No," Casso said, a sly grin creasing his face. "I didn't shoot him in the head. I was in somebody's house. You'd make a mess that way. I shot him a couple of times. I didn't torture the kid. Maybe I shot him ten, twelve times. I gave Louie and Steve I think $45,000 for delivering him to me."

Brooklyn District Attorney Charles Hynes was then interviewed. "I've seen organized corruption cases but the allegations that two cops were hit men in addition to giving up people for hits is absolutely shocking," Hynes said.

The clip of Eppolito in *Goodfellas* was played, followed by a shot of the cover of *Mafia Cop*. Bradley reported that Gaspipe Casso had been deemed an unreliable witness and his cooperation agreement had been breached by prosecutors. But only after an ex-cop named Tommy Dades "helped break the case wide open" did prosecutors start to believe Casso's stories about Eppolito and Caracappa.

Next came a Bradley interview of Dades.

"You sat for months by yourself poring through records, computer files, phone logs?" he asked.

"I would go over as much information as I could, to try to come up with a mistake that they made here, a mistake they may have made there."

"Was there a moment when you said, 'I got them'?"

"There was a moment that got me very excited, that I knew I was on the right track," Dades said.

Bradley reported that Dades had discovered how Caracappa had run a search on an NYPD database for a man named Nicky Guido.

EXIT OLDHAM

The obsession with who should get credit for the arrests obscured and infected the ongoing investigation of the case, which, now that a trial loomed, rapidly took on greater urgency. The first order of business was continuing to debrief Burton Kaplan. For prosecutor Robert Henoch, the process required a stringent protocol. Over the months to follow, he would get to know Kaplan's life story in as much detail as humanly possible. Yet Oldham was increasingly isolated. He didn't want to sit in a room and listen to Henoch ask Kaplan one question after another. Henoch was good at giving orders. Oldham was terrible at taking them.

"The other guys were resentful because I wasn't doing my share of the shit work," Oldham said. "But I'd been doing it for years. I thought I had equity in the case. Among other things, we fought about the Eddie Lino charge. Henoch thought we needed to do a DNA test on the watch found down the road from Lino's car, to see if it was Caracappa's. I disagreed. I told him it wasn't Steve's watch. I was in Major Case with Caracappa at the time of the Lino hit. I knew Steve wouldn't wear a cheap watch like a Pulsar. His taste ran more to the expensive—he wore suits hand-tailored in Hong Kong. More to the point, if you run a DNA swipe on the watch and it comes back negative, then it looks to the jury like you don't know what you're doing."

The claim that Tommy Dades had "made" the case upset investigators in the Eastern District as well as many in the Brooklyn DA's office. Dades had quit six months before the arrest of Caracappa and Eppolito; he had left of his own volition. He had nothing to do with Kaplan, before or during or after his proffer. The assertion that Dades "made" the case was absurd to many insiders. But tensions remained between those involved, as frequently occurred in the rough and tumble of New York City OC cases. Much of the dispute inside the Eastern District revolved around semantics. What did "making" the case mean? What *was* the "case"? Was it "made" when Kaplan flipped, or did "making" the case demand the yearlong investigation to corroborate Kaplan and then present the evidence to the jury? To a large extent, the term meant different things to different investigators and lawyers. For Oldham, the case was "made" when Kaplan agreed to talk. There was an enormous amount of work to be done, but once Kaplan agreed to divulge the actions of Eppolito and Caracappa the key pieces of the puzzle had been put in place. For Robert Henoch and his team of attorneys inside the Eastern District, "making" the case meant securing a conviction. Both definitions of "making" a case were arguably valid.

The task of placing the case before a jury fell to Henoch, and his two associates, Mitra Hormozi and Daniel Wenner. Kaplan's narration of events was critical, and his testimony would make or break the trial, but it was also vital that every shred of evidence that corroborated Kaplan, including Caracappa's check of the wrong Nicky Guido, be amassed, structured, and prepared for presentation to a jury. In addition, other witnesses would have to be interviewed and prepared.

The lead resources for Henoch in the months after the arrest were Bobby Intartaglio and Joel Campanella, both experts on organized crime. Oldham chafed. He and Henoch started to argue even more. Oldham had chosen Henoch, and now Oldham felt pushed to the margins.

"The Caracappa and Eppolito case was an orphan for years," Oldham said. "Many people wanted to get them but no one thought it could be done. The FBI and DEA wouldn't put any resources into it. Mark Feldman gave it to the Brooklyn DA's office. But once the case was made, there was a gold rush. Everyone wanted to jump on the bandwagon. It was getting crowded and I wanted off."

Oldham was also caught up in other cases. He got a letter from an inmate in the New York state system named Oswaldo Medea saying he wanted to talk about the murder of a police officer in the past. "I researched his claim and I couldn't find a murder of a police officer that was unsolved. The NYPD claimed we had solved every murdered officer

case but two. Then I realized that the NYPD had absorbed the New York
Housing Police in 1995. The cop Medea was talking about was a housing
cop, so he wasn't technically a cop. I brought Medea down from Attica.
He was doing multiple life sentences. He was a very scary guy. Wiry and
mean, you could see he would kill you if he got riled. Another inmate had
told me he had twenty-three bodies. Medea told me it was actually more
like forty. He was very serious about being who he was. Medea had a code
of honor. He said he would snitch on himself but no one else. He admitted he killed the cop. It was a coup, closing an old murder of a police officer. All Medea wanted for his cooperation was to spend ten years in
federal prison in Florida. He knew he was never getting out, but he
wanted to retire to a cell in a warm-weather state. In return we would
close the murder of a police officer, which means something to my kind.
We don't like open police murders. They send the wrong message. Every
cop wants to close those cases, even if takes thirty years. But the front
office wouldn't sign off on the deal. They didn't want it to seem like the
government was rewarding Medea's behavior.

"The fights were enervating. I was feeling depleted—not just physically
but like my beliefs were out of date. They called us dinosaurs around the
office, the law enforcement counterparts to Burt Kaplan and the last of the
old-school hard cases. The office politics were killing me. I knew I wasn't
going to get better cases than Louie and Steve, and a guy who professed
to have killed forty people plus a cop. On the flip side, it couldn't get any
worse. For the first time in the Eastern District I was being told what to
do. I was told to stay away from organized crime cases. I was ending up
where I began when I first came to the Major Case Squad and Caracappa
locked me out of the Organized Crime Homicide Unit. Working on
Steve and Louie didn't win me any friends. The opposite.

"The years had taken a toll. Detectives will tell you there is only so
much murder and misery you can take. There comes a time when you
either submit and you will be diminished if you stay on the job, or you get
out and try something else in life. I decided it was time to retire. I was
done. I was finished. Tired, worn-out, ready for a new challenge."*

---

* When he decided to tell his account of the investigation of Caracappa and
Eppolito, Oldham didn't quite know how to present himself to potential publishers.
He had no literary agent, and his tendency to mumble and speak obliquely did not
suggest that he was ready for prime time. Eventually, of course, he found an interested
publisher—the publisher of this book.

A BODY APPEARS

On the morning of March 31, 2005, three weeks after the arrest of Caracappa and Eppolito, NYPD helicopters hovered above a parking lot on
Nostrand Avenue in the Flatbush section of Brooklyn. Below, Dr.
Bradley Adams from the Office of the Chief Medical Examiner excavated
the earth underneath a covered parking shed. A leading forensic anthropologist, tasked during the nineties with exhuming the remains of more
than fifty American servicemen buried during the Korean and Vietnam
wars, the youthful and earnest scientist diligently sifted through the soil
looking for evidence of disturbance. Adams dug slowly, carefully, using
his hands and a masonry trowel in the sandy silt and clay. Signs of digging,
or compaction, would indicate that he was looking in the right spot.
The only clue Adams had was a report that a body was buried in the earth
under one of the parking sheds.

The lead had come from a tiny, seemingly insignificant document
buried inside an NYPD murder file nearly twenty years old. Going
through the evidence boxes related to the 1987 homicide of Frank Santora
Jr., the cadre had come across Santora's phone book. At the time, Burton
Kaplan was being debriefed by Henoch in a New Jersey motel. During
the proffer sessions, Kaplan had said that when Caracappa and Eppolito
snatched Jimmy Hydell in the fall of 1986, they had taken him to a parking lot in order to transfer him to the trunk of their car for the handoff to
Casso at the Toys 'R' Us at the end of Flatbush Avenue. Kaplan remembered that Santora and Eppolito had a connection inside the Brooklyn lot
where they had taken Hydell that day. It was noticed that Santora's telephone book contained an entry for "Pete's tow truck" and two numbers,
one in Brooklyn, the other in Pennsylvania. Oldham and his cadre colleagues tracked down the numbers and found they led to a parking lot on
Nostrand Avenue in Brooklyn. Further inquiries had identified a man
named Pete Franzone as the operator of the lot in the eighties.

On the day Caracappa and Eppolito were arrested in Las Vegas,
Henoch had instructed FBI Special Agent Michael Wolf to approach
Franzone and inquire about his knowledge of the two retired NYPD
detectives. Panicked, Franzone denied any connection. He was terrified
that Special Agent Wolf was, in fact, an impersonator sent by Caracappa
and Eppolito to see if Franzone would rat on them—and kill him if he
did. After Wolf left, Franzone picked up the yellow pages and called the

first attorney he saw in the book, Alan Abramson, a lawyer who just happened to be a former assistant district attorney for the Brooklyn DA. Franzone told Abramson that a man was buried under a concrete slab in one of the parking sheds he used to manage. Abramson convinced Franzone that he needed to tell law enforcement what he knew about the two "mafia cops" making headlines at the time.

On April 1 Dr. Adams returned to the site and began excavation in an adjacent garage. The FBI Evidence Response Team brought a small backhoe to expedite the process. A large block of concrete formed the floor of the garage. The slab was removed. As he began to dig, Dr. Adams quickly saw indications of white material flecked in the soil. He thought it was lime, a substance believed by many to speed the process of decomposition—when in fact the chemical composition slows insect activity and therefore keeps a body intact longer. He began to dig with great care. As he went deeper he encountered a piece of black fabric. Dr. Adams probed further, the hole reaching down three and then four feet. The soil was extremely loose. Moving his hands through the earth, Dr. Adams felt the shape of a shoulder blade. Gently removing the remaining dirt, he revealed the decomposed corpse of a man lying in the fetal position, his head bent and arms and legs folded under his torso.

The pit measured twenty-nine inches in diameter and was precisely five feet deep. Dr. Adams removed the body. The man's head was disconnected, part of normal decomposition, and stuck in a plastic Shop Rite shopping bag. The remnant of a yarmulke clung to his head. His wrists were tied behind his back. He was wearing rubber galoshes over his shoes, indicating he had been killed in the winter. A wallet was removed from his pocket. The American Express card inside was for one Isidor A. Greenwald of Blue River Gems Inc. He had been shot twice in the back of the head. One slug exited through his forehead. The other slug exited through his left eye. For nearly two decades, this had been the unmarked grave of the jeweler Israel Greenwald.

BEFORE THE JUDGE

The federal courthouse of New York City's Eastern District is located at the foot of the Brooklyn Bridge. It is a landmark for both sides of the organized crime industry—gangsters and cops. Over the decades, hundreds of Brooklyn wiseguys have entered the courthouse's revolving doors, some acquitted and returned to the streets, the vast majority convicted and transported on a Bureau of Prisons bus to a penitentiary on the outskirts of a town in middle America.

In their first appearance in court, Caracappa and Eppolito seemed dazed as they emerged from the holding cells. The two former detectives had been held in Las Vegas and then transferred to Atlanta and from there to Brooklyn and the Metropolitan Detention Center. Both men appeared shaken as they gazed at the onlookers packed in the gallery. Caracappa was sickly, pale, and disoriented. Eppolito appeared in worse condition. Dressed in prison garb—T-shirt, cotton slacks, slip-on sneakers—Eppolito had the pallor of a man at death's door.

Judge Jack Weinstein stared back at them with cold solemnity. Eighty-three years old, tall, still muscular, his face distinguished by a hawkish nose and prominent eyebrows, Weinstein was arguably the best trial judge in the country. A longtime professor at Columbia University and author of an authoritative text, *Weinstein on Evidence,* he had been appointed to the bench in 1967 by President Lyndon Johnson. In the decades since, he had established a reputation for maverick decisions, often of a liberal bent, and a courtroom manner that moved quickly from courtly gentility to sharp irritability. The august cadences of his voice suggested the dispassionate grandeur of the late actor John Houseman. Born in Wichita, Kansas, in 1922, Weinstein had been raised in Brooklyn and in the thirties appeared as an actor on Broadway, in productions of *Subway Express* and *I Love an Actress,* as well as auditioned for a part in the 1928 production of *Peter Pan* starring famed lesbian actress and theatrical *impresario* Eva Le Gallienne.

Judge Weinstein was no innocent. During his teenage years, he drove a truck on the docks of Brooklyn, exposing him to the criminal forces that controlled the commercial underworld and shaped Gaspipe Casso, junior and senior. Weinstein had served as a submarine officer in the Pacific during World War II. In the final days of the conflict, after the attacks on Hiroshima and Nagasaki and the subsequent Japanese surrender, Weinstein's submarine got an enemy ship in its sights while on patrol. The war was over but hostilities had not officially ceased. The captain of the American submarine trained his torpedo sights on the ship. Weinstein, a junior officer, asked if it was necessary to sink the ship—and kill the men aboard. The captain replied that he was still under orders. The ship was struck, and the crew perished. The experience seared Weinstein, and provided the impetus for a lifelong interest in the existential question of what a man with power should do when literal adherence to the letter of the law seemed to thwart justice. It would be a question that would find its way into the fates of the men who now appeared before him.

Vigorous in his great age, often rising with the dawn to row or swim in Long Island Sound near his suburban home, Weinstein remained perhaps the most prolific judge in the Eastern District. Intellectually, he was the equal of any sitting judge in the country—and known for wanting to be known as such. As he heard both criminal and civil matters, as do all federal trial judges, many of Weinstein's decisions were animated by the dilemmas created when courts are confronted by large social questions. For years Weinstein refused to enforce draconian mandatory drug sentences, which frequently imprisoned low-level mules and couriers caught with small amounts of narcotics for decades. He had been instrumental in the creation of class-action lawsuits, deciding cases involving veterans of the Vietnam War who had been exposed to Agent Orange, illnesses caused by asbestos, and the impact of antidepressants on mental health. Over the years, hundreds of writs for habeas corpus—claims of convicts saying they had been unjustly convicted—had piled up in the dockets of the judges in the Eastern District, a backlog thought impossible to clear. Single-handedly, Judge Weinstein took all of the claims and worked through more than five hundred in one year. Most were frivolous but approximately a dozen inmates had their claims vindicated. He was, in sum, a man of Olympian talent and industry, fearsomely independent in habit and mind.

Like all Brooklyn judges, Judge Weinstein had encountered his share of organized crime cases. Over the years members of all five New York crime families had appeared before him, as had the various populations of the OC industry in Brooklyn—criminals, cops, reporters, attorneys, judges. It had been Jack Weinstein who had tried the case of Vincent Chin Gigante in 1996.* In a profile by the *New York Times* after the Gigante conviction, it was noted that at trial Weinstein had finally managed to get Gigante to stop wearing pajamas and a bathrobe and to dress appropriately for court. "To liberals," said the article, "Weinstein is the emblem of the 1960's notion that the country's problems can be solved by good intentions and that the legal system can be a tool for reform. To conservatives, he is the epitome of judicial power run amok." A legal scholar

---

* It was in that proceeding that Gaspipe Casso had hoped to testify for the government, and thereby qualify for a light sentence. Weinstein was also close with Judge Eugene Nickerson, the federal court eminence whom Casso had plotted to kill while he was in the MCC awaiting his own trial on RICO charges.

from Yale Law School was quoted saying of Weinstein, "He thinks of himself as a man who can integrate the formal requirements of the law with the practical requirements of justice." He is known in legal circles for his prodigious ego; the *New York Times* reported that a courthouse joke about the judge went, "God has been seeing a psychiatrist lately because He thinks He is Jack Weinstein." Friends of Weinstein's were interviewed, and it was said that beneath the gruff, confident exterior he did not believe he had lived up to his own goals in life. Evelyn, his wife of nearly sixty years, who worked as a psychiatric social worker, said that she didn't recognize the person lionized by his colleagues. "I always think he doesn't think he's done enough," she said.

United States v. Stephen Caracappa and Louis Eppolito would be Judge Weinstein's last great case, perhaps drawing more worldwide media attention than any matter that had ever come before him. It was a trial Weinstein was uniquely qualified to oversee for many reasons, not least of which because he had a long-standing and intimate awareness of the criminal career of Burton Kaplan. In the early seventies and again in the early eighties, Weinstein had tried and sentenced Kaplan. Kaplan's wife and daughter, Eleanor and Deborah, had gone before Weinstein to plead for leniency. In 1973, Kaplan had written to Weinstein from Lewisburg Federal Prison seeking leniency. "I have never been involved in any violence in any form, physical or verbal, in my life," Kaplan wrote. "I detest it and all it stands for." Weinstein, it may be assumed, remembered this as "the cops" stood before him.

In a series of pretrial decisions, Weinstein appeared to live up to his reputation for liberality on the bench. The statute of limitations and the five-year time limit to bring a RICO prosecution troubled him in particular. The government's case was weak, Weinstein said, and there were significant problems with the way that the indictment was structured. Tying criminal acts in the eighties and early nineties in New York City to the criminality in Las Vegas in 2004 strained the plain meaning of the words of the law, Weinstein said. Henoch argued that the acts in New York and Las Vegas were connected for several reasons. The core players were the same. Eppolito continued to utilize his mob bona fides to make money for himself and Caracappa. They continued to commit crimes together, when the opportunity arose. They continued to associate with each other, in the pursuit of lawful and unlawful enterprises.

The scope of the case the government could present had to be determined. Over the years, Oldham had collected voluminous evidence regarding the character of the two cops. Caracappa had been known as

"Stevie Aces" as a young man on Staten Island, caught during a burglary on a lumber yard. While Caracappa was partnered with Eppolito in the Brooklyn Robbery Squad, they had stuck up bodegas with paper bags over their heads, according to Kaplan. The evidence, if presented to a jury, would form the basis for a judgment about the kind of man Caracappa was—despite his illustrious career on the NYPD.

The same was true for Eppolito. *Mafia Cop* was a study in the character of Eppolito—reading its glorification of violence, crime, and the mafia was not likely to endear him to a jury. Within the dozens of hours of recorded conversations with accountant Steven Corso in Las Vegas, Eppolito had proved himself to be an ardent racist. He talked about "niggers" nearly as constantly as he avowed his love for violence and killing. If this information became evidence in a trial, the prejudicial effect would be enormous. Eppolito would be a deeply unsympathetic character—especially to a jury likely to include a significant number of African-Americans.

Weinstein leaned heavily in favor of the defense. He decided to disallow "character evidence." This meant the two retired detectives would not be allowed to call witnesses to prove what exemplary members of the force they had been. If such evidence was submitted by the defense, it would "open the door" to the prosecution countering the testimony with their proof of Caracappa and Eppolito's bad character. Thus, the contents of *Mafia Cop* were excluded from trial. The tapes of recorded conversations in Las Vegas between Corso and Caracappa and Eppolito were to be edited to only the portions that bore directly on proof of guilt of the charges that they had trafficked narcotics and laundered money. Weinstein effectively split the difference, Solomon-like, forcing both sides to concentrate on the substance of the indictment.

Even with the strict limits placed on the government, Henoch proposed putting one hundred witnesses on the stand against Caracappa and Eppolito. The trial would last three to four months, Henoch told Weinstein.

The judge rejected the notion.

"Rethink your trial strategy," Weinstein said testily. He would not countenance the prosecution putting on a case that veered away from the charges. Many judges permitted the government to shape their evidence as they pleased, affording the defense the same opportunity. The approach appeared fair, but too often trials got out of control if attorneys were given too much leeway. Henoch was forced to cast a critical eye over his evidence. "What I was going to leave out was as important as what I was going to put in," Henoch recalled. "We reconfigured the indictment in order to more accurately reflect Steve and Louie's criminal scheme. The focus was properly placed on them, and less on *cosa nostra*. The two of them were their own criminal enterprise. Associates like Frank Santora, Burton Kaplan, Gaspipe Casso, Steven Corso, and Guido Bravatti came and went in their conspiracy, but the enterprise was ongoing. The case law was solid that a RICO enterprise can consist of two people. It had been done before. It wasn't that novel in that regard. We aimed to capture the essence of who they were and what they did."

BRUCE AND EDDIE FOR THE DEFENSE

Twenty thousand pages of documents were delivered to the defense attorneys by the federal government during pretrial discovery. They included the FBI debriefings of Anthony Casso, Al D'Arco, Fat Pete Chiodo, and other relevant gangster records; surveillance tapes from Kaplan's Staten Island warehouse; and hundreds of hours of recorded conversations in Las Vegas between Corso and Eppolito and Caracappa.

A bail hearing was held in June 2005. After three months in custody, Eppolito's skin was ghostly and his swept-back pompadour white. The weight he had carried for decades, the sag of a glutton, had begun to disappear. He was fifty pounds lighter than on the evening of the bust at Piero's in Vegas. Aged fifty-seven, he looked a decade older and seemed even more disoriented as he smiled at the faces in the gallery. Caracappa, on the other hand, had regained his bearings. He moved slowly and precisely, staring with black eyes at the press. If incarceration had weakened Eppolito, making him into a pitiable figure, it had turned Caracappa stone cold.

The prosecution opposed the application for bail. Despite the age and ill health of the defendants, Henoch argued, they represented a threat to the public. Weinstein decided to grant Caracappa and Eppolito bail. The terms were onerous. The security required was $5 million. The two men would remain at all times in the houses of local relatives: Caracappa with his mother on Kramer Street on Staten Island, and Eppolito with his brother-in-law on Long Island. Telephone conversations would be conducted only with their attorneys and members of their family. All calls would be recorded and monitored by the government. Both men would wear ankle bracelets with an electronic tracking device to ensure they did not leave their houses. In order to prepare their defense, they were permitted to go to and from their attorneys' offices to review evidence and plan strategy.

"The risk of flight might have appeared minimal," Oldham said. "They were two old guys with dodgy health. But I figured one of them was going to run. I know I'd probably hit the road. Weinstein was a smart old dog, but he was not predictable in any way."

As Eppolito left court that spring day, walking into the shove and shout of the fifty-strong scrum of cameras and reporters trying to make breaking news, he lifted the leg of his argyle elastic-waisted leisure pants and displayed the ankle bracelet. Caracappa did not come out through the public exit. He was allowed to leave the courthouse using a back way, to avoid the frenzy.

Granting bail was an indication that events might be turning in favor of the defense, perhaps decisively. During the summer Eppolito arrived at court surrounded by an entourage of relatives, including his wife and daughter Andrea. He answered questions from reporters and eagerly protested his innocence. The entire case was a frame-up, he said. Stopping at the security checkpoint inside the courthouse, the gregarious and confident Eppolito greeted the court security guards running his possessions through X-ray machines. The guards were retired NYPD cops, some of whom had served with Eppolito. The entire case was an outrageous mistake, Eppolito's manner said, and he clearly imagined himself still to be a member in good standing of the fraternal order of former cops with the NYPD shield on their pinkie-finger rings.

Caracappa, by contrast, arrived alone, or in the company of former Major Case detective Jack Ryan. He kept his counsel, never saying a word or exchanging pleasantries. He was as aloof and austere as he had been fifteen years earlier, when Oldham arrived at Major Case.

The defense's accumulated victories were due to the representation of Eppolito and Caracappa by two of the leading defense lawyers in the country. Bruce Cutler and Eddie Hayes were flamboyant, well-known figures in New York. During preliminary proceedings, as fall turned to winter, Cutler and Hayes arrived for hearings at the courthouse wearing fedoras and trench coats with collars roguishly upturned against the chill. Longtime friends, the two lawyers had deep connections; Cutler had been a groomsman in Hayes's wedding and was godfather to his only daughter. Although wildly different personalities, the pair hosted a legal affairs cable chat show called *Cutler & Hayes*.

In New York criminal defense attorneys constituted their own tribe, complete with history, ethos, and ancient animosities. The religion of the

New York criminal defense bar dictated that certain traditions needed to be upheld. The government, it was to be repeated ad infinitum, was to be suspected and resisted at every turn. The belief system had been shaped to a large degree by RICO. The law invited the possibility for abuse, in the hands of hell-bent investigators and prosecutors. RICO changed the entire idea of criminality in ways that have still not been fully understood. Guilt by association, hearsay, the use of cooperators who have a great deal of self-interest in striking a deal to save their skins—they are all legitimate concerns. The system is subject to abuse in new and unpredictable ways. The law was being used to fight terrorism. To the extent that the "war on terrorism" involves legal concepts, RICO provides dangerous precedent when applied to networks of association only superficially understood by law enforcement. Religion, ethnicity, and culture can be conflated with conspiracy and criminalized.

The creed of the defense bar had outward manifestations as well. The esthetic demanded that a leading attorney adopt a trademark affectation that branded him in the public consciousness. Cutler was the bald, barrel-chested brawler who didn't just defend mobsters—he was friend, champion, and fellow traveler, in sympathy if not in fact. Hayes was the quick-witted, light-footed dandy. Wearing bespoke suits and handmade shoes, extremely proud of his appearances on various "best-dressed" lists, Hayes traded on a mixture of blarney and full disclosure about his less than charitable motives in practicing law. He had represented clients ranging from Anna Wintour, editor of *Vogue* magazine, to Robert De Niro, and the estate of Andy Warhol. Both lawyers admitted to suffering bouts of depression. "Melancholia," Cutler called it. Hayes freely allowed that he wept openly and often and uncontrollably.

To top-shelf criminal attorneys like Cutler and Hayes, the law was only one aspect of a big-time, media-saturated New York City trial. An overall attack needed to be decided upon. What narrative would be related to the public and the jury? How might the defendants be prosecuted? How might the defense prosecute the prosecution? Cutler and Hayes concentrated on the large-scale critical matters: strategy, cross-examination of government witnesses, media relations. But trial work required legal research, drafting motions, understanding the intricacies of arcane precedents and laws. Such details were not handled by lawyers like Cutler and Hayes. Each man needed a book-smart co-counsel attorney, and each happened to prefer a blonde: Bettina Schein, who ably filled that position for Cutler, and former NYPD deputy commissioner of trials Rae Koshetz, who was Hayes's aide-de-camp.

As a courtroom performer, Bruce Cutler was the personification of a mobster lawyer. Adopting a tone of high drama, Cutler described his role as a defense attorney as that of a "roving paladin," a term derived from the twelve peers of Charlemagne's court and meant to refer to a medieval knight of virtue and valor blessed with magical powers to salve wounds with a touch. Cutler had represented Chinese gangsters from the Flying Dragons, mobsters in the Windows Case, Hell's Angels bikers from Quebec, and an NYPD police officer in the infamous Morgue Boys case. But he had gained the largest measure of his fame during the trials and travails of Gambino boss John Gotti—the "career maker," Cutler wrote in his autobiography, *Closing Argument: Defending (and Befriending) John Gotti and Other Legal Battles I Have Waged.* In the late eighties, he had represented Gotti for two acquittals, one state and one federal, verdicts that led to the nickname of "The Teflon Don." Over the years, Cutler had frequently met with Gotti at the Ravenite Social Club. In *Closing Argument* Cutler described accompanying Gotti on the mob boss's "walk-and-talks": "As I sauntered through Little Italy alongside him, turning left now onto Spring Street, I felt singularly alive, as though I were worthy, as though I could get the job done. I would learn that he made everyone feel that way."

Cutler's close identification with Gotti had resulted in the government succeeding in having him excluded from representing his longtime client in the 1992 trial that ended in conviction and a life sentence for the erstwhile Teflon Don. During those proceedings, Cutler was ordered by Judge Eugene Nickerson ("His Majesty," according to Cutler) to refrain from talking to the press during the trial. Cutler had continued to defend the Gambino crime boss, granting interviews to all of New York's major newspapers, as well as to *60 Minutes* and *Nine Broadcast Plaza*—where he appeared on a panel with Louis Eppolito to defend the mafia. "I went after the Eastern District of New York prosecutors," Cutler wrote in *Closing Argument,* "accusing them of bad faith and of manufacturing a case against John with the purchased assistance of self-avowed murderers; worse, I called them a 'sick and demented lot,' 'McCarthyites' who'd 'orchestrated' a conspiracy to 'get' John. I'd suggested to one reporter that it would be 'John Gotti today—you [the public] tomorrow.' In short, I'd told the truth." Cutler was found guilty of contempt of court and sentenced to house arrest, followed by three years of probation and six hundred hours of community service. In October 2005, as the trial of Caracappa and Eppolito neared, Henoch had sought a similar gag order against Cutler and Hayes. The two attorneys had discussed the forthcoming trial on their cable television show, with Cutler claiming the defense would win, "knock on wood," and saying that the indictment was "legally defective." The motion was denied—and Cutler continued to hold forth to the press.

Eddie Hayes, by contrast, had little interest in wiseguy cases. He did, however, have an avowed interest in the prospects of Eddie Hayes. "What's in it for Eddie?" was the first question he asked himself when considering taking on a client. The week before the trial began, Eddie Hayes published his autobiography, *Mouthpiece: A Life in—and Sometimes Just Outside—the Law*. Dedicated to novelist Tom Wolfe, who found in Hayes the inspiration for the defense lawyer Tommy Killian in *The Bonfire of the Vanities,* Hayes's book tells the tale of his rise from childhood under the rule of an abusive alcoholic father in working-class Queens to the heights of Manhattan society.*

Why did Hayes take on the case? His practice was thriving and he didn't need the money. There were powerful attractions, however. Hayes had remained close to cop culture since his days as a Bronx prosecutor, developing ties with a number of leading detectives in the Major Case Squad—and meeting Oldham during his Biggie Smalls rap investigation, when Hayes represented Sean "Puff Daddy" Combs at the height of hip-hop violence. Most of the allegations against Caracappa were not new, nor were they believed by many detectives who were friends of Caracappa and were convinced the case was the result of a mob-concocted conspiracy against an OC colleague. Hayes also craved the action of a trial that promised to be one for the ages. The wave of publicity couldn't hurt sales of his book, and, for the first time, Hayes would team up with his old friend Bruce Cutler. Hayes had represented Caracappa in 1994, when Casso's allegations first surfaced, so he would be seeing the job through to the end.

And then there was the substance of the case—especially Burton

---

* *Mouthpiece* offered a surprisingly intimate portrait of Hayes's interior life, from bouts of depression to descriptions of sexual escapades. As a prosecutor in the Bronx during the crime-plagued seventies, he wrote that he often spent his nights in libertine midtown Manhattan clubs like Studio 54. "This was when transgender operations were still very new," Hayes wrote in *Mouthpiece*. "I didn't know what was going to happen when I brought someone I'd met in one of those places home with me one night. She was gorgeous and I had seen her in clubs for months. When I took her attractive, tight-fitting dress off, I saw she had the whole deal! She had worked hard and gone through great pain to turn herself from an effeminate guy from Spanish Harlem into a beautiful woman. I was game. I was too ill at ease for it to be a great sexual experience, but what I liked about New York at that time was that you could go out and something was always going to happen, something you couldn't begin to predict."

Kaplan and the government's use of cooperating witnesses. In *Mouthpiece,* Hayes wrote of growing up as an Irish Catholic kid in Queens. He and his friends all held the same beliefs, Hayes wrote. "Chief among these was the idea that the worst thing you can do is rat out a friend, and that if you did you would (and should) be killed . . . The Irish don't rat. Bounce them off the wall for a week and they won't tell you a thing."

THE TORMENT OF BARRY GIBBS

The arrest of Caracappa and Eppolito and coverage of the ongoing pre-trial hearings summoned ghosts from the city's past. A New York attorney named Barry Scheck, who had once been part of O. J. Simpson's defense team, recognized the name of Louis Eppolito. Scheck had been instrumental in founding the Innocence Project, a legal clinic run out of the Benjamin N. Cardozo School of Law that was dedicated to using DNA evidence to exonerate the wrongly convicted. One of the Innocence Project's cases involved a convict named Barry Gibbs. In 1988, Gibbs had been found guilty of the murder of Virginia Robertson, a twenty-seven-year-old black woman with prostitution convictions and a drug abuse problem. Her body had been found dumped in the weeds next to the Belt Parkway in Brooklyn. She had been wearing a rust-colored fur coat and there were rope burns around her neck. Detective Louis Eppolito from the Six-Three ended up with the case.

At the time, Gibbs had worked for the U.S. Postal Service for seventeen years. He, too, had a substance abuse problem. Gibbs had recently had an "encounter" with Robertson. Gibbs worked nights at a Brooklyn deli. Detective Eppolito came into the deli one night and took a can of soda from the refrigerator and drank it. He put the empty can on the counter. "You got a problem with me?" Eppolito asked Gibbs defiantly. "Yeah," Gibbs said. "You didn't pay for the soda." Eppolito threw money on the counter and left.

Two days later he was back. He put Gibbs in the backseat of his car with no explanation and took him to the Six-Three precinct house. There Eppolito showed Gibbs photographs of Robertson. He asked Gibbs if he knew her. Gibbs said no. Polaroids were taken of Gibbs and he was placed in a holding cell. Eppolito arranged for a lineup, and Gibbs agreed to submit to it, but when he saw the other participants he balked. None looked like him; all the men were much shorter and bore no resemblance. Gibbs was instructed to sit.

Convicted of murder as a result of Detective Eppolito's investigation, Gibbs had protested his innocence ever since. He had been framed, he said. The plea was common in prisons, but Gibbs had an unusually interesting case, Scheck believed. Gibbs had been convicted primarily on the say-so of a single eyewitness and the testimony of a jailhouse informant who swore that Gibbs had confessed to him in jail. "Each of the key pieces of evidence was incredibly weak," Oldham said. "Eyewitnesses need to be corroborated if a verdict is going to be reliable. Jailhouse informants make up stories all the time. If a prisoner knows a cop is after a guy, he'll write a novel about him. If a cop is dirty, all he has to do is drop a hint about his perp and the jailhouse will fill with canaries singing a cappella about the guy. Reading the homicide file, the Gibbs case was a monument to bad detective work."

But Scheck had been unable to have the case revived in the courts. He lacked DNA or any scientific evidence upon which he could base an appeal. The news of Eppolito's arrest rang a bell. Scheck recalled Eppolito had been the detective leading the investigation into Gibbs. Scheck didn't have to tell Gibbs. The name Louie Eppolito was branded on Gibbs's mind. As he wasted away in state prison, Gibbs had seen Detective Eppolito a number of times in the years since his conviction. Watching the movie *Goodfellas,* he caught sight of Eppolito in a bit role. Sitting in the common room in jail, he saw Eppolito promoting *Mafia Cop* on the *Sally Jessy Raphael Show.* At five in the morning on the day after Eppolito's arrest, Gibbs had heard a broadcast describing the arrest of two NYPD "mafia cops"—and heard the name Louie Eppolito. Gibbs had screamed with joy, "There is a God!"

During the search of Eppolito's house in Las Vegas, the NYPD's file on the Robertson murder was discovered in Eppolito's cabinet, setting into motion a review of the case. At the same time, Scheck contacted prosecutors in the Eastern District. In the spring, a DEA agent interviewed the eyewitness who had claimed to see Gibbs kill Virginia Robertson. Peter Mitchell, an ex-Marine, told the DEA and the press a story Eppolito would later deny. Mitchell said he had been out jogging on the day of the murder. He called the police after he saw a man dragging a body to the side of the road. According to Mitchell, Eppolito brought him to the 63rd Precinct and threatened him. If Mitchell didn't testify against Gibbs, the heavyset detective reportedly said, he would plant drugs in the home of Mitchell's mother and arrest her for possession of narcotics. Being a black man in Brooklyn, Mitchell was aware of the power of a corrupt cop.

Eppolito's capture gave Gibbs new hope. On September 30, 2005,

Alan Feuer reported in the *New York Times* that upon hearing of the arrest, "Mr. Gibbs raised his hands over his head, rubbing them gleefully together, then brought them down in a prayerful gesture." Gibbs said he was going to eat lobster tail and crab meat. "I knew I was innocent," Gibbs told reporters, "I just had to make people believe me."

The next day, the *New York Post* followed up on the Gibbs story with the headline, "Slain Gal's Ma: 'I'll Fight to Lock Up That Liar.'" Virginia Robertson's seventy-eight-year-old mother told the *Post* Detective Eppolito had given her false comfort at the time of her daughter's murder. Mrs. Robertson's husband was a retired Brooklyn cop. On the day of her daughter's death, Robertson's mother told the *Post*, Eppolito had come to her home to tell her the news. Informing the family of a homicide victim of the death of a loved one was a particularly melancholy duty for any police officer. Eppolito told the shocked and grieving mother that her daughter had talked to him, saying she hadn't meant to die like this.

"But Virginia Robertson had been found dead," Oldham said. "Eppolito had responded to a DOA. He had never had an opportunity to talk to the victim. He was turning the awful reality of a murder into a chance to aggrandize himself, be the hero cop, always at the center of his own drama. He was telling a story that was supposed to assuage the pain of the Robertsons. He would solve the case. Eppolito had promised to catch the killer. Barry Gibbs was his instrument of justice—no matter what Gibbs hadn't done. As long as Eppolito got another medal, it didn't matter."

The Robertsons had found closure with Gibbs's conviction, it seemed, until the arrest of Eppolito brought to life the death of their daughter. "Eppolito is a liar," Mrs. Robertson told the *Post*. "How can dead people talk?" she asked in despair.

Eppolito vehemently denied the allegation. Cutler told the *Post* that Eppolito was "more upset" about the accusation than any of the other crimes he was charged with. "It cut to the core, angered, and frustrated him more so than anything else," Cutler said. Eppolito had been instructed by Cutler not to speak to the media, but he was convinced of his ability to convince others of his innocence, and while leaving a hearing in the Brooklyn federal courthouse, he told a group of journalists that he had not framed Gibbs for the Robertson murder. He had taken the murder file from the records of the Six-Three for a good reason, he said. "I had that file in my house because I was going to write a television show about the case," Eppolito said.

A WEAKNESS

The last legal question outstanding before a trial could commence was the most important—and most difficult. From the beginning, Judge Weinstein was troubled by the issue of the time limits in RICO cases. "It's a very thin connection between the end of the acts of these defendants in New York and what was happening in Las Vegas," Weinstein told the prosecutors. "The weight of the evidence is not strong, particularly in the light of the statute of limitations."

In response, Henoch altered the legal thesis underlying the RICO charges. At first, it had been alleged that the criminal enterprise to which Caracappa and Eppolito belonged was the Luchese family. The amended prosecution case said that Caracappa, Eppolito, and Kaplan constituted their own racketeering enterprise. If Eppolito and Caracappa constituted a miniature mafia, then the crime wave of the eighties and early nineties could be tied to their ongoing criminal activity in Las Vegas.

Weinstein's admonitions to the prosecution about the statute of limitations caused a commotion in the press. Weinstein's statements about the "weakness" of the case was only meant to refer to the statute of limitations, not to the factual allegations regarding murder, kidnapping, obstruction of justice, and the rest. Many reports conflated the two aspects of the case. The defense filed a motion to dismiss the charges and a hearing was held. Weinstein listened patiently to the legal arguments. The motion was denied. It became clear that the statute of limitations was the lone cause of Weinstein's criticism of the government's case. The charges against the two former NYPD officers were "horrendous," Judge Weinstein said. It was "vital for the public" to be allowed to try a "case which raises such serious doubts about the police department." "The defendants are entitled to put the government to proof regarding such grave insinuations." Weinstein glowered over his reading glasses. "This case has to be tried, and it will be tried."

THE AUTHORS APPEAR

At ten o'clock on the morning jury selection was to commence, there was no sign of Louis Eppolito. Hours late, he arrived. His failure to appear in federal court on time seemed to Eppolito of little consequence. In the hallway he explained to reporters that there had been a massive backup in traffic coming from Long Island, where he was staying with relatives. He had no access to a cell phone so he hadn't been able to send word that the Brooklyn-Queens Expressway had been turned into a parking lot.

Judge Weinstein was not interested in Eppolito's excuse. "Arrest that man," the judge snarled at the sight of Eppolito. Startled, Eppolito was placed in handcuffs by marshals. Faced with forfeiture of his parole, Eppolito appeared terrified as Cutler explained the circumstances to the judge. The aged Weinstein, it was apparent to observers, was capable of sudden and unexpected mood swings. He sternly admonished Eppolito not to be late again, and renewed the terms of his bail.

After the hearing, seasoned *Daily News* reporter and ex-cop John Marzulli shared the elevator down to the ground floor with Eddie Hayes. "Off the record," Marzulli asked, "was there a moment when you thought maybe Louie made a run for it?"

Hayes laughed. "I thought maybe he had a heart attack, to the tell the truth," Hayes said.

Jury selection in *United States v. Stephen Caracappa and Louis Eppolito* began with a pool of more than one hundred potential jurors gathered in the large ceremonial court on the second floor of the federal courthouse in Brooklyn. The walls were lined with oil portraits of distinguished jurists from the past. A forty-two question form was distributed. "Do you believe there are such entities as organized crime families, La Cosa Nostra, or the Mafia?" those present were asked. "Have you read the book, *Mafia Cop: The Story of an Honest Cop Whose Family Was the Mob*?" Weinstein addressed the assembled citizenry. "The trial will be dull and tedious at times," he said. "But for many of you it will be the most interesting experience of your life."

A parade of potential jurors formed before the bench, all of whom sought to escape their duty. Their claims ranged from financial hardship— jurors would be paid $40 per day—to the need to care for family members. Judge Weinstein heard the pleas with limited patience. "I'm nervous," said one man. "I'm scared," said another. A middle-aged woman was shaking as she sat down. Weinstein allowed them all to leave. "Why would the defendant hire a mob lawyer? No offense, Mr. Cutler," a beefy man asked, securing his dismissal.

The final jury consisted of a cross-section of metropolitan New York's polyglot, with an overrepresentation of black women—six of the twelve empaneled. The majority was drawn from Staten Island, Brooklyn, Queens, and Long Island, strongholds for law-and-order jurors. "Defendants want a particular kind of juror, as a rule, depending on their own racial and social profile. The prosecution want the opposite. In this case there was no clear way to know what kind of jury either side wanted. A bias against the police cut both ways. Caracappa and Eppolito were allegedly two dirty cops, so if you were inclined to believe police could be criminals—if you had directly experienced police corruption—then you would be open to the idea of two cops working as hit men for the mafia. But dirty cops needed to be caught. It was a wash. Prejudice for or against cops was going to matter a lot less than facts. Proof was what the government needed. Reasonable doubt was all the defense had to raise."

Days before the trial was to begin, Caracappa's attorneys issued a subpoena to compel the production of the manuscript for this book. The subpoena demanded Simon & Schuster hand over to the defense all materials pertaining to the publishing agreement, notes taken by Oldham related to the investigation, and the book proposal written by the authors. In particular, the subpoena sought any documents regarding the visit by Oldham and Joe Ponzi to Burt Kaplan at the Metropolitan Detention Center in their attempt to get him to cooperate. Such details were "highly relevant to the defense of this case," the defense's letter to Judge Weinstein said. "Moreover, in light of Oldham's self-professed leading role in the investigation, the particulars of his deal with the publisher to write a self-aggrandizing book are highly relevant to the exploration of his motives to propel the investigation of this matter to indictment and conviction of the defendants, his potential bias, and the possibility that exculpatory material is lurking in notes and memoranda that he might have held back for publication at a later time."

Judge Weinstein heard a motion to quash the subpoena argued for the publisher by Elizabeth McNamara, an attorney retained by Simon & Schuster. The authors were summoned from the gallery to answer questions. Judge Weinstein asked why the defense didn't simply call Oldham to testify if it wanted to know what had transpired during Oldham's encounters with Kaplan, instead of making an end run and trying to compel a publisher to provide confidential material.

"I understood the gambit," Oldham recalled. "The defense wasn't going to call me. I wasn't going to help them get Steve and Louie off by testifying. But there was a chance I could help them by not testifying. One of the defense theories was that I had concocted the whole case in order to write a book and cast myself as the hero. There was one small problem—the evidence. The argument was flimsy, to be kind. They needed the jury to believe an evil detective had dreamed up a diabolical plot against two innocent law-abiding officers of the law."

Judge Weinstein had little patience for these arguments. The matter was an "open-and-shut quash motion," he said. Freedom of the press required that the defense's attempt to obtain the publisher's confidential materials be rebuffed. If the defense wished to question Oldham about his interrogation of Kaplan or any matter related to the case or the publication of the book, all it had to do was subpoena Oldham as a witness.

"Judge Throws 'Book' at Mob Cops' Defense" read the headline in the *New York Post* the next day.

"EVERYBODY GETS CAUGHT"

Not long before, *60 Minutes* once again became a player in the case. This time the CBS show claimed the exclusive of an interview with the aggrieved Stephen Caracappa. Ed Bradley spoke to Caracappa in the Manhattan law offices of Eddie Hayes. Caracappa said he was speaking on behalf of Eppolito, who had declined the offer to be interviewed.

"Caracappa was willing to go on television and talk about the case," Oldham said. "But he wasn't going to stand up in court and answer any questions that Henoch might ask him because he would surely be cut to shreds. He'd probably take the Fifth within seconds. As for the idea that Eppolito declined the interview request, to me it only indicated the degree to which Caracappa controlled Eppolito. Steve wouldn't let Louie make a move without his say-so. That was why Caracappa was looking over the movie deal Corso proposed in Las Vegas. Ed Bradley wasn't going to ask Caracappa any of the hard questions.

"Even after the arrest, Eppolito was unpredictable." He had been instructed by Cutler not to talk to the press but at every court appearance he stopped and held a press conference, as if protesting his innocence loudly and often enough would make it so. There was no way Caracappa was going to let Eppolito represent them on the most popular newsmagazine on the air."

Given the opportunity to put forward his case, Caracappa opted for a defense of outright and outraged denial. The charges were ridiculous, Caracappa told Bradley. "Anybody who knows me knows I love the police department," Caracappa said. "I couldn't kill anybody. I shot a guy once on the job and I still think about it. It bothers me."

A portion of the 1998 interview of Casso with *60 Minutes* was aired. "I have two detectives that work the major squad team for the New York City Police Department," Casso had told Bradley in 1998.

"What were their names?" Bradley had asked Casso in the clip.

"Lou Eppolito and Steve—Steve—I can't—he's got a long last name. Cappa—"

"Caracappa?"

"Yeah," Casso had said to Bradley. "Caracapra, whatever it is. I can't say it all the time, you know. Louie's a big guy, he works out. Steve is a small, skinny guy."

In the 1998 footage, Casso had described the kidnapping of Jimmy Hydell in 1986 and the delivery of the still-living Hydell to Casso in the Toys 'R' Us parking lot. "At that time, I gave Louie and Steve, I think, $45,000. They wanted to kill him for me. They were going do whatever I wanted with him."

On the 2006 broadcast Caracappa looked at Bradley impassively and calmly denied knowing Hydell and Casso. He claimed that he didn't know why Casso would lie but speculated that it might be "to save himself."

The former OCHU expert assigned to collect intelligence on the Luchese family neglected to mention that he had spent the best part of a decade studying the inner workings of Casso's crime family. Running the name Nicky Guido through the system, as the cadre's investigation had discovered, was a fact Caracappa did not dispute. Bradley asked incredulously if Caracappa was claiming that the records search and the subsequent murder of the wrong Nicky Guido were merely a coincidence. Caracappa said he ran countless names during his career. The check on Guido was properly documented in NYPD files, Caracappa claimed—excluding the fact that the search had been disguised by putting the name in a cluster of other names Caracappa was running in an unrelated case.

"I was a New York City detective for twenty-three years," Caracappa said. "We don't go around killing people. I did not kill Eddie Lino. I'm not a cowboy."

Being a member of the police force did not automatically make you a good guy, Bradley said. There were a number of instances of cops who became killers.

Caracappa agreed.

"That's not a good answer, to say, 'I didn't do it because I'm on the job,'" Bradley said.

"It's my answer because I have pride in myself, Mr. Bradley," Caracappa said. "I wouldn't put my life in jeopardy, my family, disgrace the badge, disgrace the city, take everything that I'd worked for my whole life and throw it away and kill somebody in the street like a cowboy. That's not my style."

"If you felt you wouldn't get caught?" Bradley asked.

"Get caught?" Caracappa asked. "Everybody gets caught. The person who did this is going to get caught."

Caracappa met the camera's gaze with steady, cold eyes. Eppolito was not the monster the newspapers portray him to be, he said, adding that they would put up evidence to show that they could not have committed the crimes. We just couldn't have done them."

On *60 Minutes,* Caracappa took his chances in the court of public opinion. On camera he attempted to come across as earnest and sincerely puzzled by the circumstances that had engulfed his life. He offered a defense of Eppolito. "If you knew Louie Eppolito and you spoke to Louie Eppolito and you spent any time with him, you would see he couldn't do that," Caracappa said. "The guy's gentle."

The face of Barry Gibbs appeared on screen. Gibbs was in late middle age, bearded, wearing a turquoise pendant, giving him the appearance of an aged hippy. He was extremely angry for being framed for the November 1986 murder of Virginia Robertson. Eppolito was shown offering his defense. "I was a very highly decorated cop," Eppolito said. "I worked very hard my whole life, and I want the people to know that I'm not the person that they are portraying me."

Ed Bradley asked Caracappa one final question. "You must know that if you get convicted on even one of these murder charges, you'll go down in history as one of the most corrupt cops in the history of the department."

"That's true, Mr. Bradley," Caracappa said. "But I won't be convicted because I didn't do this. I won't — " He stopped himself. "I didn't do it, so I'm not going to be convicted. I won't have that on my epithet."

In all likelihood Caracappa meant to say "epitaph," which is a memorializing inscription on a tombstone. An "epithet" is a term of revilement or contempt. A slip of the tongue, perhaps.

The appearance was the first and last time the former Major Case Squad detective spoke publicly about the case.

CHAPTER SIXTEEN

TRIAL FOR THE AGES

Monday, March 13, 2006, was a cold and windy late winter day. Dozens of reporters and television crews from New York and around the country and the world gathered in the chill outside the federal courthouse in downtown Brooklyn as the protagonists in *United States v. Stephen Caracappa and Louis Eppolito* arrived for the first day of trial. For years the building had been covered in scaffolding as a new office tower was constructed. The scaffolding came down and the structure was opened as the trial of the detectives began. Set apart from the foot traffic in downtown Brooklyn, the courthouse finally had a grand façade to match the dramas that unfolded within it. Other high-profile organized crime cases were being tried or pending—the erstwhile Teflon Don's son John Gotti Jr., Bonanno wiseguy and beauty salon owner Vinny "Gorgeous" Basciano. But those cases were a sideshow compared to the trial of the "mafia cops."

The gallery in Judge Jack Weinstein's fourth-floor court was packed shoulder to shoulder. The rear rows were set aside for law enforcement, and some of the men in the cadre from the Brooklyn DA's office were in attendance, including Joe Ponzi and Bobby Intartaglio. Two rows of press were shoved tightly into the front rows. Staying clear of the courthouse because he was a potential witness, and following his longstanding practice of avoiding days in court as much as possible, Oldham was a notable absence.

In keeping with the scarcely believable accusations, the number of book projects attached to the case seemed to grow with each passing week. In the *New York Times,* reporter Alan Feuer's coverage wryly emphasized the bizarre book bonanza. Tommy Dades had entered into a deal, with rumored Hollywood movie rights attached, collaborating with Brooklyn Assistant District Attorney Mike Vecchione. Jimmy Breslin, the noted New York City columnist and author of the classic mob novel *The Gang That Couldn't Shoot Straight,* was said to be working on a book about the case. Sitting next to Breslin was Jane McCormick, the former Vegas girl-around-town who had paid Eppolito her life savings to write the screenplay of her life. She had flown from Minnesota to witness the trial for the autobiography she was now writing. Beside McCormick was Louie Eppolito Jr., Eppolito's son from his first marriage. Louie junior, with a shaved head and a quiet manner, worked in a vitamin warehouse in New Jersey. His life partner Rob Gortner ran a dog-grooming salon in a quaint rural village in New Jersey. The younger Eppolito was said to be seeking a deal to write a book with a reporter from the *Philadelphia Inquirer* that would focus on his relationship with his father. Greg B. Smith of the *Daily News* was contracted to write a book on the case. Finally, sitting quietly in a corner of the court, professor Jefferey Morris from Touro College Law Center in Huntington, New York, was in the midst of a decade-long scholarly study of Judge Weinstein's life on the bench. In addition to this, the judge, both defense attorneys, and one of the defendants were all authors of books.

As Judge Weinstein called the court to order, the room bristled with anticipation. Opening statements were to be given first by the prosecution and then the counsel for each defendant. Mitra Hormozi spoke for the government. The usual pecking order in a RICO prosecution with three attorneys on the case was for the junior-most lawyer to give the opening statement, the second-most senior to handle the closing statement, and the lead, in this case Henoch, to make the final argument and have the last say to the jury—the rebuttal summation. The last was considered the most difficult, with no real time for preparation, and therefore the most desirable.

But Henoch had asked his second in command, Hormozi, to present the opening statement. Setting the tone of the trial was critical to success. Hormozi's appearance was in stark contrast to the onslaught of blood and betrayal she described. Disarmingly attractive, with large eyes and dark hair pulled back in a ponytail, Hormozi looked like an intelligent, pretty, and diligent young attorney—hardly the vicious government lawyer conspiring to frame two NYPD cops that defense counsel Bruce Cutler and Eddie Hayes hoped to convince the jury she was. Her voice was sweet and innocent, but her address was strong and unblinking and direct as she described the crimes of Caracappa and Eppolito. Hormozi began with the morning that Israel Greenwald disappeared forever. He was late for work, Hormozi told the jury, but before he left his young daughter at the bus stop for the last time, Israel Greenwald put his briefcase down, walked back to Michal, and gave her a final kiss—the last time she would ever see her father.

Next came Bruce Cutler. In and out of court, his approach was a unique combination of bombastic Brooklyn grandiloquence spiced with an exceedingly courtly manner. If Cutler appeared to be playing a role it was because he was, in fact, acting—even as he represented a failed actor in Louis Eppolito. In *Closing Argument* Cutler described his experience acting the part of a crooked attorney in the Robert De Niro film *15 Minutes* and acting as defense counsel. "My style is to adopt the role of my client before the jury," Cutler wrote. "Most lawyers don't need to do this. I do. In order to get motivated, to enter the zone of indignation, sorrow, or elation I seek, I need to feel that I am portraying someone other than who I really am. Call me a method lawyer. My courtroom style is a performance, acting."

Prowling around the courtroom, Cutler offered disdain for the gangsters who had become informants and would be called as witnesses, thereby destroying the traditions of the mafia. "The so-called mafia had rules that were torn asunder years ago," Cutler declaimed. "It has no cachet now. It's desultory and decadent and filled with lowlives who run to mommy when they're in trouble. They wet their pants and run to mommy—the federal government." Cutler said that Eppolito could have been a mobster, if he had so desired. But he did not follow the path of his father and his grandfather. "Louie did as Teddy Roosevelt did," Cutler said. "He joined a priesthood. He eschewed his father's life. Lou said no. Not for me. *Not. For. Me.* He had the courage to say no."

Eppolito joined "the blue gang," making a meager salary and dedicating himself to law and order, Cutler continued. "He received medals for honor, bravery, and valor, risking his life for you and me. His chest wouldn't hold all the medals, as big as his chest was." Eppolito had even written a book about his life, Cutler said. The title Eppolito gave the work was "Man in the Middle." Cutler said the publisher redubbed it with the more commercial, oxymoronic name *Mafia Cop*. "Louie Eppolito was out, proud, and unashamed," Cutler emoted. "But for the book, there would be no case."

Eddie Hayes was impeccably attired in a pinstriped Savile Row bespoke suit as he rose to make his opening statement. The essence of the case, he said, was a plot by gangsters to undermine law enforcement by concocting elaborate fantasies about detectives and federal agents collaborating toward nefarious ends. "Gangsters learned that the best way to get themselves out of trouble and keep their money was to turn on the people who were chasing them. Steve Caracappa was high on that list." The prosecution would try to portray Caracappa as a cold-blooded killer, Hayes said. It was a challenge Stephen Caracappa relished taking up, Hayes said. The defense was not afraid of the evidence the government would present.

"Bring it on," Hayes said.

RUNNING THE BULLS

The government's trial strategy was to begin with a quotidian Christmas Day twenty years earlier. Henoch aimed to put a human face on the case, to display to the jury that the case was not a mob melodrama, nor a book deal opportunity, nor the premise for a feature film. The prosecution was going to tell a true crime story with victims, blood, and suffering—a reality that required the jury to look through the obvious sensationalism to see why the case mattered. The first witness was Sergeant Michael Cugno, who was a newly minted patrol cop assigned to the Seven-Two in 1986. That day Officer Cugno had responded to a radio run to 499 17th Street in the Windsor Terrace section of Brooklyn in the middle of Christmas celebrations. Cugno found a young man slumped in the front seat of a new red Nissan Maxima. The young man was covered in blood and he was not breathing. Cugno was shown a photograph of the crime scene, nearly twenty years old now. He recalled the scene well, he said. Nicky Guido was his first homicide. The lights were lowered and a murder scene photograph of Guido was displayed on a large screen using an overhead projector. The jury turned to see the dead young man with his new white winter coat crimson with blood.

The next witness was Pauline Pipitone, the mother of the dead man. An elderly Italian woman, stooped and walking slowly, she entered with her eyes downcast. She testified that her son had gone to Catholic school in Brooklyn, worked for the telephone company, and liked baseball and bowling. He had never gotten in trouble with the law. Christmas dinner in 1986 had started with the family gathering at noon. Her son had been given the white winter coat as a present. She had given her boy a golden crucifix necklace. Guido had wanted to show his uncle his new car. "I started washing the dishes while Nicholas went outside," she testified. "My brother-in-law came in screaming, 'They shot Nicholas.' I went over to the car and his heart was beating. I went to touch his hands and his fingertips were cold." Mrs. Pipitone said her husband had taken the death of their son very badly. Heartbroken, he died three years later, Pipitone testified. Silence fell upon the courtroom as she looked around with bewildered grief, casting her eyes on Caracappa and Eppolito, and then dropping her head.

Tone established, Henoch then threw the jury into the criminal culture of the case. Luchese wiseguy Little Al D'Arco emerged through the door behind Judge Weinstein's bench, the entrance reserved for criminals and witnesses under government protection. D'Arco was a small, wiry, angry man, in the mold of Jimmy Cagney playing the lippy bad guy in classic gangster films from the thirties like *Little Caesar*—the movie that gave RICO its name.

"Al D'Arco was put on to give the jury the mafia background," Henoch recalled. "It was important that the jury get used to hearing from criminals, if Kaplan was going to be credible. Burt was a bad guy but he wasn't as bad as D'Arco. Little Al would absorb the body blows from Cutler and Hayes. He had testified in ten mob trials so he was experienced. It would give me the chance to see how the cross-examination would go. I wanted to know if the old bombastic Bruce Cutler was going to appear, shouting and carrying on, or if he was going to put on a more muted presentation. I wanted to see what the judge was going to allow. I didn't want to minimize D'Arco's crimes. I was going to make him out to be the murderer he was. Some federal prosecutors try to sugarcoat their witnesses. Not in an illegal or unethical way—just to play it down. I do the opposite. I learned this when I was doing state cases for the Manhattan DA in the Homicide Investigation Unit. I would tell juries that the case was about the murder of a drug dealer. It will involve violent criminals and drug dealers because those are the kinds of people who know the most about violent crime and drug dealing. Wall Street brokers testify in an insider-dealing case, nurses in medical malpractice suits. The same thing applies to violent crime."

D'Arco explained the structure of the mafia to the jury, familiarizing them with the organization and basic terminology. But it was D'Arco's description of the intimate and corrupting relationship between the mob and law enforcement that provided the substance and surprise of his evidence. The entire world of organized crime was awash in rumors, treachery, and double dealing. Access to a source inside the government was not unusual for senior and successful gangsters. During the eighties, Colombo wiseguy Wild Bill Cutolo had uniformed NYPD officers on his payroll, D'Arco testified. Luchese Steve Crea had a DEA special agent working for him. Sal Avellino, the Long Island garbage carting Luchese, paid a government agent in the Gambino task force squad, D'Arco said. But no one was as connected as Vic Amuso and Gaspipe Casso. The Luchese boss and underboss had informants with unrivalled access to the most sensitive law enforcement intelligence. Amuso and Casso had been very careful about keeping the identities of their source inside law enforcement from their colleagues in the Luchese family. It was the same story D'Arco had told the FBI more than fifteen years earlier when he flipped and went into the Witness Protection Program. Amuso and Casso called their source "the bulls," D'Arco said, the mob term for NYPD detectives. The "bulls" were paid $4,000 a month, D'Arco said, but he didn't know the names or any identifying details about them.

In October 1991, D'Arco's revelations had been documented in FBI 302s, which had then been provided to the defense as part of pretrial discovery. On cross-examination, Bruce Cutler demanded to know why D'Arco was using the term "bulls" during his testimony when the word appeared nowhere in the 302s. Tempers quickly rose as D'Arco and Cutler argued about the ability of gangsters to tell the truth. The obvious explanation for the discrepancy between D'Arco's testimony about "the bulls" and the term "law enforcement sources" in the 302s was that D'Arco did not write the 302s himself. FBI agents, with little sense of the streets of New York and idioms, took the proffered particulars and turned mob lingo into prose that could be understood by lawyers in distant offices who had no clue how gangsters actually spoke.

"Did you have any moral compunction?" Cutler asked D'Arco, describing his years as a killer on behalf of Gaspipe Casso. The question was bellowed with indignation.

"Keep your voice down, pal," D'Arco said.

"Wouldn't you agree with me—"

"I wouldn't agree with you on anything," D'Arco interrupted.

"You okayed the induction of your son Joseph into the mafia," Cutler said.

"You're twisting my words around," D'Arco snapped. "I remember you at [a restaurant called] Taormina with all the crew there and you drank with them and ate with them and never picked up the tab."

Taking the bait, Cutler was red with fury as he prowled around the courtroom loudly calling out questions and trying to turn D'Arco's defiance into advantage for the defense. D'Arco matched Cutler's anger, threatening to turn the proceedings into chaos. The questions were leading nowhere, it seemed, other than toward further screaming.

"I can yell louder than you!" D'Arco shrieked at Cutler.

"Enough," Judge Weinstein yelled at Cutler. "Your cross-examination is finished."

"The defense was on the defense from the start," Henoch recalled. "They expected a conventional mob prosecution, with a procession of convicted criminals like Fat Pete Chiodo and Georgie Neck Zappola appearing on the stand to the tell the jury about their life of crime and Casso's 'cops.' That wasn't the way it was going to go. The judge wanted me to pare my case back. It was a blessing in disguise. I wanted the jury to focus on what happened. I wanted the jury to focus on the defendants, not the character of government witnesses. I wasn't going to put on a mob case—I was going to put on a corrupt cop case."

Henoch used the analogy of judo to describe his approach. The word *judo* translates from the Japanese as "the way of giving way." Instead of meeting force with force, in judo a combatant invites and allows the strengths of his opponent to work to his advantage. Instead of fighting the characterization of his witnesses as despicable killers and mobsters, bribed with the promise of leniency to lie for the government, Henoch readily admitted D'Arco's pedigree as a villain—as he did for all of the cooperators he put on the stand. Using the egos of defense attorneys in a productive way was also one of Henoch's aims. There was no point in fighting Cutler and Hayes as they clashed with cooperators. Calling upon the jury to hear his gangster witnesses with a degree of skepticism matched to their criminal pasts, Henoch believed, worked to his advantage. All the more reason to listen carefully to what they had to say to determine if it was credible.

THE EAGLE TAKES THE STAND

The first government witnesses had proved valuable to the prosecution but Burton Kaplan, all knew, was the case. Setting up his testimony was critical. NYPD Detective Thomas Limberg was called. For sixteen years, Limberg had been assigned to a joint task force investigating organized crime in New York City. Limberg's specific assignment was the Luchese family—the family Caracappa also worked on. Pretrial, Hayes had suggested that Kaplan was a secret cooperator before he flipped against Caracappa and Eppolito. To rebut the argument up front, Limberg testified that Kaplan had refused to cooperate when he was arrested in 1996 and had never cooperated to his knowledge. Detective Limberg told the court that Kaplan's telephone book had been seized twice during arrests over a period of more than a decade. The contents of the phone book were vital to the case. Limberg read out the names Kaplan had listed: Bonanno member Jerry Chilli, former Luchese boss Vic Amuso, with his inmate number in Terre Haute, Indiana, as well as someone named "Marco."

Henoch had spent months preparing Kaplan, and as the vicissitudes of the case continued to unfold during the year before trial, Kaplan had remained very reluctant to testify. Kaplan felt genuinely unhappy cooperating, unlike many who take pleasure in finally coming clean. Henoch had continued to reassure Kaplan—and perhaps himself, as well—as Kaplan vented about feeling terrible as a rat. Flipping Burt was not a done deal, Henoch believed, until the moment Kaplan stood before the court, raised his right hand, and swore to tell the truth, the whole truth, and nothing but the truth.

On the third day of the trial, Kaplan appeared from the wooden door behind Judge Weinstein's bench to a hushed gallery. Eppolito twitched his head and neck and swallowed hard, a tic that would be repeated for the remainder of the proceedings. Caracappa's face remained impassive but alert. Kaplan was wearing a blue suit. He was small, trim, bald, and wore thick eyeglasses. His voice was steady, his words clipped and spoken in a Brooklyn accent. Seventy-two years old, he testified that his health was not good. Among his ailments had been two minor strokes, three detached retinas, prostate cancer, high blood pressure, and Reynaud's disease.

On the stand Kaplan appeared calm, collected, despite the fact that his entire adult life had been dedicated to avoiding precisely this moment. Ratting represented the lowest form of human endeavor to Kaplan. Monotone, matter-of-fact, able to describe the murder of a mob informant in the same tone of voice as he used when he talked about distributing Disco brand jeans, it was easy for an observer to misapprehend Kaplan's state of mind. "Kaplan didn't seem especially troubled that he had become, in his old age, exactly the sort of turncoat that he and his associates aimed to kill," Ben McGrath reported for the *New Yorker*.

In a typical case, Henoch believed, the jury gave their undivided attention to each witness for three to five minutes before they started to tune out. With Kaplan, Henoch figured he had ten minutes to get the essence of the case across to the jury. At that moment, at the onset of the main part of the prosecution's case, the key was to establish that there was no doubt whatsoever that Kaplan had an intimate relationship with the two defendants.

Henoch asked Kaplan to identify anyone in the court he recognized.

Kaplan pointed across the courtroom: Louie Eppolito and Stephen Cara-cappa.

"Did you have a business relationship with Mr. Eppolito and Mr. Caracappa?" Henoch asked.

"Yes."

"Can you please tell the jury what the nature of that business relationship was?"

"They brought me information about wiretaps, phone taps, informants, ongoing investigations, and imminent arrests."

"What did you do for them in exchange for that information?"

"I paid them."

"Can you tell the jury, sir, at the time you had the relationship with Mr. Eppolito and Mr. Caracappa, where were they employed?"

"New York Police Department."

Henoch's first thematic strand, long planned, came next.

"Sir," Henoch asked Kaplan, "have you ever been to Mr. Caracappa's residence?"

"Yes," Kaplan replied.

"Where is it?"

"In Manhattan, on 22nd Street," Kaplan said.

The exchange seemed innocuous, especially for a jury trying to get their bearings in a complex RICO case, but it contained the kernel inside the seed of truth that Henoch would nurture during the weeks to come.

"Did Mr. Caracappa have pets inside that apartment?" Henoch asked Kaplan. The question derived from the fact that Oldham had remembered that Caracappa complained about cat hair on his suit when they worked for Major Case at the same time. It was a small but telling fact. Details contained their own drama.

"He had two cats," Kaplan said.

"Did you ever meet any of Mr. Caracappa's family members?" Henoch asked.

"I met his wife."

"What's her name?"

"Monica."

It was an unlikely approach to a mob murder trial, Henoch recalled, but the evidence was aimed at attacking the defense that Caracappa and Eppolito were being framed by mobsters. "One of the purposes of spending so much time with Kaplan was to mine his knowledge of the lives of Steve and Louie and organized crime, and to find out as many details as possible about his relationship with them," Henoch said. "Kaplan knew where Steve lived in Manhattan, and the precise address on East 22nd Street. He knew what floor he lived on. Kaplan knew where Steve's mother lived on Staten Island. How would a seasoned career criminal know where a hero cop's mother lived, and be able to describe in detail a cemetery near that hero cop's house? How would he know the hero cop's sister-in-law took care of his mother on occasion? Caracappa was quiet, unassuming, and cautious. He wasn't a public figure, with information about his life readily available. The jury could see that Kaplan was confident in his facts. The jury could see that he had to have had a relationship with Caracappa and Eppolito. He knew too much. Kaplan's tiny bits of information were daggers in the heart of a defense that Caracappa and Eppolito didn't know Kaplan. We wanted to make it preposterous for either defense attorney to claim his client had no relationship with Burton Kaplan."

Henoch had Kaplan review for the jury his brushes with the law, including two trials, five convictions, and civil proceedings involving his business vending knockoff designer wear. Kaplan said he had pled guilty to paying a group of Mexican inmates $1,000 in Allenwood Federal Prison Complex to assault another inmate. Kaplan explained the transaction to the jury. "That's part of what prison life is all about," he said. As a result of his guilty plea for the assault, and despite his cooperation with the government in this case, Kaplan had been sentenced to thirty days in "the hole" in Allenwood.

"Do you know Tommy Dades?" Henoch asked.

"No," Kaplan replied.

Before trial there had been speculation in the press that Kaplan had been a secret informant for the FBI for many years. Kaplan flatly denied the accusation. He had been approached more than ten times over the years by authorities seeking his cooperation, but had always refused.

"Was the standard practice, in your experience, that every time you were arrested some law enforcement official would try to get you to cooperate?" Henoch asked.

"Every time."

"In 2004 you actually began to cooperate. Is that correct?"

"Correct."

"Can you please tell the jury what changed your mind?"

"Definitely," Kaplan said. "I was in jail nine straight years. I was on the lam two and a half years before. In that period of time I seen an awful lot of guys that I thought were stand-up guys go bad, turn, and become informants. As I told Steve the night I left to go on the lam, I asked him if he could guarantee that Louie would stand up. Steve said he could do that. But after nine years I felt they were going to be indicted by the state in this case, and I didn't think they would stand up. I was tired of going to jail by myself. I would be at the defense table right now, and Steve and Louie be would sitting up here on the stand."

"Did your family have any sway over you in your decision to cooperate?" Henoch asked.

"Yes and no," Kaplan testified. "My wife and daughter have been asking me to cooperate from the first day, and I didn't do it. My daughter adopted a boy from Russia, and he's two and a half years old now. I wanted to be able to spend some time with him. But I can't honestly say I did this for my family. I did it, in all honesty, because I felt I was going to be made the scapegoat in this case."

From an objective point of view, Kaplan's explanation made little sense. The targets of the investigation were Caracappa and Eppolito, not Kaplan, who was already in prison and would remain there until he died. "But it was the truth that Kaplan told himself," Oldham recalled. "Even after he flipped, Kaplan didn't want to admit to the court, or to himself, that he had caved. Criminals frequently come up with contorted reasons for their cooperation that allow them to maintain a fig leaf of dignity. Kaplan didn't want to allow that Joe Ponzi or I had anything to do with his decision. Between the lines, though, you can hear what really motivated Kaplan. His wife, his daughter, and finally the realization that he was standing up for two dirty cops who would never do the same thing for him—especially Eppolito."

For the next two days, Kaplan told the jury his life story, from the first trips he took with his father to the racetrack and his early gambling addiction to his collaboration with the Lucheses and Gaspipe Casso. Kaplan said he had not been in contact with Casso since Casso's arrest in 1993. Casso's son still lived in a house that Kaplan owned but Kaplan had served an eviction notice on the son and the matter was still the subject of dispute.

Despite the passage of years, Kaplan's version of events matched Casso's in virtually every aspect. One exception was the murder of the wrong Nicky Guido. Casso claimed he had paid "the cops" for the address of the wrong Nicky Guido. According to Kaplan, Caracappa and Eppolito didn't give Casso the address. Kaplan said that they wanted to be paid to run the license plate, and Casso turned them down, believing "the cops" were being greedy. "The inconsistency with Casso might seem problematic but factual discrepancies can be the best thing for the credibility of an informant or witness," Oldham noted. "For the jury, if the accounts of every witness match perfectly, if every fact fits seamlessly, it can seem like the witnesses are lying, or colluding to create a story. Memory is not perfect. Synapses don't fire. All of us remember events in fragments. Like the color of the Plymouth Detectives Caracappa and Eppolito were driving at the time of the Hydell kidnapping. Was it gray, or blue, or green? All three versions existed in people's memories but there was no definitive proof which it was. Did that mean that Caracappa and Eppolito were not searching Staten Island and Brooklyn in an American-made automobile picked to look like a nondescript unmarked police car? Did it mean they didn't kidnap Hydell and serve him up for Casso to brutally murder? No. The same was true for Nicky Guido. Whether or not Casso paid for the address, Caracappa did the search and Nicky Guido was killed. The jury heard the evidence."

"At some later point, did you have a conversation with Mr. Eppolito about the wrong Nicky Guido being killed?" Henoch asked.

"Yes."

"What did Mr. Eppolito say to you?"

"He told me Gas should have paid the money and he would have got the right guy."

"I HOPE MY DAD IS INNOCENT"

During lunch breaks, a procession of the principal players in the case made their way across Cadman Plaza to the Plaza Diner. Caracappa remained in the courthouse, eating his lunch in the cafeteria with Jack Ryan, the former Major Case Squad detective working for the defense. Eppolito, by contrast, strolled with an entourage of his family, usually stopping to grant walk-and-talk interviews to the reporters camped outside. One member of Eppolito's family did not form part of his inner circle. Louis Eppolito Jr., a thoughtful and gentle thirty-six-year-old, was the only child of his father's first marriage.

"Kaplan appears to be believable," Eppolito junior said over lunch.

"He seems very, very smart," said Rob Gortner, Eppolito's partner.

"I hope my dad is innocent," the younger Eppolito told a listener. "I want to believe it. I'm here to find the truth. I need to hear the evidence. I need to make my own decision."

That morning, before proceedings began, he had gotten to speak with his father alone for the first time since the arrest. They had embraced,

Louis junior said. "I told him I love him. He said he loves me and appreciates me coming here. Of course he denies it to me. He says he's innocent. He says it's lies, lies, lies. I'm not the kind of person to say, 'Okay, Daddy.' He's extremely defensive. I told him I will be there for him throughout. He said, 'I ain't going anywhere.'"

After lunch, Kaplan's testimony continued. He described the aftermath of the murders of Jimmy Hydell and the wrong Nicky Guido. Kaplan said that Casso had decided he wanted to kill Sammy the Bull Gravano, the prominent member of the Gambinos, the family that had tried to kill Casso in 1986. Frankie Santora Jr. and Detectives Caracappa and Eppolito agreed to take up the contract, Kaplan testified. Payment would only be forthcoming upon completion of the job. The trio tailed Gravano to and from work. Weeks passed and they were still looking for a clear shot at Gravano.

"Did there come a time that you found out what happened with respect to that contract?" Henoch asked.

"Yes. Frankie junior told me," Kaplan testified.

"What did Frankie junior tell you?"

"That the three of them followed Gravano to his house. They surveilled his construction company on Stillwell Avenue, and they also staked out Tali's Bar and Grill on 18th Avenue, where Gravano hung out. Frankie junior told me that they stopped surveilling Gravano because a detective who knew Louie or Steve came up to them in a car and started a conversation with them, asking how you doing, what are you doing here. They said they are just there to meet somebody. They didn't think they should go to that spot anymore. They followed Gravano to his house and from his house on a lot of occasions, but they could never catch him alone. They told me he was always dropped off by people or picked up by people in other cars. They didn't have a chance to fulfill the contract."

"Did you tell Casso anything about that?"

"I gave him a word-by-word explanation of what Frankie told me."

"What did Casso say to you about that?"

"'Okay,' he said. 'If they want to keep it, they can keep it. If they want to give it up, they can give it up and we will try ourselves.'"

Soon after that Frankie Santora Jr. was shot and killed during the murder of Carmine Variale. The connection with the NYPD was now lost, it seemed. If the matter had been dropped by Caracappa and Eppolito the conspiracy would have ended. But the money was too attractive, and easy. Weeks after the murder of Santora, Kaplan testified, he got a phone call from Frankie Santora Jr.'s wife.

"After the conversation with Ms. Santora, did there come a time that you had a meeting with Mr. Eppolito?"

"Yes."

"Where did you meet with Mr. Eppolito?"

"In Mrs. Santora's house."

"Can you tell the jury about how long after the murder of Frank Santora the meeting was that you had with Mr. Eppolito?"

"I would say within a month. I went to Frankie's house and I sat down in his dining room with Louie at the table. Frankie's wife went into another room. Louie says, 'I'm pretty sure you know who I am.' I said, 'Yes, I know who you are. I have seen you on a few occasions. You're Frankie's cousin.' He said yes. He asked me if I had a desire to continue the business that we were doing together."

"What did you take that to mean?"

"Continue what I was doing with Frankie, but directly with Louie. Continue getting information."

"Was there any discussion about paying for that information?"

"At that point he said, 'I think we could make this simple. We could make this a business arrangement.' He said, 'You could put me and my partner on a four-thousand-a-month pad and we'll give you everything that we get on every family, any bit of information we get about informants, about ongoing investigations, wiretaps, and imminent arrests.'"

Kaplan wanted to think it over. Eppolito gave Kaplan his home phone number and Caracappa's beeper number. Kaplan gave Eppolito his beeper number and the number for a phone line he had installed in his daughter's bedroom. The number was given to only a few of his most trusted associates—Casso, Tommy Galpine, and now Detective Louis Eppolito.

Kaplan lived six blocks away from the Santora residence. He walked out of the house from the meeting and along the driveway. There was a man sitting in a car with his chin resting pensively on his palm. Kaplan didn't know his name but he recognized him as Eppolito's partner. In court, he looked across the room in the direction of the defendants' table and indicated Caracappa.

"After that conversation with Mr. Eppolito, did you contact anyone?" Henoch asked.

"Yes," Kaplan said.

"Who did you contact?"

"Anthony Casso."

"Did you have a conversation with Casso about what you and Eppolito had discussed?"

"Yes. I told him that I had a meeting with Louie Eppolito, at Frankie's house, and that he suggested that if we wanted to continue we could do it on a more businesslike basis. He would want—he would like, he didn't want—four thousand a month. He would do everything he could to give me information at all times, whenever it became available. Louie said that his partner worked in a task force and that there's a lot of information that he came across. He was in meetings with the FBI and that that would all become part of the four thousand a month. The only exception would be murder contracts. They would be above that."

"So the four thousand a month was supposed to cover what?"

"Information."

"What type of information?"

"Imminent arrests, wiretaps, bugs, ongoing investigations."

"As of the time of this meeting, had Nicky Guido already been killed?"

"Yes."

"What about Jimmy Hydell, had he already been kidnapped?"

"Yes."

"What about jeweler number two, had he already been killed?" Henoch asked, referring to Israel Greenwald.

"Yes."

Henoch asked what Casso's reply had been to the proposal made by Caracappa and Eppolito. The new arrangement carried risks, with Kaplan in a direct relationship with the cops and Casso therefore one step closer to the perils they represented. But the partnership had already proved invaluable.

Kaplan recalled his conversation with Casso. "I said, 'Well, so far they've been real good to you.' He says, 'Yes, I agree with that. Let's do it.'"

"What conditions did Casso place on the agreement?"

"He said, 'Tell them if they want to do this, and we go forward on it, that they have to work exclusively for us. We don't want them giving information to other guys in other families, and possibly have a problem back from it which will eventually come back to us.'"

"Do you know, or did you know at that time, whether it was against mafia protocol to use policemen in this manner?"

"No, I didn't know it then."

"Did you discuss methods of contacting with one another?"

"Yes."

"Can you tell the jury were there any codes or numbers that you decided to use?"

"When I would call his house, I would always use the name 'Marco,' and if I beeped, he had given me a beeper number for Steve, and I agreed to use my prefix in my home phone number, 259, and put that behind the beeper so he would know it was me."

An arrangement was established for meetings. Kaplan lived on 85th Street in Brooklyn. Kaplan would know when Eppolito was coming to see him. If there was no reason to cancel the meeting Kaplan left the porch light on in front of his house. Eppolito would arrive at ten at night. He would tap on Kaplan's front window. Kaplan would let him in the front door. If Kaplan's wife was asleep, they would stay in the living room for their conversations. If she was awake, they would go back to the rear of the house where his daughter had once lived.

As Kaplan testified, the names of victims and heists long since forgotten and seemingly unconnected were brought back to life. Otto Heidel, the Bulova watch job, Tiger Management. Kaplan's command of the facts was impressive. Jurors began to steal looks at Eppolito as Kaplan continued to describe power struggles inside the Luchese family and Casso's violent solutions to dysfunction. Caracappa and Eppolito had been central players, as Casso's hired informants. Over the years, remembered Kaplan, they met in a number of other places as well. Rest areas on the Southern State Parkway and the Long Island Expressway were often used. Eppolito was married, and he had three children by his second marriage, but he also had a lover. Kaplan said she had lived on 84th Street in Bensonhurst, and they met at her place as well. Kaplan couldn't recall her name but said she had a dog and a teenage son. Eppolito came alone, for the most part. Kaplan dealt nearly always with Eppolito. Until he got greedy.

"Louie and I had a big argument. Louie said he wanted to meet Gaspipe. I said, 'Louie, that don't make no sense. Why do you want to do that?' He said, 'We've been so good with our information, I think we deserve more money.' I said, 'That isn't going to happen. You are not going to meet him.' He says, 'I'm willing to stand on one side of the door. He could be on the other side of the door. We don't have to see each other.' I said, 'Louie, that isn't going to happen.' He got a little indignant with me. We had an argument. If you look at Mr. Eppolito, he's three times my size. I pushed him out the door to my house and we had an argument. I said, 'Don't ever come back to my house anymore.'"

"What happened after that?"

"About a month later, Steve Caracappa came to my house with a box of cookies. He says, 'Is it okay if we talk?' And I says, 'Sure.' I like

Steve. I liked him then. I like him now. I know I am not doing him any good by being a rat, but I always liked him."

In court, Caracappa threw down his pen and looked around the court with indignation, as if to ask how a man could be permitted to tell such outrageous lies. Eppolito's eyes were bloodshot and his jaw clenched. He continually swallowed and twitched his head. From that time forward, Kaplan said, he met with Caracappa. The pair convened at the cemetery at the end of Kramer Street on Staten Island near Caracappa's mother's house. It was during these meetings that Kaplan asked Caracappa to help locate Anthony DiLapi by contacting DiLapi's parole officer. Kaplan testified that he was concerned that a written letter would create a record that might later be uncovered. Caracappa told him not to worry; he would put DiLapi's name in a list of half a dozen others involved in a real investigation, obscuring his intention. Caracappa provided one address for DiLapi. After DiLapi escaped the first attempt by Casso's hit squad, Caracappa furnished another address in L.A.

DiLapi was then killed, Kaplan stated flatly.

Two jurors turned and stared directly at Caracappa.

On and on Kaplan continued, relentlessly detailing the attacks on Fat Pete Chiodo, Bruno Facciola, and Eddie Lino. "Marco" was the code name in Kaplan's phone book employed to disguise the contact numbers for Caracappa and Eppolito. Henoch entered the phone book into evidence. The exhibit was displayed to the jury. Henoch had Kaplan identify and explain how he had scratched out 212-616-0631 and 917-420-0150—the first number for Caracappa in Staten Island, the second his beeper number—to camouflage them.

During the weeks leading up to the Lino homicide, Kaplan said, Caracappa and Eppolito had asked Kaplan to ask Casso for untraceable guns. "Jesus," Casso had complained to Kaplan, "don't those guys do anything for themselves?" A revolver and an automatic were supplied as murder weapons. Kaplan testified that he had been in the New York Eye and Ear Infirmary at the time of Lino's death recovering from eye surgery. Eppolito came to see Kaplan there.

"I've got good news," Eppolito said to Kaplan. "We got him."

"What do you mean?" Kaplan asked.

"We killed him," Eppolito said, taking out two newspaper photographs of the scene of the crime. Eppolito told Kaplan that Caracappa had done the shooting. A former soldier, Caracappa was the better shot, Kaplan testified. Kaplan passed along payment, received in a box from

Casso. The amount was $70,000 in cash, five thousand more than had been agreed. Kaplan thought Casso was testing him to see if he was honest. Kaplan returned the excess and conveyed the balance to his two "cops."

In the early nineties, Kaplan testified, Eppolito came to see Kaplan at his home on 85th Street. "Just before he moved to Las Vegas, he pulled up in front of my house. He had his wife with him. Louie rang the bell and I came to the door. I believe it was a Saturday, and my wife and I came to the door, both of us, and Louie said, 'Come outside. Come outside. I want you to see the van I bought.' And I came outside and very honestly I was shocked. It was white, pure white, and I felt very conspicuous standing out on the sidewalk with Louie, him being a retired detective and me being a criminal, with this big white van and on a Saturday afternoon with a lot of people driving by. I didn't say that to him, but I was nervous. I said, 'Louie, it's a beautiful van' and I did what most people did at that time. I went in my pocket—I used pay phones a lot—where I had two, three dollars' worth of quarters. I threw it on the floor of the car, which meant good luck."

"Was Mr. Eppolito with anyone that day?"

"Yes, he was with Fran."

The departure of the Eppolitos for Las Vegas did not cease Kaplan's contact with his "cops." Kaplan continued to deal with Caracappa after he retired from the NYPD and took a job with the 14th Street Business Improvement District. Kaplan testified that after the arrest of Casso in 1993, he was not concerned that the conspiracy between Caracappa and Eppolito and Casso would be revealed. "If anyone in the world was a stand-up guy, I thought it was Mr. Casso," he said. The phone call from his attorney Judd Burstein a year later, saying that Casso had snitched, took Kaplan completely by surprise. That evening, before going on the lam, Kaplan said he went to see Caracappa at his apartment on East 22nd Street.

"I felt that the only way the government would take someone like Casso as a cooperator who had so much baggage—I knew he had many, many bodies, I knew about twenty-five at the time—unless he could give them something sensational back," Kaplan said.

"What was the sensational thing that you were referring to?"

"The relationship between Steve, Louie, I, Frankie junior, and Casso," Kaplan said.

VIVA LAS VEGAS

On the lam first in Ensenada, Mexico, then Oregon, and finally Las Vegas, Kaplan testified, he had kept in contact with Caracappa and Eppolito, both then living in Las Vegas. Henoch entered into evidence the pieces of identification Kaplan had acquired as he constructed the identity of "Barry Mayers." Kaplan told the court that during this time he lent Eppolito money from his marijuana business to help the retired detective finance the purchase of his dream house. Kaplan described for the jury the interior of Eppolito's study on Silver Bear Way, including the glass display case of knives. Financial stability had been a constant theme in Kaplan's dealings with Eppolito, he told the court.

"On occasion Louie came to me and said he needed to borrow money and I said, 'I don't understand you, Louie. Do you have any bad habits?' And he said, 'No, I don't gamble, and I don't do drugs.' I said, 'How come you're always in trouble with money? You are getting—your end is two thousand a month plus you have your salary.' He says, 'I collect snakes, very expensive snakes and it costs a lot of money to feed them and a lot of money to buy them. I like doing things like that.' Louie always wore three, four chains and five rings on his fingers. I tried to preach to him as an older guy that he should be more conscious of the way he spends his money and stop getting himself under pressure all the time."

"Did you ever have a conversation with Mr. Caracappa about Mr. Eppolito's money habits?" Henoch asked.

"Yes," Kaplan said.

"What did Mr. Caracappa tell you?"

"We were in the cemetery on Staten Island near his mother's house on a Saturday. I broached the subject about the conversation I had had with Louie. Steve said that since he had known Louie, Louie had always been in trouble with money and he was always into Steve for six, eight, ten thousand dollars at a time. He said that there was a time in their relationship when they got desperate for money—"

"Objection," Hayes said, rising to his feet.

"Sustained," Judge Weinstein said.

"Just what Mr. Caracappa said?" Henoch asked.

"He said that there was a time that they had to put bags over their—"

Eddie Hayes leapt to his feet again. "Objection," he called.

The jury had no way to know, but this was a reference to evidence that in the late seventies, when Caracappa and Eppolito were partners in the

Brooklyn Robbery Squad, they told Kaplan that on occasion they had put paper bags over their heads and stuck up bodegas to make cash on the side. The allegation did not go directly to proof of the RICO conspiracy, but it had powerful implications for the jury in determining the characters of Caracappa and Eppolito. Judge Weinstein had ruled such character evidence inadmissible.

"Sustained," Judge Weinstein said. "Strike it."

Kaplan testified about his various business dealings in Las Vegas, including the proposed deal with Caracappa's wife to sell a punching bag on the QVC shopping channel, which they hoped might be endorsed by George Foreman. For only the second time in the trial, Caracappa's face took on an expression other than stoicism. He appeared angry and disgusted as he muttered to himself. "The son of a bitch has brought my wife into this thing," he said audibly enough to be heard in the press seats.

Kaplan described his return to New York City, after the government had determined not to use Casso as a witness and Kaplan hoped the heat had been turned down on the "cops" investigation. Kaplan's subsequent arrest on the marijuana charges led to a downward spiral resulting in the conviction of Kaplan and Tommy Galpine. Kaplan explained to the jury that he repeatedly refused to cooperate with law enforcement. He described his encounters with Oldham, first in Allenwood with DEA Special Agent Mark Manko, and later in the MDC in Brooklyn with Ponzi. The session in the MDC was the beginning of the end of Kaplan's resistance. "I had my lawyer come and visit me in Brooklyn," Kaplan testified of his response to that session. "I told him about all the visits I was getting. I told him I was thinking of cooperating. I wanted to talk it over with my family. I wanted him to be aware of the fact that I was considering cooperating."

Kaplan said again that he had become convinced the investigation Oldham and the cadre had undertaken was going to result in indictments. Kaplan didn't want to wind up on the wrong side of the law, once again. "It was a very, very hard decision for me, but I made it."

Henoch had Kaplan explain the terms of his proffer agreement to the jury. The benefits he might receive, if any, would be determined by a federal judge, not prosecutors from the Eastern District. Kaplan had not been able to dictate terms, as he initially hoped. "Did anyone ever suggest to you any answer to questions when they were asked of you?" Henoch asked.

"No."

"Did anyone ever tell you to change any of your answers?"

"No."

Henoch was finished, for now. "No further questions, Your Honor."

EDDIE JABS

Fast Eddie Hayes led for the defense. Always tightly wound, with the high-energy manner of a Queens-raised speed-tawker salesman, Hayes began his questioning of Kaplan with a few jabs and feints. Did Kaplan lie to a Hasidic businessman about the murder of Israel Greenwald by saying he had gone on a "long vacation"? Kaplan agreed he had. What about forfeiture of assets under the cooperation agreement, Hayes wanted to know, suggesting that Kaplan had money squirreled away the government didn't know about. Kaplan stated that he had no hidden assets or significant amount of money.

Hayes asked Kaplan if he'd been close friends with Amuso and Casso. "That's true."

"And you went and you helped Mr. Casso on a number of occasions by supplying him with information, having people killed, isn't that right?"

"That's correct."

"What did they do for you, what did Mr. Casso do for you?"

"Mr. Casso didn't do anything for me specifically because of that, but Mr. Casso lent me large amounts of money for my businesses in the past years."

"Casso was, as you describe it, a homicidal maniac?"

"That's true, that's my belief."

"Would you describe yourself, Mr. Kaplan, as an intelligent man?"

"I don't really think I'm intelligent. I think I'm an average human being. If I was really intelligent I wouldn't be sitting in this chair at this time. I'm not being sarcastic, I'm being honest."

"You're not in the chair because you're stupid, you're in the chair because you're a thief, right, and a killer?"

"I'm in the chair because I'm a criminal."

Under scrutiny from Hayes, Kaplan said that in the best year of his marijuana business he had sold between 12,000 and 15,000 pounds, netting a personal profit of millions. Hayes then asked about Kaplan's former business partner, Ray Fontaine. Oldham had always been suspicious of Kaplan's account of the sudden disappearance of Fontaine in the eighties. Fontaine had been involved in disputes with pot dealers Kaplan supplied who'd warned Downtown Burt that Fontaine was destroying their monopoly by selling pot to other mobsters. If there was a major chink in the armor of Burt Kaplan's testimony—if the defense had uncovered a fact not known to the prosecution—it would appear now.

"Ray Fontaine went on a long vacation, didn't he?" Hayes asked.

"No, no," Kaplan said. "Ray Fontaine left his house and somebody, I imagine, grabbed him."

"And killed him?"

"I don't know if they killed him or not."

"But he's never been seen again?"

"Ray was like my brother. I love him."

Hayes dropped the line of questioning, without adding any evidence or catching Kaplan in a contradiction. The gambit had failed to injure Kaplan's credibility, crossing a major hurdle for the prosecution. Hayes turned to Kaplan's descent into a life of crime. Kaplan agreed that he had behaved reprehensibly toward his wife and daughter due to his gambling addiction. "I was a very sick individual," Kaplan said. Hayes asked if inviting mob figures like Christy Tick Furnari and Anthony Casso to his daughter's wedding in the eighties had been a wise or decent thing to do. Kaplan's daughter had then just graduated from law school, and clerked for criminal defense attorney Jerry Shargel. Kaplan said there was the real possibility that she would defend accused criminals such as himself. "Like you do," Kaplan said to Hayes. Under questioning from Hayes, Kaplan said that he had lost a great deal of his daughter's respect but he loved her dearly. "I love her more than death," Kaplan testified.

Hayes ranged around the courtroom, moving from the lectern to the well in front of the judge's bench and back behind the defense tables. His physical restlessness was matched by the lack of an overarching point to his questioning. He changed topics unpredictably, as if searching for a tiny opening—any opening—in an impenetrable wall of cold hard fact. In reply, with cold precision, Kaplan recited what he knew, neither more nor less. The testimony of Burton Kaplan was compelling for the sheer consistency of his calculated, violent deviance. Kaplan maintained a level of discipline anyone could respect. Kaplan was a worker. He didn't do drugs, cheat on his friends, or stay out until all hours of the night in bars with his buddies. To the contrary. Kaplan considered himself a stand-up guy and a man of his word. Kaplan was a working-class Jew from Brooklyn, son of a straight-arrow store owner who died young. Kaplan shaped his life during the rise of the mafia but he didn't follow the familiar pattern of dissipation. Kaplan kept his self-respect. Above all he possessed an ascetic's charm. He was a loyal friend to his inner circle, legal and illegal.

On the stand, Kaplan's evidence was unrelentingly credible. His life story was filled with improbable incidents and characters. In the early eighties, he testified that he had tried to turn an African hair cream export business into a Quaalude factory. He told the jury he had attempted to fence Peruvian passports in Hong Kong in the early nineties. Stolen diamonds from Burkina Faso, knockoff Disco jeans, women's leisure suits in Las Vegas: Kaplan's career as a criminal ranged far and wide in scope and ambition. Testifying, Kaplan was plainly very honest, perhaps not with himself and the way he treated his family over the years, but on the stand there were no elisions or evasions. The more questions Hayes asked Kaplan, the more he displayed his knowledge of the "cops," and the more damning the case against Hayes's client became. Kaplan was honest about his brutality, and he was brutally honest.

Hayes ended with Kaplan's meetings with Caracappa and Eppolito in Las Vegas.

"If we believe you, that you hired Eppolito and Caracappa to do all these murders, right, why don't they kill you?" Hayes asked.

"Why don't who kill me?" Kaplan replied.

"Eppolito and Caracappa."

"Believe me, that was on my mind. That's why I had my girlfriend come with me and sit in the car so she could observe Louie when I met them the first time."

"You then met them by yourself?" Hayes asked.

"No, I never met them by myself. I only met Steve by myself and I was taken there by my girlfriend. She waited in the car."

"If they already killed all these people, what stops them from killing you and your girlfriend?"

"I personally think that Steve and I had a lot of affection for each other," Kaplan testified. "I've had a lot of affection for Louie over the times, except for when we had a falling out. I don't think they would have killed me. As a matter of fact, they made a statement to me that when Casso was trying to kill me, they said if he ever does kill you, we will kill him and if he's not around, we'll kill his son. So, they loved me. I believed they loved me."

Caracappa stared directly ahead, into the middle distance, his eyes ringed by red.

BRUCE RAGES

Bruce Cutler rose, in the decidedly formal manner he employed in court. Kaplan began by acknowledging a personal connection to Cutler. In the seventies, when Kaplan received his first conviction in a trial before Judge Weinstein, his defense attorney was a well-known ex-cop and highly regarded criminal lawyer named Murray Cutler.

"Your father represented me in a case with Judge Weinstein many, many years ago," Kaplan said. "Your father was a very nice man," Kaplan said.

"Mr. Kaplan," Cutler said, "I have to go to work on you a little bit."

"That's your job, counselor."

If Hayes was a fox, sniffing around the case and looking for holes, Cutler was the hedgehog. The truism of British philosopher Sir Isaiah Berlin, taken from the ancient Greek poet Archilochus, refers to two kinds of people. The fox races in many directions at once, seeing contradictions and complexities, avoiding grand theories about life or the law. Hayes was the personification of an attorney who inhabited relative truths, seeking to raise reasonable doubt in the minds of jurors with charm and a hundred tiny factual quibbles and inconsistencies and implications. The hedgehog is the embodiment of a person who holds to a single, totalizing truth. For Cutler that truth was that RICO prosecutions were innately corrupt and unjust. The government degraded itself by making deals with killers, offering rewards to habitual liars and thieves, and turning the centuries-old traditions of the common law into a mockery of justice. Gangsters who became cooperators were morally, spiritually, and legally despicable, unreliable, and dishonorable. What was at stake, Cutler wanted the jury to believe, was the sanctity of the legal system itself. Believing the word of confessed killers like Casso and Kaplan against that of upstanding NYPD detectives such as Caracappa and Eppolito was an outrage and an injustice.

"About how many meetings would you say you have had with Mr. Henoch from the time you decided to fully cooperate?" Cutler asked.

"I would say over thirty," Kaplan said.

The meetings lasted approximately five hours, Kaplan testified. The total number of hours Henoch had spent with Kaplan was in excess of one hundred and fifty, Cutler calculated.

"I had a lot of crime to confess," Kaplan said.

"And a lot of information to give?"

"True."

Cutler asked if Kaplan had seen newspaper accounts in 1994 of the allegations made by Casso against Caracappa and Eppolito. Kaplan said he had not; he was already on the run in Mexico. Kaplan said he was aware of the publicity the crimes had attracted in New York City at the time—just as they had during the trial now.

"Prior thereto, Lou Eppolito had written a book," Cutler said. "You knew that Louie had written a book?"

"Yes," Kaplan replied. "At one point he gave me a copy of the book and he signed it, 'To my good friend Burt.' When I got arrested, I had my wife throw it away."

Cutler reviewed the basic outline of Kaplan's early life story: Brooklyn childhood, gambling debts, mob connections. "You are seventy-two now, and I am not quibbling with you, but you made a choice in your life at some point to live this illicit life?"

"Shame on me," Kaplan said. "But I did that. I admit to it."

Cutler turned to Kaplan's first major criminal activity: acting as an accessory after the fact to murder in driving the body of a homicide victim from New York to Connecticut at the direction of an ex-cop turned criminal. Kaplan was twenty-nine years old at the time, Cutler noted.

"As I look at my life in retrospect," Kaplan testified, "I did a lot of unsettling things."

"I am not passing judgment," Cutler said. "I am just trying to unravel these things as best I can. Did you have a moral compunction, a hesitation, to say, 'Wait a minute, I've got a dead body in my car. What am I, losing my mind?'"

"If you want me to answer that question, I trembled all the way up to Connecticut in the car by myself. I was scared to death."

Cutler began to dissect the evidence Kaplan had given to Henoch. Cutler ran through the voluminous list of gangsters who had flipped and become informers over the years. By contrast, Cutler contended, Kaplan's old and dear friend Christy Tick Furnari had "stood up" and refused to snitch, thus remaining in Allenwood well into his eighties. Such silence was "old-school," Cutler said, and Kaplan agreed that there were old-school gangsters left.

"You testified that one of the reasons you signed a cooperation agreement was you didn't want to be a scapegoat?" Cutler asked.

"That's true."

"You felt that the state authorities would charge Stephen and Lou and they would point to you?"

"I said that."

"But they didn't charge Stephen and Lou in state court?"

"Because they were indicted in federal court."

"They didn't charge Stephen and Lou, you know that? They're not pointing their fingers at you, Mr. Kaplan. You don't see them pointing their fingers at you."

"In what way, counsel?" Kaplan asked. "Meaning they're not on the witness stand?"

"Meaning they are not on the witness stand. You are."

"Because I was first, counselor," Kaplan said.

"My point exactly," Cutler said.

"I made a very, very tough decision."

"You also said and part of the reason was, you would agree with me, you didn't want to be in jail anymore?"

For Kaplan, admitting to the disgrace of ever wanting to get out of prison was too much to ask. Kaplan would not admit such a thing to himself—let alone Bruce Cutler.

"That's not true," Kaplan said.

"I understand, I understand."

"Please don't say it, it's not true," Kaplan said.

Stoicism in the face of a long prison sentence was part of the ethos of career criminals like Furnari and Kaplan. But that didn't mean Kaplan had meekly accepted his pot conviction. In 2003, Kaplan had filed a motion to have his 1997 conviction in the marijuana case overturned. The grounds Kaplan had come up with constituted one of the oldest, most common refuges for convicted criminals trying to find a way out of trouble. Kaplan claimed his legal representation at trial had been incompetent. Kaplan, like countless convicts before him, had turned the blame on his attorneys as a desperate last resort.

Outraged at the attack on the honor of fellow defense attorneys, Cutler read sections from Kaplan's motion protesting his innocence of the crimes he had been convicted of. The basis for the claim of the poor legal representation was slight and the chances of success were slim. But Kaplan had approached his affidavit with determination. "It was clear to me from the pressure the government tried to impose on me that the government was willing to go to virtually any length to make me crack in the hope of bringing me on board to have me serve as a substitute for Anthony Casso," Kaplan's motion claimed.

Confronted in court by Cutler now, Kaplan did not attempt to minimize, hedge, or deflect the evidence.

"I was fighting for my life at the time," Kaplan testified.

The motion had not been adjudicated at the time Kaplan decided to flip in the summer of 2004.

"Would the outcome have affected your decision to cooperate?" Cutler wanted to know.

"Objection," Henoch said. "It calls upon the witness to speculate."

"Overruled," Judge Weinstein said.

The question was read back to Kaplan.

"Yes," he said.

Once again, invited into a trap by Cutler, Kaplan refused to fall for the ruse. It was implausible to say that having his marijuana conviction overturned, and potentially being freed on bail while a retrial was pending, would not have an impact on Kaplan's thinking. Of course it would. As a witness, Kaplan was frank and appeared to have nothing to hide. He told Cutler that Casso had tried to interject in Kaplan's motion. Ever vengeful, trapped in solitary confinement with nothing but time on his hands to dream up plots to gain revenge, or even a little attention, Casso had tried to hire attorney David Schoen himself to thwart Kaplan's efforts. After Kaplan flipped and agreed to testify, Kaplan said, he had dropped his appeal, even though the matter had still not been decided.

"I didn't want to be on both sides of the law," Kaplan said.

"Did you cooperate because you hoped for something in return?" Cutler asked, his voice rising in indignation.

"I agree," Kaplan said.

"A reduction in sentence?"

"I would agree," Kaplan said. "I'm hoping for a low sentence."

Cutler's voice started to rise as he recited the procedure Kaplan would undergo after his testimony was complete. The Eastern District would submit a letter to Kaplan's sentencing judge within thirty days. During the cross-examination, Cutler had managed to maintain a controlled atmosphere. Now, however, as Kaplan's testimony neared the end, Cutler's sense of moral disgust was matched by a sense of urgency. Goading Kaplan into a mistake, or a display of anger, would weaken the weight of his testimony, perhaps.

"Are you sorry for the misery, death, and destruction you caused?" Cutler demanded. "Did you testify as to that?"

"No," Kaplan replied.

Kaplan had grown more and more irritable as Cutler implied that Kaplan had ulterior motives for flipping. Kaplan again insisted his main reason for becoming a cooperating witness was that he was convinced

Eppolito would try to make a deal and leave Kaplan as the one sitting at the defense table facing trial on multiple murder counts. It had happened to him before, in the marijuana case, and he wasn't going to let it happen again. "I felt Louie would cooperate against me, and he might be able to get Steve to go along," Kaplan testified yet again.

The tone between the two men was contentious. Cutler, it emerged, was moving toward a subject that had been ruled inadmissible by Judge Weinstein prior to the trial. While being questioned by federal authorities, Kaplan had failed to pass a lie detector test when asked if he was becoming a cooperator in order to get into the witness security program. Weinstein ruled that the defense could not ask about lie detector tests because they are not admissible as a matter of law. Cutler began to ask a question about the lie detector test when he was interrupted simultaneously by Henoch and Judge Weinstein.

"I won't have that," Weinstein said sternly. "Your cross-examination is finished."

Cutler seemed astonished at the turn in events. His cross-examination of Little Al D'Arco had likewise devolved into a shouting match called to an end by the judge. "I'm used to being upbraided," Cutler said to his fellow attorneys. "But not cut off."

The prosecution had the opportunity to ask Kaplan questions to clarify or amplify answers given during cross-examination. Redirect was generally used for the government to attempt to rehabilitate a witness who had suffered at the hands of defense attorneys. There was little need to be concerned about such contradictions or weaknesses. Henoch asked Kaplan how he had concealed his meetings with "the cops." Using the code name Marco, only calling from pay phones, and rendezvousing late at night in a Staten Island cemetery had seemed sufficient, Kaplan said.

Hayes rose to again cross-examine Kaplan. How was it, Hayes wanted to know, that in all the years Kaplan had met with Eppolito and Caracappa he had never been surveilled by law enforcement officials who routinely followed known organized crime figures like Kaplan? Had not Kaplan led the FBI to Casso in 1994, as Casso believed when he ordered the hit on Kaplan? The implication was that Kaplan had deliberately arranged to have Casso arrested, which Kaplan flatly denied. "In all honesty," Kaplan said, "I'm a very good driver. I'm good at watching my mirrors and making U-turns. That's why Casso never got to kill me."

As Eppolito listened to Kaplan's testimony, the veneer of defiance he had adopted from the beginning of the trial slowly started to disappear. Before the proceedings started, it had seemed that the defense had an excellent opportunity of prevailing. Caracappa and Eppolito had completely denied conspiring with Kaplan. But how could Kaplan know so much about the two NYPD detectives, in such detail, with such convincing recall? He had testified that Eppolito's wife, Fran, used to dye her hair blond. Kaplan knew that Eppolito had a girlfriend, with an apartment in Bensonhurst, where they met on occasion. Kaplan knew Eppolito collected snakes and expensive knives. Listening, Eppolito pulled at his collar to give himself breathing room. One of the courtroom artists drawing sketches during the trial for newspapers and television news had noted the drastic physical transformation of Eppolito during the days Kaplan gave evidence. His flesh was wan, his shoulders were sloping, and there were large black bags under his eyes. "He looks like an ice-cream cone," she said as she drew his portrait. "Slowly melting away."

After three days on the stand, Kaplan was finally done. His testimony had stunned the court. He was a devastating witness, it was agreed in the press room and among courtroom watchers. Cross-examination had failed to find a flaw in his account of the conspiracy with Caracappa and Eppolito. For seasoned watchers, the performance gave rise to conversations about the most impressive testimony ever given in a Brooklyn courtroom. Kaplan, it was agreed, had been the most convincing organized crime witness any observer could recall. "The Joe DiMaggio of mob snitches," Jimmy Breslin called Kaplan. If anyone would know, it was Breslin.

Still, there was no way to be sure of Kaplan's impact on the jury. Could Henoch and the team from the Eastern District turn the testimony of Downtown Burt into convictions?

CHAPTER SEVENTEEN

CORROBORATION

The next two weeks would put the prosecution's case to the test. The amount of evidence compiled by the government was enormous. Thirty-four witnesses, dozens of exhibits, including murder scene photographs, old NYPD documentation, and audiotapes of Caracappa and Eppolito conniving to deal drugs and launder money in Las Vegas. The evidence was direct and concrete. Some witnesses testified to specific matters to buttress the testimony of Kaplan in ways that underscored his credibility on small questions, like the number of cats kept by the Caracappas on East 22nd Street. Others were aimed at the broad sweep of cop and mob culture.

Instead of adopting a strictly chronological and linear narrative form, Henoch employed a style that contained order but not the kind found in a conventional book or film. Even though subjective evidence as to character was banned, all of the evidence the government entered was designed to construct a portrait of two NYPD detectives that would lead a jury to believe beyond reasonable doubt they committed the heinous crimes they were charged with.

The first witness after Burton Kaplan stood down was Detective Gary Ward, a retired NYPD officer. Ward had responded to the scene where the body of murder victim Bruno Facciola had been discovered in August 1990 with a bird shoved in his mouth, signifying his status as a rat who had "sung." A photograph was entered into evidence. Next came Detective Felix Sciannamen, a thirty-nine-year veteran of the force and a partner of Eppolito's in the Six-Three in the eighties. Detective Sciannamen recalled the cramped quarters in the detective squad room, with officers having easy access to each other's files, and Eppolito's flamboyant tastes in gold jewelry. After Anthony Casso was shot in September 1986, Sciannamen testified, he had accompanied Detective Eppolito to the NYPD pound to search Casso's car. Traces of drugs were found in the car. Eppolito discovered a key ring with a safe deposit key from a bank in

Canada, which was vouchered. In his testimony, Kaplan had said that Casso was eager to retrieve the key from his impounded car, explaining Eppolito's interest in searching for it despite having no legitimate connection to the case.

A man named Tom Knierim, who worked for the 14th Street Business Improvement District in the nineties when Caracappa was in charge of security, testified that the phone number Burton Kaplan had in his book under the name "Marco" was in fact the same as the beeper number Caracappa had been given by the BID. Paul Smith, a retired investigator with the New Jersey Attorney General's Office, testified that he had been involved in surveillance of the suspected mob-related company called Tiger Management in 1989. The operation was shared with the NYPD—particularly with Detective Kenny McCabe, whom Smith trusted implicitly. McCabe had died before the trial and thus could not testify but had told Oldham that he was certain Caracappa pumped him for information on matters like the Tiger Management surveillance.

Victoria Vreeland, an investigator with the New Jersey Attorney General's Office on her very first assignment as a law enforcement official during the surveillance of Tiger Management, took the stand next. On April 19, 1989, she testified, she watched from a motel window across the road as a man driving in a recreational vehicle entered the property of Tiger Management. Vreeland had observed in amazement as the man searched in the same places where law enforcement technicians had placed listening devices only days earlier. The prosecution entered into evidence videotape from that day. The silent black-and-white footage showed a fat, hairy, middle-aged man dressed in an undershirt and wearing a fedora—a cartoon version of a gangster, circa 1989—climbing telephone poles and scuttling in and out of the mobile home as he found the government's listening devices. Ironically, as he uncovered the audio surveillance, the man was oblivious to the fact that he was being recorded by video cameras, lending an air of farce to the man's brazen behavior.

With every witness, Hayes and Cutler probed for inconsistencies, hoping to cast doubt on some corner of the case in the hope of convincing the jury that if one piece was dubious none of the evidence could be relied upon. Eddie Hayes was an expert on the NYPD, and close to many Major Case Squad detectives, but his questions yielded few, if any, concessions from the witnesses, or comfort for the accused. As the prosecutors constructed the case, well-known criminal defense attorneys frequently stopped by to watch. Jerry Shargel, once Kaplan's attorney and employer of Kaplan's daughter as a law clerk, was an eminence in the defense bar with a beard and designer tortoiseshell glasses. Bald with a full silver-tinged beard, Shargel had been Bruce Cutler's co-counsel when he won acquittals for John Gotti in the 1980s. Shargel responded to press inquiries about the problems the government might face in prosecuting crimes that were fifteen and twenty years old saying, "It's a big risk. RICO doesn't cover sporadic and disconnected criminal behavior." During Kaplan's testimony Shargel told the *Guardian* that if the charges were true, "it has to be the rawest breach of a police officer's duty perhaps in history."

Each morning, Judge Weinstein set aside time to hear motions from the prosecution and defense. One week into the trial, Henoch rose to call Burton Kaplan's former defense attorney Judd Burstein to the stand. The testimony Burstein would provide would detail conversations he had had with Kaplan in 1994 and again in 1996 regarding the cooperation of Anthony Casso and Kaplan's relationship with Casso and former detectives Caracappa and Eppolito. Henoch said the evidence would rebut the suggestion by the defense that Kaplan had made up his story of the cops while in prison in a desperate bid to get out early and alive.

Ordinarily, such evidence would be inadmissable as hearsay—Burstein would be testifying about what Kaplan had said about Caracappa and Eppolito, not about a conversation he was directly involved in. Federal rules of evidence provided for limited exceptions. Always in command of his courtroom, Weinstein handled the legal arguments with dispatch. Burstein had come forward and approached the government with his evidence, not the other way around, Weinstein noted. His client, Burt Kaplan, had waived attorney-client privilege. By suggesting that Kaplan had a motive to lie when he flipped in 2004, he ruled, the defense had "opened the door" for the prosecution to lead evidence showing Kaplan had made earlier statements consistent with his current testimony. In this case that meant Kaplan's conversations with Burstein about being the "go-between" for Casso and Caracappa and Eppolito, which occurred in 1994 and 1996, might be taken by the jury to show that Kaplan's evidence was credible. Any ambiguity in the law must be decided in favor of the defense, Weinstein added, so anything that Kaplan had said to Burstein subsequent to his arrest in 1996 would not be admitted, a distinction that severely restricted the government—but allowed Burstein to re-create for the jury the sequence of events that sent Kaplan on the run when Casso flipped in 1994.

Outside the court, Cutler and Hayes were plainly outraged that a member of their fraternal order of defense attorneys was assisting the government—worse, Burstein had *volunteered* to help the enemy. Attorneys would wind up in the Witness Protection Program, Hayes said. No one could recall such a legal oddity. Hayes said he wanted to be able to ask Burstein about large amounts of cash Kaplan had paid him over the years. There was a financial motive, Hayes told Judge Weinstein, for Burstein to come forward and support Kaplan's testimony. Weinstein was appalled by the accusation against Burstein.

"I'm not going to subject a distinguished member of this bar to that harassment," he told Hayes.

"I've never seen this before," Hayes sighed.

Burstein was in his early fifties, a prosperous attorney who had quit criminal practice to represent civil clients in the mid-nineties. From the mid-eighties he had represented Kaplan in matters ranging from an alleged heroin importation conspiracy to Kaplan's scheme to sell Peruvian passports to Hong Kong businessmen. When Casso flipped in the spring of 1994, Burstein testified that he had contacted Kaplan immediately. He knew the pair were close. "You didn't have to be Sherlock Holmes to know Mr. Kaplan might have some legal difficulties," Burstein testified. When Casso's cooperation became public that year, revealing the role of Caracappa and Eppolito in the murder of Eddie Lino, there was no mention in the press of Burton Kaplan's role, or even his name. If Kaplan had concocted the story, there was no way he could have known what he knew when he contacted Burstein in the spring of 1994. "Mr. Kaplan told me it was a big problem for him. He said he was the go-between for Lino and for other matters. The sum and the substance was that there was more than one murder."

"Did Mr. Kaplan say he was the go-between for Anthony Casso and a federal agent?" the prosecution asked.

"Absolutely not," Burstein said. "It was cops."

Eddie Hayes winced. In the summer of 2005, Burstein testified, he saw a piece on the case on the television show *Dateline NBC*. From his knowledge of Kaplan, Burstein deduced that Kaplan must be cooperating with the government against Caracappa and Eppolito. He contacted the Eastern District and said that if Kaplan waived attorney-client privilege, he, Burstein, would be willing to tell them about Kaplan's prior statements regarding his conspiracy with Caracappa and Eppolito. For years, Burstein had suggested to Kaplan that it was in his interests to cooperate, but his client had refused.

"Burt Kaplan had this ethic about not cooperating against other people," Burstein testified.

In cross-examination, Eddie Hayes asked if Burstein had considered the possibility that Kaplan might use the information about Casso's cooperation to kill Casso's family, or warn others in the mafia. Burstein testified that he didn't consider Kaplan an organized crime figure— perhaps naïvely. "It never crossed my mind that this guy had a propensity for violence." Hayes's anger at Burstein flared as he asked, with outrage, if Burstein had been aware of the murder of Israel Greenwald. Burstein blandly replied no.

Cutler had known Burstein since the early eighties, when they first worked together. "People liked you, Judd, and they trusted you," Cutler said. "Didn't you at one time open a big office with green furniture and a machine that served cappuccino coffee?"

"It almost bankrupted me," Burstein replied.

Cutler asked if Burstein was aware that Kaplan and Casso had met thirty-five to forty times when Casso was on the lam in the early nineties. It was during this time, Cutler suggested, that the pair had come up with the idea of framing Caracappa and Eppolito. Standing next to the jury box, Cutler bent deeply to the floor and scooped and gathered air into his hand to express the lack of substance to the plan that the villains had come up with against two innocent hero cops. "They *concocted* some scheme," Cutler said, voice rising. "Concocted some scheme," Cutler bellowed.

Burstein did not answer.

THE DELUGE

Before the arrest of Caracappa and Eppolito, Oldham and the cadre had gathered a significant amount of evidence. After the arrests, as Henoch took control of the investigation and turned it into a prosecution, an even larger cargo of corroborative evidence had been collected. In state cases, there was a legal requirement that evidence given by criminal accomplices be independently corroborated. RICO had no equivalent provision. Kaplan's evidence could convict, in and of itself. But while corroboration wasn't technically necessary, it was a practical imperative.

Detective Steven Rodriguez from the NYPD Criminal Records Division took the stand to testify. He was a twenty-three-year veteran who had been promoted to first grade, highly unusual honor for an officer who had an inside job pushing paper. Rodriguez was an expert on NYPD recording systems. He explained to the jury how the department kept track of all information requests run by members of the force at the time. Detectives had to provide their tax identification number. It was a kind of fingerprint inside the NYPD. The point was to ensure there was a paper trail. The only permitted use of the system was for official purposes.

Detective Rodriguez told the jury that searches in the Identification Section resulted in the production of a criminal history sheet for the name of the person in question that listed criminal pedigree, aliases, a description, and contact information. Officers could make a request by telephone or in person. A record of all checks were mailed monthly to commanders in the units throughout the force to verify that the checks were being used properly. The only permitted purpose for a check was in pursuit of an investigation or for an official reason. Members of the service were strictly forbidden from using the database of the NYPD for personal reasons, to do favors, or, of course, in return for money.

In the courtroom, the lights were dimmed and Exhibit 23A was put up on the projector. A Request for Information at 10:30 a.m. on November 4, 1986, by Detective George Terra was shown. The check was for a man named Nicholas Guido. The date of birth of the Nicky Guido in question was January 29, 1957. Terra, then an investigator with the Brooklyn DA, was assigned to the investigation of the string of murders and drug deals committed by Robert Bering and Jimmy Hydell in the summer and fall of 1986.

The next exhibit was a Request for Information from the Major Case Squad from November 11, 1986. The tax identification number of the detective making the request was 862810—Detective Stephen Caracappa. There were two names in the search: Felix Andrugar and Nicky Guido, both done under "Case Number 341." The date of birth for the Nick Guido requested was different from the one Terra had sought. This Nick Guido was born on February 2, 1960—the date of birth of the young man shot and killed on Christmas Day 1986. It was the search that Tommy Dades had found in the files Oldham had given him. "Caracappa had run Nicky Guido—the wrong Nicky Guido," Oldham said. "There were simply no circumstances under which Caracappa would have run a search on the Nicky Guido who worked for the telephone company and lived a quiet, innocent life. The person processing the request had no way to check on the case number provided by the detective. It was taken on faith that the detective was giving a valid case number. The weakness in the system was that it trusted but had no way of verifying.

"Caracappa could be confident that the Guido search was lost in the maze of names and taxpayer identification numbers of all the different detectives from all of the squads and precincts in the city. He bet that the NYPD's filing system was a sinkhole. He didn't expect me to carry his personnel file around for nearly a decade. He didn't expect Tommy Dades to find the search. He thought the past was past and in this case it wasn't."

The jury learned that Caracappa had misused the system on numerous occasions. Later in November 1986 he had run the name Nick Guido again. This time the search was disguised within a list of four other names to make the name Guido appear to be attached to a larger investigation. The field of names included in the report would include the right Nicky Guido (born in 1957), who was then on the run from Casso and living in Florida. Caracappa had also run the record of Peter Savino, the Genovese associate secretly informing for the government in the Windows Case. Detectives Caracappa and Eppolito, it may be remembered, had told Casso that Savino was an informant but the Lucheses had been unable to convince Vincent Chin Gigante and the Genoveses to murder him.

Detective Rodriguez testified that it was even discovered that Caracappa had searched the criminal record of "Monica Singleton." She was born on July 5, 1950, and no case number was attached to the request. Why had he searched her name? This was the woman Caracappa was about to marry.

On cross-examination Hayes pointed out that Caracappa had followed proper NYPD procedures on the searches, filling in the requests according to protocol. Detective Rodriguez agreed. Hayes said that Caracappa would have to be "a falling-down moron" not to know that there would be a permanent record of his search for Nicky Guido. Rodriguez had no reply. Hayes suggested it would be easy for a detective to get the permission of his boss to run the name of his wife to find out if she had a criminal record. The question seemed to astonish Detective Rodriguez. "There were no circumstances that would allow the NYPD Criminal Records Division, or any officer in the force, to misuse criminal history sheets," Oldham said. "The suggestion was absurd."

SECRET LIVES

The pace of the prosecution case quickened as a series of witnesses were called, each with a particular purpose, each adding another brick to the wall Henoch and his team were building. Investigators followed up on Kaplan's tip that Detective Eppolito had kept a lover for half a dozen years in the eighties. Cabrini Cama appeared in court wearing a tight-fitting brown pantsuit, her hair teased up and caught in a black bow. Eppolito's wife, Fran, stared silently ahead as Cama said she had lived with her teenage son and dog in an apartment on 84th Street in Bensonhurst, within the confines of the Six-Three, Eppolito's precinct at the time. She said she had met Detective Caracappa approximately ten times over the years in which she carried on the illicit affair with Eppolito. Cama pointed across the court and identified Caracappa and Eppolito. She said Eppolito had met with Burton Kaplan at her apartment—the men went to another room to speak. A photo array with six late-middle-aged, balding white men was introduced. Cama picked out number four, Burton Kaplan. On cross-examination, Cutler got Cama to testify that Eppolito was "a nice guy" who had left "old feelings" behind when he moved to Las Vegas. Hayes tried to elicit testimony that she often went out with Eppolito and other cops. But she replied, "It was always Louie and Steve." Caracappa was polite and a gentleman, she said.

Eppolito's nervous twitch, which had become pronounced during Kaplan's testimony, was now accompanied by repeated gulping.

The next witness, Betty Hydell, was dressed in black, wearing glasses, her hair white. She sat on the witness stand and caught sight of Eppolito and gave a sharp intake of breath through her teeth. Three women who accompanied her sat in the gallery on the verge of tears. A picture of Jimmy Hydell was displayed on the overhead projector. She told the court about the day of October 18, 1986. She said Jimmy was going to Brooklyn; he didn't tell her why. She described going outside to confront the two men circling the block. There was a big one, with black hair and gold necklaces, and a little one, dressed in a dark suit. When the big one, the driver, pulled out his badge, she said she grew angry. "You should let people know who you are and what you're doing," she testified that she had said. "If you're a cop why are you hiding?" She said Jimmy called her that afternoon to say he would be home for dinner. He never came home. His body has never been recovered. Betty Hydell did not testify about the *Sally Jessy Raphael Show,* or identify Caracappa and Eppolito. The "golden nugget" was not introduced as evidence. The defense had no questions for Betty Hydell.

Onward the prosecution marched, relentlessly accumulating territory. Rodolfo Wazlawik, an elderly man long the superintendent at 12 East 20th Street, testified that Steve and his wife, Monica, lived in apartment 10A, one floor down from the penthouse. The phone number was 420-0150, the same number entered in Kaplan's phone book.

Before trial Hayes had suggested to the authors of an article in *Vanity*

Fair magazine and in press conferences that the defense would reveal evidence that Kaplan had secretly been an informant for the FBI for many years. The FBI Special Agent who had run Otto Heidel as an informant for more than a decade now took the stand. Patrick Colgan, retired and white-haired, testified that he had chased Kaplan for decades—for his entire twenty-eight-year career. Once a month, he estimated, he knocked on Kaplan's door and tried to convince him of the merits of working for the FBI. The two exchanged social pleasantries, and Kaplan was unfailingly polite. But he refused to cooperate. Kaplan showed no sign of weakness, and he never appeared to so much as consider Colgan's offers.

In cross-examination Hayes suggested that if Kaplan was such an attractive target for the FBI, why was there never any evidence of him interacting with Caracappa and Eppolito? Colgan responded that Kaplan made frequent appearances in surveillance footage. He came and went from known organized crime locations—the 19th Hole, El Caribe, Allenwood penitentiary. But Kaplan had never been the "target" of an FBI operation.

In point of fact, the notion that Kaplan had been Colgan's snitch was preposterous. He was not asked on the stand, but after he testified he told why. In 1997, after Kaplan and Galpine had been convicted in the pot case, Kaplan had contacted Special Agent Colgan. Kaplan was in the Metropolitan Correctional Center awaiting sentencing, and facing twenty years, or more, if he didn't get a sentence reduction. Colgan, who had retired from the FBI a few months earlier, agreed to see Kaplan at the MCC. They shared small talk, as they had countless times before. "We had a good conversation," Colgan recalled. "We always did. We asked after each other, the family, the usual. Burt wanted to know how to mitigate or get out of his sentence. I laid it out for him. First, you have to get a new attorney. Then, I told Burt, he needed to cough everything up. I said, 'You're not going to get a pass. I will get you a United States attorney and a private attorney and you will have to tell them everything you know.' Burt said, 'Pat, you know I can't do that.' He didn't have to say what he meant. It was understood. If he talked, Burt would be dead in jail, and his family would be dead on the outside. I told him there was no way he was going to sway a judge if he didn't do what I said. I knew Burt had a great deal of knowledge. I didn't know how much. I had no idea about Caracappa and Eppolito. I did know that Burt was *never* an informant before he started to talk in 2004. He didn't know where to turn to get a lesser sentence, and if he was a cooperator he would have known where to go and what to say. He would have had proof of prior cooperation. I was shocked when he flipped. I was sure he would take his secrets to the grave."

TOMMY SINGS

Tommy Galpine was big, simple, and slow, a forty-nine-year-old high school dropout and career criminal, Brooklyn born and raised. He sported a large mustache. Appearing in court in a brown sports coat, he testified that he had met Kaplan when he was sixteen years old. Since that time, he had been in Kaplan's thrall, as errand boy, apprentice, and finally partner in crime. Galpine had assisted Kaplan in legitimate business, trucking leisure suits and designer jeans and velour sweat suits around the city. He had also aided Kaplan in illegitimate commerce, bootlegging clothes, fencing stolen goods, dealing drugs. Galpine had been convicted with Kaplan in the marijuana case and sentenced to sixteen years—192 months, he specified. He had served nine years. Galpine cited his precise release date, with time reduced according to the guidelines, as April 26, 2011.

From the witness stand, Galpine identified Eppolito sitting at the defense table. Galpine had not seen Eppolito since the early nineties, the last time he had given him cash on Kaplan's behalf. He said Kaplan had introduced him to Eppolito in approximately 1988. Before then, Kaplan had told Galpine about his dealings with NYPD officers. Kaplan called them "the bulls," Galpine said, a common street expression referring to detectives.

Galpine testified that he had known Anthony Casso since the mid-seventies, when they had been introduced by Kaplan. Over the years he had often taken "things" to Casso for Kaplan: money, paperwork, messages. "I run around," Galpine said. "I do things. I'm a doer, I'm not a talker." Galpine lived near Casso and they had prearranged meeting places: a car wash on Utica Avenue, a parking lot in a shopping mall, the Golden Ox Chinese restaurant in Mill Basin—the same place Casso had been shot by Jimmy Hydell in 1986. Galpine testified that the evening Casso was shot he had been driving a gold Lincoln Town Car that Kaplan had given him and registered under Progressive Distributors, one of his clothing companies. After Casso was nearly killed, Kaplan gave Galpine a manila envelope and told him to take it to Casso. The envelope contained the NYPD DD-5s for the investigation of the shooting of Gaspipe Casso. The men named therein were the men about to face the wrath of Casso: Jimmy Hydell, Bob Bering, Nicky Guido. The next instruction Galpine received from Kaplan was to retrieve a Ford Fury from Patty Testa's used car lot. The car was meant to appear to be a police car. "The cops" were going to use the car to hunt down Jimmy Hydell. "The car was very cop-looking," Galpine testified. So convincing was its appearance that as Galpine drove to deliver the car he was hailed by a young man on the sidewalk who wanted help and thought Galpine must be NYPD.

There were minor discrepancies in the testimony of Kaplan and Galpine. Kaplan said he had given the manila NYPD folder with the DD-5s to Casso himself; Galpine said he delivered it to Casso for Kaplan. The inconsistency was significant, perhaps, but it could be seen by the jury to only buttress the case against Caracappa and Eppolito. Galpine corroborated Kaplan in small and large matters. Galpine said he remembered Otto Heidel from the Bulova watch job pulled by the Bypass gang. Kaplan had fenced a large number of the watches through Gaspipe Casso. Heidel came to Kaplan's warehouse on Staten Island, Galpine said, with a Luchese named Georgie Zappola. Heidel was a smart aleck, Galpine said. Only a few days after the Bulova job, as members of the Bypass gang were getting arrested and suspicions were aroused that Heidel was a rat, Kaplan told Galpine to wipe their fingerprints from the watches. When Heidel was gunned down on Casso's orders after playing a game of paddleball, Galpine testified that he had come into possession of a cassette tape that "the cops" had given to Kaplan. Kaplan told Galpine to destroy the tape. Instead, Galpine said he had played part of the tape one day as he drove to Pennsylvania. The recording was of a debriefing session. Law enforcement officials were getting information from a criminal who was cooperating—from a snitch. Galpine said he wasn't supposed to listen to the tape, and it made him nervous to defy Kaplan's instructions, but curiosity got the better of him. The names mentioned weren't familiar, but he did remember the name of the man being interviewed. It was Otto Heidel. The tape was corroboration of the information provided by Detectives Caracappa and Eppolito about Heidel's cooperation.

It was the practice of Kaplan and Galpine to talk every night to review the events of the day, he said. Once, Galpine testified, he went to Kaplan's house and was told he couldn't come inside. "The cops" were in the house, Kaplan told Galpine, and he didn't want them to meet. Another time, Galpine came into Kaplan's house to discover he was in the kitchen with a large man wearing gold chains around his neck and an NYPD pinkie ring. Kaplan introduced the man as "Louie."

"Tommy is like a son to me," Kaplan told Eppolito.

The next time Galpine saw Detective Eppolito was in the Caribbean resort of Martinique or St. Martin—he couldn't remember which island he flew to. Kaplan had given Galpine $10,000 with the instruction to give it to Eppolito. The year was 1988. Galpine testified he flew Continental out of Newark Airport. The round trip was completed in a single day, there and back. Before he left on vacation, Eppolito had approached Kaplan and asked if he would be willing to send him money if he ran short while he was away. He was taking his three children and mother-in-law on a vacation, and his American Express was maxed out. During his testimony, Kaplan had said he offered to give Eppolito the money before he left, but Eppolito insisted he would only take the money if he needed it.

Galpine testified that Eppolito was waiting for him at the airport. Eppolito wanted the money to purchase a time-share. Eppolito and Galpine sat together for an hour during Galpine's layover. Eppolito suggested Galpine stay for dinner, or perhaps overnight. Galpine told him he had to return to New York; he had no interest in befriending the corrupt detective. The danger of the association was evident to Galpine, even if Eppolito appeared to believe such business could be conducted cordially.

During the lunch break in Galpine's testimony, a rumor circulated through the courthouse that Gaspipe Casso had contacted the prosecutors. Casso, people whispered, wanted to testify in the case. He was said to have recanted the version of events he told the FBI in 1994 and *60 Minutes* in 1998. The attempted intervention threatened to upend the trial; there was no way to know what Casso might say if he testified for the defense. "Prisoners like Casso are constantly trying to find a way to get back in the game," Oldham said. "They are locked away for the rest of their lives. In our society people don't think what that really means—the tedium and despair. At the least, Casso would get a change of scenery if he came to testify. He would get a ride on an airplane. He would get to see New York City."

As Eppolito walked across Cadman Plaza toward the Plaza Diner, where he regularly ate lunch, he stopped to give an interview to a news radio reporter.

"Do you want to see Mr. Casso on the stand?" the reporter asked.

"Absolutely," Eppolito said.

"You have no fear of him up there on the stand?"

"I've never been afraid of anything in my life," Eppolito said. "He's not going to bother me."

"You're not worried he could incriminate you further and change his story again?"

"If he does, he does. That's the way it goes."

"What do you think of Bruce Cutler's defense?"

"I have faith in Bruce," Eppolito said. "I always have. I always will."

"What do you want people to know today?" the reporter asked. "That you were set up?"

"To me it's an obvious frame," Eppolito said, referring to Galpine's inability to recall which island he went to. "It's blatant to me. Have you ever got on a plane and not known where you went? Has anyone ever got on a plane and not known where they went?"

Yet the trip to the islands was a provable, concrete fact, and testimony after lunch showed why. Even though nearly twenty years had passed, records could be checked to see if Eppolito or Galpine were in the Caribbean at the time in question, or if Eppolito had purchased a time-share. Joel Campanella had investigated Tommy Galpine's alleged day trip. Campanella had put a "travel query" out for Tommy Galpine for that time period. The search was to see if a Certified Travel Record had been generated by Customs for Galpine. The records were created if a passenger paid for his ticket with cash, or traveled back and forth from a destination alone on the same day. And, indeed, Galpine had been flagged by immigration and Customs officials on April 13, 1989. He had flown to and from St. Martin, the exquisite tiny island located in the Caribbean just where the Antilles curve to the south. Henoch introduced into evidence an application for a time-share membership purchase in the Royal Islands Club in St. Martin on April 11, 1989, by Louis and Fran Eppolito. And on April 13, 1989, as Henoch displayed to the jury, Galpine had flown to St. Martin—two days after the Eppolitos had treated themselves to the Royal Islands time-share.

Cutler's cross-examination of Galpine began by focusing on Galpine's extensive criminal history.

"It's something I did with my life," Galpine responded. "I had a choice." Asked about his decision to talk, Galpine said he never expected to cooperate. "I thought I would never be here, but I am." Cutler countered that his testimony was aimed at obtaining a "Rule 35 letter," recommending his early release from prison. Galpine said he had confessed to committing many crimes, including a large number he had never been charged with and that the government had no idea about, including murder. "I told them everything. And along with that came Louis Eppolito."

Cutler pounded his elbow on the lectern, startling those in attendance with the ferocity of the blow. He bellowed, "That is the ticket! Implicating Lou Eppolito!"

"I try to be a fair guy, to tell the truth," Galpine said. "All those lies in my life got me nowhere."

Next, Eddie Hayes took his turn at Galpine.

Heroin dealing was despicable, a destructive force in minority neighborhoods throughout the city, Hayes said.

"I didn't think about it," Galpine said. "I'm not looking to play it down. I did a lot of stupid things in my life."

"Why would anyone believe that anyone capable of dealing heroin was not capable of lying so they can go home?" Hayes asked. Hayes was imploring the jurors with his eyes. The contention Hayes was making was that each successive witness was lying to try to gain a personal benefit. By the middle of the second week, with half a dozen names still on the government witness list, the effort was increasingly forlorn. Galpine didn't reply; the question was rhetorical. "No further questions," Hayes said.

The redirect by Henoch was brief but effective. "Are you lying for Burt Kaplan?" Henoch asked in the redirect.

"No," said Galpine.

Galpine testified that when he saw the report on television that Detectives Caracappa and Eppolito had been arrested, he knew Kaplan must have decided to cooperate. Like Kaplan, Galpine had refused to cooperate when he was arrested on the marijuana trafficking charges in 1996. Law enforcement had tried to convince him to testify against Kaplan. Galpine rejected any deal. But with Kaplan's cooperation Galpine knew he was next. Galpine said he considered his options carefully. He had six years left in his sentence. He was still young enough to construct a new life. If he were indicted and convicted of further charges, on the basis of Kaplan's testimony, he would never get out of prison. Galpine was taken by the authorities to New York City. He met with his attorney, and he met with the FBI, DEA, and prosecutors. Galpine refused to cooperate. He had no idea that Kaplan had specifically included him in the deal he struck with the Eastern District. Kaplan's wife, Eleanor, came to see him and asked what he was going to do. Galpine said he was going to rely on the Fifth Amendment and refuse to answer questions on the grounds that it would tend to incriminate himself.

Once again, Galpine was backed into a corner. "It seemed like I was going to get more time for this," he testified. "There was no way I wasn't going to be charged with obstruction of justice or pulled into the conspiracy."

Henoch called Joel Campanella, the only member of the cadre to take the stand. Campanella described the protocol Henoch used for debriefing sessions with Kaplan and Galpine. The point was to get the story from the witness, Campanella testified, not to feed it to him. Incidents would not be suggested, or locations named, or identities disclosed. No reports or documents or notes were shown to cooperators. Specific questions were asked, without naming the individuals involved, so the cooperator couldn't confirm the version he thought the government wanted to hear. Campanella testified that he had been involved in the many debriefing sessions with Kaplan and Galpine. Campanella had sought medical records showing that Kaplan had been a patient at the New York Eye and Ear Infirmary on 14th Street on the day after Eddie Lino was murdered. The fact confirmed Kaplan's testimony, as to his whereabouts. It was where Eppolito had gone to see Kaplan to tell him the Lino job was complete.

THE UNMARKED GRAVE

The murder of Israel Greenwald had hung over the trial from the first words of the prosecution's opening statement. Henoch and his team now turned to the final pieces of evidence, and the path that had led them to a parking shed on Nostrand Avenue in Brooklyn. The first witness called was Tammy Ahmed, the daughter of Frank Santora Jr.; she was a quiet and shy woman in her mid-thirties who had the appearance of being a suburban mother. Her father was a co-conspirator with Caracappa and Eppolito in the deal with Kaplan and Casso. Santora had been shot and killed on Bay 8th Street in 1987. She said she had been very close to him and often went with him as he drove around Brooklyn doing business. After the murder, she testified, her father's cousin, Detective Eppolito, came to their house two or three times a month, sometimes with his girlfriend, Cabrini Cama, sometimes with Caracappa. Photographs from her Sweet Sixteen birthday party were produced. The event included entire tables filled with wiseguys, many of them later murder victims. Ahmed testified that there were only two members of the NYPD present at the event at Pisa Caterers on 86th Street in Bensonhurst—Stephen Caracappa and Louis Eppolito.

"My father didn't like the police very much," she testified. "The police weren't his favorite subject."

Sitting at the defense table, Eppolito smiled. On the stand, Ahmed carefully and insistently refused to make eye contact with Eppolito. Ahmed said that as best she could recall, she was present only once when Detective Caracappa talked with her father. Burton Kaplan had been a friend of her father's, she said, and she recalled buying jeans from his Brooklyn warehouse after her father was released from prison in the mid-eighties.

Investigators for the Eastern District had come to Tammy Ahmed a few months earlier and she had gone through the remnants of her father's possessions. One relic she had kept was his phone book. The pages were projected on the screen for the jury. Kaplan's number was in the book, along with Eppolito's Long Island, work, and "private" number. "Steve (Lou friend)" was listed. There was also an entry for "Pete's tow truck." The number referred to a man who had appeared in a photograph at her Sweet Sixteen and that she only knew as "Pete from the gas station."

Tammy Ahmed's testimony finished, the next witness, Peter Franzone, appeared from behind Judge Weinstein's bench looking terrified. Franzone was a man who had kept a secret a very long time. It was Franzone who had led investigators to the decomposed body of Israel Greenwald the previous April. Franzone was so petrified of testifying against Caracappa and Eppolito he had given up his identity and gone into the Witness Protection Program. At Franzone's request, Judge Weinstein asked the court artists making sketches of witnesses not to draw Franzone's likeness. A small nondescript man, with a mustache and salt and pepper hair parted on the side, he would have little trouble blending into a crowd. Face cast downward to avoid eye contact, Franzone swore to tell the truth, even as he shook with fear. He said he had quit school in the sixth grade, at the age of sixteen. He could not read. He said he got in trouble with the law as a young man. When he was nine years old he broke into a recycling plant with a group of his friends. The heist netted Franzone $65. He took the proceeds to Coney Island where he blew his wad on roller-coaster rides and a cowboy hat. At fourteen he was caught stealing a car. The second offense led to him being sent to a reformatory school in upstate New York. There Franzone learned to weld. When he came out of reform school and returned to Brooklyn he took a job in a wrecking yard salvaging car parts. As a young man he drove a Chinese laundry truck and fixed flat tires at a gas station. A stint as a tow truck driver on Flatlands Avenue gave Franzone a start. Mustering the money and courage to strike out on his own, Franzone then started his own company, Valiant Towing.

In 1979, Franzone rented property at 2232 Nostrand Avenue. The location was in the far reaches of Brooklyn. In the mid-eighties a customer came to him with an Oldsmobile damaged in a rear-end accident. Frank Santora Jr. wanted the car repaired. Franzone had met Santora briefly years earlier when he was working for a local gas station. Franzone was a neighborhood guy with an interest in cars. Santora told Franzone he was a "salesman" but avoided questions involving details about his work. Whatever he did for a living, Santora had the spare time to spend a couple of afternoons every week loafing around Franzone's lot while his Oldsmobile was worked on. The inference was obvious, though, especially given the white Cadillac that Santora drove. The two men became friendly. Santora had the time to go on tow jobs with Franzone. Santora invited Franzone to his home for Christmas dinner. Franzone met Santora's wife and young daughter, Tammy.

Franzone's towing and parking business was modest. The operation included nineteen enclosed parking garages running in a row in the rear of his office shed and repair workshop. There were an additional seventy-five open-air parking spaces on the lot. The garages and outdoor spaces were rented by the month. Located near a railroad track and facing the busy commercial strip of Nostrand Avenue, the shed housing the office was only large enough to accommodate a tow truck dispatcher and parking lot attendant. Over the years Franzone testified he encountered problems with local kids climbing the fence and stealing hubcaps. He installed 150-watt fluorescent lights near the collision shop, spotlights over the garages, and placed a large mercury light at the end of the lot to illuminate the premises. He allowed a homeless man to live in a van in the back in order to scare away local kids. The shed was equipped with multiple windows to allow attendants to clearly see people coming and going. His business was open twenty-four hours a day, year round.

Valiant Towing was located less than a mile from the Six-Three precinct house. Soon after Franzone took on the job of repairing Santora's Oldsmobile, his "salesman" client introduced Franzone to a detective in the Six-Three. That day Detective Louis Eppolito pulled up, beeped his horn, and double-parked on Nostrand Avenue in front of Franzone's property. Santora called Franzone over to introduce him. "This is my cousin," Santora said. Eppolito was heavyset, wearing gold chains around his neck, and sporting a thick mustache. In the weeks that followed, Franzone met Eppolito a few more times with Santora. The cousins were close, although one was a cop and the other was a "salesman" who didn't appear to have to work for a living. Eppolito rented one of Franzone's parking sheds. Business arrangements were informal for Franzone, a simple man unable to cope with the routines of written contracts, record keeping, legal documentation. His wife kept the books. Eppolito took space number ten. He told Franzone not to enter his name in any records. Eppolito paid $50 a month in rent, a lower price than paid by the general public. The detective parked a maroon Chrysler four-door in the garage;

it looked like an old highway patrol car that had been repainted. Whenever he encountered Eppolito, Franzone testified, he only spoke in monosyllabic "yes" and "no" despite Eppolito's compulsion to be familiar and talkative.

Franzone had been summoned to court to testify about a particular day in the mid-eighties. He told the court he couldn't recall the date precisely. It was winter, he testified, toward the end of 1985, or perhaps early in 1986. In the late afternoon, when it was still light outside, Franzone saw Detective Eppolito pull into the lot in the maroon Dodge or Chrysler and drive to the rear of the lot. Eppolito backed up so that his car was aimed toward the parking shed he rented. A few moments later, Franzone caught sight of a shadow moving out of the corner of his eye. The windows in the shed allowed him to keep track of movements everywhere in his domain—from Nostrand Avenue, or the back by the railroad tracks. Franzone turned and saw Santora approaching with two men. One of the men was thin and wearing a trench coat with his collar up. Franzone got a good look at the man. He was white with dark hair, a mustache, and his face was pocked with small pits. Between Santora and the other man there was a third man. The man in the middle was wearing a skullcap, or yarmulke. He was dressed in a blue pinstripe suit. The threesome walked in lockstep, shoulder to shoulder, giving the man in the middle no chance of escape.

Before the judge and jury, Henoch now measured the distance Franzone had stood from the men using a tape measure. He was about fifteen feet away, with a clear view of the men for approximately twenty seconds. Franzone testified that Santora undid the lock on Eppolito's parking shed and opened the door and the three men stepped inside. Santora closed the door behind them. Twenty minutes or half an hour passed, Franzone said. When the door opened only two men emerged. Santora closed the door and he and the thin man in the trench coat walked by Franzone again—and again he got a direct look at his face, despite his raised collar and bent head. The man in the yarmulke didn't emerge. Five seconds later Eppolito, who had been parked opposite his parking shed throughout this time, drove past Franzone and pulled onto Nostrand Avenue.

After a few minutes, Frank Santora Jr. returned in his white Cadillac. Santora told Franzone he wanted to show him something. Franzone followed Santora to Eppolito's parking garage. It was still daylight outside. Santora opened the door. Franzone's eyes adjusted to the darkness inside. He made out the shape of a man lying on the floor. Santora turned on the light. Franzone was staring at the body of the man wearing the yarmulke.

"You got to help me bury the body," Santora said. "You're an accessory."

Franzone stared at the dead man. He knew nothing about him: no name, background, why he had been murdered. Franzone did know that Louie Eppolito was a detective in the Six-Three. Eppolito had stood lookout during the murder. Franzone had no idea who the third man was, but he knew Santora and had just seen what he was capable of doing. Santora was a murderer with an NYPD detective as accomplice and protection. Franzone knew he was in deep trouble, and believed he had nowhere to turn.

"If you tell anybody," Santora said, "I'll kill you and your fucking family."

Franzone testified that Santora told Franzone to wait. Santora opened and then closed the garage door, leaving Franzone with the body. Santora returned with two shovels, two bags of cement, and jugs of white lime powder. Franzone started digging. There was a thin layer of cement but it had been broken by the weight of cars resting on it. The earth underneath was loose and sandy. Franzone dug and dug. Santora was talking to him but Franzone didn't listen. All Franzone could think about was the trouble he was in. He was convinced no one would believe him if he said a police officer had been involved in the murder. As he reached a depth of five feet, Franzone stopped. He thought Santora was going to shoot him and leave him in the hole along with the other man.

"I was too scared to go to the police," Franzone told the jury. "Who would believe me? They would probably call Louis Eppolito and say you've got a guy here saying you killed someone. They would get me and kill me, or lock me up and get someone in jail to kill me. I was scared for my wife and children. I didn't tell anyone—not my wife, not no one."

Oldham said, "Once he had been compromised by Santora, Caracappa, and Eppolito, Franzone was at their mercy. For years Louie Eppolito hid his police-style sedan in the shed he rented from Franzone. There is no way to know for sure but there's good reason to ask whether he was parking on top of Israel Greenwald's remains."

Franzone next saw the thin man who had been with Santora that day at a Sweet Sixteen party for Santora's daughter Tammy. Detective Eppolito came to Franzone's table and said hello. Franzone introduced his wife. The mousy garage owner was terrified of the outsized cop. The entire scene terrified him—Santora, Eppolito, the thin man in the trench coat from "that day" who was standing behind Eppolito at the party. They had killed and gotten away with it. Franzone reasoned they could easily do the same to him. He had not wanted to attend the Sweet Sixteen party, he testified, but he was afraid failure to come would offend Santora. Franzone thought it might signal he was not reliable—they might think Franzone was talking to the cops.

On the night of February 13, 1987, one year after Israel Greenwald had been killed, Franzone was working in the dispatch shed when the telephone rang. It was Frank Santora Jr. calling. Franzone knew that Santora was in the collision shop only a few yards away. Franzone had let Eppolito and Santora into the shop. Another car, a brown Cadillac with two passengers, had backed into the shop. Franzone saw two more people arrive. He stayed in the shed, as far from Eppolito and Santora as possible. The week before, Franzone's wife had given birth to a son. As a gesture of celebration, Santora had presented the couple with a garbage bag filled with baby clothes. Franzone threw the infant outfits away. He didn't want his son wearing anything that had come from Santora. On the phone, Santora wanted to know how to turn the heat down in the shop. The area was extremely hot. Franzone told him to turn the toggle on the pipes but Santora couldn't find the right switch. Franzone made the short walk to the collision shop.

Walking in, Franzone saw two men wrapping a dead man in a brown canvas tarp. The tarp was tied with rope, trussed like a slab of roast beef. "Oh, my God," Franzone said, terrified again. Franzone was told to help the two men lift the body into the trunk of the brown Cadillac.

Franzone had no idea who the men were, and he never saw them again. The dead man was a wiseguy named Pasquale Varialle. His body was found at five in the morning on St. Valentine's Day in front of a church by patrol officer Sylvia Cantwell. Varialle's hands were tied behind his back, as Greenwald's had been. The body was on the sidewalk, with snow drifting over the tarp in front of a Catholic church located in the heart of the Six-Three—the stomping grounds of Detective Eppolito.

Franzone said that Santora and Eppolito continued to frequent the garage until Santora was gunned down. Santora's wife called Franzone's wife to tell her that Frankie had been killed. Peter Franzone remembered being happy and relieved. But he was still worried about Eppolito. Franzone testified that he went to Santora's wake. "I wanted to let them know I wasn't going to tell nobody," he said.

There was a hush in the court as Judge Weinstein took a break in the proceedings. During the trial there had been many moments when the case against Caracappa and Eppolito appeared devastating. Franzone's testimony was yet another. But it had a different sense, qualitatively and quantitatively. There was no conceivable way Franzone had concocted the story to frame the two cops. The body of Israel Greenwald, compounded by the testimony of Burton Kaplan regarding the murder of the jeweler, was powerful corroboration. Franzone was simple-minded, nearly childish in his guilelessness. A year after Santora had died, Franzone sold the business and took a job as a maintenance man for a city-owned building. He had lived quietly until March 2005, when he saw the newspaper reports detailing the arrests of Caracappa and Eppolito. After agreeing to talk with prosecutors, he and his wife had quit their jobs and gone into hiding. He had forfeited his benefits and pension with the city, the main reason he had taken the job seventeen years earlier. He was still out of work.

The cross-examination by Eddie Hayes concentrated on the cut of the trench coat worn by the third man—his client, Caracappa. Was it single-breasted or double-breasted, with large or small lapels? Hayes questioned Franzone about the skin blemishes the third man had—inviting the jury to look at Caracappa and see that he had no pockmarks. He questioned the distances from which Franzone had seen the third man, implying his testimony was dubious.

Hayes, an avid gardener, attempted to show that Franzone could not have dug the hole with the spade because of the length of the handle but the demonstration was unconvincing. In the hallway on the fourth floor during a recess, Hayes insisted to reporters that there was no way Franzone could have pierced the hard cold earth with a small handheld spade in the dead of winter. The cold froze the ground, Hayes said, making it extremely difficult to dig a few inches let alone the five feet Franzone claimed to have reached that night.

But when Dr. Bradley Adams was called to testify about the uncovering of Greenwald's body, he flatly contradicted Hayes's theory. The earth is only frozen for the first few inches, Adams averred. On the stand, Franzone confirmed that the earth was loose and he had not found it particularly difficult work to dig the hole—not with Santora supervising.

Cutler followed Hayes in his cross-examination. He started his questioning at full force, standing at the lectern and shouting at Franzone. "Maybe you were more involved in the murder than just digging the grave?"

"No," Franzone said quietly.

"We rely upon you," Cutler said, with evident distaste. "Did it bother you?"

"Of course it bothered me," Franzone said. "I was too scared to do anything about it."

Cutler displayed the photograph of Franzone at Tammy Ahmed's Sweet Sixteen party on the overhead projector. A slight smile creased Franzone's face as he sat with the other guests.

"You don't look afraid to me," Cutler said, pacing back and forth across the courtroom, his outrage gathering. He asked, "Did you call your wife and say, 'Dear, I'm going to be late for dinner, I'm burying a body'?" Cutler slammed his hand on the lectern and shouted, at the top of his lungs, "Burying a body is the most despicable, most loathsome thing a man can do."

The next witness rolled into court in a wheelchair. Joseph Pagnatta was elderly, frail, fraught as he looked around the packed court. Pagnatta worked as a parking lot attendant. He testified that he had been employed by Triple P Parking at 2232 Nostrand Avenue since the mid-eighties. He had worked for Franzone as a tow truck dispatcher as well. Pagnatta had not seen or spoken to Franzone since 1991. Pagnatta now told the jury he had been introduced to Eppolito by Franzone in the late eighties. "Louie" was how Franzone referred to Eppolito. Pagnatta said he had once washed Eppolito's car and the detective gave him a $20 tip, at the time a memorably large amount of money, the kind of money palmed out by mob high-rollers. The car Eppolito parked at the lot looked like an unmarked police car.

THE EMBEZZLER'S TALE

Steven Corso, the crooked accountant who had worked for the FBI in Las Vegas, arrived in court dressed in a blue suit and silk tie, his face tanned and ruddy. According to the terms of the cooperation agreement Corso had entered into with the federal government, he said he was required to testify truthfully. He told the tale of his downfall, from the theft of his clients' money in New York to falsely filing income tax returns for strippers at the Crazy Horse Too nightclub in Las Vegas. Corso testified that he had pled guilty to wire fraud and attempted income tax evasion, and had been sentenced to five years for each count, but had not been incarcerated, pending his continued cooperation.

Corso was a deeply unsympathetic figure—a dissipated fifty-year-old embezzler and heavy gambler who had cheated on his wife, lied to his clients, stolen millions of dollars, and single-handedly destroyed a thriving accounting firm. The dislike of him was palpable in the courtroom. His response was defiant indifference. Corso's reason for appearing in court was naked self-interest. He stared blankly at Eppolito and Caracappa as he recited the criminal conspiracies he had concocted to entice the two retired detectives—and that they had eagerly leapt at.

The story told by Corso on the stand was sordid, as was the storyteller. But Corso's tale didn't have to be taken on his word. He told the court that he had worn a secret listening device to record conversations with more than two hundred people. More than a thousand hours of conversations had been taped with various underworld figures in Las Vegas. The conversations with Caracappa and Eppolito were played on the court audio systems. The clink and chatter of busy restaurants were audible, but so were the voices of Corso, Eppolito, and Caracappa.

Corso had played the part of a dirty New York accountant fascinated by the mafia. The two retired NYPD cops appeared to him to be precisely what they were: men willing to do anything to make a buck. Caracappa and Eppolito, in turn, had tried to play Corso for a fool, thinking they could make major money—maybe millions—from a man willing to finance Eppolito's appalling scripts.

Walking to the Plaza Diner at lunch, Eppolito continued to talk to reporters. He said he was feeling confident. Bruce Cutler was a great attorney, Eppolito said. During the lunch break on Corso's second day of testimony, after Corso had described how he introduced the idea of drugs to their dealings in Las Vegas, Eppolito was stopped by a skinny man in the hallway on the fourth floor. The man said he was a friend of Eppolito's "from the neighborhood." The two men exchanged greetings and a grimace about the predicament Eppolito found himself in. The man said he had come to court to display his support. Eppolito thanked him, lamenting the testimony of Burt Kaplan and other organized crime figures who had become cooperators. "Nobody knows how to be a man no more," Eppolito said.

The cross-examination of Corso was commenced by Cutler with indignation. He pointed out that Corso had managed to transform the theft of more than $5 million into a sweetheart deal with the government. Corso was not in prison and no charges were outstanding against him. Cutler ran through the sums stolen from various clients.

"Honor," Cutler declaimed. He held one hand in the air as if communicating with a greater power about the disgrace presented by Corso. "You dishonored yourself and your profession and your country. You stole for the worst reasons. Indifference. Callousness. Greed."

"What I did was absolutely wrong," Corso said.

Despite such honesty, Corso remained glib, cocky, his tan somehow repugnant. "Sure," he replied to repeated questions about his various schemes and conspiracies. But that didn't mean he was lying. There was tape-recorded evidence of Eppolito agreeing to have his son procure the drugs. The jury listened to Eppolito's profanity-laced grandiosity. "Listening devices are a potent investigative tool," Oldham said. "If you captured a man saying something on tape, there is simply no way for him to deny it. From the tapes, Caracappa and Eppolito clearly had no idea in the world that Corso was conspiring with the FBI but they were biting hook, line, and sinker."

The next morning, Eddie Hayes again lobbied the press gallery. There were seven black jurors, Hayes said, and they had good reason to hate the FBI. He was going to run a "Washington defense," he said. The reporters assigned to cover the Eastern District every day, John Marzulli from the *Daily News* and Zach Haberman from the *New York Post,* rolled their eyes at Hayes's antics.

Cutler's continued cross-examination addressed the specifics of the moral outrages he had addressed the day before. Corso had failed to pay federal income tax even as he cooperated with the FBI from 2002 to 2004. Exhibits were entered into evidence: Corso's resignation as a CPA, lawsuits started by Corso's defrauded clients, correspondence showing that Corso had contested the underlying wrong in stealing from his clients as recently as August 2004. Cutler turned to the last recorded conversation between Corso and Eppolito. It was from March 3, 2005, about a week before Caracappa and Eppolito were arrested in front of Piero's. Corso was trying to draw Guido Bravatti further into his web of deceit. Suddenly supposedly indifferent to the money offered through Corso, Eppolito tried to extricate his son from the drug dealing conspiracy he had insinuated the young man into in the first place.

"I got a panic call from my son," Eppolito said to Corso. "Don't call him or Guido anymore. They don't exist."

"Why?" Corso asked Eppolito.

"I told him not to," said Eppolito.

Cutler stopped reading from the transcript. "I ask you, Mr. Corso, isn't it a fact that Lou was upset about you meeting with his son?"

But there was no way to contest the fact that Eppolito had sent his son to deal drugs.

To present the human side of Caracappa, and the inhumane side of

Corso, Eddie Hayes's junior counsel Rae Koshetz portrayed Corso as a man preying on an unsuspecting extended family. Koshetz suggested that Corso's expression of interest in Eppolito's youngest daughter was part of the deal. Corso begged to differ. "My impression was that if the deal went through, if the money came through, he would recommend me to his daughter."

Koshetz presented her client as an avuncular suburbanite entrapped by a conniving con man. Corso had only met Caracappa three times, she said, all of them only weeks before Caracappa was arrested. Corso agreed. Were the Hollywood stars coming to Las Vegas Corso's "concoction," she asked incredulously, contrived and executed by Corso without FBI connivance? The insinuation was that such a scenario was not only improbable but unbelievable. Corso testified that he alone had come up with the idea. Nothing Koshetz asked was directly exculpatory, or answered the taped evidence. Had the entire "designer drug" gambit been invented by Corso, she wanted to know. Corso blandly stated that it was.

"A motivated cooperator can be a very effective undercover," Oldham knew from many years' experience. "When I worked Born to Kill in the early nineties in the Major Case Squad, Tinh was full of ideas how to get Cow Pussy and the others. Once a cooperator gets inside the skin of a conspiracy—inside 'the closeness,' as Caracappa called it—he starts to sense the predilections and the possibilities. How far would Eppolito go? Would Caracappa get the jitters? As much as the FBI monitored their dealings, only Corso could see the faces and draw the inferences. Corso was highly motivated. Corso had presented Caracappa and Eppolito with choices. Scrub away all the psychobabble and conjecture about what lies in the heart of man, and what you are left with is the human truth that life is about making choices. Crime is about making choices. Sitting at dinner with Caracappa and Eppolito, Corso was adding items to the menu. They were the ones who ordered."

When Corso told Caracappa he had contacts who would be interested in having armed protection while in Las Vegas, Koshetz said, wasn't it true that Caracappa refused to take up the business. "I'm not licensed," Caracappa said to Corso. "I don't have insurance." Corso protested that Caracappa suggested at least two illegal protection opportunities. Invisibly, incrementally, Koshetz was flirting with catastrophe.

On redirect, Henoch went directly for the jugular. In attempting to portray Caracappa as an upstanding and outstanding police officer and man, Koshetz had raised the question of his character. Henoch now questioned Corso about government allegations that Caracappa had made references to Corso about using drugs as an undercover narcotics agent in New York.

Before Corso could answer, Hayes leapt to his feet. "The question is only related to this drug deal," he said plaintively.

Henoch replied that Rae Koshetz had "opened the door" to character evidence. If the defense wished to elicit testimony that Caracappa did not use drugs, Henoch argued, it was only fair that the government have the opportunity to try to show that the opposite was the case. The jury was instructed to ignore the exchange, but they had heard every word.

GASPIPE'S LAST GASP

For years, Anthony Casso had been imprisoned in Supermax in Florence, Colorado, one hundred miles south of Denver. Constructed in the mid-nineties in response to the murder of two prison guards in Marion, Illinois, the thirty-seven-acre Supermax complex was built into the side of a mountain. The facility was a study in extreme punitive incarceration. Prisoners were housed in small soundproof cells with a concrete desk, bed, and stool. The thirteen-inch black-and-white television only played religious and anger-management programming. Prisoners were locked down twenty-three hours a day. Visitors, if permitted, had to come to the inmate's cell, denying even the slight satisfaction of a change in physical surroundings. Meals arrived through a slot in each cell door. The only rays of natural light to reach the inmates came in a tiny exercise area known as "the dog run." Casso's fellow inmates constituted a who's who of dangerous criminals, including the Unabomber, Theodore Kaczynski; Terry Nichols from the Oklahoma City bombing; and Ramzi Ahmed Yousef, leader of the 1993 attack on the World Trade Center. Surrounded by twelve-foot-high razor wire and monitored by countless motion detectors, pressure pads, and attack dogs, no one has ever escaped from Supermax. Remaining sane presents the primary challenge in an environment designed to grind down even the most determined prisoner.

In July 2005, a couple of months after the arrest of Caracappa and Eppolito in Las Vegas, a letter addressed to the United States Attorney for the Eastern District, Roslynn Mauskopf, had arrived in the mail. The two-page letter handwritten in a tidy script was from Gaspipe Casso. Stuck in Supermax, Casso was hoping to ingratiate himself with prosecutors and perhaps find a way to insert himself in the process of preparing for the trial of Stephen Caracappa and Louis Eppolito. If Casso were used by prosecutors, there was the chance he could strike a deal and receive a reduction in sentence, or at least an easing of the wretched isolation of solitary confinement in Supermax.

"I have nothing but the deepest respect for the work you are doing," Casso wrote. The letter recited his grievances against the government. But in the light of the coming trial of Caracappa and Eppolito, Casso had a proposal. "One would think at this critical point a truce would be declared for us to unite," Casso wrote. "If it's all for justice."

The Eastern District never replied to his letter.

By March 2006, as his chance to inject himself into the trial evaporated, Casso had changed his mind. The defense had been asked repeatedly if they were going to call Casso as a witness, even as the rumor had circulated in the courthouse that Casso had recanted his accusations against the "crystal ball." In the middle of the final week of the trial Casso dropped a bomb on the proceedings. A letter addressed to Assistant U.S. Attorney Mark Feldman arrived, headed "Sworn Statement," and dated March 4, 2006. The author of the letter was Gaspipe Casso.

"I, Anthony Casso, hereby confess to have personally participated as part of a three man team that shot and killed Eddie Lino in Brooklyn's Gravesend section. Detectives Eppolito and Caracappa are falsely being accused of this crime."

The letter continued to state that Detectives Caracappa and Eppolito had never supplied confidential information to the Lucheses, or participated in the abduction of Jimmy Hydell. Written from the confines of Supermax, it represented a desperate last gasp. Casso wanted to appear useful to either the defense or prosecution—to someone, anyone.

"Although, I do concede, that the Luchese family, has for decades, received confidential information, from other law enforcement officials, and New York, Federal Bureau of Investigation agents, as well. This fact, should be documented, with the Justice Department, during my three and a half years of phenomenal, substantial assistance."

The defense submitted a motion for mistrial. To date, the trial had not gone well for the two former NYPD detectives. Any change in momentum, no matter how improbable, was preferable to watching prosecutors continue to build peaks on mountains of evidence already accumulated.

In order for the defense to determine if calling Casso was advisable, even at such a late hour, a telephone conference with Casso was arranged for lunch the following day, to be made from a conference room in the U.S. attorney's offices in Pierrepont Plaza. As lead counsel, Cutler and

Hayes did not participate in the call. The two defense lawyers went to the Plaza Diner with a reporter from the *New Yorker* working on an article about the trial. There was little chance Casso would say anything of exculpatory value, Cutler and Hayes believed. Casso had suggested he would reveal the whereabouts of Jimmy Hydell's body in return for leniency—a suggestion that repulsed Bruce Cutler. The two men sent their co-counsel, Rae Koshetz and Bettina Schein. Told that prosecutors were listening to the call, Casso asked for them to be excluded from the conversation. Prosecutors Feldman and Henoch left the room. Casso asked if the defense attorneys had been shown the letter he sent the government. They said they had.

"The prosecution is about to rest and the case will sum up on Monday," Schein said. "So the timing is propitious."

Casso said he had tried to contact Eddie Hayes a number of times before the trial began. He wrote to the government only after Hayes failed to respond to Casso's calls. Casso explained that he had been following the case through the news media. From the press, he had learned that Al D'Arco and Burt Kaplan had testified.

"I can't see how either attorney could honestly and wholeheartedly cross-examine them people without speaking to me first and learning the truth."

Casso did not dispute the general allegations against Caracappa and Eppolito. The role of the "crystal ball" in multiple murder counts went uncontradicted. He only took issue with two specific counts in the indictment.

"I would have given the defense lawyers the right questions to ask D'Arco on the stand," Casso said. "I proved to the government D'Arco is a liar over and over again. This is why I got the life sentence, not because I did something in the unit in Otisville or whatever the government claims were the reasons. This is why they kept me here and they keep the media away from me—they keep everybody away from me. They don't allow nobody to see me."

Gaspipe Casso recounted a convoluted tale in which he purported to implicate not just Caracappa and Eppolito but also FBI agents and a third detective.

"There was a newspaper article that came out in the *Post* that claimed the information came from these two detectives," Schein said, referring to Eppolito and Caracappa.

"I didn't know where they got Eppolito's name and the other guy's name back in '94," Casso said. "But I found out where they got the names from when I was in Otisville. It was another government witness in Otisville. He is the one that brought up their names whenever the hell he got arrested."

"Who is that?" Koshetz asked.

"Fat Sal Miciotta," Casso said. "When I met him in Otisville he started explaining to me how the agents had him trying to go after cops. They wired him up to get cops. This is how he was giving them names. But he was lying to them. He was lying to the feds. Wherever he got their names I don't know, but I heard he implicated not only them but other detectives too."

Reached at an undisclosed location, in a suburb of the city where he works in sales and service, Miciotta said he wasn't surprised that Casso would attempt to put him in the middle of the case. "How could I possibly concoct a story like that? What was in it for me? What ax did I have to grind? Was I in the Luchese family? I met Eppolito once, in Six-Two Precinct on Bath Avenue after I killed Larry Champagne Carrozza. Eppolito let me off on a murder. Eppolito was a guy who could be had. But that was all I knew about this.

"If you ask me, the government was never going to let Casso out. The prosecutors knew he was a serial killer, not a gangster. Casso thought he had the system played. He's a great manipulator. He was that way all of his life. He thought he was going to testify against Chin Gigante, do five years, and then go somewhere and set up shop again. He was recruiting guys to meet him when he got out. He was going to start his own little crime family someplace. Some unsuspecting town somewhere would become the marijuana and cocaine capital of the country.

"You spend time, enough time, in isolation like Supermax—and I did five years of solitary after my dispute with Casso—it changes who you are. Sitting in a cell by yourself is very lonely. Solitary has a huge psychological effect. You're in total despair 24/7. It's very depressing. It runs down your immune system. You start to suffer from physical illnesses. You feel claustrophobic. I've been out six years and I can still feel the effects. I take medication for anxiety. To have a guard come by and ask how you're doing was the highlight of the day—to hear a human voice. There is a little flap on the door where they shove your tray of food through. They lock that, too. You don't control the lights. Half the time the sink didn't work, or the toilet was backed up. I wished for death all the time. I was suicidal but I had no way of doing it. Holding anyone like that, under those conditions, is inhumane. Even Casso. It leaves a man demented. Casso can't tell the difference between reality and the fantasy he lives in."

During the telephone conference call between Brooklyn and Supermax in Colorado, the subject of Miciotta was dropped without comment by Schein and Koshetz. They turned to the matter of Casso's relationship with Burt Kaplan. "I can tell you everything about Burton Kaplan," Casso said. "Burton Kaplan is saying on the stand what I want him to say on the stand. I was supposed to be part of this. Right after I got sentenced, I did an interview with *60 Minutes.* I did the interview to make amends with the government, to show them I was on their side. I would testify against the cops."

Casso said he and Kaplan had dreamt up the entire story about Cara-cappa and Eppolito. They used their wives to carry messages providing details about the scheme. Casso's wife had a phobia about prisons but Casso ordered her to visit Kaplan and convince him to become a cooper-ator and frame two randomly selected NYPD officers. "When Kaplan flipped months later, after my wife seen him, he brought this story to the agents and they were tickled pink. Now they turn around, the agents, and they brought forward two guys in the 'witsec' unit who told Kaplan I went and hired these two guys to kill him. They put it in Kaplan's head that I had tried to kill him to get Kaplan to go against me. Now he wanted to go alone because they put the idea in his head. Jerry Capeci who writes that column put two names of guys who said I was going to kill Kaplan in one of his articles. I wrote to him that I was never looking to hurt Kaplan. This way they got Kaplan on their side one hundred per-cent and they can still take out their revenge against me and keep me in here. That's how it worked out."

"Would you testify to this if we called you as a witness?" Schein asked.

"Without a doubt," Casso said. "The government told my lawyer you don't want me as a witness because I'm accused of thirty-six murders. That is a farce, too. That is a number they made up."

"We have to get back to court now but certainly this information has been—" Ms. Schein paused. "We appreciate you taking the time to call."

"I wish youse luck," Casso said.

Eppolito spoke for the first time. "Anthony, this is Lou Eppolito. Thank you very much."

The mistrial motion was denied. Calling Casso to testify for the defense had been an option open to Cutler and Hayes since the outset, Weinstein ruled. Casso's attempted intervention would not be allowed to throw the proceedings into disarray. The only conceivable benefit Casso could hope to receive for testifying would come from the government. Putting him on the stand offered the real possibility that he would contradict himself, yet again, and testify in detail about his dealings with the "crystal ball." The gamble had been too great for the government for more than a decade. Casso was too risky for the defense now. Calling an admitted "homicidal maniac" as witness for two self-styled distinguished and utterly innocent retired NYPD detectives was unlikely to prove exculpatory in the eyes of twelve citizens from the tough-minded streets of New York.

THE DEFENSE

In RICO cases often little if any defense is presented. It is common that no witnesses are called by the accused or exhibits entered into evidence. The defense consists of casting doubt on the prosecution. But in the lead-up to the trial the members of the defense team had said they would put on evidence to show that the government's accusations were nothing more than a product of lies invented by gangsters like Kaplan and Casso. For weeks Judge Weinstein had repeatedly asked the defense for a list of the witnesses they intended to call. No list had been furnished by Hayes or Cutler. On *60 Minutes* before the trial Caracappa had claimed the defense would provide evidence that exonerated the two men. Caracappa said they would prove to the jury and the world that they could not have committed the crimes. Caracappa had spent months in Hayes's office meticulously going through dozens of boxes provided by the government as part of the discovery process. The defense was entitled to see every document produced or found during the course of the investigation, including any information that was exculpatory or contradictory. Eppolito had attended the research sessions on occasion but characteristically Caracappa had been the man in control of these activities.

The defense, it turned out, was practically nonexistent. Detective Les Shanahan had been Caracappa's partner in the OCHU. They were friends. Shanahan, like the few other former NYPD detectives who came to court each day and sat in the row behind Caracappa, had remained loyal to his old partner. "It was his nature," Oldham said. "Les was a great guy. I loved Les."

Called by Eddie Hayes, Detective Shanahan testified he had been working with Caracappa the night before Eddie Lino was murdered. He said that the two Major Case detectives had been assigned to act as a security detail for a radical Jewish leader named Meir Kahane, who was shot to death while speaking before the founding conference of a Zionist organization at a midtown hotel. He was pronounced dead at Bellevue

Hospital on Manhattan's East Side, just above 26th Street. Caracappa and Shanahan wound up working his murder and pulled an all-nighter (as did Oldham, too, while working the same case). They had worked thirty-six hours straight. Both were exhausted. Like most NYPD cops, Shanahan lived in the suburbs. After they signed off duty that morning, he had to drive home. Detective Caracappa lived on East 22nd Street, a five-minute walk from the hospital. Or perhaps Shanahan had dropped him off; Caracappa didn't like driving and rarely drove himself. Hayes's line of questioning was meant to create an alibi for Caracappa. But Eddie Lino was not killed until that evening.

"Alibi evidence that left a seven-and-a-half-hour gap opportunity was no alibi evidence at all," Oldham said. "When Henoch asked Shanahan how long it would take to drive from Manhattan to the Belt Parkway, he didn't want to answer. Les said he didn't know if the ten miles or so could be driven in seven and a half hours. He didn't want to say that there was simply no way he could testify that Caracappa didn't have ample opportunity to have killed Eddie Lino. Caracappa could go home, have a five-hour nap, get up, shower, shave, meet up with Eppolito, and make it to Brooklyn in plenty of time. Les Shanahan standing up for his old friend in his hour of need was admirable, in many ways, but Shanahan wasn't going to lie for Caracappa."

"The defense of Stephen Caracappa rests," Eddie Hayes said.

Bruce Cutler rose somberly on behalf of Eppolito. A few days earlier, Eppolito had arrived in court carrying a battered moving box. Inside the box were plaques and ribbons and medals Eppolito had accumulated during his time on the NYPD. The box contained the sum of Eppolito's career on the force, and had formed the basis of his public persona. But to enter the awards into evidence would amount to leading character evidence and "open the door" to the prosecution putting in evidence about the ways that Eppolito had actually performed as a law officer. In a hearing without the jury present, Judge Weinstein had gone through the contents of the box deciding what would be admissible. Only a few of the medals and honors were permitted. The question of *Mafia Cop* had arisen. Cutler wanted the jury to see the entire dust jacket, with words on the back and on the inside flaps praising Eppolito as a heroic detective. Weinstein would not allow the ploy. If Eppolito wished the jury to see as evidence his book *Mafia Cop,* only the front of the dust jacket would be allowed. Thus the cover was snipped with a pair of scissors. The book that promised to be Eppolito's undoing was finally presented but the jury would only have the cover of the book to judge.

Cutler read out Eppolito's various awards to the jury. It took less than fifteen minutes. He called no witnesses. He ended by reading aloud the title of Eppolito's book. "*Mafia Cop: The Story of an Honest Cop Whose Family Was the Mob*," he said. "The defense rests."

THE JURY GETS THE CASE

A defense motion to dismiss the charges on the basis that the RICO counts were barred by the statute of limitations was turned down summarily by Judge Weinstein. "Denied in whole, as to all counts, as to both defendants," Weinstein said. There was a further motion to dismiss based on the late intervention of Anthony Casso and the defense's inability to call him as a witness because notice had been so short and so close to the end of the trial. Eddie Hayes was absent for the hearing, having traveled to California on another matter, a move that visibly annoyed Judge Weinstein. Weinstein asked Caracappa if he had consented to his attorney's absence, and if he accepted the attenuated representation Hayes's travel created. Caracappa nodded and said he had no problem with Hayes being away at that critical moment. Talking on the phone from his room in the Hotel Bel-Air, a five-star luxury boutique hotel in Los Angeles, Hayes argued that he would have conducted the defense differently had he known of Casso's letters to the prosecution. Hayes said he wanted to talk to Casso before deciding whether to call him as a witness.

"I'm not going to give Casso a trip to New York City unless you're going to call him," Weinstein said. Weinstein explained the perils of calling Casso to Caracappa, in order to forestall a later claim by Caracappa that he didn't understand the risks. Casso might change his mind on the stand and try to curry favor with the prosecution, Weinstein said. The only benefit Casso could receive would be from the government, Weinstein said. Arrangements were made for Hayes to have a telephone conference with Casso. On the following Monday, Hayes informed the court the defense would not call Casso as a witness. The letters Casso had written were not admissible, the judge ruled, because they were rank hearsay. The second motion to dismiss was denied. The case would go to the jury.

Summations were spread over two days. The prosecution went first. The third member of Henoch's team, Daniel Wenner, spoke for the government. His presentation was dull but comprehensive as he went over the legal aspects of the case the jury needed to consider. The statute of limitations had been satisfied, he said, by the ongoing pattern of racketeering acts of Caracappa and Eppolito. The defendants had not withdrawn from the conspiracy, by renouncing their involvement or ceasing to associate with their co-conspirators, but had continued it by trying to conceal the conspiracy. Wenner went through the different counts in detail. He pointed out that Caracappa had taken a day off on the date Israel Greenwald disappeared in 1986, explaining that Caracappa was a newlywed and it was just before Valentine's Day so the money would have come in handy. As Wenner marched through the facts, Eppolito gave his head tiny shakes in disagreement, while Caracappa continued to stare stolidly ahead. Hayes rested his head on the defense table, while Cutler had his face buried in his hands.

Speaking for Caracappa, Hayes began, eyes afire with passion. "What evil fate put this man in this chair?" he asked the jury, gesturing toward his client. "It was evil that put him in that chair. Not good. Evil." Hayes appeared to be on the verge of tears. He said Caracappa had led a good life. He had no vices, no infidelities. He had no motive to become a criminal. "Steve Caracappa risked his life one hundred thousand times for you," he told the jury. The entire prosecution was a Washington, D.C.–inspired plot to frame two NYPD detectives. "In all of history, this case had the best investigators working on it," Hayes claimed. "How many times have we seen things happen behind the scenes in Washington, D.C., that put good men and good women at risk?"

Peppering the jury with questions and assertions, Hayes said Burton Kaplan had lied about the ownership of the house Casso's family lived in in Mill Basin in order to collect the $900,000 the property was worth. Kaplan dealt in blood diamonds from a poor African country, "holding the people in poverty and despair." Hayes pointed to Kaplan's attempt to deal heroin, the "smelly" nature of the relationship between Kaplan and Judd Burstein, and the improbability of a detective of Caracappa's pedigree making a mistake as elementary as searching for the wrong Nicky Guido. "We know that Stephen Caracappa is a good person, an exceptional person, an exemplary person."

Nearly a month into the trial, April's warm weather had arrived in New York City. Bruce Cutler wore a blue suit with a powder blue pocket puff and expensive loafers as he stood to address the jury. Manila folders were neatly lined up on the table. Cutler was in a state of deep concentration as he began. "My mentors—the people that Judd Burstein walked away from—considered court a temple of justice," he said. Cutler read the jury different definitions of *justice.* He then defined *spring* as a season of hope. He defined *hope* as "the desire or search for a future good." Cutler continued, "I have a hope in this case that there will be a day—a turning point, if you will—when the likes of D'Arco, Casso, Kaplan, Corso, and Franzone will not be allowed into a court of law. Criminal lawyers will rise and be considered a kind of nobility because of their commitment to justice."

The timid grave digger of Israel Greenwald, Peter Franzone, in particular, had raised the ire of Cutler. He was a cretin, Cutler said, a lowlife and a liar. "I looked up the definition of *Franzone* in the dictionary, where I start all my work," Cutler said. "I didn't look up his name but I looked up *gnome.* G-N-O-M-E." Franzone was "one of a race of dwarflike creatures who live underground and guard treasure hoards." Real detectives would have charged Franzone with murder, Cutler said, not given him a pass so he could flash his "pearly whites" on the witness stand. "The whole portrayal was a fake, a canard." Franzone had no reason to be afraid of Eppolito. Cutler said that Eppolito's photographs were on the walls of Chinese and Italian restaurants in the Six-Three. "Everyone knew Lou because of his service and his efforts," Cutler said, explaining why Franzone would single out his client. All the cooperators in the case were inherently evil, bereft of life, villains. "They're not reliable," Cutler said. "They're not dependable. They're only out for themselves. Even their lies are not honest."

Fond of asides, Cutler told the jury that he had lost fourteen and a half pounds during the trial, lying awake at night thinking about the case. He said his father had once taken him to the film *Bridge on the River Kwai,* a World War II prisoner-of-war classic set in Burma. The bridge in the movie, Cutler told the jurors, was built on a base of mud, not solid rock. "Burton Kaplan is the bridge in this case from Casso to us," he said. "If you build a bridge on mud, the first train that comes along will bring the bridge down."

Before and during the trial, the question of how to deal with the relationship between Kaplan and Caracappa and Eppolito had haunted the defense. How to explain NYPD detectives dealing with a known OC figure like Kaplan? Once it was admitted that the two defendants were friendly with him, it became difficult to deflect the criminal aspects of their interactions. Henoch had made it impossible, as he had hoped, for Eppolito to deny outright any knowledge of Kaplan. Caracappa could maintain that façade, and Hayes had ignored the matter during his summation. The proof of the financial transactions in Las Vegas compelled Eppolito and Cutler to concede the point and give the jury some explanation. First, Cutler allowed that Kaplan had lent Eppolito money. Cutler said Kaplan lived a double, triple, or quadruple life. "Burt Kaplan had a veneer of legitimacy. Policemen got friendly with him. Lou didn't see the other side. Lou didn't know the other side. The money Kaplan gave to Lou wasn't stamped as marijuana money. The money was given to Lou in appreciation for who Lou Eppolito is. Kaplan extended money for a time-share and a house in Nevada."

Cutler turned to the testimony given by Steven Corso. "He sauntered into court in a fancy suit with a tan and looking like he didn't have a care in the world," Cutler said. "He didn't misappropriate funds. He stole money. He had a rapacious greed, a lack of honor, dignity, and care." The jury leaned back in their seats as Cutler implored them to aim for a larger sense of good in the "temple of justice." "The federal government sent Corso to casinos and strip clubs to meet fakes, phonies, and idiots, who tell him things like they're the boss of Las Vegas," Cutler said. "There is no boss of Las Vegas." The city was the world of grand illusion, Cutler said. Corso was "a coyote in Central Park eating the chicks. He was a thieving, low-living scurvy. Lou was no match." Eppolito had set himself up as a writer. He talked gangster to Corso as a form of writing, creating the illusion that he was a gangster who knew "Donut Joe" and "Pastrami Benny."

"Lou had no intent to violate any laws," Cutler said. "He had no intent to launder any money. Lou said to Corso, 'I'm not afraid to die.' And then came the final dagger. DEA agent Ken Luzak, at the arrest, said to Lou, 'It's been a long time coming.' Lou supposedly said, 'I know.'" Cutler paused before the jury box. He bent his head, choking back tears, and he began to speak in the first person as if he were Louis Eppolito talking directly to the twelve men and women who would decide his fate. "I know what the life of my father was like," Cutler-as-Eppolito sobbed. "I know what the life of my uncle was like. I know what my life was like. I know you've been after me. Come, and take me!" Cutler put his hands out, as if to be placed in handcuffs. Snapping out of his trance, Cutler returned to his own voice.

"He's in your hands," he said to the jury.

During an intermission, Jimmy Breslin admired Cutler's performance, even as he doubted its effectiveness. "I've seen it before," Breslin said. "Bruce is good, God bless him. I've seen him defend John Gotti like he was Saint Peter."

Henoch had the final word. He clearly relished the opportunity. "If you're a cop you can't associate with known criminals," Henoch said. "You have to report it." Hayes and Cutler were two of the best-known defense attorneys in the country, he said, but they can't explain the truth that lies in the details of the case. "If you make a great speech, but you don't talk about details, something is wrong," Henoch said. He offered eleven examples of evidence that couldn't be refuted, from Kaplan's knowledge of Eppolito's huge knife collection in Las Vegas to Tommy Galpine's trip to the Caribbean coinciding with Eppolito's purchase of a time-share. Every time the investigation went deeper into the facts, more detailed corroboration emerged. Cross-examination had revealed nothing the jury didn't know. The mystery of the motive of Caracappa and Eppolito was simple, Henoch said. The pair made a total of $375,000 from Casso—"that we know of." They were bound together in their "closeness," or "this thing of ours." If Stephen Caracappa was an exceptional person, Henoch asked, then why was not a single character witness called by the defense? Hayes objected. Weinstein overruled him: summation was argument and lawyers had broad discretion to argue as they pleased. "Truth is not always pretty, but it's always perfect," Henoch told the jury. "The truth is perfect and it's beautiful."

There was no government conspiracy, Henoch said, or else why wouldn't Mitra Hormozi simply urge a witness to lie and fabricate? Franzone didn't come forward as part of a huge mob conspiracy. The government found him. As for the charge that the government was trolling for Eppolito and Caracappa in Las Vegas, the pair had found Corso, not the other way around. "What would a hero cop say when Steven Corso throws drugs out there?" Henoch asked the jury. "What would you say? These men jumped right into the drug deal and they aided and abetted it. They set it up. The government didn't go after Tony Eppolito. Caracappa and Eppolito insulated themselves. Eppolito got his son to get the drugs because he wouldn't touch them himself."

Henoch turned to the statute of limitations question. The legal question represented a danger for the prosecution, if the jury decided as a matter of fact that the crimes from the eighties and early nineties were too remote in time from the Las Vegas charges from 2004 and 2005. "We gave Caracappa and Eppolito an out," Henoch said. "They could have walked away from Corso. That would be evidence of withdrawal. But there is no evidence of withdrawal—not a smidgen. They said to Corso, 'We bring you into our family, our closeness, and we don't want to get hurt.'"

THE VERDICT

The jury retired to a small room in the back of Judge Weinstein's chambers on the fourth floor. On the first day, the jury asked for access to evidence. Speculation about the significance of this was rife in the hallway, where attorneys and reporters and family members of the victims and accused stood in small packs mostly observing a funereal silence. Eddie Hayes said he was optimistic, even though he said everyone else seemed to think "the cops" were going down hard and fast.

On the second day, the jury asked for further read-backs of evidence. Eppolito's daughter Deanna worried her rosary beads. Eddie Hayes was carrying a book titled *God in Search of Man* by Abraham Joshua Heschel, a history of Judaism he had borrowed from Henoch. Caracappa paged through the book and ate fruit-flavored LifeSavers.

On April 6, just after lunch, word spread that the jury had reached a verdict. The court was packed to overflowing as the twelve jurors entered, none of them meeting the gaze of Caracappa or Eppolito. It took nearly half an hour for the entirety of the charged crimes to be put to the jury and for the jury to give its verdict. On all counts, for both defendants, the result was the same. "Guilty," "guilty," "guilty," the word was repeated by the forewoman of the jury in a calm and even voice.

After the first "guilty," the U.S. marshals assigned to the court blocked the exits. At the end Caracappa and Eppolito both stood. The men took off their belts and ties and emptied their pockets on the defense table. Eyes welling with tears, Hayes embraced Caracappa, whose face was drained of color and whose hands were shaking. Eppolito turned forlornly to his family. The air of confusion he had the first day he was arraigned returned to his face, now accompanied by a look of real fear.

After the verdict, Eddie Hayes told reporters that Caracappa had told him everything would be all right. " 'You did the best you could,' he told me," Hayes said. "So that's it." Deanna Eppolito was defiant, declaring that her father was innocent. Lou Eppolito Jr. had appeared increasingly sad as the trial proceeded and the evidence continued to mount. "I will be there for my father," he told reporters. "I love him." Israel Greenwald's daughters, Yael and Michal, stopped in the corridor of the fourth floor outside the court to talk to reporters. "We are grateful that justice has been done," Michal said through tears. "This is closure for us."

When the verdict was announced, Oldham didn't feel triumphant. He'd put a lot of men away on life sentences and was all too aware that his life's work amounted to men waiting to die in prison. Now it appeared Eppolito and Caracappa would join them.

"I felt no victory, no gladness, no happiness. I like the hunt, but not the kill."

CHAPTER EIGHTEEN

THE RULE OF LAW

On June 5, 2006, the sentencing hearing for Caracappa and Eppolito was held in Judge Weinstein's court.* Before sentencing, relatives of their victims presented statements. Leah Greenwald went first. Israel Greenwald's wife described the devastation Caracappa and Eppolito had inflicted on their lives. "What happened to us was like a chain reaction," she said. "Husband and father missing, confusion and chaos, emotional stress, weakness, pain, nightmares, feelings of abandonment, loss of income, hard labor, loss of time, loss of joy, pain, pain, and pain." Her husband was only thirty-four when he vanished, she said, leaving his wife and their eight- and ten-year-old daughters with no explanation for his disappearance. Thrown into poverty, the Greenwalds had lived in a series of apartments in Brooklyn, one only two blocks away from Israel Greenwald's unmarked grave on Nostrand Avenue. "My daughters wanted to know why I wasn't doing more to find their beloved father," she said. Michal Greenwald, the elder daughter, now a beautiful young woman, recounted the deprivation of life without a father. "For thirty thousand dollars?" she asked Caracappa and Eppolito. "Is that what his life was worth?" The Greenwalds had been enveloped by pity and fear, she said. "You thought you could get away with it and you almost did. You made

---

*As Eppolito and Caracappa awaited their sentencing hearing, the very man who had triggered the chain of events that led to their murderous conspiracy with Luchese underboss Gaspipe Casso was himself arrested and charged with loan-sharking, extortion, and drug dealing. Twenty years earlier, Mickey Boy Paradiso had taken out a contract on Casso, hiring Jimmy Hydell and his incompetent crew for the hit—a failed gambit that provoked Casso's revenge and the killing spree that cascaded decades forward in time. Jerry Capeci's "Gangland" column of May 25, 2006, reported the indictment of Paradiso, the Gambino gangster who had once smacked John Gotti in the face during an argument and lived to tell the tale. "I'll kill him, I'll cut his fucking throat," Paradiso was caught saying on an FBI tape. "When I get mad I'm a different person. I don't rationalize."

sure this story would stay hidden and forgotten. And it was. But you underestimated the power of a child's innocent prayer."

The two former detectives looked directly and intently at Michal Greenwald, as if to drink in her sorrow and anger, not as a sign of remorse but as part of their continuing performance as honest officers of the law now wrongfully convicted. Caracappa appeared toughened by his time in prison, and remained silent. Eppolito had grown a goatee—facial hair Cutler had instructed him to shave off before trial.

The final gathering of the people whose lives had been caught in the destructive force of Caracappa and Eppolito was both melancholy and angry. The grief of the victims' families and the denials of Caracappa and Eppolito created palpable hostility in the courtroom. Danielle Lino, the twenty-eight-year-old daughter of Eddie Lino, dressed entirely in black. Betty Hydell, led through the back of the building to avoid the photographers in front of the courthouse, was wearing large black sunglasses to hide her eyes as she quietly wept. On the left side of the court, reserved for law enforcement, sat Joe Ponzi and Bobby Intartaglio. Oldham was in the public gallery, in the back row sitting by himself, eyes wet.

"When I came to the Major Case Squad I wanted to work for victims, not drug dealers ripped off by police impersonators," Oldham recalled. "I had no idea I would be chasing down cops preying on the people they were paid to protect. The families had a right to be angry—law enforcement betrayed them. The criminal justice system had been perverted. In the end, we got Caracappa and Eppolito, police impersonators who were true policemen. The system succeeded, despite itself."

The defense had submitted letters imploring the judge to overturn the jury's verdict, a prospect that seemed extremely unlikely. A Nevada couple, a doctor and nurse who were acquaintances of the Caracappas and Eppolitos in Las Vegas, wrote to Judge Weinstein to express shock and dismay. "Stephen was an extremely decent friend and neighbor and avid race-walker, bike racer, and sometimes weightlifter," the letter said. "Hardly a habitué of the Las Vegas nightlife, he was usually to be seen only when he was exercising or socializing in the small compound where we all lived." A letter from an NYPD officer was entered into the record registering his desire to see the conviction reversed. "I know firsthand the elements that are needed to be pieced together before taking a man's freedom," the officer wrote. "When I am interviewing an alleged victim I look for facts, I look for evidence, I look for witnesses."

Eppolito's younger daughter, Deanna, wrote to beg Weinstein to let her father return home. "My father is the most hardworking, dedicated man to his family and friends that God ever put on earth," she wrote. "Anyone who walks the beat in NYC knows the legend of Louis Eppolito—the cop and detective." Finally, predictably, the ever desperate Gaspipe Casso wrote in support of his former collaborators, declaring the verdict to be based on "misleading evidence" and "purely mistaken identities by government witnesses." Casso quickly turned to the true subject of his mercy plea: Gaspipe Casso. "Your Honor, I can assure you that I am in no way the monstrous person the government had their witnesses portray me to be."

Since the arrest, Oldham had speculated that Eppolito was likely to flip and turn on Caracappa. Cooperating would provide Eppolito no personal benefit. Confessing would mean he would spend the rest of his life in prison, disgraced as a policeman and as a man. He would no longer be his daughter's "hero." "But Eppolito might be able to save his son's life. Tony Eppolito was a young man with no criminal history. Judging from the evidence on the surveillance tapes in Las Vegas, the son's motivation in making the drug deal was to please his father. Like so many sons, the younger Eppolito had been caught up in the self-serving fantasies of his father. I figured Eppolito would spare his son the wages of his own sins. I know I would have. Tony Eppolito would soon face trial on federal charges of selling narcotics. His father was determined to clear his name, no matter how hopeless the cause or the price to be paid by his son."

EXIT BRUCE AND FAST EDDIE

Within weeks of his conviction, Eppolito fired Bruce Cutler and claimed his representation had been incompetent. The willingness to turn on others that had made Kaplan nervous about relying on Eppolito emerged as his plight became truly hopeless. To the surprise of many, Caracappa soon followed suit. Statements made during the trial about their enduring faith in the two famous defense attorneys now became accusation and character assassination. Claiming ineffective assistance of counsel was a common tactic for convicts who had run out of options—Kaplan himself had launched the same proceeding against Judd Burstein and others who defended him in the marijuana case.

Eppolito was now represented by an attorney named Joseph Bondy, whose specialty was getting lesser sentences for convicted defendants. Federal sentencing guidelines were voluminous, prescribing the mitigating and exacerbating factors to be considered by a judge when imposing punishment. Bondy marketed himself as an expert at constructing the life story of an accused in order to best impress the judge that the convict was the victim of a difficult childhood, mental illness, or substance addiction. Bondy called himself a "humanizer." The child of mild-mannered Bronx schoolteachers, Bondy had aspired to be a mob lawyer since early in life. For a time, he had even rented the same small corner office in a building on Broadway opposite City Hall that Bruce Cutler had once occupied. Bondy was still relatively unknown, and Eppolito was by far the highest-profile client he had ever taken on.

At the sentencing hearing, Bondy would not have the chance to tell the tale of a repentant Louis Eppolito, raised by an abusive and murderous father; Eppolito had displayed no regret for his crimes. The entire case, Eppolito maintained, was a concoction by Gaspipe Casso and Burton Kaplan. The crimes his client was convicted of couldn't be worse, Bondy admitted to Judge Weinstein. Bondy then said that Judge Weinstein himself had expressed skepticism about the strength of the government's case.

"Your Honor has pointed out that this was a thin case, with barely enough evidence to go to a jury," Bondy said.

Weinstein interrupted Bondy. "No," he said, curtly. "The only issue from the outset was with respect to the statute of limitations. There has been no doubt and there is no doubt that the murders and other crimes were proven beyond a reasonable doubt. That has never been an issue."

Bondy was taken aback. Confusion about the substance of the accusations and the legal questions about the statute of limitations had plagued the trial from the onset. Weinstein had finally clarified the matter from the bench. Guilt had been determined, decisively and overwhelmingly, leaving only the legal question of RICO statutory limitations.

"Does the defendant wish to make a statement?" the judge asked Eppolito.

"Yes, sir," Eppolito said.

The press was seated in the jury box. After trial, jury charge, and finally conviction, the only audience left for Eppolito to attempt to convince was the court of public opinion—and that meant the media. Sitting in the two rows of leather swivel seats used by the jury during the trial, reporters from the major dailies, news radio, and local television channels listened as Eppolito began his appeal. He spoke in the present tense, as if he were still a member of the NYPD.

"I have been a police officer for twenty two and a half years," Eppolito said. "I know the feelings that every single family had here today. I han-

dled as a detective many, many homicides and I know how they feel
from inside their guts. Sometimes I'm the one that goes to the house and
knocks on the door and tells them there has been a death in the family."
Eppolito paused. He looked around the court, arms outstretched plead-
ingly. "I don't know what I'm allowed to do or what I'm allowed to say.
Of course, it comes from my heart. I would invite the Greenwalds, the
Linos, the Hydells to come and visit me in jail, let me tell them the story.
I was not allowed to do that. I had no opportunity to do that."

"I don't want to hear that," Weinstein warned angrily.

"If I was afforded the opportunity to talk to these families, if it was
okay, if they wanted to sit with me and ask me and I could prove to them,
I think I would prove to them I didn't hurt anybody ever. My first seventeen years as a police officer I went to work with broken fingers, broken hands, stab wounds. I never missed a day's work. It is when I had my
first heart attack I couldn't work. After I had my heart attack I started
writing and I could find out I was able to write and tell a story."

In the gallery, a man rose. Barry Gibbs was wearing dark sunglasses, a
Hawaiian shirt, and a turquoise necklace.

"Remember me?" Gibbs shouted. "Remember, Mr. Eppolito?"

Eppolito and everyone in the court turned to Gibbs.

"Remove him," Weinstein ordered the marshals.

"You framed me!" Gibbs yelled. "Do you remember what you did to
me? Barry Gibbs! Do you remember? I had a family, too. You remember
what you did to my family? You don't remember what you did to my
family and to me? Remember what you did to me? Me! Do you remember?"

Gibbs was led out of the court by marshals. Eppolito addressed the
gallery, as if he was before a theatrical audience. "As far as Mr. Gibbs was
concerned, he also was afforded the same opportunity I was and he went
before a jury and he had a very good attorney who fought for him."

In *Mafia Cop*, Eppolito wrote of clandestine meetings with mobsters.
He wrote of socializing with organized crime figures, in deliberate and fla-
grant disregard of NYPD rules. For years he admired the values of
organized crime, praising the mafia on national television. In court he now
claimed such events had never occurred, and that he had never held such
views. Where was a photograph of Eppolito in a social club or bar? he
asked. Where were the phone taps? Explanations for Eppolito's conviction tumbled out. The entire case had been constructed on a false premise, he said, based on a frame concocted by Kaplan and Casso. Once
investigators had decided the guilt of Caracappa and Eppolito, facts had

been forced to fit the theory. "When they lock on to something, like I did as a detective, it stays there. Selectively they said what they want. It was selective and I'll prove it to the court on a later date," he claimed.

Eppolito continued, "I worked hard, I had three children, married to the same lady all these years. I never ever, ever did anything ever that I would have to embarrass my children. Yet in the last two years, when this all broke, I was willing to go to the government, sit there and have them ask me any questions they could. I was willing to take my polygraph test. I took the so-called DNA test. Anything that was asked of me I did. I just was not able to sit down and present a case because I found it was so flawed to me. I was a detective, I wasn't a guy who worked on a truck, I know how these things are. I worked cases with the government. I worked cases with the state. I worked cases with the city. I have been before judges and I have said to them there is no reason for me to lie.

"I didn't need $30,000 to harm Mr. Greenwald. I never heard Mr. Greenwald's name in my life. When they mentioned it when we were incarcerated in Las Vegas, I said, 'I never heard of a person like that, I never heard of the human being, I never heard of these times.' They said, 'Oh, you spoke to this guy.' I never had access to them. I never had access to files or who it was. When I heard this I said to people, 'This is coming down on me because of who I am, who I was, not because of what I've done.' I've always maintained my honesty, my integrity. I tried so hard. But I said to the government show me a piece of paper, a picture of me in a bar, in a club. Where did I meet an organized crime figure? Where was my phone? My phone was open, I was in the phone book.

"I have a family. I would feel the same way these people do. I could feel the hate and the sorrow. Your Honor, I've always felt that's why I became a cop. I had to live down my father. My father was a member of the Gambino crime family. I was already crucified with the name before I had an opportunity. I turned my back on organized crime so much, I just turned my back on it. I had no respect for them. I had no liking for them. I turned down every opportunity to speak to me. I was never associated or around them. The one thing that I was so proud of as a human being, whether it is in jail or home or whether it is anywhere—the one thing that I have to go to my grave with—is I was one hell of a cop.

"I've always maintained my honesty, my integrity," Eppolito continued, his voice increasing in urgency. "I tried so hard. I apologize for having to speak for the first time until all this happened. I can hold my head up high. I never done any of this. To Mrs. Hydell, Otto Heidel's daughter, Mrs. Lino, and Mrs. Greenwald, please call the judge. If I can't convince you I'm innocent, I will apologize. I didn't do any of these crimes at all."

Eppolito sat before a silent courtroom.

Weinstein asked Caracappa if he had anything to say to the court. Caracappa half stood.

"My lawyer will speak for me," he said, sitting again.

Daniel Nobel, the attorney appointed by the court to represent Caracappa, noted that no one from Caracappa's family was present. "Your Honor, there are no members of his family here today, not because they don't want to be, but because they could accurately anticipate the atmosphere of the courtroom today."

Nobel referred to the letters submitted by Caracappa to the court. "Members of the family and individuals who have known Mr. Caracappa over the last fifteen years expressed the same thing, Your Honor," Nobel said. "They knew this man well, they knew him in varying circumstances over a long period of time. They knew him in a way that the kind of secrets that have been alluded to here just could not have been."

Prosecutor Robert Henoch then addressed the court. "The government's position is that a sentence of life imprisonment is the only sentence that will satisfy the statutory objectives of sentencing under the United States Code," he said. "In this case, Your Honor, it is the only sentence that will serve justice and it is our position that it is the correct sentence and it is the sentence we're asking Your Honor to impose." Henoch continued, "Caracappa and Eppolito are unremorseful and unrepentant. An overwhelming case was amassed by the investigators."

Judge Weinstein needed no time to reach his conclusion. He issued a sentence of life in prison. In addition, the government would be entitled to seize $1 million in assets, effectively bankrupting Caracappa and Eppolito. "It's hard to visualize a more heinous offense," Judge Weinstein said. "The characteristics of the defendants are revealed by the nature of their crimes. A heavy sentence is required to promote respect for the law and to deter the conduct of people in a like position. It is needed to deter conduct of the defendants as late as 2005 and 2006. It is necessary to protect the public from further crime by these defendants. No crime has come before this court with a similar severity."

There was one catch. Imposition of the sentence would have to await the outcome of the motion to overturn the conviction based on the statute of limitations and the alleged incompetency of Bruce Cutler and Eddie Hayes. A hearing on the matter was scheduled for June. Caracappa and Eppolito would remain in custody until the motion had been decided.

LOUIE'S DAY IN COURT

No longer representing their former clients but themselves, Eddie Hayes and Bruce Cutler reacted with outrage to the accusations. "I showed him what kind of man I am, and he showed me what kind of man he is," Hayes said in an interview in his midtown office. Hayes had taken the case because he thought it would be easy to win—the evidence appeared flimsy and the conspiracy improbable. But then he had encountered the phenomenon of Burton Kaplan on the witness stand—followed by the onslaught of evidence gathered by the cadre. "You can fight through a certain amount of evidence, but after a while it becomes impossible," Hayes said. "The weight is too great. Steve taking a day off when Israel Greenwald was killed, the phone numbers of Steve and Louie in Kaplan's phone book, after all the facts pile up you can't convince a jury that the whole thing is unreliable." Hayes took consolation in the fact that the *New York Times* had quoted a juror saying Hayes's performance in court had been "extraordinary."

"To accuse a fighter of walking away from a fight, that is what is so insulting," Cutler told the *Washington Post*. "This is the most offensive thing that has ever happened to me in my life." Bondy was a "guttersnipe lawyer," Cutler said, and Eppolito just another convict looking for someone to blame. "Desperate men make desperate allegations in desperate times," Cutler said to the New York papers.

The competency hearing was held in early June. In the slow-motion train wreck that the case had become, Bondy's brief seemed little more than a forlorn footnote. Assisted by his own young female blond aide-de-camp attorney, Bondy would not be denied his moment in the spotlight, even if it meant ridiculing his former role model, Bruce Cutler, and disregarding the basic civilities of the fraternity of the criminal bar. "Defense counsel spent the majority of Mr. Eppolito's closing argument speaking about himself, including the fact that he lost over fourteen pounds during the trial, loved Brooklyn as a borough of bridges and churches, and was an admirer of the great Indian Chief Crazy Horse." Bondy's lengthy legal memorandum portrayed a dysfunctional relationship between Cutler and his client. "Counsel consistently refused to read Mr. Eppolito's notes, listen to his comments, or otherwise allow him to participate meaningfully in his own defense." Cutler had also failed to interview Casso or call him as a witness.

Bondy had the opportunity to put Eppolito's desperate revisionist theories before the court. He then called his only witness.

"Louis Eppolito calls Louis Eppolito," Bondy declared.

Eppolito took the stand, dressed in a suit and tie, a convicted murderer swearing to tell the truth upon pain of perjury charges—small disincentive given his pending life sentence. From the witness stand, Eppolito described how he had learned of the allegations made by Casso and had come to engage Bruce Cutler. In March 1994, he testified, his co-author for *Mafia Cop*, journalist Bob Drury, had called him to ask if he would be willing to talk to mob reporter Jerry Capeci.

"I said yes," Eppolito said. "Jerry got on the phone and asked me if I ever heard of or knew a person named Anthony Casso. I told him I heard the name but I don't know him, I never met him. He says, 'Would you be surprised if I told you that he was a member of the Luchese crime family, he was now testifying on the government's behalf, and he had mentioned that you were a killer of Eddie Lino?' I thought it was a joke. I says, 'You're kidding me, right?' He says, 'No.' I says, 'I don't even know who Eddie Lino is, I never met the man, I don't know who he is.' He says, 'Did you do that killing with Steve Caracappa?' I says, 'Steve?' I says, 'That's insane.' Steve and I didn't even work together, we have not worked together, at that time, since 1979."

Eppolito testified that he hung up and made two calls. First he called Caracappa. Next he called Bruce Cutler. Eppolito had known Cutler since the mid-seventies, when Cutler was a prosecutor for the Brooklyn DA. Despite the tabloid headlines in 1994, Cutler had managed to assist Eppolito in avoiding any criminal charges in the matter for more than a decade—a fact omitted in Bondy's questioning. After Eppolito was arrested in front of Piero's in Las Vegas, he had engaged Cutler once again—telling his wife Cutler was "the only man who could save me." When the two men met at the MDC in New York City to plan Eppolito's defense, Cutler began to question his client about specific facts, asking particularly if he knew Burton Kaplan. "I knew the man," Eppolito testified. "I knew him and I had a relationship with him. I would buy my clothes from him. I says, 'What does Burt Kaplan have to do with this case?' He says, 'He's one of the main witnesses against you.' I says, 'This is nonsense. I know the man. I buy my clothes from him.' I says, 'Bruce, I got to take the stand.' I says, 'I see what's going on here, I know what's going on now.'"

Developing the defense before trial, Cutler told Eppolito he would have him testify, if it seemed necessary, but he had in mind another approach. Cutler told Eppolito that there was a good chance of success because of RICO's time limitations. The suggestion upset Eppolito, he testified. "I have to apologize the way I say it, but I said to Mr. Cutler, 'I don't give a damn about the statute of limitations. They're telling me that I killed people, that I kidnapped people. I never did any of that. I want to clear myself from every single charge here. I'm not just worried about getting off on some legal technicalities.'"

Eppolito testified that Cutler refused to let him testify, under the threat of no longer representing him. Eppolito said he was terrified Cutler would quit if he demanded to take the stand. When the defense was called to present its list of witnesses, Eppolito claimed he had physically expressed his exasperation at not being able to give evidence. "I had my two hands and I hit the table and I says, 'I'm not going to allow this to happen. I have people who I wanted to testify for me and I want to take that stand. I'm the only one that could tell the truth about what is being told about me.'"

"What was the response of Mr. Cutler at that time?" Bondy asked.

"'You're not, you're not taking that stand,'" Eppolito said. "He gave me a story. He says to me, 'They can ask you any questions they want.' I says, 'I don't care what they ask me, I don't care where they go, I don't care what they say.'"

Eppolito said he was convinced that if he testified he could have countered the prosecution's evidence. Why then, with his life on the line, did he not demand to testify?

"I was afraid," Eppolito said.

"Afraid of what?" Bondy asked.

"I was afraid of the judge."

During the trial, Eppolito had repeatedly boasted to reporters that nothing and no one had ever scared him. Now Eppolito claimed he would rather face conviction on multiple racketeering murder counts than risk raising the ire of an eighty-four-year-old judge. Eppolito explained that his fear stemmed from the day that he had been late for court because he had been trapped in traffic. "When I got in, I had run the block and I was nervous and sweaty, and the judge said, 'Marshal, arrest him. His bail is revoked.' At that time I was—I was scared. I didn't want to attempt to ask the judge, and I didn't know what to do."

"Eppolito kept stammering apologies to the judge while he testified," Oldham recalled. "He couldn't look at Weinstein. Even when he was saying he was sorry he couldn't look at him. It was clear to me that much of what he said in his book about his father beating him had a huge impact on Louis. He beat people down as a cop, but he was fearful of authority. He wanted to be someone in authority—and when he was, he abused that authority. Shit rolls downhill. Eppolito had choices in life, as does everyone, but Fat the Gangster left lasting scars on him. He was the playground bully caught out. He was plainly petrified—and I don't blame him for that. But it was like none of what had happened had actually happened. It was intensely depressing. Eppolito had to know what he had done.

"Caracappa by contrast didn't say anything. He didn't look at Eppolito, the judge, or the gallery. Caracappa wasn't going to ruin his chances for a retrial by taking the stand. Everything Eppolito said on the stand could be used against him if there was another trial. Eppolito was just hammering one last nail into his own coffin. Caracappa was no such fool. Caracappa wasn't going to create a record of lying under oath. If Eppolito went far enough, there was the chance that Caracappa could move to demand a separate trial to avoid being tainted by prejudicial and inflammatory statements made by Eppolito. To the bitter end, when he had been tried, convicted, and sentenced, Caracappa stayed quiet and played the system. Letting Eppolito hang himself might work to Caracappa's advantage."

As Eppolito's explanations grew less believable, so did his attacks on Cutler's judgment. Eppolito testified that Cutler had not allowed him to participate in creating his own defense. At lunch at the Plaza Diner during the trial, Eppolito said, Cutler refused to talk to him, saying that he prepared for court by remaining focused. Eppolito said he wanted to call Casso as a witness after his last-ditch attempted intervention in the trial, against the advice of Cutler. "All of a sudden there's a letter saying we didn't do it," Eppolito claimed, incorrectly, of Casso's letter. "Well, is this man psychotic only when the government says he's a psychotic, or is he crazy all the time? For three years he says I did it, now he says I didn't. Bring him on the stand and let him tell the story. If he's a liar, he's a liar. I'm not afraid of what he was going to say. I was never afraid of anybody in my life. I'm not afraid of being confronted. Just because you say it don't mean it's the truth."

On cross-examination, Henoch mowed down Eppolito's proclamations. Eppolito had spent twelve years as a detective in Bensonhurst and Flatbush, but he claimed to have no knowledge of the location of the parking lot on Nostrand Avenue, or to have ever kept a car there, or to have met Peter Franzone, or the two other men who had said they knew Eppolito from the lot. For decades Eppolito had claimed to be the eleventh most decorated cop in the history of the NYPD, but now he allowed that was a "fallacy." The two Medals of Honor he had won were only "honorable mentions," not the actual awards, he allowed under questioning. Eppolito agreed that Cutler had won many victories before trial, including getting the judge to agree to exclude prejudicial evidence the government had sought to introduce—like the allegation Eppolito had sold mug shots, robbed corner stores in the seventies, and accepted a bribe from Sammy the Bull Gravano not to investigate the murder of Frank Fiala in the Six-Two Precinct.

On the stand, Eppolito admitted that Kaplan had come to the home of his girlfriend, Cabrini Cama.

"Had you testified you were prepared to offer an explanation as to why you met covertly with Mr. Kaplan in Miss Cama's apartment?" Henoch asked.

"Yes."

"And it was because you were buying jeans from Mr. Kaplan?"

"Buying suits and I was buying shirts. It was almost impossible to get—I couldn't go to Macy's or Sears. I was a 20 shirt, a 54 jacket, a 36 pants."

"And the one guy you could buy suits from in Brooklyn was a Luchese family associate closely associated with Anthony Casso?"

"No, he's the one guy that would switch the pants with the jacket. I would get a smaller pants with a bigger jacket."

Henoch turned to *Mafia Cop*. Eppolito said the original manuscript titled "The Man in the Middle" had been changed and edited. Henoch read Eppolito excerpts from the book. One involved taking the prisoner named Bugs and dunking his head repeatedly in a bucket filled with ammonia while Eppolito was partners with Caracappa. Eppolito claimed the quote was taken out of context.

"You bragged about basically torturing a suspect?" Henoch asked.

"Absolutely."

"Knowing that that is not lawful for you to do so?"

"Never happened," Eppolito testified.

"Assuming for the sake of argument you were asked about that in front of the jury, how do you think that would have played out for them?"

"I think if I told them the truth and what happened, I think they would have been fine with it."

Henoch read another passage. The incident described in *Mafia Cop* involved Detective Eppolito being insulted by a wiseguy. He went into his locker in the precinct house, the book said, grabbed his (illegal) sawed-off, double-barreled shotgun, and went to a mob social club in search of

"Frankie Carbone." Henoch read, "I spotted Frankie sitting at a card table, walked up behind him, stuck the barrel in his mouth, and ordered him to his feet. 'Bye motherfucker' was all I said and he lost his whole insides. As I backed him into a wall I watched the stain in his pants get bigger and bigger. Suddenly I knew what it felt like to be my father. I was walking like a wiseguy, talking like a wiseguy, the power surge was comparable to what I felt at times as a cop yet somehow different, as if the police worked on AC current and the Mafia on DC."

"You're not allowed to do that as a cop, fair to say?" Henoch asked. "That would not be something lawful?"

"Who said I'm not allowed to do that?" Eppolito asked.

Henoch read another section from *Mafia Cop*, where Eppolito threatened to murder a man, leave his body in the trunk of a car to rot, and then find it and lead the NYPD investigation into the homicide himself.

"You thought that that was okay for a jury to know, in a case where you were being accused of being corrupt, and accused of abusing your police power, that you actually admitted doing that in a book you wrote?" Henoch asked.

"It actually happened, yeah. I would tell the jury the truth. I was a tough guy. It was the seventies. That is what the procedures were."

"You told him you were going to kill him and put him in a trunk?"

"That's just talk."

Eppolito seemed to believe that declaring himself a liar was somehow exculpatory. All a judge and jury needed to do was tease apart the lies that were only lies, Eppolito apparently proposed, and lies that were *lies*. He applied the same line of reasoning to all the mobster conniving and bragging caught on tape in Las Vegas in 2004 and 2005. Eppolito wasn't a "real, real gangster," he told the court, despite the audio evidence of him telling Corso precisely that. Eppolito was only playing a part for Corso's benefit. Caracappa and Eppolito took Steven Corso for a chump, Eppolito said. Corso lapped up the tough-guy talk and the New York gangster act.

"Mr. Caracappa was helping me make Corso feel like he was more important than what he was," Eppolito testified. "He liked being around tough guys and wiseguys, and I ate it up. I tried to pull him into me. I wanted him to invest in my films."

Eppolito's testimony was a bewildered mix of mob melodrama, deception, and unconscious confession. The scams he ran writing screenplays, charging large sums to write unproducible drivel, was an honest business, he said. He tried to explain how it worked, with a crooked smile. The money he was paid by people who hired him to write their life stories was not really "paid" to him. It was only a sum given to him against the future windfall the subject would receive when the script was sold to Hollywood. Eppolito kept the money, of course, but this did not mean he was being "paid." Eppolito also testified that he used the prospect of dating his daughter as yet another lure for Corso. The threats of violence he related to Corso, including taking up a hatchet to murder a recalcitrant tradesman, were true or false depending on the circumstances, Eppolito testified.

"Is it fair to say that you lie about anything if it would benefit you?" Henoch asked.

Eppolito appeared delighted by the question, as if he could finally state a self-evident truth. "As long as it will help me get my movies made."

"Down the rabbit hole and through the looking glass," Alan Feuer wrote in the *New York Times*, describing the hearings in Judge Weinstein's court. The ironies and fantasies and surrealities rapidly mounted. Caracappa and Eppolito were conning Corso by exploiting his fascination with the mafia, according to Eppolito, even while Corso tempted the pair to their ruination with a con. Caracappa's lawyer claimed that the government had turned Eppolito into the most effective witness and potent weapon against Caracappa. "The more Eppolito testified, the more it became clear that Cutler was absolutely right in refusing to put Eppolito on the stand," Oldham recalled. "Eppolito would have been the best witness the prosecution could have hoped for."

DEFENDING THE DEFENSE

Henoch, meanwhile, was placed in the odd position of defending his former adversaries, Cutler and Hayes, in order to protect the hard-won verdict. The next witness was Bruce Cutler—a defense attorney defending himself. Before Cutler took the stand, Judge Weinstein warned Bondy that by calling his own former attorney Eppolito was waiving his protection against self-incrimination in any future proceeding, including any prior crimes he had committed. Bondy agreed.

On the stand, Cutler recited his prodigious professional qualifications. During more than twenty-five years on the bar, he had been involved in many of the biggest criminal cases in the country, including his famously successful representation of John Gotti.

"I've been fortunate," Cutler said.

Bondy asked if Cutler had ever made a mistake during a trial. "Trial work is an art, not a science," Cutler replied. "You improvise, adapt, overcome. There's nobody like me."

Bondy asked about Cutler's cross-examination of Al D'Arco. Judge Weinstein had halted the questioning with Cutler in full oratorical flight. "You lost control," Bondy said.

"I never lose control," Cutler said. "My intention as a defense lawyer, always, is to pulverize the government's case. My goal is to pulverize and eviscerate."

"Did you attempt to put on a defense case?" Bondy asked.

"That's my defense: attack. Most of my cases, after the government's witnesses are eviscerated, I sum up and I win."

The case against Caracappa and Eppolito involved the worst crimes Cutler had ever encountered. "If I thought Lou was involved in any of them, I never would have represented him," Cutler said.

Cutler allowed that Henoch had surprised him with his tactics by truncating the case. Not calling Fat Pete Chiodo and proscribing D'Arco's testimony largely took the subject of the mafia out of the trial. "The government had Kaplan with his fake hair and his fake teeth and his lies," Cutler said. He had never heard of Burt Kaplan before Caracappa and Eppolito were arrested. He expected Kaplan to be one of many witnesses. "Not that he was going to be the sine qua non of the case," Cutler testified.

Bondy asked why Cutler had gone to lunch with the reporter from the *New Yorker* instead of attending the meeting in which Cutler's co-counsel and Eppolito had the phone call with Casso. "I didn't want to hear this devil, this Tasmanian Devil's voice," Cutler said. "I knew he had been dangling the Hydell body in front of the government. At the end of the call Lou thanked him and it bothered me."

"I don't want to hear anymore about Casso," Judge Weinstein said. "It is clear that any responsible attorney would not call Casso."

Bondy waded through the record of the trial attempting to show Cutler's poor decision making as an attorney. Cutler explained that he had to be careful not to "open the door" to character evidence, given Eppolito's repeated racist remarks and recounted tales of violence. As ineffective and pompous as Cutler's speechifying may have seemed at the trial, under Bondy's questioning a logic to Cutler's seemingly fevered defense emerged. After Eppolito's testimony, Cutler seemed downright reasonable.

"There was a day, Mr. Bondy, when lawyers worked together," Cutler said. He turned to Judge Weinstein. "Are you going to have lunch today, judge?" he asked. "It's the only thing I want."

Lunch was taken.

Upon resumption of the proceedings, Bondy raised the subject of Cutler's relationship with Eppolito.

"I had a little chat with him before trial," Cutler said. "Act like a man. Dress properly. Shave that goatee. I don't hold hands. I don't play footsie. I don't need you to help me. I'm helping you. Things were all right with Lou, but I sensed I couldn't console him or hold his hand and I think he needed it."

Cutler testified about his refusal to deal with Eppolito in the Plaza Diner, where he ate breakfast ("a half a cup of coffee, a banana, and some orange juice") at a separate table from Eppolito and family. The subject of Eppolito taking the stand had never come up, Cutler said, except for perhaps once.

"I've got to protect Lou above all else because he doesn't protect himself," Cutler said. "After dissecting the evidence, including Lou's book, I'm not sure I'm strong enough, but if I could have, I would have tackled him—not literally, figuratively."

"Did you ever consider calling William Oldham or Tommy Dades?" Bondy asked.

"I had no intention of calling either as a defense witness," Cutler replied.

Weinstein interjected. "The defendant's excuse for not bringing his desire to testify to the attention of the court is ludicrous," Weinstein observed. "The defendant's immorality and lack of credibility lead the court to ignore his testimony on any point. The defendant received an excellent defense."

Eddie Hayes was next, but he was nowhere to be found. The court learned that Hayes had traveled to Florida to visit his eighty-two-year-old mother but was expected momentarily. While the court waited, Bondy read excerpts from Hayes's memoir, *Mouthpiece,* regarding his dealings with the NYPD and long friendship with Cutler. Hayes arrived dressed in a pink-and-white-striped polo shirt and wearing a characteristic grin. Bondy had called Hayes and so began the direct examination. Hayes testified that he and Cutler had known each other for thirty years. Bondy wanted to know if Hayes recollected Eppolito's efforts to be allowed to take the stand in his own defense. Hayes did not.

"You never heard Mr. Eppolito insist on testifying?" Bondy asked.

"Never," Hayes replied.

The proceedings descended into farce as Bondy continued to call witnesses in the hope of convincing the court of Eppolito's desire to testify despite Weinstein's explicit refutation of the argument. Weinstein continued to give Bondy room to create a record for a possible appeal, but the judge's skepticism was readily apparent. Eppolito's daughter, Andrea, his foremost spokesperson and advocate, swore that her father had banged the steering wheel in frustration driving away from the court after the telephone call with Casso. "He won't take a fucking phone call," she said her father said of Cutler. "He won't read my notes."

While Bondy seemed convinced he was gaining a legal advantage, Daniel Nobel was more realistic. Caracappa's attorney had informed his client that there was little likelihood the convictions would be overturned. The *Daily News* reported, "Nobel said outside court that he had advised his client there was 'a snowball's chance in hell' of Weinstein throwing out the verdict."

On Caracappa's behalf, Nobel re-called Eddie Hayes, now testifying against his former client. As Nobel tried to cast doubt on Hayes's command of the intricacies of RICO, Hayes corrected and clarified Nobel's own characterizations of the law. Nobel asked Hayes why he did not place the statute of limitations argument more forcefully before the jury. Hayes replied that it was not a good strategy to tell the jury that the two defendants were guilty of a string of horrific crimes while they were NYPD detectives but should be acquitted because the charges had come too late. Nobel imagined an opening statement that Hayes might have given to a jury. Nobel imagined himself giving such an opening, bellowing to a nonexistent jury about the statute of limitations and the need to not convict even if they were guilty.

"It would take some nerve to make that argument before a jury, especially with former detective defendants," Hayes said.

"I would not expect a counsel of such eminence to make such an opening," Weinstein said. "It's absurd."

A MAN FOR ALL SEASONS

On Friday, June 30, 2006, a sleepy afternoon at the federal courthouse, Judge Jack Weinstein issued a seventy-seven page judgment in the case of the *United States v. Stephen Caracappa and Louis Eppolito*. The legal determination was one of the most important in Weinstein's distinguished career. The publicity it would attract would be vast. It was an opportunity for the veteran judge, friend of Bobby Kennedy and lifelong New York liberal, to make a statement that would reach the largest possible audience. The "mafia cops" case was suddenly back in the headlines.

"The evidence presented at trial overwhelmingly established the defendants' participation in a large number of heinous and violent crimes, including eight murders," Weinstein began. "While serving as New York City police detectives, the defendants used their badges not in service of the public, but in aid of organized crime. They kidnapped, murdered, and assisted kidnappers and murderers, all the while sworn to protect the public against such crimes."

Judge Weinstein reviewed the factual history of the case. In reciting the underlying criminal acts in detail he created a record that the guilt of Caracappa and Eppolito had been proven beyond reasonable doubt. There were two sets of criminal conduct, Weinstein wrote. From 1986 until the early nineties, Caracappa and Eppolito had been "employed" by Gaspipe Casso through his agent Burton Kaplan. These offenses constituted "the New York acts." The crimes related to money laundering and narcotics trafficking, which transpired in Las Vegas in 2004 and 2005, were "the Nevada acts." The "thin" connection between these two acts had caused Weinstein concern from the outset, he wrote. For a RICO case to fall within the time limits of the law, the two acts had to form a single "pattern." But the necessity of a trial, for the defendants to clear their name or the government to prove its case, had overcome Weinstein's misgivings about the statute of limitations.

"The government's overwhelming case was skillfully presented with credible witnesses and supporting interlocking documents and other proof of each of the racketeering acts charged," Weinstein wrote. Kaplan had testified convincingly and methodically about the formation of the conspiracy and the New York acts, he said.

"Although co-conspirator Anthony Casso did not testify at the trial, he was a constant ethereal presence," Weinstein wrote. "At no time did either party indicate that it desired to call Casso. His unreliability, capriciousness, and potential danger as a witness who could turn toward either side as quickly as a weathervane on a blustery day was well-known to all." Cutler's decision not to call Casso as a witness was not only strategically sound, but wise, noted the judge. "Calling Casso would have been an unmitigated disaster," Weinstein said. "Up until the final days of the trial, Casso had done nothing but implicate the defendants, even making eleventh-hour attempts to assist the government."

The claim of inadequate representation was baseless, said the judge. "While there may be disagreement as to the value of the sometimes baroque style of these two attorneys, they were clearly skilled, dedicated to their clients, and enormously hardworking." As for Eppolito's claim that he was denied the right to testify in his own defense, this was also dismissed by the judge. Eppolito had been a police officer for more than twenty years. The notion that he didn't know he could assert his right to take the stand was risible. Regardless, even if he had testified the verdict would not have been changed.

"On the contrary, Eppolito's testimony at the hearing made it overwhelmingly clear that his testimony at the trial would have proven a disaster to himself and his co-defendant. In addition to describing himself, under oath, as a man who would lie to get what he wanted, Eppolito gave numerous examples of times when he had lied or embellished in order to further his career or image. He discussed his own racism at great length, volunteering a long list of racial slurs that he said he often used; admitted to having placed a sawed-off shotgun in the mouth of a man who had insulted his mother, expressing disbelief when the prosecutor asked him whether he knew such an act was illegal; and confessed to having removed files from the police department without permission. On cross-examination, he repeatedly volunteered more self-damaging information than was necessary to answer the prosecution's questions. As for his testimony regarding the crimes with which he was charged, it appears that, aside from a general denial of involvement, Eppolito had little to say. Although Eppolito claimed that he had told his counsel that he could refute the charges against him, his testimony at the hearing gave no indication that was the case."

Repeatedly stressing the guilt of Caracappa and Eppolito, Judge Weinstein then put the case back in the news around the world. Throughout the judgment Weinstein drew a bright-line distinction between facts and the law. In the verdict, the jury had been asked as a matter of fact if the statute of limitations requirement had been met by the prosecution. The jury found, as fact, that the conspiracy was ongoing and satisfied the statute of limitations rule.

Weinstein disagreed, as a matter of law.

It was not an unprecedented move for the judge. Weinstein had done the same thing during the trial of Vincent "Chin" Gigante in 1997. The jury found Gigante guilty of conspiring to murder John Gotti. Despite the jury's verdict, Weinstein overturned the conviction on the grounds that it was time-barred under RICO. In this new judgment, he quoted himself in the Gigante case. "Conspiracy theory provides federal prosecutors with a powerful flail to unseat criminals, a weapon so effective that many potential state prosecutions are shifted to federal court by frustrated district attorneys. Yet its very effectiveness requires care that it is not utilized to commit injustice."

The trial of Caracappa and Eppolito involved crimes that dated back twenty years. But it was taking place in a contemporary context. The trial attracted enormous interest. Front pages were commanded, Hollywood movies contemplated, books prepared for publication. The eighty-four-year-old Weinstein, in what would probably be his last judgment in a case of such public magnitude, turned to the broadest notions of justice. Those who knew him well and those who had closely watched him during the trial felt a sense that he had known all along where the case was heading. Judge Weinstein attempted to thread the needle. The public good of the trial and conviction of the cops had been achieved. Weinstein now turned to the limitation of the government's power.

The government's case stretched the conspiracy law to the breaking point, Weinstein wrote. Decades-old crimes could not be joined with three completely unrelated criminal acts committed years later in another geographical area and under different circumstances. The evidence was insufficient to support the jury's verdict.

"It will undoubtedly appear peculiar to many people that heinous criminals such as the defendants, having been found guilty on overwhelming evidence of the most despicable crimes of violence and treachery, should go unwhipped of justice. Yet our Constitution, statutes, and morality require that we be ruled by law, not by vindictiveness or the advantages of the moment. If we are to be ruled by the law, we must be limited by its protections. As Justice Oliver Wendell Holmes reminded us, it is a 'less evil that some criminals should escape than that the government should play an ignoble part.' Even during the great emergency of the Civil War, the court rejected the theory that the rule of law could be twisted to meet the exigencies of the moment. In 1866, the Supreme Court wrote, 'The constitution of the United States is a law for rulers and people, equally in war and in peace, and covers with the shield for its protection all classes of men, at all times, and under all circumstances. No doctrine, involving more pernicious consequences, was ever invented by the wit of man than that any of its provisions can be suspended during any of the great exigencies of government.' And, as John Locke declared in his Second Treatise of Government—and as the events of the last century have illustrated—'wherever Law ends, Tyranny begins.'"

Weinstein ended with a literary quotation, a touch of éclat at the end of a case that had from the first revolved around the written word. The reference was from *A Man for All Seasons*. The play was produced on Broadway in 1961, the dawn of the golden age of liberal democracy in America, when the Kennedy administration was dubbed "Camelot" after the court of King Arthur and the Broadway play of the same name. *A Man for All Seasons* was a play about ancient concerns. The subject was Henry VIII and his desire to be made head of the Church in order to grant himself a divorce. Sir Thomas More, friend of the king but chancellor of England, must decide whether to grant the king's request. Faced with overwhelming power, More stood by the law and refused to accept the king's claim to the Church. The dialogue quoted by Weinstein is written in a style both antique and modern.

"What would you do?" More asks the zealot William Roper. "Cut a great road through the law to get after the Devil?"

"I'd cut down every law in England to do that!" Roper exclaims.

"Oh?" More asks. "And when the law was down, and the Devil turned round on you, where would you hide, Roper, all the laws being flat? This country's planted thick with laws from coast to coast—man's laws, not God's—and if you cut them down—and you're just the man to do it—do you really think you could stand straight upright in the winds that would blow then? Yes, I'd give the Devil the benefit of law, for my own safety's sake."

Weinstein concluded that the sanctity of law and justice transcended the guilt of Caracappa and Eppolito. In the age of the government's war on terror, the rule of law was in peril, Weinstein intimated. In such a time of danger, the government had to be watched to see that it did not stretch the meaning of words and statutes to suit its purposes, no matter how just the cause appeared.

In the end, Judge Weinstein held, the devil himself must be granted the benefits of the rule of law, as should Louis Eppolito and Stephen Caracappa.

The verdict was overturned.

THE BROTHERHOOD

The government immediately announced it would appeal the ruling, an action that would take months. As the fall turned to winter in 2006, the fates of Caracappa and Eppolito hung in legal limbo. Their convictions had been vacated, yet they were guilty of murder. The evidence said so. A jury said so. The esteemed judge said so.

No longer convicted of any crimes, Caracappa and Eppolito would remain in prison pending the outcome of the government's appeal. Bail was denied by Judge Weinstein. "Defendants have a high incentive to flee, given that they have been publicly shamed—and as a result, will be ostracized—after a trial at which they were proven guilty of heinous criminal acts," Weinstein wrote.

Eppolito continued to maintain his innocence. Granting an interview to *Daily News* reporter Greg B. Smith, he said, "I thought this was all a very well-thought-out plan. It was a perfect frame. There's no more perfect frame than this."

Caracappa remained silent.

In public statements, the Brooklyn District Attorney's Office announced that if Caracappa and Eppolito were eventually found to have no criminal liability in federal court, New York state authorities would pursue murder and kidnapping charges against the two former NYPD detectives. In the state, there was no statute of limitations on murder and kidnapping prosecutions. For those who had followed the case and were convinced of the guilt of Caracappa and Eppolito, this news was welcome and reassuring: if convicted on state charges, Stephen Caracappa and Louis Eppolito, both aged beyond their years, would nearly certainly spend the rest of their lives behind bars.

Housed in the same cell, the first fissure in their relationship appeared during the hearing where bail was denied, when Caracappa asked that he be taken out of his cell with Eppolito and permitted to live in the general prison population. Caracappa did not say if the request was to escape the monotony of twenty-three-hour-a-day lockdown, or to finally rid himself of his association with Louis Eppolito, aka *Mafia Cop*.

After the guilty verdicts were announced, Oldham was invited to speak to a group of retired NYPD detectives. Known as the Knights of the Round Table, the group met once a month to talk about old times and listen to true-crime cop stories from the present and the past. The meeting to which Oldham was invited was held at Pete's Tavern, an old pub in Gramercy Park in Manhattan known for its literary history and the hundreds of signed pictures of sports and entertainment figures that covered its walls.

As Oldham donned a dark blue shirt and suit he felt weary. The wear and tear on him from the case showed in his eyes, and like many ex-cops, he was having difficulty adjusting to retirement. As he dressed, he wondered about the nature of the invitation. He had grown so used to people telling him that they didn't want to hear about the case that he had been a little taken aback by the interest from the detectives' group. The invitation had come from a retired police captain named John McMahon.

Now in his late sixties, McMahon was gregarious and energetic, and had become a defense attorney after leaving the police department.

Oldham kissed his daughters good-bye and headed for his car. The drive to Gramercy Park was short, and he approached the meeting not knowing what to expect. Despite the victory, the prosecution of Caracappa and Eppolito had not been a popular cause inside many circles in the NYPD, both active duty and retired. "A lot of guys thought the whole case made the department look bad. Some thought criminals shouldn't be used to testify against cops. Most didn't want to know too much. An entire generation of law enforcement had been fooled by Caracappa and Eppolito. Men who had dedicated their lives to saving lives and catching criminals had two killers walking among them. That generation was dying, too. Kenny McCabe, a legend, had passed away that winter. Other guys were getting sick or old."

Pete's Tavern was a step or two up from the usual police haunts—it served an excellent steak, a good red wine. Oldham had worked as Jacques Chirac's bodyguard on a visit to Pete's in the late eighties when Chirac was mayor of Paris before he became president of France. When Oldham arrived he saw that the tavern had not changed much in nearly twenty years, which was not surprising, as it had opened in 1864.

The lunch meeting was held in a room upstairs from the main bar. Two dozen retired NYPD detectives had gathered. Prime rib and roasted potatoes were served. Oldham had never belonged to an organization like the Knights of the Round Table. In the NYPD he had been an outsider from the beginning. He did not expect a hero's welcome, nor did he expect open resentment and anger. When Oldham entered, a former Major Case colleague got to his feet and walked out. Oldham wasn't shocked. He and the former colleague had never gotten along in a department where people often clashed, rivalries arose, and disagreements about guilt and innocence were commonplace. The reaction of the others surprised Oldham—the last twist in a case that had contained so many.

"Few of the cops in the room wanted to confront the fact that two of their fellow detectives were killers. Eppolito maybe. But Steve Caracappa? A first-grade detective and stand-up guy? Caracappa had been convicted by a jury of his peers of murdering, kidnapping, selling crystal meth—and selling out his friends, partners, and society. The evidence had been declared overwhelming by the most experienced judge in the country. For some of the cops in Pete's Tavern it was easier—less painful—to fall back on the old assumptions and excuses, the ones that created the problem in the first place. The general sentiment was that the feds were cop haters. That Burt Kaplan was a liar. One old guy said he'd heard that I was a bum and that Steve and Louie were innocent. That attitude was exactly what Caracappa and Eppolito had preyed upon. Detectives supposedly trained to not make assumptions were incapable of imagining two of their own capable of murder. It contradicted their way of seeing the world, and themselves. They didn't want to know the facts.

"I knew that some detectives had taken the time to familiarize themselves with the case. Detective Chuck Siriano, who served with Caracappa and me in the Major Case Squad, had read the entire transcript of Kaplan's testimony. Chuck saw how convincing Kaplan's evidence was—the detail, the texture, the command of facts. Chuck lay awake for nights playing back events in his mind—the shooting of Dominic Costa, the times that he had been out on surveillance and Caracappa knew of his whereabouts, the time he was certain wiseguys had followed him on his way home. It was torture thinking about the betrayal. I knew the feeling.

"As the hostility in the room rose, I started to get angry. I couldn't help wondering what the hell these detectives wanted. For Caracappa and Eppolito to get away with murder so the reputation of the NYPD wouldn't be dirtied? For Israel Greenwald to still lay buried under a concrete slab on Nostrand Avenue so they could eat their meat and potatoes at Pete's Tavern in peace? I was tired of being told by my brother detectives that they didn't want to hear about the case. They should have been applauding the work of the cadre. A bunch of old New York City detectives—men just like them—went out and made one of the best cases in years. Not the young, clean-cut federal agents who couldn't find their way home without a map. Old guys like me who drink too much and don't follow the rules but run their cases to the ground—detectives who want to know the truth, no matter where it leads, no matter how hard it is to take."

While others couldn't contain their hostility, Oldham's host, retired captain John McMahon, remained a gentleman throughout. "I told the men that I would stay until the last of them left, if anyone wanted to talk about the case," Oldham remembered. "Some guys stayed. They wanted to hear the story of Louie and Steve. I told them how it began. I told them how I got to the Major Case Squad by nearly getting killed by a police impersonator in the Three-Four. How I wanted to be a go-to detective, like Caracappa. How I knew there was something wrong with Caracappa the first time I met him."

ACKNOWLEDGMENTS

Writing a big, sprawling tale such as this requires the help of a multitude. We are grateful for the assistance of people drawn from the many walks of the world of organized crime in New York City—gangsters, detectives, federal agents, defense attorneys, prosecutors, reporters. We would like to thank, in particular, Detectives Stefano Braccini, George Slater, Mike Connelly, Joseph Keenan, and Chuck Siriano for their insights and memories. Without DEA Special Agent Eileen Dinnan there would have been no case. Retired Special Agent Patrick Colgan enabled us to re-create the world of cooperators from the perspective of the FBI. Brooklyn DA Chief Investigator Joe Ponzi not only helped break the case, he helped make this book. We would like to recognize the contributions of three of the best detective investigators, Tommy Dades, Bobby Intartaglio, and George Terra.

The fingerprints of Zoe Alsop, ace researcher and now intrepid reporter, are on every page of this book. Her commitment was complete, no matter how difficult the challenges, and so are our gratitude and admiration.

Former Colombo capo Big Sal Miciotta shared an enormous amount of his hard-earned wisdom about the ways of wiseguys. No one knows the underworld better. Janie McCormick generously trusted us with a small part of her story, in the hope it will help others. Jerry Capeci's "Gangland" (www.ganglandnews.com) and Selwyn Raab's *Five Families* were invaluable resources. Three reporters covering the trial were unfailingly generous with their time and notebooks: John Marzulli of the *New York Daily News*, Zach Haberman of the *New York Post*, and Alan Feuer of the *New York Times*. Legendary New York City journalist Jimmy Breslin was a source of wisdom and amusement. Professor Jefferey Morris helped provide a portrait of Judge Jack Weinstein. Steve Wick, the *Newsday* reporter who played a role in keeping the case alive, was kind enough to let us recount the story he originally broke. Seamus Conlan, great photojournalist and friend, provided enormous assistance in compiling the images for this book.

Defense attorney Eddie Hayes, a New York City original, understood the value of the written word and a good story. Gerry Labush, Esq., aided us in an early and critical phase and we are grateful for his efforts. Elizabeth McNamara and Peter Karanjia of Davis, Wright & Tremaine provided outstanding legal representation and review. Assistant U.S. Attorney Robert Henoch was generous with his time and beyond all expectation in his effort to assist in ensuring this account is as accurate and comprehensive as possible.

Jody Hotchkiss, literary agent and all around good guy, was a steady hand throughout the voyage, and Gay Salisbury ably managed the launch. Extraordinary efforts were made by extraordinary people at Scribner. We are grateful for the attention, enthusiasm, and professionalism of Carolyn Reidy, Susan Moldow, Nan Graham, John Fulbrook, Emily Remes, Suzanne Balaban, and Caroline Walker. Karen Thompson, Paul Whitlach, Katy Sprinkel, Erich Hobbing, and Kathleen Rizzo gave their all to turn the manuscript into a book on deadline and we thank them for their hard work.

Our editor, Colin Harrison, deserves more thanks than an acknowledgment can provide. This book was commissioned by Colin, himself an accomplished novelist, and he guided it through every stage of development from conception to delivery. *The Brotherhoods* truly is his baby. Whatever merits it might have are due to his vision and passion. The shortcomings are all ours.

G. L. writes, "I would like to thank the excellent editors I have had the good fortune to work with over the years—Paul Tough, Anne Collins, Jim Nelson, Barbara Jones, John Gillies, Vera Titunik, and the irreplaceable and much missed Art Cooper and Barbara Epstein. To that number I now add Colin Harrison, who took a big risk and dared me to write my first book. Paul McHugh, Merrily Weisbord, and Murray Sayle, mentors each in their own fashion, gave the invaluable gift of believing in me. To my friends Elyce and Andy Arons, Andrea Moss and Norm Magnusson, Srinivas Krishna, Charlie Foran, Scott Anderson, Tara Farrell—and the many others who helped maintain my sense of humor and perspective—I am in your debt. I was raised to love words and books and for that I thank my loving mother, Mary, my writer father, Bruce, and Pam Lawson and Ted Wood. Lorraine and Chandran Kaimal were the best help a son-in-law could ask for. Zoe became my friend through this book and for that I am thankful. To William Oldham, collaborator and great detective, I thank you for your story. My deepest gratitude goes to my three great loves for their sacrifices, strength, and sweet smiles — Maya, Lucy, Anna."

W. D. O. writes, "First, I want to thank our editor, Colin Harrison, a sweetheart. My agent, Jody Hotchkiss, a real guy in an otherwise strange business. Thank you to my old partners, without whom I am only half my self, S/A Dan Kumor, Detective George Slater (retired), Detective Mike Connolly (retired), Detective John Ross (retired), and you Steph. Kelly Moore, a one and only. John and Laura. My friends Willie Rashbaum, Allen Towbin, Bim (Gilbert Oakley), and Maureen Walsh and others. Thank you to Bacon and Paula, you helped me live. Dave Lubitz, I don't know why. Guy Lawson, a truly talented writer and now a good friend. Zoe Alsop, who pushed us down the path when we needed it. My mother, Nan. Andrea, thank you for the beautiful children and the good times. I hope all is well."

CREDITS

1. Courtesy of William Oldham
2. Courtesy of William Oldham
3. From *Mafia Cop* by Louis Eppolito
4. From *Mafia Cop* by Louis Eppolito
5. From *Mafia Cop* by Louis Eppolito
6. From *Mafia Cop* by Louis Eppolito
7-19. Courtesy of the U.S. Attorney's Office
20. Ramin Talaie/*The New York Times*/Redux
21-33. Courtesy of the U.S. Attorney's Office
34. Bryan Smith/*New York Daily News*
35. Ron Antonelli/*New York Daily News*
36. Photo by Ken Schles

ABOUT THE AUTHORS

Guy Lawson is an award-winning investigative journalist whose articles on war, crime, culture, and law have appeared in the *New York Times Magazine, GQ, Harper's,* and many other publications.

William Oldham is a decorated twenty-year veteran of the NYPD and a retired investigator for the U.S. Department of Justice. He is the president of Cadre Investigations, a private investigative agency in New York City.